T0178605

Lecture Notes in Computer Science 13703

More information about this series at https://link.springer.com/bookseries/558

Tiziana Margaria · Bernhard Steffen (Eds.)

Leveraging Applications of Formal Methods, Verification and Validation

Adaptation and Learning

11th International Symposium, ISoLA 2022
Rhodes, Greece, October 22–30, 2022
Proceedings, Part III

 Springer

Editors
Tiziana Margaria ⓘ
University of Limerick, CSIS and Lero
Limerick, Ireland

Bernhard Steffen ⓘ
TU Dortmund
Dortmund, Germany

ISSN 0302-9743 ISSN 1611-3349 (electronic)
Lecture Notes in Computer Science
ISBN 978-3-031-19758-1 ISBN 978-3-031-19759-8 (eBook)
https://doi.org/10.1007/978-3-031-19759-8

Introduction

As General and Program Chairs we would like to welcome you to the proceedings of ISoLA 2022, the 11th International Symposium on Leveraging Applications of Formal Methods, Verification and Validation held in Rhodes (Greece) during October 22–30, 2022, and endorsed by EASST, the European Association of Software Science and Technology.

Returning to the traditional in-person event, ISoLA 2022 provided a forum for developers, users, and researchers to discuss issues related to the adoption and use of rigorous tools and methods for the specification, analysis, verification, certification, construction, testing, and maintenance of systems from the point of view of their different application domains. Thus, since 2004 the ISoLA series of events has served the purpose of bridging the gap between designers and developers of rigorous tools on one side, and users in engineering and in other disciplines on the other side. It fosters and exploits synergetic relationships among scientists, engineers, software developers, decision makers, and other critical thinkers in companies and organizations. By providing a specific, dialogue-oriented venue for the discussion of common problems, requirements, algorithms, methodologies, and practices, ISoLA aims in particular at supporting researchers in their quest to improve the practicality, reliability, flexibility, and efficiency of tools for building systems, and users in their search for adequate solutions to their problems.

The program of ISoLA 2022 consisted of a collection of special tracks devoted to the following hot and emerging topics:

1. Rigorous Engineering of Collective Adaptive Systems
   (Organizers: Rocco De Nicola, Stefan Jähnichen, Martin Wirsing)
2. Programming: What is Next?
   (Organizers: Klaus Havelund, Bernhard Steffen)
3. X-by-Construction meets Runtime Verification
   (Organizers: Maurice H. ter Beek, Loek Cleophas, Martin Leucker, Ina Schaefer)
4. Automated Software Re-Engineering
   (Organizers: Serge Demeyer, Reiner Hähnle, Heiko Mantel)
5. Digital Twin Engineering
   (Organizers: John Fitzgerald, Peter Gorm Larsen, Tiziana Margaria, Jim Woodcock, Claudio Gomes)
6. SpecifyThis - Bridging gaps between program specification paradigms
   (Organizers: Wolfgang Ahrendt, Marieke Huisman, Mattias Ulbrich, Paula Herber)
7. Verification and Validation of Concurrent and Distributed Heterogeneous Systems
   (Organizers: Marieke Huisman, Cristina Seceleanu)
8. Formal Methods Meet Machine Learning
   (Organizers: Kim Larsen, Axel Legay, Bernhard Steffen, Marielle Stoelinga)
9. Formal methods for DIStributed COmputing in future RAILway systems
   (Organizers: Alessandro Fantechi, Stefania Gnesi, Anne Haxthausen)

10. Automated Verification of Embedded Control Software
    (Organizers: Dilian Gurov, Paula Herber, Ina Schaefer)
11. Digital Thread in Smart Manufacturing
    (Organizers: Tiziana Margaria, Dirk Pesch, Alan McGibney)

It also included the following the embedded or co-located events:

- Doctoral Symposium and Poster Session (Sven Jörges, Salim Saay, Steven Smyth)
- Industrial Day (Axel Hessenkämper, Falk Howar, Hardi Hungar, Andreas Rausch)
- DIME Days 2022 (Tiziana Margaria, Bernhard Steffen)

Altogether, the proceedings of ISoLA 2022 comprises contributions collected in four volumes:

- Part 1: Verification Principles
- Part 2: Software Engineering
- Part 3: Adaptation and Learning
- Part 4: Practice

We thank the track organizers, the members of the program committee, and their reviewers for their effort in selecting the papers to be presented, the local Organization Chair, Petros Stratis, and the EasyConferences team for their continuous precious support during the entire period preceding the events, and the Springer for being, as usual, a very reliable partner for the proceedings production. Finally, we are grateful to Christos Therapontos for his continuous support for the Web site and the program, and to Steve Bosselmann for his help with the editorial system EquinOCS.

Special thanks are due to the following organizations for their endorsement: EASST (European Association of Software Science and Technology) and Lero - The Irish Software Research Centre, along with our own institutions - TU Dortmund and the University of Limerick.

We wish you, as an ISoLA participant, lively scientific discussions at this edition, and also later, when reading the proceedings, valuable new insights that contribute to your research and its uptake.

October 2022   Bernhard Steffen
                                                             Tiziana Margaria

Organization

Program Committee Chairs

Margaria, Tiziana   University of Limerick and Lero, Ireland
Steffen, Bernhard   TU Dortmund University, Germany

Program Committee

Ahrendt, Wolfgang   Chalmers University of Technology, Sweden
Cleophas, Loek   Eindhoven University of Technology (TU/e),
                                         The Netherlands
De Nicola, Rocco   IMT School for Advanced Studies, Italy
Demeyer, Serge   Universiteit Antwerpen, Belgium
Fantechi, Alessandro   Università di Firenze, Italy
Fitzgerald, John   Newcastle University, UK
Gnesi, Stefania   ISTI-CNR, Italy
Gomes, Claudio   Aarhus University, Denmark
Gurov, Dilian   KTH Royal Institute of Technology, Sweden
Havelund, Klaus   Jet Propulsion Laboratory, USA
Haxthausen, Anne   Technical University of Denmark, Denmark
Herber, Paula   University of Münster, Germany
Hessenkämper, Axel   Schulz Systemtechnik GmbH, Germany
Howar, Falk   TU Dortmund University, Germany
Huisman, Marieke   University of Twente, The Netherlands
Hungar, Hardi   German Aerospace Center, Germany
Hähnle, Reiner   TU Darmstadt, Germany
Jähnichen, Stefan   TU Berlin, Germany
Jörges, Sven   FH Dortmund, Germany
Lamprecht, Anna-Lena   University of Potsdam, Germany
Larsen, Kim   Aalborg University, Denmark
Larsen, Peter Gorm   Aarhus University, Denmark
Legay, Axel   UCLouvain, Belgium
Leucker, Martin   University of Lübeck, Germany
Mantel, Heiko   TU Darmstadt, Germany
Margaria, Tiziana   University of Limerick and Lero, Ireland
McGibney, Alan   Munster Technological University, Ireland
Pesch, Dirk   University College Cork, Ireland
Rausch, Andreas   Clausthal University of Technology, Germany

Saay, Salim	University of Limerick, Ireland
Schaefer, Ina	Karlsruhe Institute of Technology, Germany
Seceleanu, Cristina	Mälardalen University, Sweden
Smyth, Steven	TU Dortmund University, Germany
Steffen, Bernhard	TU Dortmund University, Germany
Stoelinga, Marielle	University of Twente, The Netherlands
Ulbrich, Mattias	Karlsruhe Institute of Technology, Germany
Wirsing, Martin	LMU Munich, Germany
Woodcock, Jim	University of York, UK
ter Beek, Maurice	ISTI-CNR, Italy

Additional Reviewers

Abbas, Houssam
Adelt, Julius
Alberts, Elvin
Arbab, Farhad
Bainczyk, Alexander
Barbanera, Franco
Beckert, Bernhard
Berducci, Luigi
Beringer, Lennart
Bettini, Lorenzo
Bhattacharyya, Anirban
Blanchard, Allan
Boerger, Egon
Bogomolov, Sergiy
Bonakdarpour, Borzoo
Bortolussi, Luca
Bourr, Khalid
Brandstätter, Andreas
Breslin, John
Broy, Manfred
Bubel, Richard
Bures, Tomas
Busch, Daniel
Chaudhary, Hafiz Ahmad Awais
Chiti, Francesco
Ciancia, Vincenzo
Cok, David
Cordy, Maxime
Damiani, Ferruccio
De Donato, Lorenzo
Demrozi, Florenc

Di Stefano, Luca
Dierl, Simon
Dubslaff, Clemens
Duchêne, Fabien
Eldh, Sigrid
Ernst, Gidon
Feng, Hao
Flammini, Francesco
Freitas, Leo
Gabor, Thomas
Gerastathopoulos, Ilias
Groote, Jan Friso
Grosu, Radu
Grunske, Lars
Hallerstede, Stefan
Hansen, Simon Thrane
Hartmanns, Arnd
Hatcliff, John
Heydari Tabar, Asmae
Hnetynka, Petr
Inverso, Omar
Jakobs, Marie-Christine
John, Jobish
Johnsen, Einar Broch
Jongmans, Sung-Shik
Kamburjan, Eduard
Katsaros, Panagiotis
Kittelmann, Alexander
Knapp, Alexander
Kosmatov, Nikolai
Kretinsky, Jan

Kuruppuarachchi, Pasindu
Köhl, Maximilan
König, Christoph
Könighofer, Bettina
Lee, Edward
Lluch Lafuente, Alberto
Loreti, Michele
Madsen, Ole Lehrmann
Massink, Mieke
Mauritz, Malte
Mazzanti, Franco
Merz, Stephan
Micucci, Daniela
Monica, Stefania
Monti, Raul
Morichetta, Andrea
Nardone, Roberto
Naujokat, Stefan
Nayak, Satya Prakash
Neider, Daniel
Niehage, Mathis
Nolte, Gerrit
Ölvecky, Peter
Pace, Gordon
Perez, Guillermo
Petrov, Tatjana
Phan, Thomy
Piterman, Nir
Pugliese, Rosario
Reisig, Wolfgang
Remke, Anne
Riganelli, Oliviero
Ritz, Fabian

Rocha, Henrique
Runge, Tobias
Santen, Thomas
Scaletta, Marco
Schallau, Till
Schiffl, Jonas
Schlatte, Rudolf
Schlüter, Maximilian
Schneider, Gerardo
Schürmann, Jonas
Seisenberger, Monika
Smyth, Steven
Soudjani, Sadegh
Spellini, Stefano
Stankaitis, Paulius
Stewing, Richard
Stolz, Volker
Tapia Tarifa, Silvia Lizeth
Tegeler, Tim
Tiezzi, Francesco
Trubiani, Catia
Tschaikowski, Max
Tuosto, Emilio
Valiani, Serenella
Van Bladel, Brent
van de Pol, Jaco
Vandin, Andrea
Vittorini, Valeria
Weber, Alexandra
Weigl, Alexander
Wright, Thomas
Zambonelli, Franco

Contents – Part III

Rigorous Engineering of Collective Adaptive Systems

Rigorous Engineering of Collective Adaptive Systems Introduction
to the 4th Track Edition 3
   Martin Wirsing, Rocco De Nicola, and Stefan Jähnichen

Correct by Design Coordination of Autonomous Driving Systems 13
   Marius Bozga and Joseph Sifakis

Neural Predictive Monitoring for Collective Adaptive Systems 30
   Francesca Cairoli, Nicola Paoletti, and Luca Bortolussi

An Extension of HybridSynchAADL and Its Application to Collaborating
Autonomous UAVs 47
   Jaehun Lee, Kyungmin Bae, and Peter Csaba Ölveczky

Discrete Models of Continuous Behavior of Collective Adaptive Systems 65
   Peter Fettke and Wolfgang Reisig

Modelling Flocks of Birds from the Bottom Up 82
   Rocco De Nicola, Luca Di Stefano, Omar Inverso, and Serenella Valiani

Towards Drone Flocking Using Relative Distance Measurements 97
   Andreas Brandstätter, Scott A. Smolka, Scott D. Stoller, Ashish Tiwari,
   and Radu Grosu

Epistemic Ensembles 110
   Rolf Hennicker, Alexander Knapp, and Martin Wirsing

A Modal Approach to Consciousness of Agents 127
   Chen Yifeng and J. W. Sanders

An Experimental Toolchain for Strategy Synthesis with Spatial Properties 142
   Davide Basile, Maurice H. ter Beek, and Vincenzo Ciancia

Toward a Kinetic Framework to Model the Collective Dynamics
of Multi-agent Systems 165
   Stefania Monica, Federico Bergenti, and Franco Zambonelli

Understanding Social Feedback in Biological Collectives with Smoothed
Model Checking 181
  Julia Klein and Tatjana Petrov

Efficient Estimation of Agent Networks 199
  Alexander Leguizamon-Robayo and Max Tschaikowski

Attuning Adaptation Rules via a Rule-Specific Neural Network 215
  Tomáš Bureš, Petr Hnětynka, Martin Kruliš, František Plášil,
  Danylo Khalyeev, Sebastian Hahner, Stephan Seifermann,
  Maximilian Walter, and Robert Heinrich

Measuring Convergence Inertia: Online Learning in Self-adaptive Systems
with Context Shifts 231
  Elvin Alberts and Ilias Gerostathopoulos

Capturing Dependencies Within Machine Learning via a Formal Process
Model 249
  Fabian Ritz, Thomy Phan, Andreas Sedlmeier, Philipp Altmann,
  Jan Wieghardt, Reiner Schmid, Horst Sauer, Cornel Klein,
  Claudia Linnhoff-Popien, and Thomas Gabor

On Model-Based Performance Analysis of Collective Adaptive Systems 266
  Maurizio Murgia, Riccardo Pinciroli, Catia Trubiani, and Emilio Tuosto

Programming Multi-robot Systems with X-KLAIM 283
  Lorenzo Bettini, Khalid Bourr, Rosario Pugliese, and Francesco Tiezzi

Bringing Aggregate Programming Towards the Cloud 301
  Giorgio Audrito, Ferruccio Damiani, and Gianluca Torta

Ensemble-Based Modeling Abstractions for Modern Self-optimizing
Systems 318
  Michal Töpfer, Milad Abdullah, Tomas Bureš, Petr Hnětynka,
  and Martin Kruliš

Formal Analysis of Lending Pools in Decentralized Finance 335
  Massimo Bartoletti, James Chiang, Tommi Junttila,
  Alberto Lluch Lafuente, Massimiliano Mirelli, and Andrea Vandin

A Rewriting Framework for Interacting Cyber-Physical Agents 356
  Benjamin Lion, Farhad Arbab, and Carolyn Talcott

Model Checking Reconfigurable Interacting Systems 373
  Yehia Abd Alrahman, Shaun Azzopardi, and Nir Piterman

Formal Methods Meet Machine Learning

Formal Methods Meet Machine Learning (F3ML) 393
  Kim Larsen, Axel Legay, Gerrit Nolte, Maximilian Schlüter,
  Marielle Stoelinga, and Bernhard Steffen

The Modest State of Learning, Sampling, and Verifying Strategies 406
  Arnd Hartmanns and Michaela Klauck

Importance Splitting in Uppaal 433
  Kim Guldstrand Larsen, Axel Legay, Marius Mikučionis,
  and Danny Bøgsted Poulsen

Verification of Variability-Intensive Stochastic Systems with Statistical
Model Checking 448
  Sami Lazreg, Maxime Cordy, and Axel Legay

Author Index 473

Rigorous Engineering of Collective Adaptive Systems

Rigorous Engineering of Collective Adaptive Systems Introduction to the 4th Track Edition

Martin Wirsing[1]([✉]), Rocco De Nicola[2], and Stefan Jähnichen[3]

[1] Ludwig-Maximilians-Universität München, Munich, Germany
wirsing@lmu.de
[2] IMT School for Advanced Studies Lucca, Lucca, Italy
rocco.denicola@imtlucca.it
[3] TU Berlin and FZI Forschungszentrum Informatik Berlin, Berlin, Germany
stefan.jaehnichen@tu-berlin.de

Abstract. A collective adaptive system consists of collaborating entities that are able to adapt in real-time to dynamically changing and open environments and changing needs. Rigorous engineering requires appropriate methods and tools to help ensure that a collective adaptive system lives up to its intended purpose. This note provides an introduction to the 4th edition of the track "Rigorous Engineering of Collective Adaptive Systems" and briefly introduces the panel discussion and its 22 scientific contributions, structured into eight thematic sessions: Design and Validation of Autonomous Systems, Computing with Bio-inspired Communication, New System Models and Tools for Ensembles, Large Ensembles and Collective Dynamics, On the Borderline between Collective Stupidity and Collective Intelligence, Machine Learning for Collective Adaptive Systems, Programming and Analysing Ensembles, and Tools for Formal Analysis and Design.

Keywords: Adaptive system · Collective system · Ensemble · Software engineering · Formal method · Rigorous method · Machine learning

1 Collective Adaptive Systems

Modern IT systems are increasingly distributed and consist of collaborating entities that are able to adapt at runtime to dynamically changing, open-ended environments and to new requirements. Such systems are called Collective Adaptive Systems (CAS) or also ensembles [18,20]. Examples of CAS are cyber-physical systems, the internet of things, socio-technical systems as well as smart systems and robot swarms.

Rigorous engineering of CAS requires devising appropriate methods and tools to guarantee that such systems behave as expected. To achieve this goal, we need to develop theories for modelling and analysing collective adaptive systems, techniques for programming and running such systems, and specific methods for adaptation, validation and verification while ensuring security, trust and performance.

T. Margaria and B. Steffen (Eds.): ISoLA 2022, LNCS 13703, pp. 3–12, 2022.
https://doi.org/10.1007/978-3-031-19759-8_1

2   Track Overview

The track "Rigorous Engineering of Collective Adaptive Systems" is a follow-up of four other successful tracks [13,19,38,39] at ISOLA 2014 [26], ISOLA 2016 [27], ISOLA 2018 [28], and ISOLA 2020 [29], respectively. The first track [38] was entitled "Rigorous Engineering of Autonomic Ensembles" and was organised within the activities of the EU-funded research project ASCENS [40]. The latter three tracks [13,19,39] addressed the same theme as this year's edition and included research results from several research approaches and projects. Also, a Special Section of the International Journal on Software Tools for Technology Transfer was devoted to the rigorous engineering of collective adaptive systems [12].

The present edition of the track comprises 22 research papers; each of which has undergone a rigorous check by at least two reviewers. During the event, a panel "On the Borderline between Collective Stupidity and Collective Intelligence" took place to discuss the relationships between human and artificial intelligence. The papers were grouped according to seven thematic sessions, viz.: Design and Validation of Autonomous Systems, Computing with Bio-inspired Communication, New System Models and Tools for Ensembles, Large Ensembles and Collective Dynamics, Machine Learning for Collective Adaptive Systems, Programming and Analysing Ensembles, Tools for Formal Analysis and Design.

3   Track Contributions

In this section, the panel discussion and the papers are briefly introduced in the order of their presentations and grouped according to the thematic sessions.

3.1   Design and Validation of Autonomous Systems

Because of their temporal and spatial dynamism, automotive collective systems are among the most difficult systems to design and validate. The three papers in this session provide novel methods for designing, monitoring, and validating autonomous systems for cars, bikes, and drones.

In their paper "Correct by Design Coordination of Autonomous Driving Systems" [6], Marius Bozga and Joseph Sifakis propose a method for the *correct by design* coordination of autonomous automotive systems. Using assume-guarantee contracts they show that it is practically possible to determine speed control policies for vehicles that are *safe by design*.

Francesca Cairoli, Nicola Paoletti, and Luca Bortolussi do not consider cars but bikes in their paper "Neural Predictive Monitoring for Collective Adaptive Systems" [10]. They present a neural-network learning-based approach, called Neural Predictive Monitoring [5], to preemptively detect violations of requirements for bike-sharing systems, e.g. having bike stations left with no bikes.

Often automotive autonomous systems or more generally distributed cyber-physical systems are virtually synchronous, i.e. they logically behave as if they were synchronous in spite of network delays, and changing execution times. In the paper "An Extension of HybridSynchAADL and Its Application to Collaborating Autonomous UAVs" [22], Jaehun Lee, Kyungmin Bae, and Peter Csaba Ölveczky discuss how to analyze virtually synchronous systems using an extension of the modelling language HybridSynchAADL [21] with compound data types and user-defined functions and illustrate the method by considering a system of collaborating drones for packet delivery.

3.2 Computing with Bio-inspired Communication

This session focuses on bioinspired computing and presents new approaches for modelling colonies of ants, flocks of birds, and flocks of drones.

The paper "Discrete models of continuous behaviour of collective adaptive systems" [14] by Peter Fettke and Wolfgang Reisig considers artificial ant systems and presents a Petri net approach for modelling the behaviour of the artificial ants, and the causal dependencies between actions, while accounting for continuous movements in discrete models.

In the paper "Modelling Flocks of Birds from the Bottom Up" [11] Rocco De Nicola, Luca Di Stefano, Omar Inverso, and Serenella Valiani propose a novel compositional specification approach for modelling and reasoning about collectives in natural systems. As an example, they incrementally build a bottom-up model of a flock of birds and use a prototype simulator for validating the model in a controlled experiment, where a flock is attacked by a bird of prey and reacts by splitting into smaller groups to reunite when the threat is over.

Andreas Brandstätter and co-authors study flocks of drones and in the paper "Towards Drone Flocking using Relative Distance Measurements" [7] they introduce a method for forming and maintaining a drone flock by considering only relative distance measurements. The proposed approach is fully distributed and can work even in GPS-denied environments.

3.3 New System Models and Tools for Ensembles

The papers of this session use modal and spatial logic-based methods to specify ensembles of knowledge-based agents, in order to formalise the consciousness of agents and synthesise strategies.

In the paper "Epistemic Ensembles" [15] Rolf Hennicker, Alexander Knapp, and Martin Wirsing study ensembles of knowledge-based agents that, unlike the agents considered in their previous work on ensembles [16,17], do not use messages to communicate. In this case, information exchange is achieved implicitly through the modification of the knowledge of the agents. Ensemble behaviour is specified in a dynamic logic with compound ensemble actions while specifications are implemented by epistemic processes.

The paper "A modal approach to consciousness of agents" [41] by Chen Yifeng and J. W. Sanders proposes a novel fundamental approach to the notions of awareness and consciousness of agents. Awareness is modelled as a modal operator which satisfies a well-chosen set of basic laws and inequalities. Consciousness is formalised as an iterated form of awareness, more specifically as awareness of awareness.

Maurice ter Beek, Davide Basile, and Vincenzo Ciancia in the paper "An Experimental Toolchain for Strategy Synthesis with Spatial Properties" [34] study the application of strategy synthesis to enforce spatial properties and present the integration of two tools, (i) Contract Automata Library that supports the composition and synthesis of strategies of games modeled in a dialect of finite-state automata, (ii) Voxel-based Logical Analyser, a spatial model checker that supports the verification of properties of (pixels of) digital images. The approach is illustrated through a basic example of the synthesis of strategies on automata that encode the motion of agents in spaces represented by images.

3.4 Large Ensembles and Collective Dynamics

This section considers the issues connected to the huge number of individuals that a CAS might have.

In the paper "Towards a Kinetic Framework to Model the Collective Dynamics of Large Agent Systems" [30], Stefania Monica, Federico Bergenti, and Franco Zambonelli instantiate the approach based on the kinetic theory of active particles [4] to model and analyse large and decentralized multi-agent systems and use it study cumulative properties of such systems by using statistical techniques that focus on the long-time asymptotic behaviour. As a case study, they show how to derive two asymptotic properties of the symmetric gossip algorithm for multi-agent systems and validate them on a multi-agent implementation of the symmetric gossip algorithm.

Julia Klein and Tatjana Petrov, in the paper "Understanding Social Feedback in Biological Collectives with Smoothed Model Checking" [36], consider biological groups and show that by experimentally observing the collective response of a chosen small set of groups it is possible: (i) to predict the collective response for any given group size and (ii) to infer the desirable group behaviours fitness function which the group robustly performs under different perturbations. They use Smoothed Model Checking, an approach based on Gaussian Process Classification, and specify the fitness function as a template temporal logic formula with unknown parameters. The framework is validated over a case study of a collective stinging defence mechanism in honeybee colonies.

Max Tschaikowski has recently proposed to obtain reliable estimates on global dynamics of agent networks from local agent behavior by replacing dependencies among agents with exogenous parameters, in order to estimate the global dynamics via agent decoupling [37]. The paper "Efficient Estimation of Agent Networks" [23], by Alexander Leguizamon-Robayo and Max Tschaikowski, introduces the notion of estimation equivalence, a model reduction technique for systems of nonlinear differential equations that allows the aforementioned decoupled model to be replaced with a smaller and easier to analyze one. The approach is validated on a multi-class epidemiological SIRS model and is shown to result in a speed-up factor proportional to the number of population classes.

3.5   Panel: On the Borderline Between Collective Stupidity and Collective Intelligence

When observing swarms we might see two different kind of behaviours:

1. the behaviour of individuals appears to be very determined and, above all, the same for all of them. All components follow the same pattern and the behaviour of the swarm as a whole is also very determined. The reaction of the swarm to unknown signals or situations is hardly predictable and rather random and often leads to chaos or even destruction. An example could be the behaviour of lemmings, which for reasons unknown at least to us, join the swarm behaviour and plunge into the sea. We would want to call that *collective stupidity*, although the word stupidity is perhaps not appropriate for a natural behaviour.
2. the behaviour of individual objects is not determined - i.e. each or everyone can do what he or she does "best" - we would call *collective intelligence* if, in the process of achieving a given goal, the feature and the behavior of each individual member of the swarm contribute to the achievement of the goal with its specific characteristics or abilities.

During the panel, Stefan Jähnichen as moderator and the panelists Tomáš Bureš, Thomas Gabor, Joseph Sifakis, Tatjana Petrov, and Franco Zambonelli vividly discussed questions such as "Do we need collective intelligent systems?", "How can we avoid "stupid" swarm behaviour?" or "Can we build systems fostering the collective intelligence of humans?"

3.6   Machine Learning for Collective Adaptive Systems

This session, consisting of four papers, one of which, for organizational reasons, was presented in the panel session. The paper in the session addresses the issues connected to sub-symbolic artificial intelligence in two complementary ways: using machine learning techniques for supporting collective adaptation and using software development process models for building machine learning systems.

In the paper Ensemble-based modeling abstractions for modern self-optimizing systems" [36], Michal Töpfer and co-authors argue that incorporating machine-learning and optimization heuristics is a key feature of modern smart systems which are to learn over time and optimize their behavior at runtime to deal with uncertainty in their environment. They introduce an extension of their ensemble-based component model DEECo [9] that enables them to use machine-learning and optimization heuristics for managing autonomic component ensembles. An example of how such a model can be beneficially used for modeling access control related problems in the Industry 4.0 settings is provided.

The paper "Attuning Adaptation Rules via a Rule-Specific Neural Network" [8] by Tomáš Bureš and co-authors discusses the use of neural networks in self-adaptive systems. In order to avoid losing some key domain knowledge and improve the learning process, a rule-specific neural network method is introduced that makes it possible to transform the guard of an adaptation rule into a rule for the neural network. The key feature is that rule-specific neural networks are composable and their architecture is driven by the structure of the logical predicates in the adaption rule in question.

To deal with unknowns often online learning is used, but the complexity of online learning increases in the presence of context shifts. In the paper "Measuring Convergence Inertia: Online Learning in Self-Adaptive Systems with Context Shifts" [1], Elvin Alberts and Ilias Gerostathopoulos propose a new metric to assess the robustness of reinforcement learning policies against context shifts and use it to assess the robustness of different policies within a specific class of reinforcement learning policies (multi-armed bandits - MAB) to context shifts. Through an experiment with a self-adaptation exemplar of a web server, they show that their approach is a viable way to inform the selection of online learning policies for self-adaptive systems.

The paper "Capturing Dependencies within Machine Learning via a Formal Process Model" [33] by Fabian Ritz and co-authors defines a comprehensive software development process model for machine learning that encompasses, in a consistent way, most tasks and artifacts described in the literature. In addition to the production of the necessary artifacts, they also consider the generation and validation of fitting descriptions in the form of specifications. They also advocate designing interaction points between standard software development processes and machine learning models throughout their entire life-cycle after initial training and testing.

3.7 Programming and Analysing Ensembles

In this session, new methods are presented for efficiently running collective adaptive systems and for analysing their quality.

The paper "On Model-based Performance Analysis of Collective Adaptive Systems" [31] by Maurizio Murgia, Riccardo Pinciroli, Catia Trubiani, and Emilio Tuosto is concerned with the analysis of performance properties of CAS. Two recently proposed approaches are considered: one is based on generalised stochastic Petri nets derived from the system specification, while the other is based on queueing networks derived from suitable behavioural abstractions. The relative merits of the two approaches are assessed also by considering a case study based on a scenario involving autonomous robots.

The paper "Programming Multi-Robot Systems with X-KLAIM" [35] by Francesco Tiezzi, Khalid Bourr, Lorenzo Bettini, and Rosario Pugliese also considers software development for robotics applications. It proposes an approach for programming Multi-Robot Systems at a high abstraction level using the programming language X-KLAIM. The computation and communication model of X-KLAIM, based on multiple distributed tuple spaces, allows programs to be coordinated by the same abstractions and mechanisms for both intra- and inter-robot interactions. The feasibility and effectiveness of the proposal are demonstrated in a realistic Multi-Robot Systems scenario.

In the paper "Bringing Aggregate Programming towards the Cloud" [2], Giorgio Audrito, Ferruccio Damiani, Gianluca Torta address the problem of running an Aggregate Programming application on a high-performance, centralized computer such as those available in a cloud environment, in order to manipulate large centralised graph-based data structures across multiple machines, dynamically joining and leaving the computation and have adaptive CAS whose computations dynamically move across the IoT/edge/fog/cloud continuum, according to availability of resources and infrastructures.

3.8 Tools for Formal Analysis and Design

This section deals with tools and examples of formal design and verification of different kind of collective systems. One considers financial systems, the other deals with cyber-physical systems, while the third one considers agents with opportunistic behaviour.

Bartoletti and his co-authors, in the article "Formal Analysis of Lending Pools in Decentralized Finance" [3] consider decentralized finance applications implemented on blockchain and advocate their formalization and verification. The main contribution is a tool for the formal analysis of lending pools, one of the most popular decentralized finance applications. The tool supports several analyses, including reachability analysis, LTL model checking, and statistical model checking. In the paper, the tool is used to search for threshold and reward parameters that minimize the risk of unrecoverable loans.

In [24] Benjamin Lion, Farhad Arbab, and Carolyn Talcott proposed a compositional approach for modelling distributed cyber-physical systems. There, cyber and physical aspects of a system are described as streams of discrete observations. In the paper in this volume, titled "A Rewriting Framework for Cyber-Physical Systems" [25], the same authors present a rewriting logic implementation of this modelling approach and illustrate it through a case study in which robots move in a common area.

The paper "Model Checking Reconfigurable Interacting Systems" [32] by Nir Piterman, Yehia Abd Alrahman and Shaun Azzopardi deals with reconfigurable multi-agent systems, namely autonomous agents, with integrated interaction capabilities that feature opportunistic interaction. The authors propose a model checker, named R-CHECK, to reason about these systems at both the individual and system levels. The tool supports a high-level input language and allows reasoning about interaction protocols and joint missions, considering reconfiguration, coalition formation and self-organization.

Acknowledgements. As organisers of the track, we would like to thank all authors and panelists for their valuable contributions, all reviewers for their careful evaluations and constructive comments, and all participants of the track for lively discussions. We are also grateful to the ISOLA chairs Tiziana Margaria and Bernhard Steffen for giving us the opportunity to organise this track and to them and Springer–Verlag for providing us with the very helpful Equinocs conference system.

References

1. Alberts, E., Gerostathopoulos, I.: Measuring convergence inertia: online learning in self-adaptive systems with context shifts. In: Margaria, T., Steffen, B. (eds.) ISoLA 2022, LNCS 13703, pp. 231–248. Springer, Heidelberg (2022)
2. Audrito, G., Damiani, F., Torta, G.: Bringing aggregate programming towards the cloud. In: Margaria, T., Steffen, B. (eds.) ISoLA 2022, LNCS 13703, pp. 301–317. Springer, Heidelberg (2022)
3. Bartoletti, M., Chiang, J., Junttila, T., Lafuente, A.L., Mirelli, M., Vandin, A.: Formal analysis of lending pools in decentralized finance. In: Margaria, T., Steffen, B. (eds.) ISoLA 2022, LNCS 13703, pp. 335–355. Springer, Heidelberg (2022)
4. Bellomo, N., et al.: What is life? a perspective of the mathematical kinetic theory of active particles. Math. Models Methods Appl. Sci. 31(9), 1821–1866 (2021)
5. Bortolussi, L., Cairoli, F., Paoletti, N., Smolka, S.A., Stoller, S.D.: Neural predictive monitoring and a comparison of frequentist and Bayesian approaches. Int. J. Softw. Tools Technol. Transfer 23(4), 615–640 (2021). https://doi.org/10.1007/s10009-021-00623-1
6. Bozga, M., Sifakis, J.: Correct by design coordination of autonomous driving systems. In: Margaria, T., Steffen, B. (eds.) ISoLA 2022, LNCS 13703, pp. 13–29. Springer, Heidelberg (2022)
7. Brandstätter, A., Smolka, S.A., Stoller, S.D., Tiwari, A., Grosu, R.: Towards drone flocking using relative distance measurements. In: Margaria, T., Steffen, B. (eds.) ISoLA 2022, LNCS 13703, pp. 97–109. Springer, Heidelberg (2022)
8. Bureš, T., et al.: Attuning adaptation rules via a rule-specific neural network. In: Margaria, T., Steffen, B. (eds.) ISoLA 2022, LNCS 13703, pp. 215–230. Springer, Heidelberg (2022)
9. Bures, T., Gerostathopoulos, I., Hnětynka, P., Keznikl, J., Kit, M., Plášil, F.: DEECO: an ensemble-based component system. In: Kruchten, P., Giannakopoulou, D., Tivoli, M. (eds.) CBSE 2013, Proceedings of the 16th ACM SIGSOFT Symposium on Component Based Software Engineering, part of Comparch 2013, Vancouver, BC, Canada, 17–21 June 2013, pp. 81–90. ACM (2013)
10. Cairoli, F., Paoletti, N., Bortolussi, L.: Neural predictive monitoring for collective adaptive systems. In: Margaria, T., Steffen, B. (eds.) ISoLA 2022, LNCS 13703, pp. 30–46. Springer, Heidelberg (2022)
11. De Nicola, R., Di Stefano, L., Inverso, O., Valiani, S.: Modelling flocks of birds from the bottom u. In: Margaria, T., Steffen, B. (eds.) ISoLA 2022, LNCS 13703, pp. 82–96. Springer, Heidelberg (2022)
12. De Nicola, R., Jähnichen, S., Wirsing, M.: Rigorous engineering of collective adaptive systems: special section. Int. J. Softw. Tools Technol. Transfer 22(4), 389–397 (2020). https://doi.org/10.1007/s10009-020-00565-0
13. De Nicola, R., Jähnichen, S., Wirsing, M.: Rigorous engineering of collective adaptive systems - introduction to the 2nd track edition. In: [28], pp. 3–12 (2018)
14. Fettke, P., Reisig, W.: Discrete models of continuous behavior of collective adaptive systems. In: Margaria, T., Steffen, B. (eds.) ISoLA 2022, LNCS 13703, pp. 65–81. Springer, Heidelberg (2022)

15. Hennicker, R., Knapp, A., Wirsing, M.: Epistemic ensembles. In: Margaria, T., Steffen, B. (eds.) ISoLA 2022, LNCS 13703, pp. 110–126. Springer, Heidelberg (2022)
16. Hennicker, R., Wirsing, M.: Dynamic logic for ensembles. In: [28], pp. 32–47 (2018)
17. Hennicker, R., Wirsing, M.: A dynamic logic for systems with predicate-based communication. In: [29], pp. 224–242 (2020)
18. Hölzl, M., Rauschmayer, A., Wirsing, M.: Engineering of software-intensive systems: state of the art and research challenges. In: Wirsing, M., Banâtre, J.-P., Hölzl, M., Rauschmayer, A. (eds.) Software-Intensive Systems and New Computing Paradigms. LNCS, vol. 5380, pp. 1–44. Springer, Heidelberg (2008). https://doi.org/10.1007/978-3-540-89437-7_1
19. Jähnichen, S., Wirsing, M.: Rigorous engineering of collective adaptive systems - track introduction. In: [27], pp. 535–538 (2016)
20. Kernbach, S., Schmickl, T., Timmis, J.: Collective adaptive systems: challenges beyond evolvability. CoRR abs/1108.5643 (2011)
21. Lee, J., Kim, S., Bae, K., Ölveczky, P.C.: HYBRID SYNCHAADL: modeling and formal analysis of virtually synchronous CPSs in AADL. In: Silva, A., Leino, K.R.M. (eds.) CAV 2021. LNCS, vol. 12759, pp. 491–504. Springer, Cham (2021). https://doi.org/10.1007/978-3-030-81685-8_23
22. Lee, J., Kim, S., Bae, K., Ölveczky, P.C.: An extension of HybridSynchAADL and its application to collaborating autonomous UAVs. In: Margaria, T., Steffen, B. (eds.) ISoLA 2022, LNCS 13703, pp. 47–64. Springer, Heidelberg (2022)
23. Leguizamon-Robayo, A., Tschaikowski, M.: Efficient estimation of agent networks. In: Margaria, T., Steffen, B. (eds.) ISoLA 2022, LNCS 13703, pp. 199–214. Springer, Heidelberg (2022)
24. Lion, B., Arbab, F., Talcott, C.L.: A semantic model for interacting cyber-physical systems. In: Lange, J., Mavridou, A., Safina, L., Scalas, A. (eds.), Proceedings of 14th Interaction and Concurrency Experience, ICE 2021, vol. 347 of EPTCS, pp. 77–95 (2021)
25. Lion, B., Arbab, F., Talcott, C.L.: A rewriting framework for cyber-physical systems. In: Margaria, T., Steffen, B. (eds.) ISoLA 2022, LNCS 13703, pp. 356–372. Springer, Heidelberg (2022)
26. Margaria, T., Steffen, B. (eds.): ISoLA 2014, Part I. LNCS, vol. 8802. Springer, Heidelberg (2014). https://doi.org/10.1007/978-3-662-45234-9
27. Margaria, T., Steffen, B.: Erratum to: leveraging applications of formal methods, verification and validation. In: Margaria, T., Steffen, B. (eds.) ISoLA 2016, Part I. LNCS, vol. 9952, pp. E1–E1. Springer, Cham (2016). https://doi.org/10.1007/978-3-319-47166-2_67
28. Margaria, T., Steffen, B. (eds.): ISoLA 2018, Part III. LNCS, vol. 11246. Springer, Cham (2018). https://doi.org/10.1007/978-3-030-03424-5
29. Margaria, T., Steffen, B. (eds.): ISoLA 2020, Part II. LNCS, vol. 12477. Springer, Cham (2020). https://doi.org/10.1007/978-3-030-61470-6
30. Monica, S., Bergenti, F., Zambonelli, F.: Towards a kinetic framework to model the collective dynamics of large agent systems. In: Margaria, T., Steffen, B. (eds.) ISoLA 2022, LNCS 13703, pp. 165–180. Springer, Heidelberg (2022)
31. Murgia, M., Pinciroli, R., Trubiani, C., Tuosto, E.: On model-based performance analysis of collective adaptive systems. In: Margaria, T., Steffen, B. (eds.) ISoLA 2022, LNCS 13703, pp. 266–282. Springer, Heidelberg (2022)
32. Piterman, N., Abd Alrahman, Y., Azzopardi, S.: Model checking reconfigurable interacting systems. In: Margaria, T., Steffen, B. (eds.) ISoLA 2022, LNCS 13703, pp. 373–389. Springer, Heidelberg (2022)

33. Ritz, F., et al.: Capturing dependencies within machine learning via a formal process model. In: Margaria, T., Steffen, B. (eds.) ISoLA 2022, LNCS 13703, pp. 249–265. Springer, Heidelberg (2022)

34. ter Beek, M., Basile, D., Ciancia, V.: An experimental toolchain for strategy synthesis with spatial properties. In: Margaria, T., Steffen, B. (eds.) ISoLA 2022, LNCS 13703, pp. 142–164. Springer, Heidelberg (2022)

35. Tiezzi, F., Bourr, K., Bettini, L., Pugliese, R.: Programming multi-robot systems with X-KLAIM. In: Margaria, T., Steffen, B. (eds.) ISoLA 2022, LNCS 13703, pp. 283–300. Springer, Heidelberg (2022)

36. Töpfer, M., Abdullah, M., Bureš, T., Hnětynka, P., Kruliš, M.: Ensemble-based modeling abstractions for modern self-optimizing systems. In: Margaria, T., Steffen, B. (eds.) ISoLA 2022, LNCS 13703, pp. 318–334. Springer, Heidelberg (2022)

37. Tschaikowski, M.: Over-approximation of fluid models. IEEE Trans. Autom. Control. **65**(3), 999–1013 (2020)

38. Wirsing, M., De Nicola, R., Hölzl, M.M.: Rigorous engineering of autonomic ensembles - track introduction. In: [26], pp. 96–98 (2014)

39. Wirsing, M., De Nicola, R., Jähnichen, S.: Rigorous engineering of collective adaptive systems - introduction to the 3rd track edition. In: [29], pp. 161–170 (2020)

40. Wirsing, M., Hölzl, M., Koch, N., Mayer, P. (eds.): Software Engineering for Collective Autonomic Systems. LNCS, vol. 8998. Springer, Cham (2015). https://doi.org/10.1007/978-3-319-16310-9

41. Yifeng, C., Sanders, J.W.: A modal approach to consciousness of agents. In: Margaria, T., Steffen, B. (eds.) ISoLA 2022, LNCS 13703, pp. 127–141. Springer, Heidelberg (2022)

Correct by Design Coordination of Autonomous Driving Systems

Marius Bozga$^{(\boxtimes)}$ and Joseph Sifakis

Univ. Grenoble Alpes, CNRS, Grenoble INP (Institute of Engineering Univ. Grenoble Alpes), VERIMAG, 38000 Grenoble, France
{Marius.Bozga,Joseph.Sifakis}@univ-grenoble-alpes.fr
http://www-verimag.imag.fr/

Abstract. The paper proposes a method for the correct by design coordination of autonomous driving systems (*ADS*). It builds on previous results on collision avoidance policies and the modeling of *ADS* by combining descriptions of their static environment in the form of maps, and the dynamic behavior of their vehicles.

An *ADS* is modeled as a dynamic system involving a set of vehicles coordinated by a *Runtime* that based on vehicle positions on a map and their kinetic attributes, computes free spaces for each vehicle. Vehicles are bounded to move within the corresponding allocated free spaces. We provide a correct by design safe control policy for an *ADS* if its vehicles and the *Runtime* respect corresponding assume-guarantee contracts. The result is established by showing that the composition of assume-guarantee contracts is an inductive invariant that entails *ADS* safety.

We show that it is practically possible to define speed control policies for vehicles that comply with their contracts. Furthermore, we show that traffic rules can be specified in a linear-time temporal logic, as a class of formulas that constrain vehicle speeds. The main result is that, given a set of traffic rules, it is possible to derive free space policies of the *Runtime* such that the resulting system behavior is safe by design with respect to the rules.

Keywords: Autonomous driving systems · Traffic rule specification · Map specification · Collision avoidance policy · Assume-guarantee contract · Correctness by design

1 Introduction

Autonomous driving systems (*ADS*) are probably the most difficult systems to design and validate, because the behavior of their agents is subject to temporal and spatial dynamism. They are real-time distributed systems involving components with partial knowledge of their environment, pursuing specific goals while the collective behavior must meet given global goals.

© The Author(s), under exclusive license to Springer Nature Switzerland AG 2022
T. Margaria and B. Steffen (Eds.): ISoLA 2022, LNCS 13703, pp. 13–29, 2022.
https://doi.org/10.1007/978-3-031-19759-8_2

Development of trustworthy *ADS* is an urgent and critical need. It poses challenges that go well beyond the current state of the art due to their overwhelming complexity. These challenges include, on the one hand, modeling the system and specifying its properties, usually expressed as traffic rules; on the other hand, building the system and verifying its correctness with respect to the desired system properties.

Modeling involves a variety of issues related to the inherent temporal and spatial dynamics as well as to the need for an accurate representation of the physical environment in which vehicles operate. Many studies focus on formalizing and standardizing a concept of map that is central to semantic awareness and decision-making. These studies often use ontologies and logics with associated reasoning mechanisms to check the consistency of descriptions and their accuracy with respect to desired properties [2,3]. Other works propose open source mapping frameworks for highly automated driving [1,16]. Finally, the SOCA method [7] proposes an abstraction of maps called zone graph, and uses this abstraction in a morphological behavior analysis.

There is an extensive literature on *ADS* validation that involves two interrelated problems: the specification of system properties and the application of validation techniques. The specification of properties requires first-order temporal logics because parameterization and genericity are essential for the description of situations involving a varying number of vehicles and types of traffic patterns. The work in [17,19] formalizes a set of traffic rules for highway scenarios in Isabelle/HOL. It shows that traffic rules can be used as requirements to be met by autonomous vehicles and proposes a verification procedure. A formalization of traffic rules for uncontrolled intersections is provided in [12], which shows how the rules can be used by a simulator to safely control traffic at intersections. The work in [10] proposes a methodology for formalizing traffic rules in linear temporal logic; it shows how the evaluation of formalized rules on recorded human behaviors provides insight into how well drivers follow the rules.

Many works deal with the formal verification of controllers that perform specific maneuvers. For example, in [11], a dedicated multi-way spatial logic inspired by interval temporal logic is used to specify safety and provide proofs for lane change controllers. The work in [18] presents a formally verified motion planner in Isabelle/HOL. The planner uses maneuver automata, a variant of hybrid automata, and linear temporal logic to express properties. In [10], runtime verification is applied to check that the maneuvers of a high-level planner conform to traffic rules expressed in linear temporal logic.

Of particular interest for this work are correct by construction techniques where system construction is guided by a set of properties that the system is guaranteed to satisfy. They involve either the application of monolithic synthesis techniques or compositional reasoning throughout a component-based system design process. There is considerable work on controller synthesis from a set of system properties usually expressed in linear temporal logic, see for example [13,21,26–28]. These are algorithmic techniques extensively studied in the field of control. They consist of restricting the controllable behavior of a system interacting with its environment so that a set of properties are satisfied. Nonetheless, their application is limited due to their high computational cost, which depends in particular on the type of properties and the complexity of the system behavior.

An alternative to synthesis is to achieve correctness by design as a result of composing the properties of the system components. Component properties are usually "assume-guarantee" contracts characterizing a causal relationship between a component and its environment: if the environment satisfies the "assume" part of the contract, the state of the component will satisfy the "guarantee" part, e.g. [4, 8, 15]. The use of contracts in system design involves a decomposition of overall system requirements into contracts that provide a basis for more efficient analysis and validation. In addition, contract-based design is advocated as a method for achieving correctness by design, provided that satisfactory implementations of the system can be found [23]. There are a number of theoretical frameworks that apply mainly to continuous or synchronous systems, especially for analysis and verification purposes [14, 20, 22]. They suffer computational limitations because, in the general case, they involve the symbolic solution of fixed-point equations, which restricts the expressiveness of the contracts [14]. Furthermore, they are only applicable to systems with a static architecture, which excludes dynamic reconfigurable systems, such as autonomous systems.

The paper builds on previous results [5] on a logical framework for parametric specification of ADS combining models of the system's static environment in the form of maps, and the dynamic properties of its vehicles. Maps are metric graphs whose vertices represent locations and edges are labeled with segments that can represent roads at different levels of abstraction, with characteristics such as length or geometric features characterizing their shape and size.

An ADS model is a dynamic system consisting of a map and a set of vehicles moving along specific routes. Its state can be conceived as the distribution of vehicles on a map with their positions, speeds and other kinematic attributes. For its movement, each vehicle has a safe estimate of the free space in its neighborhood, according to predefined visibility rules. We assume that vehicle coordination is performed by a *Runtime* that, for given vehicle positions and speeds on the map, can compute the free spaces on each vehicle's itinerary in which it can safely move.

We study a safe control policy for ADS, which is correct by design. It results from the combination of two types of assume-guarantee contracts: one contract for each vehicle and another contract for the *Runtime* taking into account the positions of the vehicles on the map. The contract for a vehicle states that, assuming that initially the dynamics of the vehicle allow it to stay in the allocated free space, it will stay in this free space. Note that the details of the contract implementation are irrelevant; only the I/O relationship between free space and vehicle speed matters. The *Runtime* contract asserts that if the free spaces allocated to vehicles are disjoint, then they can be allocated new disjoint free spaces provided they have fulfilled their contract.

We build on this general result by specializing its application in two directions. First, we show that it is possible to define speed policies for vehicles that satisfy their assume-guarantee contract. Second, we show that it is possible to define free space policies for the *Runtime* enforcing safety constraints of a given set of traffic rules. We formalize traffic rules as a class of properties of a linear temporal logic. We provide a method that derives from a given set of traffic rules, constraints on the free spaces chosen by the *Runtime* such that the resulting system behavior is safe with respect to these rules. This is the main result of the paper establishing correctness by design of general *ADS*, provided that their components comply with their respective contracts.

The paper is structured as follows. In Sect. 2, we establish the general framework by introducing the basic models and concepts for the representation of maps. In Sect. 3, we introduce the dynamic model of *ADS* involving a set of vehicles and a *Runtime* for their coordination. We show how a correct by design safe control policy is obtained by combining assume-guarantee contracts for the vehicles and the *Runtime*. In Sect. 4, we study the principle of speed policies respecting the vehicle contract and show its application through an example. In Sect. 5, we formalize traffic rules as a class of formulas of a linear temporal logic and show how it is possible to generate from a set of traffic rules free space policies such that the system is safe by design. Section 6 concludes with a discussion of the significance of the results, future developments and applications. The proofs of technical results are available in the long version of the paper [6].

2 Map Representation

Following the idea presented in [5], we build contiguous road segments from a set $\mathcal{S}$ equipped with a partial concatenation operator $\cdot : \mathcal{S} \times \mathcal{S} \to \mathcal{S} \cup \{\bot\}$, a length norm $\|.\| : \mathcal{S} \to \mathbb{R}_{\geq 0}$ and a partial subsegment extraction operator $.[.,.] : \mathcal{S} \times \mathbb{R}_{\geq 0} \times \mathbb{R}_{\geq 0} \to \mathcal{S} \cup \{\bot\}$. Thus, given a segment s, $\|s\|$ represents its length and $s[a,b]$ for $0 \leq a < b \leq \|s\|$, represents the sub-segment starting at length a from its origin and ending at length b. Segments can be used to represent roads at different levels of abstraction, from intervals to regions. In this paper, we consider $\mathcal{S}$ as the set of curves obtained by concatenation of line segments and circle arcs, for representing roads of a map as depicted in Fig. 1.

We use metric graphs $G \stackrel{def}{=} (V, \mathcal{S}, E)$ to represent maps, where V is a finite set of *vertices*, $\mathcal{S}$ is a set of segments and $E \subseteq V \times \mathcal{S}^{\star} \times V$ is a finite set of *edges* labeled by *non-zero length* segments (denoted $\mathcal{S}^{\star}$). For an edge $e = (v, s, v') \in E$ we denote $^{\bullet}e \stackrel{def}{=} v$, $e^{\bullet} \stackrel{def}{=} v'$, $e.s \stackrel{def}{=} s$. For a vertex v, we define $^{\bullet}v \stackrel{def}{=} \{e \mid e^{\bullet} = v\}$ and $v^{\bullet} \stackrel{def}{=} \{e \mid {}^{\bullet}e = v\}$. We call a metric graph *connected* (resp. *weakly connected*) if a path (resp. an undirected path) exists between any pair of vertices.

We consider the set $Pos_G \stackrel{def}{=} V \cup \{(e, a) \mid e \in E, 0 \leq a \leq \|e.s\|\}$ of *positions* defined by a metric graph. Note that positions $(e, 0)$ and $(e, \|e.s\|)$ are considered equal respectively to positions $^{\bullet}e$ and $e^{\bullet}$. We denote by $p \xrightarrow{s}_G p'$ the existence of an s-labelled *edge ride* between succeeding positions $p = (e, a)$ and $p' = (e, a')$ in the same edge e whenever $0 \leq a < a' \leq \|e.s\|$ and $s = e.s[a, a']$. Moreover, we denote by $p \overset{s}{\leadsto}_G p'$ the existence of an s-labelled *ride* between arbitrary positions

p, p', that is, $\leadsto_G \stackrel{def}{=} (\rightarrow_G)^+$ the transitive closure of edge rides. Finally, we define the distance d_G from position p to position p' as 0 whenever $p = p'$ or the minimum length among all segments labeling rides from p to p' and otherwise $+\infty$ if no such ride exists. Whenever G is fixed in the context, we will omit the subscript G for positions Pos_G, distance d_G, and rides $\rightarrow_G$ or $\leadsto_G$.

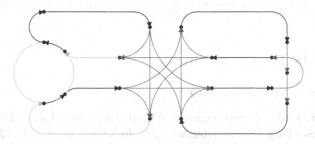

Fig. 1. A map with junctions (blue edges) and a merger vertices (red edges) (Color figure online)

A connected metric graph $G = (V, \mathcal{S}, E)$ can be interpreted as a map, structured into roads and junctions, subject to additional assumptions:

- we restrict to metric graphs which are 2D-consistent [5], meaning intuitively they can be drawn in the 2D-plane such that the geometric properties of the segments are compatible with the topological properties of the graph. In particular, if two distinct paths starting from the same vertex v, meet at another vertex v', the coordinates of v' calculated from each path are identical. For the sake of simplicity, we further restrict to graphs where distinct vertices are located at distinct points in the plane, and moreover, where no edge is self-crossing (meaning actually that distinct positions (e, a) of the same edge e are located at distinct points).
- the map is equipped with a symmetric *junction* relationship $\times$ on edges E which abstracts the geometric crossing (or the proximity) between edges at positions other than the edge end points. This relationship is used to define the *junctions* of the map, that is, as any non-trivial equivalence class in the transitive closure of $\times$. Actually, junctions need additional signalisation to regulate the traffic on their edges (e.g., traffic lights, stop signs, etc.). In addition, we assume a partial ordering $\prec_j$ on the set of vertices to reflect their static priorities as junction entries.
- to resolve conflicts at merger vertices, i.e., vertices with two or more incident segments which do not belong to a junction, we assume that the map is equipped with a static priority relationship. Specifically, for a vertex v, there is a total priority order $\prec_v$ on the set of edges $\overset{\bullet}{v}$. This order reflects an abstraction of the static priority rules associated with each of the merging edges (e.g., right-of-way, yield-priority, etc.).
- every edge e is associated with a maximal speed limit $e.v \in \mathbb{R}_{\geq 0}$.

In the remainder of the paper, we consider a fixed metric graph $G = (V, \mathcal{S}, E)$ altogether with the junction relationship $\times$, static priorities $\prec_v$ and edge speed limits as discussed above. Also, we extend the junction and priority relationships from edges to their associated positions, that is, consider $(e_1, a_1) \sim (e_2, a_2) \overset{def}{=} e_1 \sim e_2$ for any relation $\sim \in \{\times, (\prec_v)_{v \in V}\}$. Finally, we denote by $r_1 \uplus r_2$ the property that rides r_1, r_2 in G are *non-crossing*, that is, their sets of positions are disjoint and moreover not belonging to the same junction(s), except for endpoints.

3   The *ADS* Dynamic Model

3.1   General *ADS* Architecture

Given a metric graph G representing a map, the state of an *ADS* is a tuple $\langle st_o \rangle_{o \in \mathcal{O}}$ representing the distribution of a finite set of objects $\mathcal{O}$ with their relevant dynamic attributes on the map G. The set of objects $\mathcal{O}$ includes a set of vehicles $\mathcal{C}$ and fixed equipment such as lights, road signs, gates, etc. For a vehicle c, its state $st_c \overset{def}{=} \langle c.p, c.\delta, c.v, c.wt, c.it \ldots \rangle$ includes respectively its *position* on the map (from *Pos*), its *displacement* traveled since $c.p$ (from $\mathbb{R}_{\geq 0}$), its *speed* (from $\mathbb{R}_{\geq 0}$), the *waiting time* (from $\mathbb{R}_{\geq 0}$) which is the time elapsed since the speed of c became zero, its *itinerary* (from the set of segments $\mathcal{S}$) which labels a ride starting at $c.p$, etc. For a traffic light lt, its state $st_{lt} \overset{def}{=} \langle lt.p, lt.cl, \ldots \rangle$ includes respectively its *position* on the map (from *Pos*), and its *color* (with values *red* and *green*), etc.

The general *ADS* model is illustrated in Fig. 2 and consists of a set of vehicle models $\mathcal{C}$ and a *Runtime* that interact cyclically with period Δt. The *Runtime* calculates free space values for each vehicle c which are lengths $c.f$ of initial rides on their itineraries $c.it$ whose positions are free of obstacles. In turn, the vehicles adapt their speed to stay within the allocated free space. Specifically, the interaction proceeds as follows:

- each vehicle c applies a *speed policy* for period Δt respecting its free space $c.f$ received from the *Runtime*. During Δt, it travels a distance $c.\delta'$ to some new position $c.p'$, and at the end of the period its speed is $c.v'$, its itinerary $c.it'$, etc. The new state is then communicated to the *Runtime*.
- the *Runtime* updates the system state on the map taking into account the new vehicle states and time-dependent object attributes. Then it applies a *free space policy* computing the tuple $\langle c.f' \rangle_{c \in \mathcal{C}}$, the new free space for all vehicles based on the current system state. The corresponding free spaces are then communicated to vehicles and the next cycle starts.

Note that the coordination principle described is independent of the type of segments used in the map, e.g. intervals, curves or regions. For simplicity, we take the free spaces to measure the length of an initial ride without obstacles on the vehicle itinerary. This abstraction is sufficient to state the basic results. We discuss later how they can be generalized for richer interpretations of the map.

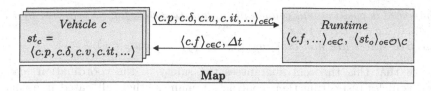

Fig. 2. General *ADS* architecture

3.2 Assume-Guarantee for Safe Control Policies

We give below the principle of a safe control policy for vehicles, which respects their allocated free space, applying assume-guarantee reasoning.

We consider the following two hypotheses. For a vehicle c, there exists a function $B_c : \mathbb{R}_{\geq 0} \to \mathbb{R}_{\geq 0}$ that gives the minimum braking distance c needs to stop from speed v, in case of emergency. Furthermore, for a non-negative distance f, let $Ahead_c(f)$ denote the ride consisting of the positions reachable on the itinerary $c.it$ from the current vehicle position $c.p$ within distance f, formally $Ahead_c(f) \stackrel{def}{=} \{p' \in Pos \mid \exists \delta \leq f.\ c.p \stackrel{c.it[0,\delta]}{\leadsto} p'\}$.

The following definition specifies a safe control policy using assume-guarantee reasoning on the components of the *ADS* architecture. We consider assume-guarantee contracts on components defined as pairs of properties A/G specifying respectively the input-output component behavior for a cycle, i.e., respectively, what the component guarantees (G) provided its environment conforms to given assumption (A).

Definition 1 (safe control policy). *A control policy is safe if*

– *each vehicle $c \in C$ respects the assume-guarantee contract:*

$$0 \leq c.v,\ B_c(c.v) \leq c.f\ /\ 0 \leq c.v',\ 0 \leq c.\delta',\ c.\delta' + B_c(c.v') \leq c.f,$$
$$c.p \stackrel{c.it[0,c.\delta']}{\leadsto} c.p',\ c.it' = c.it[c.\delta', -]$$

– *the Runtime respects the assume-guarantee contract:*

$$\wedge_c 0 \leq c.\delta \leq c.f,\ \uplus_c Ahead_c(c.f - c.\delta)\ /\ \wedge_{c \in C} c.f' \geq c.f - c.\delta,\ \uplus_{c \in C} Ahead_c(c.f')$$

The policy is the joint enforcement of safe speed policies for vehicles and safe free space policies for the *Runtime*. Vehicle safe speed policies require that if a vehicle can brake safely by moving forward within its allocated free space at the beginning of a cycle, then it can adapt its speed moving forward within this space. *Runtime* safe free space policies require that if the free spaces of the vehicles are non-crossing at the beginning of a cycle, then it is possible to find new non-crossing free spaces for the vehicles provided they move forward in their allocated free space.

Theorem 1. *Safe control policies preserve the following invariants:*

- *the speed is positive and compliant to the free space, for all vehicles, that is,*
  $\bigwedge_{c \in C} 0 \leq c.v \wedge B(c.v) \leq c.f,$
- *the free spaces are non-crossing, that is,* $\biguplus_{c \in C} Ahead_c(c.f).$

Note that this theorem guarantees the safety of the coordination insofar as the vehicles respecting their contracts remain in their allocated free spaces which are non-crossing by construction. Nevertheless, the result leaves a lot of freedom to vehicles and the *Runtime* to choose speeds and non-crossing free spaces. In particular, two questions arise concerning these choices. The first question is whether the system can reach states where no progress is possible. One can imagine traffic jam situations, for example when vehicles do not have enough space to move. The second question is whether free space choices can be determined by traffic rules that actually enforce fairness in resolving conflicts between vehicles. This question is discussed in detail in Sect. 5.

4   Speed Policies Abiding by the Vehicle Contract

In this section, we show that it is possible for vehicles to compute speed policies in accordance with their contract.

The behavior of each vehicle is defined by a controller, which given its current speed and its free space, computes the displacement for Δt so that it can safely move in the free space. Such safe speed policies have been studied in [24,25].

We illustrate the principle of safe speed policy with respect to f considering that each vehicle is equipped with a controller that receives a free space value and adjusts its speed adequately. For the sake of simplicity, assume the controller can select among three different constant acceleration values $\{-b_{max}, 0, a_{max}\} \in \mathbb{R}$ respectively, the negative value $-b_{max}$ for decreasing, the zero value for maintaining and the positive value a_{max} for increasing the speed. At every cycle, the controller will select the highest acceleration value for which the vehicle guarantee holds as defined by its contract in Definition 1. Nonetheless, an exception applies for the very particular case where the vehicle stops within the cycle, which cannot be actually handled with constant acceleration.

The proposed speed policy defines the new speed v' and displacement δ' using a region decomposition of the safe $v \times f$ space (that is, where $v \geq 0$ and $f \geq B(v)$) as follows:

$$
v', \delta' \stackrel{def}{=}
\begin{cases}
0, f & \text{if } f \geq B(v), f - v\Delta t < B(v), v - b_{max}\Delta t < 0 \\
v - b_{max}\Delta t, \ v\Delta t - b_{max}\Delta t^2/2 \\
\quad \text{if } f \geq B(v), f - v\Delta t < B(v), v - b_{max}\Delta t \geq 0 \\
v, \ v\Delta t \text{ if } f - v\Delta t \geq B(v), f - v\Delta t - a_{max}\Delta t^2/2 < B(v + a_{max}\Delta t) \\
v + a_{max}\Delta t, \ v\Delta t + a_{max}\Delta t^2/2 \\
\quad \text{if } f - v\Delta t - a_{max}\Delta t^2/2 \geq B(v + a_{max}\Delta t)
\end{cases}
\tag{1}
$$

Intuitively, the regions are defined such that, when the corresponding acceleration is constantly applied for Δt time units, the guarantee on the vehicle is provable given the assumptions and the region boundary conditions.

Moreover, the vehicle position and the itinerary are updated according to the travelled distance by taking $c.p'$ such that $c.p \overset{c.it[0,c.\delta']}{\rightsquigarrow} c.p'$ and $c.it' = c.it[c.\delta', -]$. Furthermore, the waiting time $c.wt$ is updated but taking $c.wt' \overset{def}{=} c.wt + \Delta t$ if $c.v = c.v' = 0$ and $c.wt' \overset{def}{=} 0$ otherwise.

Proposition 1. *The region-based speed policy respects the safety contract for vehicles if the braking function is $B(v) = v^2/2b_{max}$.*

Note that the speed policy works independently of the value of the parameter Δt, which is subject only to implementation constraints, e.g., it must be large enough to allow the controlled electromechanical system to realize the desired effect. A large Δt may imply low responsiveness to changes and jerky motion, but will never compromise the safety of the system.

The proposed implementation of the speed policy is "greedy" in the sense that it applies maximum acceleration to move as fast as possible in the available space. We could have "lazy" policies that do not move as fast as possible, and simply extend the travel time. We have shown in [24] that the region-based speed policy approaches the optimal safety policy, i.e., the one that gives the shortest travel time, when we refine the choice of acceleration and deceleration rates in the interval $[-b_{max}, a_{max}]$.

5 Free Space Policies Implied by Traffic Rules

In this section, we study free space safety policies for a given set of global system properties describing traffic rules. We formalize traffic rules as a class of linear temporal logic formulas and provide a method for computing free space values for vehicles that allow them to meet a given set of traffic rules.

5.1 Writing Specifications of Traffic Rules

Given a map G and a set of objects $\mathcal{O}$, we specify traffic rules as formulas of a linear time logic of the following form, where $\square$ is the *always* time modality and N is the *next* time modality:

$$\square \; \forall c_1. \; \forall o_2 ... \forall o_k. \; \phi(c_1, o_2, \ldots, o_k) \implies \mathsf{N} \; \psi(c_1, o_2, \ldots, o_k) \tag{2}$$

A rule says that for any run of the system, the satisfaction of the precondition ϕ implies that the postcondition ψ holds at the next state. Both ϕ and ψ are boolean combinations of state predicates as defined below. Furthermore, we assume that ψ constrains the speed of a single vehicle c_1 for which the property is applicable, and which we call for convenience the *ego* vehicle.

The rules involve state predicates ϕ in the form of first-order assertions built from variables and object attributes (denoting map positions, segments, reals, etc.) using available primitives on map positions (e.g., rides $\rightsquigarrow$, edge rides

$\rightarrow$, distance d, equality $=$), on segments (e.g., concatenation and subsegment extraction), in addition to real arithmetic and boolean operators.

Moreover, we define auxiliary non-primitive *location* and *itinerary* predicates proven useful for the expression of traffic rules. For a vehicle $c \in C$ and x either an object $o \in \mathcal{O}$, a vertex u or an edge e of the map, we define the predicates $c@x$ (c *is at* x), $c \rightarrow x$ (c *meets* x *along the same edge*), $c \rightsquigarrow x$ (c *meets* x) as in Table 1. Furthermore, for a vehicle $c \in C$ and non-negative δ let $c.p \oplus_c \delta$ denote the future position of c after traveling distance δ, that is, either $c.p$ if $\delta = 0$ or the position p' such that $c.p \xrightarrow{c.it[0,\delta]} p'$. We extend $\oplus_c$ to arbitrary future positions of c by taking $(c.p \oplus_c \delta) \oplus_c \delta' \overset{def}{=} c.p \oplus_c (\delta + \delta')$ and we consider the total ordering $\leq_c$ defined as $c.p \oplus_c \delta \leq_c c.p \oplus_c \delta'$ if and only if $\delta \leq \delta'$.

Table 1. Location and itinerary predicates.

	$c@x$	$c \rightarrow x$	$c \rightsquigarrow x$
$x = o$	$c.p = o.p$	$\exists \delta. \; c.p \xrightarrow{c.it[0,\delta]} o.p$	$\exists \delta. \; c.p \xrightarrow{c.it[0,\delta]}{\rightsquigarrow} o.p$
$x = u$	$c.p = u$	$\exists \delta. \; c.p \xrightarrow{c.it[0,\delta]} u$	$\exists \delta. \; c.p \xrightarrow{c.it[0,\delta]}{\rightsquigarrow} u$
$x = e$	$\exists a. \; c.p = (e,a)$	$\exists \delta. \; \exists a > 0. \; c.p \xrightarrow{c.it[0,\delta]} {}^\bullet e \wedge$ $c.p \xrightarrow{c.it[0,\delta+a]}{\rightsquigarrow} (e,a)$	$\exists \delta. \; \exists a > 0. \; c.p \xrightarrow{c.it[0,\delta]}{\rightsquigarrow} {}^\bullet e \wedge$ $c.p \xrightarrow{c.it[0,\delta+a]}{\rightsquigarrow} (e,a)$

We define the semantics of state predicates ϕ in the usual way, by providing a satisfaction relation $\sigma, st \vdash \phi$, where σ is an assignment of free variables of ϕ and st is a system state. A complete formal definition can be found in [5]. The semantics of rules is defined on pairs $\sigma, [st^{(t_i)}]_{i \geq 0}$ consisting of a function σ assigning objects instances to object variables of the formulas and a run $[st^{(t_i)}]_{i \geq 0}$ for a finite set of objects $\mathcal{O}$. For initial state $st^{(t_0)}$ we define *runs* as sequences of consecutive states $[st^{(t_i)}]_{i \geq 0}$ obtained along the cyclic *ADS* execution as described in Sect. 3.1 and parameterized by the sequence of time points $t_i \overset{def}{=} t_0 + i \cdot \Delta t$, that is, equal to the time for reaching the ith system state.

We provide examples of traffic rules in Table 2. We restrict ourselves to safety rules that characterize boundary conditions that should not be violated by the driver controlling the vehicle speed. Therefore, the preconditions characterize potential conflict situations occurring at intersections as well as other constraints implied by the presence of obstacles or speed rules, e.g., traffic lights or speed limit signals. The preconditions may involve various itinerary and location predicates and constraints on the speed of the ego vehicle. Moreover, the latter are limited to constraints maintained by the vehicle and involving braking functions in the form $B_c(c.v) \# k$ where k is a distance with respect to a reference position on the map and $\#$ is a relational symbol $\# \in \{<, \leq, =, \geq, >\}$. Furthermore, the postconditions involve two types of constraints on the speed of the ego vehicle: either speed regulation constraints that limit the distance to full stop, that is

Table 2. Traffic rules

---

1   enforcing safety distance between following vehicles c_1 and c_2:

$\quad \Box \; \forall c_1. \; \forall c_2. \; c_1 \leadsto c_2 \implies N \; B_{c_1}(c_1.v) \leq d(c_1.p, c_2.p)$

2   coordination within all-way-stop junctions:

(i)   safe braking of vehicle c_1 approaching a stop so_1

$\quad \Box \; \forall c_1. \; \forall so_1. \; c_1 \to so_1 \implies N \; B_{c_1}(c_1.v) \leq d(c_1.p, so_1.p)$

(ii) vehicle c_1 obeys a stop sign when another vehicle c_2 crosses the junction

$\quad \Box \; \forall c_1. \; \forall so_1. \; \forall c_2. \; c_1 so_1 \wedge c_1.v = 0 \wedge c_2.v > 0 \wedge c_1.p \times c_2.p \implies N \; c_1.v = 0$

(iii) if two vehicles c_1, c_2 are waiting before the respective stops so_1, so_2

and c_2 waited longer than c_1 then c_1 has to stay stopped

$\quad \Box \; \forall c_1. \; \forall so_1. \; \forall c_2. \; \forall so_2. \; c_1 so_1 \wedge c_1.v = 0 \wedge c_2 so_2 \wedge c_2.v = 0 \wedge$

$\qquad c_1.p \times c_2.p \wedge c_1.wt < c_2.wt \implies N \; c_1.v = 0$

(iv) if two vehicles c_1, c_2 are waiting before the respective stops so_1, so_2 the same

amount of time and c_2 is at an entry with higher priority then c_1 has to stay stopped

$\quad \Box \; \forall c_1. \; \forall so_1. \; \forall c_2. \; \forall so_2. \; c_1 so_1 \wedge c_1.v = 0 \wedge c_2 so_2 \wedge c_2.v = 0 \wedge$

$\qquad c_1.p \times c_2.p \wedge c_1.wt = c_2.wt \wedge so_1.p \prec_j so_2.p \implies N \; c_1.v = 0$

3   coordination using traffic-lights:

if vehicle c_1 meets a red traffic light lt_1, it will remain in safe distance

$\quad \Box \; \forall c_1. \; \forall lt_1. \; c_1 \to lt_1 \wedge lt_1.color = red \wedge B_{c_1}(c_1.v) \leq d(c_1.p, lt_1.p)$

$\qquad \implies N \; B_{c_1}(c_1.v) \leq d(c_1.p, lt_1.p)$

4   priority-based coordination of two vehicles c_1 and c_2 whose itineraries

meet at merger vertex u:

(i)   if c_2 cannot stop at u then c_1 must give way

$\quad \Box \; \forall c_1. \; \forall c_2. \; \forall u. \; c_1 \to u \wedge B_{c_1}(c_1.v) \leq d(c_1.p, u) \wedge$

$\qquad c_2 \to u \wedge B_{c_2}(c_2.v) > d(c_2.p, u) \implies N \; B_{c_1}(c_1.v) \leq d(c_1.p, u)$

(ii) if c_1, c_2 are reaching u and c_1 has less priority than c_2 then c_1 must give way

$\quad \Box \; \forall c_1. \; \forall c_2. \; \forall u. \; c_1 \to u \wedge B_{c_1}(c_1.v) = d(c_1.p, u) \wedge c_1.p \prec_u c_2.p \wedge$

$\qquad c_2 \to u \wedge B_{c_2}(c_2.v) = d(c_2.p, u) \implies N \; B_{c_1}(c_1.v) \leq d(c_1.p, u)$

5   enforcing speed limits for vehicle c_1:

(i)   if c_1 is traveling in an edge e then its speed should be lower than the speed limit

$\quad \Box \; \forall c_1. \; \forall e. \; c_1 e \implies N \; c_1.v \leq e.v$

(ii) if c_1 is approaching an edge e then it controls its speed so that it complies

with the speed limit at the entrance of e

$\quad \Box \; \forall c_1. \; \forall e. \; c_1 \to e \implies N \; B_{c_1}(c_1.v) \leq d(c_1.p, {}^\bullet e) + B_{c_1}(e.v)$

$B_{c_1}(c_1.v)$, or speed limitation constraints requiring that the speed $c_1.v$ does not exceed a given limit value.

Note the difference with other approaches using unrestricted linear temporal logic, with "eventually" and "until" operators, to express traffic rules, e.g. [5]. We have adopted the above restrictions because they closely characterize the vehicle safety obligations in the proposed model. Furthermore, as we show below, traffic rules of this form can be translated into free space rules that can reinforce the policy managed by the *Runtime*.

5.2   Deriving Free Space Rules from Traffic Rules

We show that we can derive from traffic rules limiting the speed of vehicles, rules on free space variables controlled by the *Runtime* such that both the traffic rules and the free space contract hold.

To express constraints on the free space variables $c.f$, we use, for vehicles c, auxiliary *limit position* variables $\langle c.\pi \rangle_{c \in C}$ such that $c.\pi = c.p \oplus_c c.f$. In other words, the limit position $c.\pi$ defines the position beyond which a vehicle should not be according to its contract. It is clear that for given $c.\pi$ and $c.p$, $c.f$ is defined as the distance from $c.p$ to $c.\pi$.

Using the limit position variables $\langle c.\pi \rangle_{c \in C}$ we can transform structurally any state formula ϕ into a free space formula ϕ_π by replacing constraints on speeds by induced constraints on limit positions as follows, for $\# \in \{<, \leq, =, \geq, >\}$ and t a non-negative real constant:

$$B_c(c.v) \# d(c.p, x) + t \qquad \mapsto \quad c.\pi \#_c \quad x \oplus_c t$$
$$c.v \# t \qquad \qquad \mapsto \qquad c.\pi \#_c c.p \oplus_c B_c(t)$$

The first case concerns speed regulation constraints bounding the limit position $c.\pi$ relatively to the position x of a fixed or moving obstacle ahead of c, that is, a stop or traffic light sign, a vehicle, etc. The second case concerns speed limitation constraints bounding $c.\pi$ relatively to the current vehicle position $c.p$ and the allowed speed.

Given a state formula ϕ, let ϕ_π be the derived formula obtained by replacing constraints on speeds by constraints on limit positions. The following theorem guarantees preservation between properties involving speed constraints and properties involving limit positions, in relation to the vehicle speed contracts.

Theorem 2. *The following equivalences hold:*

$$(i) \quad \phi \iff (\exists\, c.\pi)_c\ \phi_\pi \wedge \bigwedge_c B_c(c.v) = d(c.p, c.\pi)$$
$$(ii)\ \swarrow\!\phi \iff (\exists\, c.\pi)_c\ \phi_\pi \wedge \bigwedge_c B_c(c.v) \leq d(c.p, c.\pi)$$

where $\swarrow\!\phi$ is the speed-lower closure of ϕ, that is, ϕ where speed constraints of the form $c.v \# t$, $B_c(c.v) \# d(c.p, x)) + t$ for $\# \in \{\geq, >\}$ are removed.

Re-calling Theorem 1 in Sect. 3.2, notice that $B_c(c.v) \leq d(c.p, c.\pi)$ is enforced by safe control policies as $d(c.p, c.\pi) = c.f$. Therefore, any property ϕ is preserved through equivalence only when all the vehicles run with the maximal allowed speed by the distance to their limit positions. Otherwise, the speed-lower closure $\swarrow\!\phi$ is preserved through equivalence, that is, only the upper bounds on speeds as derived from corresponding bounds on limit positions.

Therefore, all traffic rules of form (2) which, for states satisfying the precondition ϕ, constrain the speed of vehicle c_1 at the next cycle according to constraint ψ, are transformed into free space rules on limit positions of the form:

$$\Box \; \forall c_1.\forall o_2...\forall o_k. \; \phi_\pi(c_1,o_2,\dots,o_k) \implies \mathsf{N}\,\psi_\pi(c_1,o_2,\dots,o_k) \tag{3}$$

Notice that the postcondition ψ_π is of the form $c_1.\pi \leq_{c_1} b_\psi(c_1,o_2,\dots,o_k)$ for a position term b_ψ obtained by the transformation of ψ.

For example, the traffic rule 1 is transformed into the free space rule: $\Box \forall c_1. \; \forall c_2. \; c_1 \rightsquigarrow c_2 \implies \mathsf{N}\, c_1.\pi \leq_{c_1} c_2.p$. The traffic rule $4(ii)$ is transformed into the free space rule: $\Box \forall c_1. \; \forall c_2. \; \forall u. \; c_1 \rightarrow u \wedge c_2 \rightarrow u \wedge c_1.\pi = u \wedge c_2.\pi = u \wedge c_1.p \prec_u c_2.p \implies \mathsf{N}\, c_1.\pi \leq_{c_1} u$.

We are now ready to define the *Runtime* free space policy based on traffic rules. Let $\mathcal{R}$ denotes the set of traffic rules of interest e.g., the ones defined in Table 2. For a current *ADS* state st and current limit positions and free spaces $\langle c.\pi, c.f\rangle_{c \in C}$ the policy computes new limit positions and new free spaces $\langle c.\pi', c.f'\rangle_{c \in C}$ as follows:

$$c.\pi' \stackrel{def}{=} \min_{\leq c} \{ \sigma b_\psi \mid [\forall c_1.\forall o_2...\forall o_k. \; \phi \implies N\psi] \in \mathcal{R}, \; \sigma[c/c_1], st \vdash \phi_\pi \}$$
$$\cup \{ e^\bullet \mid \exists a < \|e\|, \; c.\pi = (e,a), \; c \rightsquigarrow e \} \tag{4}$$
$$c.f' \stackrel{def}{=} \delta \text{ such that } c.p \oplus_c \delta = c.\pi' \tag{5}$$

Actually, that means computing for every vehicle c the new limit position $c.\pi'$ as the nearest position with respect to $\leq_c$ from two sets of bounds. The first set contains the bounds σb_ψ computed for all the free space rules derived from the traffic rules in $\mathcal{R}$ and applicable for c at the given state st. The second set contains the endpoint $e^\bullet$ of the edge e where the current limit position $c.\pi$ is located. It is needed to avoid "jumping" over $e^\bullet$, even though this is allowed by application of the rules, as $e^\bullet$ may be a merger node and should be considered for solving potential conflicts. Then, we define the new free space $c.f'$ as the distance δ from the current position $c.p$ to the new limit position $c.\pi'$ measured along the itinerary of c.

Note that if the free space policy respects the assume-guarantee contract of the *Runtime* from Definition 1 then it will moreover guarantees the satisfaction of all traffic rules from $\mathcal{R}$ where both the pre- and the postcondition ϕ and ψ are speed-lower closed formulas. First, conformance with respect to the contract is needed to obtain the invariants $B_c(c.v) \leq c.f = d(c.p, c.\pi)$ according to Theorem 1. Second, these invariants ensure preservation through equivalence between speed-lower closed formula and derived formula on limit positions, according to Theorem 2. Third, the free space policy ensures the satisfaction of the derived free space rules, that is, by construction it chooses limit positions ensuring postconditions ψ_π hold whenever preconditions ϕ_π hold. As these formulas are preserved through equivalence, it leads to the satisfaction of the original traffic rule.

5.3 Correctness with Respect to the Free Space Contract

We prove correctness, that is, conformance with the assume-guarantee contract of Definition 1, of the free space policy obtained by the application of the traffic rules from Table 2 excluding the one concerning traffic lights. For this rule we need additional assumptions taking into account the light functioning and the behavior of the crossing vehicles.

First, we assume that the vehicle braking dynamics are compatible with the speed limits associated with the map segments, that means:

- for any edge e leading to a junction (and henceforth a stop sign) or a merger vertex holds $B_c(e.v) \leq \|e\|$, for any vehicle $c \in C$ (see Fig. 3(a)),
- for any consecutive edges e_1, e_2 holds $B_c(e_1.v) \leq \|e_1\| + B_c(e_2.v)$, for any vehicle $c \in C$ (see Fig. 3(b)) i.e., between two consecutive speed limit changes, there is sufficient space to adapt the speed.

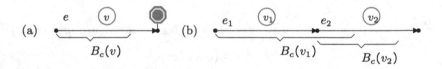

Fig. 3. Explaining restrictions on speed limits

Second, we call an ADS state $\langle st_o \rangle_{o \in \mathcal{O}}$ *consistent with limit positions* $\langle c.\pi \rangle_{c \in C}$ iff for every vehicle $c \in C$:

- the limit position is ahead of the current vehicle position, that is, $c.p \leq_c c.\pi$,
- there is no stop sign located strictly between the current vehicle position and the limit position, that is, $c.p <_c so.p <_c c.\pi$ does not hold for any stop so,
- the limit position conforms to the speed limits of the current edge (e_1) and next edge (e_2) on the itinerary of c, that is, $d(c.p, c.\pi) \leq B_c(e_1.v)$ and $d(c.p, c.\pi) \leq d(c.p, {}^\bullet e_2) + B_c(e_2.v)$.

Proposition 2. *The free space policy respects the safety contract for the* Runtime *provided the initial* ADS *state is consistent with initial limit positions.*

6 Discussion

The paper studies results for the correct by design coordination of ADS based on assume-guarantee contacts. The coordination follows a two-step synchronous interaction protocol between vehicles and a *Runtime* that, based on the distribution of vehicles on a map, computes the corresponding free spaces. A first result characterizes safe control policies as the combination of assume-guarantee contracts for vehicles and the *Runtime*. This result is then specialized by showing how policies consistent with their respective contracts can be defined for vehicles and the *Runtime*. In particular, for vehicles, we provide a principle for defining speed policies and, for the *Runtime*, we compute free space policies that conform to a set of traffic rules. The results are general and overcome the limitations of a posteriori verification. They can be applied to *ADS* involving a dynamically changing number of vehicles. In addition, they rely on a general map-based environment model, which has been extensively studied in [5]. Control policies for vehicles and the *Runtime* can be implemented efficiently. In particular, the speed policy has been tested in various implementations [24,25] and found to be not only safe, but also closer to the optimum when refining the space of possible accelerations.

Note that the results can be extended with slight modifications to maps where the segments are curves or regions to express traffic rules involving properties of two-dimensional space, for example for passing maneuvers. For example, if we consider region maps, their segments will be regions of constant width centered on curves. Itineraries, free spaces and $B(v)$ will be regions. The relationship $B(v) \leq f$ becomes $B(v) \subseteq f$ and the addition of lengths of segments should be replaced by the disjoint union of the regions they represent. The speed control policy will remain unchanged in principle but will need a function computing the distance travelled in a region. Finally, the runtime verification of the disjointness of free spaces may incur a computational cost depending on the accuracy of the region representation.

The presented results provide a basis for promising developments in several directions. One direction is to extend the results to achieve correctness by design for general properties. We have shown that traffic rules, which are declarative properties of vehicles, can be abstracted into safety constraints on free spaces. In this way, we solved a simple synthesis problem by transforming a "static" constraint on vehicle speed into a "dynamic" constraint on shared resources.

An interesting question that should be further investigated, is whether the method can be extended to more general properties involving the joint obligation of many vehicles. For example, we can require that for any pair of vehicles c_1 and c_2 that are sufficiently close, the absolute value of the difference between their speeds is less than a constant k, i.e., $|c_1.v - c_2.v| \leq k$. This can be achieved by a free space constraint that gives more free space to the vehicle with the lower speed, assuming that vehicle speed policies are not "lazy" and use as soon as possible the available space.

For general properties involving more than one vehicle, it seems realistic to translate them directly into free space constraints that will enforce the constraints processed by the *Runtime* to ensure the safe control policy. In particular, in addition to safety properties, we could devise free space policies that optimize criteria such as road occupancy and uniform separation for a given group of vehicles e.g. platoon systems studied in [9]. Note that achieving non-blocking control is such a property that involves the application of occupancy criteria.

Another direction is to move from centralized to distributed coordination with many runtimes. It seems possible to partition traffic rules according to the geometric scope of their application, e.g., a specific runtime could control access to each junction. Finally, the *Runtime* can be used as a monitor to verify that the vehicle speed policies of an *ADS* are safe and respect the given traffic rules.

References

1. ASAM OpenDRIVE® - open dynamic road information for vehicle environment. Technical report V 1.6.0, ASAM e.V., March 2020. https://www.asam.net/standards/detail/opendrive
2. Bagschik, G., Menzel, T., Maurer, M.: Ontology based scene creation for the development of automated vehicles. In: Intelligent Vehicles Symposium, pp. 1813–1820. IEEE (2018)
3. Beetz, J., Borrmann, A.: Benefits and limitations of linked data approaches for road modeling and data exchange. In: Smith, I., Domer, B. (eds.) EG-ICE. LNCS, vol. 10864, pp. 245–261. Springer, Cham (2018). https://doi.org/10.1007/978-3-319-91638-5_13
4. Benveniste, A., et al.: Contracts for system design. Found. Trends Electron. Des. Autom. **12**(2–3), 124–400 (2018)
5. Bozga, M., Sifakis, J.: Specification and validation of autonomous driving systems: a multilevel semantic framework. CoRR abs/2109.06478 (2021). https://arxiv.org/abs/2109.06478
6. Bozga, M., Sifakis, J.: Correct by design coordination of autonomous driving systems. CoRR abs/2205.10037 (2022). https://doi.org/10.48550/arXiv.2205.10037
7. Butz, M., et al.: SOCA: domain analysis for highly automated driving systems. In: ITSC, pp. 1–6. IEEE (2020)
8. Chatterjee, K., Henzinger, T.A.: Assume-guarantee synthesis. In: Grumberg, O., Huth, M. (eds.) TACAS 2007. LNCS, vol. 4424, pp. 261–275. Springer, Heidelberg (2007). https://doi.org/10.1007/978-3-540-71209-1_21
9. El-Hokayem, A., Bensalem, S., Bozga, M., Sifakis, J.: A layered implementation of DR-BIP supporting run-time monitoring and analysis. In: de Boer, F., Cerone, A. (eds.) SEFM 2020. LNCS, vol. 12310, pp. 284–302. Springer, Cham (2020). https://doi.org/10.1007/978-3-030-58768-0_16
10. Esterle, K., Gressenbuch, L., Knoll, A.C.: Formalizing traffic rules for machine interpretability. In: CAVS, pp. 1–7. IEEE (2020)
11. Hilscher, M., Linker, S., Olderog, E.-R., Ravn, A.P.: An abstract model for proving safety of multi-lane traffic Manoeuvres. In: Qin, S., Qiu, Z. (eds.) ICFEM 2011. LNCS, vol. 6991, pp. 404–419. Springer, Heidelberg (2011). https://doi.org/10.1007/978-3-642-24559-6_28
12. Karimi, A., Duggirala, P.S.: Formalizing traffic rules for uncontrolled intersections. In: ICCPS, pp. 41–50. IEEE (2020)
13. Kress-Gazit, H., Pappas, G.J.: Automatically synthesizing a planning and control subsystem for the DARPA urban challenge. In: CASE, pp. 766–771. IEEE (2008)
14. Mavridou, A., Katis, A., Giannakopoulou, D., Kooi, D., Pressburger, T., Whalen, M.W.: From partial to global assume-guarantee contracts: compositional realizability analysis in FRET. In: Huisman, M., Păsăreanu, C., Zhan, N. (eds.) FM 2021. LNCS, vol. 13047, pp. 503–523. Springer, Cham (2021). https://doi.org/10.1007/978-3-030-90870-6_27
15. Meyer, B.: Applying "design by contract". Computer **25**(10), 40–51 (1992)

16. Poggenhans, F., et al.: Lanelet2: a high-definition map framework for the future of automated driving. In: ITSC, pp. 1672–1679. IEEE (2018)
17. Rizaldi, A., Althoff, M.: Formalising traffic rules for accountability of autonomous vehicles. In: ITSC, pp. 1658–1665. IEEE (2015)
18. Rizaldi, A., Immler, F., Schürmann, B., Althoff, M.: A formally verified motion planner for autonomous vehicles. In: Lahiri, S.K., Wang, C. (eds.) ATVA 2018. LNCS, vol. 11138, pp. 75–90. Springer, Cham (2018). https://doi.org/10.1007/978-3-030-01090-4_5
19. Rizaldi, A., Keinholz, J., Huber, M., Feldle, J., Immler, F., Althoff, M., Hilgendorf, E., Nipkow, T.: Formalising and monitoring traffic rules for autonomous vehicles in Isabelle/HOL. In: Polikarpova, N., Schneider, S. (eds.) IFM 2017. LNCS, vol. 10510, pp. 50–66. Springer, Cham (2017). https://doi.org/10.1007/978-3-319-66845-1_4
20. Saoud, A., Girard, A., Fribourg, L.: Assume-guarantee contracts for continuous-time systems. Automatica **134**, 109910 (2021)
21. Schwarting, W., Alonso-Mora, J., Rus, D.: Planning and decision-making for autonomous vehicles. Annu. Rev. Control Robot. Auton. Syst. **1**, 187–210 (2018). https://doi.org/10.1146/annurev-control-060117-105157
22. Sharf, M., Besselink, B., Molin, A., Zhao, Q., Johansson, K.H.: Assume/guarantee contracts for dynamical systems: theory and computational tools. CoRR abs/2012.12657 (2020)
23. Sun, M., Bakirtzis, G., Jafarzadeh, H., Fleming, C.: Correct-by-construction: a contract-based semi-automated requirement decomposition process. CoRR abs/1909.02070 (2019)
24. Wang, Q., Li, D., Sifakis, J.: Safe and efficient collision avoidance control for autonomous vehicles. In: MEMOCODE, pp. 1–6. IEEE (2020)
25. Wang, Q., Zheng, X., Zhang, J., Sifakis, J.: A hybrid controller for safe and efficient collision avoidance control. CoRR abs/2103.15484 (2021). https://arxiv.org/abs/2103.15484
26. Waqas, M., Murtaza, M.A., Nuzzo, P., Ioannou, P.: Correct-by-construction design of adaptive cruise control with control barrier functions under safety and regulatory constraints (2022). https://arxiv.org/abs/2203.14110
27. Wongpiromsarn, T., Karaman, S., Frazzoli, E.: Synthesis of provably correct controllers for autonomous vehicles in urban environments. In: ITSC, pp. 1168–1173. IEEE (2011)
28. Wongpiromsarn, T., Topcu, U., Murray, R.M.: Receding horizon temporal logic planning. IEEE Trans. Autom. Control **57**(11), 2817–2830 (2012)

Neural Predictive Monitoring for Collective Adaptive Systems

Francesca Cairoli[1]([✉]), Nicola Paoletti[2,3], and Luca Bortolussi[1]

[1] Department of Mathematics and Geosciences, University of Trieste, Trieste, Italy
francesca.cairoli@units.it
[2] Department of Computer Science, Royal Holloway, University of London, London, UK
[3] Department of Informatics, King's College London, London, UK

Abstract. Reliable bike-sharing systems can lead to numerous environmental, economic and social benefits and therefore play a central role in the effective development of smart cities. Bike-sharing models deal with spatially distributed stations and interact with an unpredictable environment, the users. Monitoring the trustworthiness of such a collective system is of paramount importance to ensure a good quality of the delivered service, but this task can become computationally demanding due to the complexity of the model under study. Neural Predictive Monitoring (NPM) [5], a neural-network learning-based approach to predictive monitoring (PM) with statistical guarantees, can be employed to preemptively detect violations of a specific requirement – e.g. a station has no more bikes available or a station is full. The computational efficiency of NPM makes PM applicable at runtime even on embedded devices with limited computational power. The goal of this paper is to demonstrate the applicability of NPM on collective adaptive systems such as bike-sharing systems. In particular, we first analyze the performance of NPM over a collective system evolving deterministically. Then, following [7], we tackle a more realistic scenario, where sensors allow only for partial observability and where the system evolves in a stochastic fashion. We evaluate the approach on multiple bike sharing network topologies, obtaining highly accurate predictions and effective error detection rules.

1 Introduction

As the urban population grows there is an increasing need for innovative technologies that will allow cities to reach a good and sustainable quality of life with an equitable distribution of resources. Given a service and an urban framework, a developer should design a solution that guarantees the quality of the service delivered. Systems with decentralised and distributed designs, comprised

This work has been partially supported by the PRIN project "SEDUCE" n. 2017TWR-CNB.

of many autonomous and interacting entities, are known as collective adaptive systems (CAS). In CAS, the user becomes part of the system design. Formal models provide detailed descriptions of the design choices of the system under study, whereas formal methods are used to analyse the effects of these choices on the safety and reliability of such a system. In general, the goal of formal verification is to check if the system satisfies a certain requirement, e.g. avoiding an undesirable or dangerous region of the state space. It is straightforward to frame verification as a reachability checking problem. Similarly, predictive monitoring (PM) focuses on the online analysis of such reachability. PM is preemptive, meaning that it aims at predicting, at runtime, if a future violation of the requirement can be reached from the current state of the system within a given time-bound. PM is invoked periodically and typically at high frequencies. Therefore, reachability needs to be determined rapidly so that the response is provided before the eventual failure occurs. Any solution to the PM problem involves a trade-off between the *accuracy* of the reachability prediction and its computational *efficiency*. The analysis must execute within strict real-time constraints and typically with limited hardware resources. Exact formal methods suffer well-known scalability issues. The general goal of this paper is monitoring the reliability of a CAS to ensure good quality of service. This is an extremely challenging task as the state space is typically large and spatially distributed. Moreover, having humans in the loop makes the behavioural analysis even more complex. In this paper, we present NPM-CAS, an adaptation of Neural Predictive Monitoring (NPM) [5] to CAS. NPM is a machine-learning-based approach to PM that builds on Conformal Predictions (CP) to provide highly accurate predictions in a highly efficient manner together with statistical guarantees over its predictions and a principled method for detecting potential prediction errors, which significantly enhances the reliability of PM estimates.

In summary, the main contributions of this paper are the following:

- We extend Neural Predictive Monitoring of [5] so that it can be applied to CAS, where the reliability of multiple agents can be synchronously monitored. The classification problem becomes a multi-output problem instead of a single-output one as in [5]: each output predicts the reliability of a single agent.
- We extend the CP framework to work under multiple-output classification problems so that we can have an agent-specific error detection rule and serve-specific statistical guarantees.
- We extend NPM to allow for stochastic dynamics. In [5] only deterministic and non-deterministic dynamics where considered. In such a scenario, the classification problem becomes a multi-class problem as states cannot be deterministically labelled as safe or unsafe.
- We evaluate the method on three different bike-sharing systems having network geometries with increasing complexities.

The paper is structured as follows. Section 2 describes the details of the bike-sharing model. Section 3 formally states the problems solved by NPM for a generic CAS. Section 4 provides the theoretical background on CP, used to quantify the predictive uncertainty and to have statistical guarantees. The results of the experimental evaluation are then presented in Sect. 5.

2   Bike Sharing System

Bike-sharing systems (BSSs) are becoming important for urban transportation. In these systems, users arrive at a station, pick up a bike, use it for a while, and then return it to another station of their choice. Each station has a finite capacity and it cannot host more bikes than its capacity. Stochasticity is due to the randomness of user choices.

2.1   Model of the System

The BSS is modeled as a Markovian system with M stations and a fleet of N bikes. Each bike can be either locked at a station i, for $i \in \{1,\ldots,M\}$, or in transit between two stations i and j, for $i,j \in \{1,\ldots,M\}$ and $i \neq j$. Station i can host at most K_i bikes. We can frame this system as a population model where individuals, the bikes, can belong to M^2 different species: *stationary bikes* $S = \{S_1,\ldots,S_M\}$ for bikes locked in a station and *transitioning bikes* $T = \{T_{i,j} \mid i \neq j\}$ for bikes moving between stations. The total number of species is thus $|S \cup T| = |S| + |T| = M^2$. The state of the system $x(t) \in \mathbb{N}^{M^2}$ counts the number of bikes in each species at time t. At each station, new users arrive at a rate λ_i, independently of the number of bikes present in that station. However, if the station has no bike available, the unhappy user leaves the system. Instead, if the station is not empty, the user picks up a bike at this station and joins the pool of riding users and the bikes move from a species in S to a species in T. We can summarize these events with a transition from S_i to $T_{i,j}$, given that the bike is moving from station i towards station j, happening with rate $\lambda_i \cdot \mathbb{I}(x_{S_i} > 0)$. The trip time between the two stations is exponentially distributed with mean $1/d_{ij}$, where d_{ij} is the distance between the two stations. After this time, the riding user wants to return the bike. If the destination has fewer than K_j bikes, the user returns the bike to this station and leaves the system. If the station has already K_j bikes, meaning if it is full, no more bikes can be returned. In this case, the user waits for a slot of that station to become available. This transition can be summarized as moving from species $T_{i,j}$ to species S_j with rate $x_{T_{ij}} \cdot \mathbb{I}(x_{S_j} < K_j)/d_{ij}$. The dynamics of the system is thus fully determined by $2M(M-1)$ reactions of the form:

$$R_1^{i,j}: \quad S_i \longrightarrow T_{i,j} \qquad \text{with rate } \lambda_i \mathbb{I}(x_{S_i} > 0),$$
$$R_2^{i,j}: \quad T_{i,j} \longrightarrow S_j \qquad \text{with rate } x_{S_j} \cdot \mathbb{I}(x_{T_{ij}} < K_i)/d_{ij}$$

for every $i \neq j \in \{1,\ldots M\}$. Let $\mathcal{R}$ denote the set of all possible reactions. The topology of the network of stations strongly influences the dynamics of the system. Figure 2 shows a very simple topology where all bikes are equidistant but each station can have a different arrival rate λ_i, meaning that some stations can be more popular than others, and a different capacity K_i.

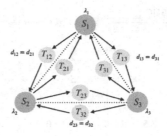

Fig. 1. BSS network with triangular topology: all bikes are equidistant but each station can have a different arrival rate λ_i and a different capacity K_i.

2.2   Dynamics of the System

The time evolution of the population model presented above can be described by the deterministic evolution of its probability mass. Let $\mathbb{P}_{x_0}(x(t) = x)$ denote the probability of finding the system in state x at time t given that it was in state x_0 at time t_0. This probability satisfies a system of ODEs known as Chemical Master Equation (CME):

$$\frac{\partial}{\partial t}\mathbb{P}_{x_0}(x(t) = x) = \sum_{j=1}^{|\mathcal{R}|}\left[f_{\mathsf{R}_j}(x - \nu_j)\mathbb{P}_{x_0}(x(t) = x - \nu_j) - f_{\mathsf{R}_j}(x)\mathbb{P}_{x_0}(x(t) = x)\right], \quad (1)$$

where ν_j is the update vector associated with reaction $\mathsf{R}_j \in \mathcal{R}$. The equation above is the Kolmogorov equation for a population process, considering the inflow and outflow probability at time t for a state x. Since the CME is a system in general with countably many differential equations, its analytic or numeric solution is almost always infeasible.

In this regard, *approximate solutions* become the only viable approach to analyse the dynamics of a complex stochastic population model. In particular, we can resort either to stochastic simulation algorithms or to deterministic fluid approximations.

Gillespie Simulation. The Gillespie stochastic simulation algorithm (SSA) [8] generates trajectories that are exact realizations of the CME (Eq. (1)). Given a certain initial state, one can take a large number of samples (trajectories) that serves as an empirical estimate of the CME that can be used to extract information about the process via statistical methods. For example, one can consider an upper and a lower quantile and obtain a credible interval over the trajectory space (Fig. 2 (right)).

Mean Field Approximation. The deterministic approximation of a stochastic population model builds on the observation that stochastic fluctuations tend to average out as the population size grows larger, i.e. when the number of interacting individuals is very large. In particular, if the state variables are scaled, so that the state evolution is independent of the population size, the dynamics

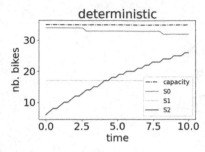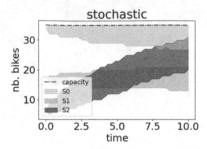

Fig. 2. Deterministic (left) and stochastic (right) trajectory for stationary bikes over the triangular topology of Fig. 1. In the stochastic version, we show the 95% credible interval over the trajectory space.

of the stochastic models is very similar to a deterministic one, described by an ODE, the well-known mean-field (MF) approximation [2,3,6,9]. Thus, in the BSS, as the number of bikes present in the system increases, the dynamics of the system tends to the following fluid ODE:

$$\frac{d\hat{x}}{dt} = \sum_{i \neq j} \frac{\nu_1^{i,j}}{M} \lambda_i \mathbb{I}(\hat{x}_{S_i} > 0) + \frac{\nu_2^{i,j}}{d_{ij}} \mathbb{I}(M \cdot \hat{x}_{S_j} < K_i), \qquad (2)$$

where $\hat{x} = \frac{x}{M}$ is the scaled state and $\nu_1^{i,j}$ and $\nu_2^{i,j}$ are the original update vectors respectively for reaction $R_1^{i,j}$ and $R_2^{i,j}$. Therefore, MF trajectories have a deterministic evolution (Fig. 2 (left)). The formalism and dynamics of the Markovian population model, presented here specifically for a BSS, can be easily applied to a generic CAS.

3   Neural Predictive Monitoring for CAS

In this section, we describe the Neural Predictive Monitoring technique for a generic CAS evolving with either deterministic or stochastic dynamics.

3.1   Deterministic Dynamics

Consider the model $\mathcal{M}_{det}$ of a CAS with state space X evolving deterministically over discrete time with time steps of width Δt. Consider a temporal horizon H, the dynamics can be described by a function $F_{det} : X \rightarrow X^H$, mapping a state $x(t)$ to a trajectory $F_{det}(x(t)) = x(t_1) \cdots x(t_H)$, where $t_j := t + j\Delta t$. The measurement process is instead modeled by a deterministic function μ mapping a state x into its observable part y, $y = \mu(x)$. The CAS is composed of N different agents and we aim at monitoring the reliability of service for each of these N agents. For instance, in the BSS the agents are the N bike stations. Reliability is modeled by considering a region D of the state space that we want to avoid, referred to as the *unsafe* or *dangerous region*. Predictive monitoring of such a system corresponds to deriving a function that approximates a given reachability specification for all the N agents, $\mathsf{Reach}(D, x, H) \in \{-1, 1\}^N$: given a state x and a set of unsafe states D, establish whether agent $i \in \{1, \ldots, N\}$ admits a trajectory starting from x that reaches D in a time H. If such a trajectory exists, $\mathsf{Reach}^{(i)}(D, x, H)$ evaluates to 1, -1 otherwise, where $\mathsf{Reach}^{(i)}(D, x, H)$ denotes the i-th component of $\mathsf{Reach}(D, x, H)$. The approximation is w.r.t. some given distribution of states, meaning that we can admit inaccurate reachability predictions if the state has zero probability.

Full Observability. We now illustrate the PM problem under the ideal assumption of full observability (FO).

Problem 1. (PM under FO). Given a CAS $(\mathcal{M}_{det}, F_{det})$ with N agents, state space X, a distribution $\mathcal{X}$ over X, a time bound H and set of unsafe states $D \subset X$, find a function $h : X \to \{-1, 1\}^N$ that minimizes the probability

$$Pr_{x \sim \mathcal{X}}\Big(h(x) \neq \mathsf{Reach}(D, x, H)\Big).$$

A state $x \in X$ is called *positive* for agent i w.r.t. a predictor h if the i-th component of $h(x)$ evaluates to 1, $h^{(i)}(x) = 1$. Otherwise, it is called *negative*.

As discussed in the next section, finding h, i.e., finding a function approximation with minimal error probability, can be solved as a supervised multi-output classification problem, provided that a reachability oracle is available for generating supervision data. The predictor h is indeed solving N classification problems at once. In [5] such a classification problem is solved using deep neural networks, which demonstrated the best performance across several other machine learning models.

Partial Observability. The problem above relies on the assumption that full knowledge about the state is available. However, in most practical applications, state information is only partial. Under partial observability (PO), we only have access to a sequence of past observations $\bar{y}_t = (y_{t-H_p}, \ldots, y_t)$ which can be generated by applying the observation function μ to the *unknown* state sequence $x_{t-H_p}, \ldots, x_t$, evolving according to F_{det}. In the following, we consider the distribution $\mathcal{Y}$ over Y^{H_p} of the observations sequences $\bar{y}_t = (y_{t-H_p}, \ldots, y_t)$ induced by state $x_{t-H_p} \sim \mathcal{X}$, dynamics given by F_{det} and observations given by μ.

Problem 2. (PM under PO). Given the system and reachability specification of Problem 1, find a function $g : Y^{H_p} \to \{-1, 1\}^N$ that minimizes

$$Pr_{\bar{y}_t \sim \mathcal{Y}}\Big(g(\bar{y}_t) \neq \mathsf{Reach}(D, x_t, H)\Big).$$

In other words, g should predict reachability values given in input only for a sequence of past observations, instead of $x(t)$, the true state at time t. In particular, we require a sequence of observations for the sake of identifiability. Indeed, for general non-linear systems, a single observation does not contain enough information to infer the state [7].

Error Detection. The predictors h and g provide approximate solutions and, as such, they can commit safety-critical prediction errors. Building on [4], we endow the predictive monitor of Problem 1 and 2 with an error detection criterion Rej. This criterion should be able to *preemptively* identify – and hence, reject – inputs where the prediction is likely to be erroneous (in which case Rej evaluates to 1, 0 otherwise). Rej should also be optimal in that it has minimal probability of errors in detection. The rationale behind Rej is that uncertain predictions are more likely to lead to prediction errors. Hence, rather than operating directly over inputs, $s \in \{x, \bar{y}\}$, the detector Rej receives in input a measure of predictive uncertainty of $f \in \{h, g\}$ about s.

Problem 3. (Uncertainty-based error detection). Given an approximate reachability predictor $f \in \{h, g\}$ for the system $(\mathcal{M}_{det}, F_{det})$ and reachability specification of Problem 1 and 2, and a measure of predictive uncertainty $u_f : S \to U^N$ over some uncertainty domain U and over a space $S \in \{X, Y^{H_p}\}$ with distribution $\mathcal{S} \in \{\mathcal{X}, \mathcal{Y}\}$, find an optimal error detection rule, $Rej_f : U \to \{0, 1\}^N$, that minimizes the probability

$$Pr_{s_t \sim \mathcal{S}} \Big(\mathbf{1}\big(f^{(j)}(s_t) \neq \mathsf{Reach}^{(j)}(D, s_t, H)\big) \neq Rej_f^{(j)}(u_f^{(j)}(s_t)) \mid j \in \{1, \ldots N\}\Big).$$

In the above problem, we consider all kinds of prediction errors, but the definition and approach could be easily adapted to focus on the detection of a specific type of error, e.g. on false negatives (the most problematic errors from a safety-critical viewpoint).

Statistical Guarantees. The general goal of Problems 1, 2 and 3 is to minimize the risk of making mistakes in predicting reachability and in predicting prediction errors, respectively. We are also interested in establishing probabilistic guarantees on the expected error rate, in the form of prediction regions guaranteed to include the true reachability value with arbitrary probability.

Problem 4. (Probabilistic guarantees). Given the system and reachability specification of Problem 1 and 2 find, for every output $j \in \{1, \ldots, N\}$, a function $\Gamma_{f^{(j)}}^\epsilon : S \to 2^{\{-1, 1\}}$, mapping an input s_t into a prediction region for the corresponding reachability value, i.e., a region that satisfies, for any error probability level $\epsilon \in (0, 1)$, the *validity* property below

$$Pr_{s_t \sim \mathcal{S}} \Big(\mathsf{Reach}^{(j)}(D, s_t, H) \in \Gamma_{f^{(j)}}^\epsilon(s_t)\Big) \geq 1 - \epsilon.$$

Among the maps that satisfy validity, we seek the most *efficient* one, meaning the one with the smallest, i.e. less conservative, prediction regions.

3.2 Stochastic Dynamics

We now consider a CAS $\mathcal{M}_{stoch}$ evolving stochastically over a state space X and over discrete time. Function $F_{stoch} : X \to \mathcal{X}^H$ describes the dynamics, over a temporal horizon H, mapping a state $x(t)$ to a random variable over the trajectory space X^H, $F_{stoch}(x(t)) = \mathbf{x}(t_1) \cdots \mathbf{x}(t_H)$. A sample

$\xi \sim F_{stoch}(x(t))$ is nothing but a trajectory over X^H. The distribution of $F_{stoch}(x(t))$ can be empirically approximated by taking a large number, P, of samples, $\bar{\xi} := (\xi_1, \ldots, \xi_P) \sim F_{stoch}(x(t))$. We evaluate the safety of state x through a function $\mathsf{StochReach}(D, x, H) \in \{-1, 0, 1\}^N$, which outputs 1 if the trajectories starting from x eventually reach D with probability higher than $(1 - \alpha)$ (x safe), -1 if D is reached with probability below α (x unsafe), 0 otherwise. These probabilities can be derived with Monte-Carlo or numerical probabilistic model checking techniques [13,14]. Predictive monitoring of such a stochastic system $(\mathcal{M}_{stoch}, F_{stoch})$ corresponds to deriving a function that approximates $\mathsf{StochReach}(D, x, H)$ w.r.t. some given distribution for x.

Problem 5. (Stochastic PM). Given an system $(\mathcal{M}_{stoch}, F_{stoch})$ with state space X, a distribution $\mathcal{X}$ over X, a time bound H and set of unsafe states $D \subset X$, find a function $h_s : X \to \{-1, 0, 1\}^N$ that minimizes the probability

$$Pr_{x \sim \mathcal{X}}\Big(h_s(x) \neq \mathsf{StochReach}(D, x, H)\Big)$$

The uncertainty-based error detection rule of Problem 3 and the statistical guarantees of Problem 4 are defined very similarly in the stochastic scenario. The main differences are that the predictive errors of Problem 3 are now defined as $\mathbf{1}\big(h_s^{(i)}(x) \neq \mathsf{StochReach}^{(i)}(D, x, H)\big)$ for $i \in \{1, \ldots, N\}$ and the predictive region $\Gamma_{h_s}^\varepsilon$ of Problem 4 is a function $\Gamma_{h_s}^\varepsilon : X \to 2^{\{-1, 0, 1\}^N}$.

3.3   Predictive Monitoring for BSS

Given a BSS modeled as in Sect. 2, we aim at predicting, from the current state of the system, if a station i is about to get full, $x_{S_i} = K_i$, or if it is soon going to be empty, $x_{S_i} = 0$. The goal of predictive monitoring is to access this information in advance, so that one can try to prevent undesirable events from happening, e.g. by using a truck to transport bikes from one station to another.

Different scenarios, with increasing complexity, can be considered. Each station constantly monitors the number of bikes available, so that measuring the number of stationary bikes is straightforward. On the other hand, when a bike is in transit, we have no exact information about where it is directed to.

We start by considering, a simplified scenario where we assume to have complete knowledge about the state of each bike. We then consider the more realistic setting in which no information about the state of transitioning bikes is available, so we must predict the future reliability of the service only from partial information.

In terms of system dynamics, we start by predicting the service reliability based on the deterministic evolution of the system, using the MF approximation. In this scenario, a state x is labelled as unsafe if the deterministic trajectory, starting from x, violates the requirement. It is labelled as safe otherwise.

We then move to a more complex scenario, where the stochasticity of the dynamics is preserved. Under these circumstances, a state x can be classified as safe, unsafe or risky. It is safe if both the lower and upper bound trajectories satisfy the requirement, unsafe if they both violate it and risky if only one of the bounds violates the requirement. Notice that, potentially, one could extend this approach to an arbitrary number of quantiles by adding a label for each quantile.

By doing so we can create a synthetic dataset by randomly sampling a pool of n initial states, $x^1(t_0) \dots, x^n(t_0)$, and by letting the system evolve from each of these states for a time H. We then use the obtained trajectories to label them as safe, unsafe or risky. As we have N stations, we are going to consider N different requirements, each state thus is associated with N labels. In other words, we separately monitor the future reliability of each station from the current state of the system. The dataset can be summarized as

$$Z' = \{(s_i, \ell_i)\}_{i=1}^n, \tag{3}$$

where $s = x(t_0)$ in case of full observability (FO) and $s = x_S(t_0)$ in case of partial observability (PO), whereas $\ell_i = (\ell_i^1, \dots, \ell_i^N)$. If the dynamics is deterministic $\ell_i^j \in \{safe, unsafe\}$. If the dynamics is stochastic $\ell_i^j \in \{safe, risky, unsafe\}$.

4   Uncertainty Quantification and Statistical Guarantees

In the following, we provide the necessary background on Conformal Prediction (CP), the technique used to quantify the uncertainty and to obtain statistical guarantees over the predictions, the two ingredients needed to solve Problem 3 and Problem 4 in both the deterministic and the stochastic scenario. In the following, we provide an intuitive explanation; we refer the interested reader to [7] for a more detailed description of the procedure. The main difference is that CP is now addressing a multi-output multi-class classification problem rather than a simple binary classification problem.

4.1   Conformal Predictions for Multi-output and Multi-class Classification

Conformal Prediction (CP) [1] is a very general approach that associates measures of reliability to any traditional supervised learning problem. NPM for CAS, presented in Sect. 3, deals with multi-output classification problems (Problem 1, 2 and 5). We thus present the theoretical foundations of CP in relation to a generic multi-class multi-output classification problem.

Let S be the input space, $L = \{l^1, \dots, l^c\}$ be the set of labels (or classes), and define $Z = S \times L^N$, where N is the number of outputs. The classification model is represented as a function $f : S \to [0,1]^{c \times N}$ mapping inputs into N vectors of class likelihoods. For each output j, the class predicted by $f^{(j)}$ corresponds to the class with the highest likelihood. In the context of NPM for CAS, the input space S can be either X, under FO, or Y^{H_P}, under PO, whereas labels L indicates the possible reachability values ($c = 2$ in the deterministic version and $c = 3$ in the stochastic version), and $f \in \{h, g, h_s\}$ is the predictor.

For a generic input s_i, we denote with $\ell_i = (\ell_i^1, \ldots, \ell_i^N)$ the vector of true labels for s_i and with $\hat{\ell}_i$ the vector of labels predicted by f. Test points, whose true labels are unknown, are denoted by s_*. The main ingredients of CP are: a set of labelled examples $Z' \subseteq Z$, a classification model f trained on a subset of Z', a *nonconformity function* $ncm_{f^{(j)}} : S \times L \to \mathbb{R}$ and a statistical test. The nonconformity function $ncm_{f^{(j)}}(s_i, \ell_i^j)$ measures the "strangeness" of an example (s_i, ℓ_i^j), i.e., the deviation between the label ℓ_i^j and the corresponding prediction $f^{(j)}(s_i)$. For ease in the notation, let ncm_j denote the nonconformity function $ncm_{f^{(j)}}$.

CP Algorithm for Multi-output Classification. Given a set of examples $Z' \subseteq Z$, a test input $s_* \in S$, and a significance level $\varepsilon \in [0, 1]$, CP computes $\Gamma_{\varepsilon,*}$, a set of N prediction regions.

1. Divide Z' into a training set Z_t, and calibration set Z_c. Let $q = |Z_c|$ be the size of the calibration set.
2. Train a model f using Z_t.
3. Define a nonconformity function $ncm_j(s_i, \ell_i^j))$ for every output $j \in \{1, \ldots, N\}$.
4. Apply the nonconformity measure to each example in Z_c

$$A_c = \left\{ \{\alpha_{ij} = ncm_j(s_i, \ell_i^j) \mid j \in \{1, \ldots, c\}\} \mid (s_i, \ell_i) \in Z_c \right\}$$

and, for each output $j \in \{1, \ldots N\}$, sort the nonconformity scores in descending order: $\alpha_{1j} \geq \cdots \geq \alpha_{qj}$.
5. For a test input s_*, compute the nonconformity scores w.r.t each output and w.r.t. each possible class:

$$A_* = \left\{ \{ncm_j(s_*, l^k) \mid k \in \{1, \ldots, c\}\} \mid j \in \{1, \ldots, N\} \right\}.$$

Then, for $j \in \{1, \ldots, N\}$ and $k \in \{1, \ldots, c\}$ compute the respective smoothed p-value

$$p_*^{(j,k)} = \frac{|\{z_i \in Z_c : A_c^{(i,j)} > A_*^{(j,k)}\}|}{q+1} + \theta \frac{|\{z_i \in Z_c : A_c^{(i,j)} = A_*^{(j,k)}\}| + 1}{q+1}, \quad (4)$$

where $\theta \in \mathcal{U}[0, 1]$ is a tie-breaking random variable. Note that $p_*^{(j,k)}$ represents the portion of calibration examples whose j-th outputs are at least as nonconforming as the tentatively labelled test example (s_*, l^k).
6. Return a set of N prediction regions (one per output)

$$\Gamma_{\varepsilon,*} = \left\{ \{l^k \in L : p_*^{(j,k)} > \varepsilon\} \mid j \in \{1, \ldots, N\} \right\}. \quad (5)$$

together with the p-values.

Note that in this approach, called inductive CP [11], steps 1–4 are performed only once, while Steps 5–6 are performed for every test point s_*.

Statistical Guarantees. The CP algorithm outputs *prediction regions*, instead of single point predictions: given a significance level $\varepsilon \in (0,1)$ and a test point s_*, its prediction region with respect to output j, $\Gamma_{\varepsilon,*}^{(j)} \subseteq L$, is a set of labels guaranteed to contain the true label ℓ_*^j with probability $1 - \varepsilon$. The rationale is to use a statistical test, more precisely the Neyman-Pearson theory for hypothesis testing and confidence intervals [10], to check if (s_*, l^k) is particularly nonconforming compared to the calibration examples. The unknown distribution of nonconformity scores, referred to as $\mathcal{Q}$, is estimated by applying ncm_j to all calibration examples, set A_c (step 4). Then the scores A_* (step 5) are computed for every possible label and every output in order to test for the null hypothesis $A_* \sim \mathcal{Q}$. The null hypothesis is rejected if the p-values associated with A_* are smaller than the significance level ε. If a label l^k is rejected for output j, meaning if it appears unlikely that $ncm_j(s_*, l^k) \sim \mathcal{Q}^{(j)}$, we do not include this label in $\Gamma_{\varepsilon,*}^{(j)}$. Therefore, given ε, the prediction region for each output contains only those labels for which we could not reject the null hypothesis. In the stochastic setting, our approach guarantees that there is a probability (w.r.t. sampling) of $1 - \varepsilon$ that our prediction region includes the correct StochReach value, i.e., whether the (stochastic) system will reach D with probability above $1 - \alpha$, below α or in-between.

Nonconformity Function. A nonconformity function is well-defined if it assigns low scores to correct predictions and high scores to wrong predictions. In multi-output classification problems, a natural choice for ncm_j, based on the underlying model f, is

$$ncm_j(s_i, l^k) = 1 - P_{f^{(j)}}(l^k | s_i), \qquad (6)$$

where $P_{f^{(j)}}(l^k | s_i)$ is the likelihood of class l^k for output j when the model f is applied on s_i. If $f^{(j)}$ correctly predicts ℓ_i^j for input s_i, the corresponding likelihood $P_{f^{(j)}}(\ell_i^j | s_i)$ is high (the highest among all classes) and the resulting nonconformity score is low. The opposite holds when $f^{(j)}$ does not predict ℓ_i^j. The nonconformity measure chosen for our experiments, Eq. 6, preserves the ordering of the class likelihoods predicted by $f^{(j)}$ for every output j.

Confidence and Credibility. Observe that, for significance levels $\varepsilon_1 \geq \varepsilon_2$, the corresponding prediction regions are such that $\Gamma_{\varepsilon_1} \subseteq \Gamma_{\varepsilon_2}$. It follows that, given an input s_* and an output j, if ε is lower than all its p-values, i.e. $\varepsilon < \min_{k=1,\ldots,c} p_*^{(j,k)}$, then the region $\Gamma_{\varepsilon,*}^{(j)}$ contains all the labels. As ε increases, fewer and fewer classes will have a p-value higher than ε. That is, the region shrinks as ε increases. In particular, $\Gamma_{\varepsilon,*}^{(j)}$ is empty when $\varepsilon \geq \max_{k=1,\ldots,c} p_*^{(j,k)}$.

The *confidence* of a point $s_* \in S$ w.r.t. output j, $1 - \gamma_*^{(j)}$, measures how likely our prediction for s_* is compared to all other possible classifications (according to the calibration set). It is computed as one minus the smallest value of ε for which the conformal region is a single label, i.e. the second largest p-value γ_*:

$$1 - \gamma_*^{(j)} = \sup\{1 - \varepsilon : |\Gamma_{\varepsilon,*}^{(j)}| = 1\}.$$

Informally, the confidence of a prediction can be interpreted as the probability that a prediction corresponds to the true label.

The *credibility* w.r.t. output j, $\kappa_*^{(j)}$, indicates how suitable the training data are to classify that specific example. In practice, it is the smallest ε for which the prediction region is empty, i.e. the highest p-value according to the calibration set, which corresponds to the p-value of the predicted class:

$$\kappa_*^{(j)} = \inf\{\varepsilon : |\Gamma_{\varepsilon,*}^{(j)}| = 0\}.$$

Intuitively, credibility quantifies how likely a given state is to belong to the same distribution of the training data.

Uncertainty Function. The higher $1 - \gamma_*^{(j)}$ and $\kappa_*^{(j)}$ are, the more reliable the prediction $\hat{\ell}_*^j$ is. Therefore, our uncertainty-based rejection criterion relies on excluding points with low values of $1 - \gamma_*^{(j)}$ and $\kappa_*^{(j)}$. We stress, in particular, the following statistical guarantee: the probability that the true prediction for s_* is exactly $\hat{\ell}_*^j$ is at most $1 - \gamma_*^{(j)}$.

The uncertainty map u_f used to quantify the predictive uncertainty of a predictor f, introduced in Problem 3, is thus defined as

$$u_f(s_*) = \{(\gamma_*^{(j)}, \kappa_*^{(j)}) \mid j \in \{1, \dots, N\}\}.$$

4.2 Uncertainty-Based Rejection Rule

Confidence and credibility measure how much a prediction can be trusted. Our goal is to leverage these two measures of uncertainty to identify a criterion to detect errors of the reachability predictor. The rationale is that every new input s is required to have values of confidence, $1 - \gamma$, and credibility, κ, sufficiently high in order for the classification to be accepted. However, determining optimal thresholds is a non-trivial task.

In order to automatically identify optimal thresholds, we proceed with an additional supervised learning approach. For this purpose, we introduce a *cross-validation strategy* to compute values of confidence and credibility, using Z_c as validation set. For every output j, the cross-validation strategy consists of removing the i-th score, $A_c^{(i,j)}$, in order to compute $\gamma_i^{(j)}$ and $\kappa_i^{(j)}$, i.e. the p-values at $s_i \in S_c$ w.r.t. output j, where $S_c = \{s \mid (s, \ell) \in Z_c\}$. In this way, we can compute confidence, $1 - \gamma^{(j)}$, and credibility, $\kappa^{(j)}$, for every point in the calibration set. For each output j, the points of the calibration set are then labelled with 1 or 0 depending on whether the classifier $f^{(j)}$ makes a prediction error over that calibration point or not. We then solve N binary classification problems by training N separate Support Vector Classifiers (SVCs) over the calibration set. These SVC optimally solve Problem 3.

Rejection Rule Refinement. As already observed in [4], predictors with very high accuracy result in over-conservative rejection rules. Intuitively, the reason is that since the number of non-zero calibration scores is limited, the p-values are less sensitive to changes in the nonconformity score. We here propose an output-specific refinement, meaning that, for each output j, we add to $A_c^{(j)}$ the points where $f^{(j)}$ predictions where rejected by $Rej^{(j)}$. By doing so, we add calibration points with informative non-zero calibration scores. However, in doing so we modify the data generation distribution of the calibration set. Thus the statistical guarantees, meaning the prediction regions, are computed w.r.t. the original calibration set.

Active Learning. The rejection rule defined above can be used as an uncertainty-based query strategy for an active learning approach, allowing the user to select the points where the predictor f is performing poorly and then add them to the training set to improve the performances of f.

5   Experiments

Implementation. The workflow can be divided into steps: (1) define the BSS models for different architectures, (2) generate the synthetic datasets Z' for both the deterministic (both under FO or PO) and the stochastic version, (3) train the NPM-CAS, (4) train the CP-based error detection rules and (5) evaluate NPM-CAS on a test set. The technique is fully implemented in Python[1]. In particular, PyTorch [12] is used to craft, train and evaluate the neural networks used to solve Problem 1, 2 and 5. The source code for all the experiments can be found at the following link: https://github.com/francescacairoli/CAS_NPM.git.

Datasets Generation. We set the number of bikes in the system to $M = 100$ for each configuration. The training set consists of $20K$ points, the calibration set consists of $10K$ points and the test set consists of $5K$ points. In the stochastic version, the upper and lower bounds are computed over samples of 200 trajectories per point. We define BSS networks with three different topologies with increasing dimensions, i.e. larger number of bike stations, and thus increasing complexity.

- *Triangular network* – Fig. 1: 3 bike stations, departure rates $\lambda_1 = 0.25$, $\lambda_2 = 0.2$, $\lambda_3 = 0.15$, distances are set to 10, station capacity K is set to 35 for each station.
- *Diamond network* – Fig. 3 *(left)*: 5 bike stations, departure rates $\lambda = 0.25$, $\lambda_a = 0.2$, $\lambda_b = 0.15$, distances are set to $a = 10$ and $b = 12$, station capacity K is set to 25 for each station.
- *Hexagon network* – Fig. 3 *(right)*: 7 bike stations, constant departure rates $\lambda = 0.2$, distances $d = 10$, constant station capacity $K = 20$.

---

[1] The experiments were performed on a computer with a CPU Intel x86, 24 cores and a 128 GB RAM and 15 GB of GPU Tesla V100.

Training Details. A grid-search approach has been used to find the best performing hyper-parameters under each configuration. In FO scenarios (both deterministic and stochastic), we use a feed-forward neural network composed of five layers with 50 neurons each, LeakyReLU activations and drop-out with probability 0.1. The last layer has a ReLU activation so to obtain positive likelihood scores that are fed into a cross-entropy loss. The training is performed for 1000 epochs over batches of size 256, using Adam optimizer with a learning rate of 0.0005.

In the PO scenario, we use one-dimensional convolutional neural networks with N channels, 128 filters of size 5, LeakyReLU activations and drop-out with probability 0.1. As before, the last layer has a ReLU activation and a cross-entropy loss. The training is performed for 400 epochs over batches of size 256, using Adam optimizer with a learning rate of 0.0005.

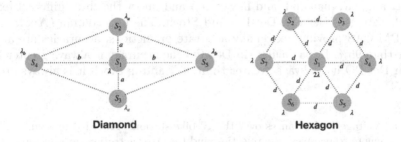

Diamond   **Hexagon**

Fig. 3. Diamond and hexagon geometries.

Computational Costs. NPM-CAS is designed to work at runtime which translates into the need for high computational efficiency together with high reliability. The time needed to generate the dataset and to train both methods does not affect the runtime efficiency of the NPM-CAS, as it is performed only once (offline). Once trained, the time needed to analyse the reachability of the current sequence of observations is the time needed to evaluate the trained neural networks, which is almost negligible (in the order of microseconds on GPU). On the other hand, the time needed to quantify the uncertainty depends on the size of the calibration set. It is important to notice that the percentage of points rejected, meaning points with predictions estimated to be unreliable, affects considerably the runtime efficiency of the methods. Therefore, we seek a trade-off between accuracy and runtime efficiency. The training phase takes from 3 to 10 hours, whereas computing a single prediction takes less than 1 microseconds. Training each SVC takes from 1 to 10 s, whereas computing values of confidence and credibility for a single point takes from 0.01 to 0.08 s.

Measures of Performance. The measures used to quantify the overall performance of the NPM-CAS are: the *accuracy* of the reachability predictor, the *error detection rate* and the *rejection rate*. We seek high accuracies and detection rates without being overly conservative, meaning keeping a rejection rate as low as possible. We also check if and when the statistical guarantees are met empirically, via values of coverage and efficiency. Efficiency is measured as the percentage of singletons in the prediction regions. We analyse and compare the performances of NPM-CAS on the three different BSS network configurations – the triangular, the diamond and the hexagon network. For each configuration, we compare the results of the deterministic version under the full observability assumption (Det-FO), the deterministic version under the partial observability assumption (Det-PO) and the stochastic version assuming full observability (Stoch).

5.1 Results

Table 1 summarizes the experimental results over the three different BSS topologies – triangular, diamond, and hexagon – and under the three different experimental settings – Det-FO, Det-PO and Stoch. The first column (**Acc.**) shows how NPM-CAS provides extremely accurate predictions, accuracies are always greater than 95%. In particular, in Det-FO the accuracy is always greater than 98%, in Det-PO it is always greater than 96% and in Stoch it is always greater than 95%.

Table 1. Average performances over the N bike stations. **Acc.** is the accuracy, **Rej.** and **det.** denote respectively the rejection and the error detection rates, whereas **Cov.** and **Eff.** respectively denote coverage and efficiency of the prediction regions (at level $\varepsilon = 0.05$).

Topology	Version	Initial results					Refinement	
		Acc.	**Rej.**	**Det.**	**Cov.**	**Eff.**	**Rej.**	**Det.**
Triangular	Det-FO	99.20	8.47	88.93	95.17	95.26	6.87	85.14
	Det-PO	98.24	11.93	96.87	95.35	95.75	9.40	94.48
	Stoch	97.55	13.05	92.02	95.13	96.07	12.03	91.51
Diamond	Det-FO	98.85	10.10	85.22	94.90	95.09	9.39	84.87
	Det-PO	96.21	19.71	92.07	94.99	97.67	14.27	89.86
	Stoch	96.38	18.12	87.05	95.16	97.92	15.93	86.21
Hexagon	Det-FO	98.02	13.12	84.09	95.13	95.81	12.28	81.37
	Det-PO	96.47	19.67	93.56	94.79	97.13	14.39	97.07
	Stoch	95.37	26.35	88.64	95.19	98.14	20.53	81.50

In column **Cov.** we observe how the CP prediction regions meet the statistical guarantees as the empirical coverage is close to the desired value of 95%. Moreover, the prediction regions show rather high efficiencies – see **Eff.** column. Efficiencies are always greater than 95%, meaning that there is no need for the CP predictor to be over-conservative in order to meet the guaranteed coverage.

Table 1 also shows the performances of the CP-based error detection rule before and after the refinement. We observe how the refinement of the error detection rule always reduces the rejection rate but it also results in slightly lower detection rates. In particular, on average over all the case studies, the rejection rate reduces from 17.41% to 13.70%, whereas the detection rate reduces from 88.78% to 83.32%. The reduction in the rejection rate is proportional to the reduction in the detection rate. This is most likely because the number of errors is rather small, resulting in highly unbalanced datasets, even after the refinement process, making the error detection phase extremely sensitive. Moreover, the refinement process changes the data generating distribution of the calibration set, meaning that the CP statistical guarantees no longer apply. Therefore, the refined solution is more efficient but less conservative than the original one and thus, its application has to be chosen wisely knowing the criticalities of the CAS at hand.

5.2 Discussion

Our results show great promise overall: the method attains very high accuracy levels (ranging from 95.37% to 99.2%), provides statistical guarantees, and effectively identifies and reject prediction errors. As expected, the performance is affected by the complexity and the dimensionality of the problem, i.e., deterministic scenarios with few agents outperform stochastic ones with a larger number of agents. As future work, we plan to systematically evaluate the scalability of our NPM approach with respect to the complexity and the dimensionality of the CAS at hand.

Moreover, our current approach handles the stochastic setting by partitioning the range of reachability probabilities into three regions, safe ($[0, \alpha]$), unsafe ($[1 - \alpha, 1]$), and "indifference" ($\alpha, 1 - \alpha$), and predicting one of these segments (a classification problem). While the method can be easily extended to support arbitrary probability partitions, a next step will be to develop a quantitative approach that directly predicts reachability probabilities rather than categorical values (a regression problem). Another open problem is dealing with partial observability in stochastic systems where state identifiability remains an issue.

Finally, a natural extension would be to apply NPM-CAS to more realistic BSS topologies, e.g., the London BSS or any other cities that make such data available.

6   Conclusions

In this paper, we presented NPM-CAS an extension of the neural predictive monitoring technique to collective adaptive systems with variable complexity. In particular, NPM-CAS works both on CAS with deterministic dynamics, under either full or partial observability, and on CAS with stochastic dynamics. The technique is experimentally tested on a bike-sharing system with network topologies with increasing complexity. Results are promising, predictions are extremely accurate and computationally efficient, thereby enabling the deployment of predictive monitoring at runtime on embedded devices with limited computational power.

References

1. Balasubramanian, V., Ho, S.S., Vovk, V.: Conformal Prediction for Reliable Machine Learning: Theory, Adaptations and Applications. Newnes, Oxford (2014)
2. Bortolussi, L.: Hybrid limits of continuous time Markov chains. In: 2011 Eighth International Conference on Quantitative Evaluation of Systems, pp. 3–12. IEEE (2011)
3. Bortolussi, L.: Hybrid behaviour of Markov population models. Inf. Comput. **247**, 37–86 (2016)
4. Bortolussi, L., Cairoli, F., Paoletti, N., Smolka, S.A., Stoller, S.D.: Neural predictive monitoring. In: Finkbeiner, B., Mariani, L. (eds.) RV 2019. LNCS, vol. 11757, pp. 129–147. Springer, Cham (2019). https://doi.org/10.1007/978-3-030-32079-9_8
5. Bortolussi, L., Cairoli, F., Paoletti, N., Smolka, S.A., Stoller, S.D.: Neural predictive monitoring and a comparison of frequentist and Bayesian approaches. Int. J. Softw. Tools Technol. Transf. **23**(4), 615–640 (2021)
6. Bortolussi, L., Hillston, J., Latella, D., Massink, M.: Continuous approximation of collective system behaviour: a tutorial. Perform. Eval. **70**(5), 317–349 (2013)
7. Cairoli, F., Bortolussi, L., Paoletti, N.: Neural predictive monitoring under partial observability. In: Feng, L., Fisman, D. (eds.) RV 2021. LNCS, vol. 12974, pp. 121–141. Springer, Cham (2021). https://doi.org/10.1007/978-3-030-88494-9_7
8. Gillespie, D.T., Petzold, L.: Numerical simulation for biochemical kinetics. In: Systems Modelling in Cellular Biology, pp. 331–354 (2006)
9. Le Boudec, J.Y., McDonald, D., Mundinger, J.: A generic mean field convergence result for systems of interacting objects. In: Fourth International Conference on the Quantitative Evaluation of Systems (QEST 2007), pp. 3–18. IEEE (2007)
10. Lehmann, E.L., Romano, J.P.: Testing Statistical Hypotheses. Springer, New York (2006). https://doi.org/10.1007/0-387-27605-X
11. Papadopoulos, H.: Inductive conformal prediction: theory and application to neural networks. In: Tools in Artificial Intelligence. InTech (2008)
12. Paszke, A., et al.: Automatic differentiation in PyTorch. In: NIPS-W (2017)
13. Younes, H.L., Simmons, R.G.: Statistical probabilistic model checking with a focus on time-bounded properties. Inf. Comput. **204**(9), 1368–1409 (2006)
14. Zuliani, P., Platzer, A., Clarke, E.M.: Bayesian statistical model checking with application to simulink/stateflow verification. In: Proceedings of the 13th ACM International Conference on Hybrid Systems: Computation and Control, pp. 243–252 (2010)

An Extension of HybridSynchAADL and Its Application to Collaborating Autonomous UAVs

Jaehun Lee[1], Kyungmin Bae[1(✉)] (iD), and Peter Csaba Ölveczky[2] (iD)

[1] Pohang University of Science and Technology, Pohang, South Korea
kmbae@postech.ac.kr
[2] University of Oslo, Oslo, Norway

Abstract. Many collective adaptive systems consist of distributed nodes that communicate with each other and with their physical environments, but that logically should operate in a synchronous way. HYBRID-SYNCHAADL is a recent modeling language and formal analysis tool for such virtually synchronous cyber-physical systems (CPSs). HYBRID-SYNCHAADL uses the Hybrid PALS equivalence to reduce the hard problem of designing and verifying virtually synchronous CPSs—with network delays, asynchronous communication, imprecise local clocks, continuous dynamics, etc.—to the much easier tasks of designing and verifying their underlying synchronous designs. Up to now HYBRIDSYNCH-AADL has lacked important programming language features, such as compound data types and user-defined functions, which made it difficult to model advanced control logics of collective adaptive systems. In this paper, we extend the HYBRIDSYNCHAADL language, its formal semantics, and its analysis tool to support these programming language features. We apply our extension of HYBRIDSYNCHAADL to design and analyze a collection of collaborating autonomous drones that adapt to their environments.

1 Introduction

Many distributed cyber-physical systems (CPSs)—including avionics [4,30] and automotive systems [27,34], and networked medical devices [3,21]—are *virtually synchronous*: They should logically behave as if they were synchronous—in each iteration of the system, all components, in lockstep, read inputs and perform transitions which generate outputs for the next iteration—but have to be realized in a distributed setting where the infrastructure guarantees bounds Γ on the clock skews, networks delays, and execution times. The design and model checking of such virtually synchronous CPSs is hard, due to communication delays, race conditions, execution times, and imprecise local clocks, and due to the state space explosion caused by interleavings.

T. Margaria and B. Steffen (Eds.): ISoLA 2022, LNCS 13703, pp. 47–64, 2022.
https://doi.org/10.1007/978-3-031-19759-8_4

The PALS ("physically asynchronous, logically synchronous") design and analysis pattern [2,30] greatly simplifies the design and verification of virtually synchronous distributed real-time system *without* continuous behaviors: It is sufficient to design and verify the much simpler synchronous design *SD*—without asynchrony, network delays, clock skews, etc.—since the corresponding distributed real-time system $PALS(SD, \Gamma)$ satisfies the same properties as *SD*. Many virtually synchronous CPSs are distributed *hybrid* systems where local controllers have continuous environments. *Hybrid PALS* [8] extends PALS to such distributed hybrid systems. However, in such systems we can no longer abstract from the time when a continuous value is sampled or when a control command is sent, both of which depend on the local controller's imprecise clock.

To make the Hybrid PALS design and verification methodology available to CPS designers, we have developed the HYBRIDSYNCHAADL modeling language and analysis tool [25,26]. Its modeling language (for modeling the synchronous designs) is an annotated sublanguage of AADL [18], an industrial modeling standard used in avionics, aerospace, automotive systems, and robotics. We have also integrated the modeling and formal model checking analysis of HYBRIDSYNCH-AADL models into the OSATE modeling environment for AADL.

In HYBRIDSYNCHAADL, controller behaviors are defined using a subset of AADL's *Behavior Annex* [19], with behaviors defined by transitions with Boolean guards, variable assignments, conditionals, loops, and so on. Mode-dependent continuous behaviors are specified using differential equations. In [25] we use the rewriting logic language Maude [16] to formalize complex control programs, and use Maude combined with SMT solving [11,32] to *symbolically* encode continuous behaviors—with all possible sampling and actuating times depending on imprecise local clocks—and provide a Maude-with-SMT semantics, as well as symbolic reachability analysis, randomized simulation, and multithreaded portfolio analysis, for HYBRIDSYNCHAADL. In [25,26] we use HYBRIDSYNCHAADL to model and analyze a collection of autonomous drones, and show that our tool in most cases outperforms the state-of-the-art hybrid systems tools HyComp [15], SpaceEx [20], Flow* [14], and dReach [22].

Up to now HYBRIDSYNCHAADL has lacked some language features that would make it much more convenient and less error-prone to model sophisticated CPSs. Since an adaptive system often consist of a large number of communicating nodes, we extend HYBRIDSYNCHAADL with *arrays* to conveniently specify and store information about multiple nodes. We also extend HYBRIDSYNCHAADL with user-definable data types and with the possibility of specifying user-defined functions as AADL *subprograms*. We extend the HYBRIDSYNCHAADL property specification language accordingly (Sect. 6). In this paper, we introduce these new features of HYBRIDSYNCHAADL (Sect. 4), and explain how its Maude-with-SMT semantics has been extended to include these features (Sect. 5).

We demonstrate the modeling and analysis convenience of this new version of our tool with a system of collaborating drones for packet delivery, where each drone adapts to the motions of the other drones for collision avoidance (Sect. 6). This case study involves multiple drone/packet components with a nontrivial connection topology, and includes complex control programs that use several subroutines and composite data types. It is therefore very difficult to specify our case study without the new programming language features of HYBRIDSYNCH-AADL. Our tool and the model of the case study are available at https://hybridsynchaadl.github.io/artifact/isola2022.

2 Preliminaries

PALS. The PALS pattern [2,30] reduces the problem of designing and verifying a distributed real-time system to the much easier problems of designing and verifying its synchronous design, provided that the underlying infrastructure guarantees bounds Γ on execution times, clock skews, and network delays. For a synchronous design SD, bounds Γ, and a period p, PALS provides the distributed real-time system $PALS(SD, \Gamma, p)$, which is stuttering bisimilar to SD.

The synchronous design SD is formalized as the synchronous composition of an *ensemble* of communicating state machines [30]. At the beginning of each iteration, each state machine performs a transition based on its current state and its inputs, proceeds to the next state, and generates outputs. All machines perform their transitions at the same time, and the outputs to other machines become inputs at the *next* iteration.

Hybrid PALS. *Hybrid PALS* [8] extends PALS to virtually synchronous CPSs with environments that exhibit continuous behaviors. The *physical environment* E_M of a machine M has real-valued parameters $\boldsymbol{x} = (x_1, \ldots, x_l)$. The continuous behaviors of $\boldsymbol{x}$ are modeled by ordinary differential equations (ODEs) that specify different *trajectories* on $\boldsymbol{x}$. E_M also defines *which* trajectory the environment follows, as a function of the last *control command* received by E_M.

The local clock of a machine M can be seen as a function $c_M : \mathbb{R}_{\geq 0} \to \mathbb{R}_{\geq 0}$, where $c_M(t)$ is the value of the local clock at time t, satisfying $|c_M(t) - t| < \epsilon$ for the maximal clock skew $\epsilon > 0$ [30]. In its ith iteration, a controller M samples the values of its environment at time $c_M(i \cdot p) + t_s$, where t_s is the *sampling time*, and then executes a transition. As a result, the new control command is received by the environment at time $c_M(i \cdot p) + t_a$, where t_a is the *actuating time*.

AADL. The *Architecture Analysis & Design Language* (AADL) is an industrial modeling standard used in avionics, automotive, medical devices, and robotics to describe an embedded real-time system [18]. AADL models describe a system of hardware and software components. Software components include: *threads* modeling the application software; *data* representing data types; *subprograms* representing subroutines; and *systems* defining top-level components.

In AADL, a component *type* specifies the component's *interface* (e.g., ports) and *properties* (e.g., periods), and a component *implementation* specifies its internal structure as *subcomponents* and *connections* linking their ports. AADL constructs may have *properties* describing their parameters, declared in *property sets.* Thread and subprogram behavior is modeled as a guarded transition system with local variables using AADL's *Behavior Annex* [19]. When a thread is activated, enabled transitions are applied until a *complete* state is reached.

Maude with SMT. Maude [16] is a language and tool for formally specifying and analyzing distributed systems in rewriting logic. A *rewrite theory* [29] is a triple $\mathcal{R} = (\Sigma, E, R)$, where (Σ, E) is an equational theory—specifying system states as an algebraic data type—with Σ a signature (declaring sorts, subsorts, and function symbols) and E a set of equations; and R is a set of rewrite rules—specifying system transitions—of the form $l : t \longrightarrow t'$ **if** *cond*, where l is a label, t and t' are terms, and *cond* is a conjunction of equations and rewrites.

A declaration   class C | $att_1 : s_1, \ldots, att_n : s_n$ declares a class C with attributes $att_1, \ldots, att_n$ of sorts $s_1, \ldots, s_n$. An *object* o of class C is represented as a term $< o : C \mid att_1 : v_1, \ldots, att_n : v_n >$ of sort Object, where v_i is the value of att_i. A *subclass* inherits the attributes and rewrite rules of its superclasses. A *configuration* is a multiset of objects and messages, and has sort Configuration, with multiset union denoted by juxtaposition.

In addition to its explicit-state analysis methods for concrete states (ground terms), Maude also provides SMT solving and *symbolic reachability analysis* for *constrained terms*, using connections to Yices2 [17] and CVC4 [13]. A constrained term is a pair $\phi \parallel t$ that symbolically represents all instances of the term t satisfying the SMT constraint ϕ. A *symbolic rewrite* on constrained terms can symbolically represent a (possibly infinite) set of system transitions [11,32].

3   Overview of HybridSynchAADL

This section gives a brief overview of the original HYBRIDSYNCHAADL language and its Maude-with-SMT semantics as defined in [25,26]; see [25] for details.

3.1   The HybridSynchAADL Modeling Language

The HYBRIDSYNCHAADL language is a subset of AADL extended with the property set Hybrid_SynchAADL. HYBRIDSYNCHAADL can specify synchronous designs of distributed controller components, (local) environment components with continuous dynamics, and interactions between controllers and environments based on imprecise local clocks and sampling and actuation times.

Discrete controllers are standard software components in the Synchronous AADL subset of AADL [7,9]. This subset includes system, process, and thread components; data components for base types; ports and connections; and thread behaviors defined in the Behavior Annex [19]. The subset in [25,26] did not include composite data types, subprograms, and arrays of components and ports.

Environments specify real-valued state variables that change continuously over time. The continuous dynamics of state variables can be declared using either ODEs or continuous real functions. An environment can have multiple *modes* for different continuous dynamics. A controller command may change the mode of the environment or the value of a state variable.

3.2 Symbolic Semantics of HybridSynchAADL

Representing HybridSynchAADL Models. Each component is represented as an object instance of a subclass of the base class Component. The attribute features denotes a set of Port objects, subcomponents denotes a set of Component objects. connections denotes its connections, and properties denotes its properties.

```
class Component | features : Configuration, properties : PropertyAssociation,
          subcomponents : Configuration, connections : Set{Connection} .
```

The type of each AADL component corresponds to a subclass of Component. The class Thread has attributes for thread behaviors, such as transitions, states, and local variables. The class Env for environments has attributes for continuous dynamics, sampling and actuating times, and mode transitions.

Ports and data components are also modeled as objects. Data components are represented as instances of the class Data, where value denotes the current value. A data content is represented as a pair $e \# b$ of an expression e and a Boolean condition b. If b is *false*, then there is no content (i.e., some "don't care" value $\perp$) in the data/port; otherwise, the value of the content is e.

```
class Data | value : DataContent .              subclass Data < Component .
op _#_ : Exp BoolExp -> DataContent [ctor] .
```

We use a *constrained object* of the form $\phi \;||\; obj$ to symbolically represent a (possibly infinite) set of object instances of obj, where $\phi(x_1, \ldots, x_n)$ is an SMT constraint and $obj(x_1, \ldots, x_n)$ is a "pattern" over SMT variables $x_1, \ldots, x_n$. Figure 1 shows an example of a thread component and its representation.

```
thread CtrlThread                          not x_b or (y_b and x_v > 0)  ||
 features                                   < ctrlThread : Thread |
   c: out event port;                          features :
   i: in data port Base_Types::Float;          < c : DataOutPort |
   o: out data port Base_Types::Float;            content : * # false, ... >
end CtrlThread;                                 < i : DataInPort |
                                                   content : 0 # y_b, ... >
thread implementation CtrlThread.impl          < o : DataOutPort |
 subcomponents                                     content : 0 # true,  ... >,
   v: data Base_Types::Float;               subcomponents :
 annex behavior_specification {**             < v : Data | value : x_v # x_b, ... >,
   states                                    transitions :
     s0: initial complete state;  s1: state;   s0 -[on dispatch]-> s1
   transitions                                 { v := (i + v) / 2 } ;
     s0 -[on dispatch]-> s1 {v := (i + v) / 2};  s1 -[v > 25]-> s0 { c ! } ;
     s1 -[v > 25]-> s0 {c!};                    s1 -[otherwise]-> s0 { o := v },
     s1 -[otherwise]-> s0 {o := v};    **};   currState : s0,
end CtrlThread.impl;                          completeStates : s0, ... >
```

Fig. 1. A thread component and a constrained term representation.

Specifying the Behavior. We define various *semantic operations* on constrained terms to specify the behavior of components, threads, environments, etc. In particular, the operation executeStep defines a symbolic rewrite relation for a "big-step" synchronous iteration of a single AADL component.

A symbolic synchronous step of the entire system is then formalized by the following rule step. A symbolic rewrite from $\{\phi \parallel obj\}$ to $\{\phi' \parallel obj'\}$ holds if there is a symbolic rewrite from executeStep($\phi \parallel obj$) to $\phi' \parallel obj'$, provided that obj has no ports and the constraint ϕ' is satisfiable.

```
crl [step]: {PHI || < C : System | features : none >} => {PHI' || OBJ'}
if executeStep(PHI || < C : System | >) => PHI' || OBJ'  /\ check-sat(PHI') .
```

Figure 2 shows the definition of executeStep and auxiliary operations for threads. In the first rule, readPort returns a map from each input port to its content; readData returns a map from each data subcomponent to its value; execTrans executes the transition system, given a *behavior configuration* BCF of local variables, port contents, data component values, and properties; writePort updates the output ports; and writeData updates the data subcomponents. In the second rule, a transition L -[GC]-> L' ACT from the current state L is chosen nondeterministically, and execAction executes the actions ACT with the guard condition GC; if the next state L' is a complete state (L' in LS), the operation ends; otherwise, execTrans is applied again. The operation execAction computes a behavior action; e.g., the third rule defines the semantics of an assignment action *id := exp*, where eval evaluates the data content D of an expression.

```
crl executeStep(
     PHI  || < C : Thread | features : PORTS,       variables : VIS, completeStates : LS,
            transitions : TRS, subcomponents : COMPS, properties : PRS, currState : L >)
 => PHI' || < C : Thread | features : writePort(FM',PORTS'),
                          subcomponents : writeData(DATA',COMPS),  currState : L' >
if {PORTS',FM} := readPort(PORTS)  /\  DATA := readData(COMPS)
/\ execTrans(PHI || {emptyVal(VIS), FM, DATA, PRS}, TRS, L, LS) => L' | FM' | DATA' | PHI' .

crl execTrans(PHI || BCF, TRS, L, LS)
 => if L' in LS then  L' | FM' | DATA' | PHI'
               else  execTrans(PHI' || {local(BCF), FM', DATA', PRS}, TRS, L', LS)  fi
if (L -[GC]-> L' ACT) ; TRS' := TRS  /\  B := guardConst(GC, L, TRS', BCF)
/\ execAction(ACT, (PHI and B) || BCF) => PHI' || {VAL', FM', DATA', PRS} .

crl execAction(ID := EXP, PHI || BCF) => PHI' || update(ID, D, BCF)
if eval(EXP, PHI || BCF) => PHI' || D .

eq update(VI, D, VAL | FM | DATA | PRS) = insert(VI,D,VAL) | FM | DATA | PRS .  --- local
eq update(PI, D, VAL | FM | DATA | PRS) = VAL | insert(PI,D,FM) | DATA | PRS .  --- port
eq update(CI, D, VAL | FM | DATA | PRS) = VAL | FM | insert(CI,D,DATA) | PRS .  --- data
```

Fig. 2. Some semantic operations for thread components.

4   An Extension of HybridSynchAADL

In this section we extend the HYBRIDSYNCHAADL modeling language in [25, 26] with the following AADL constructs: struct and array data types, arrays of components and ports, and subprograms.

Composite Data Types. We now support (nested) *struct* and *array* types defined in the Data Modeling Annex [33] of AADL. They are declared as user-defined data components annotated with `Data_Model` properties representing the details of the data types. In particular, the property `Data_Model::Data_Representation` denotes the representation of a data type, such as `Struct` and `Array`.

```
data Vector
 properties
   Data_Model::Data_Representation => Struct;
   Data_Model::Base_Type => (
     classifier (Base_Types::Float),
     classifier (Base_Types::Float));
   Data_Model::Element_Names => ("x", "y");
 end Vector;

data VectorArray
 properties
   Data_Model::Data_Representation => Array;
```

```
   Data_Model::Base_Type =>
     (classifier (Vector));
   Data_Model::Dimension => (5);
 end VectorArray;


data TwoDimIntArray
 properties
   Data_Model::Data_Representation => Array;
   Data_Model::Base_Type => (
     classifier (Base_Types::Integer));
   Data_Model::Dimension => (10, 20);
 end TwoDimIntArray;
```

Fig. 3. Examples of composite data types in AADL.

Figure 3 shows examples of struct and array data types. Vector is a struct type with two floating-point elements x and y, declared using `Data_Model` properties. VectorArray is a one-dimensional array of Vector, and TwoDimIntArray is a two-dimensional array of integers, where the sizes of array dimensions are declared using `Data_Model::Dimension`. In AADL, array indices begin with 1.

Arrays of Components and Ports. In AADL, multiple instances of the same component type can be declared as an array of the component type. For example, the system component `Top.impl` in Fig. 4, contains an array of Agent (of size 3) and an array of Tower (of size 2), where both components Agent and Tower have an array ip of input ports (of size 3).

The connections between arrays of components/ports are declared with the properties `Connection_Set` and `Connection_Pattern`. A connection set specifies a list of individual connections using array indices. A connection pattern uses a predefined list of frequently used connection sets. For example, the connection C1 in Fig. 4 uses a connection set: each pair $[\texttt{src=>}(i,j)\texttt{; dst=>}(k,l)\texttt{;}]$ specifies a connection from output port ot$[i]$ of subcomponent agent$[j]$ to input port ip[k] of subcomponent tower[l]. The connection C2 uses a connection pattern: output port sd of agent[i] connects to input port ip[j] of agent[k], where $i = j$ (One_To_One) and each j is related to all k's (One_To_All).

```
system Agent                    system implementation Top.impl
  features                        subcomponents
    ip: in data port Vector [3];    agent: system Agent [3];    tower: system Tower [2];
    sd: out data port Vector;     connections
    ot: out data port Vector [2];   C1: port agent.ot -> tower.ip;
end Agent;                          C2: port agent.sd -> agent.ip {Connection_Pattern
                                        => ((One_To_One, One_To_All));};
system Tower                      properties
  features                          Connection_Set =>
    ip: in data port Vector [3];      ([src=>(1,1);dst=>(1,1);], [src=>(2,1);dst=>(1,2);],
end Tower;                            [src=>(1,2);dst=>(2,1);], [src=>(2,2);dst=>(2,2);],
                                      [src=>(1,3);dst=>(3,1);], [src=>(2,3);dst=>(3,2);])
system Top                          applies to C1;
end Top;                        end Top.impl;
```

Fig. 4. Arrays of subcomponents and features.

Subprograms. In AADL, subprograms represent sequentially executable code. Subprogram components can have data parameters to pass and return values. Parameters can be input, output, or both input and output, where input parameters are readable and output parameters are writable. Subprogram components can also have data subcomponents to indicate local temporary variables.

In HYBRIDSYNCHAADL, subprogram behavior is modeled using guarded transitions written in the Behavior Annex in a way similar to thread behavior. The execution of a subprogram starts in its initial state and ends in a final state. A subprogram has one initial state and one or more final states. Subprograms can be called within threads and subprograms (including recursively).

```
subprogram getDist              subprogram implementation getDist.11
  features                        annex behavior_specification {**
    p: in parameter Vector;         states
    q: in parameter Vector;           s0: initial state;    s1: final state;
    d: out parameter                transitions
        Base_Types::Float;            s0 -[]-> s1 {d := abs(p.x - q.x) + abs(p.y - q.y)};    **};
end getDist;                    end getDist.11;
```

Fig. 5. A subprogram getDist.

Figure 5 shows a subprogram getDist which computes the distance between two vectors, given by the input parameters p and q, and returns the value to the caller using the output parameter d. The implementation getDist.11 returns the rectilinear distance between input parameters p and q using a single transition from the initial state s0 to the final state s1.

5   Extending the Semantics of HYBRIDSYNCHAADL

This section presents the Maude-with-SMT semantics for the new features introduced in Sect. 4 by extending the original semantics of HYBRIDSYNCHAADL. As those features extend the discrete subset of HYBRIDSYNCHAADL, we have only changed the part for discrete controllers in the original semantics. In particular, the definition of execAction is significantly changed to support subprograms and assignment actions with nested struct/array targets.

5.1   Representation of the Additional Features

An array content is represented as a term $array(1 \mapsto d_1; 2 \mapsto d_2; \ldots; n \mapsto d_n)$ of sort ArrayContent, where the i-th element is data content d_i. Likewise, a struct content is represented as $struct(c_1 \mapsto d_1; c_2 \mapsto d_2; \ldots; c_n \mapsto d_n)$ of sort StructContent, where the element c_i is d_i. Array and struct contents can be nested, since ArrayContent and StructContent are subsorts of DataContent.

Arrays and array connections of components and ports are *fully instantiated* in our representation. Figure 6 shows an example of a Maude representation of Top.impl in Fig. 4. Component arrays agent and tower, and port array ip are instantiated as concrete objects. Array connections, declared using a connection set and a connection pattern, are also instantiated as concrete connections.

```
< TopInstance : System |                connections :
  features : none,                        agent[1] .. ot[1] --> tower[1] .. ip[1];
  subcomponents :                         agent[2] .. ot[1] --> tower[1] .. ip[2];
    < agent[1] : System | ... >           agent[3] .. ot[1] --> tower[1] .. ip[3];
    < agent[2] : System | ... >           agent[1] .. ot[2] --> tower[2] .. ip[1];
    < agent[3] : System | ... >           agent[2] .. ot[2] --> tower[2] .. ip[2];
    < tower[1] : System | ... >           agent[3] .. ot[2] --> tower[2] .. ip[3];
    < tower[2] : System | features :      agent[1] .. sd --> agent[1]. ip[1];
      < ip[1] : DataInPort | content :    agent[1] .. sd --> agent[2]. ip[1];
         struct(x |==> 0 # true ;         agent[1] .. sd --> agent[3]. ip[1];
                y |==> 0 # true), ... >    ...
      < ip[2] : DataInPort | ... >         agent[3] .. sd --> agent[3]. ip[3];
      < ip[3] : DataInPort | ... >, ... >, properties : none >
```

Fig. 6. Maude representation of the System component Top in Fig. 4.

Subprograms are represented as instances of the class Subprogram, similar to Thread. The attribute args denotes the list of parameters; transitions denotes the set of transitions; currState denotes the current state; finalStates denotes the final states; and variables denotes the local variables and their types.

```
class Subprogram | args : List{FeatureId},  transitions : Set{Transition},
                   currState : Location,    finalStates : Set{Location},
                   variables : Map{VarId,DataType},
subclass Subprogram < Component .
```

A parameter of a subprogram is represented as an instance of a subclass of the class `Param`. The `features` attribute of the class `Subprogram` includes a set of `Param` objects instead of `Port` objects. Notice that `features` includes an unordered set of parameters, and `args` defines the argument order of them.

```
class Param | type : DataType,  properties : PropertyAssociation .
class InParam .     class OutParam .     class InOutParam .
subclass InOutParam < InParam OutParam < Param .
```

We define the function `subprogram` that returns a subprogram instance from its fully qualified name (automatically synthesized by code generation).

5.2   Semantic of Composite Data Types

We extend the definitions of the two operations `eval`—evaluating expressions—and `executeAction`—executing actions—for struct and array data types. For `eval`, we define the cases for struct expressions $exp.id$ and array expressions $exp'[exp]$. For `executeAction`, we define the case of an assignment action that includes (nested) struct and array expressions on the left-hand side.

The following rule defines the case of struct expressions $exp.id$ for `eval`. Given a constrained behavior configuration PHI $||$ BCF (including local variables, port contents, data component values, and properties), we first evaluate the struct data content of exp and then choose the element id from the content:

```
crl eval(EXP . CI, PHI || BCF) => PHI' || D
if eval(EXP, PHI || BCF) => PHI' || struct(CI |==> D ; STR) .
```

Similarly, for array expressions $exp'[exp]$, we first evaluate the index data content $e \# b$ of exp and the array data content of exp'. Because e may be a symbolic expression (not an integer constant), we nondeterministically choose the i-th element from the array data content with the constraint $i = e$.

```
crl eval(EXP'[EXP], PHI || BCF) => (PHI'' and B and I === E) || D
if eval(EXP,  PHI || BCF)  => PHI' || E # B
/\ eval(EXP', PHI' || BCF) => PHI'' || array(I |==> D ; ARR) .
```

Consider an assignment action $a.x[1].y := e$ with a nested struct/array target. The intuitive behavior is as follows. We first evaluate the "top" data content of a, e.g., $td = struct(x \mapsto array(1 \mapsto struct(y \mapsto \ldots; \ldots); \ldots); \ldots)$. We then update the sub-content of td at the "position" indicated by ".$x[1].y$" with e.

The following rules specify the above behavior. The function `evalPos` returns the top identifier and a position; e.g., `evalPos`$(a.x[1].y, nil)$ returns the pair $\{a, (.x)[1](.y)\}$. The substitution operation $td[pos \leftarrow d](\phi \parallel bcf)$ computes a new data content obtained by replacing the content of position pos with d.

```
crl execAction(TARGET := EXP, PHI || BCF) => assign(TARGET, D, PHI' || BCF)
if eval(EXP, PHI || BCF) => PHI' || D .

crl assign(TARGET, D, PHI || BCF) => PHI' || update(ID, TD', BCF)
if {ID, POS} := evalPos(TARGET, nil) /\ eval(ID, PHI || BCF) => PHI'' || TD
/\ TD [POS <- D] (PHI'' || BCF) => PHI' || TD' .
```

5.3   Semantics of Subprogram Calls

We define `executeAction` for subprogram calls $f!(exp_1, \ldots, exp_n)$ as follows. We first obtain the subprogram instance for f, and evaluate the parameters based on the caller's behavior configuration. We then use `execTrans` to execute the subprogram's transition system with a new behavior configuration. Finally, we update the caller's behavior configuration based on the output parameters.

```
crl executeAction(F!(EXPS), PHI || BCF) => retOutParams(OM, FM', PHI' || BCF)
if < O : Subprogram | features : PARAMS, properties : PRS,  args : PIS,
                      transitions : TRS, finalStates : LS,
                      variables : VIS,   currState : L > := subprogram(F)
/\ {OM, FM} := outParams(EXPS, PIS, PARAMS, none, empty)
/\ {FM'', PHI''} := inParams(EXPS, PIS, PARAMS, BCF, {FM, PHI})
/\ execTrans(PHI'' || {emptyVal(VIS), FM'', empty, PRS}, TRS, L, LS)
   => L' | FM' | empty | PHI' .
```

The operation `outParams` returns the output targets `OM` in the argument list. After the call ends, these targets are updated with the values assigned to the output parameters during subprogram execution. The operation `outParams` also returns initial contents `FM` (with no value `bot`) for the output parameters.

```
eq outParams((EXP,EXPS), PI PIS, < PI : OutParam | type : TY > PARAMS, OM, FM)
 = outParams(EXPS, PIS, PARAMS, insert(PI,EXP,OM), insert(PI,bot(TY),FM)) .
eq outParams((EXP,EXPS), PI PIS, < PI : Param | > PARAMS, OM, FM)
 = outParams(EXPS, PIS, PARAMS, OM, FM) [owise] .
eq outParams(nil, nil, none, OM, FM) = {OM, FM} .
```

The operation `inParams` evaluates the values of the input expressions in the argument list using `eval`. Notice that the initial contents generated by `outParams` are updated with the evaluated values for input-output parameters.

```
eq inParams((EXP,EXPS), PI PIS, < PI : InParam | > PARAMS, BCF, {FM, PHI})
 = inParams(EXPS, PIS, PARAMS, BCF, evalInParam(EXP, BCF, {FM, PHI})) .
eq inParams((EXP,EXPS), PI PIS, < PI : Param | > PARAMS, BCF, {FM, PHI})
 = inParams(EXPS, PIS, PARAMS, BCF, {FM, PHI}) [owise] .
eq inParams(nil, nil, none, BCF, {FM, PHI}) = {FM, PHI} .

crl evalInParam(EXP, BCF, {FM, PHI}) => {insert(PI,D,FM), PHI'}
if eval(EXP, PHI || BCF) => PHI' || D .
```

Finally, the operation `retOutParams` updates the output parameter targets (generated by `outParams`) with the values assigned to the output parameters. If no value is assigned to an output parameter, the target is not updated.

```
ceq retOutParams((PI |-> TARGET, OM), FM, PHI || BCF) = retOutParams(OM, FM,
     assign(TARGET, D, PHI || BCF)) if D := data(FM[PI]) /\ hasValue(D) .
eq retOutParams(empty, FM, PHI || BCF) = PHI || BCF .
```

6   Case Study: A Packet Delivery System

This section shows how HYBRIDSYNCHAADL can be used to design and analyze a collection of collaborating autonomous drones, taking into account network delays, clock skews, execution times, continuous dynamics, etc. The new features supported by HYBRIDSYNCHAADL make it easy to specify and analyze multiple instances of components with complex control programs.

6.1   System Description

We consider a packet delivery system adapted from [36]. As illustrated in Fig. 7, there are drones, packets, and charging stations. A drone picks up a packet and transports it to its destination. Drones use energy when moving and can recharge at charging stations. Each drone exchanges its position with other drones to adapt its movement to the motions of the other drones.

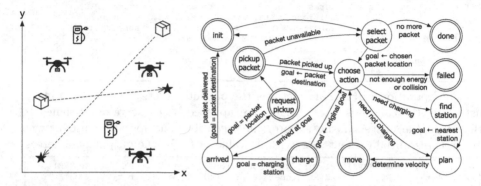

Fig. 7. Packet delivery system.   **Fig. 8.** Control logic of drones.

The continuous dynamics of the i-th drone is specified by the ODEs $\dot{x}_i = v_i$ and $\dot{e}_i = -h \cdot |v_i|$, where x_i, v_i, and e_i denote its position, velocity, and energy, respectively, and h denotes the energy consumption rate. The controller samples the drone's position, velocity, and energy at its sampling time, and gives a new velocity value to the environment at its actuating time.

Figure 8 shows the control logic of drones, where double circles indicate complete states (see Sect. 2), and `init` denotes the initial state. The controller uses a state variable `goal` to indicate the drone's target, such as a packet location, a packet destination, or a charging station location. The drone's behavior is determined in state `choose_action`, based on the current values of state variables (including `goal`) and the sampled position and energy from the environment.

A new velocity is calculated in state `plan` to move towards the current `goal` while adapting to the motions of the other drones. In this paper, we use this adaptation framework to implement a simple collision avoidance technique: each drone has a priority, and when a potential collision is detected (e.g., the distance between two drones is below a certain threshold), a drone with lower priority must yield to a drone with higher priority.

6.2   The HYBRIDSYNCHAADL Model

Figure 9 shows the top-level system component that contains `Drone` and `Packet` component arrays. We model the locations of charging stations as a constant array. The period, maximal clock skew, and sampling and actuating times are declared using `Hybrid_SynchAADL` properties. A drone can send a request to a packet (connection `C1`) and its position to the other drones (connection `C3`), and a packet can reply its destination to a drone (connection `C2`). In this section, we consider a packet delivery system with three drones and two packets.

```
system PacketDelivery
end PacketDelivery;

system implementation PacketDelivery.impl
  subcomponents
    drone: system Drone[3];
    packet: system Packet[2];
  connections
    C1: port drone.req -> packet.req;
    C2: port packet.dest -> drone.dest;
    C3: port drone.oPos -> drone.iPos
      {Connection_Pattern =>
        ((One_To_One, One_To_All));};
  properties
    Hybrid_SynchAADL::Synchronous => true;
    Period => 100ms;
    Timing => Delayed applies to C1,C2,C3;
```

```
Hybrid_SynchAADL::Max_Clock_Deviation => 5ms;
Hybrid_SynchAADL::Sampling_Time => 20ms..25ms;
Hybrid_SynchAADL::Response_Time => 40ms..45ms;

Connection_Set => ([src=>(1,1); dst=>(1,1);],
  [src=>(1,2); dst=>(2,1);],
  [src=>(1,3); dst=>(3,1);],
  [src=>(2,1); dst=>(1,2);],
  [src=>(2,2); dst=>(2,2);],
  [src=>(2,3); dst=>(3,2);]) applies to C1;
Connection_Set => ([src=>(1,1); dst=>(1,1);],
  [src=>(2,1); dst=>(1,2);],
  [src=>(3,1); dst=>(1,3);],
  [src=>(1,2); dst=>(2,1);],
  [src=>(2,2); dst=>(2,2);],
  [src=>(3,2); dst=>(2,3);]) applies to C2;
end PacketDelivery.impl;
```

Fig. 9. A top level component in HYBRIDSYNCHAADL.

A `Packet` component chooses one of the drones that have sent the request, and sends its destination to the selected drone. A `Drone` contains a controller and an environment connected to each other using ports. The environment declares the continuous dynamics of the drone's position, velocity, and energy mentioned above. We assume that a drone moves in a two-dimensional space. The controller also communicates with the outside components using `Drone`'s ports.

Figure 10 shows part of the HYBRIDSYNCHAADL specification for a controller thread that implements the control logic of Fig. 8. It contains several state variables, such as `goal` for the current target and `chargeStation` for the charging station locations. It also uses several subprograms, such as `chkClose` to check whether the drone is too close to other drones with higher priority. The entire HYBRIDSYNCHAADL specification of our model is given in the report [24] and is available at https://hybridsynchaadl.github.io/artifact/isola2022.

6.3 Formal Analysis

We are interested in analyzing whether all drones complete their tasks (i.e., going to state `done`) within a certain time, e.g., 10 seconds. This can be expressed as the following invariant property using HYBRIDSYNCHAADL's property specification language. We analyze this property up to bound 10,100 ms.

```
thread DroneThread
 features
    req: out data port Base_Types::Boolean[];
    dest: in data port Vector[];
    oPos: out data port Vector;
    iPos: in data port Vector[];
    ...
 end DroneThread;

thread implementation DroneThread.impl
 subcomponents
    goal: data Vector;
    chargeStation: data VectorArray;
    packetPos: data VectorArray;
    ...
 annex behavior_specification {**
  variables
    cur: Vector;  ...
  states
    init: initial complete state;
    ...
  transitions
    ...
    plan -[]-> move {
      chkClose.impl! (cur, iPos,..., close);
      if (close) set_hover! elsif ...     };
    ...
 **};
 end DroneThread.impl;
```

```
subprogram chkClose
 features
    p: in parameter Vector;
    pos: in parameter VectorArray;
    cand: in parameter BooleanArray;
    size: in parameter Base_Types::Integer;
    thld: in parameter Base_Types::Float;
    output: out parameter Base_Types::Boolean;
 end detectCollision;

subprogram implementation chkClose.impl
 annex behavior_specification {**
  variables
    d: Base_Types::Float;
    i: Base_Types::Integer;
    r : Base_Types::Boolean;
  states
    s0: initial state;   sf: final state;
    s1: state;
  transitions
    s0 -[]-> s1 { r := false; i := 1 };
    s1 -[r = false and i <= size]-> s1 {
      getDist.l1! (p, pos[i], d);
      r := d < thld and cand[i];
      i := i + 1
    };
    s1 -[otherwise]-> sf { output := r };
 **};
 end detectCollision.impl;
```

Fig. 10. A controller thread in HYBRIDSYNCHAADL ('...' indicates omitted parts).

```
invariant [complete] :
  ?initial ==> (not clock.time >= 10000) or ?allDone in time 10100 ms;
```

The above propositions `allDone` and `initial` are declared as follows. The keyword `const` is used to introduce a `VectorArray` constant p. The declaration of `allDone` includes universal quantification over array index i, which is a new feature of HYBRIDSYNCHAADL proposed in this work. Notice that there are infinitely many initial states satisfying `initial`.

```
const p:VectorArray = [{x:2.7, y:0.9}, {x:1.0, y:2.3}, {x:12.0, y:12.0}];

proposition [allDone]: forall i in {1,2,3}. drone[i].ctrl.proc.thrd @ done;
proposition [initial]: forall i in {1,2,3}.
  abs(drone[i].env.x - p[i].x) < 0.3 and abs(drone[i].env.y - p[i].y) < 0.3;
```

We find a counterexample by randomized simulation in one minute: a collision occurs after five iterations (500 ms), since the subprogram `chkClose` in Fig. 10 does not consider clock skews and sampling/actuating times. As mentioned, each drone's position is sampled from the environment at some time in the sampling time interval, also perturbed by a clock skew. The calculation of `chkClose` is not precise enough without considering these values.

We therefore modify the implementation `DroneThread.impl` to mitigate this problem as follows. When invoking `chkClose`, we use an extra padding value depending on the maximal clock skew and sampling/actuating time intervals given in the corresponding `Hybrid_SynchAADL` properties. With this change, no counterexample of `allDone` is found in three hours using randomized simulation.

Furthermore, we verify that no such counterexample exists up to bound 500 ms using symbolic reachability analysis for the invariant property `safety`, which takes about 95 minutes. The proposition `failure` states that some drone has gone into the `failed` state, and the invariant property `safety` states that no such `failure` is possible within bound 500 ms.

```
invariant [safety]: ?initial ==> not ?failure in time 500 ms;
proposition [failure]: exists i in {1,2,3}. drone[i].ctrl.proc.thrd @ failed;
```

7 Related Work

PALS is a synchronizer for CPSs without continuous behaviors, and is therefore related to time-triggered architectures (TTA) [23], but typically allows shorter periods, etc. See [6,35] for comparisons between PALS and TTA. MSYNC [6] generalizes both TTA and PALS (and its multirate extension Multirate PALS [5]). Unlike Hybrid PALS, neither of these take continuous behaviors into account.

Synchronous AADL [7,10] and Multirate Synchronous AADL [9] also use AADL to define synchronous PALS designs, but do not consider continuous behaviors. As mentioned above, this work extends HYBRIDSYNCHAADL in [25, 26] with features making it easy to specify complex systems, and demonstrate the extended version of the language and analysis tool on a new case study.

Unlike other hybrid extensions of AADL, e.g., [1,12,28,31], HYBRIDSYNCH-AADL supports the specification of complex controllers using (a subset of) AADL's expressive Behavior Annex, and we also consider (virtually synchronous) CPSs—with clock skews, network delays, etc. (using the Hybrid PALS equivalence). See [25, Sect. 10] for a more detailed discussion of related work.

Our case study is based on the simple packet delivery system example in [36]. Unlike the original model where drones discretely move on a grid, our model considers the continuous movements of drones and imprecise local clocks.

8 Concluding Remarks

HYBRIDSYNCHAADL is an AADL-based modeling language and formal analysis tool for sophisticated virtually synchronous (distributed) CPSs—with complex controllers, imprecise local clocks, and continuous behaviors—that is fully integrated into the OSATE tool environment for AADL. Control programs are defined using (a significant subset of) AADL's intuitive and expressive Behavior Annex, and continuous behaviors are given by differential equations. Furthermore, the performance of our tool compares favorably with (less expressive) state-of-the-art hybrid systems analysis tools.

In this paper we have extended HYBRIDSYNCHAADL with (AADL) features for data types, arrays, and user-defined functions/subprograms. This should make the modeling of complex CPSs—including adaptive CPSs—significantly more convenient and less error-prone. We have introduced the language extensions (including to the property specification language), have extended the Maude-with-SMT formal semantics of HYBRIDSYNCHAADL with the new features, and have illustrated the convenience of the extended language by modeling and analyzing a complex collection of packet-delivery drones that adapt to the movements of other drones to avoid collision.

Acknowledgments. We thank the organizers of the Rigorous Engineering of Collective Adaptive Systems track for inviting us to present this work at ISOLA 2022, and the reviewers for helpful comments. This work was partly supported by the National Research Foundation of Korea (NRF) grants funded by the Korea government (MSIT) (No. 2021R1A5A1021944 and No. 2022R1F1A1074550).

References

1. Ahmad, E., Larson, B.R., Barrett, S.C., Zhan, N., Dong, Y.: Hybrid Annex: an AADL extension for continuous behavior and cyber-physical interaction modeling. In: Proceedings of the ACM SIGAda Annual Conference on High Integrity Language Technology (HILT 2014). ACM, NY (2014)
2. Al-Nayeem, A., Sun, M., Qiu, X., Sha, L., Miller, S.P., Cofer, D.D.: A formal architecture pattern for real-time distributed systems. In: Proceedings of the RTSS, pp. 161–170. IEEE (2009)
3. Arney, D., Jetley, R., Jones, P., Lee, I., Sokolsky, O.: Formal methods based development of a PCA infusion pump reference model: generic infusion pump (GIP) project. In: HCMDSS-MDPnP, pp. 23–33. IEEE (2007)
4. Bae, K., Krisiloff, J., Meseguer, J., Ölveczky, P.C.: Designing and verifying distributed cyber-physical systems using Multirate PALS: an airplane turning control system case study. Sci. Comput. Program. **103**, 13–50 (2015)
5. Bae, K., Meseguer, J., Ölveczky, P.C.: Formal patterns for multirate distributed real-time systems. Sci. Comput. Program. **91**, 3–44 (2014)
6. Bae, K., Ölveczky, P.C.: MSYNC: a generalized formal design pattern for virtually synchronous multirate cyber-physical systems. ACM Trans. Embedd. Comput. Syst. **20**(5s), 1–26 (2021)
7. Bae, K., Ölveczky, P.C., Al-Nayeem, A., Meseguer, J.: Synchronous AADL and its formal analysis in Real-Time Maude. In: Qin, S., Qiu, Z. (eds.) ICFEM 2011. LNCS, vol. 6991, pp. 651–667. Springer, Heidelberg (2011). https://doi.org/10.1007/978-3-642-24559-6_43
8. Bae, K., Ölveczky, P.C., Kong, S., Gao, S., Clarke, E.M.: SMT-based analysis of virtually synchronous distributed hybrid systems. In: Proceedings of the HSCC, pp. 145–154. ACM, NY (2016)
9. Bae, K., Ölveczky, P.C., Meseguer, J.: Definition, semantics, and analysis of multirate synchronous AADL. In: Jones, C., Pihlajasaari, P., Sun, J. (eds.) FM 2014. LNCS, vol. 8442, pp. 94–109. Springer, Cham (2014). https://doi.org/10.1007/978-3-319-06410-9_7

10. Bae, K., Ölveczky, P.C., Meseguer, J., Al-Nayeem, A.: The SynchAADL2Maude tool. In: de Lara, J., Zisman, A. (eds.) FASE 2012. LNCS, vol. 7212, pp. 59–62. Springer, Heidelberg (2012). https://doi.org/10.1007/978-3-642-28872-2_4

11. Bae, K., Rocha, C.: Symbolic state space reduction with guarded terms for rewriting modulo SMT. Sci. Comput. Program. **178**, 20–42 (2019)

12. Bao, Y., Chen, M., Zhu, Q., Wei, T., Mallet, F., Zhou, T.: Quantitative performance evaluation of uncertainty-aware Hybrid AADL designs using statistical model checking. IEEE Trans. Comput.-Aided Des. Integr. Circuits Syst. **36**(12), 1989–2002 (2017)

13. Barrett, C., et al.: CVC4. In: Gopalakrishnan, G., Qadeer, S. (eds.) CAV 2011. LNCS, vol. 6806, pp. 171–177. Springer, Heidelberg (2011). https://doi.org/10.1007/978-3-642-22110-1_14

14. Chen, X., Ábrahám, E., Sankaranarayanan, S.: Flow*: an analyzer for non-linear hybrid systems. In: Sharygina, N., Veith, H. (eds.) CAV 2013. LNCS, vol. 8044, pp. 258–263. Springer, Heidelberg (2013). https://doi.org/10.1007/978-3-642-39799-8_18

15. Cimatti, A., Griggio, A., Mover, S., Tonetta, S.: HyComp: an SMT-based model checker for hybrid systems. In: Baier, C., Tinelli, C. (eds.) TACAS 2015. LNCS, vol. 9035, pp. 52–67. Springer, Heidelberg (2015). https://doi.org/10.1007/978-3-662-46681-0_4

16. Clavel, M., et al.: All About Maude - A High-Performance Logical Framework. LNCS, vol. 4350. Springer, Heidelberg (2007). https://doi.org/10.1007/978-3-540-71999-1

17. Dutertre, B.: Yices 2.2. In: Biere, A., Bloem, R. (eds.) CAV 2014. LNCS, vol. 8559, pp. 737–744. Springer, Cham (2014). https://doi.org/10.1007/978-3-319-08867-9_49

18. Feiler, P.H., Gluch, D.P.: Model-Based Engineering with AADL: An Introduction to the SAE Architecture Analysis and Design Language. Addison-Wesley, USA (2012)

19. França, R., Bodeveix, J.P., Filali, M., Rolland, J.F., Chemouil, D., Thomas, D.: The AADL Behaviour Annex – experiments and roadmap. In: Proceedings of the ICECCS 2007. IEEE (2007)

20. Frehse, G., et al.: SpaceEx: scalable verification of hybrid systems. In: Gopalakrishnan, G., Qadeer, S. (eds.) CAV 2011. LNCS, vol. 6806, pp. 379–395. Springer, Heidelberg (2011). https://doi.org/10.1007/978-3-642-22110-1_30

21. Kim, C., Sun, M., Mohan, S., Yun, H., Sha, L., Abdelzaher, T.F.: A framework for the safe interoperability of medical devices in the presence of network failures. In: Proceedings of the 1st ACM/IEEE International Conference on Cyber-Physical Systems (ICCPS), pp. 149–158 (2010)

22. Kong, S., Gao, S., Chen, W., Clarke, E.: dReach: δ-reachability analysis for hybrid systems. In: Baier, C., Tinelli, C. (eds.) TACAS 2015. LNCS, vol. 9035, pp. 200–205. Springer, Heidelberg (2015). https://doi.org/10.1007/978-3-662-46681-0_15

23. Kopetz, H., Bauer, G.: The time-triggered architecture. Proc. IEEE **91**(1), 112–126 (2003)

24. Lee, J., Bae, K., Ölveczky, P.C.: An extension of HybridSynchAADL and its application to collaborating autonomous UAVs (2022). http://hybridsynchaadl.github.io/artifact/isola2022/techrep.pdf

25. Lee, J., Bae, K., Ölveczky, P.C., Kim, S., Kang, M.: Modeling and formal analysis of virtually synchronous cyber-physical systems in AADL. Int. J. Softw. Tools Technol. Transfer (2022). https://doi.org/10.1007/s10009-022-00665-z

26. Lee, J., Kim, S., Bae, K., Ölveczky, P.C.: HYBRID SYNCHAADL: modeling and formal analysis of virtually synchronous CPSs in AADL. In: Silva, A., Leino, K.R.M. (eds.) CAV 2021. LNCS, vol. 12759, pp. 491–504. Springer, Cham (2021). https://doi.org/10.1007/978-3-030-81685-8_23
27. Leen, G., Heffernan, D., Dunne, A.: Digital networks in the automotive vehicle. Comput. Control Eng. J. **10**(6), 257–266 (1999)
28. Liu, J., Li, T., Ding, Z., Qian, Y., Sun, H., He, J.: AADL+: a simulation-based methodology for cyber-physical systems. Front. Comput. Sci. **13**(3), 516–538 (2018). https://doi.org/10.1007/s11704-018-7039-7
29. Meseguer, J.: Conditional rewriting logic as a unified model of concurrency. Theor. Comput. Sci. **96**(1), 73–155 (1992)
30. Meseguer, J., Ölveczky, P.C.: Formalization and correctness of the PALS architectural pattern for distributed real-time systems. Theor. Comput. Sci. **451**, 1–37 (2012)
31. Qian, Y., Liu, J., Chen, X.: Hybrid AADL: a sublanguage extension to AADL. In: Proceedings of the Internetware 2013. ACM, NY (2013)
32. Rocha, C., Meseguer, J., Muñoz, C.: Rewriting modulo SMT and open system analysis. J. Log. Algebr. Methods Program. **86**(1), 269–297 (2017)
33. SAE International: Architecture analysis and design language (AADL) annex volume 2: Annex B: Data modeling annex (2011)
34. Steiner, W., Bauer, G., Hall, B., Paulitsch, M., Varadarajan, S.: TTEthernet dataflow concept. In: 2009 Eighth IEEE International Symposium on Network Computing and Applications, pp. 319–322. IEEE (2009)
35. Steiner, W., Rushby, J.: TTA and PALS: formally verified design patterns for distributed cyber-physical systems. In: 2011 IEEE/AIAA 30th Digital Avionics Systems Conference, pp. 7B5–1. IEEE (2011)
36. Talcott, C., Arbab, F., Yadav, M.: Soft agents: exploring soft constraints to model robust adaptive distributed cyber-physical agent systems. In: De Nicola, R., Hennicker, R. (eds.) Software, Services, and Systems. LNCS, vol. 8950, pp. 273–290. Springer, Cham (2015). https://doi.org/10.1007/978-3-319-15545-6_18

Discrete Models of Continuous Behavior of Collective Adaptive Systems

Peter Fettke[1,2]([✉]) [iD] and Wolfgang Reisig[3] [iD]

[1] German Research Center for Artificial Intelligence (DFKI), Saarbrücken, Germany
peter.fettke@dfki.de
[2] Saarland University, Saarbrücken, Germany
[3] Humboldt-Universität zu Berlin, Berlin, Germany
reisig@informatik.hu-berlin.de

Abstract. Artificial ants are "small" units, moving autonomously on a shared, dynamically changing "space", directly or indirectly exchanging some kind of information. Artificial ants are frequently conceived as a paradigm for collective adaptive systems. In this paper, we discuss means to represent continuous moves of "ants" in discrete models. More generally, we challenge the role of the notion of "time" in artificial ant systems and models. We suggest a modeling framework that structures behavior along causal dependencies, and not along temporal relations. We present all arguments by help of a simple example. As a modeling framework we employ HERAKLIT; an emerging framework that already has proven its worth in many contexts.

Keywords: Systems composition · Data modeling · Behavior modeling · Composition calculus · Algebraic specification · Petri nets

1 Introduction

Some branches of informatics take processes in nature as a model for unconventional classes of algorithms. In particular, numerous variants of "swarm intelligence" have been and are being studied to a large scale, with specialized conference series, journals, etc., e.g. *International Conference on Swarm Intelligence (ICSI)*, and *International Journal of Swarm Intelligence Research (IJSIR)*. What many of these approaches have in common, is the assumption of a number of artificial ants, i.e. "small" units, moving autonomously around on a shared, dynamically changing "space", directly or indirectly exchanging some kind of information.

This kind of behavior needs an adequate representation, i.e. it must be modeled in a formal framework, as a basis for implementation, for proving correctness, for studies of complexity, and many other tasks.

T. Margaria and B. Steffen (Eds.): ISoLA 2022, LNCS 13703, pp. 65–81, 2022.
https://doi.org/10.1007/978-3-031-19759-8_5

In the following, we discuss fundamental assumptions and questions of modeling such systems. In particular, we discuss means to represent continuous moves of "ants" in discrete models. More generally, we challenge the role of the notion of "time" in artificial ant systems and models. We show that time-based models do not adequately represent the causal dependencies in such systems. Instead, we suggest a modeling framework that structures behavior along causal dependencies, and not along temporal relations.

We present all arguments by help of a simple example, i.e., ants moving up and down a bar. This example already exhibits numerous fundamental problems of the area. As a modeling framework we employ HERAKLIT [2,3]; an emerging modeling framework that already has proven its worth in many contexts, and shows its utility also in the context of artificial ants.

2   Running Example: Ants on a Bar

Here we start out with an informal description of ants on a bar. We identify three kinds of events.

2.1   The Behavior of Ants on a Bar

Assume a bar and some ants, moving up and down the bar, as in Fig. 1. An ant, moving towards the right end of the bar, and its right neighbor moving left, will eventually meet at some point on the bar. In this case, both ants swap direction of movement. A right moving ant without right neighbor will eventually drop down from the bar, and so will drop down a left moving ant without a left neighbor. Ants cannot get ahead of each other.

Fig. 1. Ants on a bar

An initial state is a set of ants on the bar, where each ant is directed left or right. For every given initial state, the ants' behavior is clear and unambiguous, generating a *run*. The ants system is the set of all potential initial states and their runs. As the above description of the ants system is intuitively clear, it should not be too difficult to model it formally. However, there is much to say about this seemingly simple endeavor.

2.2 Events of the Ants' System

We start with the quest of modeling single runs. Starting in a given initial state, three types of events may occur:

1. Two ants i and j meet. As a shorthand we write "a i j" for this event.
2. An ant i drops down on the left edge of the bar. As a shorthand we write "b i" for this event.
3. An ant i drops down on the right edge of the bar. As a shorthand we write "c i" for this event.

Occurrence of an event causes a fresh state.

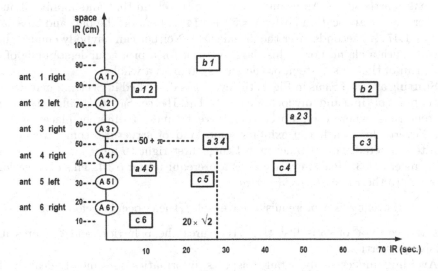

Fig. 2. The continuous model of behavior

3 Conventional Models of the Ants' Behavior

There are several more or less different ways to represent the behavior of ants, embedding events into a temporal framework, and structuring the behavior along the flow of time. We consider four such representations and show what they have in common.

3.1 The Continuous Model of a Run of the Ants System

Figure 2 models a behavior of the ants in the style of classical mechanical engineering: a Cartesian plain is spanned, with real numbers for time and for space in its x- and y-axis, respectively. An initial state S_0, reached at time $t = 0$, is outlined as follows: For each ant i, an ellipse, inscribed $A\,i\,l$ or $A\,i\,r$, describes the initial position on the bar of ant i, as well as its orientation, left or right. For example, ant 1 is the leftmost ant, oriented rightwards.

Figure 2 shows a typical behavior of the events of the ants system. Any real number of the x-axis of Fig. 2 denotes a point in time, and any real number of the y-axis denotes a point in space on the bar, where an event may occur. For example, the "$c\,6$" inscribed box indicates the event of ant number 6 dropping down the right edge of the bar. The "$a\,3\,4$" inscribed box indicates that ants 3 and 4 meet.

The model in Fig. 2 encompasses infinitely many, in fact more than countably many potential states apt to cope with "real time". However, for the understanding of the functionality of a system, the aspect of "real time" is often irrelevant and makes little sense. An example would be the claim that ants number 3 and number 4 meet at location $50 + \pi$ ($= 50 + 3.14\ldots$) cm on the bar, and $20 \times \sqrt{2}$ ($= 20 \times 1.47\ldots$) seconds after the initial state. Neither can anybody empirically measure such a claim, nor is this claim relevant for a proper understanding of a single run of the ants system, or the ants system as a whole.

Starting at state S_0 as in Fig. 2, the events as described in Sect. 2.2 may occur at any point of time and any location on the bar. Hence, S_0 yields infinitely many different runs, where events occur at different times at different places on the bar. Nevertheless, each run exhibits some kind of structure: some events are definitely ordered. For instance, ant 4 turns first right to meet ant 5, and then left to meet ant 3. Hence, event $a\,4\,5$ is a prerequisite for $a\,3\,4$. This observation gives rise to the *causality requirement*:

$$\text{If event } e \text{ is a prerequisite for event } f, \text{then } e \text{ occurs before } f. \qquad (1)$$

It is the concept of causality, that structures the behavior, and captures its decisive properties.

Avoiding unnecessarily detailed aspects, informatics does mostly deals with *discrete* models. A discrete model of behavior describes behavior by help of finitely many or countably many states and events, where an event updates a given state. This is aspired in different ways, most prominently the following three ones.

3.2 The Grid Model

The grid model spans a grid in the plane, e.g. the integer grid as in Fig. 3. This grid cuts time and space into intervals. In each state of the system, each ant occupies a square of the grid. Upon an event, each ant is assumed to move right to the next time interval, and coincidently moving up or down to a neighbored space interval, or to remain at its position. Consequently, ants meet or drop down from the bar at the grid's crossings. This is what cellular automata and most implementations of ant algorithms do. Resnick suggests a programming language, based on the grid model [10].

For a fixed initial state, the grid model does not define a unique run: depending on the choice of the grid, two events may be mapped to the same or to

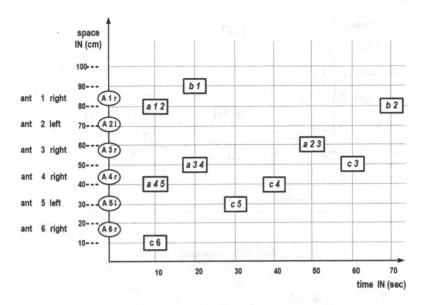

Fig. 3. The grid model of behavior

different points of the grid, i.e. two pairs of ants are considered as meeting in time coincidently (at different points of space on the bar), or in a sequence. Any such mapping of events onto grid points is acceptable, provided the causality requirement (1) holds in a slightly revised form:

$$\text{If } e \text{ is a prerequisite for } f, \text{ then the time component of } e$$
$$\text{must be smaller than the time component of } f. \tag{2}$$

This is in fact the case in Fig. 3. As a further example, the event $c6$ indicates that ant number 6 just drops down at the right edge of the bar, without meeting any other ant. Consequently, $c6$ may be mapped to any of the seven grid points of time.

3.3   The Numbering Model

As a second possibility, one just numbers the ants' meetings, such that the causality requirement holds in the varied formulation:

$$\text{If } e \text{ is a prerequisite for } f,$$
$$\text{then the number of } e \text{ must be smaller than the number of } f. \tag{3}$$

For the above initial state S_0, Fig. 4 shows an example for this model of behavior. There are various different acceptable numberings. For example, the numberings 2 and 4 of the events $a45$ and $b1$ may be swapped.

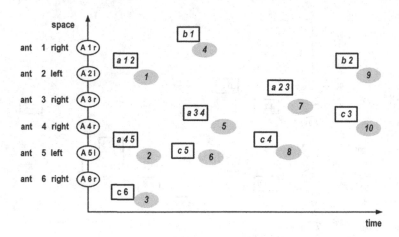

Fig. 4. The numbering model

3.4 The Lockstep Model

Behavior can also be modeled as to proceed in lockstep, i.e. in a sequence of steps, where each step is a set of events. Figure 5 shows the ants' behavior as a sequence of four steps, for the above initial state S_0. Again, the causality requirement must hold is a varied form:

$$\text{If } e \text{ is a prerequisite for } f, \text{ then the step including } e \\ \text{must occur in the lockstep sequence before the step including } f. \tag{4}$$

Again, the running example generates not a unique lockstep sequence.

3.5 The Uniqueness Problem

For the given initial state S_0, the continuous model of Sect. 3.1 as well as each of the above three discrete models cause various different runs. The runs all differ w.r.t. the time at which events occur. The assumption of time is the structuring principle of these runs. However, "time" come from outside the ant system. In forthcoming Sect. 4, we strive at a discrete, yet unique model of the ants' run, without outside structuring principles. But first we shed light onto the causality requirement (1) that occurs in some way in all models ((2), (3), (4)). This requirement induces an order on the events of a run.

3.6 Weak Orderings of Events

All above models of single runs (i.e. the continuous, the grid- the numbering- and the lockstep-model) order the evens of a run along the x-axis, representing the intuitive notion of time in various forms: as real numbers, discrete number intervals, integers, or just discrete, finite order. In all these models, events are either ordered in time, or they occur at the same time. This ordering is a *weak ordering* on the events: for three events e, f, and g always holds:

If e and f are not ordered, and f and g are not ordered,

then also e and g are not ordered. $\qquad(5)$

For example, $a\,1\,2$, $a\,4\,5$ and $c\,6$ occur at time 10 in the grid, as well as in the first step of the lockstep run. Generally, a partial order, namely a transitive and irreflexive relation, is a weak ordering, if the complement of its symmetric closure is transitive. Consequently, any version of order that is motivated by the intuitive notion of "time" is a weak order, because in a temporally motivated order, unorder means "occurring at the same time". And "occurring at the same time" is intuitively definitely transitive.

4   The Causal Model of the Ants' Runs

Here we suggest a behavioral model that contrasts the above time-based model: A run is no longer structured along time, but along causality. It turns out, that the induced order is no weak order anymore.

4.1   The Order of Events

As an alternative to ordering events by temporal aspects, we start out with a closer look at the causality requirement, as stated in (1): "If event e is a prerequisite for event f, then e occurs before f". Here, "to be a prerequisite of ..." is a certainly a transitive relation:

If e is a prerequisite for f, and if f is a prerequisite for g,

then e is a prerequisite for g. $\qquad(6)$

This implies that "to be a prerequisite of ..." is a partial order. In the sequel, we denote it as an *event order*. Figure 7 shows the event order for the run of the ants system, starting in state S_0. Graphically, each arrow begins at a direct prerequisite of the event at the arrow's end. Order on events induced by transitivity is not depicted. In Fig. 7, $c\,5$ is unordered with $a\,3\,4$, as well as with $a\,2\,3$. But $a\,3\,4$ is ordered with (i.e. smaller than) $a\,2\,3$. Formulated more generally, if e no prerequisite for f, and if f is no prerequisite for g, then e may very well be a prerequisite for g. In technical terms, this means:

In general, causal order is no weak ordering. $\qquad(7)$

This contrasts the temporally motivated orders of (1) to (4).

We intend to employ event orders as a model of runs. This rises the problem of identifying states in a run. There is no way to insert global states into a partial order that is not weakly ordered. Nevertheless, wishing to embed single runs into behavioral system models, some aspects of states are inevitable.

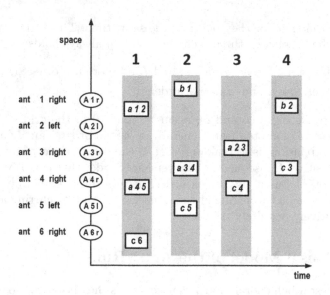

Fig. 5. The lockstep model

4.2 Local States and Steps

To include aspects of states into an event order, we pursue the idea of local states. For example, the initial state S_0 of the ants system, as in Figs. 2, 3, 4, and 5 consists of local states, one for each ant.

We construct local states as suggested in the framework of the HERAKLIT [2]: a local state is a proposition, usually a predicate p together with an item or a tuple t, where p applies to t. For example, let A be the predicate "directed ants on the bar". This predicate applies to the tuple $(1, r)$ in the initial state S_0 of the ants system. This kind of propositions is usually written $A(1, r)$. In graphical representations we skip the brackets. Hence, the initial state S_0 of the ants system is a set of local states, each of which is shaped "A i j", with $i = 1, \ldots, 6$, and $j \in \{l, r\}$.

A local step is an occurrence of an event, together with the event's effect on local states. Each step updates some of the local states. For example, Fig. 6(a) shows the local step of meeting of ants 1 and 2, and their swapping of direction. This figure shows the cause and effect of event $a\,4\,5$ to the local states $A\,4\,r$ and $A\,5\,l$: they both are updated to $A\,4\,l$ and $A\,5\,r$, respectively. Any kind of global state is not necessary to specify event $a\,4\,5$. Correspondingly, Fig. 6(b) shows the meeting of ants 3 and 4.

According to Fig. 7, the event $a\,4\,5$ is a prerequisite for $a\,3\,4$, because ant 4

1. starts to the right (local state $A\,4\,r$),
2. then swaps to $A\,4\,l$ (jointly with ant 5),
3. then returns back to $A\,4\,r$, (jointly with ant 3).

Figure 6(c) shows the combined behavior of $a\,4\,5$ occurring before $a\,3\,4$.

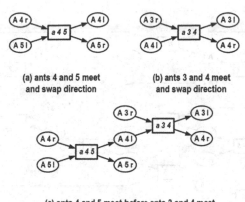

(a) ants 4 and 5 meet
and swap direction

(b) ants 3 and 4 meet
and swap direction

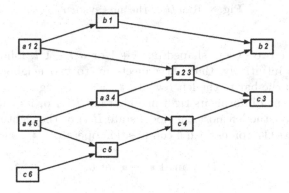

(c) ants 4 and 5 meet before ants 3 and 4 meet.

Fig. 6. Events and their composition

Fig. 7. Event order

4.3 The Run Starting at State S_0

Figure 8 shows the run U of the ants system, starting in the initial state S_0. Besides the predicate "A", the run U employs further predicates, used to describe causes and effects of ants to drop down left and right: Local states $B\,i$ state that ant i is the leftmost ant, hence i is the next ant expected to drop down to the left; $L\,i$ states that ant i has dropped down left. Accordingly, $C\,i$ stated that ant ant i is the rightmost ant, hence next ant expected to drop down to the right; $R\,i$ states that ant i has dropped down right. The gray background displays a HERAKLIT module, with interfaces on its left and right margin.

4.4 Composing the Run U from the Ants' Behavior

As each single ant contributes to the run U, one may ask for the contribution of each single ant to U. Figure 9 shows the contribution of ants $1, \ldots, 6$, as HERAKLIT modules, "ant i" ($i = 1, \ldots, 6$). For each ant i, the module of i starts

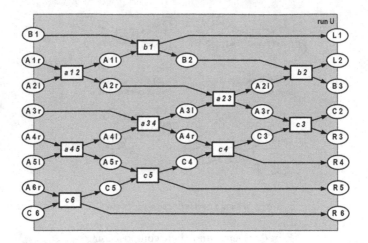

Fig. 8. Run U of the ants system

with zero, one or two events shaped $a\ i\ i+1$ or $a\ i-1\ i$, followed by $b\ i$ or $c\ i$. This means intuitively, that ant i meets up to two neighbored ants, and then drops down the bar to the left (event $b\ i$) or to the right (event $c\,i$). Before dropping down, ant i informs its right neighbor ant $i+1$ or its left neighbor ant $i-1$ that it is now the leftmost ant (local state $B\ i$) or the rightmost ant (local state $C\ i$). HERAKLIT comes with a composition operator "•", such that we can write:

$$U = \text{ant } 1 \bullet \cdots \bullet \text{ant } 6. \tag{8}$$

5   Modeling the Bar with Ants

In the definition of runs, replacing temporal order by event order is a fundamental step. It raises the question of how to cope with the new version of runs, how such runs are generated by a kind of system model, etc. In the rest of this paper, we model the ants system itself, we discuss the composition of system models and runs, and we discuss a schematic representation for ant systems.

5.1   The Model of the Ants System

Figure 10 shows the ant system as a module in the HERAKLIT framework [2]. The places on its left and right margin are the left and right interface of the module, collecting the dropped down ants. Essentially, this figure shows a high-level Petri net. Its initial marking represents the local state components of the initial state S_0. As usual for such Petri nets, in a given marking, a transition is enabled with respect to a *valuation* of the involved variable, i. For example, in marking S_0, transition "a" is enabled with $i = 1$ (representing the event $a\,1\,2$), but not with $i = 2$. This way, each transition of Fig. 10 causes a set of steps. A run (such as

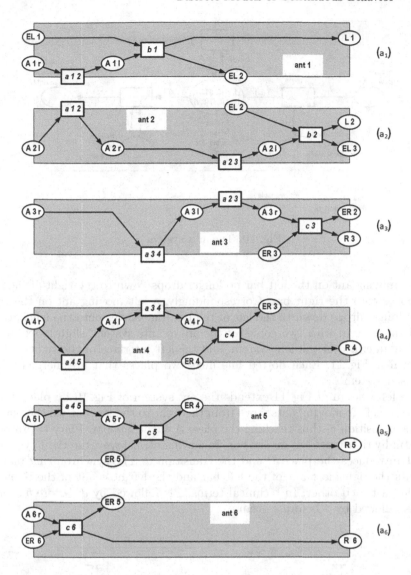

Fig. 9. Each ant's behavior

in Fig. 8) is a run of the system, if each step of the run can be conceived as a step of the system, and if the initial state of the run fits the initial system state. For Fig. 10, this applies to the run U of Fig. 8. Formal details of the notion of a run of a system are presented in [2].

5.2   Composing Two Bars

As an exercise showing the elegance and technical simplicity of the HERAKLIT approach, we consider the case of two bars, a left and a right one, linked together.

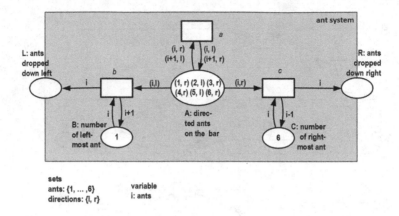

Fig. 10. The ants system

A right moving ant on the left bar no longer drops down to the right of the bar, but moves onto the right bar. Correspondingly, a left moving ant on the right bar no longer drops down to the left of the bar, but moves onto the left bar. We model this system with two copies of the above ants system, slightly extending the right interface of the left system, and the left interface of the right system, as shown in Fig. 11. Each dotted line links two places that are merged in the composed system.

The left system of Fig. 11 extends the ant system of Fig. 10 by place L and transition e. Left-moving ants move from the right to the left bar via the place L and the transition e, thus reaching the place A of the left bar. Place C protocols the actually rightmost ant on the bar. In a symmetrical way, the right system of Fig. 11 introduces the place R and the transition d. The synchronizing place S prevents the rightmost ant of the left bar and the leftmost ant of the right bar to slide past each other. In technical terms, c is followed by d, before b occurs. Or b is followed by e before c occurs.

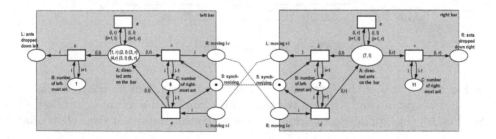

Fig. 11. Composing two bars

Ignoring the dotted lines, the composed system can be written in HERAKLIT as

$$\text{left bar} \bullet \text{right bar.} \tag{9}$$

It is interesting to study the composition of runs of the composed system. As initial state, for the left system we assume the state as in Fig. 8. The right system contains initially only one ant, oriented to the left. In the run of Fig. 12, ant 6 moves from the left to the right bar, meeting ant 7 on the right bar. Both ants swap direction: ant 6 returns to the left bar, and ant 7 eventually drops down to the right of the right bar. Ant 6 meets ant 5 on the left bar, swaps direction, etc. Eventually, ants $3, \ldots, 7$ are dropped down to the right of the right bar. Ants 1 and 2 take no notice at all from the newly attached bar, and drop down to the left of the left bar. In Fig. 12, the transitions of the right module are shaded.

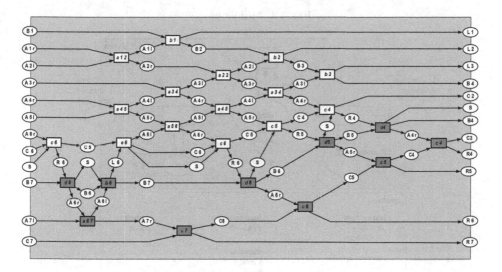

Fig. 12. Composed run

5.3 Composing Many Bars

The case of composing two bars can systematically be extended to any number of bars. To this end we employ a middle bar, as in Fig. 13. For example, composition of five bars can be written in HERAKLIT as

$$\text{left bar} \bullet \text{middle bar} \bullet \text{middle bar} \bullet \text{middle bar} \bullet \text{right bar.} \tag{10}$$

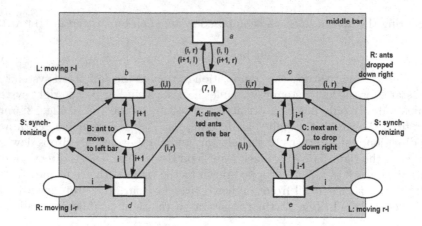

Fig. 13. Middle bar

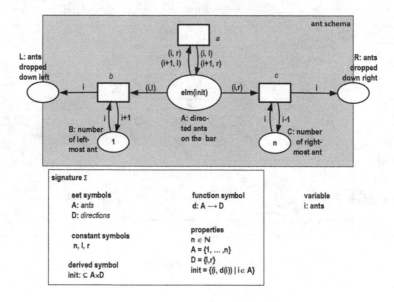

Fig. 14. The ant schema

6   A Schematic Representation of Ants Systems

Figure 10 shows an ant system with a fixed initial state, consisting of six ants, each of which is oriented either to the left or to the right. Now we strive at a representation that covers any number of ants, and any orientation of each ant. We achieve this by help of well-established concepts of general algebra [11], as used in algebraic specifications such as *CASL*, *VDM*, *Z*, etc. The inscriptions of Fig. 10 represent elements of a set of ants and a set of directions.

Figure 14 includes a signature, Σ, some typed symbols for sets, constants and functions, and four properties. As usual in algebraic specifications, an instantiation of Σ assigns each symbol a corresponding set, constant, or function, such that the required properties are respected. Thus, an instantiation of Σ is structure, denoted as a Σ-structure. For example, Fig. 10 includes an instantiation of the signature Σ of Fig. 14: The symbols A and D are instantiated by the sets $\{1, \ldots, 6\}$ and $\{l, r\}$. The constant symbol n is instantiated by the integer 6. The symbols l and r are instantiated by themselves. The instantiation of the function symbol d is a function that is implicitly given by the initial marking of the place A. Summing up, each instantiations of Σ specifies an ant system.

The initial marking of the place A deserves particular attention. One may be tempted to use the symbol "init" as symbolic initial marking. According to the signature Σ, an instantiation would instantiate "init" as a set ants of directed ants, as one initial token. This is, however, not what we want. Instead, we want each element of the set ants to be a token. In logical terms, with the place A denoting the predicate "directed ants on the bar", we want not to state "A(ants)", but

$$\forall a \in \text{ants} : A(a). \tag{11}$$

Using the HERAKLIT framework, we denote this by the inscription "elm(init)" in the place A.

7 Related Work

On the background of classical automata theory and transition systems, a run (i.e. a single behavior) of a discrete system is a set of activities, totally ordered along the evolution of time. Each activity updates a (global) state, with a state containing all what is the case at a distinguished point in time. C.A. Petri challenged this "interleaving semantics" since the 1960ies, and suggested non-sequential processes as a model for single runs of any kind of discrete systems [8]. In this view, a run is a set of activities, partially ordered by causal dependencies. Such partial orders have been suggested for many models, in particular for interacting sequential systems. Typical such contributions include [1,4,5,7,9] and may others. But partial order semantics never prevailed. Its technical costs were considered to outperform the gained insight.

The HERAKLIT framework with its composition operators used above, however reduces the technical burden drastically and reveals further insight. In particular, composition of systems yields exponentially many interleaving runs, but only quadratically many partially ordered runs. The number of runs of a composed system $A \bullet B$ is in general exponentially bigger than the number of runs of A and B. The corresponding number of partially ordered runs is only quadratically bigger.

Our discussion of weak orderings in Sect. 3.6 reflects the discussion of measurement in several scientific fields as discussed by e.g. [6]: typically it is argued that measurement means that attributes of objects, substances, and events can reasonably be represented numerically such that the observed order of objects etc. is preserved in the numerical representation. In other words, any reasonable kind of measurement yields totally ordered results if different objects has to be represented by different numbers; and weakly ordered results if different objects can be represented by the same number. So, it comes without surprise that the behavioral models of Sect. 3.1, 3.2, 3.3 and 3.4 define weak orderings.

8   Conclusion

With this paper, we intend to raise a number of questions, without claiming full-fledged answers:

- The fundamental question: Is it possible for each system with timing aspects, to separate time and functionality? If yes, does this separation always yield better insight into the system, or better methods to prove aspects of correctness? If no, can properties of systems be identified, that would characterize this distinction?
- To which extent does our chosen modeling technique, HERAKLIT, limit or bias the representation of functionality?
- How is the notion of time in real world systems related to the treatment of time in models, and in implementations: In informatics we frequently tend to assume continuous or discrete time to "exist" and to be "measurable" without much of effort. Sects. 3.2, 3.3 and 3.4 show that this assumption is not justified, and the above question is far from trivial. Before discussing e.g. meeting points of ants with different velocities, it must be clarified how those notions will be fixed in the model.

We suggest to base this kind of questions on the notion of causality. This offers a larger degree of mathematical expressiveness, because causality orders the events of a run not necessarily by a weak ordering (as time based models usually do), but by a more general partial order. We suggest this as a beginning of a theoretical framework for any kind of modeling of collective adaptive systems. This implies new development processes, property preserving verification, refinement, composition etc.

Acknowledgment. We deeply appreciate the careful and thoughtful hints and comments of the referees.

References

1. Degano, P., Nicola, R.D., Montanari, U.: A distributed operational semantics for CCS based on C/E systems. Acta Inform. **26**, 59–91 (1988)
2. Fettke, P., Reisig, W.: Handbook of HERAKLIT (2021). HERAKLIT working paper, v1.1, 20 September 2021. http://www.heraklit.org
3. Fettke, P., Reisig, W.: Modelling service-oriented systems and cloud services with HERAKLIT. In: Zirpins, C., et al. (eds.) ESOCC 2020. CCIS, vol. 1360, pp. 77–89. Springer, Cham (2021). https://doi.org/10.1007/978-3-030-71906-7_7

4. Korff, L.R., Korff, M.: Concurrency = interleaving concurrency + weak conflict. Electron. Notes Theoret. Comput. Sci. **14**, 204–213 (1998)
5. Koutny, M.: Partial order semantics of box expressions. In: Valette, R. (ed.) ICATPN 1994. LNCS, vol. 815, pp. 318–337. Springer, Heidelberg (1994). https://doi.org/10.1007/3-540-58152-9_18
6. Krantz, D.H., Luce, R.D., Suppes, P., Tversky, A.: Foundations of Measurement, Volume I, Additive and Polynomial Representations. Academic Press, Cambridge (1971)
7. Lamport, L.: Time, clocks and the ordering of events in a distributed system. Commun. ACM **21**(7), 558–564 (1978)
8. Petri, C.A.: Non-sequential processes. Technical report ISF-77-5, Gesellschaft für Mathematik und Datenverarbeitung, St. Augustin, Federal Republic of Germany (1977)
9. Reisig, W.: Partial order semantics versus interleaving semantics for CSP—like languages and its impact on fairness. In: Paredaens, J. (ed.) ICALP 1984. Lecture Notes in Computer Science, vol. 172, pp. 403–413. Springer, Heidelberg (1984). https://doi.org/10.1007/3-540-13345-3_37.pdf
10. Resnick, M.: Turtles, Termites, and Traffic Jams. MIT Press, Cambridge (1994)
11. Sanella, D., Tarlecki, A.: Foundations of Algebraic Specification and Formal Software Development. Springer, Heidelberg (2012). https://doi.org/10.1007/978-3-642-17336-3

Modelling Flocks of Birds
from the Bottom Up

Rocco De Nicola[1], Luca Di Stefano[2,3], Omar Inverso[4],
and Serenella Valiani[1(✉)]

[1] IMT School of Advanced Studies, Lucca, Italy
serenella.valiani@imtlucca.it
[2] Univ. Grenoble Alpes, Inria, CNRS, Grenoble INP, LIG, Grenoble, France
[3] University of Gothenburg, Gothenburg, Sweden
[4] Gran Sasso Science Institute (GSSI), L'Aquila, Italy

Abstract. We argue that compositional specification based on formal languages can facilitate the modelling of, and reasoning about, sophisticated collective behaviour in many natural systems. One defines a system in terms of individual components and local rules, so that collective behaviours emerge naturally from the combined effect of the different actions of the individual components. With appropriate linguistic constructs, this can yield compact and intuitive models that are easy to refine and extend in small incremental steps. In addition, automated workflows implemented on top of this methodology can provide quick feedback, thereby allowing rapid design iterations. To support our argument, we consider flocking, a well-known example of emergent behaviour in collective adaptive systems. We build a minimalistic bottom-up model of a flock of birds incrementally, discussing specific language constructs as we go along. We then describe a prototype simulator, and use it to validate our model in a controlled experiment, where a flock is attacked by a bird of prey. The flock effectively reacts to the attack by splitting into smaller groups and regathering once the threat subsides, consistently with both natural observations and previous models from the literature.

1 Introduction

The organization of complex systems in nature, such as flocks of birds, colonies of ants, schools of fish, swarms of insects, and many more, has long since been attracting considerable interest. Researchers with different background have been resorting to different mathematical frameworks in order to study these phenomena. For instance, *flocking*, where a group of birds exhibits coherent patterns of collective motion, has been modelled using graph theory [24], distributed control laws [32], and statistical mechanics [3].

This way of modelling is not always practical because it relies on general-purpose formalisms that may not be very intuitive to use, in addition to the fact that the system needs to be modelled as a whole, regardless from its natural

Work partially funded by MIUR project PRIN 2017FTXR7S IT MATTERS (Methods and Tools for Trustworthy Smart Systems).

T. Margaria and B. Steffen (Eds.): ISoLA 2022, LNCS 13703, pp. 82–96, 2022.
https://doi.org/10.1007/978-3-031-19759-8_6

structure and often by artificially introducing some kind of central control. In contrast, in different disciplines, including epidemiology, ecology, economics, and social sciences [5,14,19,33], there seems to be a growing interest towards *compositional* approaches where the model focusses on the individual components rather than on the whole system.

Along these lines, in this paper we advocate a *bottom-up* approach based on formal specification languages. One defines the system of interest in terms of individual components and local rules. The collective behaviour of the system as a whole is not specified explicitly, but can be observed to emerge from the combined effect of the different actions of the components. This can be of significant help to reproduce sophisticated collective dynamics intuitively, and, when combined with appropriate linguistic constructs, can yield compact and intuitive specifications that are easy to refine. The adoption of a formal language allows implementing automated workflows for simulation or formal analysis that can provide feedback quickly, thereby allowing rapid design iterations.

To illustrate our point, we develop a model of a flock by gradually defining the individual behaviour and features of a bird. As we progressively refine it, we aim at keeping the behaviour of individual birds as decentralized as possible. We write our increasingly complex models in an existing language [7], which we gradually extend with new constructs that keep the specifications compact and intuitive. Once the model is fully refined, we simulate the evolution of a flock obtained by composing a number of birds together, and show that it displays interesting collective features. Namely, when birds are attacked by an external bird of prey, they are able to first escape from it, and then reassemble into a coherent flock when they are no longer under threat. This kind of collective behaviour reflects the one emerging from other models in the literature, but relies on a rather simple model.

The rest of this paper is structured as follows. We define our model of flocking behaviour and discuss tailored linguistic constructs for the specification language in Sect. 2. We describe our experimental setup for simulation and our controlled experiment in Sect. 3. We discuss related work in Sect. 4. Lastly, in Sect. 5 we report some final remarks and discuss potential directions for future work.

2 Specification

In this section, we develop a simplified model that resembles the dynamics of a flock. We start from describing a set of very simple birds, and then show how this description can be extended to implement our desired dynamics. As we do so, we also extend the modelling language itself with new constructs, aiming to keep the specifications succinct and intuitive.

Description of a Bird. Each bird in the flock can be described by two properties, namely its *position* and its *orientation* of movement. We model the former through a pair of coordinates (x, y) and the latter as a pair of integers $(dirx, diry)$ representing a heading vector. This description allows to represent both the direction of the bird's displacement, i.e., the angle subtended by the

---

Listing 1: Baseline agent modelling.

```
1  agent Bird {
2      Interface =
3          x: 0..G;
4          y: 0..G;
5          dirx: −D..D + 1;
6          diry: −D..D + 1
7
8      Behaviour = Move; Behaviour
9      Move = {
10         x ← x + dirx;
11         y ← y + diry
12     }
13 }
```

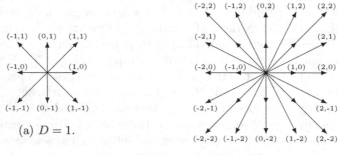

(a) $D = 1$.

(b) $D = 2$ (some labels omitted for readability).

Fig. 1. Possible heading vectors that a bird can assume for different values of D

heading vector, and the bird's velocity, represented by the length of the heading vector.

Listing 1 shows how we can model the above description.[1] In the first subsection (lines 2–6) we define the *interface* of the agent, where we define and initialize its observable features, or *attributes*. Attributes x and y are initialized non-deterministically and can assume any value corresponding to a valid coordinate on a grid that represents the arena where the flock is located. The grid is a square with edges of length G, thus the possible values vary from 0 to $G − 1$ included (lines 3–4). The initial values of dirx and diry range over $[−D, D]$ (lines 5–6). We use D to denote the maximum displacement along each coordinate of the grid: note that, as D increases, so does the number of possible heading vectors, as shown in Fig. 1. The actual initial value of each attribute is chosen non-deterministically.

---

[1] In this paper, we present condensed, human-readable versions of the full, machine-readable specifications. These are available at https://github.com/labs-lang/labs-examples/tree/isola2022/isola2022.

Listing 2: Alignment.

```
1  agent Bird
2    Interface = ...
3
4    Behaviour = Move; Behaviour
5    Move = {
6      p := pick 1;
7      dirx ← dirx_p;
8      diry ← diry_p;
9      x ← x + dirx;
10     y ← y + diry
11   }
12 }
```

Behaviour of a Bird. As for the *behaviour* of birds, let us initially model a system in which each bird simply moves along its heading vector set in the initial state, without ever changing it.

Listing 1 shows how to model such a behaviour. It is expressed through the recursive definition at line 8 that states that each agent repeatedly carries out the actions described in the **Move** process. More in detail, the statement $x \leftarrow x + dirx$ at line 10 updates the attribute x, which represent a component of the position of the agent, with the evaluation of the expression $x + dirx$, i.e., the new position that the agent reaches by moving along its heading vector. Attribute y is updated similarly (line 11). Currently, we assume that agents never reach the edge. Please note that each assignment is executed atomically, but sequences of assignments may be subject to interleaving. To prevent interleaving between the assignments of the different agents, i.e. to execute multiple assignments atomically, these must be enclosed in curly brackets, as shown in lines 9–12.

Alignment. The specification introduced above does not lead to any kind of collective behaviour, as birds simply ignore each other and keep moving in their own, fixed directions. Therefore, we now have to specify birds that are somehow influenced by other flockmates. Indeed, it is commonly held that flocking behaviour is a result of a combination of local interaction mechanisms [13, 29]. We start by considering *alignment*, i.e., the property whereby each bird adjusts its own direction according to that of its neighbours. A trivial method for achieving this is to let each bird imitate the heading of another bird in the flock. To model this behaviour, each bird must then be able to "watch" other birds and observe their heading.

Listing 2, lines 6–8 show the changes needed to implement the behaviour described above. We omit the interface for clarity, as it is the same as that of Listing 1. Before proceeding, we must stress that, although agents are anonymous to each other, they do have a concept of *identity*. This is provided internally by an *identifier* (id) that is unique to every agent in the system, performing a function

Listing 3: Cohesion.

```
 1  agent Bird {
 2     Interface = ...
 3
 4     Behaviour = Move; Behaviour
 5     Move = {
 6        p := pick 1;
 7
 8        a_x := x_p + ω · dirx_p;
 9        a_y := y_p + ω · diry_p;
10        sgn_x := 0 if x = a_x else (−1 if x > a_x else 1);
11        diff_x := d((x, 0), (a_x, 0));
12        ... (Same for sgn_y, diff_y)
13        a_dirx := sgn_x · (D:2 if diff_y > diff_x else D);
14        a_diry := sgn_y · (D:2 if diff_y < diff_x else D);
15
16        dirx ← (dirx + a_dirx) : 2;
17        x ← x + dirx
18        ... (Same for diry, y)
19     }
20  }
```

similar to that of the keywords *this* or *self* in many general-purpose programming languages. The fact that agents have identifiers allows us to introduce a new operator, by which an agent can non-deterministically select other agents in the system: namely, at line 6, the instruction p := **pick** 1 selects the id of another agent and stores it into a *local* variable p. In general, **pick** k returns k distinct identifiers that are guaranteed to be different from that of the agent doing the selection. We use the operator := to denote assignments to local variables; these are implicitly declared upon their first assignment.

Now that the bird has the identifier of an agent stored in p, it can read its heading vector by using the syntax $\text{dirx}_p, \text{diry}_p$. In this specification, the bird simply replaces its own heading vector by that of p (lines 7–8), and then moves by updating its own position (lines 9–10).

Cohesion. It is evident that birds in a real flock do not simply tend to move along the same direction, but also get close to each other and try to remain cohesive. However, the model of birds seen so far is not refined enough to display this kind of behaviour. In fact, two birds in distant positions will at best assume a coherent direction of movement, but this will not bring them closer to each other. Therefore, we now modify the behaviour described above in order to obtain both alignment and cohesion of the flock. Each bird first selects another bird of the flock; then, observing its direction, estimates the position where the selected bird will be in the future, and steers towards that position.

Listing 3 shows how to model this behaviour. Notice that, from now on, we use a **if** c **else** b to denote the ternary operator that evaluates to a when

Listing 4: Flock dispersion and birds collision.

```
1  agent Bird {
2    Interface = ...
3
4    Behaviour = Move; Behaviour
5    Move = {
6      p := pick 1;
7      pIsIsolated := forall Bird b, (b = p) or d((x_p, y_p), (x_b, y_b)) > δ;
8      appId := id if pIsIsolated else p;
9
10     a_x := x_appId + ω · dirx_appId;
11     sgn_x := 0 if x = a_x else (−1 if x > a_x, else 1);
12     diff_x := d((x, 0), (a_x, 0));
13     ... (Same for a_y, sgn_y, diff_y)
14     a_dirx := sgn_x · (D:2 if diff_y > diff_x else D);
15     a_diry := sgn_y · (D:2 if diff_y < diff_x else D);
16
17     dirx ← (dirx + a_dirx) : 2;
18     diry ← (diry + a_diry) : 2;
19     posFree := forall Bird b, (x_b ≠ x + dirx) or (y_b ≠ y + diry);
20     x ← x + dirx if posFree else x
21     y ← y + diry if posFree else y
22   }
23 }
```

condition c holds and to b otherwise; the syntax $a : b$ denotes integer division with rounding; and $d((x_1, y_1), (x_2, y_2))$ denotes the Manhattan distance between two points, i.e., $|x_1 - x_2| + |y_1 - y_2|$. After picking the bird p to be approached (line 6), we estimate its position after ω steps (lines 8–9). Then, we determine an approach vector (a_dirx, a_diry) pointing towards that position. We compute this vector component-wise at lines 10–14: we omit the instructions for the y-component for sake of brevity. Lastly, we compute the bird's new heading vector as the average of its current one and the approach vector (line 16). This gives the bird a bit of inertia for a more realistic movement.

Avoiding Flock Dispersion and Collisions. The specifications outlined so far may still cause undesired outcomes. For instance, the flock may disperse instead of compacting: this may occur when birds decide to approach other birds that are separated from the rest of the flock. Additionally, we may end up with collisions, i.e., two or more birds sharing the same grid location. To avoid the former, we need to provide birds with the capability of checking whether a bird is isolated. Similarly, to avoid collision, the bird has to check whether a location is free before moving.

In Listing 4, we refine our specifications as described above. At line 7, we check whether bird p is isolated, i.e., its distance from all other birds is greater than a parameter δ. To perform this check, quantified predicates are introduced,

---

Listing 5: Fleeing from a predator.

```
1  agent Predator { ... }
2
3  agent Bird {
4    Interface = ...
5
6    Behaviour = Move; Behaviour
7    Move = {
8      p := pick 1 Bird;
9      ...
10     a_diry := sgn_y · (D:2 if diff_y < diff_x else D);
11
12     e := pick 1 Predator;
13     e_x := x_e + ν · dirx_e;
14     esgn_x := 1 if x ≥ e_x else − 1;
15     ediff_x := d((x, 0), (e_x, 0));
16     ... (Same for e_y, esgn_y, ediff_y)
17     e_dirx := esgn_x · (D:2 if ediff_y > ediff_x else D);
18     e_diry := esgn_y · (D:2 if ediff_y < ediff_x else D);
19
20     e_dist := d((x, y), (e_x, e_y));
21     f_dirx := e_dirx if e_dist < λ else a_dirx;
22     dirx ← (dirx + f_dirx) : 2;
23     ... (Same for f_diry, diry)
24     posFree := forall Bird b, (x_b ≠ x + dirx) or (y_b ≠ y + diry);
25     x ← x + dirx if posFree else x
26   }
27 }
```

---

allowing to predicate over the attributes of all agents, or some agent, of given types. The bird will only approach p if it is not isolated; otherwise, it will continue along its current direction (line 8). Similarly, at lines 19–21, the bird only moves to the position pointed at by its heading vector if that position is free, i.e., if no other bird is currently there; otherwise, it stays in its current location.

Fleeing from a Predator. Until now, we have considered a flock that is unperturbed by external threats. We now want to consider one that may be threatened, for instance, by a bird of prey. This means that birds should be able to recognize a predator and flee from it when it gets too close. At the same time, the flocking dynamics that we have gradually introduced so far should be preserved.

Listing 5 shows the implementation of this new kind of flock. Please notice that we refine the **pick** operator introduced in Listing 2 by making it typed. For instance, at line 8 the bird selects another member of the flock, and then performs the same operations seen in Listing 4. We omit some of the instructions for sake of brevity. Similarly, at line 12 the bird selects a Predator, and then evaluates its distance from itself. If this distance is too small, the bird will not perform its

---

Listing 6: Constraints.

```
1  assume {
2     GridCentre = forall Bird b,
3        x_b > 490 and x_b ≤ 510 and y_b > 490 and y_b ≤ 510
4     DifferentPositions = forall Bird b1, forall Bird b2,
5        b1 = b2 or x_b1 ≠ x_b2 or y_b1 ≠ y_b2
6     DirectionNotNull = forall Bird b, dirx_b ≠ 0 or diry_b ≠ 0
7  }
```

---

usual approach to its flockmate; instead, it will flee from the predator. We model this fleeing behaviour by computing a repulsive heading vector (e_dirx, e_diry) and letting the bird follow it if the predator is closer than a given parameter λ.

3   Simulation Results

The aim of this section is to understand whether the specifications provided so far allow the flock to remain compact. We set up an experimental scenario in which all birds start from non-deterministically chosen positions in a small area, and a single bird of prey flies through the centre of this area, threatening the flock. We aim at showing that the attack of the predator perturbs the flock, which becomes scattered, and that the flock manages to regroup once the predator leaves.

Let us first assume that all agents are placed within an *arena*, modelled as a 1024×1024 square. If the birds could initially assume any position within the arena, they could be very scattered. Instead, we want the birds to start close to each other, as an unperturbed flock would be. Similarly, we want birds not to start from the same position as others, nor to be stationary (i.e., with a null heading vector).

Listing 6 shows how to model these initial constraints, by listing them into a new section of the specifications titled **assume**. Each constraint is expressed through a quantified predicate, like those seen in Sect. 2. Lines 2–3 establish that birds can only be placed in a 20×20 sub-grid at the centre of the arena. Please note that, due to this initial configuration and the limited number of steps we will analyse, it never occurs that the flock reaches the edges of the arena. Lines 4–5 state that two agents cannot assume the same initial position. Finally, line 6 prescribes non-null heading vectors for every bird.

Listing 7 specifies the predator agent. Our predator has the same attributes as the birds in the flock: a position (x, y) and a heading vector $(dirx, diry)$. We give it a very simple behaviour, such that it moves in a straight line along its initial heading vector. To ensure that a predator intersects the flock, the initial position and the heading vector are given determined values (lines 3–6). We give the predator a longer heading vector than those of flock birds, modelling the fact that it moves faster. The predator's behaviour is shown at lines 8–12 and is exactly like the one seen in Listing 1, modelling movement in a straight line.

As mentioned earlier, our aim is to check whether the flock preserves cohesion after an attack. Specifically, as the predator closes in on the flock, birds will flee

---

Listing 7: Predator specifications.

```
1  agent Predator {
2    Interface =
3      x: 480;
4      y: 480;
5      dirx: 3;
6      diry: 3
7
8    Behaviour = Move; Behaviour
9    Move = {
10     x ← x + dirx;
11     y ← y + diry
12   }
13 }
```

Listing 8: Specifying a cohesion requirement.

```
1  check {
2    Cohesion = after B forall Bird b1, forall Bird b2,
3      id_b1 = id_b2 or d((x_b1, y_b1), (x_b2, y_b2)) ≤ k
4  }
```

$$\text{Cohesion} = \textbf{after } B \textbf{ forall } \text{Bird b1}, \textbf{forall } \text{Bird b2},$$
$$\text{id}_{b1} = \text{id}_{b2} \textbf{ or } d((x_{b1}, y_{b1}), (x_{b2}, y_{b2})) \leq k$$

---

from it and thus the distance between any two of them will increase. We want to study whether this distance manages to decrease again after the predator leaves. Listing 8 shows the formalization of this property within another section of the specifications, titled **check**. The property described above is shown at line 3. Here, **after** B denotes that the predicate, which asserts that any two birds are not farther apart than a parameter k, should hold B steps after the initial state. In LTL [27], this construct would be expressed as X^B, i.e., a sequence of B applications of the "next" operator X.

To quickly assess whether our flock is capable of displaying this kind of behaviour, we implemented a *simulation* workflow (Fig. 2) that produces random traces of our specification. Intuitively, we perform a structural encoding of our specifications into a sequential imperative program [10], and then feed the program into a reachability analysis tool to produce one or more random traces of a desired length. These traces are then automatically translated into the specification syntax and shown to the user. The simulation traces that we generate this way also contain information about the satisfaction of properties included in the specification.

To improve the performance of this workflow, we introduce a *concretization* step before feeding the program to the back end. This step is a source-to-source transformation in which we replace nondeterministic assignments in the program with deterministic assignments to *concrete* values, randomly-chosen among the feasible ones. Specifically, we concretize the initial values of the agents' attributes (based on their initial values and on the contents of the **assume** section), the agents' scheduling, and the identifiers returned by **pick** statements. This way, we

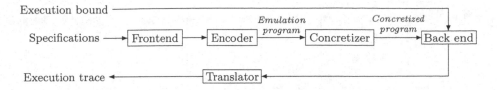

Fig. 2. Workflow to simulate our specifications

Table 1. Parameters in our model and their values used in the simulation process

Name	Description	Value
B	Bound for the cohesion property	600
D	Maximal absolute value of heading vector components for birds	2
G	Size of the arena	1024
k	Maximal distance to satisfy the cohesion property	40
δ	Isolation distance	32
λ	Safe distance from predator	32
ν	Used to estimate the future position of the predator	2
ω	Used to estimate the future position of the bird to approach	14
	Number of Bird agents	29
	Number of Predator agents	1

partially resolve nondeterminism upfront, alleviating the workload of the back end and leading to faster generation of traces. To implement this workflow, we extended SLiVER,[2] a tool originally aimed at formal verification of collective systems [10,11]. Namely, we added support for the new constructs described in Sect. 2, adapted its program generator to the simulation use case, and implemented the concretization step.

Table 1 sums up the parameters in our models and their values in our simulations, as well as the composition of the system. Notice that we use B both as the bound of the cohesion property and as the desired length of our simulations. We assume round-robin scheduling: thus, every trace is a sequence of *epochs* in which each agent performs exactly one action. It is worth recalling that, in this context, an atomic block is regarded as a single action. In our view, this assumption, though demanding, is reasonable when modelling a real-world system. Furthermore, it is significantly weaker than the implicit synchrony assumptions of other models [2,29], in which all agents are required to evolve in *lockstep*. In fact, this requirement implies that the future state of individual agents depends on the current state of the whole system, and that state changes happen simultaneously for all agents.

Figure 3 shows the visual representation of a trace generated through this simulation process. Each bird is represented by a triangle pointing in the direction

---

[2] https://github.com/labs-lang/sliver/.

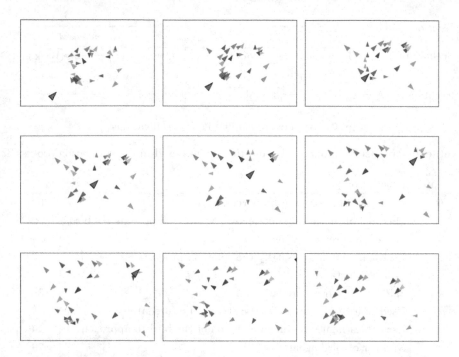

Fig. 3. A trace generated through simulation. The predator is the red triangle with black outline (Color figure online)

of its heading vector; the predator is the larger, red triangle with black outline. Notice that, in this trace, birds are never in the same position, and overlapping triangles are merely an artefact of the visualization. As we expected, the trace shows that the predator attack does introduce a certain amount of dispersion in the flock as birds move to avoid the threat; however, birds are eventually able to regroup and reorient themselves coherently, satisfying the property that we specified in Listing 8. As a final remark, we should stress that our simulation workflow helped us throughout the specification process: for instance, they made us realize the potential for flock dispersion in Listing 3, guiding us to develop the more refined Listing 4.

4 Related Work

Models of flocking behaviour in the literature rely either on equational modelling, using for instance differential equations [34], discrete-time dynamics [2,29] or statistical mechanics [3]; on decentralized control laws, either developed ad-hoc [35] or synthesized from a centralized controller [23]; or on language-based specifications, such as the ones presented in this work.

An advantage of language-based approaches is that models can be gradually refined, or compared against each other, with little effort. For instance, the framework of [20] has been used to model different predator tactics (such as attacking the centroid of the flock, the nearest prey, or the most isolated one) and different versions of flocking behaviour: simulations show that preys with a more individualistic behaviour are more likely to get caught, while more social flocks provide better chances of survival [8].

Formal specification languages also enable exhaustive exploration of the state space, which can provide strong guarantees about the behaviour of a system, or find subtle bugs that are hard to detect through simulations alone. As an example, the *alpha algorithm* [36], which was supposed to make a flock of scattered agents aggregate in a small region of space, has been found to be incorrect [1,18] by verifying models of the algorithm written in ISPL [22] or NuSMV [6]. Emulation programs may similarly enable formal analysis of high-level specification by means of structural encodings towards lower-level languages, allowing to reuse different existing verification technologies [10,12].

Bottom-up and simulation-aided design is also common in the engineering of robot swarms and related classes of robotic systems [4]. In this context, robots are typically programmed at the individual level, using either general-purpose languages such as C++ or Python, or higher-level, domain-specific formalisms [9,25], possibly relying on existing robotic middleware such as ROS [28]. The resulting programs are evaluated by simulating the robots under one of several available simulation platforms [17,26,30] to empirically check whether the swarm exhibits an adequate collective behaviour. These platforms also support physical simulations, allowing to check how real-world phenomena (like gravity, collisions, etc.) may interfere with the agents. These kinds of interactions with the environment are out of the scope of this work, but it might be worthwhile to integrate these platforms into our simulation workflow.

5 Conclusion

In this work, we have considered the natural collective behaviour known as flocking, and we have shown how compositional models can help reasoning about the individual dynamics that lead to its emergence. To this end, we gradually refined an extremely simple individual behaviour into a more elaborate, but still rather compact and intuitive, final specification. This specification allows a flock of birds to display some interesting collective features. By feeding it to an automated simulation workflow, we indeed showed that the birds are able to counter the threat of a predator by splitting into smaller groups that reassemble once the danger subsides. This successfully reproduces the behaviour observed both in real-life flocks and in other models [2].

We are considering several interesting directions for future work on this subject. Our simulation workflow is still experimental and, while it does simulate the model of Sect. 2 well, we do not expect it to work in every scenario. For instance, specifications that contain guarded statements may be hard to simulate, since some concretizations may fail to satisfy some guards and thus make it impossible to produce a trace of the desired length. To work around these issues, we plan to customize the back end so that we can modify the concretization constraints until a valid trace is obtained.

We intend to complement the simulation-based approach shown in this work with exhaustive state space exploration techniques that may formally prove the emergence of desired collective features, regardless of the initial state or the system or the specific interactions between agents. We may achieve this by adapting existing techniques based on verification of emulation programs [10], possibly extending them to support expressive temporal logics such as LTL [27]. This goal may also benefit from a more rigorous formalization of the linguistic constructs introduced in Sect. 2, which is also reserved for future work. Since the cost of exhaustive analysis may be prohibitive for very large system, we plan to further extend our simulation workflow to enable lightweight formal methods, such as statistical model checking [31], allowing us to at least obtain statistical evidence on the correctness of these systems. Our framework's capability to check for property satisfaction during simulation can be seen as a rudimental form of runtime verification [21]. Extending this capability to larger classes of monitorable properties [15] is also planned as future work.

We can trivially parallelize our simulation workflow by running it on multiple machines at once; moreover, we might further improve performances by implementing distributed techniques in the back end [16]. Working in these two directions may allow us to generate large numbers of traces for massive systems. Generating effective visualizations from a textual trace is also essential to support the design process. So far, our automated visualization tool (which we used, for instance, to generate Fig. 3) is tailored to the flocking case study: building a more generic framework, or integrating our workflow into existing simulation platforms, would be interesting contributions.

References

1. Antuña, L., Araiza-Illan, D., Campos, S., Eder, K.: Symmetry reduction enables model checking of more complex emergent behaviours of swarm navigation algorithms. In: Dixon, C., Tuyls, K. (eds.) TAROS 2015. LNCS (LNAI), vol. 9287, pp. 26–37. Springer, Cham (2015). https://doi.org/10.1007/978-3-319-22416-9_4
2. Ballerini, M., et al.: Interaction ruling animal collective behavior depends on topological rather than metric distance: evidence from a field study. Proc. Natl. Acad. Sci. 105(4), 1232–1237 (2008). https://doi.org/10.1073/pnas.0711437105
3. Bialek, W., et al.: Statistical mechanics for natural flocks of birds. Proc. Natl. Acad. Sci. 109(13), 4786–4791 (2012)
4. Brambilla, M., Ferrante, E., Birattari, M., Dorigo, M.: Swarm robotics: a review from the swarm engineering perspective. Swarm Intell. 7(1), 1–41 (2013). https://doi.org/10.1007/s11721-012-0075-2
5. Cederman, L.E.: Endogenizing geopolitical boundaries with agent-based modeling. Proc. Natl. Acad. Sci. 99(Suppl 3), 7296–7303 (2002). https://doi.org/10.1073/pnas.082081099
6. Cimatti, A., et al.: NuSMV 2: an OpenSource tool for symbolic model checking. In: Brinksma, E., Larsen, K.G. (eds.) CAV 2002. LNCS, vol. 2404, pp. 359–364. Springer, Heidelberg (2002). https://doi.org/10.1007/3-540-45657-0_29

7. De Nicola, R., Di Stefano, L., Inverso, O.: Multi-agent systems with virtual stigmergy. Sci. Comput. Program. **187**, 102345 (2020). https://doi.org/10.1016/j.scico.2019.102345

8. Demsar, J., Lebar Bajec, I.: Simulated predator attacks on flocks: a comparison of tactics. Artif. Life **20**(3), 343–359 (2014). https://doi.org/10.1162/ARTL_a_00135

9. Desai, A., Saha, I., Yang, J., Qadeer, S., Seshia, S.A.: DRONA: a framework for safe distributed mobile robotics. In: ICCPS (2017). https://doi.org/10.1145/3055004.3055022

10. Di Stefano, L., De Nicola, R., Inverso, O.: Verification of distributed systems via sequential emulation. ACM Trans. Softw. Eng. Methodol. **31**(3), 1–41 (2022). https://doi.org/10.1145/3490387

11. Di Stefano, L., Lang, F.: Verifying temporal properties of stigmergic collective systems using CADP. In: Margaria, T., Steffen, B. (eds.) ISoLA 2021. LNCS, vol. 13036, pp. 473–489. Springer, Cham (2021). https://doi.org/10.1007/978-3-030-89159-6_29

12. Di Stefano, L., Lang, F., Serwe, W.: Combining SLiVER with CADP to analyze multi-agent systems. In: Bliudze, S., Bocchi, L. (eds.) COORDINATION 2020. LNCS, vol. 12134, pp. 370–385. Springer, Cham (2020). https://doi.org/10.1007/978-3-030-50029-0_23

13. Emlen, J.T.: Flocking behavior in birds. Auk **69**(2), 160–170 (1952)

14. Finkelshtein, D., Kondratiev, Y., Kutoviy, O.: Individual based model with competition in spatial ecology. SIAM J. Math. Anal. **41**(1), 297–317 (2009). https://doi.org/10.1137/080719376

15. Francalanza, A., Aceto, L., Ingolfsdottir, A.: On verifying Hennessy-Milner logic with recursion at runtime. In: Bartocci, E., Majumdar, R. (eds.) RV 2015. LNCS, vol. 9333, pp. 71–86. Springer, Cham (2015). https://doi.org/10.1007/978-3-319-23820-3_5

16. Inverso, O., Trubiani, C.: Parallel and distributed bounded model checking of multi-threaded programs. In: 25th Symposium on Principles and Practice of Parallel Programming (PPoPP), pp. 202–216. ACM (2020). https://doi.org/10.1145/3332466.3374529

17. Koenig, N., Howard, A.: Design and use paradigms for Gazebo, an open-source multi-robot simulator. In: IEEE/RSJ International Conference on Intelligent Robots and Systems (IROS), vol. 3, pp. 2149–2154. IEEE (2004). https://doi.org/10.1109/IROS.2004.1389727

18. Kouvaros, P., Lomuscio, A.: A counter abstraction technique for the verification of robot swarms. In: 29th Conference on Artificial Intelligence (AAAI), pp. 2081–2088. AAAI (2015)

19. Kuylen, E., Liesenborgs, J., Broeckhove, J., Hens, N.: Using individual-based models to look beyond the horizon: the changing effects of household-based clustering of susceptibility to measles in the next 20 years. In: Krzhizhanovskaya, V.V., et al. (eds.) ICCS 2020. LNCS, vol. 12137, pp. 385–398. Springer, Cham (2020). https://doi.org/10.1007/978-3-030-50371-0_28

20. Lebar Bajec, I., Zimic, N., Mraz, M.: Simulating flocks on the wing: the fuzzy approach. J. Theor. Biol. **233**, 199–220 (2005). https://doi.org/10.1016/j.jtbi.2004.10.003

21. Leucker, M., Schallhart, C.: A brief account of runtime verification. J. Log. Algebraic Program. **78**(5), 293–303 (2009). https://doi.org/10.1016/j.jlap.2008.08.004

22. Lomuscio, A., Qu, H., Raimondi, F.: MCMAS: an open-source model checker for the verification of multi-agent systems. Int. J. Softw. Tools Technol. Transf. **19**(1), 9–30 (2015). https://doi.org/10.1007/s10009-015-0378-x

23. Mehmood, U., Roy, S., Grosu, R., Smolka, S.A., Stoller, S.D., Tiwari, A.: Neural flocking: MPC-based supervised learning of flocking controllers. In: Goubault-Larrecq, J., König, B. (eds.) FoSSaCS 2020. LNCS, vol. 12077, pp. 1–16. Springer, Cham (2020). https://doi.org/10.1007/978-3-030-45231-5_1

24. Olfati-Saber, R.: Flocking for multi-agent dynamic systems: algorithms and theory. IEEE Trans. Autom. Control **51**(3), 401–420 (2006). https://doi.org/10.1109/TAC.2005.864190

25. Pinciroli, C., Beltrame, G.: Buzz: an extensible programming language for heterogeneous swarm robotics. In: IEEE/RSJ International Conference on Intelligent Robots and Systems (IROS), pp. 3794–3800. IEEE (2016). https://doi.org/10.1109/IROS.2016.7759558

26. Pinciroli, C., et al.: ARGoS: a modular, parallel, multi-engine simulator for multi-robot systems. Swarm Intell. **6**(4), 271–295 (2012). https://doi.org/10.1007/S11721-012-0072-5

27. Pnueli, A.: The temporal logic of programs. In: 18th Annual Symposium on Foundations of Computer Science (FOCS), pp. 46–57. IEEE (1977). https://doi.org/10.1109/SFCS.1977.32

28. Quigley, M., et al.: ROS: an open-source robot operating system. In: ICRA Workshop on Open Source Software (2009)

29. Reynolds, C.W.: Flocks, herds and schools: a distributed behavioral model. In: Proceedings of the 14th Annual Conference on Computer Graphics and Interactive Techniques, SIGGRAPH 1987, Anaheim, California, USA, 27–31 July 1987, pp. 25–34. ACM (1987). https://doi.org/10.1145/37401.37406

30. Rohmer, E., Singh, S.P.N., Freese, M.: V-REP: a versatile and scalable robot simulation framework. In: IEEE/RSJ International Conference on Intelligent Robots and Systems (IROS), pp. 1321–1326. IEEE (2013). https://doi.org/10.1109/IROS.2013.6696520

31. Sen, K., Viswanathan, M., Agha, G.: Statistical model checking of black-box probabilistic systems. In: Alur, R., Peled, D.A. (eds.) CAV 2004. LNCS, vol. 3114, pp. 202–215. Springer, Heidelberg (2004). https://doi.org/10.1007/978-3-540-27813-9_16

32. Shi, H., Wang, L., Chu, T.: Flocking of multi-agent systems with a dynamic virtual leader. Int. J. Control **82**(1), 43–58 (2009). https://doi.org/10.1080/00207170801983091

33. Stiglitz, J.E., Gallegati, M.: Heterogeneous interacting agent models for understanding monetary economies. East. Econ. J. **37**(1), 6–12 (2011). https://doi.org/10.1057/eej.2010.33

34. Toner, J., Tu, Y.: Flocks, herds, and schools: a quantitative theory of flocking. Phys. Rev. E **58**(4), 4828–4858 (1998). https://doi.org/10.1103/PhysRevE.58.4828

35. Vásárhelyi, G., et al.: Outdoor flocking and formation flight with autonomous aerial robots. In: IEEE/RSJ International Conference on Intelligent Robots and Systems (IROS), pp. 3866–3873. IEEE (2014). https://doi.org/10.1109/IROS.2014.6943105

36. Winfield, A.F.T., Liu, W., Nembrini, J., Martinoli, A.: Modelling a wireless connected swarm of mobile robots. Swarm Intell. **2**(2–4), 241–266 (2008). https://doi.org/10.1007/s11721-008-0018-0

Towards Drone Flocking Using Relative Distance Measurements

Andreas Brandstätter[1]([envelope]) [iD], Scott A. Smolka[2], Scott D. Stoller[2] [iD],
Ashish Tiwari[3] [iD], and Radu Grosu[1] [iD]

[1] Research Division for Cyber-Physical Systems, TU Wien, Vienna, Austria
`andreas.brandstaetter@tuwien.ac.at`
[2] Department of Computer Science, Stony Brook University, New York, USA
[3] Microsoft, Redmond, USA

Abstract. We introduce a method to form and maintain a flock of
drones only based on relative distance measurements. This means our
approach is able to work in GPS-denied environments. It is fully distributed and therefore does not need any information exchange between
the individual drones. Relative distance measurements to other drones
and information about its own relative movement are used to estimate
the current state of the environment. This makes it possible to perform
lookahead and estimate the next state for any potential next movement.
A distributed cost function is then used to determine the best next action
in every time step. Using a high-fidelity simulation environment, we show
that our approach is able to form and maintain a flock for a set of drones.

Keywords: Drones · Quadcopters · Flock · Swarm · Distributed
controller

1 Introduction

Flocking is a fundamental flight-formation problem. Birds flock for a variety
of reasons, including foraging for food, protection from predators, communal
warmth, and for mating purposes. Starling flocks can also perform high-speed
pinpoint maneuvers, such as a 180° turn [1]. Some types of flocks in nature
have distinct leaders, such as queen bees, and queen ants. Other swarms are
formed by animals that do not have a permanently defined leadership, such as
starlings or herrings. Although flocking is a well-studied problem mathematically
[6,7,14,18], its realization using actual drones is not nearly as mature (but see
[22,25]).

Drone swarms, a quintessential example of a multi-agent system, can carry
out tasks that cannot be accomplished by individual drones alone [5]. They can,
for example, collectively carry a heavy load while still being much more agile
than a single larger drone [12,15]. In search-and-rescue applications, a swarm
can explore unknown terrain by covering individual paths that jointly cover

T. Margaria and B. Steffen (Eds.): ISoLA 2022, LNCS 13703, pp. 97–109, 2022.
https://doi.org/10.1007/978-3-031-19759-8_7

the entire area [3,8,16]. While flocking provides a number of advantages over individual flight, it also poses a significant challenge: the need for a distributed control mechanism that can maintain flock formation and its stability [17]. These collective maneuvers can be expressed as the problem of minimizing a *positional cost function*, i.e., a cost function that depends on the positions of the drones (and possibly information about their environment). In our formulation, every agent is identical, which means there is no designated leader.

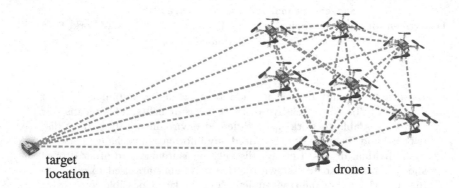

target
location

drone i

Fig. 1. Our distributed controller forms and maintains a flock based on relative distance measurements to other agents of the flock. The target location is shown in blue. Distance measurements for drone i to other drones and to the target location are shown in orange. (Color figure online)

To work with such a positional cost function, an absolute localization system is needed. This can be an optical or radio-based system for indoor applications or GPS-based localization for outdoor scenarios. In this work, we study the problem for scenarios that lack an absolute localization system (GPS-denied environments). We only have the ability to measure the distance to other drones and to measure the acceleration and rotational velocity of the own drone using an onboard Inertial Measurement Unit (IMU). For flock formation, we observe that the positional cost function can be replaced by a function based solely on relative distances. This obviates the need for absolute localization. We propose a method to simultaneously learn properties of the environment (inter-agent distance changes), while at the same time maintaining the flock formation solely on relative distance information.

In this paper, we address the following **Challenge Problem:** *Design a distributed controller that forms and maintains a flock based solely on inter-agent distance measurements.*

To solve this problem, we introduce a method to estimate changes of the environment based on the observed changes for previous movements and thereafter use this information to minimize the cost-function over a set of candidate positions. We build upon our previous work that introduced Spatial Predictive

Control (SPC) [4] to select the best next action from the set of candidate positions. However we have a substantially different problem here, since we have limited observation capability: in the previous work [4], absolute positions of all the drones were available; whereas in this work we can only measure relative distances. This also changes our possibilities how to apply SPC: whereas in the previous work it was possible to optimize the direction based on the cost function's gradient, we need to do a search on possible candidate positions in all directions in this work.

Our agent's observations consist of its own acceleration in three-dimensional space, rotational velocity along three axes, and the relative distance to other agents, as well as the distance to a fixed target location (as shown in Fig. 1). (The target location is currently only used to counteract drifting tendencies of the whole flock.) There is no communication or central coordination, which makes our approach fully distributed. Our flocking objective is formulated as a cost function (see Sect. 2.2) which is based on these distance measurements. The corresponding action of each agent is a relative spatial vector, to which the drone should move, to minimize its cost function's value.

Paper Outline: Section 2 describes our cost function for flocking with target seeking and related performance metrics. Section 3 introduces our method to represent environmental knowledge and thereafter describes our distributed flocking controller. Section 4 presents the results of our experimental evaluation. Section 5 considers related work. Section 6 offers our concluding remarks.

2 Drone Flocking

This section starts with background on flocking, introduces our cost function for flocking with target seeking, and then presents metrics to assess the quality of a flocking controller.

2.1 What Is a Flock?

A set of agents, D, is in a flock formation if the distance between every pair of agents is range bounded; that is, the drones are neither too close to each other nor too far apart. Our approach to flock formation is based on defining a cost function such that the agents form a flock when the cost is minimized. The requirement that the inter-agent distance is range bounded is encoded as the first two terms of our cost function, namely the *cohesion* and *separation* terms shown in the next section. Note that the Reynolds rules for forming a flock [18] also include a term for aligning the drone's velocities, apart from the cohesion and separation terms. By not including velocity alignment term, we potentially allow a few more behaviors, such as circling drones, but some of those behaviors are eliminated by our third term, namely the *target seeking* term. The effects of these terms are illustrated in Fig. 2.

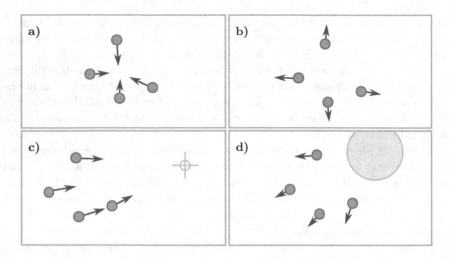

Fig. 2. Directional movements (indicated by arrows) induced by cost-function terms: **a**: *Cohesion*, **b**: *separation*, **c**: *target seeking*, and **d**: *obstacle avoidance* (not implemented in our method yet).

2.2 Cost Function

Consider drones i and j, where $i, j \in D$. Let d_{ij}, when it appears in the local cost function of drone i, denote the distance between drone i and drone j as it appears to drone i; this may differ from the actual distance due to sensing error. Similarly l_i denotes the distance between drone i and the fixed target location p_{tar}. In all cases, distances are measured from the drone's center of the mass. Let r_{drone} denote the radius of each drone (specifically the radius of the circumscribed sphere including propellers). In our formulation for the cost function, drone i has access to distances of only a subset $H_i \subseteq D$ of drones, namely its local neighbors. Hence, we define a local cost function, parameterized by i, which uses only the distances to drones in H_i. However for now we only consider the case for global neighborhood, which is $H_i = D$. We plan to extend our experiments also to local neighborhood as future work (see Sect. 6). Let d_{H_i} denote the tuple of distances from drone i to drones in H_i. The cost function c we use in this paper is defined for every drone $i \in D$ as in Eq. (1).

$$c(d_{H_i}, l_i) = c_{coh}(d_{H_i}) + c_{sep}(d_{H_i}) + c_{tar}(l_i) \tag{1}$$

The value of the *cohesion* term increases as drones drift apart, and the *separation* term increases as drones get closer. Each term has a weight, denoted by a subscripted ω.

Cohesion Term:

$$c_{coh}(d_{H_i}) = \omega_{coh} \cdot \frac{1}{|H_i|} \cdot \sum_{j \in H_i} d_{ij}^2 \tag{2}$$

Separation Term:

$$c_{sep}(d_{H_i}) = \omega_{sep} \cdot \frac{1}{|H_i|} \cdot \sum_{j \in H_i} \frac{1}{max(d_{ij} - 2r_{drone}, \hat{0})^2} \tag{3}$$

Here $\hat{0}$ denotes a very small positive value. The function $max(., \hat{0})$ ensures the denominator remains nonzero, especially because sensor noise can cause distance measurements to have errors.

To prevent the flock from moving in random directions, we currently use a *target seeking* term with a fixed target location, denoted by p_{tar}, for the entire flock. Here l_i denotes the distance between the center of drone i and the fixed target location p_{tar}.

Target Seeking Term:

$$c_{tar}(l_i) = \omega_{tar} \cdot l_i^2 \tag{4}$$

With only *cohesion* and *separation*, the whole flock would form and move in random directions and random locations in absolute world coordinates. This would make it of limited use in any real-world scenario. Our *target seeking* term avoids this behaviour. All drones use the same target location; thus, this last term assumes shared global knowledge of the target. The control algorithm will still be fully distributed. A way to avoid having a fixed target location would be to designate one of the drones as the leader of the flock. This leader could be equipped with additional sensors to get information about its absolute position, allowing it to employ a different control scheme. We leave that investigation for future work.

2.3   Flock-Formation Quality Metrics

We define two quality metrics to assess the quality of the flock formation achieved by a flocking controller. To compute these quality metrics, we assume to have access to full ground truth information about the absolute positions of the drones. The position (center of mass) of drone i is denoted by p_i.

Collision Avoidance: To avoid collisions, the distance between all pairs of drones distance(D) must remain above a specified threshold distance$_{thr}$. We define the metric for the minimum distance between any pair of drones as follows:

$$\text{distance}(D) = \min_{i,j \in D; i \neq j} \|p_i - p_j\| \tag{5}$$

$$\text{distance}(D) \geq \text{distance}_{thr} \tag{6}$$

We set distance$_{thr} = 2 \cdot r_{drone} + r_{safety}$, where r_{safety} is a safety margin.

Compactness: Compactness of the flock is determined by the flock *radius*. Radius is defined as the maximum distance of any drone from the centroid of the flock:

$$\text{radius}(D) = \max_{i \in D} \left\| \frac{\sum_{j \in D} p_j}{|D|} - p_i \right\| \tag{7}$$

The drones are said to be in a compact flock formation if $\text{radius}(D)$ stays below some threshold radius_{thr}; otherwise the drones are too far apart, not forming a flock.

$$\text{radius}(D) \leq \text{radius}_{thr} \tag{8}$$

The value for radius_{thr} is picked based on the drone model and other parameters governing the flock formation problem. We set it to $\text{radius}_{thr} = \frac{F \cdot r_{drone}}{\sqrt[3]{|D|}}$, where we use the drone radius r_{drone} to incorporate the physical size and multiply by a factor F.

3   Distributed Flocking Controller Using Relative Distances

In our distributed approach to flock formation, each drone picks the best action at every time step. The action here is a target displacement vector. Each drone picks the optimal displacement vector for itself by looking ahead in different spatial directions and finding a location that would minimize the cost *if this drone moved there*. To perform this search, each drone needs capability to *estimate* the relative distances to other drones when it moves to different potential target locations. To perform this estimation, each drone stores some measurements from past time steps, which is described in Sect. 3.1. Thereafter, Sect. 3.2 shows how this stored knowledge is used by each drone to estimate relative distances of other drones for different possible displacements of itself.

3.1   Environmental Knowledge Representation

We describe the procedure from the perspective of Drone i. The "environment" for Drone i consists of the current distances to the neighboring drones (and the fixed target), as this is all the information Drone i needs to evaluate the cost function. To represent the knowledge of the environment, Drone i keeps two matrices, a $(k \times 3)$-matrix N and a $(k \times (|D|+1))$-matrix P for some $k \geq 3$. The j-th row of N is a displacement vector for Drone i. The j-th row of P is a vector of change in distances of every other drone and the target to Drone i (as seen by Drone i when it moved by displacement vector in j-th row of N). In particular, P_{lj} is the change in distance of Drone j (or target if $j = |D| + 1$) as seen by Drone i when it moved by the vector N_{l*}. The notation N_{l*} denotes the l-th row vector of matrix N. Let us see how the matrices N and P are generated.

   Each drone is capable of measuring its own acceleration vector in three dimensions $\vec{a}_i$. By integration, the velocity vector $\vec{v}_i$ can be derived. Drone i constructs the matrices N and P as follows:

1. Save the observations of time instant t. Let $d_{ij,t}$ denote the distances to Drone j, and let $l_{i,t}$ denote the distance to the fixed target, at this time instant t (as obtained from the sensors).

$$d_{ij,t} = d_{ij} \,|\, j \in H_i, t \tag{9}$$

$$l_{i,t} = l_i \,|\, t \tag{10}$$

2. Integrate velocity vector to keep track of its own position changes, which gives the displacement vector $\vec{u_i}$:

$$\vec{u_i} = \int_{t-\Delta t}^{t} \vec{v_i}\, dt \tag{11}$$

3. If the norm of the change in position is larger than a threshold $\|\vec{u_i}\| > s_{thr}$, calculate the changes in distances as follows:

$$\bar{d}_{ij} = d_{ij,t} - d_{ij,t-\Delta t} \tag{12}$$

$$\bar{l}_i = d_{i,t} - d_{i,t-\Delta t} \tag{13}$$

Here $d_{ij,t-\Delta t}$ denotes the observed distance of Drone j at the previous time instant $t - \Delta t$. If the length of the displacement vector is smaller than the threshold, we go back to Step (1).

4. Add the displacement vector $\vec{u_i}$ of Drone i as a row vector in matrix N and add the vector $\langle \bar{d}_{i1}, \ldots, \bar{d}_{i|D|}, \bar{l}_i \rangle$ as a row vector in matrix P. Note that we have assumed here that the neighborhood H_i of Drone i is the full set D, but the details can be easily adapted to the case when $H_i \subset D$.

5. The process starts again at (1) and we thus keep adding rows to the matrices N and P.

In this way, the matrix P reflects the available knowledge of how the distances to other drones and to the target change when Drone i moves along vector $\vec{u_i}$. Note that this data gets stale as time progresses, and the newly added rows clearly have more relevant and current information compared to the rows added earlier. Furthermore note that $\vec{u_i}$ is obtained by double integration and therefore it is prone to acceleration sensing errors, and also numerical errors. This influence is however limited, since integration times Δt are also small.

When the procedure above is followed, the matrices N and P keep getting bigger. Let N_{l*} denote the l-th row vector of matrix N. Let N_{a*}, N_{b*}, N_{c*} denote three displacement (row) vectors taken from the (most recent rows in) matrix N such that they are linearly independent – that is, they are all different from each other ($N_{a*} \neq N_{b*} \neq N_{c*}$), nonzero ($N_{a*} \neq \vec{0}$, $N_{b*} \neq \vec{0}$, $N_{c*} \neq \vec{0}$), and not in a common plane (($N_{a*} \times N_{b*}) \cdot N_{c*} \neq \vec{0}$). These three vectors form a basis in the three-dimensional space. Using a basis transform it is therefore possible to estimate the change for distances for any movement vector $\vec{u}$. Specifically, if

$$\vec{u} = \lambda_a \cdot N_{a*} + \lambda_b \cdot N_{b*} + \lambda_c \cdot N_{c*} \tag{14}$$

then we can compute the estimated change in distances of each of the other drones, $\bar{d}(\vec{u})$, and the target, $\bar{l}(\vec{u})$ for this displacement $\vec{u}$ as follows:

$$\langle \bar{d}(\vec{u}), \bar{l}(\vec{u}) \rangle = \lambda_a \cdot P_a + \lambda_b \cdot P_b + \lambda_c \cdot P_c \tag{15}$$

(addition and multiplication in Eq. (15) are applied element-wise on the vectors).

We have shown how the three vectors N_{a*}, N_{b*}, N_{c*} can be used to infer the expected change for any displacement vector $\vec{u}$ for Drone i. To ensure that three different vectors with meaningful data are present, our controller employs some optimizations in addition to the procedure described above. A special startup procedure with random movements is used to collect initial data. The three vectors (N_{a*}, N_{b*}, N_{c*}) and their associated data in P are continuously updated to avoid outdated information. However, a vector is only considered if the threshold s_{thr} is exceeded within a certain time limit. This avoids updates when the drone is moving very slowly over longer time-periods. To get the best quality of the prediction for any displacement $\vec{u}$, it is desirable to have the vectors (N_{a*}, N_{b*}, N_{c*}) ideally, but not necessarily, orthogonal to each other. This also influences which row (vector) gets replaced in the matrices N and P. As soon as one of the vectors gets outdated, a random movement in an orthogonal direction might be triggered to enhance the knowledge representation.

3.2   Distributed Flocking Controller

We now describe our control approach based on the cost function introduced in Sect. 2.2 and on the environmental knowledge representation described in Sect. 3.1.

The set of candidate positions Q is defined as follows:

$$Q = \left\{ \begin{pmatrix} x \\ y \\ z \end{pmatrix} \mid x \in \{-\epsilon_Q, 0, \epsilon_Q\}, y \in \{-\epsilon_Q, 0, \epsilon_Q\}, z \in \{-\epsilon_Q, 0, \epsilon_Q\} \right\} \qquad (16)$$

This gives a set of 27 points on a equally spaced three dimensional grid. The spacing distance of this grid is ϵ_Q. Over this set Q the best action q_{next} is searched by minimizing the cost function c:

$$q_{next} = \underset{q \in Q}{\operatorname{argmin}} \{ c(\widehat{d}_i(q), \widehat{l}_i(q)) \} \qquad (17)$$

If two candidate positions q_1 and q_2 both have the same minimum value for the cost function c, our implementation of argmin takes the last one based on the implementation of the enumeration. The function $\widehat{d}_i(q)$ estimates the distances to drones, where $\widehat{l}_i(q)$ estimates the distance to the target, if the action q is applied. For each $q \in Q$, the vector $\widehat{d}_i(q)$ (and the value $\widehat{l}_i(q)$) is calculated by first computing the estimates of the *change vector* $\bar{d}_i(q)$, and the change $\bar{l}_i(q)$ using Eq. 15. Now the distances can be estimated by just adding the estimated change to the currently measured distances d_{i*} and l_i:

$$\widehat{d}_i(q) = d_{i*} + \bar{d}_i(q) \qquad (18)$$

$$\widehat{l}_i(q) = l_i + \bar{l}_i(q) \qquad (19)$$

Each drone minimizes its local cost function (Eq. 17) in order to recompute the desired set-point at every time step. As we similarly did in [4], this set-point is then handed off to a low-level controller that controls the thrust of the drone's motors so that it steers towards this set-point.

4   Experiments

We evaluated our method using simulation experiments. The goal of the experiments was to investigate and demonstrate the ability to form and maintain a stable flock while holding position at a target location.

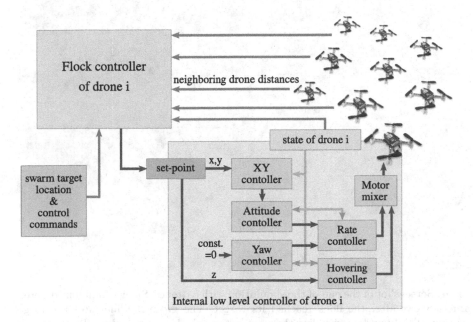

Fig. 3. The ROS-node of the SPC controller for drone i receives distance measurements to neighboring drones and control messages (e.g. swarm target location, start/stop command). It outputs the set-point for the internal low level controller.

4.1   Simulation Experiments

As a simulation framework, we use *crazys* [20], which is based on the *Gazebo* [11] physics and visualization engine and the Robotic Operating System (ROS) [23]. Our algorithm is implemented in C++ as a separate ROS node. As shown in Fig. 3, it receives the measured distances to neighboring drones, and control messages, such as the target location or a stop command, from the human operator. It calculates the best next action according to Eqs. (16)–(19). The parameter ϵ_Q is determined empirically and fixed throughout the whole simulation. Auxiliary functions, like hovering at the starting position, and landing after the experiments are finished, are also implemented in this node.

In order to evaluate the control mechanism and its implementation, we fixed the target location, as described above. This avoids drifting behaviour of the whole flock, which could not be detected by relative distance measurements in any way. Simulations were done with flocks of size $|D| = 5$, 9, and 15. Figure 4 shows a screenshot of a simulation with 5 drones. All simulations use global neighborhood ($H_i = D$) for now.

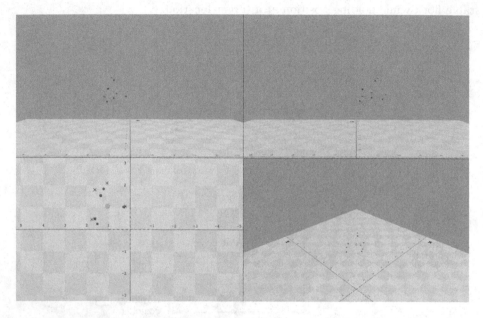

Fig. 4. Screenshot of the end of the simulation with 5 drones. Shown from four different camera views after the flock reached its target. The green dot indicates the target location. The blue dots visualize the next action which is supplied to the lower level controller. (Color figure online)

4.2   Results

Early results show that our approach is able to properly form and maintain a flock with only relative position measurements. Figure 5 shows performance metrics over time for a simulation with 5 drones. The analysis of the quality metrics for *collision avoidance*, and *compactness* show that our control approach successfully maintains a stable flock (threshold $distance_{thr}$ is only violated for very short moments). Note that these results are already obtained before extensive controller tuning. Using carefully adjusted values for ω_{coh} and ω_{sep} should lead to even better results and maintain the threshold throughout the whole simulation.

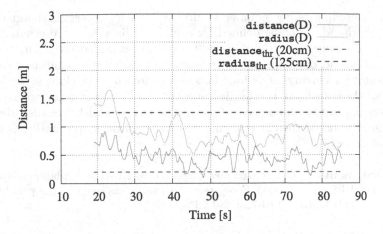

Fig. 5. Quality metrics for simulation with 5 drones. Threshold $distance_{thr}$ for collision avoidance is satisfied most of the time. After settling in, the swarm radius remains below the threshold $radius_{thr}$, thus showing the ability to form a compact flock in the simulation. (Quality metric recordings start at $t = 19\,s$ after initialization procedure).

5 Related Work

Reynolds [18] was the first to propose a flocking model, using cohesion, separation, and velocity alignment force terms to compute agent accelerations. Reynolds' model was extensively studied [9] and adapted for different application areas [5]. Alternative flocking models are considered in [13,14,17,21,24], and [19]. In all these approaches, absolute position measurements and/or inter-agent communication were available. In our work, we only work with relative distance measurements and a fully distributed formulation.

In addition to these largely theoretical approaches, in [25] and [22], flocking controllers are implemented and tested on real hardware. However, the approach of [22] involves the use of nonlinear model-predictive control (NMPC). In contrast to our work, [25] also requires the velocity of neighboring drones.

6 Conclusions

We introduced a method to control a flock only based on relative position measurements to neighboring drones, and demonstrated its utility on the drone flocking problem. We performed simulation experiments using a physics engine with a detailed drone model. Our results demonstrated the ability to form and maintain a flock, and hold its position on a target location.

Future Work

As we currently have only intermediate results of the experiments with limited number of agents, we plan to do more extensive testing with a wide set of different scenarios, including larger number of drones, and local neighborhood ($H_i \subset D$). Neighborhood might be defined by euclidean distance, or alternatively by topological distance, as introduced in [2]. As further directions of future work, we plan to extend our approach with obstacle avoidance capabilities. We also plan to test it for moving target locations and various path tracking scenarios. To prepare for the transfer to real hardware we plan to introduce sensor noise in the simulation and test the robustness of our method to cope with such disturbances. As next goal it should then be implemented on real drones, specifically, *Crazyflie 2.1*- quadcopters [10].

Acknowledgments. R.G. was partially supported by EU-H2020 Adaptness and AT-BMBWF DK-RES and CPS/IoT Ecosystem. This work was supported in part by NSF grants CCF-1954837, CCF-1918225, and CPS-1446832.

References

1. Attanasi, A., et al.: Emergence of collective changes in travel direction of starling flocks from individual birds' fluctuations. J. Roy. Soc. **12**, 20150319 (2015)
2. Ballerini, M., et al.: Interaction ruling animal collective behavior depends on topological rather than metric distance: evidence from a field study. Proc. Natl. Acad. Sci. **105**(4), 1232–1237 (2008). https://doi.org/10.1073/pnas.0711437105
3. Boggio-Dandry, A., Soyata, T.: Perpetual flight for UAV drone swarms using continuous energy replenishment. In: 2018 9th IEEE Annual Ubiquitous Computing, Electronics Mobile Communication Conference (UEMCON), pp. 478–484 (2018). https://doi.org/10.1109/UEMCON.2018.8796684
4. Brandstätter, A., Smolka, S.A., Stoller, S.D., Tiwari, A., Grosu, R.: Multi-agent spatial predictive control with application to drone flocking (extended version) (2022). https://doi.org/10.48550/ARXIV.2203.16960
5. Chung, S.J., Paranjape, A.A., Dames, P., Shen, S., Kumar, V.: A survey on aerial swarm robotics. IEEE Trans. Rob. **34**(4), 837–855 (2018). https://doi.org/10.1109/TRO.2018.2857475
6. Cucker, F., Smale, S.: Emergent behavior in flocks. IEEE Trans. Autom. Control **52**(5), 852–862 (2007). https://doi.org/10.1109/TAC.2007.895842
7. Cucker, F., Smale, S.: On the mathematics of emergence. Japan. J. Math. **2**(1), 197–227 (2007). https://doi.org/10.1007/s11537-007-0647-x
8. Câmara, D.: Cavalry to the rescue: Drones fleet to help rescuers operations over disasters scenarios. In: 2014 IEEE Conference on Antenna Measurements Applications (CAMA), pp. 1–4 (2014). https://doi.org/10.1109/CAMA.2014.7003421
9. Eversham, J., Ruiz, V.F.: Parameter analysis of Reynolds flocking model. In: 2010 IEEE 9th International Conference on Cyberntic Intelligent Systems, pp. 1–7 (2010). https://doi.org/10.1109/UKRICIS.2010.5898089
10. Giernacki, W., Skwierczyński, M., Witwicki, W., Wroński, P., Kozierski, P.: Crazyflie 2.0 quadrotor as a platform for research and education in robotics and control engineering. In: 2017 22nd International Conference on Methods and Models in Automation and Robotics (MMAR), pp. 37–42 (2017). https://doi.org/10.1109/MMAR.2017.8046794
11. Koenig, N., Howard, A.: Design and use paradigms for gazebo, an open-source multi-robot simulator. In: 2004 IEEE/RSJ International Conference on Intelligent Robots and Systems (IROS) (IEEE Cat. No.04CH37566), vol. 3, pp. 2149–2154 (2004). https://doi.org/10.1109/IROS.2004.1389727

12. Loianno, G., Kumar, V.: Cooperative transportation using small quadrotors using monocular vision and inertial sensing. IEEE Rob. Autom. Lett. **3**(2), 680–687 (2018). https://doi.org/10.1109/LRA.2017.2778018

13. Martin, S., Girard, A., Fazeli, A., Jadbabaie, A.: Multiagent flocking under general communication rule. IEEE Trans. Control Netw. Syst. **1**(2), 155–166 (2014). https://doi.org/10.1109/TCNS.2014.2316994

14. Mehmood, U., et al.: Declarative vs rule-based control for flocking dynamics. In: Proceedings of the 33rd Annual ACM Symposium on Applied Computing, SAC 2018, pp. 816–823. Association for Computing Machinery, New York (2018). https://doi.org/10.1145/3167132.3167222

15. Michael, N., Fink, J., Kumar, V.: Cooperative manipulation and transportation with aerial robots. Auton. Robot. **30**(1), 73–86 (2011). https://doi.org/10.1007/s10514-010-9205-0

16. Michael, N., et al.: Collaborative mapping of an earthquake damaged building via ground and aerial robots. In: Yoshida, K., Tadokoro, S. (eds.) Field and Service Robotics. STAR, vol. 92, pp. 33–47. Springer, Heidelberg (2014). https://doi.org/10.1007/978-3-642-40686-7_3

17. Olfati-Saber, R.: Flocking for multi-agent dynamic systems: algorithms and theory. IEEE Trans. Autom. Control **51**(3), 401–420 (2006). https://doi.org/10.1109/TAC.2005.864190

18. Reynolds, C.W.: Flocks, herds and schools: a distributed behavioral model. In: Proceedings of the 14th Annual Conference on Computer Graphics and Interactive Techniques, SIGGRAPH 1987, pp. 25–34. Association for Computing Machinery, New York (1987). https://doi.org/10.1145/37401.37406

19. Schwager, M.: A Gradient optimization approach to adaptive multi-robot control. Ph.D. thesis, Massachusetts Institute of Technology (2009). https://dspace.mit.edu/handle/1721.1/55256

20. Silano, G., Aucone, E., Iannelli, L.: CrazyS: a software-in-the-loop platform for the Crazyflie 2.0 nano-quadcopter. In: 2018 26th Mediterranean Conference on Control and Automation (MED), pp. 1–6 (2018). https://doi.org/10.1109/MED.2018.8442759

21. Soria, E., Schiano, F., Floreano, D.: The influence of limited visual sensing on the Reynolds flocking algorithm. In: 2019 Third IEEE International Conference on Robotic Computing (IRC), pp. 138–145 (2019). https://doi.org/10.1109/IRC.2019.00028

22. Soria, E., Schiano, F., Floreano, D.: Predictive control of aerial swarms in cluttered environments. Nat. Mach. Intell. **3**, 545–554 (2021). https://doi.org/10.1038/s42256-021-00341-y

23. Stanford Artificial Intelligence Laboratory et al.: Robotic operating system (2018). https://www.ros.org

24. Tanner, H.G., Jadbabaie, A., Pappas, G.J.: Stability of flocking motion. Technical report, University of Pennsylvania (2003). https://www.georgejpappas.org/papers/boids03.pdf

25. Vásárhelyi, G., Virágh, C., Somorjai, G., Nepusz, T., Eiben, A.E., Vicsek, T.: Optimized flocking of autonomous drones in confined environments. Sci. Robot. **3**(20) (2018). https://doi.org/10.1126/scirobotics.aat3536

Epistemic Ensembles

Rolf Hennicker[1], Alexander Knapp[2], and Martin Wirsing[1(✉)]

[1] Ludwig-Maximilians-Universität München, Munich, Germany
{hennicker,wirsing}@ifi.lmu.de
[2] Universität Augsburg, Augsburg, Germany
knapp@informatik.uni-augsburg.de

Abstract. An ensemble consists of a set of computing entities which collaborate to reach common goals. We introduce epistemic ensembles that use shared knowledge for collaboration between agents. Collaboration is achieved by different kinds of knowledge announcements. For specifying epistemic ensemble behaviours we use formulas of dynamic logic with compound ensemble actions. Our semantics relies on an epistemic notion of ensemble transition systems as behavioural models. These transition systems describe control flow over epistemic states for expressing knowledge-based collaboration of agents. Specifications are implemented by epistemic processes that are composed in parallel to form ensemble realisations. We give a formal operational semantics of these processes that generates an epistemic ensemble transition system. A realisation is correct w. r. t. an ensemble specification if its semantics is a model of the specification.

1 Introduction

An ensemble [13] is formed by a collection of agents which run concurrently to accomplish (together) a certain task. For that purpose agents must collaborate in some way, for instance by explicit interaction via message passing [8,9]. In the context of the epistemic approach considered here collaboration is based on the knowledge that agents have about themselves, about other agents and about their environment. Any change of knowledge caused by an action of one agent may influence the behaviour of other agents. Hence interaction is implicit. This is related to the ideas of autonomic component ensembles where coordination is achieved via knowledge repositories in which information is stored and from which information is retrieved; see, e.g., [5].

We propose a dynamic logic for specifying properties of epistemic ensembles. Our semantic models are labelled transition systems with atomic ensemble actions as labels. Labelled transitions model two aspects, (i) the control flow of an ensemble and (ii) changes of epistemic information caused by the epistemic effect of an agent action. To model the latter we introduce an epistemic state operator which assigns to each ensemble state s of the system an epistemic state $\Omega(s)$ modelling the current epistemic information available in the ensemble. Note that different ensemble states can carry the same epistemic information, in particular if a non-epistemic agent action is performed. Then a transition between the two has a pure control flow effect. The set of

T. Margaria and B. Steffen (Eds.): ISoLA 2022, LNCS 13703, pp. 110–126, 2022.
https://doi.org/10.1007/978-3-031-19759-8_8

ensemble states is restricted to states which are reachable by system transitions from the initial ones. This reflects our intuition that we want to consider ensembles as dynamic processes.

The restriction to reachable states and the ability to model control flow in the semantics is a crucial difference to public announcement logic (PAL) and dynamic epistemic logic (DEL); see, e.g., [6]. Instead of stating requirements for ensemble behaviours these logics are more appropriate for the verification of pre- and postconditions of given epistemic programs. [12] was one of the motivations for our work; it proposes to describe structural properties of ensembles with epistemic logic. An approach which deals with control flow as well are the knowledge-based programs in [7]. The semantic basis are system runs and the interpretation of knowledge tests inside the programs needs a circular procedure by relying on possible system runs at the same time.

After recapitulating basic notions of epistemic logic and epistemic actions in Sect. 2, we present our proposal to specifications of epistemic ensembles in Sect. 3 and provide a (formal) semantics for them in Sect. 4. In Sect. 5 we present an approach to realise epistemic ensemble specifications by a set of concurrently running epistemic processes and we define a correctness notion for such realisations. We finish in Sect. 6 with some concluding remarks.

2   Epistemic Logic and Epistemic Actions

We provide the basis for the epistemic treatment of ensembles considered later on. First, we summarise basic notions of epistemic logic. Then, we provide a summary of epistemic actions and adjust the definitions for their use in epistemic ensemble development. More details can be found in the literature, for instance [3,6].

2.1   Epistemic Logic

An *epistemic signature* (P, A) consists of a set P of *propositions* and a finite set A of *agents*. The set $\Phi_{P,A}$ of *epistemic formulæ* φ over (P, A) is defined by the following grammar:

$$\varphi ::= \text{true} \mid p \mid \neg\varphi \mid \varphi \vee \varphi \mid K_a \varphi$$

where $p \in P$ and $a \in A$. The epistemic formula $K_a \varphi$ is to be read as "agent a *knows* φ". As usual, we write false for $\neg$true, $\varphi_1 \rightarrow \varphi_2$ for $\neg\varphi_1 \vee \varphi_2$, and $\varphi_1 \wedge \varphi_2$ for $\neg(\neg\varphi_1 \vee \neg\varphi_2)$.

For each $a \in A$, $\Phi_{P,A}^a$ denotes the set of all purely propositional connections (including true and hence false) of epistemic formulæ starting with the modality K_a. These formulæ focus on the knowledge of agent a. The set $\Phi_{P,A}^a$ is defined by the following grammar:

$$\varphi^a ::= \text{true} \mid \neg\varphi^a \mid \varphi^a \vee \varphi^a \mid K_a \varphi$$

with $\varphi \in \Phi_{P,A}$. An *epistemic structure* $K = (W, R, L)$ over (P, A) consists of a set W of *worlds*, an A-indexed family $R = (R_a \subseteq W \times W)_{a \in A}$ of epistemic *accessibility relations*, and a *labelling* $L : W \rightarrow \wp P$ which determines for each world $w \in W$

the set of propositions valid in w. The accessibility relations of epistemic structures are assumed to be equivalence relations. For any $a \in A$, $(w, w') \in R_a$ models that agent a cannot distinguish the two worlds w and w'.

An *epistemic state* over (P, A) is a pointed epistemic structure $\mathfrak{K} = (K, w)$ over (P, A) where $w \in W$ determines an actual world. The class of all epistemic states over (P, A) is denoted by $EpiSt(P, A)$.

For any epistemic signature (P, A) and epistemic structure $K = (W, R, L)$ over (P, A) the *satisfaction* of an epistemic formula $\varphi \in \Phi_{P,A}$ by K at a point $w \in W$, written $K, w \models \varphi$, is inductively defined as follows:

$$K, w \models \text{true}$$
$$K, w \models p \iff p \in L(w)$$
$$K, w \models \neg\varphi \iff \text{not } K, w \models \varphi$$
$$K, w \models \varphi_1 \vee \varphi_2 \iff K, w \models \varphi_1 \text{ or } K, w \models \varphi_2$$
$$K, w \models \mathsf{K}_a \varphi \iff K, w' \models \varphi \text{ for all } w' \in W \text{ with } (w, w') \in R_a$$

Hence, an agent a knows φ at point w if φ holds in all worlds w' which a cannot distinguish from w. For an epistemic state $\mathfrak{K} = (K, w)$ and for $\varphi \in \Phi_{P,A}$, $\mathfrak{K} \models \varphi$ means $K, w \models \varphi$.

Example 1. We consider a (strongly simplified) victim rescue ensemble from a case study [11] of the ASCENS-project [14,15]. In the ensemble an agent, called V, is a victim who is to be supposed to be rescued by an agent R. There is one atomic proposition h indicating that the victim needs help and this is true in the actual world. The victim knows this but the rescuer does not. This situation is represented in the following diagram by the epistemic state (K_0, w_0), where, indeed, R cannot distinguish between the actual world w_0 and the possible world w_1:

The self-loops represent reflexivity of the accessibility relations. Note that $(K_0, w_0) \models \mathsf{K}_V h$ but $(K_0, w_0) \models \neg\mathsf{K}_R h$ and $(K_0, w_0) \models \neg\mathsf{K}_R \mathsf{K}_V h$.   □

Let $K_1 = (W_1, R_1, L_1)$, $K_2 = (W_2, R_2, L_2)$ be two epistemic structures over (P, A). A *bisimulation* between K_1 and K_2 is a relation $B \subseteq W_1 \times W_2$ such that for all $(w_1, w_2) \in B$ and all $a \in A$ the following holds:

1. $L_1(w_1) = L_2(w_2)$,
2. for each $w_1' \in W_1$, if $(w_1, w_1') \in R_{1,a}$ then there is a $w_2' \in W_2$ such that $(w_2, w_2') \in R_{2,a}$ and $(w_1', w_2') \in B$, and
3. for each $w_2' \in W_2$, if $(w_2, w_2') \in R_{2,a}$ then there is a $w_1' \in W_1$ such that $(w_1, w_1') \in R_{1,a}$ and $(w_1', w_2') \in B$.

Two epistemic states $\mathfrak{K}_1 = (K_1, w_1)$ and $\mathfrak{K}_2 = (K_2, w_2)$ over (P, A) are *bisimilar*, written $\mathfrak{K}_1 \approx \mathfrak{K}_2$, if there exists a bisimulation B between K_1 and K_2 such that $(w_1, w_2) \in B$.

The following lemma is a well-known result from epistemic logic; see, e.g., [3,6].

Lemma 1 (Invariance of epistemic formulæ). *Let $\mathfrak{K}_1$ and $\mathfrak{K}_2$ be epistemic states over (P, A) such that $\mathfrak{K}_1 \approx \mathfrak{K}_2$. Then, for any $\varphi \in \Phi_{P,A}$, $\mathfrak{K}_1 \models \varphi$ if, and only if, $\mathfrak{K}_2 \models \varphi$.* □

The converse is also valid for image-finite epistemic structures $K = (W, R, L)$, i.e., if for each world $w \in W$ and agent $a \in A$ there exist only finitely many pairs $(w, w') \in R_a$. Note that finiteness of A does not imply image finiteness of epistemic structures over (P, A); a counterexample is given in [6, p. 227].

2.2 Epistemic Actions

Epistemic logic deals with static aspects of knowledge captured by epistemic formulæ and their interpretation in epistemic states. A fundamental concept to support dynamic changes of knowledge is public announcement logic (PAL [3]) where knowledge about an epistemic state (formalised by a formula) can be announced to all agents. This may affect the knowledge of the agents leading to a new epistemic situation. More elaborated epistemic actions, like completely private and semi-private announcements, were also considered and a general proposal to model epistemic actions in terms of so-called action models was set up in [2]. In our approach action models will be called action structures in order to avoid confusion with the models of ensemble specifications later on.

An *epistemic action structure* $U = (Q, F, pre)$ over (P, A) consists of a set of *action points* Q, an A-indexed family $F = (F_a \subseteq Q \times Q)_{a \in A}$ of epistemic *action accessibility relations*, and a *precondition* function $pre : Q \to \Phi_{P,A}$. We assume again that the accessibility relations are equivalences. In the literature, action points are also called "events". For any agent a, $(q, q') \in F_a$ models that agent a cannot distinguish between occurrences of q and q'. For $q \in Q$, the epistemic formula $pre(q)$ determines a condition under which q can happen.

An *epistemic action* over (P, A) is a pointed epistemic action structure $\mathfrak{u} = (U, q)$ over (P, A) where $q \in Q$ determines an actual action point. The set $\mathcal{A}_{P,A}$ of *epistemic actions with (non-deterministic) choice* over (P, A) is defined by

$$\alpha ::= \mathfrak{u} \mid \alpha + \alpha$$

where $\mathfrak{u} = (U, q)$ is an epistemic action over (P, A). The precondition of an epistemic action with choice is given by $pre(\mathfrak{u}) = pre(q)$, $pre(\alpha_1 + \alpha_2) = pre(\alpha_1) \vee pre(\alpha_2)$.

Example 2. (a) *Public announcement* of an epistemic formula $\varphi \in \Phi_{P,A}$ to all agents in A is modelled by the epistemic action $(U_{pub,\varphi}, \mathsf{k})$ where

$$U_{pub,\varphi} = (Q_{pub}, F_{pub}, pre_{pub,\varphi})$$

with $Q_{pub} = \{\mathsf{k}\}$, $F_{pub,a} = \{(\mathsf{k}, \mathsf{k})\}$ for all $a \in A$, and $pre_{pub,\varphi} = \{\mathsf{k} \mapsto \varphi\}$. There is only one action point k and hence any agent in A considers only the occurrence of k possible. According to the precondition of k the action can only be executed in an epistemic state $\mathfrak{K}$ where the announced formula φ holds. The epistemic action $(U_{pub,\varphi}, \mathsf{k})$ is graphically represented by the following diagram.

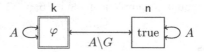

(b) *Private announcement* of an epistemic formula $\varphi \in \Phi_{P,A}$ to a group $G \subseteq A$ of agents is modelled by the epistemic action $(U_{priv,G,\varphi}, \mathsf{k})$ graphically represented by the following diagram:

$$A \circlearrowleft \boxed{\varphi} \; \mathsf{k} \xleftarrow{A \backslash G} \boxed{true} \; \mathsf{n} \circlearrowright A$$

The action structure $U_{priv,G,\varphi}$ has two action points k and n. Point k represents that the announcement of φ happens which should only be the case if φ holds in the current epistemic state and therefore $pre(\mathsf{k}) = \varphi$. Only agents in the group G can recognise this event. All other agents consider it possible that nothing happened which is represented by n. This should not have a proper precondition and therefore $pre(\mathsf{n}) = true.$[1]   □

The effect of an epistemic action on an epistemic state is defined by the product update as constructed in [1]. First, we define the product update of an epistemic structure by an epistemic action structure and then we use this for the product update of their pointed versions. The *product update* of an epistemic structure $K = (W, R, L)$ over (P, A) and an epistemic action structure $U = (Q, F, pre)$ over (P, A) is the epistemic structure $K \lhd U = (W', R', L')$ over (P, A) with

$$W' = \{(w, q) \in W \times Q \mid K, w \models pre(q)\},$$
$$R'_a = \{((w, q), (w', q')) \in W' \times W' \mid (w, w') \in R_a, \ (q, q') \in F_a\} \text{ for all } a \in A,$$
$$L'(w, q) = L(w) \text{ for all } (w, q) \in W'.$$

According to the definition of the relations R'_a the uncertainty of an agent a in a world (w, q) is determined by the uncertainty of a about world w and its uncertainty about the occurrence of q. Note that the relations R'_a are again equivalence relations and therefore the product update for epistemic structures is well-defined.

Let $\mathfrak{K} = (K, w) \in EpiSt(P, A)$ be an epistemic state and $\mathfrak{u} = (U, q)$ be an epistemic action over (P, A). If $\mathfrak{K} \models pre(\mathfrak{u})$ then the *product update* of $\mathfrak{K}$ and $\mathfrak{u}$ is defined and given by the epistemic state $\mathfrak{K} \lhd \mathfrak{u} = (K \lhd U, (w, q)) \in EpiSt(P, A)$.

The semantics of each epistemic action with choice $\alpha \in \mathcal{A}_{P,A}$ is given by a set of relations $[\![\alpha]\!] \subseteq EpiSt(P, A) \times EpiSt(P, A)$ between epistemic states inductively defined by:

$$[\![\mathfrak{u}]\!] = \{(\mathfrak{K}, \mathfrak{K} \lhd \mathfrak{u}) \mid \mathfrak{K} \models pre(\mathfrak{u})\},$$
$$[\![\alpha_1 + \alpha_2]\!] = [\![\alpha_1]\!] \cup [\![\alpha_2]\!], \text{ i.e. union of relations.}$$

Note that for each $\alpha \in \mathcal{A}_{P,A}$ and $\mathfrak{K} \in EpiSt(P, A)$ it holds: There exists a $\mathfrak{K}' \in EpiSt(P, A)$ such that $(\mathfrak{K}, \mathfrak{K}') \in [\![\alpha]\!]$ if, and only if, $\mathfrak{K} \models pre(\alpha)$.

---

[1] We do not consider here completely private announcements where the agents not in G would not consider it possible that the announcement happened. To model this case one would need non-symmetric accessibility relations.

Example 3. We consider the victim rescue example from Example 1 and instantiate private announcement of Example 2(b) to the case in which it is privately announced to R that V knows that h holds. Thus we consider the epistemic action $(U_{priv,\{R\},K_V h}, k)$ represented by the following diagram where V does not know whether R got an announcement:

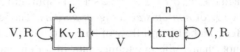

We apply this action to the epistemic state (K_0, w_0) in Example 1. The product update yields the epistemic state $(K_1, (w_0, k))$ shown, without reflexive accessibility edges, below. The world (w_1, k) does not appear since $(K_0, w_1) \not\models K_V h$ which is the precondition of k.

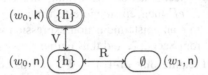

Note that $(K_1, (w_0, k)) \models K_R K_V h$ but $(K_1, (w_0, k)) \models \neg K_V K_R K_V h$, i.e. R knows that V knows that h holds, but V does not know that R knows this.

If we apply the epistemic action $(U_{priv,\{R\},K_V h}, n)$ to (K_0, w_0) we obtain the epistemic state $(K_1, (w_0, n))$. Note that $(K_1, (w_0, n)) \models \neg K_R K_V h$.   □

The next lemma shows that bisimulation is preserved by application of epistemic actions; see, e.g., [6].

Lemma 2. *Let $\mathfrak{K}_1$ and $\mathfrak{K}_2$ be epistemic states over (P, A) such that $\mathfrak{K}_1 \approx \mathfrak{K}_2$ and let $\mathfrak{u}$ be an epistemic action over (P, A). Then $\mathfrak{K}_1 \lhd \mathfrak{u}$ is defined, if and only if, $\mathfrak{K}_2 \lhd \mathfrak{u}$ is defined and then it holds $\mathfrak{K}_1 \lhd \mathfrak{u} \approx \mathfrak{K}_2 \lhd \mathfrak{u}$.*   □

We generalise Lemma 2 to epistemic actions with choice. The proof is straightforward by induction on the form of α.

Lemma 3. *Let $\mathfrak{K}_1$ and $\mathfrak{K}_2$ be as in Lemma 2 such that $\mathfrak{K}_1 \approx \mathfrak{K}_2$ and let α be an epistemic action with choice. Then, for any $\mathfrak{K}_1'$ with $(\mathfrak{K}_1, \mathfrak{K}_1') \in [\![\alpha]\!]$, there exists $\mathfrak{K}_2'$ with $(\mathfrak{K}_2, \mathfrak{K}_2') \in [\![\alpha]\!]$ such that $\mathfrak{K}_1' \approx \mathfrak{K}_2'$; the converse holds for any $\mathfrak{K}_2'$ with $(\mathfrak{K}_2, \mathfrak{K}_2') \in [\![\alpha]\!]$.*   □

3   Epistemic Ensemble Specifications

An ensemble is formed by a collection of agents which run concurrently to accomplish (together) a certain task. For that purpose agents must collaborate in some way, for instance by explicit interaction via message passing [8,9]. In the context of the epistemic approach considered here collaboration is based on the knowledge that agents have about themselves, about other agents and about their environment. Any change of knowledge caused by an action of one agent may influence the behaviour of other agents. Hence interaction is implicit.

Formally, an *agent action* is given by an action name e to which an agent $o(e)$ is associated, the "owner" of e, who is able to execute that action. An *epistemic ensemble signature* $\Sigma = (P, A, E)$ consists of an epistemic signature (P, A) and a set E of agent actions such that for each $e \in E, o(e) \in A$. The set E is split into a set eE of *epistemic agent actions* and a set nE of *non-epistemic agent actions*. The idea is that any agent action may have an effect on the control flow of an ensemble. The non-epistemic agent actions, however, do not change the epistemic state of an ensemble while epistemic agent actions in general do.

The *epistemic effect* of an agent action $e \in E$ is formalised by a relation $eeff(e) \subseteq EpiSt(P, A) \times EpiSt(P, A)$ between epistemic states over (P, A). For non-epistemic agent actions $e \in nE$ we define $eeff(e) = \{(\mathfrak{K}, \mathfrak{K}) \mid \mathfrak{K} \in EpiSt(P, A)\}$. The non-epistemic agent actions are specific actions depending on the application at hand. For epistemic agent actions $e \in eE$ their epistemic effect must be explicitly defined. For this purpose we associate to e an epistemic action expression with choice $\alpha \in \mathcal{A}_{P,A}$, whose semantics is clear from Sect. 2.2, and thus define $eeff(e) = [\![\alpha]\!]$. Moreover, we set $pre(e) = pre(\alpha)$ and require that $pre(e) \in \Phi_{P,A}^{o(e)}$. This constraint expresses that an epistemic agent action with owner a should have a precondition which concerns, and hence can be tested, by a; similarly to the knowledge tests of knowledge-based programs in [7]. Thus the epistemic action expressions in Sect. 2.2. will be used as primitives to define the epistemic effect of higher level epistemic actions for agents.

In this paper we assume given, for each epistemic signature (P, A), the following set of epistemic agent actions from which particular instantiations can be chosen for a concrete ensemble signature.

Public Announcement By an Agent: This action is a special case of public announcement such that the announcement is performed by an agent a "inside" the system. As a consequence, agent a does not simply announce a formula φ but it must indeed know φ and must announce that, i.e. $\mathsf{K}_a \varphi$. Formally, for each $a \in A$ and $\varphi \in \Phi_{P,A}$, public announcement by a is denoted by the epistemic agent action $pub^a(\mathsf{K}_a \varphi)$ over (P, A) with owner $o(pub^a(\mathsf{K}_a \varphi)) = a$. The epistemic effect of this action is defined by $eeff(pub^a(\mathsf{K}_a \varphi)) =_{\text{def}} [\![(U_{pub,\mathsf{K}_a \varphi}, \mathsf{k})]\!]$ where the latter is the epistemic public announcement action in Example 2(a) with semantics defined by product update as described in Sect. 2.2. Note that $pre(pub^a(\mathsf{K}_a \varphi)) = pre(U_{pub,\mathsf{K}_a \varphi}, \mathsf{k}) = \mathsf{K}_a \varphi \in \Phi_{P,A}^a$.

Reliable Private Sending: In this case there is an agent a who knows the validity of a formula φ and sends the information that it knows φ, i.e. $\mathsf{K}_a \varphi$, to another agent b. The sending is reliable, i.e. the information will be received by b and agent a knows that. Formally, for each $a, b \in A$ and $\varphi \in \Phi_{P,A}$, reliable private sending is denoted by the epistemic agent action $snd_{\text{rel}}^{a \to b}(\mathsf{K}_a \varphi)$ over (P, A) with owner $o(snd_{\text{rel}}^{a \to b}(\mathsf{K}_a \varphi)) = a$.

The epistemic effect of this action can be modelled as a special case of private announcement to a group of agents where the group is $\{a, b\}$ and the announcement is $\mathsf{K}_a \varphi$. Hence, we define $eeff(snd_{\text{rel}}^{a \to b}(\mathsf{K}_a \varphi)) =_{\text{def}} [\![(U_{priv,\{a,b\},\mathsf{K}_a \varphi}, \mathsf{k})]\!]$; see Example 2(b). Obviously, $pre(snd_{\text{rel}}^{a \to b}(\mathsf{K}_a \varphi)) = \mathsf{K}_a \varphi \in \Phi_{P,A}^a$ where $a = o(snd_{\text{rel}}^{a \to b}(\mathsf{K}_a \varphi))$.

Lossy Private Sending: In this case there is again an agent a who knows the validity of a formula φ and sends the information $K_a \varphi$ to another agent b. But this time the sending is unreliable and the information may get lost. Formally, for each $a, b \in A$ and $\varphi \in \Phi_{P,A}$, lossy private sending is denoted by the epistemic agent action $snd_{los}^{a \to b}(K_a \varphi)$ over (P, A) with owner $o(snd_{los}^{a \to b}(K_a \varphi)) = a$.

For defining the epistemic effect of $snd_{los}^{a \to b}(K_a \varphi)$ we proceed as follows: Let $U_{priv,\{b\},K_a \varphi}$ be the epistemic action structure of Example 2(b) instantiated by $\{b\}$ and $K_a \varphi$. Let $(U_{priv,\{b\},K_a \varphi}, k)$ and $(U_{priv,\{b\},K_a \varphi}, n)$ be the corresponding epistemic actions. The first action expresses that after a has sent the information $K_a \varphi$, agent b has received it, but a (and all other agents) do not know this; they consider it possible that the information did not arrive. The second action expresses that after the sending of $K_a \varphi$ by agent a, agent b has not received anything and b knows that. Hence, the information is lost, and a (and all other agents besides b) do not know whether the information has arrived or not. The effect of lossy private sending must capture both possibilities. Therefore, it is modelled by a non-deterministic choice of the two actions, either the information is received or not. The sender does not know what happened and the receiver knows the sent information if, and only if, it has received it. Formally, we define

$$eeff(snd_{los}^{a \to b}(K_a \varphi)) =_{\text{def}} [\![(U_{priv,\{b\},K_a \varphi}, k) + (U_{priv,\{b\},K_a \varphi}, n)]\!].$$

Then, $pre(snd_{los}^{a \to b}(K_a \varphi)) = pre((U_{priv,\{b\},K_a \varphi}, k) + (U_{priv,\{b\},K_a \varphi}, n)) = pre(U_{priv,\{b\},K_a \varphi}, k) \vee pre(U_{priv,\{b\},K_a \varphi}, n) = (K_a \varphi \vee \text{true}) \in \Phi_{P,A}^a$.

In the following we assume that $\Sigma = (P, A, E)$ is an epistemic ensemble signature. To specify global behaviours of ensembles performed by concurrently running agents we must consider ensemble actions which are formed by various combinations of agent actions. Therefore, the agent actions in E are considered as atomic ensemble actions while complex ensemble actions are formed by using the standard operators of dynamic logic which are test ($\varphi?$), non-deterministic choice ($+$), sequential composition (;) and iteration (*). The set $\mathcal{E}_\Sigma$ of *compound ensemble actions* over Σ is defined by the following grammar:

$$\pi ::= e \mid \varphi? \mid \pi + \pi \mid \pi; \pi \mid \pi^*$$

where $e \in E$ is an agent action and $\varphi \in \Phi_{P,A}$. If E is finite, we write "some" for the compound action obtained by combing with "$+$" all elements of E and, for $e \in E$, we write $-e$ for the compound ensemble action obtained by combing with "$+$" all elements of $E \setminus \{e\}$.

Ensemble formulæ are used to specify properties of ensembles. They extend the formulæ of epistemic logic in Sect. 2.1 by including modalities with (compound) ensemble actions which allow us to specify the dynamic aspects of global ensemble behaviours. The set Ψ_Σ of *epistemic ensemble formulæ* over $\Sigma = (P, A, E)$ is defined by the following grammar:

$$\psi ::= \varphi \mid \neg\psi \mid \psi \vee \psi \mid \langle \pi \rangle \psi$$

where $\varphi \in \Phi_{P,A}$ and $\pi \in \mathcal{E}_\Sigma$. The formula $\langle \pi \rangle \psi$ is to be read as "in the current ensemble state it is possible to execute π leading to an ensemble state where formula ψ holds". The abbreviations from epistemic logic are extended to epistemic ensemble logic. Furthermore, we abbreviate $\neg \langle \pi \rangle \neg \psi$ by $[\pi]\psi$ which is to be read as "each execution of π in the current ensemble state leads to an ensemble state where the formula ψ holds".

Using the shorthand notations for compound actions for finite E, we can specify safety properties with $[\text{some}^*]\psi$; deadlock freeness is expressed by $[\text{some}^*]\langle \text{some} \rangle \text{true}$. Liveness properties like "whenever an action e has happened, an action f can eventually occur", can be expressed by $[\text{some}^*; e]\langle \text{some}^*; f \rangle \text{true}$. We can also express that an action f must never occur when action e has happened before by $[\text{some}^*; e; \text{some}^*; f]\text{false}$.

Definition 1 (Ensemble specification). *An* ensemble specification $Sp = (\Sigma, Ax)$ *consists of an ensemble signature Σ and a set $Ax \subseteq \Psi_\Sigma$ of ensemble formulæ, called* axioms *of Sp.*   □

Example 4. We provide a requirements specification $Sp_{vr} = (\Sigma_{vr}, Ax_{vr})$ for victim rescue ensembles. The epistemic ensemble signature Σ_{vr} consists of the proposition h, of the two agents V and R, of the two epistemic agent actions $snd_{los}^{V \to R}(K_V\,h)$, $snd_{rel}^{R \to V}(K_R\,h)$ with owners $o(snd_{los}^{V \to R}(K_V\,h)) = V$ and $o(snd_{rel}^{R \to V}(K_R\,h)) = R$, and two non-epistemic agent actions $stop, rescue$ with owners $o(stop) = V$ and $o(rescue) = R$. We use a lossy information transfer from V to R since the idea is that the rescuer is moving around in an exploration area and cannot get information when it is outside the victim's range. The information transfer from R to V is reliable, since we assume that once the rescuer is informed it will be close enough to the victim. For a victim rescue ensemble we require the following properties expressed by the two axioms (1) and (2) of Ax_{vr}:

– "Whenever the victim performs a lossy sending to the rescuer that it knows that h is valid, i.e. the victim needs help, it is eventually possible that the rescuer knows this."

$$(1)\quad [\text{some}^*; snd_{los}^{V \to R}(K_V\,h)]\langle \text{some}^* \rangle K_R\,h$$

– "Whenever the rescuer has not yet rescued the victim but knows that the victim needs help, it is eventually possible that the rescuer rescues the victim."

$$(2)\quad [(-rescue)^*]K_R\,h \to \langle \text{some}^*; rescue \rangle \text{true}$$

This specification can be generalised in many ways, for instance to more rescuers taking into account that it is sufficient that only one rescuer goes for rescuing.   □

4   Semantics of Epistemic Ensemble Specifications

We will now turn to the semantics of epistemic ensemble logic and ensemble specifications. Our semantic models are labelled transition systems with atomic ensemble actions (i.e. agent actions) as labels. Labelled transitions model two aspects, (i) the control flow of an ensemble and (ii) changes of epistemic information caused by the epistemic effect of an agent action. To model the latter we introduce an epistemic state operator which assigns to each ensemble state s of the system an epistemic state $\Omega(s)$. Ensemble states could be modelled by pairs $s = (ctrl, \mathfrak{K})$ where $ctrl$ is an explicit control state and $\mathfrak{K}$ is an epistemic state; then the state operator would be the projection to the second component, i.e. $\Omega(s) = \mathfrak{K}$. Our definition leaving control states implicit is, however, more general.

Of course, ensemble transitions must respect (up to bisimilarity) the epistemic effect of actions, which is expressed by condition 1a below. Conversely, if an epistemic ensemble action is enabled in an ensemble state, then all epistemic effects of the action must be present (up to bisimilarity) in the transition system, which is expressed by 1b. This reflects that the choice of the effect of a (non-deterministic) epistemic action is made by the system environment, not by the agents of the ensemble.

Note that different ensemble states can carry the same epistemic information, in particular if a non-epistemic agent action is performed. Then a transition between the two has a pure control flow effect. The set of ensemble states is restricted to states which are reachable by system transitions from the initial ones which is expressed by condition (2) below. This reflects our intuition that we want to consider ensembles as processes with significant dynamic behaviour. The restriction to reachable states and the ability to model control flow in the semantics is a crucial difference to dynamic epistemic logic; see, e.g., [6].

Definition 2 (Epistemic ensemble transition system). *Let $\Sigma = (P, A, E)$ be an epistemic ensemble signature. An epistemic ensemble transition system (EETS) over Σ is a tuple $M = (S, S_0, T, \Omega)$ such that*

- *S is a set of ensemble states and $S_0 \subseteq S$ is the set of initial ensemble states,*
- *$T = (T_e \subseteq S \times S)_{e \in E}$ is an E-indexed family of transition relations T_e, and*
- *$\Omega : S \to EpiSt(P, A)$ is an epistemic state operator*

such that the following two conditions are satisfied:

1. *For all $s \in S$ and $e \in E$, if there exists $s' \in S$ with $(s, s') \in T_e$, then*
   (a) *there exist $\mathfrak{K}, \mathfrak{K}' \in EpiSt(P, A)$ such that $\Omega(s) \approx \mathfrak{K}$, $\Omega(s') \approx \mathfrak{K}'$, and $(\mathfrak{K}, \mathfrak{K}') \in eeff(e)$,*
   (b) *for any $(\mathfrak{K}, \mathfrak{K}'') \in eeff(e)$ there exists $(s, s'') \in T_e$ with $\Omega(s) \approx \mathfrak{K}$ and $\Omega(s'') \approx \mathfrak{K}''$.*
2. *For all $s \in S$ there are $s_0 \in S_0$, $e_1, \ldots, e_n \in E$ $(n \geq 0)$ and $(s_i, s_{i+1}) \in T_{e_i}$ for $0 \leq i < n$ such that $s_n = s$.*

The class of epistemic ensemble transition systems over Σ is denoted by $Str(\Sigma)$. $\quad\square$

We write $s \xrightarrow{e}_M s'$ for $(s, s') \in T_e$. This relation is extended to compound epistemic ensemble actions $\pi \in \mathcal{E}_\Sigma$ by the following inductive definition:

$$s \xrightarrow{\varphi?}_M s' \iff \Omega(s) \models \varphi \text{ and } s = s'$$

$$s \xrightarrow{\pi_1 + \pi_2}_M s' \iff s \xrightarrow{\pi_1}_M s' \text{ or } s \xrightarrow{\pi_2}_M s'$$

$$s \xrightarrow{\pi_1 ; \pi_2}_M s' \iff \text{there exists } s_1 \text{ with } s \xrightarrow{\pi_1}_M s_1 \text{ and } s_1 \xrightarrow{\pi_2}_M s'$$

$$s \xrightarrow{\pi^*}_M s' \iff \text{there exist } n \geq 0, s = s_0, s_1, \ldots, s_{n-1}, s_n = s' \text{ with}$$

$$s_i \xrightarrow{\pi}_M s_{i+1} \text{ for all } 0 \leq i < n$$

For any epistemic ensemble signature Σ, the *satisfaction* of an epistemic ensemble formula $\psi \in \Psi_\Sigma$ by an EETS $M = (S, S_0, T, \Omega)$ over Σ at a state $s \in S$, written $M, s \models_\Sigma \psi$, is inductively defined as follows:

$$M, s \models_\Sigma \varphi \iff \Omega(s) \models \varphi$$

$$M, s \models_\Sigma \neg\psi \iff \text{not } M, s \models_\Sigma \psi$$

$$M, s \models_\Sigma \psi_1 \vee \psi_2 \iff M, s \models_\Sigma \psi_1 \text{ or } M, s \models_\Sigma \psi_2$$

$$M, s \models_\Sigma \langle\pi\rangle\psi \iff \text{there exists } s' \in S \text{ with } s \xrightarrow{\pi}_M s' \text{ such that } M, s' \models_\Sigma \psi$$

M *satisfies* an epistemic ensemble formula $\psi \in \Psi_\Sigma$, written $M \models_\Sigma \psi$, if $M, s_0 \models_\Sigma \psi$ for all initial states $s_0 \in S_0$.

For the box, $M, s \models_\Sigma [\pi]\psi$ means that whenever π is executed by the ensemble a state s' is reached in which ψ holds. Note that, if $\pi = e$ is an atomic ensemble action such that the precondition $pre(e)$ does not hold in $\Omega(s)$, then $M, s \models_\Sigma [e]\psi$ holds since there is no execution of e in state s.

Example 5. A connection to public announcement logic [3] can be drawn as follows: Consider the ensemble signature $\Sigma = (P, A, E)$ with an arbitrary epistemic signature (P, A) and E consisting of all public announcements of the form $pub^a(\mathsf{K}_a \varphi)$ with $a \in A$. As semantic model we take the special EETS $M_{\mathrm{PAL}} = (EpiSt(P, A), EpiSt(P, A), T, \Omega)$ where the ensemble states are just the epistemic states over (P, A), all states are initial, $T = (T_{pub^a(\mathsf{K}_a \varphi)} \subseteq EpiSt(P, A) \times EpiSt(P, A))_{pub^a(\mathsf{K}_a \varphi) \in E}$ with $T_{pub^a(\mathsf{K}_a \varphi)} = eeff(pub^a(\mathsf{K}_a \varphi))$ are the semantic transitions for public announcements, and Ω is the identity. Then, for any ensemble state s of M_{PAL}, i.e. epistemic state $(K, w) \in EpiSt(P, A)$, and any epistemic ensemble formula $\psi \in \Psi_\Sigma$ we have $M_{\mathrm{PAL}}, (K, w) \models \psi$ if, and only if, (K, w) satisfies ψ in the sense of public announcement logic. $\square$

More generally, dynamic epistemic logic with arbitrary epistemic actions (U, q) such that $pre(q)$ has the form $\mathsf{K}_a \varphi$ and $o(U, q) = a \in A$ can be similarly interpreted by an EETS. Note, however, that in these cases no control information can be captured since ensemble states are just epistemic states. Therefore instead of stating requirements for ensemble behaviours these logics are more appropriate for the verification of pre- and postconditions of programs represented by compound ensemble actions where ensemble formulas have the shape $pre \rightarrow [\pi]post$.

Definition 3 (Semantics of epistemic ensemble specifications and refinement). *Let* $Sp = (\Sigma, Ax)$ *be an epistemic ensemble specification. A model of Sp is an EETS over* Σ *which satisfies all axioms of* Ax. *The semantics of Sp is given by its model class*

$$\mathrm{Mod}(Sp) = \{M \in Str(\Sigma) \mid M \models \psi \text{ for all } \psi \in Ax\}.$$

An epistemic ensemble specification $Sp' = (\Sigma, Ax')$ *is a* refinement *of Sp if* $\mathrm{Mod}(Sp') \subseteq \mathrm{Mod}(Sp)$. $\square$

As an equivalence for epistemic ensemble transition systems we use *EETS-bisimulation* which is defined as expected.

Definition 4 (Epistemic ensemble bisimulation). *Let* $\Sigma = (P, A, E)$ *be an epistemic ensemble signature and* $M_1 = (S_1, S_{1,0}, T_1, \Omega_1)$ *and* $M_2 = (S_2, S_{2,0}, T_2, \Omega_2)$ *be two EETSs over* Σ. *An* EETS-bisimulation *between* M_1 *and* M_2 *is a relation* $EB \subseteq S_1 \times S_2$ *such that for all* $(s_1, s_2) \in EB$ *and all* $e \in E$ *the following holds:*

1. $\Omega_1(s_1) \approx \Omega_2(s_2)$,
2. *for each* $s'_1 \in S_1$, *if* $s_1 \xrightarrow{e}_{M_1} s'_1$ *then there is an* $s'_2 \in S_2$ *such that* $s_2 \xrightarrow{e}_{M_2} s'_2$ *and* $(s'_1, s'_2) \in EB$, *and*
3. *for each* $s'_2 \in S_2$, *if* $s_2 \xrightarrow{e}_{M_2} s'_2$ *then there is an* $s'_1 \in S_1$ *such that* $s_1 \xrightarrow{e}_{M_1} s'_1$ *and* $(s'_1, s'_2) \in EB$.

M_1 *and* M_2 *are* EETS-bisimilar, *written* $M_1 \sim M_2$, *if there exists an EETS-bisimulation* EB *between* M_1 *and* M_2 *such that for each* $s_1 \in S_{1,0}$ *there exists an* $s_2 \in S_{2,0}$ *with* $(s_1, s_2) \in EB$ *and, conversely, for each* $s_2 \in S_{2,0}$ *there exists an* $s_1 \in S_{1,0}$ *with* $(s_1, s_2) \in EB$. $\square$

It is easy to prove, by induction on the form of compound ensemble actions, that conditions (2) and (3) above can be propagated to compound ensemble actions $\pi \in \mathcal{E}_\Sigma$. As a consequence, it is straightforward to prove, by induction on the form of epistemic ensemble formulæ, that satisfaction is invariant under EETS-bisimulation. The base case follows from Lemma 1. The converse of the theorem is also valid for image-finite EETS.

Theorem 1 (Invariance of epistemic ensemble formulæ). *Let* M_1 *and* M_2 *be EETS over the same epistemic ensemble signature* Σ *such that* $M_1 \sim M_2$. *Then, for any* $\psi \in \Psi_\Sigma$, $M_1 \models \psi$ *if, and only if,* $M_2 \models \psi$.

5   Epistemic Ensemble Realisations

Ensemble specifications describe requirements for systems of collaborating entities from a global point of view. For the realisation of ensembles we must take a local view and define a single behaviour for each agent. For this purpose, we introduce an *epistemic process language* over an epistemic ensemble signature $\Sigma = (P, A, E)$ which allows us to describe the local behaviour of each agent $a \in A$ as a sequential process P_a in accordance with the following grammar:

$$P_a ::= \mathbf{0} \mid e_a.P_a \mid \varphi_a \supset P_a \mid P_{a,1} + P_{a,2} \mid \mu X . P_a \mid X$$

where $\mathbf{0}$ represents the inactive process, $e_a.P_a$ prefixes P_a with an agent action $e_a \in E$, $\varphi_a \supset P_a$ is a guarded process, $P_{a,1} + P_{a,2}$ denotes the non-deterministic choice between processes, $\mu X . P_a$ models recursion, and X is a process variable.

The following constraints apply to the syntax of processes: First, in a prefix $e_a.P_a$ the owner of e_a must be a, i.e. $o(e_a) = a$. Secondly, each agent a, or, more precisely, its process, shall only use guards concerning the agent's own knowledge. We thus require $\varphi_a \in \Phi_{P,A}^a$; see Sect. 2.1. A similar constraint is applied to epistemic programs in [7].

Definition 5 (Epistemic ensemble realisation). *For an epistemic ensemble signature* $\Sigma = (P, A, E)$, *an* epistemic ensemble realisation *over* Σ *is a pair* $Real = (\{P_{0,a} \mid a \in A\}, \mathfrak{K}_0)$ *where* $\{P_{0,a} \mid a \in A\}$ *is a set of sequential processes over* Σ, *one for each agent* $a \in A$, *and* $\mathfrak{K}_0 \in EpiSt(P, A)$ *is an initial epistemic state of the ensemble.* □

The semantics of an epistemic ensemble realisation is given in terms of en epistemic ensemble transition system. In this case the ensemble states are pairs $s = (ctrl, \mathfrak{K})$ consisting of a global control state $ctrl$ and an epistemic state $\mathfrak{K} \in EpiSt(P, A)$ capturing the current epistemic information of the ensemble. The control state $ctrl$ holds the current (local) execution state of each agent represented by a process expression. Thus $ctrl$ is a mapping that attaches to each $a \in A$ a sequential process $ctrl(a) = P_a$. When an agent a moves from one state P_a to another state P_a' the control state $ctrl$ must be updated accordingly which is denoted by $ctrl[a \mapsto P_a']$.

In contrast to the loose semantics of ensemble specifications, an ensemble realisation $Real = (\{P_{0,a} \mid a \in A\}, \mathfrak{K}_0)$ determines a unique epistemic ensemble transition system. It has a single initial ensemble state $s_0 = (ctrl_0, \mathfrak{K}_0)$ where the control state $ctrl_0$ assigns to each agent a its process definition $P_{0,a}$, i.e. $ctrl_0(a) = P_{0,a}$ for all $a \in A$. Then, starting in s_0, an epistemic ensemble transition system is generated by the structural operational semantics rules in Fig. 1. For each ensemble state $s = (ctrl, \mathfrak{K})$ of the system the epistemic state operator is defined by $\Omega(ctrl, \mathfrak{K}) = \mathfrak{K}$.

The first five rules, from (action prefix) to (recursion), describe how single processes evolve in the context of an epistemic state which (i) may change when the process performs an agent action and (ii) is used for the evaluation of guards. We use the symbol "$\hookrightarrow$" for transitions on the process level. Transitions on the ensemble level are denoted by "$\rightarrow$". Rule (ensemble) says that whenever a single agent process moves from a local process state P_a to state P_a' changing the epistemic state from $\mathfrak{K}$ to $\mathfrak{K}'$ the whole ensemble evolves accordingly.

Definition 6 (Semantics of an epistemic ensemble realisation). *The semantics of an epistemic ensemble realisation* $Real = (\{P_{0,a} \mid a \in A\}, \mathfrak{K}_0)$ *over an ensemble signature* Σ *is the epistemic ensemble transition system*

$$\llbracket Real \rrbracket = (S, \{s_0\}, T, \Omega)$$

over Σ *where the initial ensemble state* s_0 *and the state operator* Ω *are explained above and the states in* S *and transitions in* T *are inductively generated from* s_0 *by applying the rules in Fig. 1. Note that* $\llbracket Real \rrbracket$ *satisfies the conditions of an EETS in Definition 2.*

□

(action prefix)	$$\dfrac{}{(e_a.P_a, \mathfrak{K}) \xrightarrow{e_a} (P_a, \mathfrak{K}')} \quad \text{if } (\mathfrak{K}, \mathfrak{K}') \in \text{eeff}(e_a)$$
(guard)	$$\dfrac{(P_a, \mathfrak{K}) \xrightarrow{e_a} (P'_a, \mathfrak{K}')}{(\varphi_a \supset P_a, \mathfrak{K}) \xrightarrow{e_a} (P'_a, \mathfrak{K}')} \quad \text{if } \mathfrak{K} \models \varphi_a$$
(choice-left)	$$\dfrac{(P_{a,1}, \mathfrak{K}) \xrightarrow{e_a} (P'_{a,1}, \mathfrak{K}')}{(P_{a,1} + P_{a,2}, \mathfrak{K}) \xrightarrow{e_a} (P'_{a,1}, \mathfrak{K}')}$$
(choice-right)	$$\dfrac{(P_{a,2}, \mathfrak{K}) \xrightarrow{e_a} (P'_{a,2}, \mathfrak{K}')}{(P_{a,1} + P_{a,2}, \mathfrak{K}) \xrightarrow{e_a} (P'_{a,2}, \mathfrak{K}')}$$
(recursion)	$$\dfrac{(P_a\{X \mapsto \mu X . P_a\}, \mathfrak{K}) \xrightarrow{e_a} (P'_a, \mathfrak{K}')}{(\mu X . P_a, \mathfrak{K}) \xrightarrow{e_a} (P'_a, \mathfrak{K}')}$$
(ensemble)	$$\dfrac{(P_a, \mathfrak{K}) \xrightarrow{e_a} (P'_a, \mathfrak{K}')}{(ctrl, \mathfrak{K}) \xrightarrow{e_a} (ctrl[a \mapsto P'_a], \mathfrak{K}')} \quad \text{if } ctrl(a) = P_a$$

Fig. 1. SOS rules for epistemic processes and ensemble realisations

Our semantic concepts lead to an obvious correctness notion concerning the realisation of epistemic ensemble specifications:

Definition 7 (Correct ensemble realisation). *Let Sp be an epistemic ensemble specification and let Real be a realisation over the same epistemic signature. Real is a* correct realisation *of Sp if* $[\![Real]\!] \in \text{Mod}(Sp)$. $\qquad\square$

Example 6. We provide a realisation for our simple robot rescue ensemble with two agents V (victim) and R (rescuer). The realisation consists of the two processes

$$P_{0,V} = \mu X . \left((\mathsf{K_V}\, h \wedge \neg \mathsf{K_V}\, \mathsf{K_R}\, h \supset snd_{los}^{V \to R}(\mathsf{K_V}\, h).X\right)$$
$$+ (\mathsf{K_V}\, \mathsf{K_R}\, h \supset stop.0))$$
$$P_{0,R} = \mathsf{K_R}\, h \supset snd_{rel}^{R \to V}(\mathsf{K_R}\, h).rescue.0$$

For the initial epistemic state of the realisation we take $\mathfrak{K}_0 = (K_0, w_0)$ as depicted in Example 1. Thus the initial ensemble state is $s_0 = (ctrl, \mathfrak{K}_0)$ with $ctrl_0(V) = P_{0,V}$, $ctrl_0(R) = P_{0,R}$ and $\Omega(s_0) = \mathfrak{K}_0$. As long as the victim does not know that the rescuer knows that the victim needs help, the victim continues sending the information $\mathsf{K_V}\, h$ to the rescuer. Notice again that this sending is lossy and hence either successful or unsuccessful. Only when the rescuer became aware of the emergency it can send, in a reliable way, its knowledge to the victim who can then stop its activity.

The EETS generated from the ensemble realisation has infinitely many ensemble states since it is possible that an unsuccessful sending from V to R happens infinitely often and hence each time an update of the previous epistemic state is performed. One can show, however, that if an unsuccessful sending happens after an unsuccessful or successful sending then the resulting epistemic state is bisimilar to the previous one. Therefore, there exists a minimal finite EETS, shown in Fig. 2, which is EETS-bisimilar to the one generated by the ensemble realisation. The epistemic effect of lossy sending is non-deterministic. The transitions from ensemble state s_0 to s_1 and the loops on s_1 and s_2 represent unsuccessful transmissions and the transitions from s_0 and from s_1 to s_2 represent successful ones. The associated epistemic states $(K_1, (w_0, \mathsf{k}))$ and $(K_1, (w_0, \mathsf{n}))$ are shown in Example 3. The epistemic state $(K_2, ((w_0, \mathsf{k}), \mathsf{k}))$ associated with the ensemble states s_3 to s_6 is computed by updating $(K_1, (w_0, \mathsf{k}))$ with the (deterministic) epistemic effect of the reliable sending from R to V.

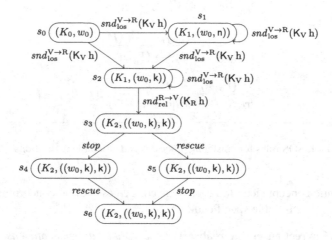

Fig. 2. EETS for the victim rescue ensemble realisation

Obviously, the EETS in Fig. 2 satisfies the axioms of the specification Sp_{vr} in Example 4. Therefore, according to Theorem 1, the bisimilar EETS generated from the epistemic ensemble realisation is a model of Sp_{vr} and thus the realisation is correct w.r.t. Sp_{vr}.   □

Two epistemic ensemble realisations $Real_1$ and $Real_2$ over the same signature are called *equivalent* if $[\![Real_1]\!] \sim [\![Real_2]\!]$. The following theorem says that for checking equivalence of epistemic ensemble realisations it is sufficient to show that their initial epistemic states are bisimilar and that the process definitions for each agent are pairwise bisimilar in the usual sense of process algebra; see e.g. [10]. We denote process bisimilarity by $\sim_p$.

Theorem 2. *Let $Real_1 = (\{P^1_{0,a} \mid a \in A\}, \mathfrak{K}^1_0)$ and $Real_2 = (\{P^2_{0,a} \mid a \in A\}, \mathfrak{K}^2_0)$ be two epistemic ensemble realisations over signature Σ. If $\mathfrak{K}^1_0 \approx \mathfrak{K}^2_0$ and $P^1_{0,a} \sim_p P^2_{0,a}$ for all $a \in A$, then $[\![Real_1]\!] \sim [\![Real_2]\!]$.*

Proof sketch. Let S_i be the ensemble states of $Real_i$ for $i = 1, 2$. We use the relation $EB \subseteq S_1 \times S_2$ such that $((ctrl_1, \mathfrak{K}_1), (ctrl_2, \mathfrak{K}_2)) \in EB$ iff $ctrl_1(a) \sim_p ctrl_2(a)$ for all $a \in A$ and $\mathfrak{K}_1 \approx \mathfrak{K}_2$. By assumption, the initial ensemble states are related by EB. We have to show that EB is an EETS-bisimulation.

Condition (1) of Definition 4 is satisfied by definition of EB. For condition (2), let $((ctrl_1, \mathfrak{K}_1), (ctrl_2, \mathfrak{K}_2)) \in EB$ and $(ctrl_1, \mathfrak{K}_1) \xrightarrow{e}_{[\![Real_1]\!]} (ctrl'_1, \mathfrak{K}'_1)$. By rule (ensemble) in Fig. 1, there is $(P_a^1, \mathfrak{K}_1) \xhookrightarrow{e} (P_a^{1'}, \mathfrak{K}'_1)$ where $P_a^1 = ctrl_1(a)$ and $P_a^{1'} = ctrl'_1(a)$. A case analysis on the form of P_a^1 yields that $P_a^1 \xhookrightarrow{e}_p P_a^{1'}$ and $(\mathfrak{K}_1, \mathfrak{K}'_1) \in eeff(e)$ where $\xhookrightarrow{e}_p$ denotes process transition. Since $\mathfrak{K}_1 \approx \mathfrak{K}_2$, it follows from Lemma 3 that there is a $\mathfrak{K}'_2$ such that $(\mathfrak{K}_2, \mathfrak{K}'_2) \in eeff(e)$ and $\mathfrak{K}'_1 \approx \mathfrak{K}'_2$. Let $P_a^2 = ctrl_2(a)$. Then $P_a^1 \sim_p P_a^2$ and therefore there exists $P_a^2 \xhookrightarrow{e}_p P_a^{2'}$ with $P_a^{1'} \sim_p P_a^{2'}$. A case analysis on the form of P_a^2 yields that $(P_a^2, \mathfrak{K}_2) \xhookrightarrow{e} (P_a^{2'}, \mathfrak{K}'_2)$ and hence, by rule (ensemble), that $(ctrl_2, \mathfrak{K}_2) \xrightarrow{e}_{[\![Real_2]\!]} (ctrl'_2, \mathfrak{K}'_2)$. Moreover, $((ctrl'_1, \mathfrak{K}'_1), (ctrl'_2, \mathfrak{K}'_2)) \in EB$.   □

6 Conclusion

We have developed a formalism for rigorous specification and realisation of ensembles based on principles of epistemic logic and epistemic actions. A crucial difference to [5, 8, 9] is that agents in epistemic ensembles do not communicate by message passing, but information exchange is achieved implicitly by changing knowledge. Another approach with implicit interaction is provided by the DEECo component and ensemble model [4]. In this case a coordinator is responsible for triggering exchange of factual knowledge which is, however, not grounded in epistemic logic.

For specifications of bigger case-studies we would need to extend our logic to allow agent types, variables and quantification over agents. For ensemble realisations we want to go a step further and represent the epistemic information, that is currently used by agent processes by accessing a global epistemic state, by local knowledge bases attached to each agent process.

References

1. Baltag, A., Moss, L.S.: Logics for epistemic programs. Synthese **139**(2), 165–224 (2004). https://doi.org/10.1023/B:SYNT.0000024912.56773.5e
2. Baltag, A., Moss, L.S., Solecki, S.: The logic of public announcements and common knowledge and private suspicions. In: Gilboa, I. (ed.) Proceedings of 7th Conference on Theoretical Aspects of Rationality and Knowledge (TARK 1998), pp. 43–56. Morgan Kaufmann (1998)
3. Baltag, A., Renne, B.: Dynamic epistemic logic. In: Zalta, E.N., Nodelman, U., Allen, C., Anderson, R.L. (eds.) Stanford Encyclopedia of Philosophy. The Metaphysics Research Lab, Stanford University (2016)
4. Bures, T., Gerostathopoulos, I., Hnetynka, P., Keznikl, J., Kit, M., Plasil, F.: DEECO: an ensemble-based component system. In: Kruchten, P., Giannakopoulou, D., Tivoli, M. (eds.) Proceedings of 16th ACM SIGSOFT Symposium on Component Based Software Engineering (CBSE 2013), pp. 81–90. ACM (2013). https://doi.org/10.1145/2465449.2465462
5. De Nicola, R., Loreti, M., Pugliese, R., Tiezzi, F.: A formal approach to autonomic systems programming: the SCEL language. ACM Trans. Auton. Adapt. Syst. (TAAS) **9**(2), 1–29 (2014). https://doi.org/10.1145/2619998

6. van Ditmarsch, H., van der Hoek, W., Kooi, B.: Dynamic Epistemic Logic. Synthese Library, vol. 337. Springer, Cham (2008). https://doi.org/10.1007/978-1-4020-5839-4

7. Fagin, R., Halpern, J.Y., Moses, Y., Vardi, M.Y.: Reasoning About Knowledge. MIT Press, Cambridge (2003)

8. Hennicker, R., Wirsing, M.: Dynamic logic for ensembles. In: Margaria, T., Steffen, B. (eds.) ISoLA 2018. LNCS, vol. 11246, pp. 32–47. Springer, Cham (2018). https://doi.org/10.1007/978-3-030-03424-5_3

9. Hennicker, R., Wirsing, M.: A dynamic logic for systems with predicate-based communication. In: Margaria, T., Steffen, B. (eds.) ISoLA 2020. LNCS, vol. 12477, pp. 224–242. Springer, Cham (2020). https://doi.org/10.1007/978-3-030-61470-6_14

10. Milner, R.: Communication and concurrency. PHI Series in computer science, Prentice Hall (1989)

11. Pinciroli, C., Bonani, M., Mondada, F., Dorigo, M.: Adaptation and awareness in robot ensembles: scenarios and algorithms. In: Wirsing, M., Hölzl, M., Koch, N., Mayer, P. (eds.) Software Engineering for Collective Autonomic Systems. LNCS, vol. 8998, pp. 471–494. Springer, Cham (2015). https://doi.org/10.1007/978-3-319-16310-9_15

12. Sürmeli, J.: Epistemic logic in ensemble specification. In: Margaria, T., Steffen, B. (eds.) ISoLA 2020. LNCS, vol. 12477, pp. 329–343. Springer, Cham (2020). https://doi.org/10.1007/978-3-030-61470-6_20

13. Wirsing, M., Banâtre, J.-P., Hölzl, M., Rauschmayer, A. (eds.): Software-Intensive Systems and New Computing Paradigms. LNCS, vol. 5380. Springer, Heidelberg (2008). https://doi.org/10.1007/978-3-540-89437-7

14. Hölzl, M., Koch, N., Puviani, M., Wirsing, M., Zambonelli, F.: The ensemble development life cycle and best practices for collective autonomic systems. In: Wirsing, M., Hölzl, M., Koch, N., Mayer, P. (eds.) Software Engineering for Collective Autonomic Systems. LNCS, vol. 8998, pp. 325–354. Springer, Cham (2015). https://doi.org/10.1007/978-3-319-16310-9_9

15. Wirsing, M., Hölzl, M., Tribastone, M., Zambonelli, F.: ASCENS: engineering autonomic service-component ensembles. In: Beckert, B., Damiani, F., de Boer, F.S., Bonsangue, M.M. (eds.) FMCO 2011. LNCS, vol. 7542, pp. 1–24. Springer, Heidelberg (2013). https://doi.org/10.1007/978-3-642-35887-6_1

A Modal Approach to Consciousness of Agents

Chen Yifeng[1] and J. W. Sanders[2]($\boxtimes$)

[1] Peking University, Beijing, China
cyf@pku.edu.cn
[2] AIMS South Africa, Cape Town, Republic of South Africa
jsanders@aims.ac.za

Abstract. An agent's awareness is modelled as a modal operator in such a way that awareness can be iterated and consciousness formalised as awareness of awareness. Agents are not necessarily human and may *a priori* be animals, organisations or software, in which setting awareness is expected to exist in degrees and so is modelled with nonnegative reals rather than just Booleans. The formalism thus expresses the degree to which an agent exhibits awareness (and so consciousness).

The context is an adaptive multi-agent system in which agents control actions, individually or in groups, and adapt ecorithmically (in the sense of Valiant) by adjusting behaviour in the short term and evolving in the very much longer term. Laws and inequalities are given and shown to be sound, but the intuition is that *awareness* 'enables' actions to form the agent's next behavioural step whilst *consciousness* provides the agent with an opportunity to adapt that behaviour.

1 Introduction

Consciousness has for long been considered beyond scientific explanation (*i.e.* not to be explicable by reduction) and instead to be an emergent property of that complex system the human brain. The fraught problem of understanding consciousness has been made no simpler by that concept cutting across neurophysiology, philosophy of the mind, physics, computer science, data science and more recently mathematics. But recent decades have heralded a fresh approach: the proposal of architectural models to account for consciousness.[1] Together with the success of machine learning (providing a candidate for artificial free will?), that has led to renewed interest in both the popular press and academic journals in the contentious question of whether or not an artificial agent can be sentient or conscious. Without a definition or even agreed properties of consciousness, how can that be answered? This work addresses that deficiency, in a modal setting.

A treatment of consciousness which does not *a priori* rule out the possibility of its application to non-humans must be general enough to embrace organisms

---

[1] A dozen such models are cited at the *Oxford Mathematics of Consciousness and Applications Network* site [19].

T. Margaria and B. Steffen (Eds.): ISoLA 2022, LNCS 13703, pp. 127–141, 2022.
https://doi.org/10.1007/978-3-031-19759-8_9

(like cells, plants and animals), organisations and artificial agents yet not be too weak when restricted to humans. For such entities we use the generic term 'agent'. We propose a Boolean notion (an agent is conscious of a feature or not), and a numerical notion (the strength of that consciousness).

We follow the usual approach when confronted with a complex concept and resort to identifying properties, or laws if possible, in place of a definition. Of course a model is still needed to show consistency of the laws, and we use as simple a model as possible. The aim of that approach is eventually to identify sufficiently many laws to characterise the concept. In the case of consciousness, where no definition seems forthcoming, it offers an enticing avenue for progress.

Our choice of laws is guided by the following intuition. An agent is aware of something that 'enables' or 'makes executable' actions under its control for use in its next step in behaviour. For instance a bird flying to its nest is aware of winds if they cause it to adjust its flight. On the other hand a person whose senses are not augmented by an appropriate receiver is unaware of radio waves since their presence 'enables' no actions within its control.

If an agent is aware of something then in some cases, identified here as those in which the agent is conscious of the thing, it uses that awareness to adapt its actions. Thus consciousness requires awareness but provides more: an opportunity for adapting the way in which the next step in behaviour is chosen. Unfortunately a definition of consciousness in those terms directly would not be observable without insight into the agent's 'mind'. So we resort to defining it in terms of iterated awareness. Thus: an agent is conscious if it is aware of its awareness (The Stanford Encyclopedia, [24]: Sect. 9.2, Reflexive Theories).

For instance a bird is conscious of fledgelings in the nest because it does not return directly to the nest, as usual, but adapts by landing first on a nearby branch. It is conscious of the flock, because it adapts its trajectory by averaging the velocities of its neighbours in the flock [5]. Thus it is not merely aware but conscious in both cases.

That intuition extends to agents many popular treatments of human consciousness. We refer to just one, by Dehaene [6], which takes human consciousness of something to mean 'the ability to report on it'. In our terms, reporting requires awareness of the thing to enable the ability to report on it, but moreover in choosing what to report the person demonstrates consciousness of it.

In this approach consciousness is necessary for adaptation, for which we follow the *ecorithm* approach of Valiant who makes a convincing case that ecorithms embody:

> ... mechanisms ... of two kinds, those that operate in individuals interacting with their environment, and those that operate via genetic changes over many generations. ... ecorithms are also construed broadly enough to encompass any process of interaction with an environment.
>
> Valiant [26], page 27.

In our context short-term adaptivity can be seen as adjustment by the agent to its environment, and long-term as evolution. As the system evolves, changes occur to the set of agents, the actions and their control by agents.

Laws of consciousness for agents must be decided without recourse to the concept of 'an agent's state of mind', and more generally eschewing anthropomorphism. Our solution is to resort, as much as possible (though not entirely), to externally observable behaviour. For instance we acknowledge that a pet dog is aware of its lead being taken from the peg in preparation for its daily walk because we observe that it wags its tail and rushes to the door. Naturally we refrain from postulating 'the dog is happy' (its state of mind).

The paper begins with our context of agents, actions, features and adaptive multi-agent systems. It motivates properties of awareness and expresses them in both Boolean and numerical forms. Then it formalises awareness and consciousness and proves soundness of the laws. After analysing properties of our adaptive mulit-agent systems, it discusses related work and draws conclusions.

2   Conscious Agents

This section provides the background to our general view of agents, the actions they perform and the features of which they may be aware. It then discusses the adaptive multi-agent systems they inhabit.

2.1   Agents

The agents we consider range from humans, other animals, plants, cells and organisations to software. They are considered not in isolation but as part of some habitat[2] which may be inhabited by various agents, but has an external environment. For instance in the local gardens we may consider birds and the things which affect them (like trees and worms). Birds exhibit a strong circadian rhythm which they exploit when deciding how to behave, but the sun and its movement which affect bird behaviour are external to the garden system. The external environment is treated as a default agent.

System actions are typically controlled by agents, individually or in groups. Care of fledgelings lies under the control of their parents whilst flocking is controlled by a group. Sunrise is controlled by the default environmental agent.

An agent is an entity in such a system having control over at least one action. The agent may be a sunflower which when growing exhibits heliotropic behaviour by tracking the sun during the day and then reorienting overnight to face east. Its movement is the combined effect of internal and external actions which result in the head tilting due to cells growing faster on the side of the stem facing the sun. Actions under the sunflower's control include the hormonal and circadian actions controlled by the plant but not solar movement; see Atamian *et al.* [1].

A rock in the garden erodes at a rate which depends on its location and composition, but as a result of action by the elements. Erosion is thus the result of environmental actions, and none under control of the rock, which is therefore not an agent.

---

[2] The term 'environment' is more commonly used to mean something external to an agent, but we are about to give 'external environment' another meaning.

Due to the generality of an agent, we cannot assume that it displays the kind of rationality assumed in logic and in particular dynamic epistemic logic. We cannot justify for instance the law that if an agent is aware of p which is stronger than q then it is also aware of q. However something of that kind holds, but with correlation instead. The pet dog is evidently conscious, from its behaviour already considered, that when its lead is taken from the peg then it is daily-walk time. We capture properties of consciousness with laws, but they are far weaker than the familiar logical laws.

2.2   Actions

The actions performed by agents either terminate or on-going and typically reactive. The former are described by postcondition with state-before, input, state-after and output. Then the precondition is defined to hold at a state-before and input if there is a state-after and output satisfying the postcondition. The latter types of action are described by safety and liveness. We try not to distinguish the two styles, thinking of an ongoing action as the iteration of a terminating action, perhaps forever.

Our descriptions of actions are not necessarily algorithmic nor even computable, but they are all state based. That allows inclusion of the view by Penrose & Hameroff (see the review by Hameroff [12]) that quantum reduction is primitive in any appropriate ecorithmic language for humans.

We use the following notation concerning an agent's control of actions. Left informal here, it has been formalised for software [21]. Suppose as given the sets *Agents* and *Actions*.

Notation 1 (Ambit). *The* ambit *of an action act : Actions is the set of agents involved in its activation:*

$$ambit(act) := \{a : Agents \mid a \text{ has some control in } act\}.$$

The set of actions in which a : Agents has control is denoted

$$\mathcal{A}_a := \{act : Actions \mid a \in ambit(act)\}.$$

For instance the ambit of a bird's return flight to its nest contains itself, and weather conditions. The ambit of its flight when flocking contains its nearest neighbours in the flock.

2.3   Features

The things in an agent's habitat which may affect its behaviour we call *features*.

For instance features in a human's habitat may include memory of birthdays past, a vision of a unicorn, a (remembered) dream, social conventions, radio waves, climate change and interactions with its pets and other humans.

In general, the definition of feature relies on domain-specific knowledge. For instance the visual range of birds extends to much higher frequencies than our own, as does the audio range of dogs. Features allow us to express concepts in terms of observable behaviour (rather than state of mind). The features of a human system may include 'the pet dog', 'its lead being taken from the peg', and 'daily walk'. A bird's features may include the state of the weather, its partner, number of fledgelings in its nest, the local flock and dawn chorus.

Notation 2 (Feature). *A feature is something which can affect system behaviour. Features are of diverse type and depend on domain knowledge, as the examples above show. As an example, the space $\mathfrak{F}$ of all features for a system of humans may be defined syntactically:*

$$Basic :: = Habitat \mid Remembered \mid Imagined \mid Dreamt$$
$$\mathfrak{F} \quad :: = Basic \mid \sim\!\mathfrak{F} \mid \mathfrak{F}\,\&\,\mathfrak{F} \mid \mathfrak{F} \rightsquigarrow \mathfrak{F} \mid \mathfrak{F} \overset{\star}{\rightsquigarrow} \mathfrak{F} \mid A_a \mathfrak{F}$$

The proposition 'feature f occurs at time t' is written $f{\downarrow}t$. Then the Boolean operations above are defined:

$$(\sim\!f){\downarrow}t := \neg(f{\downarrow}t) \qquad\qquad f \text{ doesn't occur at } t$$
$$(f\&g){\downarrow}t := (f{\downarrow}t) \wedge (g{\downarrow}t) \qquad f, g \text{ both occur at } t$$
$$(f \rightsquigarrow g){\downarrow}t := (f{\downarrow}t) \Rightarrow (g{\downarrow}t) \qquad g \text{ occurs at } t \text{ if } f \text{ does}$$
$$(f \overset{\star}{\rightsquigarrow} g){\downarrow}t := (f{\downarrow}t) \Rightarrow (\exists u{\geq}t \cdot g{\downarrow}u) \quad g \text{ occurs with or after } f \text{ at } t.$$

Of course the implications $\rightsquigarrow$ and $\overset{\star}{\rightsquigarrow}$ hold if their antecedents fail.

The absence of the absence of f is the same as the occurrence of f: $\sim$ is an involution. However an agent may be aware of neither $f{\downarrow}t$ nor $(\sim\!f){\downarrow}t$. $\&$ is commutative, associative and idempotent. $\rightsquigarrow$ and $\overset{\star}{\rightsquigarrow}$ are transitive. As usual duality (de Morgan's Law) may be used to define the analogue of disjunction as $\sim((\sim\!f)\,\&\,(\sim\!g))$, representing occurrence of at least one of f and g.

Not all features are relevant to an agent at a particular time and those which are have different levels of relevance. For instance you react immediately if your peripheral vision registers an approaching lion. For us features sensed from the habitat seem dominant, usually justified in terms of survival. But we, and many other animals, are also strongly aware of social conventions and experience, which we classify under 'Remembered'. Evidently different animals have quite different strengths of social sense.

A feature is said to 'enable' any action whose precondition it establishes. Our systems also require a more general version, eventual enabledness, in which the precondition is established eventually. For example, having fledgelings in the nest enables the parental action of feeding them and eventually enables the various parental actions of mentoring/overseeing their leaving the nest and flight.

Definition 1 (Enables). *Assume act is an action. We say that a feature $f : \mathfrak{F}$ enables act if it establishes the precondition of act. Pointwise by time,*

$$f \operatorname{\mathbf{En}} act := f \rightsquigarrow \operatorname{pre}(act).$$

More generally f eventually enables an action which is enabled some time in future:

$$f \operatorname{\mathbf{En^+}} act := f \overset{\star}{\rightsquigarrow} \operatorname{pre}(act).$$

2.4   Multiagent Systems

The systems of agents we consider are adaptable multi-agent transition systems but with the notion of control and ambit of an action as basic. Agents are distinguished in our systems, as we have observed, by belonging to the ambit of at least one action. Recall that the habitat's environment is expressed as a default agent.

Definition 2 (System). *A system* $S := (Agents, Actions)$ *is composed of a set Agents of agents, one representing the* environment, *and a set Actions of* actions, *each having an ambit. Agents have disjoint state spaces and interact by actions. So the state of S is the disjoint union of the states of the agents and each act* $\in$ *Actions has locus of control ambit(act)* $\subseteq$ *Agents and type, on each interaction in general,*

$$act : (States \times Input) \leftrightarrow (States \times Output) .$$

An agent responds to features in its habitat by behaving in some way. We take agent behaviour to be observable, although its causes may not be. Indeed human behaviour results from survival, pleasure, social pressure and 'free will'. Cell behaviour supports homeostasis. Government behaviour concerns running the country in response to its electorate, whilst dictatorship does not take into account the electorate! All have observable steps in behaviour.

A feature may enable many of an agent's actions. But at any time the agent may perform only some of them. Typically the choice is routine or even, we'd say, subconscious. For instance one can drive under normal conditions on 'auto pilot' and be aware of changing gear only if something untoward occurs in which case one needs to react spontaneously.

Thus an agent chooses actions routinely if aware of the features which enable them. But in special conditions, of 'deep awareness' which we identify with consciousness, the agent is aware that it is aware of certain features and must adapt its choice of action. Thus we identify consciousness of a feature with awareness of awareness of it, and consider that to result in the agent's adapting its choice of action.

Our systems adapt at two levels. At the system level that results from 'long term' changes; for example of a bird to climate change in its habitat. At the agent level that is due not only to incremental response to long-term changes but also to inter-agent, social, interactions. We return to this in Sect. 5.

3   Appreciating Awareness

We consider Boolean laws and numerical inequalities for the awareness, $(A_a f) \!\downarrow\! t$, by agent a of feature f at time t. Throughout we consider just a single agent and seek laws reducing awareness of a compound feature to awareness of simpler features, taking into account the consequences, under correspondence theory of modal logic, for the semantics.

For example in the Boolean model, awareness of f at t should imply that the proposition $f{\downarrow}t$ holds:

$$(A_a f){\downarrow}t \implies f{\downarrow}t . \tag{1}$$

Naturally the converse fails: an agent is aware of only certain features from its habitat.

Law (1), modal logic's Law T, implies by correspondence theory that the accessibility relation in the Kripke semantics is reflexive. It also implies that no time lag is required for a to become aware of $f{\downarrow}t$.

Numerically, if a is aware of $f{\downarrow}t$ then the strength of that awareness should equal the strength of $f{\downarrow}t$ (at the same time). We write that:

$$|(A_a f){\downarrow}t| = |f{\downarrow}t| . \tag{2}$$

Concurrency. Recall that $(f\&g){\downarrow}t = (f{\downarrow}t) \wedge (g{\downarrow}t)$. So is awareness of $(f\&g){\downarrow}t$ equivalent to awareness of $f{\downarrow}t$ and $g{\downarrow}t$ independently?

The former holds if $(f\&g){\downarrow}t$ enables some action. But the latter holds if individually each feature enables an action, which is not necessarily the same due to the usual difference between pointwise and uniform behaviour gained by interchanging quantifiers. So we expect only implication to hold:

$$(A_a f){\downarrow}t \wedge (A_a g){\downarrow}t \Rightarrow (A_a(f\&g)){\downarrow}t . \tag{3}$$

A slightly contrived counterexample to the converse is provided by an agent which requires *two-factor authentication* from users before giving them access to some information. It enables user access if presented with the feature consisting of an ID plus two passwords. But if presented with an ID and a single password it does nothing. So the converse of (3) fails.

By comparison if only *single-factor authentication* were required then of course (3) would hold. But in neither case would the agent necessarily be conscious; it responds, so is aware, but with a strict strategy. A firewall, which requires two-factor authentication and which 'attacks' users submitting single passwords, would be conscious if its attack were developed *ad hom*, indicating flexibility of response.

Intuitively, the strength of awareness of a concurrent combination should be bounded above by the stronger of the strengths of f and g, and below by the weaker. Using $\sqcap$ and $\sqcup$ for min and max of numbers rerspectively:

$$|(A_a f){\downarrow}t| \sqcap |(A_a g){\downarrow}t| \le |(A_a(f\&g)){\downarrow}t| \le |(A_a f){\downarrow}t| \sqcup |(A_a g){\downarrow}t|. \tag{4}$$

Consequence. The fundamental Law K of Modal Logic is

$$\Box f \wedge \Box(f \implies g) \implies \Box g.$$

In terms of A_a that relies on an agent to appreciate when one feature is stronger than another which, as already discussed, is unrealistic for agents in general. But replacing the first occurrence of $\implies$ by $\leadsto$ leads to a plausible Boolean law:

$$(A_a f){\downarrow}t \wedge (A_a(f{\leadsto}g)){\downarrow}t \implies (A_a g){\downarrow}t. \tag{5}$$

By comparison with Law (3), we expect awareness of $f{\downarrow}t$ and $g{\downarrow}t$ to imply awareness of $(f{\leadsto}g){\downarrow}t$:

$$(A_a f){\downarrow}t \wedge (A_a g){\downarrow}t \implies (A_a(f{\leadsto}g)){\downarrow}t . \tag{6}$$

For strength, reasoning as for concurrency,

$$|(A_a{\sim}f){\downarrow}t| \sqcap |(A_a{\sim}g){\downarrow}t| \leq |(A_a(f{\leadsto}g)){\downarrow}t| \leq |(A_a f){\downarrow}t| \sqcup |(A_a g){\downarrow}t|. \tag{7}$$

Absence and Dual. Features f and $\sim f$ cannot occur simultaneously, by the meaning of $\sim$. So in the Boolean model an agent can not be aware of both $f{\downarrow}t$ and $(\sim f){\downarrow}t$:

$$(A_a f){\downarrow}t \implies \neg((A_a{\sim}f){\downarrow}t). \tag{8}$$

The modal dual of A_a we write ∇_a.

Definition 3 (Dual). *If at time t agent a is not aware of the absence of a feature, then the feature is considered to be feasible from a's point of view:*

$$(\nabla_a f){\downarrow}t := (\sim(A_a{\sim}f){\downarrow}t){\downarrow}t .$$

Our Boolean version of modal logic's Law D follows from Law (8):

$$(A_a f){\downarrow}t \implies (\nabla_a f){\downarrow}t. \tag{9}$$

By correspondence theory accessibility in a Kripke semantics is serial.

Numerically, from that we expect:

$$|(A_a f){\downarrow}t| \leq |(\nabla_a f){\downarrow}t|. \tag{10}$$

Consciousness. Consciousness implies awareness by definition, confirmed by Law (1):

$$(A_a(A_a f){\downarrow}t){\downarrow}t \implies (A_a f){\downarrow}t. \tag{11}$$

But not conversely, as for (1), since then there would be no difference between awareness and consciousness. By correspondence theory accessibility in a Kripke semantics is not transitive.

Numerically, from that we expect:

$$|(A_a(A_a f){\downarrow}t){\downarrow}t| \leq |(A_a f){\downarrow}t|. \tag{12}$$

Time. Awareness of a feature $f{\downarrow}t$ fades with time after t unless it is refreshed in some way. For instance driving home I am careful to select reverse gear to leave the parking lot and may be aware of the first couple of gear changes. But by the time I reach home I am unaware of having changed gear *en route* unless something untoward required me to pay particular attention.

Thus the strength of awareness of f in the future is at most its strength now, unless the awareness is refreshed. We expect the inequality: provided $\neg(A_a f){\downarrow}u$,

$$\forall u > t \cdot |(A_a f){\downarrow}u| \leq |(A_a f){\downarrow}t|. \tag{13}$$

If $(A_a f){\downarrow}u$ then the law holds only if $(A_a f){\downarrow}t$ too, in which case equality holds.

4   Soundness

In this section we continue with a single agent's perspective and define a simple model, define awareness with respect to it and show the foregoing laws to be sound. We write $\mathbb{T}$ for the time domain which we now assume is $\mathbb{N}$.

Recall that an agent is not aware of all features in its habitat, but for those of which it is aware, it is aware with a certain strength. For instance in Definition 2 the default strengths of the basic features for humans might be ranked

$$|Habitat| > |Remembered| > |Imagined| > |Dreamt|. \tag{14}$$

Indeed our survival depends on quick responses to threatening features in our habitat, but we are guided by memory in particular of social mores. For now we simplify and consider features to have the same strength, using feature strength to define strength of awareness.

The strength of a feature at time t is 1 if occurs at t and otherwise is inversely proportional to the length of time before t since it occurred.

Definition 4 (Strength). *The length of time before or at t when feature f last occurred is a minimum of lengths of time:*

$$\tau(f,t) := \sqcap\{t-n \mid t \geq n, \ f{\downarrow}n, \ \forall m : (n,t] \cdot \neg(f{\downarrow}m)\}.$$

Thus it is zero if $f{\downarrow}t$. We adopt the convention that it is ∞ if f has not occurred up till t.

The strength $|f{\downarrow}t|$ *of feature f at time t is defined to be inversely proportional to the length of time $\tau(f,t)$:*

$$|f{\downarrow}t| := (1 + \tau(f,t))^{-1},$$

where as usual $1 + \infty = \infty$ and $\infty^{-1} = 0$. Thus it is 1 if the feature occurs at t.

We also adopt a convention for successor and predecessor strengths, for use below. Suppose strength $d = (1+e)^{-1}$ where $e : \mathbb{N}^{\infty}$. Then the successor *is $d^+ := e^{-1}$ if $e > 0$ and undefined for $e = 0$. The* predecessor *is $d^- := (2+e)^{-1}$ for any $e : \mathbb{N}$.*

The strength of a combined feature is not readily expressed in terms of the individual strengths so the only bounds are simple:

Lemma 1 (Feature strength). *The strength of a feature lies in $[0,1]$ and satisfies*

1. $(\sim)$ $\ |(\sim f, t)| < 1 \ iff \ |(f, t)| = 1.$
2. $(\&)$ $\ |(\sim f, t)|^+ \sqcap |(\sim g, t)|^+ \ \leq \ |(f \& g, t)| \ \leq \ |(f, t)| \sqcup |(g, t)|.$
3. $(\leadsto)$ $\ |(\sim g, t)|^+ \ \leq \ |(f \leadsto g, t)| \ \leq \ |(g, t)|.$

Next awareness is formalised as follows. First we define when an agent is aware of a feature at a given time, and then in that case the strength of awareness.

Definition 5 (Awareness). *Agent a is* aware *of feature $f : \mathfrak{F}$ at time $t : \mathbb{T}$ if at that time f enables some action at least partially within a's control:*

$$(A_a f){\downarrow}t := \exists act : \mathcal{A}_a \cdot (f \operatorname{\mathbf{En}} act){\downarrow}t. \tag{15}$$

Using instead $\mathbf{En}^+$ gives the notion of eventual awareness. *The set of features of which a is aware at time t is denoted $\mathfrak{A}_a(t)$.*

The strength of awareness of feature $f : \mathfrak{A}_a(t)$ is defined to be the strength of f at time t (without delay):

$$|(A_a f){\downarrow}t| := |f{\downarrow}t|. \tag{16}$$

Definition 6 (Consciousness). *Agent a is* conscious *of feature f at time $t : \mathbb{T}$ if it aware of f at t and moreover immediately aware that it is aware:*

$$(C_a f){\downarrow}t := (A_a((A_a f){\downarrow}t)){\downarrow}t. \tag{17}$$

The strength at time u of consciousness is simply the strength of that awareness of 'awareness at time t':

$$|(C_a f){\downarrow}t| := |(A_a((A_a f){\downarrow}t)){\downarrow}t|. \tag{18}$$

The Boolean laws rely on the following result.

Lemma 2 (Closure). *The space $\mathfrak{A}_a(t)$ of features of which a is aware at t is closed under $\&$, $\rightsquigarrow$ and $\overset{\leftrightarrow}{\rightarrow}$ but not $\sim$.*

Proof. For the typical case of $\&$ we reason:

$f, g \in \mathfrak{A}_a(t)$
$\equiv$ definition of $\mathfrak{A}_a(t)$
$A_a(f, t) \wedge A_a(g, t)$
$\equiv$ Definition 5 of awareness
$\exists F, G : \mathcal{A}_a \cdot (f \operatorname{\mathbf{En}} F){\downarrow}t \wedge (g \operatorname{\mathbf{En}} G){\downarrow}t$
$\Rightarrow$ $f \& g \in \mathfrak{F}$, and H discussed below
$\exists H : \mathcal{A}_a \cdot (f \& g \operatorname{\mathbf{En}} H){\downarrow}t$
$\Rightarrow$ Definition 5 again
$A_a(f \& g, t)$
$\equiv$ definition of $\mathfrak{A}_a(t)$ again
$f \& g \in \mathfrak{A}_a(t).$

Since both f, g occur at t they are consistent so $f \& g \in \mathfrak{F}$. The action H may be taken to be any nondeterministic choice of the two actions which results in being either F or G, the choice being resolved at a lower level of detail.[3] Any such choice H satisfies

$$\mathrm{pre}(H) = \mathrm{pre}(F) \vee \mathrm{pre}(G)$$

---

[3] For instance a choice of probability p may be attributed to the environment and F chosen with probability p (and G with probability $1-p$).

so $f \& g$ enables H as required. Furthermore $H \in \mathcal{A}_a$ because

$$ambit(H) = ambit(F) \cup ambit(G)$$

and $a \in ambit(F) \cap ambit(G)$.

For $\sim$ we observe that if $f \in \mathfrak{A}_a(t)$ then by Definition 1 $f(s){\downarrow}t$. By definition of $\sim$ and the assumption that at most one of f and $\sim f$ occur at any time, $(\sim f){\downarrow}t$ cannot hold, so again the definition ensures $\sim f \notin \mathfrak{A}_a(t)$. $\square$

The next result establishes soundness of both Boolean and numerical laws.

Theorem 1 (Correctness). *The laws (1) to (13) from Sect. 3 hold.*

Proof. The Boolean laws in Sect. 3 not already established, (1), (3), (5) and (6) follow from simple arguments using the Closure Lemma.

For the numerical laws, the proof of Law (4) is typical. We reason:

$|(A_a(f \& g)){\downarrow}t|$

$=$ Definition 4

$|(f \& g){\downarrow}t|$

$=$ Definition 5 with appropriate $d : \mathbb{N}$

$1/(1+d)$.

Now $(f \& g){\downarrow}t$ iff both $f{\downarrow}t$ and $g{\downarrow}t$ by Definition 2. So d, the time to the most recent occurrence of both f and g, is bounded above by the time to the more recent of f and g which is:

$$|(f \& g){\downarrow}t| \leq |f{\downarrow}t| \sqcup |g{\downarrow}t|$$
$$= |(A_a f){\downarrow}t| \sqcup |(A_a g){\downarrow}t|.$$

It is bounded below by the first occurrence of either f or g which is one more than the most recent occurrence of either $\sim f$ or $\sim g$:

$$|(f \& g){\downarrow}t| \geq |(\sim f){\downarrow}t|^+ \sqcap |(\sim g){\downarrow}t|^+$$
$$= |(A_a \sim f){\downarrow}t|^+ \sqcap |(A_a \sim g){\downarrow}t|^+.$$

We infer Law (4). $\square$

5 Adaptivity

In this section we reflect on the kinds of system agents inhabit.

Our agents adapt both in the short term and very much longer term and so fit, as already observed, squarely with Valiant's ecorithms [26]. Short-term, day-to-day, adaptations we regard as adjustments and long-term adaptations as evolutionary. But our approach supports both, without any need for an inverse limit which would imply some limit to evolution, which seems implausible.

In terms of multi-agent systems, adjustments can be incorporated in the description of the system because they are predictable and so state can be expanded to include changes. That is analogous to an aware agent not needing to change its manner of choosing the next step in behaviour. However evolution is not predictable and so state must be expanded and actions updated. In retrospect at any time the current system can be seen as a more comprehensive but non-adaptive system using the Myhill-Nerode construction [18] to construct states as equivalence classes of sequences of actions.

Considering that representation of an adaptive system retrospectively as a (non-adaptive) system, the changes satisfy a 'causality' (or non-magic) invariant. In the space-time of Physics, an event x can affect only those events in its future *light cone* $C^+(x)$. Events in the past cone $C^-(x)$ require 'retro causality' and those in its future but outside $C^+(x)$ require 'superluminal' communication.

For adaptive systems, a realistic causality condition is more complicated because connectivity is not homogeneous and some communications are synchronous whilst others are asynchronous. Because the relation $\mathbf{En}^+$, of eventual enabledness, is transitive it can be used to define an analogue of light cones.

Definition 7 (Cones). *If act : Actions then the future and past cones of act consist respectively of all actions which it eventually enables, and which eventually enable it:*

$$C^+(act) := \{act' : Actions \mid pre(act) \, \mathbf{En}^+ \, act'\}$$
$$C^-(act) := \{act' : Actions \mid pre(act') \, \mathbf{En}^+ \, act\}.$$

An agent is stable *at some point in the evolution of an adaptive system if further interactions do not change it: subsequently its state space and the actions entirely under its control remain unchanged.*

Our adaptive systems satisfy the invariant that changes occur only as restricted by future cones.

6   Related Work and Progress

Boolean laws for awareness, and hence for consciousness (seen as awareness of awareness), have been proposed as have inequalities for its strength. They have been shown to be sound, in spite of the reflexivity required for consciousness, in a very simple model.

The driving intuition has been that awareness 'enables' actions to form an agent's next behavioural step whilst consciousness provides an opportunity for an agent to adapt its way of deciding that behaviour. It seems difficult to formulate those ideas in observable (*i.e.* falsifiable) terms which is why we have resorted to laws and inequalities.

We know of no similar work, either law-based or in terms of choice of next behavioural step. Recent work seems to concentrate on architectural models which exhibit consciousness, and mostly for humans [19]. Influential examples are the Global Workspace Theory, GWT, of Baars [2] and the related Conscious Turing Machine, CTM, [4] of the Blooms. Those base the selection from many alternatives of one for consciousness by ranking whilst our approach is less specific: an agent is conscious if it needs or is offered the chance to adapt the protocol for its behaviour. An interesting alternative based entirely on network density is the work of Grindrod, [10,11].

Early computational-based work stems from Johnson-Laird's general analogy between mind and computer [16]. In those terms remembered and subconscious features may be thought of as being like random-access memory. When a feature is 'downloaded' afresh from memory, it enters 'local store', and so the agent's awareness. That provides a computational analogy with caching which has been made explicit in different ways by GWT and CTM.

The origins of the computational approach to system evolution go back to Barricelli's experiments [3] and Ray's *Tierra* [20], extremely early and restricted precursors of Valiant's ecorithms [26]. Of importance in the evolutionary setting will be Hoffman's work on Computational Evolutionary Perception, CEP, [13] which overturns the naive interpretation of 'what we see is what's out there', by considering its use to the observer. Similar ideas will apply to an arbitrary agent and all features, and be essential in quantifying our approach further.

Tononi's Information Integration Theory, IIT, [25], provides a measure of consciousness but in view of the computational complexity of its evaluation, current interest appears to be in its simulation. To be a model of what the brain does, it must be feasible computationally.

There is much work on awareness in adaptive system theory, from which the reader may like to compare [14,15].

The generality of our agents means that they are not necessarily rational, so we are unable to exploit work on dynamic epistemic logic. Relaxed notions of modal awareness, necessary for reasoning by logical agents who lack logical omniscience and have only bounded computational ability, have been introduced by Fagin & Halpern [7]. They refine Levesque's idea [17] of 'explicit' and 'implicit' belief (the latter being the logical closure of the former), and show how to achieve the result within a Kripke semantics adapted to include time.

Our approach can be thought of as formalising and extending to agents that of Dehaene [6]. There are many more recent popular books by experts on consciousness than we can refer to, as well as several fine youtube videos. The topic seems recently to have captured popular interest.

This work suffers several deficiencies. Features have been assumed to have the same strength, though it is simple to assign them weights when defining feature strength, depending on their basic constituents, subject to say (14). The definition of awareness of features has made no attempt to relate features, which seems likely in reality but would require currently unknown structure on $\mathfrak{F}$.

A single agent has been considered. Realistically different agents have different strengths which could be incorporated in the definition of strength of awareness by a. That agent weight would vary with evolution during which species 'search' anti-entropically for a niche with lower potential energy, but expending both energy and time in the process. Consciousness acts to break a barrier and initiate an entropy-increasing run of awareness. The connection of this with 'free energy' [22,23] is an enticing topic of further work which would incorporate recent advances in understanding the evolution of awareness (for instance Graziano [9]) and consciousness (for instance Ginsburg & Jablonka [8]).

We have not considered higher-order awareness beyond the degree 2 to define consciousness. One of the benefits of our approach is the possibility of doing so to explain subconscious and anomalous behaviour like blindsight (The Stanford Encyclopedia, [24]: Higher-order Theories of Consciousness).

The incorporation of more general, nonlinear, time would make the theory more realistic, as would the inclusion of probability of actions and the observation that consciousness does not seem to be independent for each feature, but to be bunched by kind of feature. Finally, the theorem implied in Sect. 5 of an adaptive system represented as a system could be formalised and simulation criteria used to establish agent consciousness.

Acknowledgments. The authors thank colleagues Professors Ronnie Becker and Hans Georg Zimmermann for wise council in early presentations of this material, and the referees for identifying obscurities and encouraging us to extend related work.

References

1. Atamian, H.S., Creux, N.M., Brown, E.A., Garner, A.G., Blackman, B.K., Harmer, S.L.: Circadian regulation of sunflower heliotropism, oral orientation, and pollinator visits. Science **353**(6299), 587–590 (2016)
2. Baars, B.J.: A Cognitive Theory of Consciousness. CUP (1998)
3. Barricelli, N.A.: Work from the 2nd half of the 50s at Princeton IAS summarised in Chapter 7 of G. Darwin Among the Machines. Penguin, Dyson (1997)
4. Blum, M., Blum, L.: A theoretical computer science perspective on consciousness, 16 November 2020. arxiv.org/ftp/arxiv/papers/2011/2011.09850.pdf
5. Cucker, F., Smale, S.: Emergent behaviour in flocks. IEEE Trans. Autom. Control **52**(5), 852–862 (2007)
6. Dehaene, S.: Consciousness and the Brain. Penguin (2014)
7. Fagin, R., Halpern, J.Y.: Belief, awareness and limited reasoning. Artif. Intell. **34**, 39–76 (1988)
8. Ginsburg, S., Jablonka, E.: The Evolution of the Sensitive Soul: Learning and the Origins of Consciousness. MIT Press, Cambridge (2019)
9. Graziano, M.S.A.: Speculations on the evolution of awareness. J. Cogn. Neurosci. **26**(6), 1300–1304 (2014)
10. Grindrod, P.: On human consciousness: a mathematical perspective. Netw. Neurosci. **2**(1), 23–40 (2017)
11. Grindrod, P., Lester, C.: Cortex-like complex systems: what occurs within?, June 2020. www.researchgate.net/publication/341901669
12. Hameroff, S.: How quantum brain biology can rescue conscious free will. Front. Integr. Neurosci. **6**, 93 (2012)
13. Hoffman, D.D., Singh, M.: Computational evolutionary perception. Perception **41**, 1073–1091 (2012)
14. Hölzl, M., Wirsing, M.: Towards a system model for ensembles. In: Agha, G., Danvy, O., Meseguer, J. (eds.) Formal Modeling: Actors, Open Systems, Biological Systems. LNCS, vol. 7000, pp. 241–261. Springer, Heidelberg (2011). https://doi.org/10.1007/978-3-642-24933-4_12

15. Hölzl, M., Gabor, T.: Reasoning and learning for awareness and adaptation. In: Wirsing, M., Hölzl, M., Koch, N., Mayer, P. (eds.) Software Engineering for Collective Autonomic Systems. LNCS, vol. 8998, pp. 249–290. Springer, Cham (2015). https://doi.org/10.1007/978-3-319-16310-9_7

16. Johnson-Laird, P.N.: The Computer and the Mind. Harvard University Press (1988)

17. Levesque, H.J.: A logic of implicit and explicit belief. In: Proceedings AAA1-84, Austin, TX, pp. 198–202 (1984). Revised and expanded: Lab. Tech. Rept. FLAIR, #32, Palo Alto, CA, 1984

18. Lewis, H.R., Papadimitriou, C.H.: Elements of the Theory of Computation, 2nd edn. Prentice-Hall, Hoboken (1998)

19. Oxford Mathematics of Consciousness and Applications Network. omcan.web.ox.ac.uk

20. Ray, T.S.: An approach to the synthesis of life. In: Boden, M.A. (ed.) (Without Appendices) The Philosophy of Artificial Life. Oxford Readings in Philosophy, pp. 111–145. OUP (1996)

21. Sanders, J.W., Turilli, M.: Dynamics of Control. UNU-IIST Report 353, March 2007

22. Solms, M., Friston, K.: How and why consciousness arises: some considerations from physics and physiology. J. Conscious. Stud. **25**, 202–238 (2018)

23. Solms, M.: The Hidden Spring: A Journey to the Source of Consciousness. W. W. Norton & Co. (2021)

24. Stanford Encyclopedia of Philosophy. The Metaphysics Research Lab, Center for the Study of Language and Information (CSLI), Stanford University, January 2014

25. Tononi, G.: An information integration theory of consciousness. BMC Neurosci. **5**, 42 (2004). 22 pages

26. Valiant, L.: Probably Approximately Correct: Nature's Algorithms for Learning and Prospering in a Complex World. Basic Books (2013)

An Experimental Toolchain for Strategy Synthesis with Spatial Properties

Davide Basile[✉][iD], Maurice H. ter Beek[iD], and Vincenzo Ciancia[iD]

Formal Methods and Tools Lab, ISTI–CNR, Pisa, Italy
{basile,terbeek,ciancia}@isti.cnr.it

Abstract. We investigate the application of strategy synthesis to enforce spatial properties. The Contract Automata Library (CATLib) performs both composition and strategy synthesis of games modelled in a dialect of finite state automata. The Voxel-based Logical Analyser (VoxLogicA) is a spatial model checker that allows the verification of properties expressed using the Spatial Logic of Closure Spaces on pixels of digital images. In this paper, we explore the integration of these two tools. We provide a basic example of strategy synthesis on automata encoding motion of agents in spaces represented by images. The strategy is synthesised with CATLib, whilst the properties to enforce are defined by means of spatial model checking of the images with VoxLogicA.

1 Introduction

Research on strategy synthesis in games is currently a hot topic, with established relations with supervisory control [3,60], reactive systems synthesis [41], parity games [57] (with recent complexity breakthroughs [27]), automated behaviour composition [44], automated planning [28] and service coordination [13]. Several academic tools have been developed [7,31–33,39,50,52,59] and applied to disparate domains, including land transport [12], maritime transport [62], medical systems [53], autonomous agents path planning [46], in which problems are modelled as games and solved using tailored strategy synthesis algorithms.

In an automata-based setting, a strategy is a prescription of the behaviour (transitions) of a particular player for all possible situations (states) that leads that player to a specific goal (final state). Typically, there are other players or an environment with different, often competing goals to account for, and the set of transitions may be partitioned into controllable (by the particular player) and uncontrollable transitions. Strategy synthesis is concerned with the automatic computation of a (safe, optimal) strategy (controller) in such a game-based automata setting.

Another hot topic concerns recent advancements in spatial model checking, which have led to relevant results such as the fully automated segmentation of regions of interest in medical images by brief, unambiguous specifications in spatial logic. The topological approach to spatial model checking of [34] is based on the Spatial Logic of Closure Spaces (SLCS) and provides a fully automated method to verify properties of points in graphs, digital images, and more recently

3D meshes and geometric structures [25,56]. Spatial properties of points are related to topological aspects such as being *near* to points satisfying a given property, or being able to *reach* a point satisfying a certain property, passing only through points obeying to specific constraints.

The tool VoxLogicA [24,36] (of which the third author is the lead developer) has been designed from scratch for image analysis. Logical operators can be freely mixed with a few imaging operators, related to colour thresholds, texture analysis, or normalisation. The tool is quite fast, due to various factors: most primitives are implemented using the state-of-the-art imaging library SimpleITK[1]; expressions are never recomputed (reduction of the syntax tree to a directed acyclic graph is used as a form of *memoisation*); operations are implicitly parallelised on multi-core CPUs. Ongoing work (cf., e.g., [26]) is devoted to a GPU-based implementation which enables a speedup of 1-2 orders of magnitude.

Returning to the topic of strategy synthesis, the tool CATLib [6,7,16] is a library (developed by the first author) for performing compositions of contract automata [15] (a dialect of finite-state automata) and synthesising either their supervisory control, their orchestration, or their choreography [13], using novel notions of controllability [9]. Scalability features offered by CATLib include a bounded on-the-fly state-space generation optimised with pruning of redundant transitions and parallel streams computations. The software is open source [7], it has been developed using principles of model-based software engineering [6] and it has been extensively validated using various testing and analysis tools to increase the confidence on the reliability of the library.

Contribution. In this paper, we propose a new approach to combine strategy synthesis and spatial model checking. We proceed in a bottom-up fashion by presenting a toolchain based on established off-the-shelf tool-supported theories. We explore the combination of CATLib and VoxLogicA, to pair the composition and synthesis functionalities of CATLib with the spatial model checking functionality of VoxLogicA. We provide a proof-of-concept example of strategy synthesis on automata encoding motion of agents in spaces represented by images[2]. The main insight is to encode an image as an automaton, whose states are the pixels of the image. These states are then interpreted as positions of an agent, and transitions to adjacent pixels represent motions of the agent. A composition of automata is thus a multi-agent system, in which each state of the composition is a snapshot of the current position of the agents in the map. A game can thus be played by a set of agents against other opponent agents, where successful states and failure states can be identified using spatial model checking of the images. The strategy is synthesised with CATLib, while the properties to enforce are defined by means of spatial model checking of the images with VoxLogicA.

---

[1] Cf. https://simpleitk.org/.

[2] In the VoxLogicA approach, images are seen as a special kind of graphs, where vertices are pixels, and edges represent proximity. Actually, the VoxLogicA family of tools can also operate on arbitrary directed graphs. Adapting the present work to the more general setting is left for future work.

The developed example is open-source and reproducible at [14]. The benefits include showing the practical applicability of these two tools, providing an original approach to strategy synthesis and spatial model checking, bridging theories and tools developed in different research areas and openings to future research goals.

Related Work. Practical application of spatial logics, including model checking, has been ongoing during the last decade. For instance, the research line originating in [48] merges spatial model checking with signal analysis. In the domain of cyber-physical systems, the approach of [65] demonstrates applications of SLCS in a spatio-temporal domain with linear time, using biographical models. An abstract categorical definition of SLCS has been given in [30]. The spatial model checking approach of SLCS and VoxLogicA has been demonstrated in case studies ranging from smart transportation [37] and bike sharing [35, 38], to brain tumour segmentation [4, 24], labelling of white and grey matter [23], and contouring of nevi [22].

Synthesising strategies (or plans/control) for the motion of agents is a widely researched problem [2, 42, 46, 47, 55, 63]. Spatial logics have been applied to this problem to investigate the synthesis of strategies from properties of spatially distributed systems specified with spatial logics [1, 49, 54]. Recently, the application domain of smart cities has been explored in [58], and the aforementioned signal-based approach has been enhanced for a hybrid approach to multi-agent control synthesis, by exploiting neural network and spatial-logical specifications in the Spatio-Temporal Reach and Escape Logic (STREL) formalism.

Differently from the above literature, we set out to integrate previously developed off-the-shelf algorithms and tools, with the aim of showing their applicability. Contract automata and their toolkit were introduced to synthesise ochestrations and choreographies of compositions of service contracts exchanging offers and requests [7, 9, 13, 15]. The interpretation of an image as an (agent) contract automaton enables to connect contract automata and CATLib with spatial model checking and VoxLogicA, showing the flexibility of both approaches.

Structure of the Paper. We start with the background on CATLib and VoxLogicA in Sect. 2. The toolchain is described in Sect. 3, whilst the experiments are reported in Sect. 4. Conclusions and future work are mentioned in Sect. 5.

2   Background

We provide some background on the formalisms and tools used in this paper.

2.1   CATLib, Automata Composition, and Strategy Synthesis

We first formally introduce contract automata and their synthesis operation. A Contract Automaton (CA) represents either a single service (in which case it is called a *principal*) or a multi-party composition of services performing actions.

The number of principals of a CA is called its *rank*. A CA's states are vectors of states of principals; its transitions are labelled with vectors of *actions* that are either *requests* (prefixed by ?), *offers* (prefixed by !), or *idle* actions (denoted with a distinguished symbol •). Requests and offers belong to the (pairwise disjoint) sets R and O, respectively. Figures 2 and 3 depict example CA. In a vector of actions there is either a single offer, or a single request, or a single pair of request and offer that match, i.e., the ith element of $\vec{a}$, denoted by $\vec{a}_{(i)}$, is $?a$, its jth element $\vec{a}_{(j)} = !a$, and all other elements are •; such vector of action is called *request*, *offer*, or *match*, respectively. Thus, for brevity, we may call action also a vector of actions. A transition is also called a request, offer, or match according to its action label. The goal of each principal is to reach an accepting (*final*) state such that all its requests (and possibly offers) are matched. In [20], CA were equipped with *modalities*, i.e., *necessary* (□) and *permitted* (◇) transitions, respectively. Permitted transitions are controllable, whilst necessary transitions can be uncontrollable or semi-controllable. Here we ignore semi-controllable transitions and consider necessary transitions to be uncontrollable. The resulting formalism is called *Modal Service Contract Automata* (MSCA).

Definition 1 (MSCA). *Given a finite set of states $Q = \{q_1, q_2, \ldots\}$, an MSCA $\mathcal{A}$ of rank n is a tuple $\langle Q, \vec{q_0}, A^r, A^o, T, F \rangle$, with set of states $Q = Q_1 \times \ldots \times Q_n \subseteq \mathcal{Q}^n$, initial state $\vec{q_0} \in Q$, set of requests $A^r \subseteq R$, set of offers $A^o \subseteq O$, set of final states $F \subseteq Q$, set of transitions $T \subseteq Q \times A \times Q$, where $A \subseteq (A^r \cup A^o \cup \{\bullet\})^n$, partitioned into permitted transitions $T^\diamond$ and necessary transitions $T^\square$, such that: (i) given $t = (\vec{q}, \vec{a}, \vec{q}') \in T$, $\vec{a}$ is either a request, or an offer, or a match; and (ii) $\forall i \in 1 \ldots n$, $\vec{a}_{(i)} = \bullet$ implies $\vec{q}_{(i)} = \vec{q}'_{(i)}$.*

Composition of services is rendered through the composition of their MSCA models by means of the *composition operator* ⊗, which is a variant of a synchronous product. This operator basically interleaves or matches the transitions of the component MSCA, but, whenever two component MSCA are enabled to execute their respective request/offer action, then the match is forced to happen. Moreover, a match involving a necessary transition of an operand is itself necessary. The rank of the composed MSCA is the sum of the ranks of its operands. The vectors of states and actions of the composed MSCA are built from the vectors of states and actions of the component MSCA, respectively.

In a composition of MSCA, typically various properties are analysed. We are especially interested in *agreement*. The property of agreement requires to match all requests, whilst offers can go unmatched.

CA support the synthesis of the most permissive controller from the theory of supervisory control of discrete event systems [29,60], where a finite state automaton model of a *supervisory controller* (called a strategy in this paper) is synthesised from given (component) finite state automata that are composed. Supervisory control theory has been applied in a variety of domains [13,21,43,45, 61,64], including healthcare. In this paper, we use the synthesis in the framework of games, whose relation with supervisory control is well known [3].

The synthesised automaton, if successfully generated, is such that it is *nonblocking, controllable*, and *maximally permissive*. An automaton is said to be *non-blocking* if from each state at least one of the *final states* (distinguished stable states representing completed 'tasks' [60]) can be reached without passing through so-called *forbidden states*, meaning that the system always has the possibility to return to an accepted stable state (e.g., a final state). The algorithm assumes that final states and forbidden states are indicated for each component. The synthesised automaton is said to be *controllable* when only controllable actions are disabled. Indeed, the supervisory controller is not permitted to directly block uncontrollable actions from occurring; the controller is only allowed to disable them by preventing controllable actions from occurring. Finally, the fact that the resulting supervisory controller is said to be *maximally permissive* (or least restrictive) means that as much behaviour of the uncontrolled system as possible is still present in the controlled system without violating neither the requirements, nor controllability, nor the non-blocking condition.

Finally, we recall the specification of the abstract synthesis algorithm of CA from [13]. This algorithm will be used to synthesise a strategy for the spatial game in the next sections. The synthesis of a controller, an orchestration, and a choreography of CA are all different special cases of this abstract synthesis algorithm, formalised in [13] and implemented in `CATLib` [6] using map reduce style parallel operations of Java Streams. This algorithm is a fix-point computation where at each iteration the set of transitions of the automaton is refined (pruning predicate ϕ_p) and a set of forbidden states R is computed (forbidden predicate ϕ_f). The synthesis is parametric on these two predicates, which provide information on when a transition has to be pruned from the synthesised automaton or a state has to be deemed forbidden. We refer to MSCA as the set of (MS)CA, where the set of states is denoted by Q and the set of transitions by T (with $T^\square$ denoting the set of necessary transitions). For an automaton $\mathcal{A}$, the predicate $Dangling(\mathcal{A})$ contains those states that are not reachable from the initial state or that cannot reach any final state.

Definition 2 (abstract synthesis [13]). *Let $\mathcal{A}$ be an MSCA, $\mathcal{K}_0 = \mathcal{A}$, and $R_0 = Dangling(\mathcal{K}_0)$. Given two predicates $\phi_p, \phi_f : T \times MSCA \times Q \to \mathbb{B}$, let the abstract synthesis function $f_{(\phi_p,\phi_f)} : MSCA \times 2^Q \to MSCA \times 2^Q$ be defined as:*

$$f_{(\phi_p,\phi_f)}(\mathcal{K}_{i-1}, R_{i-1}) = (\mathcal{K}_i, R_i), with$$
$$T_{\mathcal{K}_i} = T_{\mathcal{K}_{i-1}} - \{\, t \in T_{\mathcal{K}_{i-1}} \mid \phi_p(t, \mathcal{K}_{i-1}, R_{i-1}) = true \,\}$$
$$R_i = R_{i-1} \cup \{\, \vec{q} \mid (\vec{q}\to) = t \in T_{\mathcal{A}}^\square, \ \phi_f(t, \mathcal{K}_{i-1}, R_{i-1}) = true \,\} \cup Dangling(\mathcal{K}_i)$$

The abstract controller is defined in Eq. 1 below as the least fixed point (cf. [13, Theorem 5.2]) where, if the initial state belongs to $R_s^{(\phi_p,\phi_f)}$, then the controller is empty; otherwise, it is the automaton with the set of transitions $T_{\mathcal{K}_s^{(\phi_p,\phi_f)}}$ and without states in $R_s^{(\phi_p,\phi_f)}$.

$$(\mathcal{K}_s^{(\phi_p,\phi_f)}, R_s^{(\phi_p,\phi_f)}) = sup(\{\, f_{(\phi_p,\phi_f)}^n(\mathcal{K}_0, R_0) \mid n \in \mathbb{N} \,\}) \tag{1}$$

CATLib. CA and their functionalities are implemented in a software artefact, called Contract Automata Library (`CATLib`), which is under continuous development [7]. This software artefact is a by-product of scientific research on behavioural contracts and implements results that have previously been formally specified in several publications (cf., e.g., [9–11,13,15–20]). CATLib has been designed to be easily extendable to support similar automata-based formalisms. Currently, it also supports synchronous communicating machines [40,51]. CATLib and the other CA tools [8] allow programmers to use CA for developing more reliable applications. In this paper, we further showcase the flexibility of CATLib by using it to synthesise strategies for mobile agents in spatial games. CATLib has been implemented using modern established technologies for building, testing, documenting, and delivering high quality source code. CATLib is tested up to 100% coverage of all lines, branches, and the strength of the tests is measured with mutation testing with top score.

2.2 VoxLogicA, Spatial Model Checking, and Image Analysis

The *Spatial Logic of Closure Spaces* (SLCS) is a modal logical language equipped with a unary 'nearness' modality and two binary operators: 'reaches' and 'is reached'. The language is interpreted on points of a spatial structure, which is, generally speaking, a *Closure Space* (cf. [34] for details). Graphs, digital images, topological spaces, and simplicial complexes are all instances of closure spaces.

Here we concentrate on the interpretation of SLCS on images. In this case, the two reachability modalities collapse and the nearness modality is a derived operator based on the reachability operator, causing a particularly simple syntax.

Definition 3. *Fix a set AP of atomic propositions. The syntax of SLCS is defined by the following grammar (where $p \in AP$):*

$$\phi ::= p \mid \top \mid \neg \phi \mid \phi \wedge \phi \mid \rho\, \phi[\phi]$$

Models of SLCS formulae, for the purpose of this paper, are the pixels of digital images; i.e., each SLCS formula induces a truth value for each point of a given digital image. In order to define the interpretation of formulae, a notion of *path* needs to be established, based on a notion of *neighbourhood* or *connectivity* of pixels. Among infinitely many possible choices, VoxLogicA normally uses the so-called '8-neighbourhood', i.e., each pixel is adjacent to 8 other pixels, namely those that share an edge or a vertex with it. Connectivity transforms the set of pixels of an image in a (symmetric) graph. Graph-theoretical paths are then well defined, and used below.

The interpretation of formulae depends upon a valuation of atomic propositions, assigning to each atomic proposition the set of points on which it holds, and assigning a direct interpretation to the symbols $p \in AP$. The meaning of the truth value $\top$ (true), negation ($\neg$), and conjunction ($\wedge$) is the usual one. A pixel x satisfies $\rho\, \phi_1[\phi_2]$ if there is a path rooted in x, reaching a pixel satisfying ϕ_1, such that all intermediate points, except eventually the extremes, must satisfy ϕ_2. We make use of the derived operator $\phi_1 \rightsquigarrow \phi_2$ which is similar to $\rho\, \phi_2[\phi_1]$, but the extremes are also required to satisfy ϕ_1. The *near* derived operator $\mathcal{N}\phi \triangleq \rho\, \phi[\neg\top]$ is true at point x if and only if there is a pixel adjacent to x where ϕ holds.

From now on we use the tool's syntax, which uses tt, &, |, !, ˜>, and N for *true*, conjunction, disjunction, negation, ⤳, and $\mathcal{N}$, respectively, permits macro abbreviations of the form let identifier = expression, function definition of the form let identifier(argument1,...,argumentN) = expression, and other constructs not needed for the scope of this paper. On images, atomic propositions can be expressions predicating over the colour components of the pixels. For instance, in our example specification (cf. Fig. 5), to characterise the pixels composing a door as the blue pixels (note that 255 is the maximum value since we are using 8-bit images), given that img denotes an image, we use:

```
let r = red(img)
let g = green(img)
let b = blue(img)
...
let door = (r =. 0) & (b =. 255) & (g =. 0)
```

Also, the tool permits global formulae that assign a truth value to models, not just pixels in isolation. These can be based on the volume(phi) primitive, that computes the number of pixels satisfying the formula phi. For instance, existential and universal quantification are defined as follows:

```
let exists(p) = volume(p) .>. 0
let forall(p) = volume(p) .=. volume(tt)
```

The type system of VoxLogicA is very simple, and comprises *numbers, Boolean values, images of numbers* (single-channel images, sometimes called *grayscale*), *images of Boolean values*, very often called *binary images* or *masks*, and ordinary *multi-channel images*. Operators are strongly typed with no type overloading. Therefore, for instance, the pixel-by-pixel *and* of two Boolean-valued images is a different operator with respect to the conjunction of two Boolean values, and it also differs from the conjunction of the Boolean value of each pixel of an image with a Boolean (scalar) constant. With some exceptions, the naming convention of operators reflects their type, having a dot on the side of the 'scalar' value (Boolean or number) and no dot on the side of the image, so for instance .&. is Boolean *and*, whereas & is pixel-by-pixel *and* of two images. With respect to Fig. 5, for instance, we have that base and img are multi-channel images, with the operators red, green, blue, extracting number-valued images from them. The definition of mrRed (a red area) contains the =. operator taking a number-valued image on the left, and a number on the right (hence the dot on the right side). In the definition of the property forbidden1, one can find an example of the use of the operator .|. which takes as arguments two Boolean values.

3   Tool Methodology

In this section, we discuss the tool methodology used to chain CATLib and VoxLogicA in order to perform strategy synthesis of spatial properties. Later, in Sect. 5, we will detail scalable techniques that can be adopted to improve the presented methodology. The diagram in Fig. 1 depicts the workflow and the various activities in which the whole process is decomposed.

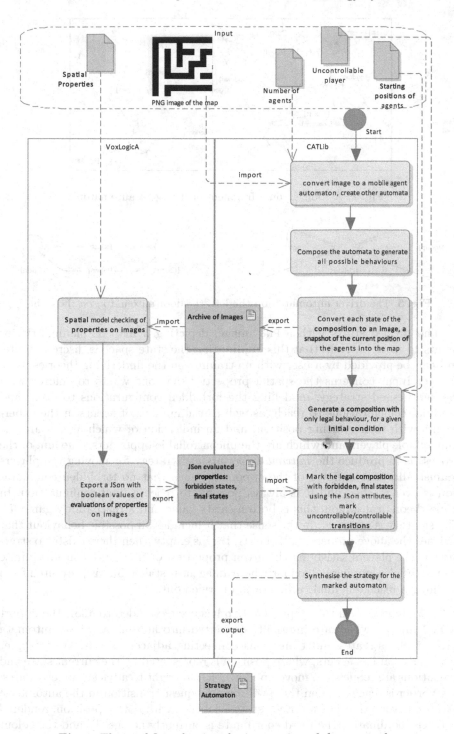

Fig. 1. The workflow showing the integration of the two tools

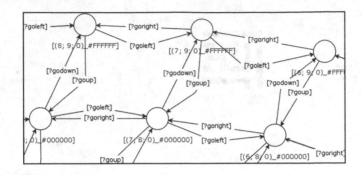

Fig. 2. A zoom-in on a fragment of the agent automaton

Fig. 3. The driver automaton on the left, the door automaton on the right

The process starts with a PNG image, depicting a map or planimetry, for agents to move in. Note that this implies that the state space is discrete, finite, and can be provided by a user with no training on the underlying theories used. Further input concerns the spatial properties that one wants to enforce with the synthesised strategy, modelling the forbidden configurations to avoid and the final configurations to reach, as well as the number of agents in the experiments with their starting position, and an indication of which agents are the controllable players and which are the uncontrollable opponents. The aim of the process is to produce the *maximally permissive* strategy for moving the players against all possible moves of the opponents, such that no forbidden configuration is ever reached and it is always possible to reach a final configuration. In game-theoretical jargon, this is both a safety game and a reachability game [5]. The strategy is maximal, in the sense that it includes all possible behaviour that satisfies the above properties. If the strategy is empty, then there exists no strategy for the players satisfying the given properties. CATLib only considers finite traces: infinite looping behaviour where an agent is stalled and is prevented from reaching a reachable final configuration is ruled out.

CATLib Activities. In this paper, CATLib has been extended to allow the import of PNG images, which are internally converted into automata. These automata have pixels as states and transitions connecting adjacent pixels. We interpret these automata as agents, whose position is represented by the current state and transitions are requests to move up, down, left, or right to adjacent pixels/states. If a border is reached, then there will be no request transition in the automaton to move beyond that border. Each state is labelled with both a position, rendered in three coordinates (the third coordinate is currently not used), and the colour of the pixel. Figure 2 depicts a small portion of an agent automaton.

Fig. 4. The state [(10; 10; 0)_#FFFFFF, (5; 7; 0)_#FFFFFF, Driver, Close] of the composition of two agents, a driver, and a door. The door is in position (2; 7) and is closed. The first agent is depicted red, the second is green, and the door is blue. The attributes of the position of the two agents are both #FFFFFF, which is the hexadecimal value for the colour white, i.e., both agents are placed on a white cell of the map. (Color figure online)

A driver automaton is used to command an agent to move in a specific direction. It is depicted in Fig. 3 (left). The driver can impose some constraints (e.g., never go down). Currently, the driver offers to move in each possible direction. The last automaton that is used models a door, which is initially closed, and which can be opened and closed repeatedly. It is depicted in Fig. 3 (right).

The first activity of CATLib thus consists of importing and creating the above automata. There can be several instances of agents and doors or different maps according to the parameters of the experiments to perform.

The second activity consists of composing these automata to generate all possible reachable configurations. As stated in Sect. 2, the composition has unicast synchronisations between offers and requests of agents (called matches), and labels that are only single moves of an agent performing an offer. Agents who perform requests can move only when paired with a corresponding offer. This type of synchronised behaviour is called agreement: all requests must be matched.

In such composition, no restriction is imposed on the agents: they are free to move over walls and doors, and even over other agents. Depending on the initial conditions, some of these configurations could result to be not useful. However, this allows to call the spatial model checker once on all possible configurations. By changing starting conditions in different experiments it is not necessary to invoke again the spatial model checker, since all possible configurations that can be generated have already been analysed offline by the spatial model checker. In the composed automaton, each state is a tuple of states of all agents (included the door and the driver). Each state can be represented as an image, a snapshot of the current configuration. For example, Fig. 4 depicts a state rendered as an image. The image is generated by colouring the starting PNG image with a red, green, and blue pixel to indicate where, respectively, the first agent, the second agent and the door are located. The door is only coloured when it is closed.

The third activity consists of generating all images for all states of the composition. These images are then passed to VoxLogicA (whose activities will be described below) to evaluate for all properties whether or not they are satisfied.

The fourth activity of CATLib consists of generating a composition with only legal behaviour. Indeed, to reduce the size of the state space, the composition of CATLib allows to avoid generating portions of the state space that are known to violate some property. In case of controllable 'bad' transitions, these will not be generated since they will be pruned by the synthesis. In case of uncontrollable 'bad' transitions, these will be generated (since they cannot be pruned) but their target state will not be visited (the synthesis will try to make these 'bad' states unreachable). Thus, once some agent is rendered as uncontrollable (by changing its transitions to uncontrollable), it cannot be stopped from reaching an illegal configuration. It follows that illegal configurations must be removed before deciding which agents are uncontrollable and which are controllable. In the experiments described in Sect. 4, the illegal moves are those where an agent is placed on top of a wall (i.e., its state has colour #000000), on top of another agent (i.e., in a state of the composition, two agents have the same coordinates), or on top of a closed door (i.e., in a state of the composition, one agent has the same coordinates as the door and the door is closed). Since these are simple invariant properties (it only suffices to check the labels of states), they can be directly checked in CATLib. VoxLogicA is used to evaluate more complex spatial properties (cf. Fig. 5). The aforementioned illegal moves are also specified in VoxLogicA under the property wrong in Fig. 5 below.

In this step it is also decided what are the initial positions of the agents, i.e., the initial state where the state-space generation starts. Depending on the given initial conditions, it is possible that some legal configuration previously generated and passed to VoxLogicA will not be generated.

Once the state space for the chosen initial conditions and legal moves is generated, it must be marked with the states that are forbidden and those that are final. This is the fifth activity of CATLib. Also, it must be decided which agents are controllable and which are not. This information is provided in part as input parameters of the experiments and in part with a JSon file computed with VoxLogicA, where each state has as set of Boolean attributes, one for each evaluated spatial property.

After all states and transitions have been marked with the required information, the strategy synthesis is performed as the final, sixth activity of CATLib. The algorithm computes the maximal behaviour of the composition (in agreement) such that it is always possible to reach a final configuration and forbidden configurations are never traversed. If the strategy is non-empty, this will provide information on the behaviour to be followed by the controllable agents to ensure that a final configuration is always reached without passing through forbidden configurations, against all possible moves of uncontrollable components.

VoxLogicA Activities. The first activity of VoxLogicA is the evaluation of the formulae representing final and forbidden states. This is done via an auxiliary python script, that takes as input the logical specification, described by a python function, whose body is constituted by an "f-string", that is a string, where python expressions enclosed in curly braces are evaluated in place, the base image (i.e., the map or planimetry where agents move), and the directory containing all the reachable configurations, encoded as images. The python script then iterates the specification, evaluating expressions where appropriate. The parameters of the python function describing the specification are the base image filename and the currently evaluated configuration, such that the specification can only

Table 1. Summary of the two experiments

	First experiment	Second experiment
Controllable	Red and green agents	Door
Uncontrollable	Door	Red and green agents
Initial state	Green agent in front of red agent	Green agent in front of red agent
Final states	Both the red and the green agent reached the exit	The door separates the green agent on the right from the red agent on the left
Forbidden states	The door separates the green agent on the right from the red agent on the left, or the red and green agents are not near each other	Both the red and the green agent reached the exit
Strategy	The red and green agents switch position before traversing the door	Empty

evaluate properties of a single configuration, using the base image to identify relevant regions (like walls).

The second activity of VoxLogicA collects all the properties that have been computed in the first activity, locally for each state, and turns them into a single source of information, in the form of a JSon file that contains a record for each state, reporting on all the properties that have been described in the specification. In order to do so, a special output mode of VoxLogicA is used, where the tool outputs a single JSon record of all the user-specified properties that have been printed or saved in the specification.

The presented methodology is a first step towards connecting CATLib and VoxLogicA. While correct, its efficiency could be improved, especially the input/output overhead. We provide details on future enhancements in Sect. 5.

4 Experiments

In this section, we describe the experiments that have been performed following the process described in the previous section. We performed two experiments, starting from the same initial conditions but with opposite controllable/uncontrollable agents and forbidden/final states. The setup and outcome of the experiments are reported in Table 1. The repository containing all data, sources, and information on how to reproduce the experiments is publicly available [14].

The PNG map image used as planimetry is a 10×10 pixels image that weighs 188 bytes. It is depicted in Figs. 1 and 4 (without coloured pixels). Since this is a preliminary exploratory study, we focus on a simple image, leaving more complex scenarios for future work.

The setup for the experiments is of two duplicate mobile agents, one door agent and one driver agent. The door agent is placed in position (2; 7) (cf. Fig. 4). Initially, the red agent is in the top left corner of the white corridor (position (1; 1)), whereas the green agent is just below the red agent (position (2; 1)) and the door is closed. The initial state is depicted in Fig. 6 (left).

The illegal moves were described in the previous section. We recall that in a legal composition, no agent moves over a wall, a closed door, or another agent.

The invocation of the composition function of CATLib is reported below. The composition is instantiated with the list of operands, namely the two agents, the driver, and the door. The second argument is the pruning predicate: if a generated transition satisfies the pruning predicate it will be pruned and not further explored. When applying the composition it is possible to specify a bound on the maximum depth of the generated automaton. In this case, the bound is set to the maximum Integer value. The two agents are instantiated with maze_tr and maze2_tr being their set of transitions, which only differ in the initial state. The property of agreement is passed as a lambda expression: transitions with a request label will be pruned. Similarly, this condition is put in disjunction with a condition checking whether the target state of the generated transition is 'bad' (i.e., an illegal transition), in which case the transition is pruned.

```
MSCACompositionFunction<String> cf = new MSCACompositionFunction<>
  (List.of(new Automaton<>(maze_tr),new Automaton<>(maze2_tr),driver,door),
   t->t.getLabel().isRequest() || badState.test(t.getTarget())));
Automaton<String, Action, State<String>, ModalTransition<String,Action,State<String>,CALabel>>
  comp = cf.apply(Integer.MAX_VALUE);
```

In the first experiment, the final and forbidden states are set according to the following definitions. Consider the specification given in Fig. 5 (cf. Sect. 2 for an introduction on the operators used therein). The final states are set to be those on the right hand side of the image passing through the corridor where the door is located (property final), and are depicted in Fig. 6 (middle). Concerning the forbidden states, we experiment with two different spatial properties to identify them. The first property (property forbidden1) is a disjunction of two sub-properties. It identifies as forbidden those states that are either illegal (property wrong) or in which the two agents are in two areas separated by the closed door, and the green agent is on the right side of the door, i.e., it can reach an escape (a final state), whereas the red agent cannot because it is blocked by the door (property greenFlees). In fact, Fig. 4 represents one of these forbidden states. The second property (property forbidden2) identifies as forbidden those states that are forbidden according to forbidden1 or in which the two agents are not close to each other, i.e., they are distant more than two pixels (negation of the property nearBy).

Finally, in this first experiment we interpret the door as uncontrollable, whereas the red and green agents are controllable. Basically, this is a scenario in which the two players are playing against an uncontrollable door. Below we list the code used to invoke the synthesis operation of CATLib. The instantiation of the operation takes as argument the property to enforce, agreement in this case, and the automaton where the synthesis is applied, called marked in this case.

```
Automaton<String, Action, State<String>, ModalTransition<String,Action,State<String>,CALabel>>
  strategy = new MpcSynthesisOperator<String>(new Agreement()).apply(marked);
```

```
load base ="{baseimage}"

load img = "{datadir}/{image}"
let r = red(img)
let g = green(img)
let b = blue(img)
let rb = red(base)
let gb = green(base)
let bb = blue(base)

let exists(p) = volume(p) .>. 0
let forall(p) = volume(p) .=. volume(tt)
let forallin(x,p) = forall( (!x) | p)

let door = (r =. 0) & (b =. 255) & (g =. 0)
let floorNoDoor = (rb =. 255) & (bb =. 255) & (gb =. 255)
let floor = floorNoDoor & (!door)
let wall = !floor

let mrRed = (r =. 255) & (b =. 0) & (g =. 0)
let mrGreen = (r =. 0) & (b =. 0) & (g =. 255)

let mrX = mrRed | mrGreen

let initial1 = exists(mrRed & ((x =. 1) & (y =. 1)))
        .&. exists(mrGreen & ((x =. 1) & (y =. 2)))
let initial2 = exists(mrRed & ((x =. 6) & (y =. 3)))
        .&. exists(mrGreen & ((x =. 1) & (y =. 4)))
let wrong = exists(mrX & wall) .|. (!. (exists(mrRed) .&. exists(mrGreen)))
let exit = (x =. 9) & (y >. 2) & (y <. 9)
let pathToExit = (floor ~> exit)
let canExit(mr) = forallin(mr,pathToExit)
let sameRoom = forallin(mrGreen,(mrGreen|floor) ~> mrRed)

let greenFlees = (!.wrong) .&. canExit(mrGreen) .&. (!.(canExit(mrRed)))
let nearby = exists(mrRed & (N N mrGreen))

let forbidden1 = greenFlees .|. wrong
let forbidden2 = forbidden1 .|. (!. nearby)

let final = exists(mrRed & exit) .&. exists(mrGreen & exit)
```

Fig. 5. VoxLogicA specification of the properties used in the experiments

The most permissive synthesised strategy consists of 684 states and 2635 transitions (recall that in each transition, only one of the agents is moving). The length of a shortest path from the initial state to a final state is composed of 33 transitions to be executed. In the initial state (Fig. 6 (left)), the green agent is in front of the red agent on the path to the exit. However, in the strategy the green agent cannot traverse the open door before the red agent. Indeed, in this case, since the door is uncontrollable, it is not possible to prevent the door from closing and separating the red agent (blocked by the door) from the green agent (who can reach the exit). This is indeed a forbidden state that the strategy must avoid. In the strategy, to overcome this problem, the two agents switch position before crossing the door. Figure 6 (right) depicts the moment where the red agent is crossing the door right after exchanging position with the green agent who is still in the corridor. Indeed, in the shortest path they switch position near the door. Note that no forbidden state occurs if the door closes after only the red

Fig. 6. On the left the initial configuration of both experiments. In the middle the final states of the first experiment (marked in violet). On the right a configuration traversed by one of the shortest paths of the first experiment's strategy, in which the red agent is crossing the door before the green agent does, thus avoiding forbidden configurations. (Color figure online)

agent has traversed it. Indeed, in this scenario the green agent is prevented from reaching an exit because it is blocked by the door. Hence, after the red agent has traversed the door, the strategy guides the green agent to safely cross the door such that they can both reach a final state.

To confirm the first experiment, we performed a second experiment by inverting the setup of the first experiment. In this second experiment, the door is controllable, whereas the green and red agents are both uncontrollable. The final states are those in which the door separates the green agent (on the right side of the door) from the red agent (on the left side of the door). These are basically the forbidden states of the first experiment. Similarly, the forbidden states in the second experiment are those states in which both the green and the red agent have reached the exit, i.e., the final states of the first experiment. The initial configuration is the same as in the first experiment. As expected, in this dual case the returned strategy is empty. Indeed, if this were not the case, then we would have a contradiction because the green and red agents have a strategy to reach the exit without being separated by the door with the red agent blocked, for every possible finite behaviour of the door.

There is no strategy for the door to reach a final configuration mainly because the door cannot ensure that the uncontrollable green agent traverses the door first. Moreover, the door cannot prevent the agents from reaching the exit by always remaining closed since (unless only the green agent has traversed the door) a final state would not be reachable.

Performance of Experiments. We conclude this section by reporting the time needed for computing various phases of the experiments and measures of the computed automata. The experiments were performed on a machine with Intel(R) Core(TM) i9-9900K CPU @ 3.60 GHz equipped with 32 GB of RAM. The time performance is reported in Table 2. We note that the synthesis is more expensive (computationally) than the composition. Indeed, as showed in Sect. 2, each iteration of the synthesis requires to compute the set of dangling states, which requires a forward and backward visit of the automaton. The marking is the most computationally expensive phase of CATLib because each marking of either a final or a forbidden state requires to search whether that state has a final or forbidden attribute in the JSon file provide by VoxLogicA.

Table 2. Time needed to perform the experiments' phases

Phase	Both experiments	
Computing the unconstrained composition	26643 ms	
Generating images	7910 ms	
Running VoxLogicA	6140 s	
Computing the legal composition	2487 ms	
	First experiment	Second experiment
Marking the composition with VoxLogicA properties and controllability	108058 ms	118291 ms
Synthesis	2942 ms	33472 ms

Table 3. Number of states, transitions and size of the automata used in the experiments

Automaton	#States	#Transitions	Size (bytes)
Agent	100	360	18723
Unconstrained composition	20000	164800	21858146
Legal composition	3200	15176	2004736
Marked composition (first experiment)	3202	17665	2339874
Marked composition (second experiment)	3202	15552	2066368
Strategy (first experiment)	684	2635	347652

Table 3 reports the number of states, the number of transitions, and the size (in bytes) of the various automata. As expected, the number of states of the agent automaton is exactly the number of pixels of the image. The largest automaton is the one with the unconstrained composition, whose number of states is the product of the states of the two agent automata and the door automaton ($100 \times 100 \times 2$). We note that the agent automaton (encoding an image as automaton) requires more space than the PNG image (188 bytes of the image against 18723 bytes of the corresponding automaton). Moreover, the legal states given the initial conditions are only a small fraction (16%) of the total number of states passed to VoxLogicA. Finally, the marked compositions for the two experiments have two additional states with respect to the legal composition, which are the added initial and final states. The number of transitions of these two automata differs according to the number of states marked as final, to which a transition to the newly added final state is added, and the number of forbidden states, to which a bad transition is added as a self-loop.

The evaluation of the given VoxLogicA specification (also reported in Table 2) takes about 530 ms per image, of which only 45 ms are spent on the actual computation; the rest is spent in file input/output, parsing the specification, and recovering the results from python. Since all the images are processed sequentially, the total analysis time for the 11562 images that are generated is therefore a bit less than two hours, which dominates the total computation time for the experiment. As discussed in Sect. 3, much of the overhead could be eliminated (cf. the Conclusion for more information).

5   Conclusion

We have discussed an integration of the tools CATLib and VoxLogicA to perform strategy synthesis on images processed with spatial model checking. Our contribution constitutes the first application of CATLib and VoxLogicA to build a framework for modelling and solving multi-agents mobile problems. The result clearly demonstrates the feasibility of a full-fledged tool chain built from CATLib and VoxLogicA and shows an original approach to combine strategy synthesis with spatial model checking. The experiments performed in this paper are still preliminary and not much thought has been given to the efficiency of the encodings, the computations, and the tool integration. Hence, this paper offers a lot of interesting opportunities for future work.

Future Work. The proof-of-concept example in this paper uses a 10×10 pixels map. Efficiency and scalability are two key issues to address in the future. Several possible scalable solutions are viable and some ideas are provided next.

In the current approach, many states are used to move agents up and down the ends of corridors (each agent has a state for each pixel of the image). However, fewer states could actually be sufficient. Relaxing the representation of an image to one where each state is a zone of the image (e.g., a corridor) rather than a pixel would drastically reduce the state space.

Another scalable solution could be to decompose a large image into smaller images. For example, the final states of the first experiment in Sect. 4 could be entering points to a new portion of the map. Several small maps could be linked together by ports for entering and exiting.

Yet another scalable solution could be to drop the requirement of a strategy to be most permissive in favour of some objective function to optimise. A near-optimal solution could be synthesised as a trace using statistics over runs, in the style of [46].

Currently, each new parameter setup requires to be implemented manually. Similarly, the various CATLib and VoxLogicA activities depicted in Fig. 1 need to be invoked manually. Future research is needed to completely automatise our proposal, providing a tool that takes as input the setup of an experiment, including the map, and outputs the synthesised strategy, if any, in a push-button way. This could result in an optimisation of the methodology presented in Sect. 3. Indeed, as shown in Sect. 4 and Table 2, currently a bottleneck is present in the processing of the images and JSon logs, mainly due to the offline processing of all images by VoxLogicA, for all possible initial conditions of the experiments. For example, the actual time spent on computing the evaluation of properties using VoxLogicA is a small fraction of its total evaluation time. The rest is spent in parsing, loading, and saving, which is repeated for each image and could mostly be eliminated. The number of images and total size of the logs could be reduced drastically by making CATLib and VoxLogicA interact online at each new experiment. In this way, there would be no need for CATLib to initially generate all possible states. Only those states that are actually reachable given the setup of the experiment at hand could be generated. This would result in far fewer images to be processed by VoxLogicA and a smaller JSon log to be parsed by CATLib in return. Concerning VoxLogicA, the input/output overhead could also be eliminated by loading several files at once in parallel, parsing the specification only once, and exploiting the recent GPU implementation [26].

Acknowledgments. Research partially funded by the MIUR PRIN 2017FTXR7S project IT MaTTerS (Methods and Tools for Trustworthy Smart Systems).

CRediT Author Statement. D. Basile: Conceptualization, Software, Formal Analysis, Investigation, Writing - Original Draft, Writing - Review & Editing. **M.H. ter Beek:** Writing - Original Draft, Writing - Review & Editing, Supervision, Funding Acquisition, Project Administration. **V. Ciancia:** Conceptualization, Software, Formal Analysis, Investigation, Writing - Original Draft, Writing - Review & Editing.

References

1. Alsalehi, S., Mehdipour, N., Bartocci, E., Belta, C.: Neural network-based control for multi-agent systems from spatio-temporal specifications. In: Proceedings of the 60th IEEE Conference on Decision and Control (CDC 2021), pp. 5110–5115. IEEE (2021). https://doi.org/10.1109/CDC45484.2021.9682921
2. Alur, R., Moarref, S., Topcu, U.: Compositional synthesis of reactive controllers for multi-agent systems. In: Chaudhuri, S., Farzan, A. (eds.) CAV 2016, Part II. LNCS, vol. 9780, pp. 251–269. Springer, Cham (2016). https://doi.org/10.1007/978-3-319-41540-6_14
3. Asarin, E., Maler, O., Pnueli, A., Sifakis, J.: Controller synthesis for timed automata. IFAC Proc. **31**(18), 447–452 (1998). https://doi.org/10.1016/S1474-6670(17)42032-5
4. Banci Buonamici, F., Belmonte, G., Ciancia, V., Latella, D., Massink, M.: Spatial logics and model checking for medical imaging. Int. J. Softw. Tools Technol. Transf. **22**(2), 195–217 (2019). https://doi.org/10.1007/s10009-019-00511-9
5. Basile, D., ter Beek, M.H., Legay, A.: Timed service contract automata. Innovations Syst. Soft. Eng. **16**(2), 199–214 (2019). https://doi.org/10.1007/s11334-019-00353-3
6. Basile, D., ter Beek, M.H.: A clean and efficient implementation of choreography synthesis for behavioural contracts. In: Damiani, F., Dardha, O. (eds.) COORDINATION 2021. LNCS, vol. 12717, pp. 225–238. Springer, Cham (2021). https://doi.org/10.1007/978-3-030-78142-2_14
7. Basile, D., ter Beek, M.H.: Contract automata library. Sci. Comput. Program. **221** (2022). https://doi.org/10.1016/j.scico.2022.102841, https://github.com/contractautomataproject/ContractAutomataLib
8. Basile, D., ter Beek, M.H.: A runtime environment for contract automata. arXiv:2203.14122 (2022). https://doi.org/10.48550/arXiv.2203.14122

9. Basile, D., et al.: Controller synthesis of service contracts with variability. Sci. Comput. Program. **187** (2020). https://doi.org/10.1016/j.scico.2019.102344

10. Basile, D., ter Beek, M.H., Di Giandomenico, F., Gnesi, S.: Orchestration of dynamic service product lines with featured modal contract automata. In: Proceedings of the 21st International Systems and Software Product Line Conference (SPLC 2017), vol. 2, pp. 117–122. ACM (2017). https://doi.org/10.1145/3109729.3109741

11. Basile, D., ter Beek, M.H., Gnesi, S.: Modelling and analysis with featured modal contract automata. In: Proceedings of the 22nd International Systems and Software Product Line Conference (SPLC 2018), vol. 2, pp. 11–16. ACM (2018). https://doi.org/10.1145/3236405.3236408

12. Basile, D., ter Beek, M.H., Legay, A.: Strategy synthesis for autonomous driving in a moving block railway system with UPPAAL STRATEGO. In: Gotsman, A., Sokolova, A. (eds.) FORTE 2020. LNCS, vol. 12136, pp. 3–21. Springer, Cham (2020). https://doi.org/10.1007/978-3-030-50086-3_1

13. Basile, D., ter Beek, M.H., Pugliese, R.: Synthesis of orchestrations and choreographies: bridging the gap between supervisory control and coordination of services. Log. Methods Comput. Sci. **16**(2) (2020). https://doi.org/10.23638/LMCS-16(2:9)2020

14. Basile, D., Ciancia, V.: Repository for reproducing the experiments. https://github.com/contractautomataproject/CATLib_PngConverter

15. Basile, D., Degano, P., Ferrari, G.L.: Automata for specifying and orchestrating service contracts. Log. Methods Comput. Sci. **12**(4) (2016). https://doi.org/10.2168/LMCS-12(4:6)2016

16. Basile, D., Degano, P., Ferrari, G.-L., Tuosto, E.: Playing with our CAT and communication-centric applications. In: Albert, E., Lanese, I. (eds.) FORTE 2016. LNCS, vol. 9688, pp. 62–73. Springer, Cham (2016). https://doi.org/10.1007/978-3-319-39570-8_5

17. Basile, D., Degano, P., Ferrari, G.L., Tuosto, E.: Relating two automata-based models of orchestration and choreography. J. Log. Algebr. Methods Program. **85**(3), 425–446 (2016). https://doi.org/10.1016/j.jlamp.2015.09.011

18. Basile, D., Di Giandomenico, F., Gnesi, S.: Enhancing models correctness through formal verification: a case study from the railway domain. In: Pires, L.F., Hammoudi, S., Selic, B. (eds.) Proceedings of the 5th International Conference on Model-Driven Engineering and Software Development (MODELSWARD 2017), pp. 679–686. SciTePress (2017). https://doi.org/10.5220/0006291106790686

19. Basile, D., Di Giandomenico, F., Gnesi, S.: FMCAT: supporting dynamic service-based product lines. In: Proceedings of the 21st International Systems and Software Product Line Conference (SPLC 2017), vol. 2, pp. 3–8. ACM (2017). https://doi.org/10.1145/3109729.3109760

20. Basile, D., Di Giandomenico, F., Gnesi, S., Degano, P., Ferrari, G.L.: Specifying variability in service contracts. In: Proceedings of the 11th International Workshop on Variability Modelling of Software-intensive Systems (VaMoS 2017), pp. 20–27. ACM (2017). https://doi.org/10.1145/3023956.3023965

21. ter Beek, M.H., Reniers, M.A., de Vink, E.P.: Supervisory controller synthesis for product lines using CIF 3. In: Margaria, T., Steffen, B. (eds.) ISoLA 2016. LNCS, vol. 9952, pp. 856–873. Springer, Cham (2016). https://doi.org/10.1007/978-3-319-47166-2_59

22. Belmonte, G., Broccia, G., Vincenzo, C., Latella, D., Massink, M.: Feasibility of spatial model checking for nevus segmentation. In: Proceedings of the 9th International Conference on Formal Methods in Software Engineering (FormaliSE 2021), pp. 1–12. IEEE (2021). https://doi.org/10.1109/FormaliSE52586.2021.00007

23. Belmonte, G., Ciancia, V., Latella, D., Massink, M.: Innovating medical image analysis via spatial logics. In: ter Beek, M.H., Fantechi, A., Semini, L. (eds.) From Software Engineering to Formal Methods and Tools, and Back. LNCS, vol. 11865, pp. 85–109. Springer, Cham (2019). https://doi.org/10.1007/978-3-030-30985-5_7

24. Belmonte, G., Ciancia, V., Latella, D., Massink, M.: VoxLogicA: a spatial model checker for declarative image analysis. In: Vojnar, T., Zhang, L. (eds.) TACAS 2019. LNCS, vol. 11427, pp. 281–298. Springer, Cham (2019). https://doi.org/10.1007/978-3-030-17462-0_16

25. Bezhanishvili, N., Ciancia, V., Gabelaia, D., Grilletti, G., Latella, D., Massink, M.: Geometric model checking of continuous space (2021). https://doi.org/10.48550/arXiv.2105.06194

26. Bussi, L., Ciancia, V., Gadducci, F.: Towards a spatial model checker on GPU. In: Peters, K., Willemse, T.A.C. (eds.) FORTE 2021. LNCS, vol. 12719, pp. 188–196. Springer, Cham (2021). https://doi.org/10.1007/978-3-030-78089-0_12

27. Calude, C.S., Jain, S., Khoussainov, B., Li, W., Stephan, F.: Deciding parity games in quasipolynomial time. In: Proceedings of the 49th Annual ACM SIGACT Symposium on Theory of Computing (STOC 2017), pp. 252–263. ACM (2017). https://doi.org/10.1145/3055399.3055409

28. Camacho, A., Bienvenu, M., McIlraith, S.A.: Towards a unified view of AI planning and reactive synthesis. In: Proceedings of the 29th International Conference on Automated Planning and Scheduling (ICAPS 2018), pp. 58–67. AAAI (2019). https://ojs.aaai.org/index.php/ICAPS/article/view/3460

29. Cassandras, C.G., Lafortune, S.: Introduction to Discrete Event Systems. Springer, Heidelberg (2006). https://doi.org/10.1007/978-0-387-68612-7

30. Castelnovo, D., Miculan, M.: Closure hyperdoctrines. In: Gadducci, F., Silva, A. (eds.) Proceedings of the 9th Conference on Algebra and Coalgebra in Computer Science (CALCO 2021). LIPIcs, vol. 211, pp. 12:1–12:21 (2021). https://doi.org/10.4230/LIPIcs.CALCO.2021.12

31. Cauchi, N., Abate, A.: StocHy: automated verification and synthesis of stochastic processes. In: Vojnar, T., Zhang, L. (eds.) TACAS 2019. LNCS, vol. 11428, pp. 247–264. Springer, Cham (2019). https://doi.org/10.1007/978-3-030-17465-1_14

32. Češka, M., Pilař, P., Paoletti, N., Brim, L., Kwiatkowska, M.: PRISM-PSY: precise GPU-accelerated parameter synthesis for stochastic systems. In: Chechik, M., Raskin, J.-F. (eds.) TACAS 2016. LNCS, vol. 9636, pp. 367–384. Springer, Heidelberg (2016). https://doi.org/10.1007/978-3-662-49674-9_21

33. Cheng, C.-H., Lee, E.A., Ruess, H.: autoCode4: structural controller synthesis. In: Legay, A., Margaria, T. (eds.) TACAS 2017. LNCS, vol. 10205, pp. 398–404. Springer, Heidelberg (2017). https://doi.org/10.1007/978-3-662-54577-5_23

34. Ciancia, V., Latella, D., Loreti, M., Massink, M.: Model checking spatial logics for closure spaces. Log. Methods Comput. Sci. **12**(4) (2016). https://doi.org/10.2168/LMCS-12(4:2)2016

35. Ciancia, V., Latella, D., Massink, M., Paškauskas, R., Vandin, A.: A tool-chain for statistical spatio-temporal model checking of bike sharing systems. In: Margaria, T., Steffen, B. (eds.) ISoLA 2016. LNCS, vol. 9952, pp. 657–673. Springer, Cham (2016). https://doi.org/10.1007/978-3-319-47166-2_46

36. Ciancia, V., Belmonte, G., Latella, D., Massink, M.: A hands-on introduction to spatial model checking using VoxLogicA. In: Laarman, A., Sokolova, A. (eds.) SPIN 2021. LNCS, vol. 12864, pp. 22–41. Springer, Cham (2021). https://doi.org/10.1007/978-3-030-84629-9_2

37. Ciancia, V., Gilmore, S., Grilletti, G., Latella, D., Loreti, M., Massink, M.: Spatio-temporal model checking of vehicular movement in public transport systems. Int. J. Softw. Tools Technol. Transf. **20**(3), 289–311 (2018). https://doi.org/10.1007/s10009-018-0483-8

38. Ciancia, V., Latella, D., Massink, M., Paškauskas, R.: Exploring spatio-temporal properties of bike-sharing systems. In: Proceedings of the Workshops at the 9th IEEE International Conference on Self-adaptive and Self-organizing Systems (SASO 2015), pp. 74–79. IEEE (2015). https://doi.org/10.1109/SASOW.2015.17

39. David, A., Jensen, P.G., Larsen, K.G., Mikučionis, M., Taankvist, J.H.: UPPAAL STRATEGO. In: Baier, C., Tinelli, C. (eds.) TACAS 2015. LNCS, vol. 9035, pp. 206–211. Springer, Heidelberg (2015). https://doi.org/10.1007/978-3-662-46681-0_16

40. Deniélou, P.-M., Yoshida, N.: Multiparty session types meet communicating automata. In: Seidl, H. (ed.) ESOP 2012. LNCS, vol. 7211, pp. 194–213. Springer, Heidelberg (2012). https://doi.org/10.1007/978-3-642-28869-2_10

41. Ehlers, R., Lafortune, S., Tripakis, S., Vardi, M.Y.: Supervisory control and reactive synthesis: a comparative introduction. Discrete Event Dyn. Syst. **27**(2), 209–260 (2016). https://doi.org/10.1007/s10626-015-0223-0

42. Fan, C., Miller, K., Mitra, S.: Fast and guaranteed safe controller synthesis for nonlinear vehicle models. In: Lahiri, S.K., Wang, C. (eds.) CAV 2020, Part I. LNCS, vol. 12224, pp. 629–652. Springer, Cham (2020). https://doi.org/10.1007/978-3-030-53288-8_31

43. Farhat, H.: Web service composition via supervisory control theory. IEEE Access **6**, 59779–59789 (2018). https://doi.org/10.1109/ACCESS.2018.2874564

44. Felli, P., Yadav, N., Sardina, S.: Supervisory control for behavior composition. IEEE Trans. Autom. Control **62**(2), 986–991 (2017). https://doi.org/10.1109/TAC.2016.2570748

45. Forschelen, S.T.J., van de Mortel-Fronczak, J.M., Su, R., Rooda, J.E.: Application of supervisory control theory to theme park vehicles. Discrete Event Dyn. Syst. **22**(4), 511–540 (2012). https://doi.org/10.1007/s10626-012-0130-6

46. Gu, R., Jensen, P.G., Poulsen, D.B., Seceleanu, C., Enoiu, E., Lundqvist, K.: Verifiable strategy synthesis for multiple autonomous agents: a scalable approach. Int. J. Softw. Tools Technol. Transf. **24**(3), 395–414 (2022). https://doi.org/10.1007/s10009-022-00657-z

47. Guo, M., Dimarogonas, D.V.: Multi-agent plan reconfiguration under local LTL specifications. Int. J. Robot. Res. **34**(2), 218–235 (2015). https://doi.org/10.1177/0278364914546174

48. Haghighi, I., Jones, A., Kong, Z., Bartocci, E., Grosu, R., Belta, C.: SpaTeL: a novel spatial-temporal logic and its applications to networked systems. In: Proceedings of the 18th International Conference on Hybrid Systems: Computation and Control (HSCC 2015), pp. 189–198. ACM (2015). https://doi.org/10.1145/2728606.2728633

49. Haghighi, I., Sadraddini, S., Belta, C.: Robotic swarm control from spatio-temporal specifications. In: Proceedings of the 55th IEEE Conference on Decision and Control (CDC 2016), pp. 5708–5713. IEEE (2016). https://doi.org/10.1109/CDC.2016.7799146

50. Kwiatkowska, M., Norman, G., Parker, D., Santos, G.: PRISM-games 3.0: stochastic game verification with concurrency, equilibria and time. In: Lahiri, S.K., Wang, C. (eds.) CAV 2020. LNCS, vol. 12225, pp. 475–487. Springer, Cham (2020). https://doi.org/10.1007/978-3-030-53291-8_25

51. Lange, J., Tuosto, E., Yoshida, N.: From communicating machines to graphical choreographies. In: Proceedings of the 42nd Annual ACM SIGPLAN-SIGACT Symposium on Principles of Programming Languages (POPL 2015), pp. 221–232. ACM (2015). https://doi.org/10.1145/2676726.2676964

52. Lavaei, A., Khaled, M., Soudjani, S., Zamani, M.: AMYTISS: parallelized automated controller synthesis for large-scale stochastic systems. In: Lahiri, S.K., Wang, C. (eds.) CAV 2020. LNCS, vol. 12225, pp. 461–474. Springer, Cham (2020). https://doi.org/10.1007/978-3-030-53291-8_24

53. Lehmann, S., Rogalla, A., Neidhardt, M., Reinecke, A., Schlaefer, A., Schupp, S.: Modeling $\mathbb{R}^3$ needle steering in Uppaal. In: Dubslaff, C., Luttik, B. (eds.) Proceedings of the 5th Workshop on Models for Formal Analysis of Real Systems (MARS 2022). EPTCS, vol. 355, pp. 40–59 (2022). https://doi.org/10.4204/EPTCS.355.4

54. Liu, Z., Wu, B., Dai, J., Lin, H.: Distributed communication-aware motion planning for networked mobile robots under formal specifications. IEEE Trans. Control. Netw. Syst. **7**(4), 1801–1811 (2020). https://doi.org/10.1109/TCNS.2020.3000742

55. Loizou, S.G., Kyriakopoulos, K.J.: Automatic synthesis of multi-agent motion tasks based on LTL specifications. In: Proceedings of the 43rd IEEE Conference on Decision and Control (CDC 2004), pp. 153–158. IEEE (2004). https://doi.org/10.1109/CDC.2004.1428622

56. Loreti, M., Quadrini, M.: A spatial logic for a simplicial complex model. arXiv:2105.08708 (2021). https://doi.org/10.48550/arXiv.2105.08708

57. Luttenberger, M., Meyer, P.J., Sickert, S.: Practical synthesis of reactive systems from LTL specifications via parity games. Acta Inform. **57**(1), 3–36 (2019). https://doi.org/10.1007/s00236-019-00349-3

58. Ma, M., Bartocci, E., Lifland, E., Stankovic, J.A., Feng, L.: A novel spatial-temporal specification-based monitoring system for smart cities. IEEE Internet Things J. **8**(15), 11793–11806 (2021). https://doi.org/10.1109/JIOT.2021.3069943

59. Meyer, P.J., Sickert, S., Luttenberger, M.: Strix: explicit reactive synthesis strikes back! In: Chockler, H., Weissenbacher, G. (eds.) CAV 2018. LNCS, vol. 10981, pp. 578–586. Springer, Cham (2018). https://doi.org/10.1007/978-3-319-96145-3_31

60. Ramadge, P.J., Wonham, W.M.: Supervisory control of a class of discrete event processes. SIAM J. Control. Optim. **25**(1), 206–230 (1987). https://doi.org/10.1137/0325013

61. van der Sanden, B., et al.: Modular model-based supervisory controller design for wafer logistics in lithography machines. In: Proceedings of the 18th International Conference on Model Driven Engineering Languages and Systems (MODELS 2015), pp. 416–425. IEEE (2015). https://doi.org/10.1109/MODELS.2015.7338273

62. Shokri-Manninen, F., Vain, J., Waldén, M.: Formal verification of COLREG-based navigation of maritime autonomous systems. In: de Boer, F., Cerone, A. (eds.) SEFM 2020. LNCS, vol. 12310, pp. 41–59. Springer, Cham (2020). https://doi.org/10.1007/978-3-030-58768-0_3

63. Sun, D., Chen, J., Mitra, S., Fan, C.: Multi-agent motion planning from signal temporal logic specifications. IEEE Robot. Autom. Lett. **7**(2), 3451–3458 (2022). https://doi.org/10.1109/LRA.2022.3146951

64. Theunissen, R.J.M., van Beek, D.A., Rooda, J.E.: Improving evolvability of a patient communication control system using state-based supervisory control synthesis. Adv. Eng. Inform. **26**(3), 502–515 (2012). https://doi.org/10.1016/j.aei.2012.02.009

65. Tsigkanos, C., Kehrer, T., Ghezzi, C.: Modeling and verification of evolving cyber-physical spaces. In: Proceedings of the 11th Joint Meeting on Foundations of Software Engineering (ESEC/FSE 2017), pp. 38–48. ACM (2017). https://doi.org/10.1145/3106237.3106299

Toward a Kinetic Framework to Model the Collective Dynamics of Multi-agent Systems

Stefania Monica[1], Federico Bergenti[2], and Franco Zambonelli[1(✉)]

[1] Dipartimento di Scienze e Metodi dell'Ingegneria, Università degli Studi di Modena e Reggio Emilia, 42122 Reggio Emilia, Italy
{stefania.monica,franco.zambonelli}@unimore.it
[2] Dipartimento di Scienze Matematiche, Fisiche e Informatiche, Università degli Studi di Parma, 43124 Parma, Italy
franco.zambonelli@unipr.it

Abstract. The investigation of the collective dynamics of multi-agent systems in terms of the study of the properties of single agents is not feasible when the number of interacting agents is large. In this case, the collective dynamics can be better examined by adopting a statistical approach that studies the long-time asymptotic properties of the system as a whole. The kinetic framework discussed in this paper can be used to study collective and emergent properties of large and decentralized multi-agent systems once single interactions among agents are properly described. Moreover, the discussed framework can be used to design how agents should interact to ensure that the resulting multi-agent system would exhibit the required collective and emergent characteristics. The discussed framework restricts the interactions among agents to message exchanges, and it assumes that the investigated properties emerge from interactions. As an example of the use of the framework, and to outline a concrete application of it, the properties of a system in which agents implement the symmetric gossip algorithm are analyzed. Analytic results obtained using the discussed framework are compared with independent simulations, showing the effectiveness of the approach.

Keywords: Collective adaptive systems · Symmetric gossip algorithm · Mathematical kinetic theories

1 Introduction

The study of the dynamics of large and decentralized multi-agent systems is an important research topic that is the basis of the studies on *collective adaptive systems* (e.g., [16]) and that finds relevant applications in various aspects of *distributed artificial intelligence* (e.g., [20]). Usually, the study of the dynamics of these systems assumes that each agent is associated with a state that changes

© The Author(s), under exclusive license to Springer Nature Switzerland AG 2022
T. Margaria and B. Steffen (Eds.): ISoLA 2022, LNCS 13703, pp. 165–180, 2022.
https://doi.org/10.1007/978-3-031-19759-8_11

dynamically to reflect, for example, observations and deliberations. The states of the agents change because of multiple causes and, in particular, because of interactions, which occur when an agent gets in touch with another agent.

Accordingly, the descriptions of how interactions change the states of the agents is central to the study of dynamics of multi-agent systems. These descriptions take into account all phenomena that describe how agents change their states, and they vary significantly according to the studied phenomena and to the peculiarities of the multi-agent system under investigation. However, when the number of agents in the considered system is large (e.g., large fleets of autonomous connected vehicles in an urban area [13,27]), the study of the dynamics of the state of each agent might not be feasible. In this case, the analysis of the *collective behavior* [22,39] of the multi-agent system as a whole is preferred, which implies focussing only on the features of the individual states that contribute to form interesting collective properties. Under the assumption that the relevant features of the states can be represented in terms of real numbers, the collective properties of multi-agent systems can be investigated using statistical approaches. Although the aggregate values that statistical approaches target are not sufficient to obtain detailed descriptions of the states of single agents, they are indeed sufficient to describe the collective and emergent dynamics of the multi-agent system as a whole.

This paper discusses the possibility of studying the asymptotic collective dynamics of large and decentralized multi-agent systems by introducing a specific instantiation of the general approach of *mathematical kinetic theories* (e.g., [4,5]), which we call *Kinetic Theory of Multi-Agent Systems (KTMAS)*. Mathematical kinetic theories are not necessarily restricted to the study of physical phenomena, and they are generally intended to investigate the collective properties of groups of interacting peers under the assumption that the relevant characteristics of a group emerge from local interactions among peers and from environmental forces. Actually, mathematical kinetic theories provide interesting results every time the characteristics of studied systems justify a statistical approach and when the interactions among peers are the main causes of the dynamics of studied systems (e.g., [30,31]). In this context, KTMAS is instead specifically designed to study the long-time asymptotic properties of large and decentralized multi-agent systems in which agents affect each other's state via message passing [6].

The major contribution of this paper is to discuss the basis of an analytic framework designed to characterize a KTMAS. The discussed framework supports descriptive and prescriptive reasoning on the long-time asymptotic properties of large multi-agent systems. As a descriptive tool, the framework can be used as an alternative to simulations that benefits from solid mathematical foundations. As a prescriptive tool, the framework supports the design of systems with desired long-time asymptotic properties. In the last part of this paper, the framework is concretely applied to the study of the collective dynamics of a system in which all agents implement the symmetric gossip algorithm [11].

This system is also analyzed using independent simulations, and the outcome of simulations is in tight agreement with the results obtained using the framework.

This paper is organized as follows. Section 2 presents the ideas behind the proposal of a KTMAS, and it reviews the discussed framework. Section 3 applies the framework to study the dynamics of a system in which all agents implement the symmetric gossip algorithm. Section 4 compares the analytic results obtained using the framework with independent simulations, showing the effectiveness of the framework. Section 5 briefly discusses related work. Finally, Sect. 6 concludes the paper and outlines future research directions.

2 The Basis of the KTMAS Framework

Mathematical kinetic theories share a common general framework designed to study the collective dynamics of groups of interacting peers (e.g., [5]). The general framework is completed with the details needed to study specific phenomena in specific contexts, and the resulting models are used to derive analytic descriptions of the collective dynamics of the studied group of peers. The general framework assumes that the properties that characterize peers change primarily because of interactions, and that groups are so large that collective and emergent properties can be adequately studied using a statistical approach. The KTMAS framework, as outlined in this section, is a specific instantiation of the general framework of mathematical kinetic theories to study large and decentralized multi-agent systems composed of agents that autonomously exchange messages. In particular, the KTMAS framework studies multi-agent systems composed of a static and large number $n \in \mathbb{N}_+$ of interacting agents, where each agent is uniquely identified by a natural number between 1 and n. Each agent has a state and, without loss of generality, it is assumed that each state can be associated with a real number $q \in Q$, where $Q \subset \mathbb{R}$ is an arbitrary interval that represents the different states an agent can assume.

Agents interact autonomously with each other in the multi-agent system. Interactions are assumed to take the form of message exchanges, and each interaction involves only two agents, so that the only considered form of interaction regards an agent r (the *receiver*) receiving a message from an agent s (the *sender*). Other forms of interaction (e.g., multicast or stigmergic [14]) can be easily mapped to message exchanges. Interactions are assumed to be mutually independent, and the semantics of an interaction depends only on the states of involved agents. Each agent can interact with any other agent in the multi-agent system, and the frequency of interactions is (roughly) constant. Since interactions are the only interesting events in the KTMAS framework, time is modeled as a sequence of discrete steps, which may not have the same duration, and each step corresponds to a single interaction that involves two agents.

The state of an agent can change only because of interactions, and interactions are modeled on the basis of how they change the states of the agents that send and receive messages. In detail, the KTMAS framework assumes that interactions are described in terms of proper *interaction rules* that link the *pre-interaction* states of involved agents with the respective *post-interaction* states.

Interaction rules are peculiar to the system under investigation, and the KTMAS framework let them unspecified until a complete model of the system is needed to actually study interesting collective and emergent properties.

In accordance with the general approach of mathematical kinetic theories, $f : Q \times [0, +\infty) \to \mathbb{R}$ is a function such that $f(q,t)\,dq$ represents the number of agents whose states are in $(q, q+dq)$ at time $t \in [0, +\infty)$. Note that f is assumed to be sufficiently regular to support the analytic developments discussed in the remaining of this paper. The number of agents in the system is

$$n = \int_Q f(q,t)\,dq, \tag{1}$$

where the dependence of n on t is dropped because the number of agents in the system is assumed to be static.

The average state of the agents at time $t \in [0, +\infty)$, denoted as $\bar{q}(t)$, is

$$\bar{q}(t) = \frac{1}{n} \int_Q q\, f(q,t)\,dq, \tag{2}$$

and the variance of the states at time $t \in [0, +\infty)$ is

$$\sigma^2(t) = \frac{1}{n} \int_Q (q - \bar{q}(t))^2 f(q,t)\,dq. \tag{3}$$

In order to study the evolution of f, and therefore, to study the dynamics of the average state and of the variance of the states, let

$$W(q_s, q_r, \hat{q}_s, \hat{q}_r)\,d\hat{q}_s\,d\hat{q}_r \tag{4}$$

be the probability per unit time that, given an agent s in state q_s and an agent r in state q_r, agent s and agent r interact and their states after the interaction fall in $(\hat{q}_s, \hat{q}_s + d\hat{q}_s)$ and $(\hat{q}_r, \hat{q}_r + d\hat{q}_r)$, respectively. Therefore, the probability per unit time that agent s and agent r interact can be computed as

$$\beta = \int_{Q^2} W(q_s, q_r, \hat{q}_s, \hat{q}_r)\,d\hat{q}_s\,d\hat{q}_r, \tag{5}$$

where the dependence of β on q_s and q_r is dropped because agents are supposed to interact at a (roughly) constant rate.

Note that previous definitions can be used to compute the loss per unit time of the agents with states in $(q_r, q_r + dq_r)$ at time t as $\mathcal{Q}^-[f]\,dq_r$, where

$$\mathcal{Q}^-[f] = \int_{Q^3} W(q_s, q_r, \hat{q}_s, \hat{q}_r) f(q_s,t) f(q_r,t)\,dq_s\,d\hat{q}_s\,d\hat{q}_r. \tag{6}$$

Similarly, the gain per unit time of the agents with states in $(q_r, q_r + dq_r)$ at time t can be computed as $\mathcal{Q}^+[f]\,dq_r$, where

$$\mathcal{Q}^+[f] = \int_{Q^3} W(\breve{q}_s, \breve{q}_r, q_s, q_r) f(\breve{q}_s,t) f(\breve{q}_r,t)\,dq_s\,d\breve{q}_s\,d\breve{q}_r. \tag{7}$$

Finally, the gain per unit time of the agents with states in $(q_r, q_r + \mathrm{d}q_r)$ at time t, as computed by (7), and the relative loss, as computed by (6), can be used to define the *collision operator* $\mathcal{Q}[f]$ as

$$\mathcal{Q}[f] = \mathcal{Q}^+[f] - \mathcal{Q}^-[f]. \tag{8}$$

The collision operator $\mathcal{Q}[f]$ expresses a balance per unit time of the agents whose states enter and exit the region of states $(q, q + \mathrm{d}q)$. Therefore, the collision operator is sufficient to express a balance equation that describes the dynamics of how states are distributed among agents

$$\frac{\partial f}{\partial t}(q, t) = \mathcal{Q}[f]. \tag{9}$$

Note that (9) is normally called *Boltzmann equation* because it is a generalization of the classic equation devised for the kinetic theory of gases by Ludwig Boltzmann in 1872. The Boltzmann equation for a group of peers is the core of all mathematical kinetic theories because it expresses the dynamics of the group once W in (4) is expressed in terms of the characteristics of the considered interactions. The explicit expression of W requires to select which phenomena to include in the description of the interactions among peers, and it is normally left unspecified in the general framework of mathematical kinetic theories. Section 3 provides an expression of W that describes how agents interact to implement the symmetric gossip algorithm. This expression is sufficient to prove the correctness of the algorithm under the assumptions of the KTMAS framework and to study the expected long-time asymptotic dynamics of the studied multi-agent system.

The Boltzmann equation provides a fine-grained characterization of the dynamics of the states of the agents, which is usually too fine-grained to be feasible for large multi-agent systems. Therefore, the study of the dynamics of the collective properties of the multi-agent system as a whole is often preferred. In order to study these collective properties, the *weak form* of the Boltzmann equation for a sufficiently regular *test function* $\phi : Q \to \mathbb{R}$ is considered

$$\int_Q \frac{\partial f}{\partial t}(q, t)\phi(q)\,\mathrm{d}q = \int_Q \mathcal{Q}[f]\phi(q)\,\mathrm{d}q. \tag{10}$$

The relevance of the weak form of the Boltzmann equation to study the collective properties of multi-agent systems can be clarified as follows. If the details of the interactions that occur in the multi-agent system are made explicit, by stating an explicit expression of W in (4), the right-hand side of (10) can be also made explicit. Therefore, for an explicit W and a fixed ϕ, the weak form of the Boltzmann equation becomes an ordinary differential equation that describes the dynamics of the collective property entailed by the chosen ϕ. For example, if $\phi(q) = q$ is chosen, (10) can be written as

$$n\frac{\mathrm{d}\bar{q}}{\mathrm{d}t}(t) = \int_Q \mathcal{Q}[f]\, q\,\mathrm{d}q, \tag{11}$$

which is the equation used in Sect. 3 to study the average state of the agents. Similarly, if $\phi(q) = (q - \bar{q}(t))^2$ is chosen, the weak form of the Boltzmann equation can be written as

$$n\frac{\mathrm{d}\sigma^2}{\mathrm{d}t}(t) = \int_Q \mathcal{Q}[f]\,(q - \bar{q}(t))^2\,\mathrm{d}q, \tag{12}$$

and this equation can be used to study the dynamics of the variance of the states of the agents. This choice of ϕ is used in Sect. 3 to prove that the variance of the states of the agents that implement the symmetric gossip algorithm tends to zero as time tends to infinity, which ensures that all agents would eventually share the same state.

3   The Case of the Symmetric Gossip Algorithm

The *distributed averaging problem* (e.g., [11]) is a well-known problem related to multi-agent systems that finds important applications, for example, in sensor networks and social networks. The motivating application in sensor networks is related to sensors that jointly measure the characteristics of physical phenomena. For example, a toy scenario to motivate the distributed averaging problem regards the sensing of the temperature of a small region of space using a network of sensors [11]. Sensors are deployed to measure the temperature of the region and, to combat minor fluctuations in ambient temperature and noise in sensor readings, sensors need to average their readings. The application in social networks is similar, and it is about *compromise* (e.g., [30]), which is one of the fundamental phenomena that govern opinion formation, and which is considered as the major force that enables decentralized consensus in multi-agent systems. In the assortment of algorithms proposed to solve the distributed averaging problem, the algorithm first proposed in [11], and called *symmetric gossip algorithm* with the nomenclature proposed in [18], can be used to describe a concrete application of the discussed KTMAS framework. The remaining of this section is devoted to apply the KTMAS framework to study the long-time asymptotic properties of systems that implement this algorithm.

3.1   Model

In the studied multi-agent systems, each agent is characterized by a state $q \in Q$, where $Q \subset \mathbb{R}$ is a known bounded interval that is assumed to be $[-1, 1]$ without loss of generality. Each agent is requested to exchange messages with other agents at a (roughly) constant rate to reach consensus on the average value of initial states. Each agent s repeatedly chooses another agent r at random and sends a message to agent r. A message from agent s to agent r contains the current state of agent s, and it is used by agent r to update its state. Given that agents update their states only upon receiving messages, the updates are based on their current states and on the states contained in the received messages.

The symmetric gossip algorithm fixes the function that an agent r uses to update its state upon receiving a message from another agent s. The adopted function is a linear combination of the current state of agent r and of the state contained in the received message. The algorithm assumes that immediately before updating its state, agent r replies with a message containing its current state, which is then used by agent s to update its state. Note that the algorithm assumes some form of synchronization because messages and related replies are supposed to contain the actual states of interacting agents. This assumption is commonly taken in the symmetric gossip algorithm, and it is considered appropriate for intended applications of the algorithm.

If agent r, in state q_r, interacts with agent s, in state q_s, the symmetric gossip algorithm requires agents to mutually exchange their current states and to update their states using the following interaction rules (adapted from [11])

$$\hat{q}_s = t_s(q_s, q_r) = q_s - \gamma(q_s - q_r)$$
$$\hat{q}_r = t_r(q_s, q_r) = q_r - \gamma(q_r - q_s),$$
(13)

where $\hat{q}_s$ and $\hat{q}_r$ are the updated states of agent s and of agent r, respectively, and $\gamma \in (0, 1)$ is a parameter of the symmetric gossip algorithm. Following the nomenclature of mathematical kinetic theories, q_s and q_r are the pre-interaction states of agent s and of agent r, respectively, while $\hat{q}_s$ and $\hat{q}_r$ are the corresponding post-interaction states. Note that the chosen interaction rules are such that, for all $q_s \in Q$ and $q_r \in Q$, $t_s(q_s, q_r) = t_r(q_r, q_s)$.

Before using the KTMAS framework to study the long-time asymptotic properties of the multi-agent systems that implement the symmetric gossip algorithm, some considerations on adopted interaction rules are needed. First, note that post-interaction states belong to interval $Q = [-1, 1]$ because the following inequalities hold

$$|\hat{q}_s| \leq (1 - \gamma)|q_s| + \gamma|q_r| \leq \max\{|q_r|, |q_s|\} \leq 1$$
$$|\hat{q}_r| \leq (1 - \gamma)|q_r| + \gamma|q_s| \leq \max\{|q_r|, |q_s|\} \leq 1.$$
(14)

Then, note that, from the adopted interaction rules, the following equality can be easily derived

$$\hat{q}_s + \hat{q}_r = q_s + q_r,$$
(15)

which implies that interactions do not modify the average state of the agents. Finally, note that each interaction reduces the distance of the states of interacting agents because $\gamma \in (0, 1)$ and the following inequality holds

$$|\hat{q}_s - \hat{q}_r| = |1 - 2\gamma||q_s - q_r| \leq |q_s - q_r|.$$
(16)

It is therefore reasonable to expect that, after a sufficiently large number of interactions, all agents would eventually tend to the same state, which is necessarily the average of the initial states. The understanding of how quickly the states of the agents tend to the average of the initial states requires further discussions, as shown in the remaining of this section.

3.2   Analytic Results

The interest now is on using the KTMAS framework to study the dynamics of the states of the agents. The following propositions accurately describe the dynamics of the states of the agents using the KTMAS framework.

Proposition 1. *The symmetric gossip algorithm described by (13) ensures that the average state of the agents in the multi-agent system is constant over time.*

Proof. The following expression is obtained by setting $\phi(q) = q$ in the weak form of the Boltzmann equation

$$n\frac{\mathrm{d}\bar{q}}{\mathrm{dt}}(t) = \beta \int_{Q^2} f(q_s,t)f(q_r,t)(t_r(q_s,q_r) - q_r)\,\mathrm{d}q_s\,\mathrm{d}q_r \tag{17}$$

after some ordinary manipulations and using the fact that, for all $q_s \in Q$ and $q_r \in Q$, $t_s(q_s,q_r) = t_r(q_r,q_s)$. Then, using the adopted interaction rules to expand $t_r(q_s,q_r)$, the previous formulation of the weak form of the Boltzmann equation becomes

$$n\frac{\mathrm{d}\bar{q}}{\mathrm{dt}}(t) = \beta\gamma \int_{Q^2} f(q_s,t)f(q_r,t)(q_s - q_r)\,\mathrm{d}q_r\,\mathrm{d}q_s. \tag{18}$$

Note that the right-hand side of the previous equation can be rewritten as

$$\beta\gamma \left(\int_Q f(q_r,t)\,\mathrm{d}q_r \int_Q f(q_s,t)q_s\,\mathrm{d}q_s - \int_Q f(q_s,t)\,\mathrm{d}q_s \int_Q f(q_r,t)q_r\,\mathrm{d}q_r \right). \tag{19}$$

Therefore, the weak form of the Boltzmann equation for $\phi(q) = q$ becomes

$$\frac{\mathrm{d}\bar{q}}{\mathrm{dt}}(t) = 0, \tag{20}$$

which ensures that the average state of the agents in the multi-agent system is constantly equal to the initial average. $\qquad\square$

Proposition 2. *The symmetric gossip algorithm described by (13) ensures that the states of all the agents tend to the same value exponentially fast as time tends to infinity.*

Proof. The variance of the states can be studied by setting $\phi(q) = (q - \bar{q})^2$ in the weak form of the Boltzmann equation, where the dependence of $\bar{q}$ on t is dropped because of Proposition 1. Therefore,

$$n\frac{\mathrm{d}\sigma^2}{\mathrm{dt}}(t) = \beta \int_{Q^2} f(q_s,t)f(q_r,t)[(t_r(q_s,q_r) - \bar{q})^2 - (q_r - \bar{q})^2]\,\mathrm{d}q_s\,\mathrm{d}q_r. \tag{21}$$

The previous equation can be simplified as follows

$$n\frac{\mathrm{d}\sigma^2}{\mathrm{dt}}(t) = \beta \int_{Q^2} f(q_s,t)f(q_r,t)[t_r^2(q_s,q_r) - q_r^2 - 2\bar{q}(t_r(q_s,q_r) - q_r)]\,\mathrm{d}q_s\,\mathrm{d}q_r. \tag{22}$$

Now, note that the term that contains $(t_r(q_s, q_r) - q_r)$ in the previous equation is proportional to the right-hand side of (17), which Proposition 1 proves to equal zero. Therefore, the previous formulation of the weak form of the Boltzmann equation can be written as

$$n\frac{d\sigma^2}{dt}(t) = \beta \int_{Q^2} f(q_s, t)f(q_r, t)(t_r^2(q_s, q_r) - q_r^2)\, dq_s\, dq_r. \tag{23}$$

The adopted interaction rules can be used to make $t_r(q_s, q_r)$ explicit in the previous equation to obtain

$$n\frac{d\sigma^2}{dt}(t) = \beta \int_{Q^2} f(q_s, t)f(q_r, t)[\gamma^2(q_r - q_s)^2 - 2\gamma q_r(q_r - q_s)]\, dq_s\, dq_r. \tag{24}$$

Simple algebraic manipulations allow obtaining the following formulation of the weak form of the Boltzmann equation for $\phi(q) = (q - \bar{q})^2$

$$n\frac{d\sigma^2}{dt}(t) = 2\beta\gamma(\gamma - 1)n\left(\int_Q f(q_r, t)q_r^2\, dq_r - n\bar{q}^2\right). \tag{25}$$

Note that the last factor of the previous equation is nothing but $n\sigma^2(t)$, and therefore, the following ordinary differential equation that describes the dynamics of the variance of the states is obtained

$$\frac{d\sigma^2}{dt}(t) = 2\beta\gamma(\gamma - 1)n\sigma^2(t). \tag{26}$$

The previous equation can be easily solved to obtain a closed-form expression of the variance of the states

$$\sigma^2(t) = \sigma_0^2 e^{-2\beta\gamma(1-\gamma)nt}, \tag{27}$$

where $\sigma_0^2 = \sigma^2(0)$ is the initial variance of the states. Note that $\gamma \in (0, 1)$, and therefore, the previous exponential function is decreasing and tends to zero as time tends to infinity. □

4   Theory Vs. Simulations

Proposition 1 ensures that the average state of a multi-agent system in which agent implement the symmetric gossip algorithm is constant over time. Proposition 2 ensures that all agents would eventually reach the same state, which equals the initial average state for Proposition 1. The following illustrative simulations are meant to compare the analytic results derived from previous propositions with the actual behavior of a multi-agent system in which agents implement the symmetric gossip algorithm. Note that an in-depth comparison between the analytic results derived from previous propositions with a simulated multi-agent system is out of the scope of this paper.

The simulated multi-agent system comprises $n = 100$ agents that implement the symmetric gossip algorithm. For each simulation, the states of the agents are initially set to random values uniformly distributed in $Q = [-1, 1]$, so that the initial variance of the states is $\sigma_0^2 = \frac{1}{3}$. Each simulation comprises $\tau = 10^3$ steps, and at every step, which corresponds to one unit of time, two agents are randomly chosen and their states are updated using (13).

Figure 1(a) shows the variance of the states for four simulations obtained using γ in $\{0.1, 0.2, 0.3, 0.5\}$. As expected, the shown variances exponentially decrease toward zero as time increases. Figure 1(b) shows the corresponding variances computed using (27) with $\beta = 2 \cdot 10^{-4}$. A quick comparison between the plots confirm that the variances obtained using simulations adequately fit the variances obtained using (27). Moreover, the plots confirm that the rate of convergence increases as γ increases. This is not surprising because the adopted interaction rules are such that the distance between the post-interaction states of two interacting agents decreases as γ increases in $(0, \frac{1}{2}]$. Note that this property of adopted interaction rules is confirmed by (27).

Figure 2 splits the plots of Fig. 1 to better compare the variances obtained using simulations with the corresponding variances computed using (27). In particular, the four plots in Fig. 2 show the variances for $\gamma = 0.1$, $\gamma = 0.2$, $\gamma = 0.3$, and $\gamma = 0.5$. The figure shows tight agreement between the variances obtained using simulations and the variances computed using (27). Actually, for a given $\gamma \in \{0.1, 0.2, 0.3, 0.5\}$, the largest distance between the variance obtained using simulations and the corresponding variance obtained using (27) are: 0.02 for $\gamma = 0.1$, 0.029 for $\gamma = 0.2$, 0.045 for $\gamma = 0.3$, and 0.038 for $\gamma = 0.5$.

5   Related Work

Besides the importance of multi-agent systems for artificial intelligence, as witnessed by the significant body of literature that originated, for example, from [23], large multi-agent systems have been recently attracting a considerable attention for their direct link with relevant applications like social networks and sensor networks. It is common opinion that large multi-agent systems have specific peculiarities, and that common methods and tools are not immediately applicable to study them (e.g., [24]). In addition, large multi-agent systems are particularly important in applications that are characterized by decentralized control (e.g., [21]). This is not surprising since decentralized control is assumed to scale for the number of agents better than centralized control, and therefore it is the most obvious choice when the number of agents is large (e.g., [40]). When studied multi-agent systems are large and decentralized, the ordinary techniques commonly used to study the dynamics of multi-agent systems (e.g., [33]) tend to become unfeasible, and the alternative approaches of *collective adaptive systems* [16] are needed. In such cases, statistical approaches seem to provide better ways to study the dynamics of multi-agent systems because they move the focus from the dynamics of single agents to the dynamics of the multi-agent system as a whole (e.g., [1,12]).

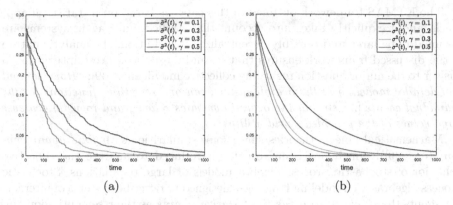

Fig. 1. Plot of (a) the variance $\tilde{\sigma}^2(t)$ obtained using simulations and (b) the variance $\sigma^2(t)$ computed using (27) for $\beta = 2 \cdot 10^{-4}$ and $\gamma \in \{0.1, 0.2, 0.3, 0.5\}$, when $n = 100$ agents whose initial states are uniformly distributed in $Q = [-1, 1]$ are considered.

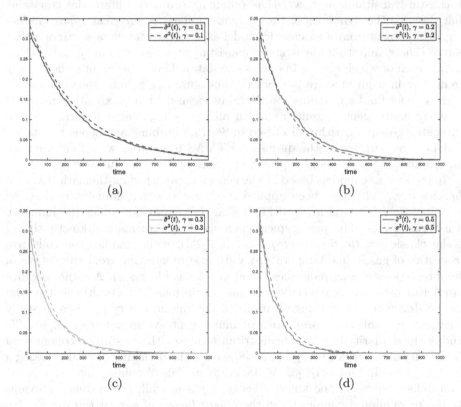

Fig. 2. Plot of the variance $\tilde{\sigma}^2(t)$ obtained using simulations (solid lines) and the variance $\sigma^2(t)$ computed using (27) with $\beta = 2 \cdot 10^{-4}$ (dashed line) for (a) $\gamma = 0.1$, (b) $\gamma = 0.2$, (c) $\gamma = 0.3$ and (d) $\gamma = 0.5$, when $n = 100$ agents whose initial states are uniformly distributed in $Q = [-1, 1]$ are considered.

The KTMAS framework outlined in this paper is based on a statistical approach, and it explicitly takes into account that studied multi-agent systems are assumed to be large and possibly decentralized. In addition, the analytic nature of the discussed framework ensures that it can be used as a prescriptive tool to answer to the major question regarding collective intelligence [39]: *"How, without any detailed modeling of the overall system, can one set utility functions for the individual agents [...] so that the overall dynamics reliably and robustly achieves large values of the provided world utility?"*

Mathematical kinetic theories share some similarities with *fluid approximation* (e.g., [9]), which has been recently introduced to analyze the collective behavior of stochastic process algebra models of large populations. Stochastic process algebras are modeling languages designed to describe systems of interacting agents that have *continuous-time Markov chains* as their semantic domain. Fluid approximation can be applied if a model contains many instances of few agent types. It works by treating as continuous the variables that count how many agents of each type are in each state, and by treating the rates of the stochastic transitions as flows, thus obtaining ordinary differential equations that describe the dynamics of the system. Similarly, *mean-field approximation* (e.g., [10]) starts from a stochastic model expressed in terms of a *discrete-time Markov chain*, and it studies systems consisting of a large number of interacting agents, each of which can be in one of few states. Then, the count of how many agents are in a given state is studied, thus obtaining a limit theorem similar to the one for fluid approximation. Notably, mean-field approximation was used to study multi-agent systems in which all agents implement a variant of the symmetric gossip algorithm discussed in Sect. 3, obtaining analogous results [3]. In-depth comparisons of the discussed KTMAS framework with fluid approximation and with mean-field approximation are reserved for future work.

In recent years, models based on the general approach of mathematical kinetic theories (e.g., [32]) have been applied to diverse research domains to describe groups of peers that interact within a shared environment under the influence of external forces. The prototypical example of a mathematical kinetic theory is the classic *kinetic theory of gases* (e.g., [25]), which studies the collective properties of gases, like temperature and pressure, starting from the details of the interactions among molecules (or atoms, for noble gases). A rather obvious parallelism between the molecules of a gas and the agents of a multi-agent system can be drawn to adopt generalizations of the kinetic theory of gases to study emergent and collective properties of multi-agent systems. For example, [35] studies the similarity between the distribution of wealth in a simple economy and the density of molecules in a gas, and [8] studies the dynamics of wealth taking a similar approach. Similarly, [31,36,38] study models of opinion dynamics using a formalism based on the kinetic theory of gases, while [30] extends previous studies on opinion dynamics using the *kinetic theory of gas mixtures* (e.g., [7]). Note that besides the general framework of mathematical kinetic theories, few results from the kinetic theory of gases can be used in the discussed KTMAS framework because the details of the collisions among molecules in gases are significantly different from those of the interactions among agents in multi-agent systems. Actually, the discussed KTMAS framework drops the assumption that agents are immersed in the physical world and that they must be characterized in terms of mechanical properties, like positions and velocities. The framework abstracts away such an assumption, and it does not treat mechanical properties specifically, thus substantially changing the developments of the framework.

Besides the multiple applications of the general approach of mathematical kinetic theories, the literature proposes several papers that document how models inspired by physics are used to study the collective properties of multi-agent systems. In the early 1990s, the term *econophysics* [15,26] was proposed to designate an interdisciplinary research field that applies methods originally developed by physicists to study economic phenomena. Similarly, the term *sociophysics* [15,19] was introduced to describe an interdisciplinary research field that uses mathematical tools inspired by physics to understand the behaviors of groups of individuals. Similar points of view have been proposed several times (e.g., [32,34]), and all proposals recognize that the long-time asymptotic properties of multi-agent systems can be studied by regarding such systems as *complex systems* [28,37]. The discussed KTMAS framework takes a similar approach, but the framework is not described in terms of an adaptation of existing formalisms. Rather, the framework outlined in this paper is constructed starting from the basic characteristics of the considered agents and multi-agent systems.

6   Conclusion

This paper discusses the possibility of working toward a complete and coherent KTMAS by outlining the basis of a KTMAS framework, which is introduced as an analytic framework to study the long-time asymptotic properties of large and decentralized multi-agent systems. In the first part of this paper, the discussed framework is motivated and described. The adopted assumptions are discussed, and an equation that describes the dynamics of the studied multi-agent systems is obtained from very general considerations regarding the effects of interactions on the states of the agents. In the second part of this paper, the framework is applied to study an illustrative distributed averaging algorithm in order to present a concrete example of the use of the framework. Note that asymmetric variants of the studied algorithm have already been proposed in the literature (e.g., [2,17]), and their study using the discussed KTMAS framework represents an interesting application of the framework reserved for future work. Also, note that a preliminary variant of the discussed KTMAS framework has already been used to study multi-agent systems in which interaction rules are nonlinear [31] or include an external random input [29].

Methodologically, the major advantages that are expected from the adoption of the discussed KTMAS framework to the study of the dynamics of large and decentralized multi-agent systems derive from the analytic nature of the framework. The analytic nature of the framework ensures that obtained results can be used both as descriptive tools to explain observations and as prescriptive tools to design the dynamics of multi-agent systems. As a descriptive tool, the framework can be used as an alternative to simulations. The validity of the results of simulations depends on how much simulations are representative of the studied multi-agent systems. On the contrary, the validity of analytic results is clearly identified by the assumptions adopted to derive them. As a prescriptive tool, the framework supports the design of multi-agent systems with desired emergent and collective properties. In fact, analytic results can be used to identify the values of parameters that ensure that the designed multi-agent system behaves as intended. With this respect, the KTMAS framework addresses the major goal of the research on collective intelligence, which regards the possibility of designing interactions to obtain desired emergent and collective properties.

Planned developments in the direction of devising a complete and coherent KTMAS involve three generalizations of the discussed framework. First, the interaction rules that govern how agents react to messages are assumed to be deterministic, while stochastic interaction rules are important when studied agents can behave erratically or experience faults. Second, the framework assumes that every agent can interact with every other agent, which is a too strong assumption in several interesting contexts. Therefore, the framework could be extended to include a, possibly dynamic and stochastic, network topology. Third, agents are often created and destroyed to serve the needs of interactions in practical multi-agent systems. However, this possibility is not yet considered in the current form of the KTMAS framework, even if mathematical kinetic theories already provide hints on allowing the studied group of peers to change dynamically.

Acknowledgements. Work supported by the Italian MUR PRIN 2017 Project *Fluidware*.

References

1. Adiga, A., Kuhlman, C.J., Mortveit, H.S., Vullikanti, A.K.S.: Sensitivity of diffusion dynamics to network uncertainty. J. Artif. Intell. Res. **51**, 207–226 (2014)
2. Asensio-Marco, C., Beferull-Lozano, B.: Fast average gossiping under asymmetric links in WSNS. In: Proceedings of the 22nd European Signal Processing Conference (EUSIPCO 2014), pp. 131–135. IEEE (2014)
3. Bakhshi, R., Cloth, L., Fokkink, W., Haverkort, B.: Mean-field analysis for the evaluation of gossip protocols. In: Proceedings of 6th International Conference on the Quantitative Evaluation of Systems (QEST 2009), pp. 247–256. IEEE (2009)
4. Bellomo, N., et al.: What is life? A perspective of the mathematical kinetic theory of active particles. Math. Models Methods Appl. Sci. **31**(9), 1821–1866 (2021)
5. Bellouquid, A., Delitala, M.: Mathematical Modeling of Complex Biological Systems. Modeling and Simulation in Science, Engineering and Technology, Birkhäuser, Basel (2006)
6. Bergenti, F., Ricci, A.: Three approaches to the coordination of multiagent systems. In: Proceedings of the ACM Symposium on Applied Computing (SAC 2002), pp. 367–372. ACM (2002)
7. Bianca, C., Dogbe, C.: On the Boltzmann gas mixture equation: Linking the kinetic and fluid regimes. Commun. Nonlinear Sci. Numer. Simul. **29**, 240–256 (2015)

8. Boghosian, B.M.: Kinetics of wealth and the Pareto law. Phy. Rev. E **89**(4), 042804 (2014)
9. Bortolussi, L., Hillston, J., Latella, D., Massink, M.: Continuous approximation of collective system behaviour: a tutorial. Perform. Eval. **70**(5), 317–349 (2013)
10. Boudec, J.Y., McDonald, D., Mundinger, J.: A generic mean field convergence result for systems of interacting objects. In: Proceedings of the 4th International Conference on the Quantitative Evaluation of Systems (QEST 2007). IEEE (2007)
11. Boyd, S., Ghosh, A., Prabhakar, B., Shah, D.: Randomized gossip algorithms. IEEE Trans. Inf. Theor. **52**(6), 2508–2530 (2006)
12. van den Broek, B., Wiegerinck, W., Kappen, B.: Graphical model inference in optimal control of stochastic multi-agent systems. J. Artif. Intell. Res. **32**, 95–122 (2008)
13. Bures, T., et al.: A life cycle for the development of autonomic systems: the e-mobility showcase. In: Proceedings of the 7th IEEE International Conference on Self-Adaptation and Self-Organizing Systems Workshops (SASOW 2013), pp. 71–76 (2013)
14. Castelli, G., Mamei, M., Rosi, A., Zambonelli, F.: Engineering pervasive service ecosystems: The SAPERE approach. ACM Trans. Auton. Adapt. Syst. **10**(1), 1:1–1:27 (2015)
15. Chakrabarti, B.K., Chakraborti, A., Chatterjee, A.: Econophysics and Socio-physics: Trends and Perspectives, Wiley, Hoboken (2006)
16. De Nicola, R., Jähnichen, S., Wirsing, M.: Rigorous engineering of collective adaptive systems: special section. Int. J. Softw. Tools Technol. Transf. **22**, 389–397 (2020)
17. Fagnani, F., Zampieri, S.: Asymmetric randomized gossip algorithms for consensus. IFAC Proc. Volumes **41**(2), 9052–9056 (2008)
18. Fagnani, F., Zampieri, S.: Randomized consensus algorithms over large scale networks. IEEE J. Sel. Areas Commun. **26**(4), 634–649 (2008)
19. Galam, S.: Sociophysics: A Physicist's Modeling of Psycho-Political Phenomena. Understanding Complex Systems, Springer, Cham (2012)
20. Garcia, A.F., de Lucena, C.J.P., Zambonelli, F., Omicini, A., Castro, J. (eds.): Software Engineering for Large-Scale Multi-Agent Systems, Research Issues and Practical Applications. Lecture Notes in Computer Science, vol. 2603. Springer, Cham (2002). https://doi.org/10.1007/3-540-35828-5
21. Goldman, C.V., Zilberstein, S.: Decentralized control of cooperative systems: categorization and complexity analysis. J. Artif. Intell. Res. **22**, 143–174 (2004)
22. Hillston, J., Pitt, J., Wirsing, M., Zambonelli, F.: Collective adaptive systems: qualitative and quantitative modelling and analysis. Dagstuhl Rep. 4(12), 68–113 (2014)
23. Huhns, M.N. (ed.): Distributed Artificial Intelligence. Pitman Publishing, London (1987)
24. Kash, I.A., Friedman, E.J., Halpern, J.Y.: Multiagent learning in large anonymous games. J. Artif. Intell. Res. **40**, 571–598 (2011)
25. Liboff, R.L.: Kinetic Theory: Classical, Quantum, and Relativistic Descriptions. Springer, Cham (2003). https://doi.org/10.1007/b97467
26. Mantegna, R.N., Stanley, H.E.: An Introduction to Econophysics: Correlations and Complexity in Finance. Cambridge University Press, Cambridge (1999)
27. Mariani, S., Cabri, G., Zambonelli, F.: Coordination of autonomous vehicles: taxonomy and survey. ACM Comput. Surv. **54**(1), 19:1–19:33 (2021)
28. Mitchell, M.: Complex systems: network thinking. Artif. Intell. **170**, 1194–1212 (2006)

29. Monica, S., Bergenti, F.: An analytic study of opinion dynamics in multi-agent systems with additive random noise. In: Adorni, G., Cagnoni, S., Gori, M., Maratea, M. (eds.) AI*IA 2016. LNCS (LNAI), vol. 10037, pp. 105–117. Springer, Cham (2016). https://doi.org/10.1007/978-3-319-49130-1_9

30. Monica, S., Bergenti, F.: An analytic study of opinion dynamics in multi-agent systems with additive random noise. Comput. Math. Appl. **73**(10), 2272–2284 (2017)

31. Monica, S., Bergenti, F.: Opinion dynamics in multi-agent systems: Selected analytic models and verifying simulations. Computational & Mathematical Organization Theory **23**(3), 423–450 (2017)

32. Pareschi, L., Toscani, G.: Interacting Multiagent Systems: Kinetic Equations and Montecarlo Methods. Oxford University Press, Oxford (2013)

33. Pynadath, D.V., Tambe, M.: The communicative multiagent team decision problem: analyzing teamwork theories and models. J. Artif. Intell. Res. **16**, 389–423 (2002)

34. Schweitzer, F.: Brownian Agents and Active Particles: Collective Dynamics in the Natural and Social Sciences. Springer, Synergetics (2003). https://doi.org/10.1007/978-3-540-73845-9

35. Slanina, F.: Inelastically scattering particles and wealth distribution in an open economy. Phy. Rev. E **69**, 46–102 (2004)

36. Sznajd-Weron, K., Sznajd, J.: Opinion evolution in closed community. Int. J. Mod. Phy. C **11**, 1157–1166 (2000)

37. Thurner, S., Klimek, P., Hanel, R.: Introduction to the Theory of Complex Systems. Oxford University Press, Oxford (2018)

38. Weidlich, W.: Sociodynamics: A Systematic Approach to Mathematical Modelling in the Social Sciences. Harwood Academic Publisher, Reading (2000)

39. Wolpert, D.H., Tumer, K.: Collective intelligence, data routing and Braess' paradox. J. Artif. Intell. Res. **16**, 359–387 (2002)

40. Ygge, F., Akkermans, H.: Decentralized markets versus central control: a comparative study. J. Artif. Intell. Res. **11**, 301–333 (1999)

Understanding Social Feedback in Biological Collectives with Smoothed Model Checking

Julia Klein[1,2]($\boxtimes$) (iD) and Tatjana Petrov[1,2] (iD)

[1] Department of Computer and Information Sciences, University of Konstanz, Konstanz, Germany
julia.klein@uni-konstanz.de
[2] Centre for the Advanced Study of Collective Behaviour, University of Konstanz, 78464 Konstanz, Germany

Abstract. Biological groups exhibit fascinating collective dynamics without centralised control, through only local interactions between individuals. Desirable group behaviours are typically linked to a certain fitness function, which the group robustly performs under different perturbations in, for instance, group structure, group size, noise, or environmental factors. Deriving this fitness function is an important step towards understanding the collective response, yet it easily becomes non-trivial in the context of complex collective dynamics. In particular, understanding the social feedback - how the collective behaviour adapts to changes in the group size - requires dealing with complex models and limited experimental data. In this work, we assume that the collective response is experimentally observed for a chosen, finite set of group sizes. Based on such data, we propose a framework which allows to: (i) predict the collective response for any given group size, and (ii) automatically propose a fitness function. We use Smoothed Model Checking, an approach based on Gaussian Process Classification, to develop a methodology that is scalable, flexible, and data-efficient; We specify the fitness function as a template temporal logic formula with unknown parameters, and we automatically infer the missing quantities from data. We evaluate the framework over a case study of a collective stinging defence mechanism in honeybee colonies.

Keywords: Social feedback · Gaussian processes · Biological collectives · Smoothed model checking

1 Introduction

Biological groups exhibit fascinating collective dynamics without centralised control, through only local interactions between individuals. Quantitative models of the mechanisms underlying biological grouping can directly serve important

© The Author(s) 2022
T. Margaria and B. Steffen (Eds.): ISoLA 2022, LNCS 13703, pp. 181–198, 2022.
https://doi.org/10.1007/978-3-031-19759-8_12

societal concerns (for example, prediction of seismic activity [22]), inspire the design of distributed algorithms (for example, ant colony algorithm [9]), or aid robust design and engineering of collective, adaptive systems under given functionality and resources, which is increasingly gaining attention in vision of smart cities [17,21]. Quantitative prediction of the behaviour of a population of agents over time and space, each having several behavioural modes, results in a high-dimensional, non-linear, and stochastic system [12]. Computational modelling with population models is therefore challenging, especially since model parameters are often unknown and repeated experiments are costly and time-consuming.

In this paper, we focus on the phenomenon of collective social feedback in biological groups, that is, how the collective behaviour adapts to changes in the group size. Examples of social adaptation include the emergence of sensing abilities through interactions and only exist at the group level [3], or, colony defence [19] or thermoregulation [8] in social insects (as altruistic behaviours that do not occur in isolated individuals), to name but a few. Understanding such social adaptation cannot be done by extrapolating from observing individuals in isolation. Computationally, the challenge of understanding how social context shapes group behaviours emerges at two levels. First, models of group-behaviours enumerating each possible social context of an individual suffer from the combinatorial explosion of states, but also from a prohibitive number of model parameters. With no simplifying assumptions, an individual within a group of size n adapts to at least n different social contexts that need to be parametrized [14,27]. While simplifying assumptions are justified for some experimental systems, they generally need to be validated for each experimental system at hand. For instance, in modelling molecular dynamics with chemical reaction networks, mass-action law assumes a linear influence of reactants' counts to reaction propensities, but this is not justified in case of animal collectives, due to a richer cognitive aspect of individuals. Second, while experimentally measuring the overall group response is significantly simpler than measuring the response of each individual within a group via continuous tracking, it still remains impossible to measure the group response for *each* group size; Instead, one must choose a set of representative group sizes. In other words, in order to find a general pattern of behaviours, it is necessary to analyse groups of many different sizes, both of small and large scale.

For the above reasons, it becomes important to develop methods that are scalable with respect to growing group size, flexible in terms of model size and parameters, and data-efficient - producing reliable results for scarce data sets. Our methodology relies on *Gaussian Processes*, a powerful Bayesian approach in Machine Learning, to learn unknown functions from data. Gaussian Processes, considered a "desired meta-model in various applications" [7], fulfil our requirements of scalability, flexibility, and data-efficiency. In addition, in contrast to other Machine Learning models, Gaussian Processes deal not only with uncertainty in the training data, but also provide guarantees of the predictions in form of credible intervals.

The contributions of this work are as follows. We assume that the collective response is experimentally observed for a chosen, finite set of group sizes. Based on such data, we propose a framework which allows to: (i) predict the collective response for any given group size, and (ii) automatically propose a fitness function that is robustly preserved under perturbations in group size. We use Gaussian Process Regression for task (i), allowing to overcome the need of conducting new experiments and analysing many large models, but still having an informed estimate of the group response. Second, we apply Smoothed Model Checking [5], a novel technique based on Gaussian Process Classification, for task (ii) to derive the fitness function a collective robustly performs by setting up a template formula and inferring the missing quantity from data to understand the social feedback mechanism of the collective. An illustrative example of the developed methods in context of elucidating social feedback in collectives is provided in Sect. 1.1. Finally, we test and evaluate the proposed methods over a real-world case study with social honeybees.

Related Work. The framework we present here is specifically inspired by the application of collective defence in honeybee colonies. Honeybees protect their colonies against vertebrates by releasing an alarm pheromone to recruit a large number of defenders into a massive stinging response [25]. However, these workers will then die from abdominal damage caused by the sting tearing loose [30]. In order to achieve a balanced trade-off towards efficient defence, yet no critical worker loss, each bee's response to the same amount of pheromone may vary greatly, depending on its social context. Our own related works [14,27] focus on extracting individual behaviours from group-level data, by hypothesising a mechanistic behavioural model and developing suitable methods for parameter inference. Here, instead, we also assume that group-level data is available, but we provide a model-free methodology with different aims - predicting the group response, and inferring the group-level fitness function. To the best of our knowledge, our method is the first application of Smoothed Model Checking towards understanding collective animal behaviour.

Methodologically, our work is inspired by the general technique of Smoothed Model Checking [5] (SMMC), implemented in the software tool U-Check [4]. SMMC was used for several applications in systems and synthetic biology. Bartocci et al. [1] propose a notion of robustness degree for stochastic biochemical circuits; They furthermore show how such robustness measure can be used for designing a biochemical circuit robustly exhibiting a certain temporal property; Specifically, the design goal is that a specific behaviour of a biological process is maintained despite uncertainties from noise or uncertain model parameters. Instead of computing the robustness degree of each sample trajectory of a system, in this work we focus on measuring the satisfaction only on steady state data and evaluate the robustness over the satisfaction distribution across different group sizes. In [2], the proposed notion of robustness is used so to optimise certain control parameters of a stochastic model to maximise the robustness of desired specifications. In [6], the authors show how to learn and design continuous-time

Markov chains (CTMCs) from observations formulated in terms of temporal logic formulae; They maximise the likelihood of parameters with the Gaussian Process Upper Confidence Bound (GP-UCB) algorithm. In contrast to the previously mentioned works, we consider a model-free approach and aim to infer a general description of the collective response based only on experimental data. Hence, we do not analyse varying model parameters, but different group sizes. In reference to inferring the fitness function, [18] propose how to infer parameters given a requirement template expressed in signal temporal logic (STL) and simulation traces of the model; The approach is based on finding the tightest valuation function to prevent getting overly conservative parameters. Our method of finding the parameter of a given template differs in selecting the value not according to the tightest valuation function, but according to a measure of variation.

1.1   Illustrative Example

We next illustrate how the methodology we develop can be used to study social influence in groups, i.e., how the group size affects the behaviour of individuals. Assume a group of n identical agents in which each individual is confronted with a task and either solves it successfully or fails, with certain probability. We further assume that, each time an agent in a group succeeds, other individuals in the group are more likely to succeed. Specifically, if the baseline probability of success is p_0, assume that the probability of succeeding with i already successful agents in the system grows with the number of successful agents according to a function $p_i = f(p_0, \alpha, i)$ (simple examples could be $p_i = p_0 + \alpha \cdot (i > 0)$, where the probability increases by α if at least one other agent in the group succeeded, or $p_i = p_0 + \alpha \cdot i$, where the probability increases linearly with the number of other successful agents). Now, if measurements are available for groups of size $1, 2$, and 10 ($n \in \{1, 2, 10\}$), inferring parameters p_0 and α clearly becomes possible from only measurements over isolated individuals (groups of size $n = 1$), and pairs of interacting individuals (groups of size $n = 2$). These two parameters, coupled with an underlying mechanistic model of interaction, would allow to predict the outcome for $n = 10$. Finally, if model-based predictions for $n = 10$ significantly differ from the experimental data for $n = 10$ – the increment parameter α differs significantly for groups of size 2 and 10 – we can conclude that the agent is aware of its social context and there is a feedback mechanism from the group that influences the individual's behaviour. Otherwise, if there is no significant difference, one may conclude that there is no influence of group size to the problem solving efficiency.

The methodology we develop here allows to predict group outcomes for any group size, with uncertainty quantification, when group measurements are available for only certain group sizes. In the context of our illustrating example, this means that one could predict measurements for groups of e.g. size $n = 3$, from measurements for $n \in \{1, 2, 10\}$. Then, the hypothesis of social feedback can be accessed by only making predictions for the model for group with $n = 3$ agents, that is dramatically smaller than the model for $n = 10$ agents (due to combinatorial explosion of the state space, models for n agents would be described by $O(2^n)$ states).

Furthermore, assume that the group aims to satisfy a certain group outcome, independently of its size. In the above example, such function may be that 'eventually, between 40% and 60% of group members succeed at solving the task'. Inferring such *fitness* function - a high-level behavioural outcome that tends to be robustly preserved under environmental perturbations - is of high importance for a biological understanding of grouping. While the qualitative form of the fitness function is often assumed by experts, quantitative parameters (e.g. the range from 40% to 60%) are typically not explored in an automated way. To this end, our second methodological contribution is automatising the search for such a fitness function from only available data measurements and a template logical formula.

2   Methods

In this section, we present the methodology based on Gaussian Processes to understand social feedback mechanisms in biological collectives. First, we describe the theoretical and mathematical background of the methods and subsequently we demonstrate how to apply these existing techniques in our framework to address the previously stated research problems. All definitions of Gaussian Processes and the corresponding regression and classification follow closely the description by Rasmussen and Williams [29].

2.1   Gaussian Process

A Gaussian Process (GP) is a generalisation of a multivariate Gaussian distribution to infinite dimension. As a non-parametric distribution over a space of functions, a GP is designed to solve regression and classification problems by approximating unknown functions. Since a GP model is data-driven, applicable without specifying the underlying distribution beforehand, and powerful even for little data, it surpasses many of the traditional regression and classification methods. The predictions of a GP are probabilistic, such that the results provide not only an estimate, but additionally a quantification of uncertainty in form of credible intervals.

Mathematically, we define a prior probability distribution directly over functions, from which the posterior distribution can be inferred when data is observed. A kernel-based probabilistic model is set up to learn relationships between observed data and make predictions about new data points. In general, a GP's characteristics are completely specified by a mean function $m(x)$ and a positive definite kernel function $k(x, x')$ for input values $x, x' \in \mathbb{R}$. Kernels are used as a similarity measure between data points and generate the covariance matrix Σ by evaluating the kernel function at all pairs of input points.

We denote matrices by capitalised letters and vectors in bold type. A subscript asterisk refers to a test set quantity.

2.2 Gaussian Process Regression

We define a GP prior $f(x) \sim \mathcal{GP}(m(x), k(x, x'))$ independent of any training data that specifies some properties of the unknown functions through the choice of the kernel function. Three of the most common kernel functions are implemented in our framework:

- *Linear kernel*: $k_{lin}(x, x') = \sigma_b^2 + \sigma^2 (x - c)(x' - c)$ with variance σ_b, scale factor σ^2 and offset c,
- *Radial Basis Function* (RBF): $k_{rbf}(x, x') = \sigma^2 \exp(-\frac{||x - x'||^2}{2\ell^2})$ with scale factor σ^2 and lengthscale ℓ, and
- *Periodic kernel*: $k_{per}(x, x') = \sigma^2 \exp(-\frac{2 \sin^2(\pi ||x - x'||/p)}{\ell^2})$ with scale factor σ^2, periodicity parameter p and lengthscale ℓ.

Beyond that, all kernels are pairwise combined by addition and multiplication to achieve higher-level structures [13].

Let X be the training data set with observed function values $\mathbf{f}$, and X_* the test data set for which we want to predict the corresponding function outputs $\mathbf{f}_*$. The joint distribution of training and test outputs is given by

$$\begin{bmatrix} \mathbf{f} \\ \mathbf{f}_* \end{bmatrix} \sim \mathcal{N}\left(\begin{bmatrix} \mu \\ \mu_* \end{bmatrix}, \begin{bmatrix} \Sigma & \Sigma_* \\ \Sigma_*^T & \Sigma_{**} \end{bmatrix} \right), \tag{1}$$

where $\mu = m(x_i)$, $i = 1, ..., n$, denotes the training mean values and analogously μ_* the test mean values. The covariance matrix Σ is evaluated at all pairs of training points, Σ_* at training and test points, and Σ_{**} at test points. The posterior distribution is obtained by conditioning the joint Gaussian prior distributions on the observations:

$$\mathbf{f}_* | X_*, X, \mathbf{f} \sim \mathcal{N}(\Sigma_*^T \Sigma^{-1} f, \ \Sigma_{**} - \Sigma_*^T \Sigma^{-1} \Sigma_*). \tag{2}$$

By evaluating the mean and covariance we derive the function values $\mathbf{f}_*$ from the posterior distribution. Computing two times the standard deviation of each test point around the mean generates 95% credible regions.

Normally distributed observational noise can be considered in the training data, $y = f(x) + \epsilon$ with $f \sim \mathcal{GP}(0, \Sigma)$ and $\epsilon \sim \mathcal{N}(0, \sigma_f^2 I)$. The noise variance σ_f^2 is independently added to each observation, $p(y|f) = \mathcal{N}(y|f, \sigma_f^2 I)$, what changes the joint distribution of training and test values to

$$\begin{bmatrix} \mathbf{y} \\ \mathbf{f}_* \end{bmatrix} \sim \mathcal{N}\left(0, \begin{bmatrix} \Sigma_y & \Sigma_* \\ \Sigma_*^T & \Sigma_{**} \end{bmatrix} \right) \tag{3}$$

with $\Sigma_y := \Sigma + \sigma_f^2 I$. Deriving the posterior distribution results in:

$$f_* | X_*, X, y \sim \mathcal{N}(\Sigma_*^T \Sigma_y^{-1} y, \ \Sigma_{**} - \Sigma_*^T \Sigma_y^{-1} \Sigma_*). \tag{4}$$

Each kernel has a number of hyperparameters that specify the precise shape of the covariance function. Optimising the kernels' hyperparameters increases the accuracy of predictions. As standard practice, we follow an empirical Bayesian approach to maximise the log marginal likelihood

$$\log p(y|X) = \log \mathcal{N}(y|0, \Sigma_y) = -\frac{1}{2}y\Sigma_y^{-1}y - \frac{1}{2}\log |\Sigma_y| - \frac{1}{2}N\log (2\pi), \quad (5)$$

where the first term is a data fit term, the second term a model complexity term, and the third term a constant. Minimising the negative log marginal likelihood with respect to the hyperparameters of a kernel gives us an optimised posterior distribution [24].

2.3 Gaussian Process Classification

Gaussian Process Classification (GPC) is applied to binary classification problems, where class labels $\mathbf{y} \in [0, 1]$ are observed for input values X. After defining a GP Prior over a suitable function space, the functional form of the likelihood is determined to approximate the posterior distribution. The goal is to get an estimate of a class probability for unknown data points from Boolean observations. The probability of belonging to a certain class at an input value x is related to the value of some latent function $f(x)$ at this location. In the first step, a GP prior is placed over the latent function $f(x)$. As we apply GPC only for multi-dimensional input, we implement the *RBF-ARD* kernel for all data sets: $k_{rbf-ard}(\mathbf{x}, \mathbf{x}') = \sigma^2 \exp(-\frac{1}{2}\sum_{d=1}^{D} \frac{||x_d - x_d'||^2}{\ell_d^2})$ for d dimensions with scale factor σ^2 and d different lengthscales ℓ_i.

The prior is squashed with the inverse probit transformation to transform real values into probabilities,

$$\Phi(z) = \int_{-\infty}^{z} \mathcal{N}(x|0, 1)dx = \frac{1}{2} + \frac{1}{2} \cdot erf \left(\frac{z}{\sqrt{2}}\right), \quad (6)$$

where erf is the Gauss error function, defined as $erf(z) = \frac{2}{\sqrt{\pi}} \int_0^z e^{-t^2} dt$ [26]. Therefore, we obtain a prior on class probabilities $\pi(x) \triangleq p(y = 1|x) = \Phi(f(x))$. Then, the distribution of the latent variable corresponding to a test case is computed with

$$p(f_*|X, \mathbf{y}, x_*) = \int p(f_*|X, x_*, \mathbf{f})p(\mathbf{f}|X, \mathbf{y})d\mathbf{f}. \quad (7)$$

This distribution contains the posterior over the latent variables as the product of a normalisation term containing the marginal likelihood, the prior and the likelihood,

$$p(\mathbf{f}|X, \mathbf{y}) = \frac{1}{p(\mathbf{y}|X)}p(\mathbf{f}|X) \prod_{i=1}^{n} p(y_i|f_i). \quad (8)$$

To increase the accuracy of the approach, the kernel's hyperparameters are optimised by minimising the negative log marginal likelihood. For predictions for a class probability we have

$$\overline{\pi}_* \triangleq p(y_* = 1|X, \mathbf{y}, x_*) = \int \Phi(f_*)p(f_*|X, \mathbf{y}, x_*)df_*. \quad (9)$$

As the observations are Boolean and the probit function is used, the corresponding likelihood is non-Gaussian and consequently the integral of the posterior distribution in Eq. 7 is intractable. Therefore, we approximate the joint posterior by a Gaussian distribution using the popular analytic approximation *Expectation Propagation* [20].

2.4   Smoothed Model Checking

When modelling biological collectives, it is often necessary to analyse uncertain stochastic systems and infer missing parameters. A novel approach based on GPC is called Smoothed Model Checking [5] (SMMC) and aims to estimate the satisfaction function of an uncertain CTMC for a specific temporal logic property. Given is an uncertain CTMC $\mathcal{M}_\theta$ with unknown parameters θ and a temporal logic property φ. For a few fixed values of θ, several trajectories of $\mathcal{M}_\theta$ are simulated and the satisfactions of φ (i.e. $\mathcal{M}_\theta \models \varphi$) collected. These observations follow a Binomial distribution and are the input to GPC. However, the algorithm of GPC is changed in such a way that it can deal with multiple observations per data point and make use of the exact statistical model. As a result, we get an accurate estimation of the satisfaction function $f_\varphi(\theta) = P(\mathcal{M}_\theta \models \varphi)$ over varying parameters θ.

In contrast to the original work, we use SMMC to estimate the satisfaction of a property not over varying model parameters, but over varying group sizes. Our application of SMMC aims to find the most plausible value of the missing quantity in a template formula to derive the fitness function. We explain the detailed workflow in Sect. 2.6.

2.5   Model Selection

Gaussian Process models are essentially defined by the chosen kernel function that determines the shape of the function to be estimated. Without prior knowledge about the shape, it is recommended to test different kernels and afterwards select the best fit. Because of only few data available, we apply Leave-One-Out Cross-Validation (LOOCV) to estimate the expected prediction error and decide for the best model. LOOCV provides reliable and unbiased estimates of the model's performance, even for small data sets [24]. In particular, the training data is split into $K = n$ folds, where n is the size of the data set. Then, for each fold $k \in \{1, ..., K\}$, the model is trained on all folds but the k-th one, and tested on the remaining ones [16].

The summary statistics of the test set gives an overall evaluation of the goodness of the model. Here, we compute the amount of error for each kernel with the Mean Squared Error (MSE),

$$MSE = \frac{\sum_i^n (y_i - f_{*_i})^2}{n} \tag{10}$$

with y_i being the observations, f_{*_i} the predictions, and n the size of the test set [24].

For GPR, we consider multiple kernel functions and use LOOCV to automatically select the best kernel. However, for GPC we always use the RBF-ARD kernel and thus only compute the MSE to evaluate the quality of the model and perform no model selection.

2.6   Problem Statement

Predict the Collective Response with GPR. In our two-folded approach, we first use GPR to predict the collective response for varying group sizes to obtain more information about the social influence within the collective. We assume to have only data about the collective response of a few group sizes available that consist of the final states of the agents. That means we can present the data as histograms counting the frequencies of different outcomes for each available group size. We extract the mean and variance of the histogram and use it as a measure of collective response, e.g. how many agents have successfully solved the task on average. Then, we apply GPR on mean values and variances with different kernels for which we optimise the hyperparameters. We select the best kernel using LOOCV, where we compare the MSE of each model. As a result, we get a prediction of the mean collective response (and variance) within a 95% credible interval for different group sizes and thus gain a better understanding of the general collective behaviour without making any previous assumptions.

Inferring the Fitness Function with SMMC. After the first part helps to understand the trend of the collective response over varying group sizes, we aim to find out how the social context influences the individual response in the second part. More precisely, we propose a general fitness function that is likely to explain the collective behaviour but contains an unknown parameter $t \in \mathbb{R}$ that specifies the exact mechanism. The fitness function is defined as a template temporal logic formula φ_t in the language Probabilistic Computation Tree Logic [15] for discrete systems, and in Signal Temporal Logic [23] for continuous systems. We expect the fitness function to describe a behaviour that is robustly performed across all group sizes n, which relates to φ_t being robustly satisfied over all n. Specifically, we set up the template formula as an atomic proposition with one unknown parameter t. To finally infer the value of t that best describes the behaviour, we choose a few equally-spaced values of t and for each of these collect the number of satisfactions of φ_t for given group sizes. Then, we run SMMC for each t individually to obtain a smooth satisfaction function of φ_t over all varying group sizes.

The resulting posterior distributions are then compared with respect to their shapes. A high mean value indicates a high satisfaction probability of the property, while a low standard deviation implies small variation across different group sizes, and therefore a robust behaviour. For our specific scenario, we compute the coefficient of variation for the posterior distribution of each t as the fraction of mean and standard deviation, $c_v(t) = \frac{\mu}{sd}$. According to the literature (e.g., [10,28]), a $c_v < 0.1$ is considered low and indicates a distribution with our desired properties, specific to the previously defined fitness function template. Finally, we select the largest value of t with $c_v(t) < 0.1$ to get the most plausible quantity of the formula and a valid fitness function the collective robustly performs. This fitness function helps to describe how the social context influences the individual's response.

3   Results

In this section we present the results of our framework on a case study discussing a social feedback mechanism found in honeybees. Biological collectives of honeybees protect their colonies against a threat by releasing an alarm pheromone that warns the other bees and leads to a recruitment of a large number of further defenders. More specifically, to successfully defend their territory, some of the bees become aggressive, decide to sting, and consequently die. During stinging, the alarm pheromone P is released and increases the aggressiveness of other bees in the colony. However, if the aggressiveness increased endlessly, eventually all bees of the population would die, which is an unreasonable assumption. Therefore, there needs to be some regulatory mechanism that prevents the colony from becoming extinct, while still being able to effectively defend against the threat. From this follows the hypothesis that the bee is socially influenced by its colony and aware of its social context, i.e., the group size. See [14] for a more detailed description of the case study and the assumptions for the associated stochastic model. To better understand the exact underlying mechanism of social feedback, we apply our methods on experimental data of this phenomenon for a few group sizes. We use Gaussian Process Regression to predict the collective response over all intermediate group sizes and learn about the trend of how the context regulates the bees' behaviour. We then aim to derive the non-trivial fitness function by setting up a plausible template formula and applying Smoothed Model Checking to automatically infer the missing quantity that explains the collective dynamics.

3.1   Data

To test our framework on real-world observations, we make use of experimental data collected at the University of Konstanz (Germany) [27]. In three experiments, groups of 1, 2, 5, 7, 10, or 15 bees were put into an arena and exposed to a threat. After a certain time, the number of stinging bees was counted which provides a measure of the collective response. This procedure was repeated several times for each population size within each experiment. Hence, we get three histograms with the frequencies of stinging bees of each population size. See Fig. 1 for the result distributions of all data sets.

3.2   Predict the Collective Response

Our data contains information about the collective response of a few selected group sizes. However, to get predictions for all other intermediate group sizes,

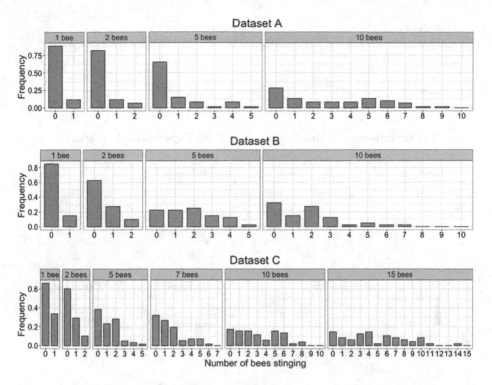

Fig. 1. Overview of experimental data from three data sets showing the frequencies of the number of stinging bees. Experiments were repeated with sample sizes $N_A = [60, 60, 60, 60]$, $N_B = [40, 40, 40, 40]$ and $N_C = [68, 68, 60, 56, 52, 48]$.

we apply GPR on the three data sets. As mentioned above, we consider the number of stinging bees as the collective response to defend the territory. We compute the mean and variance of each histogram, corresponding to the mean and variance of stinging bees for each population size, and use these values as input to the algorithm. Noise, computed as the 95% credible interval, is added to each data point to account for observation errors and limited sample sizes [31]. Then, we run GPR for each implemented kernel and combination of two kernels with optimised hyperparameters. As a result, we get the posterior predictive distribution of the collective response for different population sizes. The best model is selected with the lowest MSE according to LOOCV and shown in Fig. 2.

We observe that the uncertainty increases for larger group sizes due to the small sample size. For a group size of one bee, there are only two outcomes of the experiment: either no bees sting, or one bee stings. In contrast, for a group size of ten bees, there are eleven possible outcomes of the experiment. Since the sample size remains the same, the uncertainty increases.

The results show that we can model different trends of collective response with the same algorithm and without specifying any previous assumptions

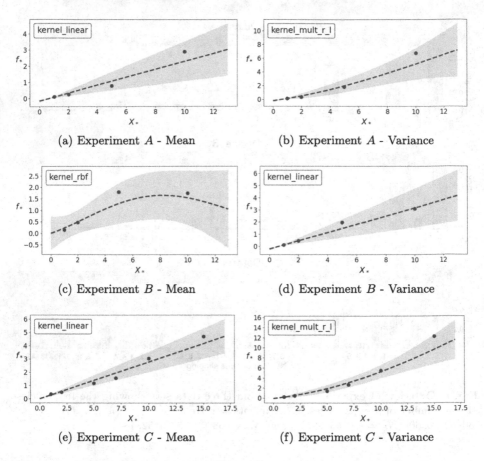

Fig. 2. Posterior distributions for mean and variance of histograms for experimental data. Points are training data points, dashed lines are predictive means and shaded areas are 95% credible regions. Best kernel according to LOOCV is written in the left upper corner with following MSEs: Experiment A - Mean: linear kernel, $MSE = 0.8882$ - Variance: multiplication of RBF and linear kernel, $MSE = 4.4019$. Experiment B - Mean: RBF, $MSE = 0.5536$ - Variance: linear kernel, $MSE = 0.1219$. Experiment C - Mean: linear kernel, $MSE = 0.2157$ - Variance: multiplication of RBF and linear kernel, $MSE = 7.3824$.

beforehand. The linear trend of the number of stinging bees in Experiment A and C is well captured, as well as the non-trivial trend in Experiment B. From these distributions we can easily infer the collective response of all other group sizes. In the case of having social feedback in a colony, we are therefore still able to get reliable estimates of the behaviour of the colony without the need of conducting new experiments. Note that predictions for group sizes outside the range of available data points are also possible, but introduce even larger uncertainties.

3.3 Inferring the Fitness Function

In the second step, we aim to get a better understanding of social feedback and how the collective behaviour adapts to changes in the group sizes. For this case study, we want to investigate if there is always a certain proportion of the population defending the whole collective. Therefore, we want to derive the most plausible quantity for the fitness function '*at least* $(100 \cdot t)\%$ *of the colony survives*' and set up the corresponding template temporal logic formula φ : $\mathbf{F}(X \geq t)$ with X being the number of surviving bees and $t \in [0, 1]$ the unknown threshold.

We select 21 equally-spaced thresholds t and analyse the satisfaction function of φ for different group sizes with SMMC with optimised hyperparameters. For each t, the inputs to SMMC are the number of observations for which the property is satisfied in each group size, read from the respective histogram. Again, we get a posterior distribution with 95% credible regions for different group sizes. Computing the coefficient of variation of the posterior distribution for all values of t gives us an estimate about the most plausible distribution with respect to the previously defined fitness function. We select the largest t with a low $c_v < 0.1$ to obtain a distribution with high mean values and little variation. This gives us the property that defines a behaviour that is robustly satisfied by the collective over all group sizes. In Fig. 3, we show on the left side the coefficients of variation c_v for different thresholds t together with the mean and standard deviation of the posterior distributions for each experiment. On the right side, we visualise the SMMC posterior of the selected value of t.

The obtained results indicate the most plausible values to be $t = 0.5$ for experiment A and B, and $t = 0.65$ for experiment C. The biological interpretation of the analysis is that, on average, $50 - 65\%$ of a honeybee colony survives when being exposed to a threat. Put differently, at least $50 - 65\%$ of a colony needs to perform a stinging response to successfully defend the territory. With this method we were able to automatically quantify the high level behavioural outcome of the collective that is robustly performed under perturbations. Furthermore, we observe that all posterior distributions capture the data well according to the low MSEs.

4 Conclusion

In this paper, we presented a framework based on Gaussian Processes to better understand the phenomenon of social feedback in biological collectives. Our contribution is two-fold: first, we predict the collective response for any given group size from only limited experimental data; Second, we derive a fitness function that is robustly preserved under perturbations in group size. On the one hand, the application of our methods helps to test the hypothesis of social feedback in a collective, when only measurements of few group sizes are available. The resulting predictions of collective response eliminate the need of conducting new experiments and analysing combinatorialy large stochastic models. Still, we get reliable results for any group size, together with a quantification of uncertainty.

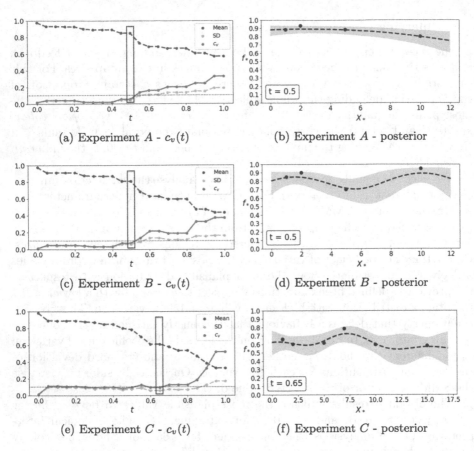

(a) Experiment A - $c_v(t)$

(b) Experiment A - posterior

(c) Experiment B - $c_v(t)$

(d) Experiment B - posterior

(e) Experiment C - $c_v(t)$

(f) Experiment C - posterior

Fig. 3. SMMC results of experimental data for the property φ : at least $(100 \cdot t)\%$ of the colony survives. Left: mean (blue), standard deviation (orange), and coefficient of variation (green) of posterior distributions over varying t are shown. Black dotted line shows the threshold $c_v = 0.1$. Black rectangle shows the values for the largest t with $c_v(t) < 0.1$. Right: SMMC posterior for selected t, points are training data points, dashed lines are predictive posterior means and shaded areas are 95% credible regions. Experiment A - $t = 0.5$ with $c_v(t) = 0.052$, $MSE = 0.0038$. Experiment B - $t = 0.5$ with $c_v(t) = 0.0731$, $MSE = 0.0136$. Experiment C - $t = 0.65$ with $c_v(t) = 0.093$, $MSE = 0.0072$. (Color figure online)

On the other hand, our framework can be used to assess the trend of social feedback in the sense of how social context influences the collective response. The missing quantities in a template logical formula (usually proposed by experts), is automatically inferred to derive a fitness function that describes the collective behaviour under group-size perturbations.

Both applications are based on Gaussian Processes, which has several key advantages compared to traditional methods. Usually, the analysis of models for larger group sizes becomes computationally infeasible due to state explosion. Gaussian Processes, as a non-parametric and model-agnostic approach, are instead scalable for any given group size and therefore particularly useful to measure the collective response with respect to growing group size. Beyond that, the analyses of our proposed methods are data-efficient and produce reliable results with uncertainty quantification even for scarce data sets. Especially when working with real-world experimental data, there are often not enough resources available to collect large amounts of data. Therefore, we decided to use Gaussian Processes that are able to find the underlying relationships between only few available data points and also provide statistical guarantees. Last, we want to emphasise the flexibility of this framework, where we not only discard any previous assumptions on the underlying model and its parameters, but further are able to use it on any related application. While we focus on understanding social feedback in honeybees in this work, other use cases of analysing collective behaviour are possible. Instead of predicting the steady state for any group size, the method could also be applied to any quantitative measurement of the collective. Accordingly, the template fitness function can be exchanged by any temporal logic formula for which we can assess the satisfaction probability, and the coefficient of variation by a different measure of robustness to suit the particular case study and research question.

Despite highlighting the power of the proposed methods, we also want to point out possible limitations. One major drawback of Gaussian Processes is the computational complexity of $O(N^3)$ [24]. In our work, we implemented all functions by hand, in order to have full control over the computations. However, using available libraries like GPyTorch [11], could speed up the calculations. Another limitation of Gaussian Processes is the extrapolation needed for larger or smaller group sizes than those available in the data set. In this case, the uncertainty quickly becomes large and the predictions imprecise. In practice, one would encourage to conduct a new experiment for much smaller/larger group sizes to counteract these high uncertainties and focus on interpolation of intermediate group sizes.

Future work will focus on exploring the full potential of the presented techniques in terms of automatically learning unknown parameters of a model or even the entire mechanisms. In general, the approach could be automatised and integrated into a probabilistic reasoning framework.

Acknowledgements. JK's research was supported by the AFF (Der Ausschuss für Forschungsfragen, EU-Anschubfinanzierung, Univ. of Konstanz), TP's research is supported by the Ministry of Science, Research and the Arts of the state of Baden-Württemberg. TP and JK were further funded by the Deutsche Forschungsgemeinschaft (DFG, German Research Foundation) under Germany's Excellence Strategy - EXC 2117 - 422037984. The authors would like to thank Francesca Cairoli, Laura Nenzi, and Wolfram Barfuss for the fruitful and inspiring discussions on the topic.

References

1. Bartocci, E., Bortolussi, L., Nenzi, L., Sanguinetti, G.: On the robustness of temporal properties for stochastic models. Electron. Proc. Theor. Comput. Sci. **125**, 3–19 (2013) 10.4204/EPTCS.125.1, https://arxiv.org/abs/1309.0866v1
2. Bartocci, E., Bortolussi, L., Nenzi, L., Sanguinetti, G.: System design of stochastic models using robustness of temporal properties. Theor. Comput. Sci. **587**, 3–25 (2015). https://doi.org/10.1016/j.tcs.2015.02.046
3. Berdahl, A., Torney, C.J., Ioannou, C.C., Faria, J.J., Couzin, I.D.: Emergent sensing of complex environments by mobile animal groups. Science **339**(6119), 574–6 (2013). https://doi.org/10.1126/science.1225883, https://www.ncbi.nlm.nih.gov/pubmed/23372013
4. Bortolussi, L., Milios, D., Sanguinetti, G.: U-Check: model checking and parameter synthesis under uncertainty. In: Campos, J., Haverkort, B.R. (eds.) QEST 2015. LNCS, vol. 9259, pp. 89–104. Springer, Cham (2015). https://doi.org/10.1007/978-3-319-22264-6_6
5. Bortolussi, L., Milios, D., Sanguinetti, G.: Smoothed model checking for uncertain continuous-time Markov chains. Inf. Comput. **247**, 235–253 (2016)
6. Bortolussi, L., Sanguinetti, G.: Learning and designing stochastic processes from logical constraints. In: Joshi, K., Siegle, M., Stoelinga, M., D'Argenio, P.R. (eds.) QEST 2013. LNCS, vol. 8054, pp. 89–105. Springer, Heidelberg (2013). https://doi.org/10.1007/978-3-642-40196-1_7
7. Chen, T., Hadinoto, K., Yan, W., Ma, Y.: Efficient meta-modelling of complex process simulations with time-space-dependent outputs. Comput. Chem. Eng. **35**(3), 502–509 (2011). https://doi.org/10.1016/j.compchemeng.2010.05.013, https://linkinghub.elsevier.com/retrieve/pii/S009813541000195X
8. Cook, C.N., Breed, M.D.: Social context influences the initiation and threshold of thermoregulatory behaviour in honeybees. Anim. Behav. **86**(2), 323–329 (2013). https://doi.org/10.1016/j.anbehav.2013.05.021
9. Dorigo, M., Birattari, M., Blum, C., Clerc, M., Stützle, T., Winfield, A.F.T. (eds.): ANTS 2008. LNCS, vol. 5217. Springer, Heidelberg (2008). https://doi.org/10.1007/978-3-540-87527-7
10. Faria Filho, D., et al.: Classification of coefficients of variation in experiments with commercial layers. Revista Brasileira de Ciência Avícola **12**(4), 255–257 (2010). https://doi.org/10.1590/S1516-635X2010000400006
11. Gardner, J.R., Pleiss, G., Bindel, D., Weinberger, K.Q., Wilson, A.G.: GPyTorch: blackbox matrix-matrix gaussian process inference with GPU acceleration. In: Advances in Neural Information Processing Systems (2018)
12. Giardina, I.: Collective behavior in animal groups: theoretical models and empirical studies. HFSP J. **2**(4), 205–219 (2008)
13. Görtler, J., Kehlbeck, R., Deussen, O.: A visual exploration of gaussian processes. Distill **4**(4), e17 (2019)
14. Hajnal, M., Nouvian, M., Šafránek, D., Petrov, T.: Data-informed parameter synthesis for population Markov chains. In: Češka, M., Paoletti, N. (eds.) HSB 2019. LNCS, vol. 11705, pp. 147–164. Springer, Cham (2019). https://doi.org/10.1007/978-3-030-28042-0_10
15. Hansson, H., Jonsson, B.: A logic for reasoning about time and reliability. Formal Aspects Comput. **6**(5), 512–535 (1994)
16. Hastie, T., Tibshirani, R., Friedman, J.H.: The elements of statistical learning: data mining, inference, and prediction. Springer series in statistics, Springer, New York, 2nd edn. (2009)

17. Hillston, J.: Challenges for quantitative analysis of collective adaptive systems. In: Abadi, M., Lluch Lafuente, A. (eds.) TGC 2013. LNCS, vol. 8358, pp. 14–21. Springer, Cham (2014). https://doi.org/10.1007/978-3-319-05119-2_2

18. Jin, X., Donzé, A., Deshmukh, J.V., Seshia, S.A.: Mining requirements from closed-loop control models. IEEE Trans. Comput. Aided Des. Integr. Circuits Syst. **34**(11), 1704–1717 (2015)

19. Kleineidam, C.J., Heeb, E.L., Neupert, S.: Social interactions promote adaptive resource defense in ants. PLoS One **12**(9), e0183872 (2017). https://doi.org/10.1371/journal.pone.0183872, https://www.ncbi.nlm.nih.gov/pubmed/28910322

20. Kuß, M.: Gaussian Process Models. Ph.D. thesis (2006)

21. Loreti, M., Hillston, J.: Modelling and analysis of collective adaptive systems with CARMA and its tools. In: Bernardo, M., De Nicola, R., Hillston, J. (eds.) SFM 2016. LNCS, vol. 9700, pp. 83–119. Springer, Cham (2016). https://doi.org/10.1007/978-3-319-34096-8_4

22. Mai, M., et al.: Monitoring pre-seismic activity changes in a domestic animal collective in central Italy. In: EGU General Assembly Conference Abstracts. vol. 20, p. 19348 (2018)

23. Maler, O., Nickovic, D.: Monitoring temporal properties of continuous signals. In: Lakhnech, Y., Yovine, S. (eds.) FORMATS/FTRTFT -2004. LNCS, vol. 3253, pp. 152–166. Springer, Heidelberg (2004). https://doi.org/10.1007/978-3-540-30206-3_12

24. Murphy, K.P.: Machine Learning: A Probabilistic Perspective. MIT press, Cambridge (2012)

25. Nouvian, M., Reinhard, J., Giurfa, M.: The defensive response of the honeybee Apis mellifera. J. Exp. Biol. **219**(22), 3505–3517 (2016)

26. Patel, J.K., Read, C.B.: Handbook of the Normal Distribution, vol. 150. CRC Press, Boca Raton (1996)

27. Petrov, T., Hajnal, M., Klein, J., Šafránek, D., Nouvian, M.: Extracting individual characteristics from population data reveals a negative social effect during honeybee defence. PLOS Comput. Biol. **18**(9), e1010305 (2022). https://doi.org/10.1371/journal.pcbi.1010305

28. Pimentel Gomes, F.: Curso de Estatística Experimental, 13th edn. Nobel, São Paulo (2000)

29. Rasmussen, C.E., Williams, C.K.I.: Gaussian processes for machine learning, 3, vol. 2. MIT Press, Cambridge (2006)

30. Shorter, J.R., Rueppell, O.: A review on self-destructive defense behaviors in social insects. Insectes Soc. **59**(1), 1–10 (2012)

31. Zhang, J., Yin, J., Wang, R.: Basic framework and main methods of uncertainty quantification. Math. Prob. Eng. **2020** (2020)

Efficient Estimation of Agent Networks

Alexander Leguizamon-Robayo and Max Tschaikowski[✉]

Aalborg University, Aalborg, Denmark
tschaikowski@cs.aau.dk

Abstract. Collective adaptive systems (CAS) are characterized by the presence of many agents and an environment which interact with each other. As a consequence, they give rise to global dynamics which cannot be analyzed by considering agents in isolation. While the *modeling* of CAS via agent (reaction) networks gained momentum, obtaining reliable forecasts is computationally difficult because parameters are often subject to uncertainty. It has been therefore recently proposed to obtain *reliable estimates* on global dynamics of agent networks from local agent behavior. To this end, dependencies among agents were replaced by exogenous parameters, allowing one thus to estimate the global dynamics via *agent decoupling*. The present work introduces the notion of *estimation equivalence*, a model reduction technique for systems of nonlinear differential equations that allows one to replace the aforementioned decoupled model by a smaller one which is easier to analyze. We demonstrate the framework on a multi-class SIRS model from epidemiology and obtain a speed-up factor that is proportional to the number of population classes.

Keywords: Agent networks · Formal estimation · Model reduction

1 Introduction

The world is full of interacting entities such as IoT devices in households, users on facebook or viruses in human bodies. By interacting with each other, agents give rise to emergent behavior, that is, global dynamics which cannot be captured by studying agents in isolation. Such systems are often referred to as collective adaptive systems (CAS). Models of CAS are attractive because they allow to make forecasts and do not hinge on the availability of a physical model. In that respect, chemical reaction networks can be seen as one of the first modeling formalisms for CAS and have been used to describe and model (bio)chemical processes by means of molecule interaction rules. In the last decades, researchers succeeded to tie the global macro dynamics, given by the famous law of mass action, to microscopic molecule interactions. Specifically, it was shown that populations of interacting agents can be modeled by a Markov chain whose average behavior coincides with the global dynamics, formally given by a set of ordinary

© The Author(s), under exclusive license to Springer Nature Switzerland AG 2022
T. Margaria and B. Steffen (Eds.): ISoLA 2022, LNCS 13703, pp. 199–214, 2022.
https://doi.org/10.1007/978-3-031-19759-8_13

differential equation (ODEs) [16]. This connection paved the way to so-called fluid approximations which allowed one to use compact ODE systems instead of large-scale agent based Markov chain models given in terms of agent networks, see [3,4,15,22] and references therein.

Models of realistic CAS depend on parameters which are often subject to finite-precision measurements or are unknown, with a possible example being the uncertain parameters in the modeling of covid-19 [13]. Reliable forecasts of nonlinear CAS models require therefore to formally estimate the nonlinear global dynamics under all possible parameterizations [1,9,14]. Unfortunately, this computationally challenging in case of nonlinear dynamics and limited to small models in general. Indeed, common nonlinear benchmarks models have usually not more than 12 ODEs, see for instance [8]. The recent work [23] proposes an estimation technique for nonlinear CAS models that exploits how agents interact with each other. By replacing dependencies among agents with uncertain external parameters, the behavior of each agent can be decoupled from that of the others and therefore analyzed efficiently. Moreover, if the external parameters have sufficiently large uncertainty ranges, local agent estimates are guaranteed to provide global agent estimates, i.e., estimates on the global dynamics.

The present work proposes to combine the estimation approach from [23] with a model reduction technique from [5,7]. More specifically, after decoupling the agents from each other using [23], the intuitive idea is to solve the decoupled system more efficiently by means of the model reduction technique [5,7]. We formalize this by introducing estimation equivalence (EE), a notion that yields estimation-preserving reductions. The EE yielding the smallest estimation-preserving reduction can be computed by means of a partition refinement algorithm which enjoys a polynomial time complexity, similarly to the partition refinement algorithms for probabilistic bisimulation [17] of Markov chains [2,11,24]. We demonstrate the applicability of the approach by reducing the estimation task of a multi-class SIRS model from epidemiology.

Further Work. To the best of our knowledge, estimation-preserving reduction techniques for *nonlinear* dynamical systems have been studied so far only in control engineering via bisimulation/abstraction [19,20,25]. These are complementary to EE because EE relies on backward differential equivalence which, in turn, is complementary to abstraction [21]. Another difference is that EE can be computed, under mild assumptions, in polynomial time, while computational bounds for obtaining abstractions of nonlinear systems have not been reported.

Outline. After setting the scene in Sect. 2, Sect. 3 introduces estimation equivalence. Section 4 instead demonstrates estimation equivalence on a multi-class SIRS model from epidemiology, while Sect. 5 concludes the paper.

Notation. For a nonempty set $\mathcal{I}$, we denote by $A^{\mathcal{I}}$ the set of all functions from $\mathcal{I}$ to A. We write $x \leq x'$ for $x, x' \in \mathbb{R}^{\mathcal{I}}$ whenever $x_i \leq x'_i$ for all $i \in \mathcal{I}$. The equality of two functions f and g, instead, is denoted by $f \equiv g$. By $\mathcal{S}$ we refer to the finite set of (agent) states. Instead, $V \in \mathbb{R}^{\mathcal{S}}$ refers to elements of the reachable set of differential equations and can be interpreted as concentrations or percentages. We write V_{α} to denote the projection of $V \in \mathbb{R}^{\mathcal{S}}$ onto the coordinate $\alpha \in \mathcal{S}$. The derivative with respect to time of a function $V \in [0;T] \to \mathbb{R}^{\mathcal{S}}$ is denoted by $\dot{V}$. At last, $\mathcal{H}, \mathcal{G}$ denote partitions of $\mathcal{S}$ and we say that $\mathcal{H}$ refines $\mathcal{G}$ whenever every block of $\mathcal{G}$ can be written as a union of blocks from $\mathcal{H}$.

2   Preliminaries

In this section we review the estimation of agent networks [23] and backward differential equivalence [5].

2.1   Estimation of Agent Networks

Agent networks can be used to efficiently approximate large-scale Markov chain models of agent populations such like, for instance, epidemics or molecule interactions.

Definition 1. *An agent network (AN) is a triple $(\mathcal{S}, \mathcal{K}, \mathcal{F})$ of a finite set of states $\mathcal{S} = \{A_1, \dots, A_{|\mathcal{S}|}\}$, a set of parameters $\mathcal{K}$ and a set of reaction rate functions $\mathcal{F}$. Each reaction rate function $\Theta_j : \mathbb{R}_{\geq 0}^{\mathcal{S} \cup \mathcal{K}} \to \mathbb{R}_{\geq 0}$*

- *describes the rate at which reaction j occurs;*
- *takes concentration and parameter vectors $V \in \mathbb{R}_{>0}^{\mathcal{S}}$ and $\kappa \in \mathbb{R}_{>0}^{\mathcal{K}}$, respectively;*
- *is accompanied by a multiset R_j of atomic transitions $A_l \to A_{l'}$, where $A_l \to A_{l'}$ states that an agent in state A_l interacts and changes state to $A_{l'}$.*

From a multiset R_j, we can extract two integer valued $|\mathcal{S}|$-vectors d_j and c_j, counting how many agents in each state are transformed during a reaction (respectively produced and consumed). Specifically, for each $1 \leq j \leq |\mathcal{F}|$, let $c_{jl}, d_{jl} \in \mathbb{N}_0$ be such that

$$c_{j,l} = \sum_{A_l \to A_{l'} \in R_j} 1 \quad \text{and} \quad d_{j,l'} = \sum_{A_l \to A_{l'} \in R_j} 1.$$

With these vectors, we can express the j-th reaction in the chemical reaction style [16] as follows:

$$c_{j,1} A_1 + \dots + c_{j,|\mathcal{S}|} A_{|\mathcal{S}|} \xrightarrow{\Theta_j} d_{j,1} A_1 + \dots + d_{j,|\mathcal{S}|} A_{|\mathcal{S}|} \tag{1}$$

We next introduce the ODE semantics of an AN.

Definition 2. *For a given AN $(\mathcal{S}, \mathcal{K}, \mathcal{F})$, a continuous parameter function $\hat{\kappa} : [0;T] \to \mathbb{R}_{>0}^{\mathcal{K}}$ and a piecewise continuous function $\delta : [0;T] \to \mathbb{R}_{>0}^{\mathcal{K}}$ such that $\delta_\alpha(\cdot) < \hat{\kappa}_\alpha(\cdot)$ with $\alpha \in \mathcal{K}$, let*

$$\mathcal{U}_\mathcal{K}^\delta := \{u : [0;T] \to \mathbb{R}_{>0}^{\mathcal{K}} \mid |u_\alpha(\cdot)| \leq \delta_\alpha(\cdot) \; \forall \alpha \in \mathcal{K} \text{ and } u \text{ is measurable}\}$$

denote the set of admissible uncertainties. Then, the reachable set of $(\mathcal{S}, \mathcal{K}, \mathcal{F})$ *with respect to* $\mathcal{U}_{\mathcal{K}}^{\delta}$ *is given by the solution set* $\{V^u \mid u \in \mathcal{U}_{\mathcal{K}}^{\delta}\}$, *where* V^u *solves*

$$\dot{V}_B^u(t) = F_B(V^u(t), \hat{\kappa}(t) + u(t))$$
$$:= \sum_{1 \leq j \leq |\mathcal{F}|} (d_{j,B} - c_{j,B})\Theta_j(V^u(t), \hat{\kappa}(t) + u(t)) \qquad (2)$$

for all $B \in \mathcal{S}$. *The reachable set at time* t *is given by* $\mathcal{R}(t) = \{V^u(t) \mid u \in \mathcal{U}_{\mathcal{K}}^{\delta}\}$.

The following example demonstrates Definition 1 and 2 in the context of an SIRS model. Recall that SIRS models are used to study the spread of infectious diseases. The population is split into different compartments: **S**usceptible, **I**nfected and **R**ecovered. This model assumes that the total population is constant. A susceptible individual can become infected. An infected individual can then recover from the infection and after its recovery become susceptible again.

Example 1. Consider the agent network $(\{S, I, R\}, \{\beta\}, \{\Theta_1, \Theta_2, \Theta_3\})$ given by

$$R_1 = \{S \to I, I \to I\}, \qquad R_2 = \{I \to R\}, \qquad R_3 = \{R \to S\},$$
$$\Theta_1(V, \kappa) = V_S V_I, \qquad \Theta_2(V, \kappa) = \kappa_\beta V_I, \qquad \Theta_3(V, \kappa) = V_R,$$

where $V = (V_S, V_I, V_R)$ and $\kappa = (\kappa_\beta)$. Let the time-varying uncertain recovery rate parameter be given by $\kappa_\beta \equiv \hat{\kappa}_\beta + u_\beta$, where $\hat{\kappa}_\beta$ denotes the nominal trajectory and $u = (u_\beta) \in \mathcal{U}_{\{\beta\}}^{\delta}$ is the uncertainty function for some positive $\delta = (\delta_\beta)$ such that $\delta_\beta < \hat{\kappa}_\beta$. The AN induces the reactions

$$S + I \xrightarrow{V_S V_I} I + I, \qquad I \xrightarrow{(\hat{\kappa}_\beta + u_\beta)V_I} R, \qquad R \xrightarrow{V_R} S, \qquad (3)$$

while the ODE system (2) is given by

$$\dot{V}_S^{u_\beta} = -V_S^{u_\beta} V_I^{u_\beta} + V_R^{u_\beta} \qquad (4)$$
$$\dot{V}_I^{u_\beta} = -(\hat{\kappa}_\beta + u_\beta)V_I^{u_\beta} + V_S^{u_\beta} V_I^{u_\beta}$$
$$\dot{V}_R^{u_\beta} = -V_R^{u_\beta} + (\hat{\kappa}_\beta + u_\beta)V_I^{u_\beta}$$

In the following, we assume that an AN $(\mathcal{S}, \mathcal{K}, \mathcal{F})$ is accompanied by a finite time horizon $T > 0$, a positive initial condition $V(0) \in \mathbb{R}_{>0}^{\mathcal{S}}$ and a Lipschitz continuous parameter function $\hat{\kappa} \in [0; T] \to \mathbb{R}_{>0}^{\mathcal{K}}$. Moreover, we require that each function Θ_j is analytic in (V, κ), linear in κ and such that $\Theta_j(V) = 0$ whenever $V_{A_l} = 0$ and $c_{j,l} > 0$, where $c_{j,l}$ is as in (1). Since atomic transitions enforce conservation of mass, the creation and destruction of agents is ruled out. This can be however alleviated by the introduction of artificial agent states, see [3].

Kolmogorov Equations. Thanks to the fact that the dynamics of an AN arise from atomic transitions, it is possible to define a continuous time Markov chain (CTMC) whose Kolmogorov equations, are closely connected to system (2).

Definition 3. *For a given AN $(\mathcal{S}, \mathcal{K}, \mathcal{F})$, define*

$$r_{B,C}(V, \kappa) = \sum_{1 \leq j \leq |\mathcal{F}| \,|\, B \to C \in R_j} \Theta_j(V, \kappa)/V_B$$

for all $B, C \in \mathcal{S}$ with $B \neq C$, $V \in \mathbb{R}_{>0}^{\mathcal{S}}$ and $\kappa \in \mathbb{R}_{>0}^{\mathcal{K}}$. Then, the coupled CTMC $(X^u(t))_{t \geq 0}$ underlying $(\mathcal{S}, \mathcal{K}, \mathcal{F})$ and $u \in \mathcal{U}_{\mathcal{K}}^{\delta}$ has state space $\mathcal{S}$ and its transition rate from state B into state C at time t is $r_{B,C}(V^u(t), \hat{\kappa}(t) + u(t))$. The coupled Kolmogorov equations of $(X^u(t))_{t \geq 0}$ are

$$\dot{\pi}_B^u(t) = f_B(\pi^u(t), V^u(t), \hat{\kappa}(t) + u(t)) \tag{5}$$

$$:= -\sum_{C:C \neq B} \left(r_{B,C}(V^u(t), \hat{\kappa}(t) + u(t))\pi_B^u(t) + r_{C,B}(V^u(t), \hat{\kappa}(t) + u(t))\pi_C^u(t) \right)$$

It can be shown that any trajectory V^u of (2) coincides with the trajectory π^u of (5) if $\pi^u(0) = V(0)$. In the context of the SIRS example, Definition 3 gives rise to the transition rates

$$r_{S,I}(V^u(t), \hat{\kappa}(t) + u(t)) = \Theta_1(V^u(t), \hat{\kappa}(t) + u(t))/V_S^u(t)$$
$$r_{I,R}(V^u(t), \hat{\kappa}(t) + u(t)) = \Theta_2(V^u(t), \hat{\kappa}(t) + u(t))/V_I^u(t)$$
$$r_{R,S}(V^u(t), \hat{\kappa}(t) + u(t)) = \Theta_3(V^u(t), \hat{\kappa}(t) + u(t))/V_R^u(t),$$

where Θ_1, Θ_2 and Θ_3 are as in Example 1. Thus, the Kolmogorov equations are

$$\dot{\pi}_S^{u_\beta} = -V_I^{u_\beta}\pi_S^{u_\beta} + \pi_R^{u_\beta}$$
$$\dot{\pi}_I^{u_\beta} = -(\hat{\kappa}_\beta + u_\beta)\pi_I^{u_\beta} + V_I^{u_\beta}\pi_S^{u_\beta} \tag{6}$$
$$\dot{\pi}_R^{u_\beta} = -\pi_R^{u_\beta} + (\hat{\kappa}_\beta + u_\beta)\pi_I^{u_\beta}.$$

In case when $\pi(0)$ is a probability measure, the Kolmogorov equations describe the transient probabilities of a Markov chain, i.e., $\pi_A(t)$ gives the probability of being in state A at time t. We will not exploit this relation here but point out that (2) can be interpreted as an ODE approximation of a Markov chain in which the number of agents is large [3,4,10]. In the case of the SIRS example, for instance, system (6) describes the stochastic behavior of a single individual in a population of many individuals whose overall behavior is given by system (4).

Decoupling. We next estimate the reachable set of an AN with respect to an uncertainty set $\mathcal{U}_{\mathcal{K}}^{\delta}$, i.e., we bound $\mathcal{R}(t) = \{V^u(t) \mid u \in \mathcal{U}_{\mathcal{K}}^{\delta}\}$ for each $0 \leq t \leq T$. To this end, we study the maximal deviation from the nominal trajectory V^0 attainable across $\mathcal{U}_{\mathcal{K}}^{\delta}$.

Definition 4. *For a given AN $(\mathcal{S}, \mathcal{K}, \mathcal{F})$ with uncertainty set $\mathcal{U}_{\mathcal{K}}^{\delta}$, let V^0 be the solution to (2) when $u = 0$. The maximal deviation at time t of (2) from V^0 is*

$$\mathcal{E}_B(t) = \sup_{u \in \mathcal{U}_{\mathcal{K}}^{\delta}} |V_B^u(t) - V_B^0(t)| \tag{7}$$

with $B \in \mathcal{S}$ and $\mathcal{E} = (\mathcal{E}_B)_{B \in \mathcal{S}}$. With this, it holds that

$$\mathcal{R}(t) \subseteq \prod_{B \in \mathcal{S}} \left[V_B^0(t) - \mathcal{E}_B(t); V_B^0(t) + \mathcal{E}_B(t) \right]$$

While the above relates the reachable set of a nonlinear system to that of a linear one, the transition rates of the coupled CTMC $(X^u(t))_{t \geq 0}$ depend on V^u. We address this by decoupling the transition rates from V^u.

Definition 5 (Decoupling). *For $\varepsilon < V^0$ and $\mathfrak{u} = (u_\mathcal{K}, u_\mathcal{S}) \in \mathcal{U}_\mathcal{K}^\delta \times \mathcal{U}_\mathcal{S}^\varepsilon$, let $(\mathcal{D}^\mathfrak{u}(t))_{t \geq 0}$ be the decoupled CTMC with rates $\left(r_{B,C}(V^0(t) + u_\mathcal{S}(t), \hat{\kappa}(t) + u_\mathcal{K}(t)) \right)_{B,C}$ and the decoupled Kolmogorov equations*

$$\dot{\pi}^\mathfrak{u}(t) = f\left(\pi^\mathfrak{u}(t), V^0(t) + u_\mathcal{S}(t), \hat{\kappa}(t) + u_\mathcal{K}(t) \right), \tag{8}$$

where f is as in Definition 3 and $\mathcal{U}_\mathcal{S}^\varepsilon$ is defined similarly to $\mathcal{U}_\mathcal{K}^\delta$ from Definition 2.

Example 2. For the AN from Example 1, the *decoupled* Kolmogorov equations (8) are given by

$$\dot{\pi}_S^\mathfrak{u} = -(V_I^0 + u_I)\pi_S^\mathfrak{u} + \pi_R^\mathfrak{u} \tag{9}$$
$$\dot{\pi}_I^\mathfrak{u} = -(\hat{\kappa}_\beta + u_\beta)\pi_I^\mathfrak{u} + (V_I^0 + u_I)\pi_S^\mathfrak{u}$$
$$\dot{\pi}_R^\mathfrak{u} = -\pi_R^\mathfrak{u} + (\hat{\kappa}_\beta + u_\beta)\pi_I^\mathfrak{u}$$

with $\mathfrak{u} \equiv (u_\mathcal{K}, u_\mathcal{S}) \equiv ((u_\beta), (u_I)) \in \mathcal{U}_\mathcal{K}^\delta \times \mathcal{U}_\mathcal{S}^\varepsilon = \mathcal{U}_{\{\beta\}}^\delta \times \mathcal{U}_{\{S,I,R\}}^\varepsilon$. This is because the transition rates of the *decoupled* CTMC are

$$r_{S,I}(V^0(t) + u_\mathcal{S}(t), \hat{\kappa}(t) + u_\mathcal{K}(t)) = V_I^0(t) + u_I(t) \tag{10}$$
$$r_{I,R}(V^0(t) + u_\mathcal{S}(t), \hat{\kappa}(t) + u_\mathcal{K}(t)) = \hat{\kappa}_\beta(t) + u_\beta(t)$$
$$r_{R,S}(V^0(t) + u_\mathcal{S}(t), \hat{\kappa}(t) + u_\mathcal{K}(t)) = 1$$

To provide an estimation of $\mathcal{E}$ using the Kolmogorov equations (8), we next define $\Phi(\varepsilon)$ as the maximal deviation from the nominal trajectory π^0 that can be attained across the uncertainties $u_\mathcal{K} \in \mathcal{U}_\mathcal{K}^\delta$ and $u_\mathcal{S} \in \mathcal{U}_\mathcal{S}^\varepsilon$.

Definition 6 (Deviation). *For a piecewise continuous function $\varepsilon < V^0$, let $\Phi(\varepsilon) = (\Phi_B(\varepsilon))_{B \in \mathcal{S}}$ be given by*

$$(\Phi_B(\varepsilon))(t) = \sup_{u_\mathcal{K} \in \mathcal{U}_\mathcal{K}^\delta} \sup_{u_\mathcal{S} \in \mathcal{U}_\mathcal{S}^\varepsilon} |\pi_B^\mathfrak{u}(t) - \pi_B^0(t)|$$

$(\Phi_B(\varepsilon))(t)$ denotes the maximal deviation of $\pi_B^\mathfrak{u}(t)$ from $\pi_B^0(t)$, where π^0 arises from $\pi^\mathfrak{u}$ in (8) if $\mathfrak{u} = 0$.

The idea is to find a positive function ε such that $\Phi(\varepsilon) \leq \varepsilon$. This ensures that $|\pi^\mathfrak{u} - \pi^0| \leq \varepsilon$ for any $\mathfrak{u} = (u_\mathcal{K}, u_\mathcal{S}) \in \mathcal{U}_\mathcal{K}^\delta \times \mathcal{U}_\mathcal{S}^\varepsilon$ and implies that $\mathcal{E} \leq \varepsilon$.

Theorem 1. *If $\Phi(\varepsilon) \leq \varepsilon$, then $\mathcal{E} \leq \varepsilon$. Moreover, if $\varepsilon^{(k+1)} := \Phi(\varepsilon^{(k)})$ for some $\varepsilon^{(0)} > 0$ and $\varepsilon^{(k)} < V^0$ for all $k \geq 0$, then $\lim_{k \to \infty} \varepsilon^{(k)} = \varepsilon$ exists and $\Phi(\varepsilon) = \varepsilon$.*

A direct consequence of Theorem 1 is that any fixed point ε^* of $\varepsilon \mapsto \Phi(\varepsilon)$ estimates $\mathcal{E}$ from above. Moreover, since $\lim_{k \to \infty} \varepsilon^{(k)}$ is finite only if $\varepsilon^{(k)} < V^0$ for all $k \geq 0$, the computation of the sequence $(\varepsilon^{(k)})_k$ can be terminated as soon as $\varepsilon^{(k)} < V^0$ is violated.

Computing the Deviation. In each step of the fixed point iteration from Theorem 1, a new value of Φ has to be computed. To this end, we have to obtain the minimal (maximal) value of each $\pi_A(\hat{t})$, where $A \in \mathcal{S}$ and $\dot{\pi}(t) = h(t, \pi(t), (u_\mathcal{K}(t), u_\mathcal{S}(t)))$ such that $(u_\mathcal{K}, u_\mathcal{S}) \in \mathcal{U}_\mathcal{K}^\delta \times \mathcal{U}_\mathcal{S}^\varepsilon$. To increase readability, we write in that what follows $u \in \mathcal{U}_{\mathcal{K} \cup \mathcal{S}}^b$ instead of $(u_\mathcal{K}, u_\mathcal{S}) \in \mathcal{U}_\mathcal{K}^\delta \times \mathcal{U}_\mathcal{S}^\varepsilon$, where $b_\alpha = \delta_\alpha$ and $b_A = \varepsilon_A$ for all $\alpha \in \mathcal{K}$ and $A \in \mathcal{S}$, respectively. Moreover, we shall write π and V instead of π^u and V^u, respectively, when the dependence on u is clear from the context.

The following mild conditions on the decoupled CTMC will be needed for the efficient computation of the minimal (maximal) value of each $\pi_A(\hat{t})$.

(A1) For any $B, C \in \mathcal{S}$ and $0 \leq t \leq T$, there exist Lipschitz continuous functions $k^{B \to C}, k_i^{B \to C} \in [0; T] \to \mathbb{R}_{\geq 0}$ such that the transition rate function $r_{B,C}$ from Definition 3 satisfies

$$r_{B,C}\big(V^0(t) + u_\mathcal{S}, \hat{\kappa}(t) + u_\mathcal{K}\big) = k^{B \to C}(t) + \sum_{i \in \mathcal{K} \cup \mathcal{S}} k_i^{B \to C}(t) u_i$$

for all $u_\mathcal{K} \in \mathbb{R}^\mathcal{K}$ and $u_\mathcal{S} \in \mathbb{R}^\mathcal{S}$.

(A2) For each $i \in \mathcal{K} \cup \mathcal{S}$, there exist unique $B_i, C_i \in \mathcal{S}$ such that $k_i^{B \to C} \neq 0$ implies $B = B_i$, $C = C_i$ and $k_i^{B \to C} > 0$.

Assumption **(A1)** requires, essentially, the transition rate functions to be linear in the uncertainties, while **(A2)** forbids the same uncertainty to affect more than one transition. The next example demonstrates that our running example satisfies condition **(A1)** and **(A2)**.

Example 3. Recall that the transition rates of the decoupled CTMC of Example 1 are given by (10). Hence, $k^{S \to I} \equiv V_I^0$, $k^{I \to R} \equiv \hat{\kappa}_\beta$ and $k^{R \to S} \equiv 1$ and **(A1)** holds true. Condition **(A2)**, instead, follows with $B_I = S$, $C_I = I$, $k_I^{S \to I} \equiv 1$ and $B_\beta = I$, $C_\beta = R$, $k_\beta^{I \to R} \equiv 1$.

Under the assumptions above, the following theorem can be shown by invoking Pontryagin's principle (aka adjoint system) [12].

Theorem 2 (Adjoint System). *Assume that (A1) – (A2) hold true and fix some $A \in \mathcal{S}$. Then, the adjoint ODE system is given by*

$$\dot{\pi}_B(t) = g_B(\pi(t), p(t), t) \tag{11}$$
$$:= f_B\big(\pi(t), V^0(t) + u_\mathcal{S}^*(t), \hat{\kappa}(t) + u_\mathcal{K}^*(t)\big)$$
$$\dot{p}_B(t) = h_B(p(t), t) \tag{12}$$
$$:= \sum_{C \in \mathcal{S}} (p_B(t) - p_C(t)) k^{B \to C}(t) - \sum_{\substack{i \in \mathcal{K} \cup \mathcal{S}: \\ B_i = B}} |p_B(t) - p_{C_i}(t)| k_i^{B \to C_i}(t) b_i(t),$$

where $B \in \mathcal{S}$ and $u_i^*(t, p(t)) = -\text{sgn}(p_{B_i}(t) - p_{C_i}(t))\mathfrak{b}_i(t)$ for the signum function sgn. If p solves (12) for the boundary condition $p_B(\hat{t}) = -\mathbb{1}_{\{A=B\}}$, then the solution $\hat{\pi}(t) = g(\pi(t), p(t), t)$ of (11) subject to $\pi(0) = V(0)$ minimizes the value $\pi_A(\hat{t})$. Similarly, the maximal value of $\pi_A(\hat{t})$ is obtained for $p_B(\hat{t}) = \mathbb{1}_{\{A=B\}}$.

Theorem 2 allows us to compute the minimal and maximal value of $\pi_A(\hat{t})$. The next example demonstrates the result in the context of the SIRS model from Example 1.

Example 4. We have seen in Example 3 that our running example satisfies the requirements of Theorem 2. In particular, if $\hat{\kappa} \equiv 1$, then (12) rewrites to

$$\dot{p}_S(t) = \big(V_I(t) + u_I^*(t, p(t))\big)\big(p_S(t) - p_I(t)\big) \tag{13}$$
$$\dot{p}_I(t) = \big(\hat{\kappa}(t) + u_\beta^*(t, p(t))\big)\big(p_I(t) - p_R(t)\big)$$
$$\dot{p}_R(t) = p_R(t) - p_S(t)$$

for $u_I^*(t, p(t)) = -\text{sgn}(p_S(t) - p_I(t))\varepsilon_I(t)$ and $u_\beta^*(t, p(t)) = -\text{sgn}(p_I(t) - p_R(t))\delta_\beta(t)$. The minimal value of, say, $\pi_I^u(\hat{t})$ can be obtained as follows. First, solve the ODE system (13) where the boundary condition is given by $p_I(\hat{t}) = -1$ and $p_S(\hat{t}) = p_R(\hat{t}) = 0$. Afterwards, using the obtained solution p, solve the ODE system (9) using the controls $u_I^*(\cdot, p(\cdot))$ and $u_\beta^*(\cdot, p(\cdot))$. Note also that we could have written $\mathfrak{b}_I(t)$ and $\mathfrak{b}_\beta(t)$ instead of $\varepsilon_I(t)$ and $\delta_\beta(t)$, respectively.

2.2 Backward Differential Equivalence

We next review backward differential equivalence (BDE) from [5,7].

Definition 7 (BDE). *Fix an ODE system $\dot{V}(t) = F(V(t), t)$ with a Lipschitz continuous vector field $F : \mathbb{R}^\mathcal{S} \times \mathbb{R}_{\geq 0} \to \mathbb{R}^\mathcal{S}$ over the set of variables $\mathcal{S}$. Moreover, for a partition $\mathcal{H}$ of $\mathcal{S}$, let $\mathcal{U}_\mathcal{H}$ denote the subspace of vectors which have common values across the blocks of $\mathcal{H}$, i.e., $\mathcal{U}_\mathcal{H} = \{V \in \mathbb{R}^\mathcal{S} \mid V_A = V_B, H \in \mathcal{H}, A, B \in H\}$. Then, $\mathcal{H}$ is called BDE whenever $F(\mathcal{U}_\mathcal{H}, t) \subseteq \mathcal{U}_\mathcal{H}$ for all $t \geq 0$.*

We shall discuss BDE on the following system

$$\dot{\pi}_A = -2\pi_A + \pi_B + \pi_C, \qquad \dot{\pi}_B = -\pi_B + \pi_A, \qquad \dot{\pi}_C = -\pi_C + \pi_A. \tag{14}$$

Intuitively, the above equations describe a CTMC with three states $\mathcal{S} = \{A, B, C\}$ such that the transition rates between A and B coincide with the rates between A and C. This symmetry of rates allows us to show that $\mathcal{H} = \{\{A\}, \{B, C\}\}$ is a BDE. Indeed, with $\mathcal{U}_\mathcal{H} = \{\pi \in \mathbb{R}^\mathcal{S} \mid \pi_B = \pi_C\}$, it follows that $F(\pi, t) \subseteq \mathcal{U}_\mathcal{H}$ for any $\pi \in \mathcal{U}_\mathcal{H}$, where $F_A(\pi, t) = -2\pi_A + \pi_B + \pi_C$, $F_B(\pi, t) = -\pi_B + \pi_A$ and $F_C(\pi, t) = -\pi_C + \pi_A$.

BDE allows one to relate the original system to a reduced system.

Definition 8 (BDE Quotient). *Let $\dot{V}(t) = F(V(t), t)$ be a Lipschitz continuous ODE system over the set of variables $\mathcal{S}$ and assume that $\mathcal{H}$ is a BDE. For each block $H \in \mathcal{H}$, pick a representative $S_H \in H$ and define the reduced system $\dot{V}^\mathcal{H}(t) = F^\mathcal{H}(V^\mathcal{H}(t), t)$ by setting $F_{S_H}^\mathcal{H}(V_{|\mathcal{H}}, t) = F_{S_H}(V, t)$ for all $H \in \mathcal{H}$ and $V \in \mathcal{U}_\mathcal{H}$, where $V_{|\mathcal{H}}$ is the restriction of V to $\mathcal{H}$.*

In the case of the BDE $\mathcal{H} = \{\{A\}, \{B, C\}\}$ of (14), we could pick as representatives A and B, meaning that A represents A, while B represents B and C. With this, $F_A^{\mathcal{H}}(\pi^{\mathcal{H}}, t) = -2\pi_A^{\mathcal{H}} + 2\pi_B^{\mathcal{H}}$ and $F_B^{\mathcal{H}}(\pi^{\mathcal{H}}, t) = -\pi_B^{\mathcal{H}} + \pi_A^{\mathcal{H}}$ and $\pi^{\mathcal{H}} \in \mathbb{R}^{\{A,B\}}$. Overall, the BDE quotient has two, while the original system three ODEs.

Remark 1. Note that for all $V \in \mathcal{U}_{\mathcal{H}}$ and $H \in \mathcal{H}$, the value $F_{S_H}^{\mathcal{H}}(V_{|\mathcal{H}}, t) = F_{S_H}(V, t)$ does not depend on the choice of the representatives $\{S_H \mid H \in \mathcal{H}\}$ when $\mathcal{H}$ is a BDE.

The next result relates the original to the reduced system.

Theorem 3 (BDE Reduction). *Let $\dot{V}(t) = F(V(t), t)$ be a Lipschitz continuous ODE system over the set of variables S, let $\mathcal{H}$ be a partition over S and pick for each block $H \in \mathcal{H}$ a representative $S_H \in H$. Then, $\mathcal{H}$ is a BDE if and only if for any solution V of $\dot{V}(t) = F(V(t), t)$ with $V(0) \in \mathcal{U}_{\mathcal{H}}$, it holds that $V_{|\mathcal{H}}$ is the solution of $\dot{V}^{\mathcal{H}}(t) = F^{\mathcal{H}}(V^{\mathcal{H}}(t), t)$ with $V^{\mathcal{H}}(0) = V(0)_{|\mathcal{H}}$.*

When applied to (14), Theorem 3 ensures that $\pi_A(t) = \pi_A^{\mathcal{H}}(t)$, $\pi_B(t) = \pi_B^{\mathcal{H}}(t)$ and $\pi_C(t) = \pi_B^{\mathcal{H}}(t)$ for all $t \geq 0$, provided that $\pi_B(0) = \pi_C(0)$. Put different, whenever $\pi_B(0) = \pi_C(0)$, the solution of the original system can be recovered from the solution of the reduced system.

We end the review of BDE by pointing out that the smallest BDE quotient, i.e. the BDE that leads to a minimal number of blocks, exists and that it can be computed in polynomial time [7].

Theorem 4 ((BDE Computation). *Given an agent network $(S, \mathcal{K}, \mathcal{F})$ and a partition $\mathcal{H}'$ of S. If the dynamics of the agent network are described by multivariate polynomials, the coarsest BDE that refines $\mathcal{H}'$ can be computed in polynomial many steps in the size of $|S|$ and $|\mathcal{F}|$.*

We end the section by pointing out that the case of general dynamics enjoys a BDE reduction algorithm too and that it relies on SMT-solvers [5].

3 Efficient Estimation of Agent Networks

We next combine the estimation technique for agent networks with backward differential equivalence from Sect. 2.

Definition 9 (EE). *For a given agent network $(S, \mathcal{K}, \mathcal{F})$, any partition $\mathcal{H}$ of S induces a partition $\mathcal{H}^a$ of the set of adjoint variables defined in Theorem 2. The induced partition is given by $\mathcal{H}^a = \{H^a \mid H \in \mathcal{H}\}$, where $H^a = \{B^a \mid B \in H\}$ and B^a denotes the adjoint variable associated to $B \in S$ as defined in (12). With this, $(\mathcal{H}, \mathcal{H}^a)$ is called estimation equivalence (EE) for $A \in S$ when $\{A\} \in \mathcal{H}$ and when $(\mathcal{H}, \mathcal{H}^a)$ is a BDE of the adjoint system from Theorem 2, i.e., $(\dot{\pi}_B(t), \dot{p}_{B^a}(t)) = (g_B(\pi(t), p(t), t), h_{B^a}(p(t), t))$ with $B \in S$.*

The estimation equivalence yields the following result.

Algorithm 1. Computing the coarsest estimation equivalence (EE) of $A \in \mathcal{S}$.

Input: Agent network $(\mathcal{S}, \mathcal{K}, \mathcal{F})$ and an arbitrary state $A \in \mathcal{S}$

   set $(\mathcal{H}, \mathcal{H}^a) = (\{\{A\}, \mathcal{S} \setminus \{A\}\}, \{\{A^a\}, \mathcal{S}^a \setminus \{A^a\}\})$

   repeat

      compute $(\mathcal{G}, \mathcal{I})$, the coarsest BDE partition that refines $(\mathcal{H}, \mathcal{H}^a)$

      compute the coarsest partition $\mathcal{H}$ that refines $\mathcal{G}$ and for which $\mathcal{H}^a$ refines $\mathcal{I}$

   until $\mathcal{H} \neq \mathcal{G}$

   return $(\mathcal{H}, \mathcal{H}^a)$

Theorem 5 (EE Reduction). *Given an agent network $(\mathcal{S}, \mathcal{K}, \mathcal{F})$ and $A \in \mathcal{S}$, assume that $(\mathcal{H}, \mathcal{H}^a)$ is an EE for $A \in \mathcal{S}$. Let further*

$$\left(\dot{\pi}^{\mathcal{H}}(t), \dot{p}^{\mathcal{H}^a}(t)\right) = \left(g(\pi^{\mathcal{H}}(t), p^{\mathcal{H}^a}(t), t), h(p^{\mathcal{H}^a}(t), t)\right)$$

be the BDE reduction of the adjoint system. Then, the minimal and maximal value of $\pi_A(\hat{t})$ can be computed by solving first $\dot{p}^{\mathcal{H}^a}(t) = h(p^{\mathcal{H}^a}(t), t)$ backwards in time and, thereafter, by solving $\dot{\pi}^{\mathcal{H}}(t) = g(\pi^{\mathcal{H}}(t), p^{\mathcal{H}^a}(t), t)$ forwards in time.

Next result ensures that the coarsest EE of A can be computed in polynomial time. Here, coarsest refers to the fact the number of blocks in the EE is minimal.

Theorem 6 (EE Computation). *Fix an agent network $(\mathcal{S}, \mathcal{K}, \mathcal{F})$ and an arbitrary $A \in \mathcal{S}$. If the dynamics of the agent network are described by multivariate polynomials, the coarsest EE of $A \in \mathcal{S}$ is computed in polynomial many steps in the size of $|\mathcal{S}|$ and $|\mathcal{F}|$ by Algorithm 1.*

We demonstrate EE on a multi-class generalization of the SIRS model with $N \geq 2$ population classes. The underlying agent network is given by $\mathcal{K} = \{\beta_1, \ldots, \beta_N\}$ and

$$
\begin{aligned}
R_1^{\nu,\mu} &= \{S_\nu \to I_\nu, I_\mu \to I_\mu\}, & \Theta_1^{\nu,\mu}(V, \kappa) &= \kappa_{\alpha_{\nu,\mu}} V_{S_\nu} V_{I_\mu}, \\
R_2^\nu &= \{I_\nu \to R_\nu\}, & \Theta_2^\nu(V, \kappa) &= \kappa_{\beta_\nu} V_{I_\nu}, \\
R_3^\nu &= \{R_\nu \to S_\nu\}, & \Theta_3^\nu(V, \kappa) &= \kappa_{\gamma_\nu} V_{R_\nu}.
\end{aligned}
$$

The time-varying uncertain recovery rate parameters are given by $\kappa_{\beta_\nu} \equiv \hat{\kappa}_\beta + u_{\beta_\nu}$, where $\hat{\kappa}_\beta$ denotes the nominal recovery rate and $|u_{\beta_\nu}| \leq b_{\beta_\nu}$ is the uncertainty satisfying $0 \leq b_{\beta_\nu} < \hat{\kappa}_\beta$. With this, the decoupled Kolmogorov equations (11) are

$$
\dot{\pi}_{S_\nu} = -\sum_\mu \hat{\kappa}_\alpha (V_{I_\mu}^0 + u_{I_\mu}^*) \pi_{S_\nu} + \hat{\kappa}_\gamma \pi_{R_\nu}
$$

$$
\dot{\pi}_{I_\nu} = -(\hat{\kappa}_\beta + u_{\beta_\nu}^*) \pi_{I_\nu} + \sum_\mu \hat{\kappa}_\alpha (V_{I_\mu}^0 + u_{I_\mu}^*) \pi_{S_\nu} \tag{15}
$$

$$
\dot{\pi}_{R_\nu} = -\hat{\kappa}_\gamma \pi_{R_\nu} + (\hat{\kappa}_\beta + u_{\beta_\nu}^*) \pi_{I_\nu}
$$

Instead, the adjoint system (12) is given by

$$\dot{p}_{S_\nu^a} = (p_{S_\nu^a} - p_{I_\nu^a}) \sum_\mu \hat{\kappa}_\alpha V_{I_\mu}^0 - |p_{S_\nu^a} - p_{I_\nu^a}| \sum_\mu \hat{\kappa}_\alpha \mathfrak{b}_{I_\mu}$$

$$\dot{p}_{I_\nu^a} = (p_{I_\nu^a} - p_{R_\nu^a})\hat{\kappa}_\beta - |p_{I_\nu^a} - p_{R_\nu^a}|\mathfrak{b}_{\beta_\nu} \qquad (16)$$

$$\dot{p}_{R_\nu^a} = (p_{R_\nu^a} - p_{S_\nu^a})\hat{\kappa}_\gamma$$

Theorem 2 ensures that picking $u_{I_\mu}^*(t, p(t)) = -\mathrm{sgn}(p_{S_\mu^a}(t) - p_{I_\mu^a}(t))\mathfrak{b}_{I_\mu}(t)$ and $u_{\beta_\nu}^*(t, p(t)) = -\mathrm{sgn}(p_{I_\nu^a}(t) - p_{R_\nu^a}(t))\mathfrak{b}_{\beta_\nu}(t)$ induces the minimum of $\pi_A(\hat{t})$ when (16) is subject to $p_A(\hat{t}) = -1$ and $p_B(\hat{t}) = 0$ for all $B \neq A$ (to obtain the maximum of $\pi_A(\hat{t})$, one replaces -1 with 1 instead).

A direct application of Theorem 2 requires us to solve a system of $6N$ whenever we wish to compute the minimum or maximum value of some $\pi_A(\hat{t})$ which, in turn, is needed to compute the value $\Phi(\varepsilon)$ for some given ε. In light of this, it is worth noting that the system (16-15) enjoys for any $1 \leq \nu_0 \leq N$ the BDE

$$\mathcal{H} = \{\{S_{\nu_0}\}, \{S_\nu \mid \nu \neq \nu_0\}, \{I_{\nu_0}\}, \{I_\nu \mid \nu \neq \nu_0\}, \{R_{\nu_0}\}, \{R_\nu \mid \nu \neq \nu_0\},$$

$$\{S_{\nu_0}^a\}, \{S_\nu^a \mid \nu \neq \nu_0\}, \{I_{\nu_0}^a\}, \{I_\nu^a \mid \nu \neq \nu_0\}, \{R_{\nu_0}^a\}, \{R_\nu^a \mid \nu \neq \nu_0\}\}, \quad (17)$$

whenever $V_{S_\nu}(0) = V_{S_\mu}(0)$, $V_{I_\nu}(0) = V_{I_\mu}(0)$, $V_{R_\nu}(0) = V_{R_\mu}(0)$ and $\mathfrak{b}_{\beta_\nu} \equiv \mathfrak{b}_{\beta_\mu}$ for all $\nu, \mu \in \{1, \ldots, N\}$. This shows that (17) is an EE for S_{ν_0}, I_{ν_0} and R_{ν_0}. Moreover, picking as representative of $\{1, \ldots, N\} \setminus \{\nu_0\}$ some arbitrary $\nu_1 \neq \nu_0$, we can see that the BDE reduction from Theorem 5 consists of 12 variables and is given for $i \in \{0, 1\}$ by

$$\dot{p}_{S_{\nu_i}^a} = (p_{S_{\nu_i}^a} - p_{I_{\nu_i}^a})\hat{\kappa}_\alpha \left(V_{I_{\nu_0}}^0 + (N-1)V_{I_{\nu_1}}^0\right) - |p_{S_{\nu_i}^a} - p_{I_{\nu_i}^a}|\hat{\kappa}_\alpha \left(\mathfrak{b}_{I_{\nu_0}} + (N-1)\mathfrak{b}_{I_{\nu_1}}\right)$$

$$\dot{p}_{I_{\nu_i}^a} = (p_{I_{\nu_i}^a} - p_{R_{\nu_i}^a})\hat{\kappa}_\beta - |p_{I_{\nu_i}^a} - p_{R_{\nu_i}^a}|\mathfrak{b}_{\beta_{\nu_i}}$$

$$\dot{p}_{R_{\nu_i}^a} = (p_{R_{\nu_i}^a} - p_{S_{\nu_i}^a})\hat{\kappa}_\gamma \qquad (18)$$

$$\dot{\pi}_{S_{\nu_i}} = -\hat{\kappa}_\alpha \left(V_{I_{\nu_0}}^0 + u_{I_{\nu_0}}^* + (N-1)(V_{I_{\nu_1}}^0 + u_{I_{\nu_1}}^*)\right)\pi_{S_{\nu_i}} + \hat{\kappa}_\gamma \pi_{R_{\nu_i}}$$

$$\dot{\pi}_{I_{\nu_i}} = -(\hat{\kappa}_\beta + u_{\beta_{\nu_i}}^*)\pi_{I_{\nu_i}} + \hat{\kappa}_\alpha \left(V_{I_{\nu_0}}^0 + u_{I_{\nu_0}}^* + (N-1)(V_{I_{\nu_1}}^0 + u_{I_{\nu_1}}^*)\right)$$

$$\dot{\pi}_{R_{\nu_i}} = -\hat{\kappa}_\gamma \pi_{R_{\nu_i}} + (\hat{\kappa}_\beta + u_{\beta_{\nu_i}}^*)\pi_{I_{\nu_i}}$$

with uncertainty functions $u_{I_{\nu_i}}^*(t, p(t)) = -\mathrm{sgn}(p_{S_{\nu_i}^a}(t) - p_{I_{\nu_i}^a}(t))\mathfrak{b}_{I_{\nu_i}}(t)$ and $u_{\beta_{\nu_i}}^*(t, p(t)) = -\mathrm{sgn}(p_{I_{\nu_i}^a}(t) - p_{R_{\nu_i}^a}(t))\mathfrak{b}_{\beta_{\nu_i}}(t)$.

Overall, the notion of EE allows us to solve the system (16-15) of size $6N$ by solving a system of constant size 12. Hence, the computation of $\Phi(\varepsilon)$ can be speed-up by a factor of $6N/12 = N/2$.

Relaxation of Symmetry Constraints. In order to apply EE, certain assumptions on uncertain parameters and initial conditions must be met. Specifically, while the requirement of common parameter intervals is mild (e.g., $\mathfrak{b}_{\beta_\nu} \equiv \mathfrak{b}_{\beta_\mu}$ for all ν, μ), the requirement on common initial conditions may be restrictive (e.g., $V_{S_\nu}(0) = V_{S_\mu}(0)$ for all ν, μ). We next present an approach that essentially drops the second requirement. The intuition is to introduce an artificial state variable that can distribute its mass across state variables with common initial conditions. As an example, let us assume that we wish to relax the constraint $V_{S_\nu}(0) = V_{S_\mu}(0)$ from above, where ν, μ. To this end, we introduce the additional agent states S_0 and S_{N+1} and the additional parameters $\eta_1, \ldots, \eta_N, \eta_{N+1}$, thus giving rise to the additional reactions $S_0 \xrightarrow{(\hat{\kappa}_\eta + u_{\eta_\nu}) V_{S_0}} S_\nu$. Assuming that $\mathfrak{b}_{\eta_{N+1}} \equiv 0$ and $\mathfrak{b}_{\eta_\nu} \equiv \mathfrak{b}_{\eta_\mu}$ for all $1 \leq \nu, \mu \leq N$, one can show that the uncertainty functions $u_{\eta_1}, \ldots, u_{\eta_N}$ determine how the mass $V_{S_0}(0)$ is distributed among $V_{S_1}, \ldots, V_{S_N}$. Additionally, if $\mathfrak{b}_{\eta_\nu} \equiv \mathfrak{b}_{\eta_\mu}$ for all $1 \leq \nu, \mu \leq N$, one can show that

$$\left(\mathcal{H} \cup \{\{S_0\}, \{S_{N+1}\}\}, \mathcal{H}^a \cup \{\{S_0^a\}, \{S_{N+1}^a\}\} \right)$$

is still a BDE, where $\mathcal{H}$ is as in (17). Thus, the extended agent network allows one to incorporate an uncertainty in the initial conditions of $V_{S_0}(0), \ldots, V_{S_N}(0)$ while preserving the original blocks of the EE.

The overall discussion generalizes as follows.

Theorem 7 (Constraint Relaxation). *Fix an agent network $(\mathcal{S}, \mathcal{K}, \mathcal{F})$ and assume that $(\mathcal{H}, \mathcal{H}^a)$ is an EE for some $A \in \mathcal{S}$. Then, for any $\{S_1, \ldots, S_N\} \in \mathcal{H}$, extend, respectively, $\mathcal{S}$ and $\mathcal{K}$ to $\mathcal{S} \cup \{S_0, S_{N+1}\}$ and $\mathcal{K} \cup \{\eta_1, \ldots, \eta_{N+1}\}$. With this and $\mathfrak{b}_{\eta_{N+1}} \equiv 0$ and $\mathfrak{b}_{\eta_\nu} \equiv \hat{\kappa}_\eta$ for all ν, this then yields, respectively, the additional reactions and the EE of A:*

$$S_0 \xrightarrow{(\hat{\kappa}_\eta + u_{\eta_\nu}) V_{S_0}} S_\nu \quad and \quad \left(\mathcal{H} \cup \{\{S_0\}, \{S_{N+1}\}\}, \mathcal{H}^a \cup \{\{S_0^a\}, \{S_{N+1}^a\}\} \right).$$

Moreover, for any small $\tau, \epsilon > 0$ there is a time-constant $\hat{\kappa}_\eta$ such that for any time-constant $u_{\eta_1}, \ldots, u_{\eta_N}$, one has that $V_{S_0}(\tau) \leq \epsilon$ and any V_{S_ν}, where $\nu = 1, \ldots, N$, receives during $[0; \tau]$

$$V_{S_0}(0) \left[\frac{\hat{\kappa}_\eta + u_{\eta_\nu}}{\sum_{\mu=1}^{N}(\hat{\kappa}_\eta + u_{\eta_\mu}) + \hat{\kappa}_\eta} \pm \epsilon \right].$$

As anticipated, the formula from Theorem 7 ensures that $V_{S_0}(0)$ can be distributed among $V_{S_1}, \ldots, V_{S_N}$ during arbitrarily short time intervals. We conclude the section by pointing out that an iterative application of Theorem 7 allows one to relax symmetry constraints across several blocks.

4 Evaluation

To compute the deviation $\Phi(\epsilon)$ for a given time horizon T, the time interval $[0;T]$ was discretized to the grid $\mathcal{T}(\Delta t) = \{0, \Delta t, 2\Delta t, \ldots, T\}$ following [23], for some step size Δt. In this way, $\Phi(\epsilon)$ is approximated at each $\hat{t} \in \mathcal{T}(\Delta t)$. As was shown in [23], finer grids lead to a better approximations. For our experiments, we picked the same values as in [23], that is, we chose as nominal parameters $\hat{\kappa}_{\alpha_{\nu,\mu}} \equiv 1.00$, $\hat{\kappa}_{\beta_\nu} \equiv 2.00$, $\hat{\kappa}_{\gamma_\nu} \equiv 3.00$, and set uncertainties to $\mathfrak{b}_{\beta_\nu} \equiv 0.03$ for all $1 \leq \nu \leq \mu \leq N$. Instead, for the sake of simplicity, the initial conditions were set to $V_{S_\nu}(0) = 4.00$, and $V_{I_\nu}(0) = V_{R_\nu}(0) = 1.00$, for all $1 \leq \nu \leq \mu \leq N$. Heterogenous initial conditions could be considered by invoking Theorem 7.

All experiments were carried out on a 4.7 GHz Intel Core i7 computer with 32GB of RAM. To solve the differential equations, MATLAB's ode45 solver was used with its default settings. The time horizon for the experiments was $T = 3.00$, in order to ensure that the simulations always reached a steady state. We chose to plot the first 10 values of N, starting from $N = 3$, to visualize the polynomial time dependence with respect to N.

The results of the experiments are summarized on Table 1 and Fig. 1. With $\mathcal{E}(t)$ denoting the maximal deviation from (4), the envelopes were computed by finding the value of $\mathcal{E}(\hat{t})$ for all $\hat{t} \in \mathcal{T}(\Delta t)$. Specifically, the upper envelope was computed by adding $\mathcal{E}(t)$ to the nominal dynamics $V^0(t)$, while the lower envelope was found by subtracting $\mathcal{E}(t)$ from the nominal trajectory. Figure 1

Table 1. Computation of estimation $\mathcal{E}(\cdot)$ of the multi-class SIRS agent networks in case of the original adjoint systems (15)-(16) and its EE-reduction (18)-(19) over grid $\mathcal{T}(\Delta t)$. It can be seen that the original estimations coincide with those obtained from the EE-reductions. Moreover, the computation times (reported in seconds) of the latter do not depend on the number of population classes N but only on the steepness, see Table 2.

| | Discretization grid $\mathcal{T}(0.03)$ | | | | Discretization grid $\mathcal{T}(0.04)$ | | | |
| | Original | | Reduced | | Original | | Reduced | |
N	$\sup_t \|\mathcal{E}(t)\|$	Time	$\sup_t \|\mathcal{E}(t)\|$	Time	$\sup_t \|\mathcal{E}(t)\|$	Time	$\sup_t \|\mathcal{E}(t)\|$	Time
3	0.040	69.4	0.040	44.0	0.040	49.4	0.040	31.9
4	0.063	100.8	0.066	42.5	0.064	75.2	0.066	32.6
5	0.103	133.0	0.103	42.8	0.103	99.5	0.103	32.8
6	0.109	173.5	0.109	43.2	0.109	131.4	0.109	33.2
7	0.114	219.2	0.114	44.9	0.113	163.2	0.113	32.8
8	0.118	276.0	0.118	45.1	0.117	200.0	0.117	33.7
9	0.120	333.5	0.120	45.6	0.120	241.5	0.120	34.2
10	0.123	383.2	0.123	46.1	0.122	282.8	0.122	34.5
11	0.125	447.4	0.125	47.1	0.124	337.2	0.124	34.9
12	0.126	521.9	0.126	48.0	0.125	389.2	0.125	35.3

shows the computed envelopes for the reduced model, where the aforementioned nominal trajectory is determined, for $i \in \{0,1\}$, by the differential equations:

$$\dot{V}^0_{S_{\nu_i}} = -\hat{\kappa}_\alpha \left(V^0_{I_{\nu_0}} + (N-1)(V^0_{I_{\nu_1}}) \right) V^0_{S_{\nu_i}} + \hat{\kappa}_\gamma V^0_{R_{\nu_i}}$$
$$\dot{V}^0_{I_{\nu_i}} = -\hat{\kappa}_\beta V^0_{I_{\nu_i}} + \hat{\kappa}_\alpha \left(V^0_{I_{\nu_0}} + (N-1)(V^0_{I_{\nu_1}}) \right) \tag{19}$$
$$\dot{V}^0_{R_{\nu_i}} = -\hat{\kappa}_\gamma V^0_{R_{\nu_i}} + \hat{\kappa}_\beta V^0_{I_{\nu_i}}$$

Table 1 reports the bounds for both the original and the reduced model. As expected, the bounds of the original and the reduced models coincide. Additionally, the bounds for grids $\mathcal{T}(0.03)$ and $\mathcal{T}(0.04)$ are reasonably close, thus justifying the choice of the discretization step $\Delta T = 0.03$. Crucially, for the original models, the run times are polynomial in the number of species classes N. As the number of classes increases, the reductions lead to a higher speed-ups, yielding in particular a speed-up factor of 10 for $N = 12$. However, there is also an increase in the run time for the reduced system with the number of species involved. We explain this by the fact that systems become steeper with larger values of N, as can be seen in Fig. 1. Indeed, a closer inspection of (18) reveals that the right-hand sides increase with N, forcing thus the numerical ODE solver to take smaller step sizes. This is also confirmed in Table 2 where the norms of the aforementioned right-hand sides are reported for increasing N.

Table 2. Steepness of the nominal trajectory $|\dot{V}^0(t)|$ with respect to the number of population classes N.

N	3	4	5	6	7	8	9	10	11	12
$\sup_t |\dot{V}(t)|$	10.0	14.0	18.0	22.0	26.0	30.0	34.0	38.0	42.0	46.0

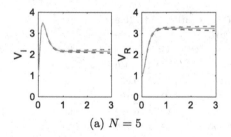
(a) $N = 5$

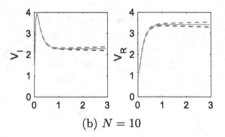
(b) $N = 10$

Fig. 1. Reachable set estimation of the reduced multi-class SIRS model (18)-(19) for different number of species over grid $\mathcal{T}(0.04)$.

5   Conclusion

We introduced estimation equivalence (EE), a technique for the efficient estimation of nonlinear models of collective adaptive systems. EE speeds-up the solution of the nonlinear estimation problem from [23] by relying on the model reduction technique from [5,7]. For a concrete model, the best EE can be computed by means of a partition refinement algorithm in the style of Paige and Tarjan [18] that enjoys polynomial time complexity when the dynamics are described by multivariate polynomials, as is often the case in biochemistry and ecology. By applying EE to a multi-class SIRS model from epidemiology, the estimation times could decreased proportionally to the number of population classes. Future work will integrate EE into the software tool ERODE [6] and conduct a large-scale evaluation of EE on published nonlinear models.

Acknowledgments. The work was partially supported by the Poul Due Jensen Grant 883901 and the Villum Investigator Grant S4OS.

References

1. Althoff, M.: An introduction to CORA 2015. In: Proceedings of the Workshop on Applied Verification for Continuous and Hybrid Systems (2015)
2. Baier, C., Engelen, B., Majster-Cederbaum, M.E.: Deciding bisimilarity and similarity for probabilistic processes. J. Comput. Syst. Sci. **60**(1), 187–231 (2000)
3. Bortolussi, L., Hillston, J.: Model checking single agent behaviours by fluid approximation. Inf. Comput. **242**, 183–226 (2015)
4. Bortolussi, L., Hillston, J., Latella, D., Massink, M.: Continuous approximation of collective system behaviour: a tutorial. Perform. Eval. **70**(5), 317–349 (2013)
5. Cardelli, L., Tribastone, M., Tschaikowski, M., Vandin, A.: Symbolic computation of differential equivalences. In: Bodík, R., Majumdar, R. (eds.) POPL, pp. 137–150. ACM (2016)
6. Cardelli, L., Tribastone, M., Tschaikowski, M., Vandin, A.: ERODE: a tool for the evaluation and reduction of ordinary differential equations. In: Legay, A., Margaria, T. (eds.) TACAS 2017. LNCS, vol. 10206, pp. 310–328. Springer, Heidelberg (2017). https://doi.org/10.1007/978-3-662-54580-5_19
7. Cardelli, L., Tribastone, M., Tschaikowski, M., Vandin, A.: Maximal aggregation of polynomial dynamical systems. Proc. Natl. Acad. Sci. **114**(38), 10029–10034 (2017)
8. Chen, X., Abraham, E., Sankaranarayanan, S.: Taylor model flowpipe construction for non-linear hybrid systems. In: RTSS, pp. 183–192. IEEE Computer Society (2012)
9. Chen, X., Ábrahám, E., Sankaranarayanan, S.: Flow*: an analyzer for non-linear hybrid systems. In: Sharygina, N., Veith, H. (eds.) CAV 2013. LNCS, vol. 8044, pp. 258–263. Springer, Heidelberg (2013). https://doi.org/10.1007/978-3-642-39799-8_18
10. Darling, R.W.R., Norris, J.R.: Differential equation approximations for Markov chains. Probab. Surv. **5**, 37–79 (2008)
11. Derisavi, S., Hermanns, H., Sanders, W.H.: Optimal state-space lumping in Markov chains. Inf. Process. Lett. **87**(6), 309–315 (2003)

12. Doncel, J., Gast, N., Tribastone, M., Tschaikowski, M., Vandin, A.: UTOPIC: under-approximation through optimal control. In: Parker, D., Wolf, V. (eds.) QEST 2019. LNCS, vol. 11785, pp. 277–291. Springer, Cham (2019). https://doi.org/10.1007/978-3-030-30281-8_16

13. Jensen, P.G., Jørgensen, K.Y., Larsen, K.G., Mikučionis, M., Muñiz, M., Poulsen, D.B.: Fluid model-checking in UPPAAL for COVID-19. In: Margaria, T., Steffen, B. (eds.) ISoLA 2020. LNCS, vol. 12476, pp. 385–403. Springer, Cham (2020). https://doi.org/10.1007/978-3-030-61362-4_22

14. Kong, H., Bogomolov, S., Schilling, C., Jiang, Y., Henzinger, T.A.: Safety verification of nonlinear hybrid systems based on invariant clusters. In: Frehse, G., Mitra, S., (eds.) HSCC, pp. 163–172. ACM (2017)

15. Kowal, M., Tschaikowski, M., Tribastone, M., Schaefer, I.: Scaling Size and Parameter Spaces in Variability-Aware Software Performance Models. In: ASE, pp. 407–417 (2015)

16. Kurtz, T.G.: The relationship between stochastic and deterministic models for chemical reactions. J. Chem. Phys. **57**(7), 2976–2978 (1972)

17. Larsen, K.G., Skou, A.: Bisimulation through probabilistic testing. Inf. Comput. **94**(1), 1–28 (1991)

18. Paige, R., Tarjan, R.: Three partition refinement algorithms. SIAM J. Comput. **16**(6), 973–989 (1987)

19. Pappas, G.J., Simic, S.: Consistent abstractions of affine control systems. IEEE Trans. Automat. Contr. **47**(5), 745–756 (2002)

20. Tabuada, P., Pappas, G.J.: Abstractions of Hamiltonian control systems. Automatica **39**(12), 2025–2033 (2003)

21. Tognazzi, S., Tribastone, M., Tschaikowski, M., Vandin, A.: Backward invariance for linear differential algebraic equations. In: CDC, pp. 3771–3776. IEEE (2018)

22. Tribastone, M.: A fluid model for layered queueing networks. IEEE Trans. Software Eng. **39**(6), 744–756 (2013)

23. Tschaikowski, M.: Over-approximation of fluid models. IEEE Trans. Autom. Control **65**(3), 999–1013 (2020)

24. Valmari, A., Franceschinis, G.: Simple $O(m \log n)$ time Markov chain lumping. In: Esparza, J., Majumdar, R. (eds.) TACAS 2010. LNCS, vol. 6015, pp. 38–52. Springer, Heidelberg (2010). https://doi.org/10.1007/978-3-642-12002-2_4

25. van der Schaft, A.J.: Equivalence of dynamical systems by bisimulation. IEEE Trans. Autom. Control **49**(12), 2160–2172 (2004)

Attuning Adaptation Rules
via a Rule-Specific Neural Network

Tomáš Bureš[1], Petr Hnětynka[1]([✉]), Martin Kruliš[1], František Plášil[1],
Danylo Khalyeyev[1], Sebastian Hahner[2], Stephan Seifermann[2],
Maximilian Walter[2], and Robert Heinrich[2]

[1] Charles University, Prague, Czech Republic
{bures,hnetynka,krulis,plasil,khalyeyev}@d3s.mff.cuni.cz
[2] Karlsruhe Institute of Technology (KIT), Karlsruhe, Germany
{sebastian.hahner,stephan.seifermann,maximilian.walter,
robert.heinrich}@kit.edu

Abstract. There have been a number of approaches to employing neural networks (NNs) in self-adaptive systems; in many cases, generic NNs/deep learning are utilized for this purpose. When this approach is to be applied to improve an adaptation process initially driven by logical adaptation rules, the problem is that (1) these rules represent a significant and tested body of domain knowledge, which may be lost if they are replaced by an NN, and (2) the learning process is inherently demanding given the black-box nature and the number of weights in generic NNs to be trained. In this paper, we introduce the rule-specific Neural Network (rsNN) method that makes it possible to transform the guard of an adaptation rule into an rsNN, the composition of which is driven by the structure of the logical predicates in the guard. Our experiments confirmed that the black box effect is eliminated, the number of weights is significantly reduced, and much faster learning is achieved while the accuracy is preserved.

Keywords: Self-adaptive systems · Adaptation rules · Machine learning · Neural networks

1 Introduction

The recent advances in neural networks and machine learning [8] led to their proliferation in various disciplines, and the field of self-adaptive systems is no exception [13]. In particular, they have found usage in approaches to control how systems of cooperating agents are formed and reconfigured at runtime [4,12].

These approaches employ neural networks to implement the self-adaptation loop, also known as the MAPE-K loop, which controls the runtime decisions in the system (e.g., to which service to route a particular request) and the runtime architectural changes (e.g., which services to deploy/un-deploy or reconfigure).

T. Margaria and B. Steffen (Eds.): ISoLA 2022, LNCS 13703, pp. 215–230, 2022.
https://doi.org/10.1007/978-3-031-19759-8_14

In typical cases, a neural network is used for the analysis and planning stages of the MAPE-K loop, replacing the traditional means of analyzing the system state and deciding on adaptation actions. These traditional adaptation mechanisms are often specified in some form of logical rules (e.g., if-then rules or a state machine with guards and actions) [6,12,16].

Using a neural network for making decisions on adaptation actions naturally means training the network for the situations the self-adaptive system is supposed to handle. Such training typically requires a large number of system behavior examples—training data in the form of observed inputs and expected adaptation actions. This approach is significantly different from the logical rules that have been traditionally used to describe adaptation actions. Due to this substantial conceptual gap between the two approaches, it is difficult to evolve an existing self-adaptive system based on some form of logical rules into a new system that uses a neural network to make adaptation decisions. Seemingly, the typical design choice is to recreate the analysis and planning stages of the MAPE-K loop from scratch.

The existing logical rules represent a significant body of domain knowledge, especially if the system has been well-functioning and tuned to its task. Thus, when replacing the logical rules with a neural network, this body of domain knowledge is often lost, which leads to severe regress. On the other hand, applying neural networks may be advantageous as they can dynamically learn completely unanticipated relationships of stochastic character. Thus, it makes the self-adaption refined to take advantage of the specific features otherwise hidden in the system and not captured in the inherently static logical rules.

Nevertheless, if logical rules are used for determining the expected actions in training data, it is not easy to train the neural network to reliably yield actions corresponding to the existing rule-based self-adaptive system in question. The main culprit is that the neural network is often built as a black box composed of generic layers (such as a combination of recurrent and dense layers). Thus, the structure of such a generic neural network does not reflect the relationships characteristic of the domain in which the self-adaptive system resides. In other words, the neural network is built as a generic one, not exploiting the existing domain knowledge about the self-adaptive system whose adaptation actions it controls.

While this genericity is inherently advantageous in empowering the neural network to "discover" ultimately unanticipated relationships, it may also hinder the ability to adequately learn because it makes the neural network relatively complex, thus potentially increasing adaptation uncertainty.

Therefore, replacing a rule-based adaptation entirely with a generic neural network-based one might be an overly drastic change that may potentially degrade the reliability of the system (at least in the short-term perspective). Moreover, it may raise legitimate concerns since generic neural networks are much less comprehensible and predictable given their black-box nature and the typically large number of weights to be trained—there is always a danger of overfitting.

In this paper, we aim to answer the following research questions: (1) how to endow an existing rule-based self-adaptation system with the ability to learn via neural networks while still benefiting from the domain knowledge encoded in the logical rules; and (2) how to scale the learning ability in a way that would allow the transition from logical rules to a neural network to be done on a step-by-step basis.

We address these research questions by introducing a rule-specific Neural Network (rsNN) method, which allows the transformation of an adaption rule to the corresponding rsNN to be done systematically. The key feature is that an rsNN is composable - its architecture is driven by the structure of the logical predicates in the adaption rule in question. Moreover, prior to the composition process, the predicates can be refined by predefined atomic"attunable" predicates, each having a direct equivalent in a primitive element of rsNN ("seed" of rsNN).

The rest of the paper is organized as follows. Section 2 presents an example that is used for motivating and illustrating rsNN. Section 3 is devoted to the key contribution of the paper—it describes the concepts and ideas of rsNN, while Sect. 4 discusses the methodology, results, and limitations of experimental evaluation. Section 5 discusses other approaches focused on employing neural networks in self-adaptation, and the concluding Sect. 6 summarizes the contribution.

2   Motivating Example

As a motivating example, we utilize a realistic yet straightforward use-case from our former project focused on security in Industry 4.0 settings[1]. The example employs the MAPE-K loop principle to dynamically reconfigure the software architecture of agents—workers (represented by components) operating jointly on a common task. In the architecture, groups of workers are determined by the access policies that allow the member workers to perform their tasks. Since these tasks are subject to changes, the access control is intertwined with dynamic, runtime modification of the software architecture.

Implementation-wise, the MAPE-K controller dynamically re-establishes the groups of workers to deal with situations in the environment—e.g., when a machine breaks down, the MAPE-K controller establishes a group of workers that communicate and collaborate to fix the machine (so that the software architecture is dynamically reconfigured). It also gives these workers the necessary access rights, e.g., to access the machine's logs and physically enter the room (workplace) where the machine is located.

In the example, we pick up a particular adaptation rule from the larger use-case in the project mentioned above, and later in Sect. 3, we will employ it to demonstrate a step-by-step transition from this static adaptation rule to the corresponding rsNN neural network.

Let us consider a factory with several workplaces where production is organized in shifts, each determined by its start and end time, during which worker

---

[1] http://trust40.ipd.kit.edu/home/.

groups, each with an assigned (the only) workplace, perform their tasks. The workers are allowed to enter the factory only at a time close to a particular shift's start and must leave soon after the shift ends. After entering, they have to pick up headgear (protective equipment) from a dispenser as a necessary condition for being permitted to enter the assigned workplace. Similarly, they are allowed to enter only the assigned workplace and only close to the shift start time (and have to leave as soon as the shift ends).

As expected in the Industry 4.0 domain, the assignment of workers to particular shifts is not static but can frequently change, and the roles of individual workers within the shift can also alternate rapidly. This leads to changes in the runtime software architecture. Consequently, the access control system of the factory cannot assign access rights statically only, thus supporting dynamic, situation-based access control.

To perform access right adaptation, the MAPE-k controller uses adaptation rules in the form of guard-actions, where the action is adding/revoking or allowing access.

Listing 1 shows an example of an adaptation rule which dynamically determines a group of workers formed for the duration of a shift, having access rights to the assigned workplace. In particular, the adaptation rule specifies whether a specific worker belongs to the group and if so, it gives the worker access to the workplace assigned for the shift.

The structure of the adaptation rule has three parts. First, there are declared data fields (in this particular case, only a single field initialized to the shift of the given worker—line 2). Second, there is a *guard*, which defines the condition when the rule is applied. This particular guard reads: To allow a worker to enter the assigned workplace, the worker needs to be already at the appropriate workplace gate (line 5), needs to have a headgear ready (line 6), and needs to be there at the right time (i.e., during the shift or close to its start or end—line 4). Finally, there is an *action* determining what has to be executed—in this case, the assignment of the *allow* access rights to the assigned workplace to the worker (line 8).

```
1  rule AccessToWorkplace(worker) {
2      shift = shifts.filter(worker in shift.workers)
3      guard {
4        duringShift(shift) &&
5          atWorkplaceGate(worker, shift.workplace) &&
6            hasHeadgear(worker)
7      }
8      action { allow(worker, ENTER, shift.workplace) }
9  }
```

Listing 1. Access to workplace rule

The predicates atWorkplaceGate, hasHeadgear, and duringShift are declared in Listing 2.

The predicate duringShift tests whether the current time is between 20 min (i.e., 1200 s) before the start of the shift and 20 min after the end of the shift. The global variable NOW contains the current time.

The atWorkplaceGate predicate mandates that the position of the worker has to be close (in terms of Euclidean distance) to the gate of the workplace assigned to the worker.

The predicate hasHeadgear checks whether the worker retrieved a headgear from the dispenser. To check this, we assume that each worker is associated with a list of related events (the events data field of the worker—line 11 in Listing 2). For instance, retrieving and returning the headgear are the events registered in the list of events upon performing the respective actions. Thus, the check of whether a worker has a headgear available is performed by verifying that after filtering the two specific event types from the list (line 12), the latest event is TAKE_HGEAR (the filtered events are sorted in descending order—line 13 and line 14).

```
1  pred duringShift(shift) {
2      shift.startTime − 1200 < NOW && shift.endTime + 1200 > NOW
3  }
4
5  pred atWorkplaceGate(worker, workplace) {
6      sqrt((workplace.gate.posX − worker.posX) ^ 2 +
7      (workplace.gate.posY − worker.posY) ^ 2) < 10
8  }
9
10 pred hasHeadgear(worker) {
11     worker.events
12     .filter(event −> event.type == (TAKE_HGEAR || RET_HGER))
13     .sortDesc(event −> event.time)
14     .first().type == TAKE_HGEAR
15 }
```

Listing 2. Predicates from Listing 1

3   Refining Adaptation Rules

The problem with the adaptation rules we presented in Sect. 1 is that their guards are too static, and thus they do not capture the domain-specific stochastic character of the data they act upon. As already mentioned in Sect. 1, we aim to employ a dedicated *rule-specific neural network* (*rsNN*) to benefit from its ability to learn from the domain characteristic data being handled. To this end, in this section, we outline the method that allows us to refine an original adaption rule to make its guard predicates "attunable" and convert the guard into an *rsNN*. In a sense, our method of employing a dedicated *rsNN* for this purpose can be viewed as paving a middle ground between the adaptation rules with static guards and the adaptation rules driven by (typically complex) generic neural networks such as in [12,17].

The main idea of our method unfolds in three stages:

1. An adaptation rule is *refined* by manually rewriting (transforming) its selected guard predicates into their attunable form—they become *attunable predicates*. This is done by applying predefined atomic attunable predicates (*aa-predicates*) listed in Sect. 3.1. These aa-predicates serve as *rsNN* seeds in

the second stage. Nevertheless, not all the guard predicates have to be transformed this way—those remain *static predicates* (their selection is application-specific).

2. We apply an automated step that generates an *rsNN* that reflects the guard of the refined adaptation rule, containing, in particular, the trainable parameters of aa-predicates as trainable weights.

3. We employ traditional neural network training using stochastic gradient descent to pre-train the trainable weights.

The result is an *rsNN* being a custom neural network, the composition of which is driven by the structure of the guard formula with aa-predicates. This neural network is pre-trained to match outputs of the original guard formula of the adaptation rule. Nevertheless, being a neural network, it can be further trained by running additional examples.

As to pre-training data, we assume there are sample traces of input data to the system, obtained either from historical data, simulation, or random sampling. We use the logical formulas of the original guard predicates over the input data to provide the ground truth (i.e., expected inputs) employed in the supervised learning of the *rsNN*.

Further, the developer has the ability to specify the learning capacity in many aa-predicates, which in turn determines how many neurons are used for its implementation in the *rsNN*.

3.1   Atomic Attunable Predicates as *rsNN* Seeds

This section provides an overview of the aa-predicates defined in the *rsNN* methods. The key idea is that these predicates serve as elementary building blocks for attunable predicates forming an adaptation rule, and at the same time, each of them is easily transformable into a building block of *rsNN*—it serves as an *rsNN* seed as defined in Sect. 3.3.

Each aa-predicate operates on a single n-dimensional input value (i.e., a fixed-sized vector). Since each aa-predicate yields a true/false value, its corresponding *rsNN* seed solves a classification task, yielding likewise true/false.

Following the type of input value domain, we distinguish between aa-predicates that operate on domains with a metric (i.e., with the ability to measure the distance between quantities) and categorical quantities where no such metric exists:

1. **Metric Quantity:** There are two types of aa-predicates defined over a metric:
   (a) Quantity lies in a one-sided interval

$$isAboveThreshold\_nD(x, min, max)$$
$$isBelowThreshold\_nD(x, min, max)$$

Here x is a value in an n-dimensional space that is compared to a learned threshold (above or below) by the corresponding *rsNN* seed. In order to control the uncertainty that is potentially induced by learning, the min and max

parameters impose the limits for the learned threshold.
(b) Quantity lies in a two-sided interval

$$hasRightValue\_nD(x, min, max, c)$$

Here it is verified whether the parameter x lies inside the learned interval of an n-dimensional space. The parameters min and max have the same meaning as in the case of the aa-predicates for a one-sided interval, while the parameter c states the learning capacity of the corresponding $rsNN$ seed; technically, this is, e.g., the highest number of the neurons in a hidden layer of the $rsNN$ seed.

2. **Categorical Quantity:** For this type of input domain, we define an aa-predicate that decides whether a categorical quantity has the right value:

$$hasRightCategories\_nD(x, m, c)$$

Here x is an n-dimensional vector of categorical values from the same domain of the size m (the number of categories). The corresponding $rsNN$ learns which combinations of categorical values in the input vector satisfy this aa-predicate. The learning capacity is determined by c.

3.2 Making Guard Predicates Attunable

In this section, we demonstrate the first stage of the $rsNN$ method (i.e., the manual rewriting of guard predicates) on the example presented in Sect. 2. We show two alternatives to such rewriting to demonstrate that a designer may choose several ways to make a predicate attunable depending on what quantities are to be the subject of future learning.

We start with the guard predicates shown in Listing 2. At first, we assume that the designer would like to rewrite duringShift to make it attunable, with the goal to learn the permitted time interval in which the access is allowed. For example, security reasons may require learning the typical behavior patterns of workers induced by the public transportation schedule. (On the contrary, in Listing 2, the interval is firmly set from 20 minutes before the shift starts to 20 minutes after the shift is over.)

We rewrite the duringShift guard predicate as shown in Listing 3: The comparison of NOW with a particular threshold is replaced by the aa-predicates isAboveThreshold and isBelowThreshold, respectively. Each of them represents a comparison against a learned threshold.

The aa-predicates isAboveThreshold and isBelowThreshold have three parameters: (1) the value to test against the learned threshold, (2) the minimum value of the threshold, (3) the maximum value of the threshold.

Since this threshold should not depend on the actual time of the shift, the times are given relative to its start and end. By assuming a worker cannot arrive earlier than one hour before the shift starts (+3600 seconds in line 2), the relative time 0 corresponds to that point in time (as computed by NOW + 3600 - shift.end).

Similarly, by assuming a worker cannot leave later than one hour after the shift ends (-3600 seconds in line 4), the relative time 0 corresponds to that point in time (as computed by NOW - 3600 - shift.end). The minimum and maximum values of the threshold correspond to the interval of 10 h (i.e., 36000 s).

```
1  pred duringShift(shift) {
2    isAboveThreshold_1D(NOW + 3600 − shift.start,min=0, max=36000)
3      &&
4    isBelowThreshold_1D(NOW − 3600− shift.end, min=−36000, max=0)
5  }
6
7  pred atWorkplaceGate(worker, workplace) {
8    sqrt((workplace.gate.posX − worker.posX) ^ 2 + (workplace.gate.posY
         − worker.posY) ^ 2) < 10
9  }
10
11 pred hasHeadgear(worker) {
12   worker.events.filter(event −> event.type == TAKE_HGEAR ||
         RET_HGER))
13                 .sortDesc(event −> event.time).first().type ==
                 TAKE_HGEAR
14 }
```

Listing 3. Guard predicates with refined duringShift by aa-predicates—one-sided intervals

The other predicates atWorkplaceGate and hasHeadgear) stay the same, as does their conjunction in the AccessToWorkplace rule.

Note that we combined static predicates with an attunable predicate. This shows that only a part of a rule can be endowed with the ability to learn while the rest can stay unchanged. At the same time, we put strict limits on how far the learning can go. In the example, these limits are expressed by the interval of 10 h which spans from one hour before the shift to one hour after the shift (assuming the shift takes 8 h). In other words, the value in the attunable predicate gained in the process of learning cannot exceed these bounds. This is useful if learning is to be combined with strict assurances with respect to uncertainty control.

As another alternative of the rule refinement, we assume the time of entry, place of entry, and the relation to the last event concerning the headgear is to be learned. Also, contrary to the variant of duringShiftin Listing 3, we assume the time of entry is not just a single interval but can be multiple intervals (e.g., to reflect the fact that workers usually access the gate only at some time before and after the shift due to the public transportation opportunities).

To capture this, we rewrite the predicates duringShift, atWorkplaceGate, and hasHeadGear as shown in Listing 4.

The guard predicate duringShift is realized using the aa-predicate hasRight-Value1D, which represents a learnable set of intervals. It has four parameters. In addition to the first three, which have the same meaning as before (i.e., value to be tested on whether it belongs to any of the learned intervals, the minimum, and the maximum value for the intervals), there is the fourth parameter capacity which expresses learning capacity. The higher it is, the finer intervals the predicate is able to learn. Since it works relative to the min/max parameters, it is unitless. Technically, the learning capacity determines the number of neurons used for training. The exact meaning of the capacity parameter is given further in Sect. 3.3.

The guard predicate atWorkplaceGate is rewritten similarly. However, as the position is a two-dimensional vector, a 2D version of the hasRightValue aa-predicate is used. The meaning of its argument is the same as in the 1D version applied for the duringShift. A special feature of atWorkplaceGate is that it is specific to the workplace assigned to the worker. (There are several workplaces where the work is conducted during a shift. Each worker is assigned to a particular work-place, and their access permission is thus limited only to that workplace.) Thus, the hasRightValue2D aa-predicate has to be trained separately for each workplace. The square brackets express this after the hasRightValue2D aa-predicate, which signifies that its training is qualified by workplace ID. Since the running example assumes that there are three workplaces in a shift, there are three aa-predicates to be trained.

The hasHeadGear guard predicate is rewritten using the hasRightCategories_1D aa-predicate which assumes 1-dimensional vector of categorical values (i.e., a single value in this case) from the domain of size 2. In this simple case, the learning capacity is set to 1.

```
1  pred duringShift(shift) {
2      hasRightValue_1D(NOW − shift.start, min=0, max=36000,
           capacity=20)
3  }
4
5  pred atWorkplaceGate(worker) {
6      hasRightValue_2D[worker.workplace.id](worker.pos,
7              min=(0,0), max=(316.43506,177.88289), capacity=20)
8  }
9
10 pred hasHeadGear(worker) {
11     hasRightCategories_1D(
12       worker.events.filter(event −> event.type == (TAKE_HGEAR ||
            RET_HGER))
13         .sortDesc(event −> event.time).take(1), categories=2,
            capacity=1
14     )
15 }
```

Listing 4. Guard predicates expressed by a two-sided interval and categorical quantity aa-predicates

3.3 Construction of *rsNN*

In this section, we formalize the second stage of the *rsNN* method, i.e., the auto-mated construction of an *rsNN* that reflects the guard of a refined adaptation rule. First, we show how to transform a logical formula into an elementary *rsNN* (*rsNN seed*) in general, and how to combine *rsNN* seeds into larger units (and how to combine these larger units as well) via transformed logical connectives. Then, we describe how the elementary logical formulas in the guard (i.e., static predicates and aa-predicates) are transformed into *rsNN* seeds.

Transforming a Logical Formula and Connectives

A logical formula $L(x_1, \ldots, x_m)$ is transformed to a continuous function $N(x_1, \ldots, x_m, w_1, \ldots, w_n) \to [0, 1]$ (i.e., a neural network), where $x_1, \ldots, x_m$ are the inputs to the logical formula (e.g., the current time, position of the worker in an aa-predicate), and $w_1, \ldots, w_n$ are trainable weights. The goal is to construct the function N and to train its weights in such a way that $L(x_1, \ldots, x_m) \Leftrightarrow N(x_1, \ldots, x_m, w_1, \ldots, w_n) > 0.5$ for as many inputs $x_1, \ldots, x_m$ as possible. By convention, we interpret $N(\ldots) > 0.5$ as *true*, while if this relation does not hold it is interpreted as *false*. Also, we use the symbol $\mathcal{T}$ to denote the transformation from the logical formula L to the continuous function N—i.e., $N(\ldots) = \mathcal{T}(L(\ldots))$.

As to logical connectives, we deviate from the traditional notion in which conjunction is defined as a product and disjunction is derived using De Morgan's laws. This is because our experiments showed that the conjunctions of multiple operands are close to impossible to train (very likely due to the vanishing gradient problem [9]). Therefore we transform conjunction and disjunction as follows (similarly to in [11]):

$$\mathcal{T}(L_1 \& \ldots \& L_k) = S\left((\mathcal{T}(L_1) + \cdots + \mathcal{T}(L_k) - k + 0.5) * p\right)$$

$$\mathcal{T}(L_1 \vee \cdots \vee L_k) = S\left((\mathcal{T}(L_1) + \cdots + \mathcal{T}(L_k) - 0.5) * p\right)$$

$$\mathcal{T}(\neg L) = 1 - \mathcal{T}(L)$$

where $S(x)$ is the sigmoid activation function defined as $S(x) = \frac{1}{1+e^{-x}}$, and $p > 1$ is an adjustable strength of the conjunction/disjunction operator. The bigger it is, the stricter the results are. However, too high values have the potential to harm training due to the vanishing gradient problem.

Transformation of a Static Predicate. A static predicate is transformed simply into a function that returns 0 or 1 depending on the result of the static predicate. Formally, we transform a static predicate $L_S(x_1, \ldots, x_m)$ to the function $N_S(x_1, \ldots, x_m)$ as follows:

$$\mathcal{T}(L_S) = \begin{cases} 0 & \text{if not } L_S(x_1, \ldots, x_m) \\ 1 & \text{if } L_S(x_1, \ldots, x_m) \end{cases}$$

Transformation of One-Sided Interval aa-Predicates. We transform an aa-predicate $isAboveThreshold(x, min, max)$ to the function $N_>(x, w_t)$ and an aa-predicate $isBelowThreshold(x, min, max)$ to the function $N_<(x, w_t)$ as follows.

$$\mathcal{T}(isAboveThreshold) = S\left(\left(\frac{x - min}{max - min} - w_t\right) * p\right)$$

$$\mathcal{T}(isBelowThreshold) = S\left(\left(w_t - \frac{x - min}{max - min}\right) * p\right)$$

where w_t is a trainable weight.

Transformation of Two-Sided Interval aa-Predicates. We base these aa-predicates on radial basis function (RBF) networks [14]. We apply one hidden layer of Gaussian functions and then construct a linear combination of their outputs. The weights in the linear combination are trainable. The training capacity c in the aa-predicate determines the number of neurons (i.e., points for which the Gaussian function is to be evaluated) in the hidden layer.

We set the means μ_i of the Gaussian function to a set of points over the area delimited by min and max parameters of the aa-predicate (e.g., forming a grid or being randomly sampled from a uniform distribution). We choose the σ parameter of the Gaussian function to be of the scale of the mean distance between neighbor points. The exact choice of σ seems not to be very important. Our experiments have shown that it has no significant effect and what matters is only its scale, not the exact value. The trainable linear combination after the RBF layer automatically adjusts to the chosen values of μ_i and σ.

For the sake of clarity, we show the transformation of

$$hasRightValue\_nD(x, min, max, c)$$

for $n = 1$ and for arbitrary n. In the 1-D case, we transform an aa-predicate $hasRightValue\_1D(x, min, max, c)$ to the function $N_{\simeq}^1(x, w_{a_1}, \ldots, w_{a_c}, w_b)$ as follows:

$$\mathcal{T}(hasRightValue\_1D) = S\left(w_b + \sum_{i=1}^{c} w_{a_i} e^{-\frac{(\mu_i - x)^2}{2\sigma^2}}\right)$$

where c is the capacity parameter of the predicate, $\mu_i \in [min, max]$ and σ are set as explained above, and $w_{a_1}, \ldots, w_{a_c}, w_b$ are trainable weights.

This is generalized to the n-D case as follows:

$$\mathcal{T}(hasRightValue\_nD) = S\left(w_b + \sum_{i_1=1}^{c} \cdots \sum_{i_n=1}^{c} w_{a_{i_1,\ldots,i_n}} e^{-\frac{|\mu_{i_1,\ldots,i_n} - x|^2}{2\sigma^2}}\right)$$

where $\mu_{i,j} \in [min_1, max_1] \times \cdots \times [min_n, max_n]$ and σ are set as explained above, x is an n-D vector, $|\cdot|$ stands for vector norm, and $w_{a_{1,\ldots,1}}, \ldots, w_{a_{c,\ldots,c}}, w_b$ are trainable weights.

Transformation of a Categorical Quantity aa-Predicate. We base this aa-predicate on a multi-layer perceptron with one hidden layer, which has the number of units equal to the capacity parameter c of the aa-predicate and is activated by the ReLU activation function.

The transformation of an aa-predicate

$$hasRightCategories\_nD(x, m, c)$$

to the function $N_{\pm}(x, w^h_{a_{1,1}}, \ldots, w^h_{a_{c,m}}, w^h_{b_1}, \ldots, w^h_{b_c}, w^o_{a_1}, \ldots, w^o_{a_c}, w^o_b)$ is defined as follows:

$$\mathcal{T}(hasRightCategories\_nD) =$$

$$S\left(w^o_b + \sum_{i=1}^{c} w^o_{a_i} \mathrm{ReLU}\left(w^h_{b_i} + \sum_{j=1}^{n}\sum_{k=1}^{m} w^h_{a_{i,j,k}} \delta_{x_j,k}\right)\right)$$

where $x \in \{1, \ldots, m\}^n$ is the n-dimensional input vector of categorical values from the same domain of size m, c is the capacity, $w^h_{i,j,k}, w^h_b$ are trainable weights of the hidden layer, $w^o_{a_i}, w^o_b$ are trainable weights of the output layer, $\delta_{i,j}$ is the Kronecker delta—i.e., $\delta_{i,j} = 1$ if $i = j$ and $\delta_{i,j} = 0$ otherwise. The ReLU function is defined as $\mathrm{ReLU}(x) = \max(0, x)$. Note that the Kronecker delta in the formula stands for one-hot encoding of the categorical input values.

3.4   Training an *rsNN*

The N function we defined as the result of the transformations in Sect. 3.3 contains trainable weights. We train these weights using supervised learning and employing the traditional stochastic gradient descent optimization.

The samples for training are taken from existing logs obtained from the system runtime or a simulation. In the case of the motivation example, each sample contains the current time, the worker id, its position, and the history of events associated with the worker. To obtain accurate outputs for supervised learning, we exploit the fact that we have the original logical formula of the guard with static predicates available. Thus we use it as an oracle for generating the ground truth for training inputs. The exact training procedure is described in [1].

After this training step, the function N can be used as a drop-in replacement for the corresponding adaptation rule. Moreover, being a neural network, it is able to digest additional samples generated at runtime—e.g., to learn from situations when the outputs of the system have been manually corrected/overridden.

4   Evaluation

We evaluated our approach by comparing the training results of *rsNNs* created by the method proposed in Sect. 3 with generic NNs comprising one and two dense layers. The complete set of necessary code and data for replicating the evaluation, as well as the experiments, detailed evaluation of results, graphs, and discussion that did not fit this paper, is available in the replication package [1].

For our motivating example, we created two datasets: (a) *random* sampled dataset, which was obtained by randomly generating inputs and using the original logical formula of the guard as an oracle; (b) *combined* dataset, which combines data from a simulation and the random dataset.

Both datasets have about $500,000$ data points.

The datasets were balanced in such a manner that half of the samples correspond to *true* and a half to the *false* evaluation of the guard of AccessToWorkplace. Additionally, to obtain more representative results for evaluation, the false cases were balanced so that each combination of the top-level conjunctions outcomes (i.e., duringShift & atWorkplaceGate & hasHeadGear) has the same probability.

The combined dataset combines false cases from random sampling and true cases from a simulation. The simulation was performed by a simulator we developed in the frame of an applied research project (Trust4.0[2]). The reason for combining these two sources is to get better coverage for all possible cases when the guard of the adaptation rule evaluates to *false*.

As the baseline generic NNs, we selected dense neural networks. Given our experiments and consultation with an expert outside our team (a researcher from another department who specializes in practical applications of neural networks), this architecture suits the problem at hand the best. Our setup comprises networks with one and two dense layers of 128 to 1024 nodes (in the case of two layers, both of them have the same amount of nodes). The dense layers use ReLU activation, and the final layer uses sigmoid. The greatest accuracy was observed when two 256-node dense layers were used; thus, this configuration was selected as the *baseline*.

Three versions of rsNNs representing our approach were built corresponding to different levels of refinement. The first two models refined only the time condition: one used the isAboveThreshold and isBelowThreshold variant (as in Listing 3)—denoted as *"time (A&B)"*, the other used hasRightValue aa-predicate (similar to Listing 3 but with hasRightValue instead of the combination of isAboveThreshold and isBelowThreshold)—denoted as *"time (right)"*. The last model refined all involved inputs (time, place, and headgear events) as outlined in Listing 4—denoted as *"all"*. To verify the properness of logical connectives redefinition (Sect. 3.3), we built a TensorFlow[3] model with no trainable weights (i.e., just rewriting the static predicates using their transformation described in Sect. 3.3). By setting $p = 10$, we achieved 100% accuracy (this value of p was then used in all other experiments).

Table 1. Comparison of accuracies of individual methods

	Baseline	Time (A&B)	Time (right)	All
Accuracy (random)	99.159%	98.878%	99.999%	99.978%
Accuracy (combined)	99.393%	92.867%	99.993%	99.575%
Number of weights	68,353	2	21	1,227

---

[2] https://github.com/smartarch/trust4.0-demo.
[3] https://www.tensorflow.org/ (version 2.4).

Table 1 presents the measured accuracies on the testing set[4] of both datasets (random and combined) after 100 training epochs, comparing *rsNNs* resulting from different refinements with the baseline. The last two models outperform the baseline in terms of accuracy. The *number of Weights* line refers to the number of trainable weights in each model. While the baseline has multiple weights (as it features two dense layers), our *rsNNs* have significantly fewer weights since their composition benefits from the domain knowledge ingrained in the adaptation rules.

The lower number of trainable parameters positively impacts the performance as it makes the models train and evaluates significantly faster whilst achieving comparable accuracy levels. We did not perform a thorough performance analysis since it heavily depends on many configuration parameters (e.g., batch size) and the actual hardware (especially whether CPU or GPU is used for the training). However, in our configurations, the proposed model was trained roughly several times (up to an order of magnitude) faster than the baseline.

5   Related Work

In the domain of adaptive systems, NNs and machine learning are used in several areas. Closely related approaches use NNs in the adaptation cycle analysis phase. Namely, in [16], neural networks are applied during the analysis and planning phase to reduce a large adaptation space. We apply *rsNN* during the same phases to refine adaptation rules, thus allowing for more flexible adaptation. Similarly, in [6], NNs are applied during the restriction of the adaptation space to achieve a meaningful system after adaptation.

In [12], NNs are used to forecast values of QoS parameters, thus allowing for the progressive selection of adaptation. A similar approach is used in [2] to predict values in sensor networks and proactively perform adaptation. Multiple machine learning algorithms, including NNs, are employed in [5] to predict QoS values again.

The approaches above target either reducing the adaptation space or adapting a system proactively. They differ from our approach as we use neural networks to relax strict conditions in an adaptive system and thus to learn new unforeseen conditions. A conceptually similar approach is [7], where machine learning approaches are utilized for training a model for rule-based adaptation. Instead of NNs, approaches like the random forest, gradient boosting regression models, and extreme boosting trees are used. Similarly, paper [3] proposes a proactive learner; however, the infrastructure is mainly discussed, and details about the used machine learning techniques are omitted. In [15], the authors propose an approach to dynamic learning of knowledge in self-adaptive and self-improving systems using supervised and reinforcement learning techniques. In [10], machine learning is used to deal with uncertainty in an adaptive system (namely in a

---

[4] We divide the data only to the training and testing set (testing set holds 10% of data). We do not need a validation set since we do not perform any hyper-parameter training.

cloud controller). Here, the proposed approach allows users to specify potentially imprecise control rules expressed with the help of fuzzy logic, and machine
learning techniques are used to learn precise rules. The approach is the complete
opposite of ours, where we start with precise rules and, via machine learning, we
reach attunable ones. A similar approach is in [18], where reinforcement learning
is also employed for generating and evolving the adaptation rules.

6   Conclusion

In this paper, we introduced the rule-specific Neural Network (*rsNN*) method
that allows for transforming the guard of an adaptation rule into a custom
neural network, the composition of which is driven by the structure of the logical
predicates in the guard. An essential aspect of *rsNN* is that by having the ability
to combine the original static predicates with attunable ones (and, in addition,
to set the training capacity of the corresponding part of *rsNN* network), one
can step-by-step proceed from a static non-trainable adaptation rule to fully
trainable one. This aspect allows for a gradual transition from the original self-
adaptive system to its trainable counterpart while still controlling the inherent
uncertainty of introducing machine learning into the system.

The aspect of being able to control the uncertainty inherent to machine
learning is a distinguishing factor of the *rsNN* method. This stems primarily
from two facts: (1) The structure of the *rsNN* generated from an adaption rule
directly relates to the composition of its predicates, and the static predicates can
be combined with attunable ones. (2) An *rsNNs* is a neural network with almost
two orders of magnitude fewer neurons than a generic neural network (e.g., a
multi-layer perceptron network with several hidden dense layers) solving the
same task. This makes the *rsNN* less prone to overfitting, which, in general, may
lead to unexpected results in real environments. Moreover, given the significant
difference in the number of neurons and thus trainable weights, rsNN networks
train much faster, as showcased in the results of the experiments. In future
work, we aim to extend the set of the predefined aa-predicates to provide a
tool for applications also featuring other than metric and categorical quantities.
Furthermore, we are looking into ways of supporting the process of gradual
transformation of static predicates into attunable ones with the aim to make
this process semi-automatic.

Acknowledgment. This work has been funded by the DFG (German Research Foundation) - project number 432576552, HE8596/1-1 (FluidTrust), supported by the Czech
Science Foundation project 20-24814J, partially supported by Charles University institutional funding SVV 260588 and the KASTEL institutional funding, and partially
supported by the Charles University Grant Agency project 408622.

References

1. Paper results replicaton package. https://github.com/smartarch/attuning-adaptation-rules-replication-package
2. Anaya, I.D.P., Simko, V., Bourcier, J., Plouzeau, N., Jézéquel, J.M.: A prediction-driven adaptation approach for self-adaptive sensor networks. In: Proceedings of SEAMS 2014, Hyderabad, India (2014)
3. Bierzynski, K., Lutskov, P., Assmann, U.: Supporting the self-learning of systems at the network edge with microservices. In: 13th International Conference and Exhibition on Smart Systems Integration Issues of Miniaturized Systems (2019)
4. Bureš, T., Gerostathopoulos, I., Hnětynka, P., Pacovský, J.: Forming ensembles at runtime: a machine learning approach. In: Proceedings of ISOLA 2020, Rhodes, Greece (2020)
5. Chen, T., Bahsoon, R.: Self-adaptive and online QoS modeling for cloud-based software services. IEEE Trans. Softw. Eng. **43**(5), 453–475 (2017)
6. Gabor, T., et al.: The scenario coevolution paradigm: adaptive quality assurance for adaptive systems. Int. J. Softw. Tools Technol. Transfer **22**(4), 457–476 (2020)
7. Ghahremani, S., Adriano, C.M., Giese, H.: Training prediction models for rule-based self-adaptive systems. In: Proceedings of ICAC 2018, Trento, Italy (2018)
8. Goodfellow, I., Bengio, Y., Courville, A.: Deep Learning. MIT Press, Cambridge (2016). https://www.deeplearningbook.org
9. Hochreiter, S., Bengio, Y., Frasconi, P., Schmidhuber, J.: Gradient flow in recurrent nets: the difficulty of learning long-term dependencies. In: A Field Guide to Dynamical Recurrent Neural Networks. IEEE Press (2001)
10. Jamshidi, P., Pahl, C., Mendonça, N.C.: Managing uncertainty in autonomic cloud elasticity controllers. IEEE Cloud Comput. **3**(3), 50–60 (2016)
11. Mańdziuk, J., Macukow, B.: A neural network performing Boolean logic operations. Opt. Memory Neural Netw. **2**(1), 17–35 (1993)
12. Muccini, H., Vaidhyanathan, K.: A machine learning-driven approach for proactive decision making in adaptive architectures. In: Companion Proceedings of ICSA 2019, Hamburg, Germany (2019)
13. Salehie, M., Tahvildari, L.: Self-adaptive software: landscape and research challenges. ACM Trans. Auton. Adapt. Syst. **4**(2), 1–42 (2009)
14. Schwenker, F., Kestler, H.A., Palm, G.: Three learning phases for radial-basis-function networks. Neural Netw. **14**(4), 439–458 (2001)
15. Stein, A., Tomforde, S., Diaconescu, A., Hähner, J., Müller-Schloer, C.: A concept for proactive knowledge construction in self-learning autonomous systems. In: Proceedings of FAS*W 2018, Trento, Italy (2018)
16. Van Der Donckt, J., Weyns, D., Quin, F., Van Der Donckt, J., Michiels, S.: Applying deep learning to reduce large adaptation spaces of self-adaptive systems with multiple types of goals. In: Proceedings of SEAMS 2020, Seoul, Korea. ACM (2020)
17. Weyns, D., et al.: Towards better adaptive systems by combining mape, control theory, and machine learning. In: Proceedings of SEAMS 2021, Madrid, Spain (2021)
18. Zhao, T., Zhang, W., Zhao, H., Jin, Z.: A reinforcement learning-based framework for the generation and evolution of adaptation rules. In: Proceedings of ICAC 2017, Columbus, OH, USA (2017)

Measuring Convergence Inertia: Online Learning in Self-adaptive Systems with Context Shifts

Elvin Alberts and Ilias Gerostathopoulos[✉]

Vrije Universiteit Amsterdam, Amsterdam, The Netherlands
{e.g.alberts,i.g.gerostathopoulos}@vu.nl

Abstract. To deal with situations not specifically designed for (unknown-unknowns), self-adaptive systems need to learn the best – or at least good enough – action to perform in each context faced during operation. An established solution for doing so is through the use of online learning. The complexity of online learning however increases in the presence of context shifts – which are typical in self-adaptive systems. In this paper, we (i) propose a new metric, *convergence inertia*, to assess the robustness of reinforcement learning policies against context shifts, and (ii) use it to assess the robustness of different policies within the family of multi-armed bandits (MAB) to context shifts. Through an experiment with a self-adaptation exemplar of a web server, we demonstrate that inertia and the accompanying interpretation of the unknown-unknowns problem is a viable way to inform the selection of online learning policies for self-adaptive systems, since it brings the influence of context shifts to the forefront. In our experiment, we found that non-stationary MAB policies are better suited to handling context shifts in terms of inertia, although stationary policies tend to perform well in terms of overall convergence.

Keywords: Online learning · Self-adaptive systems · Non-stationary · Convergence inertia

1 Introduction

Self-adaptive systems (SAS) are able to react to changes in their environment and internal state to ensure a number of adaptation goals related to e.g. application performance, resource consumption, and failure avoidance [12]. While adaptation is mostly used to address known-unknowns, i.e. situations that one anticipates and designs a specific action/policy for, a highly challenging yet realistic class of SAS has to deal with unknown-unknowns, i.e. situations that are not entirely anticipated by the system designers [14]. Such situations can lead to a suboptimal system state where adaptation goals are no longer met. To deal with unknown-unknowns, SAS can apply online learning, i.e. learn the appropriate adaptation action at runtime out of a set of available actions.

T. Margaria and B. Steffen (Eds.): ISoLA 2022, LNCS 13703, pp. 231–248, 2022.
https://doi.org/10.1007/978-3-031-19759-8_15

Online learning in SAS typically takes the form of a reinforcement learning (RL) policy that continuously applies an action and monitors its reward (in terms of overall utility of the system after the action is performed). For instance, an action may be to add or remove servers of a web application; the reward could be measured as the number of requests that can be timely served. After applying a number of actions, the RL policy gradually builds up the knowledge of which action to apply to maximize system utility.

A problem that arises when using RL for online learning in a SAS is that the SAS may undergo several context shifts during the learning phase. Following the web application example, the number of user requests may increase or decrease. Context shifts affect the reward distributions, which can interfere with the learning process as this is based on associating actions with reward values. Interference may have a positive effect if it reinforces prior knowledge and speeds up the convergence of the policy or a negative effect if it contradicts learned knowledge and slows down convergence. An example of the latter is a context shift that causes a previously optimal action to become suboptimal. In that case, the convergence to the new optimal action will be hampered because of the prior knowledge accumulated suggesting the previous optimal. We refer to this difference in the speed of convergence as *inertia*, as there is a resistance towards realizing the optimal relative to a clean start, specific to each policy.

In this paper, we focus on inertia and its effects on online learning in self-adaptive systems. In particular, we formulate the inertia metric and propose a way to measure it general to any (even non-RL) policy. To investigate its effects, we perform an experimental study using a number of RL policies belonging to the multi-armed bandits (MAB) family [13], which is a simplified category of RL algorithms. Our experiment uses SWIM [18], a SAS exemplar provided by the self-adaptive systems community that simulates an elastic web application. We compare several MAB policies that can deal with context shifts and the related inertia they incur in different ways: by just ignoring the change, by greedily exploring or assuming stationarity, by considering only a limited window of time in the past when evaluating actions, or by maintaining separate knowledge bases for a set of learned contexts through side information.

Our results show that stochastic policies that operate under the assumption of stationarity, such as UCB Tuned [2], can deceivingly converge well despite context shifts. However, when inertia is measured it is clear that non-stationary policies are better suited to handling context shifts. By quantifying the inertia an educated decision can be made when choosing RL policies for SAS systems which deal with non-stationary environments.

2   Background and Running Example

2.1   Online Learning in Self-adaptive Systems

Online learning has been proposed to remedy design uncertainty in self-adaptive systems (SAS) [9,17]: instead of trying to enumerate all the possible situations – triggers for adaptation – and the corresponding actions, the idea is to let the system try out different actions in different situations and learn *at runtime* which action is the most appropriate in each situation.

With respect to the Monitor-Analyse-Plan-Execute over Knowledge (MAPE-K) loop typically used for structuring the self-adaptation logic [8] of a SAS, online learning can be employed within the Plan phase. In this setup, there exists a MAPE-K loop that monitors the managed system, analyzes the monitored data to determine whether a change is needed, plans the change and executes it (Fig. 1). This is done by using system models and/or rules shared via the common Knowledge base. If the planner has no available plans for a situation, it invokes online learning with a certain time budget (horizon) to generate such plan. Online learning then uses the Monitor and Execute phases of the outer loop and, instead of reacting to conditions by changing the system at runtime, it proactively performs actions to assess and rank them at runtime.

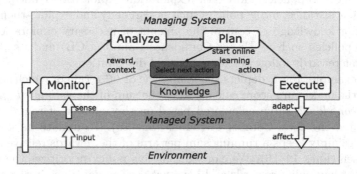

Fig. 1. Online learning invoked by the Plan phase of a self-adaptive system.

In this work, we focus specifically on the multi-armed bandits family of RL algorithms to perform online learning and compare their capability to learn optimal actions while the system undergoes context shifts. MAB policies are not considered 'full' RL [21], in that they only consider a single state. This entails that every action only affects its immediate reward (and not that of other actions), as there is no transition in states due to the action. Where the assumption of a single state can be placed on the system MAB policies provide sufficient solutions. These solutions are importantly also more accessible, and less complex and thus lightweight.

2.2   Overview of Multi-armed Bandits

Multi-armed bandit (MAB) algorithms or *policies* (used henceforth) are a class of RL algorithms that deals with choosing between a set of k options called *arms* [13]. Formally, this setting corresponds to a Markov Decision Process with a single state and k actions. Compared to general RL, actions in MAB are assumed to not influence future states of the environment. As in general RL, an MAB policy balances *exploration* with *exploitation*: it tries to explore arms to gain knowledge about them while at the same time use the best-known arm regularly enough to exploit the knowledge it has already gained. Each arm has an associated reward whose value at a time t is not known prior to selecting it. Arms are selected sequentially and their rewards are gradually revealed; an MAB policy prescribes which arm should be selected at each round. MAB policies try to minimize the *regret* they incur, i.e. the reward lost relative to that of the best arm at each round. Equivalently, they try to maximize the cumulative reward over all rounds. Formally, given k arms and sequences of rewards $X_{i,1}, X_{i,2}, ...$ associated with each arm i, the regret R_n of a policy after n plays $I_1, ..., I_n$ is [4]

$$R_n = \max_{i=1,...,k} \sum_{t=1}^{n} X_{i,t} - \sum_{t=1}^{n} X_{I_t,t}$$

Different MAB policies address the exploration-exploitation tradeoff in different ways. For instance, *naive* policies such as ϵ-greedy and explore-then-commit rely on prior knowledge to control the amount of necessary exploration, while *stochastic* policies such as Upper Confidence Bound (UCB) and its variations assume that rewards follow certain statistical distributions.

As an example, Fig. 2 depicts the main logic of UCB Tuned, which selects the arm with the maximum score calculated as the sum of the *estimated mean* (line 7) and a *confidence* value calculated based on the number of rounds the arm is played and the total number of rounds (line 10). To update its knowledge, UCB Tuned simply keeps a running sum per arm of the rewards received and the times chosen (lines 14–16). We can see that this policy prioritizes the selection of arms that have high rewards and have not used many times in the past.

```
1  class UCBTN(Bandit):
2    def get_next_arm(self):
3      return max(self.arms, key= lambda arm: self.get_score(arm))
4
5    def get_score(self, arm):
6      cum_rew, cum_sq_rew, n_k = self.knowledge[arm]
7      est_mean = cum_rew / n_k
8      est_variance = (cum_sq_rew / n_k) - square(est_mean)
9      V_k = est_variance + sqrt(2 * (log(self.round)/n_k))
10     confidence = sqrt((log(self.round)/n_k) * V_k)
11     return est_mean + confidence
12
13   def update_knowledge(self, reward):
14     self.knowledge[self.last_action][CUM_REWARD]+=reward
15     self.knowledge[self.last_action][CUM_SQ_REWARD]+=square(reward)
16     self.knowledge[self.last_action][N_K]+=1
```

Fig. 2. Python snippet of the UCB Tuned policy.

Certain MAB policies are specifically developed to deal with non-stationary environments and also consider the influence of context shifts on reward values. Representatives of the former are the Sliding Window and Discounted UCB policies [11], which perform UCB over a window of the last τ specified rounds or discount rewards by a factor γ as they age, respectively. A representative of *contextual MAB* is EXP4 [3], a policy that uses a number of experts (instances of MAB policies), each able to deal with a certain context. When a context shift occurs, the policy eventually learns which expert to listen for that context to choose the next arm.

2.3 Running Example: SWIM

SWIM [18] is a 'Simulator for Web Infrastructure and Management' representing at a high level the management of server infrastructure for a fictitious web location. The simulator allows real web traces to be replayed in simulated time, making it possible to adapt to hours of web traffic in a span of minutes. The behavior of SWIM is determined by two variables, its dimmer value and the number of servers deployed. The latter's maximum can also be configured by the user, while the dimmer is on a scale of [0,1] with the increments being user configured as well. The dimmer value determines the rate at which advertisements are included in the responses to requests, here we opt to always include ads in every response. In our experiment reported in Sect. 4 we use SWIM mostly as-is having added the ability to embed Python code to take advantage of simulated time rather than interacting with it in an external real-time fashion [1].

Strictly speaking, in SWIM the assumption of having an action influence only its immediate reward does not hold: some actions trigger a temporary secondary state where the servers have a backlog of requests to process. We have engineered as a part of our solution a means to detect this state and 'clean' the backlog to return to the original state the learners interact with. Where relevant we will refer to this change as the 'cleaning trick'.

3   Dealing with Context Switches in Online Learning

Unknown unknowns are a recognized challenge in self-adaptive systems research [14]. This entails the existence of environmental changes that are unanticipated due to a failure of imagination. These unanticipated events matter most when they interfere with achieving *explicit* (quantifiable in the degree to which they have been achieved) adaptation goals. For the purposes of MAB/RL policies such a goal can be interpreted as a 'reward' which evaluates choices made. Changes in the environment naturally influence the reward, even within anticipated scenarios e.g. circumstances dictate whether adaptation A or B is best. This closed feedback loop enables policies to learn which choices are suited to the environment. However, naive policies expect some stationarity, that over infinite time there is a singular optimal choice of which can be learned. To learn about these choices there is some degree of exploration which is traded off with exploiting the best learned choice.

A problem arises when learned knowledge is abruptly invalidated. Learned choices will continue to be made by a policy based on false pretenses. This is different from a stochastic setting which may cause noise in the evaluation of choices. In the stochastic setting it is held that each choice has an unchanging true mean which in infinite time can be discovered by the policy. In a non-stationary environment these true means shift i.e. the reward-generating functions per arm change. The abrupt invalidation is what we refer to as a shift to a new context. This is one way in which the unknown-unknowns problem manifests itself in online learning. The response of a learner to this abrupt change is to (slowly) learn the new reward functions. The speed of this learning will depend on the accrued knowledge from the previous context and the policy-specific interaction with it. Combining these two factors is what we propose to measure and refer to as a policy's *inertia*.

We will now formalize the necessary concepts to determine the inertia. An RL learner or policy has a (potentially finite) horizon H of interactions (rounds) with which to interact with the environment. We consider the horizon to be divisible into a set R of time ranges indicated in square braces: $R = \{[s, e] | s, e \in \mathbb{Z} \wedge s < e \wedge e \leq H\}$, where s is the starting point of the time range and e the ending point. To evaluate the RL policy's performance within a time range $[s, e]$ a typical measure is convergence i.e. the frequency of choosing the optimal action – we denote this as $\mathrm{conv}([s, e])$. Given that, we calculate inertia as the difference in convergence between two time ranges that have starting points $s1$ and $s2$ (with $s1 < s2$) and the same duration d:

$$\mathrm{inertia}(s1, s2, d) = \mathrm{conv}([s2, s2 + d]) - \mathrm{conv}([s1, s1 + d])$$

The main idea is that if the two time ranges belong to the same context $c1 \subset R$ (blue context in Fig. 3), inertia provides a measure of how much the convergence of a policy in a context $c1$ is affected by other contexts occurring before it, compared to the "cold start" convergence obtained by setting $s1$ to 0 in the above formula.

Fig. 3. Graphical representation of re-occuring context in inertia calculation.

For instance, if the convergence of a policy in the first occurrence of a context $c1$ is 60% and its convergence in the re-occurrence of $c1$ is 20%, the policy's inertia w.r.t. $c1$ is equal to -40%. Negative inertia values indicate a negative effect of context shifts; the larger negative values, the more negatively a policy is affected by context shifts. Clearly, inertia values depend both on the policy used and on the particular setting – number and magnitude of context shifts.

In this paper, we focus on the way MAB policies deal with the negative effects of context shifts and measure and compare their inertia. For MABs, at each sequential round, one of the k arms available to the learner is chosen. The policy π maps previously chosen arms and their rewards to a new arm choice. Formally, it is a tuple $\pi = (H, I, X)$ where the *horizon* H is the number of total interactions with the environment, and the sequences I and X are the arms it learns to choose and the rewards received for each arm, respectively. The length or number of rounds of a time range is given by $\text{len}([s, e])) = e - s$. Given the above, convergence in MABs is measured as [21]:

$$\text{conv}([s, e]) = \frac{T_{i^*}([s, e])}{\text{len}([s, e])} \quad \text{where } i^* = \text{argmax } X_{i,t} \text{ for a given } [s, e] \in R.$$

with T_i referring to the number of times a particular arm i is chosen within a time range.

We will now closely examine and compare potential solutions to the problem of dealing with accrued inertia within the realm of MAB policies. In particular, we cover the following potential solutions to the problem:

Stationary/Naive Policies: Stationary and naive MAB policies operate under the assumption of a singular true mean to be learned per arm. Therefore, they do not anticipate context shifts as we describe them. The ability to realize a new optimal choice due to a shift is dictated by that exploration rate of the policy. Policies which are 'stochastic bandits' tend to have more higher exploration rates as they expect noise to obfuscate the means. When the context shifts, this is interpreted as noise, the previous context's reading were all noise deviating from the 'true' choice of the new context. This holds until the last context it faces. The crux is that the contexts need to last long enough to overcome the 'deviations' from the previous context to realize the true choice. If contexts change often then the policy is left chasing different true choices without ever converging to any of them. Policies also tend to reduce the exploration rate over time i.e. there is an assumption that the policy becomes more certain about each choice the more it has sampled it. This assumption does not hold for a context shift as the distribution being sampled from has essentially changed; it stands to reason then that as time progresses stationary policies become worse at handling context shifts. The stationary policies used in this paper are ϵ-greedy and UCB Tuned [2]. ϵ-greedy has a hyperparameter ϵ which dictates its rate of exploration. UCB Tuned uses the 'confidence' in the true means per arm to decide its exploration rate.

Non-stationary Policies: These policies are designed with context shifts in mind. They achieve this by operating with knowledge which has an expiry date. There is a continuous disregard for older knowledge with the aim of operating based on the most recent findings. This is in the hope that when a context shift does happen, the readings from the new context start to outweigh that of the previous. If the new context is short-lived and there is a return to the previous then some knowledge of that context is still held. The prevalent issue is how quickly older knowledge should be discarded. This depends on some estimation of the frequency of changes to take place. When improperly tuned, one risks not being able to converge and exploit a context as adequately as a stationary policy or approximate a stationary policy by not recognizing context shifts in a timely manner. Discounted UCB [11] is used to represent a non-stationary policy for the experiment to follow. Its hyperparameter is a discount factor which lessens the weight of older knowledge in decision-making.

Contextual Policies: Contextual learners use 'side information' to recognize contexts. Stationary and strictly non-stationary policies, as covered in the previous two paragraphs, have the side effect of overwriting previous knowledge. This is due to the fact that they are *nonassociative*. Contextual policies instead associate side-information with learned knowledge to maintain distinct behavior per context. In essence, they learn a policy rather than an action. This eliminates the need to estimate prior the frequency of context shifts as with non-stationary policies. However, the stipulation of available side information is not a light one and restricts application to SAS systems. Depending on the policy this side information is expected in different forms. Two important contextual policies are LinUCB [15] and EXP4 [3]. For LinUCB side information are 'features' which may characterize contexts. For this paper EXP4 is used. Side information is used at design time to inform the selection and potential training of experts. In this paper side information is used to determine the number of expected contexts, with there then being one expert pre-trained per context. It is also an option to have these experts be untrained should no prior access to the expected contexts be available. The policy learns to associate each expert with its corresponding context at runtime.

4 Experiments

We have conducted an experiment aiming to answer the following research questions: **RQ1**: To what extent do different context lengths affect the convergence rate after a shift? Following from this, **RQ2**: How does convergence inertia compare as an indicator of a policy's ability to handle non-stationary environments?

In the experiment, two shifts take place between two distinct contexts A and B, with the pattern ABA. Each context has a different optimal arm choice with stationary but noisy reward distributions supporting each arm. We specifically focus on three scenarios which differ in the number of rounds each context in the sequence is active. Within each scenario, the policies are exposed to the same environment. Based on these policy-specific behavior these environments influence the knowledge accumulated which influences the inertia measured.

4.1   Setup

In our experiment, we use the SWIM exemplar and focus on arms that correspond to different numbers of servers: 3, 8, 13. These values are chosen to both cover the level of traffic that will be experienced in different contexts as well as provide a wider range of reward values. Without spreading out the reward values the suboptimality gaps between the options hinder the ability of the learner to distinguish options. To be able to better interpret the effect of each policy, all configurations have a dimmer value of 1.0 (i.e., always serving ads). The reward function used to evaluate each arm is based on the utility function originally included with SWIM [18] and is adapted to (i) always have the server cost manifested in the reward, (ii) introduce weights among the objectives, and (iii) introduce an upper response time threshold to have the minimum potential reward reflect the maximum, as described in our earlier work [1]. All three of these serve to increase the accuracy of reward values in evaluating the adaptations.

In terms of policies, we use the Random policy to serve as a baseline, ϵ-greedy as an extended baseline as it has fixed exploration rates as well as as a representative of stationary policies alongside UCB Tuned [2]. Further, Discounted UCB [11] represents a non-stationary policy and EXP4 [3] a contextual policy (solving non-stationarity through association).

For the purposes of the experiment we vary the length of time that the contexts A and B are active within the pattern ABA. We use two lengths, $X = 6600$ s and $Y = 1200$ s which correspond to 110 and 20 rounds respectively as each round is after a 60 s evaluation period. The two lengths represent a number of rounds in which each policy should converge towards the optimal are and should not respectively. Convergence is calculated as defined in Sect. 3. A policy has converged when the convergence is $\geq \frac{\lceil k/2 \rceil}{k}$ of sequential time ranges of fixed chosen length. In our case of 3 arms, it is then when the optimal arm has a convergence of ≥ 0.66. We refer to the first A in the sequence as first context, B as second context, and the second A as the third context.

Every scenario ends with a sequence of Y rounds, this is as we measure the effect of inertia which is relevant directly after the shift. We now elaborate on each chosen scenario:

- XXY: By having two longer contexts of X, the policies have sufficient time to converge to the optimal arms of the first two contexts. This should demonstrate the effect of an equal amount of rounds in influencing behavior learned in the first context.
- XYY: By having a longer context first context followed by a shorter experience of the second non-repeating context, we expect to see the learner be biased towards learning the third context (which is the same as the first). It is then interesting to see whether this holds for the policies we choose.
- YXY: By giving little time with the first context which returns after the second we expect an opposite effect of XYY. Policies may be able to still use the short first context experience to their advantage in the third context, but this may be at the cost of converging in the second context (which is $\geq 70\%$ of the scenario).

Context A and B both have uniformly distributed (noisy) traffic levels centered around 60 and 80 request/s respectively, fluctuating within a range of 10% both ways. We know empirically that the former can be handled with at least 3 servers, while the latter can be handled with 5 servers or more. Each policy is run 30 times per scenario, with the results shown being the average over those 30. This is to account for slight variation which is generated in the service capacity of the servers in SWIM, as well as those policies (like ϵ-greedy) which use a random factor in their decision logic. As covered in Sect. 3, inertia plays a role when context shifts happen. As defined, inertia is the difference in convergence over the same number of rounds between learning from scratch and learning after one or more context shifts. For example, if 20 rounds of context A from a clean start results in a convergence factor of 0.70 and after some arbitrary number of rounds of another context the same 20 rounds of context A have a convergence factor of 0.40 then the inertia is -0.30. Thus, negative values indicate a relatively poorer convergence than starting from scratch and vice versa.

4.2   Results

For Table 1 we are specifically interested in how the policies fare as a result of the shift in context. By experiencing these rounds inertia in realizing the optimal arm accumulates. The amount of inertia created depends directly on the policy as we control for environmental factors. We consider an ideal policy one which can finely balance the interests of converging to potentially long contexts (X) yet use knowledge from even short-lived contexts (Y) in case they reoccur. The policy would have low inertia yet high convergence.

The reward distributions of the previous context(s) influence the knowledge each policy builds. The actual knowledge is dictated by the arms the policy's behavior as it chooses arms at each round. Besides the arms chosen, the total number of elapsed rounds can also have an influence. It is clear from the results in both Tables 1 and 2 that the hyperparameters play a significant role. For each policy, the hyperparameter can be translated into greediness. Most straightforward is ϵ-greedy, which is more greedy the lower its ϵ value is as it explores less. UCB Tuned is a stationary policy meaning it assumes the optimal arm will not change, and therefore progressively more greedily converges towards the optimal arm with the rate depending on collected knowledge. As the γ value of Discounted UCB increases, it approximates UCB Tuned, thus for lower values of γ it is less greedy. For EXP4 the learning rate η dictates how greedily new knowledge is used to decide which expert it should listen to.

The greediness across policies is a double-edged sword. As Table 2 indicates, UCB Tuned makes use of its greediness to achieve a high weighted average of convergence. However, as results in the appendix[1] clarify, this is mostly due to its high convergence in the first two contexts. The convergence rates suggest that the policy can easily eliminate the third choice (optimal in no contexts) and begin achieving $\frac{2}{3}$ convergence, as good as random between two choices. As

---

[1] https://github.com/EGAlberts/ISOLABandits/blob/main/ISOLA/_appendix.pdf.

Table 1. Inertia based on difference in convergence.

Policy	Hyper-parameter	Convergence first 20 (Y)	Inertia XXY	Inertia XYY	Inertia YXY	AVG inertia
Random ϵ-greedy (stationary)	n/a	0.34	0.01	−0.04	0.00	−0.01
	$\epsilon = 0.30$	0.60	−0.50	0.21	−0.40	−0.23
	$\epsilon = 0.40$	0.52	−0.38	0.20	−0.30	−0.16
	$\epsilon = 0.50$	0.51	−0.36	0.17	−0.29	−0.16
	$\epsilon = 0.60$	0.48	−0.27	0.09	−0.24	−0.14
	$\epsilon = 0.70$	0.47	−0.20	0.06	−0.22	−0.12
	$\epsilon = 0.80$	0.46	−0.22	0.00	−0.19	−0.14
UCB Tuned (stationary)	n/a	0.50	−0.50	−0.19	−0.25	−0.31
Discounted UCB (non-stationary)	$\gamma = 0.89$	0.40	0.00	0.01	0.00	0.00
	$\gamma = 0.92$	0.40	0.02	0.02	0.03	**0.02**
	$\gamma = 0.97$	0.45	0.04	0.03	0.07	**0.05**
	$\gamma = 0.99$	0.49	0.06	−0.18	0.06	−0.02
	$\gamma = 0.995$	0.50	−0.17	−0.25	−0.07	−0.16
	$\gamma = 0.997$	0.50	−0.47	−0.21	−0.15	−0.28
EXP4 (contextual)	$\eta = 0.04$	0.41	−0.22	0.09	−0.29	−0.14
	$\eta = 0.10$	0.44	−0.36	0.16	−0.42	−0.21
	$\eta = 0.20$	0.40	−0.33	0.26	−0.38	−0.15
	$\eta = 0.40$	0.44	−0.37	0.19	−0.41	−0.20
	$\eta = 0.60$	0.46	−0.40	0.27	−0.45	−0.19
	$\eta = 0.80$	0.50	−0.45	0.17	−0.47	−0.25

time progresses it attempts to converge towards the best of these two. A policy like ϵ-greedy does so immediately based on whichever comes out higher, this is also clear from the tables in the appendix. However, UCB Tuned is a stochastic policy and thus expects some noise which at times may suggest one choice being better than another despite their true means. It therefore needs to have enough confidence in a choice before it chooses to converge to it. The first shift from A to B aids in this by enlarging the gap between the two arms across scenarios. This leads to a minimum convergence of 0.80 in the second context, being highest (0.97) when the most time is afforded in XXY as can be seen in the appendix.

Discounted UCB anticipates that there may be shifts in the optimal arm. However it clearly does so at a cost, its robustness towards shifts directly influences its convergence towards an arm within the context. The Discounted UCB hyperparameter values which are not too close to UCB Tuned perform best when it comes to inertia, yet poorly when it comes to actually converging. This is a clearcut indicator of inertia corresponding to the ability to handle non-stationary environments. What is key to choosing between a non-stationary and stationary policy expectation a user has of the system and what is can afford. With a

Table 2. Weighted averages of convergence per scenario.

Policy	Hyperparameter	XXY	XYY	YXY	Average
Random	n/a	0.34	0.32	0.33	0.33
ϵ-greedy (stationary)	$\epsilon = 0.30$	0.59	0.70	0.44	0.58
	$\epsilon = 0.40$	0.56	0.67	0.42	0.55
	$\epsilon = 0.50$	0.54	0.60	0.39	0.51
	$\epsilon = 0.60$	0.48	0.54	0.37	0.46
	$\epsilon = 0.70$	0.44	0.50	0.36	0.43
	$\epsilon = 0.80$	0.41	0.43	0.35	*0.40*
UCB Tuned (stationary)	n/a	0.72	0.64	0.67	**0.68**
Discounted UCB (non-stationary)	$\gamma = 0.89$	0.40	0.39	0.42	*0.40*
	$\gamma = 0.92$	0.43	0.42	0.44	0.43
	$\gamma = 0.97$	0.50	0.50	0.53	0.51
	$\gamma = 0.99$	0.64	0.56	0.63	0.61
	$\gamma = 0.995$	0.67	0.60	0.65	0.64
	$\gamma = 0.997$	0.68	0.62	0.65	**0.65**
EXP4 (contextual)	$\eta = 0.04$	0.48	0.47	0.54	0.50
	$\eta = 0.10$	0.51	0.53	0.59	0.54
	$\eta = 0.20$	0.54	0.60	0.61	0.58
	$\eta = 0.40$	0.56	0.61	0.62	0.60
	$\eta = 0.60$	0.57	0.64	0.62	0.61
	$\eta = 0.80$	0.57	0.65	0.65	0.62

significant consistent frequency of shifts, averaging a convergence rate of ~ 0.50 becomes more attractive when compared to stationary policies. One needs to look no further than high effect of inertia on UCB Tuned, also reflected in its average convergence in the third context of only 0.18 (in the appendix) which is worse than even random selection. The challenge with using Discounted UCB is the necessity to tune it, the success of which depends on possibly unrealistic assumption one knows how many shifts will take place.

Contextual Bandits such as EXP4 seek to remedy this by accounting directly for the existence of multiple contexts. In theory, if no switches take place, EXP4 would at little cost behave as well as a stationary policy, while when facing changes pivoting to another expert with which to handle the new context. There remains a hyperparameter to tune however which is how eagerly it listens to a specific expert. Here we see the same trade-off as with other hyperparameters: switching experts too greedily (higher η) yields higher convergence, but also more inertia. This underlines that a more associative policy e.g. LinUCB may fare better as it removes the need for greed through classification. Yet, the assumption on side information accompanying such a policy would outgrow a fair comparison to the other policies we consider.

Figure 4 shows the convergence factor of three selected policies over time, and the random policy as a baseline. The moments of context shifts are represented by the dashed lines, effectively dividing the plot into segments. The inertia per policy can be derived by focusing on the change in line trends after each shift. Figure 4a clearly shows the commitment of UCB Tuned to the optimal arm of the second context, and the consequence of this as the third context begins. In Fig. 4b, the second context is short-lived seeing a reduced effect on the third context's convergence, and so too the positive reinforcement in UCB Tuned's choice to converge allowing to better adapt to the third context. Lastly, Fig. 4c shows Discounted UCB's behavior clearly as it closely approximates the stationary UCB Tuned yet can handle the switch to the third context more gracefully. Throughout the plots it is clear that EXP4 varies between being twice as indecisive as a stationary policy as in Fig. 4b (due to its internal two stationary policies in the form of experts), and committing too heavily to one expert which is mimicking UCB Tuned as in Figure 4c.

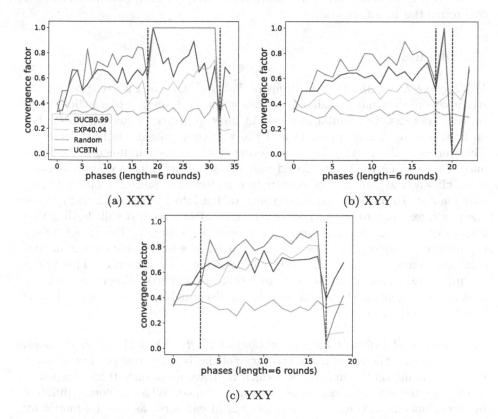

Fig. 4. Convergence calculated over phases. The number of rounds in cases XXY and YXY slightly deviates due to the cleaning trick.

Coming back to the research questions, we can answer **RQ1** as follows: It is clear that the longer a policy is exposed to a given context, the better it converges when that context reappears. For UCB Tuned, specifically, a greater factor than the length of individual contexts is the overall number of elapsed rounds. Over all policies, measuring performance through convergence rewards greed. Greedier policies converge heavily in their presumed contexts and outweigh their poor performance in other contexts when compared to non-stationary policies. This suggests at face-value that greedy, stationary, policies perform best despite context shifts. **RQ2**'s answer shows that this is not actually the case when considering the big picture. Low inertia values are an indicator of average high convergence. Therefore the metric exposes undesirable behavior which otherwise is awarded by the traditional measure of convergence. When we take both inertia and convergence into account then a policy such as Discounted UCB with $\gamma = .99$ is shown to be a policy with more desirable long-term performance than e.g. UCB Tuned when dealing with frequent context shifts. A direct study of such a long-term scenario elucidating the consequences of poor inertia would concretize this in future work.

5   Discussion

Finding the Right Measure to Compare Policies: One of the struggles in our study was to determine a fair way to assess the performance of a policy under shifting contexts. Our initial idea was to use the degree of convergence to the optimal arm to compare policies and the way they progress in their learning. This serves well enough when considering stationary environments. However, once non-stationarity is introduced and realistic conditions are approximated more closely, the evolution of convergence is disrupted since the optimal arms may change. To measure the convergence taking into account such disruptions, one could refer e.g. to the average convergence after a context shift leading to a disruption. Alternatively, we chose to explore calculating the difference between the degree of convergence after a disruption relative to the convergence in that same environment with no prior knowledge (what we call inertia). This brings the influence of context shifts to the forefront in the metric. Where convergence is agnostic to context shifts besides it being disrupted by their presence, inertia is specific to their occurrence.

Performance of Different Policies in Context Shifts: Through our experiment, we confirm that the use of non-stationary policies is not a 'one size fits all' solution: depending on the magnitude (which we leave unexamined) and frequency of change, the policies need to be separately tuned. When exploring different hyperparameters in tuning the policies, inertia can serve as a useful metric for the success of policies specifically in handling context shifts. We did observe that the inertia of non-stationary policies is quite sensitive to the hyperparameter value chosen. Non-stationary policies such as UCB Tuned did not perform well in terms of accrued inertia (although they could reap the benefits of early convergence in longer contexts and overall have good performance when looking at the weighted average of their convergence).

How to Select a Policy: Our study shows that non-stationary environments do not necessarily call for non-stationary policies. In the end, it really depends on the effects of inertia (large or small) and on how much large inertia effects can be tolerated in a system. Some systems may be robust to policies which respond to context shifts by making continuous sequences of poor decisions as a stationary policy like UCB Tuned does. For these systems, stationary policies may be a more informed choice since they converge more greedily than non-stationary ones (as also our results confirm). However, if a system cannot tolerate periods when the policy performs very poorly (suffering from large negative inertia effects) then non-stationary policies are a more reasonable choice since they better balance convergence speed with inertia effects.

Convergence Inertia Beyond MAB: Inertia is a metric that is not specific to MAB policies, but can be applied to any online planning strategy. Online planning requires knowledge which will inform policy behavior. This behavior is made time-sensitive due to the potential of context shifts. Inertia can be used to then also compare policies across paradigms and serve as a unifying metric to distinguish them. For example, a solution may recognize context shifts and choose to restart the learning process after every shift. This would result in an inertia of zero. This can be compared to an MAB policy which already has knowledge of the new context through seeing it before and therefore has a positive inertia, performing better than starting from nothing.

6   Related Work

According to a recent survey on the application of machine learning approaches for self-adaptive systems [7], reinforcement learning is a popular choice when it comes to online (or interactive) learning. Within reinforcement learning, most approaches have used temporal difference solutions such as Q-learning [9,17], while recently value-based reinforcement learning has also been employed [16,19]. In contrast, the application of MAB policies is less investigated.

Uses of MAB in SAS: In one of the first approaches that mapped a self-adaptation problem to MAB, Cabri et al. focused on endowing a multi-agent system with self-expression [5]. In particular, each collaboration pattern to expressed becomes an arm to be explored/exploited. In their work, they used three collaboration patterns, namely client/server, peer-to-peer, and swarm-based; measured reward in terms of observed application performance; and proposed and compared two custom strategies for maximizing the reward. While interesting, their approach neither considers out-of-the-box MAB policies with proven theoretical guarantees nor the specific problem of unknown-unknowns and associated convergence inertia.

Porter et al. employed MAB-based online learning to build distributed emergent software [20]. In their approach, an arm is a composition configuration that specifies which components will run and where. Their online learning approach uses UCB1 to evaluate different configurations at runtime. Distinct environment classes are identified at runtime each with its own instance of UCB1. We believe that our work is complementary: Rather than externally imposing stationarity through environment classes, we evaluate policies that can inherently deal with environment switches, even if such switches are only indirectly considered (via their effect on rewards).

Dealing with Unknown-Unknowns in SAS: Kinneer et al. also tackle the issue of unknown-unknowns with applied to a system closely related to SWIM. Rather than using RL, the authors use genetic algorithms with 'plan reuse', reusing previous knowledge for newer generations [10]. Compared to our work, their end-result is more applied, while the MAB policies we use are in principle generalizable to any architecture-based SAS.

Cardozo and Dusparic extend context-oriented programming to automatically codify contexts and associate strategies to handle them at runtime [6]. They do so by using RL options, a form of reinforcement learning which uses sequences rather than individual basic actions as the options to explore/exploit. These options are gathered by processing the execution trace at runtime. Key to their work is that system metrics are combined to explicitly define contexts, this is comparable to the solution by Porter et al. mentioned above. Our work differs in that we directly use RL to choose all actions, and do not require the overhead associated with COP to handle non-stationary environments.

7   Conclusion

In this paper, we focused on online reinforcement learning (RL) in self-adaptive systems as a technique to deal with unknown-unknowns – situations that the systems are not specifically designed for. We zoomed in on the problem of dealing with context shifts that interfere with the learning process by slowing down the convergence of RL policies. We proposed a new metric, convergence *inertia*, to capture such negative effect in the comparison of RL policies and performed an experimental study comparing RL policies belonging to the family of multi-armed bandits (MAB) in online learning of actions of a self-adaptive web server. We found that non-stationary policies are better suited to handling context shifts in terms of inertia, although stationary policies tend to perform well in terms of overall convergence. In the future, we would like to experiment with non-MAB RL policies (such as Q-learning) to better understand and assess the way they incur inertia. We would also like to use different self-adaptive systems to be able to better generalize our results.

References

1. Alberts, E.G.: Adapting with Regret: Using Multi-armed Bandits with Self-adaptive Systems. Master's thesis, University of Amsterdam (2022). https://scripties.uba.uva.nl/search?id=727497
2. Auer, P., Cesa-Bianchi, N., Fischer, P.: Finite-time analysis of the multiarmed bandit problem. Mach. Learn. **47**(2), 235–256 (2002). https://doi.org/10.1023/A:1013689704352
3. Auer, P., Cesa-Bianchi, N., Freund, Y., Schapire, R.E.: The nonstochastic multi-armed bandit problem. SIAM J. Comput. **32**(1), 48–77 (2002). https://doi.org/10.1137/S0097539701398375
4. Bubeck, S.: Regret analysis of stochastic and nonstochastic multi-armed bandit problems. Found. Trends® Mach. Learn. 5(1), 1–122 (2012). https://doi.org/10.1561/2200000024
5. Cabri, G., Capodieci, N.: Applying multi-armed bandit strategies to change of collaboration patterns at runtime. In: 2013 1st International Conference on Artificial Intelligence, Modelling and Simulation, pp. 151–156. IEEE, Kota Kinabalu (2013). https://doi.org/10.1109/AIMS.2013.31
6. Cardozo, N., Dusparic, I.: Auto-cop: adaptation generation in context-oriented programming using reinforcement learning options. CoRR abs/2103.06757 (2021)
7. Gheibi, O., Weyns, D., Quin, F.: Applying machine learning in self-adaptive systems: a systematic literature review. ACM Trans. Auton. Adapt. Syst. **15**(3), 1–37 (2021). https://doi.org/10.1145/3469440
8. Kephart, J., Chess, D.: The vision of autonomic computing. Computer **36**(1), 41–50 (2003)
9. Kim, D., Park, S.: Reinforcement learning-based dynamic adaptation planning method for architecture-based self-managed software. In: 2009 ICSE Workshop on Software Engineering for Adaptive and Self-Managing Systems, pp. 76–85 (2009). https://doi.org/10.1109/SEAMS.2009.5069076, iSSN: 2157–2321
10. Kinneer, C., Coker, Z., Wang, J., Garlan, D., Goues, C.L.: Managing uncertainty in self-adaptive systems with plan reuse and stochastic search. In: Proceedings of the 13th International Conference on Software Engineering for Adaptive and Self-Managing Systems, pp. 40–50. ACM, Gothenburg (2018). https://doi.org/10.1145/3194133.3194145
11. Kivinen, J., Szepesvári, C., Ukkonen, E., Zeugmann, T. (eds.): ALT 2011. LNCS (LNAI), vol. 6925. Springer, Heidelberg (2011). https://doi.org/10.1007/978-3-642-24412-4
12. Krupitzer, C., Roth, F.M., VanSyckel, S., Schiele, G., Becker, C.: A survey on engineering approaches for self-adaptive systems. Perv. Mob. Comput. **17**, 184–206 (2015). https://doi.org/10.1016/j.pmcj.2014.09.009. Feb
13. Lattimore, T., Szepesvári, C.: Bandit Algorithms, 1st edn. Cambridge University Press, Cambridge (2020). https://doi.org/10.1017/9781108571401
14. de Lemos, R., et al.: Software engineering for self-adaptive systems: a second research roadmap. In: de Lemos, R., Giese, H., Müller, H.A., Shaw, M. (eds.) Software Engineering for Self-Adaptive Systems II. LNCS, vol. 7475, pp. 1–32. Springer, Heidelberg (2013). https://doi.org/10.1007/978-3-642-35813-5_1
15. Li, L., Chu, W., Langford, J., Schapire, R.E.: A contextual-bandit approach to personalized news article recommendation. In: Proceedings of the 19th International Conference on World Wide Web - WWW 2010, p. 661 (2010). https://doi.org/10.1145/1772690.1772758, arXiv: 1003.0146

16. Metzger, A., Kley, T., Palm, A.: Triggering proactive business process adaptations via online reinforcement learning. In: Fahland, D., Ghidini, C., Becker, J., Dumas, M. (eds.) BPM 2020. LNCS, vol. 12168, pp. 273–290. Springer, Cham (2020). https://doi.org/10.1007/978-3-030-58666-9_16

17. Metzger, A., Quinton, C., Mann, Z.A., Baresi, L., Pohl, K.: Feature-model-guided online learning for self-adaptive systems, vol. 12571, pp. 269–286 (2020). https://doi.org/10.1007/978-3-030-65310-1_20, arXiv: 1907.09158

18. Moreno, G.A., Schmerl, B., Garlan, D.: SWIM: an exemplar for evaluation and comparison of self-adaptation approaches for web applications. In: Proceedings of the 13th International Conference on Software Engineering for Adaptive and Self-Managing Systems, pp. 137–143. ACM, Gothenburg (2018). https://doi.org/10.1145/3194133.3194163

19. Palm, A., Metzger, A., Pohl, K.: Online reinforcement learning for self-adaptive information systems. In: Dustdar, S., Yu, E., Salinesi, C., Rieu, D., Pant, V. (eds.) CAiSE 2020. LNCS, vol. 12127, pp. 169–184. Springer, Cham (2020). https://doi.org/10.1007/978-3-030-49435-3_11

20. Porter, B., Rodrigues Filho, R.: Distributed emergent software: assembling, perceiving and learning systems at scale. In: 2019 IEEE 13th International Conference on Self-Adaptive and Self-Organizing Systems (SASO), pp. 127–136 (2019). https://doi.org/10.1109/SASO.2019.00024, iSSN: 1949–3681

21. Sutton, R.S., Barto, A.G.: Reinforcement Learning: An Introduction. MIT press, Cambridge (2018)

Capturing Dependencies Within Machine Learning via a Formal Process Model

Fabian Ritz[1](✉)(iD), Thomy Phan[1], Andreas Sedlmeier[1], Philipp Altmann[1],
Jan Wieghardt[2], Reiner Schmid[2], Horst Sauer[2], Cornel Klein[2],
Claudia Linnhoff-Popien[1], and Thomas Gabor[1]

[1] Mobile and Distributed Systems Group, LMU Munich, Munich, Germany
`fabian.ritz@ifi.lmu.de`
[2] Technology, Siemens AG, Munich, Germany

Abstract. The development of Machine Learning (ML) models is more than just a special case of software development (SD): ML models acquire properties and fulfill requirements even without direct human interaction in a seemingly uncontrollable manner. Nonetheless, the underlying processes can be described in a formal way. We define a comprehensive SD process model for ML that encompasses most tasks and artifacts described in the literature in a consistent way. In addition to the production of the necessary artifacts, we also focus on generating and validating fitting descriptions in the form of specifications. We stress the importance of further evolving the ML model throughout its lifecycle even after initial training and testing. Thus, we provide various interaction points with standard SD processes in which ML often is an encapsulated task. Further, our SD process model allows to formulate ML as a (meta-) optimization problem. If automated rigorously, it can be used to realize self-adaptive autonomous systems. Finally, our SD process model features a description of time that allows to reason about the progress within ML development processes. This might lead to further applications of formal methods within the field of ML.

Keywords: Machine learning · Process model · Self-adaptation · Software engineering

1 Introduction

In recent software systems, functionality is often provided by *Machine Learning* (ML) components, e.g. for pattern recognition, video game play, robotics, protein folding, or weather forecasting. ML infers a statistical model from data, instead of being programmed explicitly. In this work, we focus on the usage of *Deep Learning* (DL) techniques, which presently are the most commonly used approaches. Figure 1 (based on [11]) gives a high-level overview how traditional software systems and ML systems are typically developed. *Software Engineering*

© The Author(s), under exclusive license to Springer Nature Switzerland AG 2022
T. Margaria and B. Steffen (Eds.): ISoLA 2022, LNCS 13703, pp. 249–265, 2022.
https://doi.org/10.1007/978-3-031-19759-8_16

(SE) for ML systems is an emerging research area with an increasing number of published studies since 2018 [11,21]. In practice, software companies face a plethora of challenges related to data quality, design methods and processes, performance of ML models as well as deployment and compliance [5,11,21]. Thus, there is a need for tools, techniques, and structured engineering approaches to construct and evolve these systems.

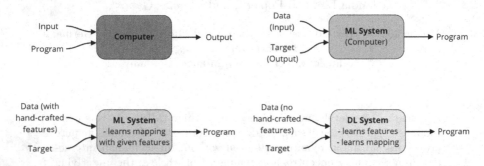

Fig. 1. Comparison of traditional software development (upper left) and ML software development (upper right). More specifically, DL systems (lower right) are a special type of ML systems (lower left): DL systems automatically learn the relevant input features and how to map these features to outputs. While this reduces the effort previously required to define features and mapping logic, it makes it more difficult to understand the rules by which DL systems make decisions. Illustration based on [11].

Software Development (SD) for ML systems typically starts with the management of data, e.g. collection and labeling. Then, repeated train-test cycles of the ML model are performed, e.g. for hyper-parameter tuning, until the expected results are obtained. After that, the ML model is deployed and monitored during operation. Feedback from operation is typically used to re-train (patch) an existing ML model or to extend the data-sets. This process is called *ML workflow* and is visualized in Fig. 2 (based on [19]). So far, a number of ML workflows and life-cycle models have been constructed in an ad-hoc manner based on early experiences of large software companies, e.g. reported by IBM [2], Microsoft [3], or SAP [27]. The respective case studies focus strongly on the ML workflow but little on the integration with existing SE processes and tools, thus not covering the entire SD process.

Then, *MLOps* [15,19] emerged as an end-to-end ML development paradigm (see Fig. 3). MLOps combines the DevOps process, i.e. fast development iterations and continuous delivery of software changes, with the ML workflow. Further collaboration between industry and academia resulted in the development of the *CRISP-ML(Q)* life-cycle model [33], which additionally contains technical tasks for quality assurance. Yet, we found existing MLOps process models and CRISP-ML(Q) lacking a clear view on the dependencies between activities and the involved artifacts.

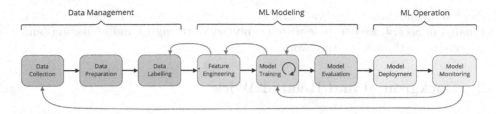

Fig. 2. Typical ML development workflow stages with activites and feedback flow. Illustration based on [19].

Another key aspect is automation. Presently, software updates (or patches) are still often performed manually by human developers or engineers. To minimize the impact of dynamic changes, agile SD paradigms such as MLOps perform smaller, faster updates through cross-functional collaboration and high automation. Ultimately, however, we might want to minimize the amount of human effort spent during SD. ML systems are able to adapt to changes via generalization and can be re-trained with little human effort. One step further, *Auto-ML* [12] is a popular tool to automate single steps of the ML workflow: the search for a suitable ML model architecture and the adjustment of the according hyper-parameters. The next advancement would be to enable automated optimization spanning over multiple steps of SD processes. One example would be to autonomously decide when to re-train an ML model that is already in production using newly collected data. Conceptually similar approaches already exist in the field of (collective) autonomic systems [36]. In practice, this would require a tight integration of quality assurance activities. Engineering trustworthy ML systems is an ongoing challenge since it is notoriously difficult to understand the rules by which these systems make decisions [18]. Adding self-optimization on SD process level will most likely increase the complexity.

To tackle these challenges, we propose a formal process model for ML that can be mapped to existing SD processes. Our process model is based on practical findings from various cooperations with industry partners on Multi-Agent Reinforcement Learning [26,29][1] and Anomaly Detection problems [23][2]. It encompasses the majority of ML-specific tasks and artifacts described in the literature in a consistent way. Further, it allows for automation spanning over multiple steps of SD processes. It is not restricted to certain feedback loops and supports self-optimization. If automated rigorously, it can be used realize self-adaptive, autonomous systems.

The remainder of the paper is structured as follows: In Sect. 2, we provide an overview of related work regarding SE for (self-) adaptive systems (Sect. 2.1), SE for ML systems (Sect. 2.2) and fundamental challenges of ML that could be alleviated through SE (Sect. 2.3). In the following Sect. 3, we visualize (Sect. 3.1) and describe (Sect. 3.2) our process model. We then present a proof of concept

---

[1] https://www.siemens.com.
[2] https://www.swm.de.

(Sect. 3.3) and provide a brief formalization of our process model (Sect. 3.4). Finally, in Sect. 4, we conclude with a summary of strengths and limitations and provide an outlook for future work.

2   Background and Related Work

Designing systems that autonomously adapt to dynamic problems is no new trend. What has changed with the emergence of modern DL techniques is the ability to handle greater state and action spaces. Still, it is often impossible to design explicit control systems that directly adapt the exactly right parameters to changed conditions (*parameter adaptation*) because there are too many and potentially unknown relevant parameters. However, it is possible to design systems which cause change on a higher level to meet the new conditions. In the literature, this concept is referred to as *compositional* [22] or *architecture-based* adaptation [9]. Following this concept, we classify a system as *self-adaptive* if it autonomously changes to meet (at least) one of the following three aspects [10]:

1. The implementation of one component is replaced by another.
2. The structure of the system changes, i.e. the relations between components change, components are added or removed.
3. The distribution of the system components changes without modification of the logical system structure, e.g. components can migrate.

Through generalization, ML systems are capable of parameter adaptation out-of-the-box and they can further be used to realize self-adaptive systems. It is already common to re-train ML models once new data is gathered during operation and then replace the deployed model with the re-trained one. Once such work-flows are fully automated, such systems are self-adaptive as per the above definition.

One key to engineer such systems will be *Verification & Validation* (V&V) activities, which shall build quality into a product during the life-cycle [1]. Verification shall ensure that the system is built correctly in the sense that the results of an activity meet the specifications imposed on them in previous activities [6]. Validation shall ensure that the right product is built. That is, the product fulfills its specific intended purpose [6]. Related to this, Gabor et al. analyzed the impact of self-adapting ML systems on SE, focusing on quality assurance [8]. They provide a general SD process description related to ML and embed it into a formal framework for the analysis of adaptivity. The central insight is that testing must also adapt to keep up with the capabilities of the ML system under test. In this paper, we build a process model around the ML life-cycle and provide insights about the interplay of SD activities and artifacts.

2.1   SE for (Self-)adaptive Systems

Researchers and practitioners have begun tackling the SE challenges of self-adaptation prior to the latest advances in DL. Influencing many later following approaches, Sinreich [32] proposed a high-level architectural blueprint to assist in delivering autonomous computing in phases. Autonomous computing aims to de-couple (industrial) IT system management activities and software products through the SD cycle. The proposed architecture reinforces the usage of intelligent control loop implementations to *Monitor, Analyze, Plan and Execute, leveraging Knowledge* (MAPE-K) of the environment. The blueprint provides instructions on how to architect and implement the knowledge bases, the sensors, the actuators and the phases. It also outlines how to compose autonomous elements to orchestrate self-management of the involved systems. As of today, the paradigms of autonomous computing have spread from IT system management towards a broad field of problems, the most prominent one being autonomous driving. Our process model is built to specifically assist the development of systems that are based on DL techniques.

To augment development processes to account for even more complex systems, Bernon et al. later proposed ADELFE [4]. Built upon RUP [17], ADELFE provides tools for various tasks of software design. From a scientific view, ADELFE is based on the theory of adaptive Multi-Agent systems: they are used to derive a set of stereotypes for components to ease modeling. Our process model also supports this architectural basis (among others), but does not require it.

In the subsequent ASCENS project [36], a life-cycle model formalizes the interplay between human developers and autonomous adaptation. It features separate states for the development progress of each respective feedback cycle. Traditional SD tasks, self-adaptation, self-monitoring and self-awareness are regarded as equally powerful contributing mechanisms. This yields a flexible and general model of an engineering process but does not define a clear order of tasks. The underlying *Ensemble Development Life Cyle* (EDLC) [14] covers the complete software life cycle and provides mechanisms for enabling system changes at runtime. Yet, interaction points between traditional SD and self-adaptation are only loosely defined. Recently, AIDL [35] specialized the EDLC to the construction of autonomous policies using Planning and Reinforcement Learning techniques. Overall, the ASCENS approach emphasizes formal verification. Correct behavior shall be proven even for adapted parts of the system. Analogous to SCoE [8], we agree a strong effort for testing is necessary when adaptation comes into play. Our process model was built with self-adaptation in mind and allows for a seamless integration of V&V activities and respective feedback loops at any point in time.

2.2 SE for ML Systems

Regarding SE for ML systems during the latest advances in DL, literature has been systematically reviewed several times [11,21]. A common conclusion is that all SE aspects of engineering ML systems are affected the non-deterministic nature of ML (even slight changes in the setup can have a drastic impact) but none of the SE aspects have a mature set of tools and techniques yet to tackle this. According to the authors, the reported challenges are difficult to classify using the established SWEBOK Knowledge Areas [6] since they are strongly tied to the problem domain. Our process model explicitly considers V&V to ensure quality of ML software independent of the problem domain.

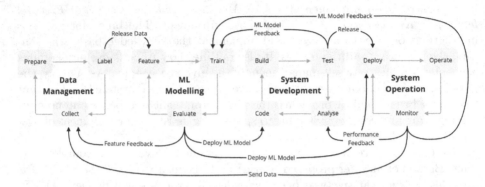

Fig. 3. Illustration of an MLOPs process model based on [19]. The ML workflow is integrated into DevOps by adding *Data Management* and *ML Modeling* to the existing *Development* and *Operations* processes and (feedback) transitions.

To identify the main SE challenges in developing ML components, Lwakatare et al. [20] evaluated a number of empirical case studies. They report a high-level taxonomy of the usage of ML components in industrial settings and map identified challenges to one of four ML life-cycle phases (*assemble data set, create model, train and evaluate model, deploy model*). These life-cycle phases can be mapped to our process model. Building upon the taxonomy of Lwakatare et al., Bosch et al. [5] propose a research agenda including autonomously improving systems. Besides data management related topics, the elements of the research agenda can be mapped to our process model.

During the recent emergence of *MLOps* (an overview is given in [15]), Lwakatare et al. [19] proposed a precise and clear variant that integrates the ML workflow into DevOps by adding the *Data Management* and *ML Modeling* to *Development* and *Operations*, effectively expanding the ML workflow to an end-to-end SD process (see Fig. 3). The resulting process model aims for automation at all stages and enables iterative development through fast feedback flow. Building on MLOps, *CRISP-ML(Q)* [33] describes six phases ranging from defining the scope to maintaining the deployed ML application. Challenges in the ML development are identified in the form of risks. Special attention is drawn to the last phase, as they state that a model running in changing real-time environments would require close monitoring and maintenance to reduce performance degradation over time. Compared to MLOps, CRISP-ML(Q) additionally considers business understanding and ties it closely to data management. However, we found MLOps and CRISP-ML(Q) lacking a precise view on the dependencies between activities and artifacts, which our process model tries to accomplish.

Finally, Watanabe et al. [34] provide a preliminary systematic literature review of general ML system development processes. It summarizes typical phases in the ML system development and provides a list of frequently described practices and a list of adopted traditional SD practices. The phases in our process model share common ground with the granular phases described in this literature review. Generally, we provide various interaction points with standard SD processes (in which ML often is an encapsulated task) by evolving the ML model throughout its life-cycle after initial training and testing.

2.3 Fundamental ML Challenges

So far, we considered emerging issues of SE when incorporating ML components. Vice versa, ML faces some fundamental challenges (besides the current technical difficulties already mentioned) that might not be solved through technical improvements alone but might require to be addressed through SE. One fundamental challenge of ML is *explainability*, i.e. methods and techniques in the application of AI such that the decisions leading to the solutions can be understood (at least) by human experts [18]. Although some approaches address explainability, e.g. by gaining post-hoc insights about the predictions [28], and proposals were made to use techniques that are explainable per default [30], most current ML models remain black boxes in the sense that even ML engineers cannot always explain why the ML models produce a certain output. Though each individual parameter within an ML model can be analyzed technically, this does not answer the relevant questions about causal relationships. This can cause legal problems in areas such as healthcare or criminal justice. More importantly, it is notoriously difficult to validate and verify these ML models, both from an engineering and an SD process point of view. Systematic guidance through the ML life-cycle to enable trustworthiness of the ML models would help.

Another fundamental challenge of ML is *efficiency*. In general, modern ML relies on DL techniques. The predictive performance of these models scales with their size, which requires the available of more training data and more computational power to optimize the risen amount of parameters. ML model complexity and the computational effort required to train these models grew exponentially during the last years [31]. Developing such ML models was only possible due to advances in hardware and algorithmic design [13]. Whether further improvements with ML can be achieved this way is uncertain. Nonetheless, re-training of state-of-the-art ML models requires significant amounts of computational resources and time. Because ML suffers from the "changing one thing changes everything" principle, it may be costly to fix issues in ML models afterwards regardless of what caused the issue in the first place. Consequently, support from SE to ensure high quality ML models upfront, e.g. through precise requirements and feedback loops, is crucial to effectively use ML in production.

3 A Process Model to Capture Dependencies Within ML

SE has given rise to a series of notions to capture the dynamic process of developing software. Opinions on which notion is the best differ between different groups of people and different periods of time. As a common ground, we assume that SD can be split into various *phases* with each phase focusing on different sets of *activities*. We acknowledge that in agile approaches to SE these phases are no longer to be executed in strict sequential order, so that phases may overlap during development. But we still regard *planning, development, deployment*, and *operations* to be useful categories to group activities in SD phases.

First of all, we model *human tasks* and *automated procedures* through activities. They may require different skill sets, rely on different (computational or human) resources, and are driven by different *key factors*. E.g., the use case analysis should be performed by business analysts and result in some form of (requirements) specification. Based on that, data scientists can select or gather suitable data for ML training. Naturally, business analysts and data scientists should collaborate closely.

Second, we model activities to result in *artifacts*, which may then be required for other activities. In the above example, the choice of data naturally depends on the problem domain, thus relies on a requirements specification. Consequently, the use case analysis resulting in the requirements specification should be finished first. Artifacts can have different types such as *data, functional descriptions* (e.g. the ML-Model), or *logical statements* (e.g. a specification, a set of hyper-parameters, or a test result indicating that a specific requirement is fulfilled by an ML model with a specific set of hyper-parameters on specific data).

Third, we capture feedback and (self-) optimization through loops that go back to earlier stages of the ML development process. This way, we take the iterative nature of ML SD into account, which consists of repeated stochastic optimization and empirical validation of the ML model at different development stages. Thus, the process model is flexible regarding the employed ML development method and considers V&V aspects. It supports manually performed hyper-parameter optimization as well as fully automated patch deployment of a model that was re-trained with data gathered during earlier live operation. Due to the vast number of possibilities, we leave the actual definition of the feedback loops open for the respective use case.

All in all, the purpose of our process model is to capture dependencies between activities and artifacts during the ML life-cycle and to close the gaps between existing SD process models and specialized ML training procedures.

3.1   Visualization

This section provides a visual representation of the proposed process model and explains concept and semantics. As to be seen in Fig. 4, the elements are arranged within a temporal dimension (x-axis) and an organizational dimension (y-axis). Within the temporal dimension, the elements are grouped by four SD phases, which allows a straightforward mapping to existing SD process models. Further right on the x-axis means later within the development process, i.e. its progress towards completion is higher. The categories within the organizational dimension are a mixture of business and technical areas. We refrain from exhaustively defining role names or responsibilities. Instead, we want to sketch the different

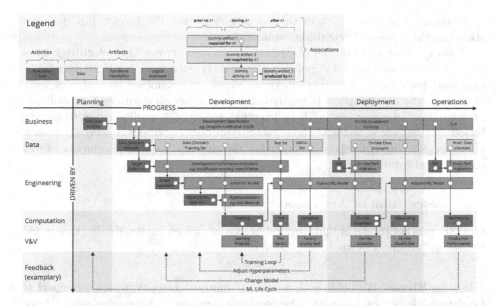

Fig. 4. Visualization of the proposed process model for the development of ML software.

key factors that drive the process forward (or limit it). As mentioned before, the overall categorization of elements within these dimensions is by no means strict and should be adapted to the respective circumstances.

We distinguish between activities, artifacts and associations. Activities include human tasks and automated procedures. Artifacts can be data, logical statements or functional descriptions. Activities always *produce* at least one artifact and can *require* other artifacts. Associations between artifacts and activities are represented by arrows. If an activity requires an artifact, a white circle connects that artifact to an arrow whose head ends on the activity. If an activity produces an artifact, a white circle connects the activity to an arrow whose head ends on that artifact.

For any progress of the development process, there exists (at least) one activity. For any activity, all activities left to it are considered completed. Vice versa, all activities right to it are not. An activity starts if all required artifacts exist. If this is the case, the respective activities are considered active by default. Activities are neither connected to other activities, nor require a dedicated trigger.

Please note that we made some trade-offs to ease readability of the visualization. First, we kept some spacing between elements on the x-axis. Thus, there are spots without activities (however, there still are associations from or towards activities). Next, there are no multiplicities on the associations. Syntactically, it does not matter if multiple artifacts are connected with an activity through one shared or multiple individual arrows. Most importantly, the size of the elements is determined by the length of their descriptions and the layout, but does not state anything about their duration in real time.

Finally, there is a number of dashed, annotated arrows in the feedback category of the organizational dimension. They start once some V&V artifacts exist and lead back to earlier points in time. These are examples for different feedback or (self-) optimization loops that define whether an iterative, a monolithic, or a mixture approach is used. In practice, we expect quality gates to decide, based on the V&V artifacts, how the SD process continues at certain points. However, this depends strongly on organizational and legal requirements as well as technical conditions.

3.2   Description of Activities

Our SD process model is built around activities, which we briefly describe in the following (grouped by their respective phase).

Planing Phase: We begin with a *use case analysis* activity, which we expect to be driven mainly by business. The resulting development (requirements) specification defines the goals in natural language. We acknowledge that this specification may change to some extent during the ML life-cycle, e.g. when the ML model is deployed at the customer's site or system later in the process. In any case, it is crucial to consider the probabilistic nature of ML when formulating the specification [11,21].

Development Phase: The first activity here is the *selection (or assembly) of the data set* based on the development specification. We assume that the resulting data set will usually be split into a training, a testing and validation part, which is indicated by dashed lines. The bottleneck and driving force here is data management. We omit activities related to data management and instead assume that suitable data is accessible in some form. How to construct data sets such that they correspond to the requirements is a challenging problem on its own [25]. In parallel, the *definition of the training target* for the ML model takes place, resulting in development performance indicators that reflect the development specification in a more technical form. E.g., a requirement may be to correctly recognize specific entities on images with a probability of more than 0.99. A suitable performance indicator could be prediction recall, where higher values are better. We consider it important to clearly distinguish between the development specification and the training target (with the respective performance indicators) for two reasons. The first one is to avoid misconceptions between business analysts and ML experts. The second one is to enable an SD process controlled curriculum, e.g. to begin training with a subset of the overall specification and once this training target is reached, it is expanded gradually until the overall requirements are met.

The following activity is the *ML model definition*. Here, the architecture of the ML model is chosen based on the data and the performance indicators. Then, the *hyper-parameter selection* activity follows, based on the initial ML model. The hyper-parameters can be algorithm-specific and also include the mathematical optimization target such as the loss in case of *Supervised Learning* (SL) and the reward in case of *Reinforcement Learning* (RL). Again, decoupling the low-level optimization target from the higher-level training target and the top-level development specification is important: deriving a suitable loss- or reward-function for a specific training target is a challenging problem on its own [29]. Also, separating reward and training target measurements allows to detect reward hacking, a known challenge of RL. Through decoupling, SD process controlled (self-) optimization can be realized here.

Then, the *training* of the ML model takes place. The current learning progress can be assessed through the history of the mathematical optimization target (loss or reward) of the ML model on the training data (or training domain in case of RL). Optionally, the training target can additionally be used to determine the learning progress during training. However, from a V&V point of view, the training target should be optimized implicitly through the mathematical optimization target. In any way, the training target will be assessed during the next, usually periodical activity: *testing* the trained ML model with the development performance indicators on the test data set (or test domain in case of RL). In practice, we expect different feedback loops from the respective test verdict to different prior activities, especially model definition and hyper-parameter selection, due to the iterative nature of ML training. This is where Auto-ML [12] comes into action. The final activity of the development phase is the *validation* (or evaluation) of the trained ML model against the development specification on the validation data set (or domain in case of RL) resulting in a "factory quality seal".

Deployment Phase: Once the validation activity is passed, we move on by leaving the controlled (maybe simulated) development environment. The trained ML model faces less controlled conditions, i.e. the individual customer's system or a physical environment. Thus, the top-level specification may now differ from the one used during development and is referred to as on-site contract. Most likely, this on-site contract is a subset of the development specification, but it may also contain some additional requirements. As the requirements and the data (or the domain) are provided by the customer, the first activity here is to *define on-site targets* and performance indicators to take the specialized on-site contract into account. Then, we expect some *on-site adaptation* of the trained ML model to take place, most likely in the form of additional re-training, followed by a on-boarding (validation) of the adapted ML model which should now fulfill the on-site contract. If significant specialization is required, on-site adaptation could be extended to a cycle similar to the train-test-cycle during the development phase. However, we consider it more likely that this is a fast, slim process step (given a thorough initial requirements engineering and training). The *onboarding* (test) of the adapted ML is the final activity during the deployment phase. Its result, the "on-site quality seal", states whether the ML model fulfills the provided on-site contract based on the provided data (or domain in case of RL).

Operations Phase: After a successful onboarding, the adapted ML model can be used in production. We expect the top-level specification to differ from the preceding on-site contract (e.g., to reflect use-case specifics recognized during onboarding), thus referring to it as SLA. We address this through a *definition of production targets* and the respective performance indicators. These are the key to meaningful *monitoring* of the ML model on production data, e.g. to detect distributional drift, which can lead to a slow degradation of performance over time. If no appropriate monitoring is present, such changes may remain undetected and can cause silent failure [33]. Also, identifying situations in which the ML model underperforms is the key for precise feedback used to train future ML models, e.g. through updated data or domain simulations.

3.3 Proof of Concept

In this section, we present a short proof of concept (POC) for our process model that was published with a different focus in [29]. This POC used a specialized RL training method that embeds functional and non-functional requirements in step-wise fashion into the reward function of a cooperative Multi-Agent system. Thus, the RL agents were able to learn to fulfill all aspects of a given specification. This POC was then compared to naive approaches, which by contrast were only able to fulfill either the functional or the non-functional requirements. Figure 5 visualizes the core of the approach with two feedback loops adjusting the training target and the reward. The third feedback loop takes into account that the environment simulation could also be adjusted. Consider that, for example, the desired collaborative task might initially be too difficult and prohibits any learning progress. In this case, training could start with a small number of simultaneously trained agents and the third feedback loop could gradually increase it, thus creating a curriculum of increasing difficulty. Although hand-crafted adaptation schedules were used in the POC, this could be realized autonomously in future applications. The physical counterpart of the environment simulation has not yet been realized, thus there is no deployment or production phase (yet).

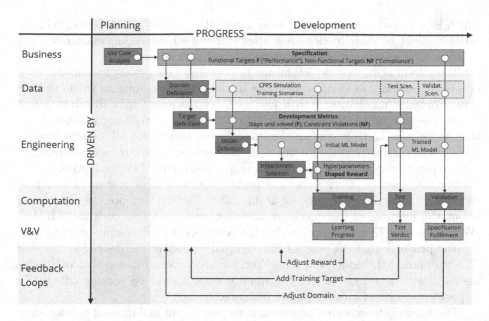

Fig. 5. Visualization of the proof of concept (POC) for our process model that was published with a different focus in [29]. Functional and non-functional requirements were embedded step-wise into the reward function of a cooperative Multi-Agent system. This enabled the RL agents to align with the provided specification.

3.4 Formalization

In the following, we briefly formalize our process model and sketch the potential we see in the application of formal methods like *Linear Time Logic* (LTL) [16].

The development process $\mathfrak{D}$ is given by a set of elements E, which can be either activities or artifacts. In both cases, an element $e \in E$ features two types of associations, i.e., to its prerequisites $pre(e)$ and the elements $post(e)$, for which it is a prerequisite. The elements and their associations we propose for our ML development process $\mathfrak{D}$ can be seen in Fig. 4.

When $\mathfrak{D}$ is executed, each of its elements can assume a single state $s^{(t)} \in \{inactive, active, done\} = S$ for each given point in time t. We thus define an instance $\mathcal{D}$ of the development process $\mathfrak{D}$ as a set of states S alongside a time line, i.e., a sequence of time points $t \in [t_{start}, t_{end}] \subseteq \mathbb{N}$: At each point in time t the process in its current state $\mathcal{D}^{(t)} : E \to S$ maps each element to one of the states mentioned before. At time point t_{start} that mapping is initialized to $D^{t_{start}}(e) = inactive$ for all e. Then, for every element e so that $\forall e' \in pre(e) : \mathcal{D}^{(t)} = active$ we can assign $\mathcal{D}^{(t+1)}(e) = active$. After an element has been *active* for at least one time step, it might switch to *done*. Note that when activities are *active*, we imagine them being executed by developers or automated procedures, and when artifacts are active, we imagine them being used in some sort of activity. Further note that we only need prerequisites to be *active* and not *done* as we assume required artifacts to further change alongside the procedures that use them, which is a deviation from what classic waterfall processes might define. Still, an artifact might be *done* immediately after starting all succeeding elements.

One of the main advantages of our formal process model is that it allows arbitrary feedback loops, which means that at any given point in time me may decide to redo any amount of elements in the process as long as we do that in sync. Formally, an element e with $\mathcal{D}^{(t)}(e) \in \{active, done\}$ may switch to *active* or *inactive* as long as all elements $e' \in post(e)$ switch to *active* or *inactive*. Note that at no point in time may an element e be *active* without all its prerequisites $pre(e)$ being *active* or *done*. Feedback loops allow us to capture a more dynamic development process while still maintaining a hierarchy of dependencies.

For any instance $\mathcal{D}$ given as a sequence of per-element states, we can now check if $\mathcal{D}$ adheres to the process $\mathfrak{D}$, i.e., $\mathfrak{D} \models \mathcal{D}$. Furthermore, we can reason about the progress of the development using common logics such as LTL [16]. We can also use LTL to postulate further constraints on development instances, e.g. the property that the process will eventually produce the desired ML model: $\Diamond \mathcal{D}(\text{"Adapted ML Model"}) = done$. Yet, we want to emphasize that other elements e with $post(e) = \emptyset$ like the quality seals should be considered equally important results of a development instance.

The immediate expected benefit of reasoning about instances of development processes might be the verification of tools and workflows ("Team A always adheres to the defined process."), the formulation of clearer process goals ("An instance of a *done* Factory Quality Seal shall occur before $t = 100$."), or the extraction of a better understanding of dependencies and correlations ("Any time the Target Definition started after Data Selection, development was successful."). But we also see further opportunities in the connection of reasoning about the process and reasoning about the product. To this end, we pay special attention to artifacts regarded as Logical Statements. Ideally, we could define requirements on the development process that reflect in certain guarantees on the software product. Using a more potent logic, e.g., we might be able to formulate a Factory Quality Seal that reads "The Basic ML Model has been trained successfully at least 3 times in a row with unchanged parameters.". If we incorporate roles into the model, which is left for future work at the moment, we might even be able to state that "Data Selection was performed by at least 2 developers with at least 10 years experience between them.", which naturally might also be part of the specification. Such quality assurance is common in engineering disciplines that are used to never being able to rely on formal proofs or extensive testing. Developing ML software is often more akin to these disciplines, which is why we regard reasoning about the process in addition to the product as so important.

4   Summary and Outlook

So far, we provided an overview of related work and challenges regarding SE for (self-) adaptive and ML systems. To tackle the challenges, we defined a process model, provided a proof of concept and a formalization. Now, we conclude by summarizing its strengths and limitations and point to future work.

Through our process model, we hope to close the gaps between existing SD process models and specialized ML training procedures. It is not restricted to certain ML techniques, i.e. it can be used for Supervised (SL), Unsupervised (UL) and Reinforcement Learning (RL). Simulated domains or environments for RL can be used analogously to data-sets for SL and UL. However, we focus on the life-cycle of the ML model, thus detailed data management activities upfront are omitted. How to construct data sets such that they correspond to certain requirements is a challenging problem on its own [25] and not (yet) covered by our approach. Yet, we believe that data management activities can be integrated straight forward. Feedback loops and V&V activities ensuring data quality can be added similarly to how we used them to ensure quality of the ML model.

Practically, our process model allows to formulate ML SD as a (meta-) optimization problem. Having human experts tailor the SD processes to the problem domain and algorithm at hand neither scales indefinitely, nor may be optimal for less well understood problem scenarios. There is a clear trend towards automation in SD with a parallel emergence of powerful optimization techniques in form of ML. Applying these methods not only on the problem level, but also on SD processes level through sequential decision making algorithms, e.g. RL or Genetic Algorithms, could enable significant progress. Further cosidering the conceptual overlap of *Ensembles* [14] and *Cooperative Multi-Agent RL* [26,29], automated ML seems suitable to realize self-adaptive, autonomous systems. Vice versa, ML should consider best practices from autonomous computing [36] on how to handle existing knowledge and how to control automated feedback loops.

Our integration of V&V acts as a quality gate when transitioning to deployment and to operation. Depending on the situation, we suggest to use evolutionary or learning methods [8,26] or Monte Carlo Based Statistical Model Checking [24] for testing. Numerical valuations [7] can distinguish systems that "barely" satisfy a specification from those that satisfy it in a robust manner. Still, we rely on a top-level specification, provided in human language, which we assume to change as the SD process progresses. The open question here is whether we can systematically define the initial specification in a way that ensures that the on-site contract and the SLA will be met.

Next, it should be possible to formulate a consistent mathematical representation of our process model, e.g. through LTL [16]. We plan to tackle this next since it would allow a validation of ML process instances that were created through meta-optimization. And finally, a key assumption is that a validation of ML processes leads to better ML software. As we also could not yet engineer an ML component's full life-cycle with the methodology proposed in this paper, both could be combined in future work.

References

1. IEEE standard for system and software verification and validation. IEEE Std. 1012–2012, pp. 1–223 (2012). https://doi.org/10.1109/IEEESTD.2012.6204026

2. Akkiraju, R., et al.: Characterizing machine learning processes: a maturity framework. In: Fahland, D., Ghidini, C., Becker, J., Dumas, M. (eds.) BPM 2020. LNCS, vol. 12168, pp. 17–31. Springer, Cham (2020). https://doi.org/10.1007/978-3-030-58666-9_2

3. Amershi, S., et al.: Software engineering for machine learning: a case study. In: 2019 IEEE/ACM 41st International Conference on Software Engineering: Software Engineering in Practice (ICSE-SEIP), pp. 291–300 (2019)

4. Bernon, C., Camps, V., Gleizes, M.P., Picard, G.: Engineering self-adaptive multi-agent systems: the adelfe methodology. In: Agent-Oriented Methodologies, vol. 7, pp. 172–202. Idea Group Publishing (2005)

5. Bosch, J., Crnkovic, I., Olsson, H.H.: Engineering AI systems: a research agenda. arxiv:2001.07522 (2020)

6. Bourque, P., Fairley, R.E. (eds.): SWEBOK: guide to the software engineering body of knowledge. IEEE Computer Society, version 3.0 edn (2014). https://www.swebok.org

7. Fainekos, G., Hoxha, B., Sankaranarayanan, S.: Robustness of Specifications and its applications to falsification, parameter mining, and runtime monitoring with S-TaLiRo. In: Finkbeiner, B., Mariani, L. (eds.) RV 2019. LNCS, vol. 11757, pp. 27–47. Springer, Cham (2019). https://doi.org/10.1007/978-3-030-32079-9_3

8. Gabor, T., et al.: The scenario coevolution paradigm: adaptive quality assurance for adaptive systems. Int. J. Softw. Tools Technology Transfer **22**(4), 457–476 (2020)

9. Garlan, D., Schmerl, B., Cheng, S.W.: Software Architecture Based Self Adaptation, pp. 31–55. Springer, Boston (2009). https://doi.org/10.1007/978-0-387-89828-5_2

10. Geihs, K.: Selbst-adaptive software. Informatik-Spektrum **31**(2), 133–145 (2008)

11. Giray, G.: A software engineering perspective on engineering machine learning systems: state of the art and challenges. J. Syst. Softw. **180**, 111031 (2021)

12. He, X., Zhao, K., Chu, X.: AutoML: a survey of the state-of-the-art. Knowl.-Based Syst. **212**, 106622 (2021)

13. Hernandez, D., Brown, T.B.: Measuring the algorithmic efficiency of neural networks. arxiv:2005.04305 (2020)

14. Hölzl, M., Koch, N., Puviani, M., Wirsing, M., Zambonelli, F.: The ensemble development life cycle and best practices for collective autonomic systems. In: Wirsing, M., Hölzl, M., Koch, N., Mayer, P. (eds.) Software Engineering for Collective Autonomic Systems. LNCS, vol. 8998, pp. 325–354. Springer, Cham (2015). https://doi.org/10.1007/978-3-319-16310-9_9

15. Kreuzberger, D., Kühl, N., Hirschl, S.: Machine learning operations (mlops): overview, definition, and architecture. arxiv:2205.02302 (2022). https://doi.org/10.48550/ARXIV.2205.02302

16. Kröger, F., Merz, S.: Temporal Logic and State Systems. Springer, Heidelberg (2008). https://doi.org/10.1007/978-3-540-68635-4

17. Kruchten, P.: The Rational Unified Process-An Introduction (2000)

18. Linardatos, P., Papastefanopoulos, V., Kotsiantis, S.: Explainable AI: a review of machine learning interpretability methods. Entropy **23**(1), 18 (2021)

19. Lwakatare, L.E., Crnkovic, I., Bosch, J.: DevOps for AI-challenges in development of ai-enabled applications. In: 2020 International Conference on Software, Telecommunications and Computer Networks (SoftCOM), pp. 1–6. IEEE (2020)

20. Lwakatare, L.E., Raj, A., Bosch, J., Olsson, H., Crnkovic, I.: A taxonomy of software engineering challenges for machine learning systems: an empirical investigation, pp. 227–243 (2019)

21. Martínez-Fernández, S., et al.: Software engineering for AI-based systems: a survey. arxiv:2105.01984 (2021)
22. McKinley, P., Sadjadi, S., Kasten, E., Cheng, B.: Composing adaptive software. Computer **37**(7), 56–64 (2004)
23. Müller., R., et al.: Acoustic leak detection in water networks. In: Proceedings of the 13th International Conference on Agents and Artificial Intelligence, vol. 2: ICAART, pp. 306–313 (2021). https://doi.org/10.5220/0010295403060313
24. Pappagallo, A., Massini, A., Tronci, E.: Monte carlo based statistical model checking of cyber-physical systems: a review. Information **11**(12), 588 (2020)
25. Paullada, A., Raji, I.D., Bender, E.M., Denton, E., Hanna, A.: Data and its (dis)contents: a survey of dataset development and use in machine learning research. Patterns **2**(11), 100336 (2021)
26. Phan, T., et al.: Learning and testing resilience in cooperative multi-agent systems. In: Proceedings of the 19th Conference on Autonomous Agents and MultiAgent Systems, AAMAS 2020 (2020)
27. Rahman, M.S., Rivera, E., Khomh, F., Guéhéneuc, Y., Lehnert, B.: Machine learning software engineering in practice: an ind. case study. arXiv:1906.07154 (2019)
28. Ribeiro, M.T., Singh, S., Guestrin, C.: "Why Should I Trust You?": explaining the predictions of any classifier. In: Proceedings of the 22nd ACM SIGKDD, KDD 2016, pp. 1135–1144. ACM (2016)
29. Ritz, F., et al.: Specification aware multi-agent reinforcement learning. In: Agents and Artificial Intelligence, pp. 3–21. Springer, Heidelberg (2022). https://doi.org/10.1007/978-3-031-10161-8_1
30. Rudin, C.: Stop explaining black box machine learning models for high stakes decisions and use interpretable models instead. Nat. Mach. Intell. **1**(5), 206–215 (2019)
31. Sevilla, J., Villalobos, P.: Parameter counts in machine learning. AI Alignment Forum (2021). https://www.alignmentforum.org/posts/GzoWcYibWYwJva8aL
32. Sinreich, D.: An architectural blueprint for autonomic computing (2006). https://www-03.ibm.com/autonomic/pdfs/AC%20Blueprint%20White%20Paper%20V7.pdf
33. Studer, S., et al.: Towards CRISP-ML(Q): a machine learning process model with quality assurance methodology. Mach. Learn. Knowl. Extract. **3**(2), 392–413 (2021)
34. Watanabe, Y., et al.: Preliminary systematic literature review of machine learning system development process. arxiv:1910.05528 (2019)
35. Wirsing, M., Belzner, L.: Towards systematically engineering autonomous systems using reinforcement learning and planning. In: Proceedings of Analysis, Verification and Transformation for Declarative Programming and Intelligent Systems (AVERTIS) (2022). https://doi.org/10.13140/RG.2.2.10618.16328
36. Wirsing, M., Hölzl, M., Koch, N., Mayer, P. (eds.): Software Engineering for Collective Autonomic Systems. LNCS, vol. 8998. Springer, Cham (2015). https://doi.org/10.1007/978-3-319-16310-9

On Model-Based Performance Analysis of Collective Adaptive Systems

Maurizio Murgia, Riccardo Pinciroli, Catia Trubiani, and Emilio Tuosto[(✉)]

Gran Sasso Science Institute, L'Aquila, Italy
{maurizio.murgia,riccardo.pinciroli,catia.trubiani,emilio.tuosto}@gssi.it

Abstract. This paper fosters the analysis of performance properties of collective adaptive systems (CAS) since such properties are of paramount relevance practically in any application. We compare two recently proposed approaches: the first is based on generalised stochastic petri nets derived from the system specification; the second is based on queueing networks derived from suitable behavioural abstractions. We use a case study based on a scenario involving autonomous robots to discuss the relative merit of the approaches. Our experimental results assess a mean absolute percentage error lower than 4% when comparing model-based performance analysis results derived from two different quantitative abstractions for CAS.

1 Introduction

Increasingly *collective adaptive systems* (CAS) crop up in many application domains, spanning critical systems, smart cities, systems assisting humans during their working or daily live activities, etc. A paradigmatic example is the use of artificial autonomous agents in rescue contexts that may put operators lives at stake [3]. The components of these systems execute in a cyber-physical context and are supposed to exhibit an *adaptive* behaviour. This adaptation should be driven by the changes occurring in the components' operational environments as well as the changes in the local computational state of each component, "collectively taken". Also, the *global* behaviour of CAS should *emerge* from the *local* behaviour of its components. Let us explain this considering the coordination of a number of robots patrolling some premises to make sure that aid is promptly given to human operators in case of accidents.

A plausible local behaviour of each robot can be:

(1) to identify accidents,
(2) to assess the level of gravity of the situation (so to choose an appropriate course of action),
(3) to alert the rescue centre and nearby robots (so to e.g., divert traffic to let rescue vehicles reach the location of the accident more quickly), and

---

Work partly funded by MIUR PRIN projects 2017FTXR7S IT MATTERS (Methods and Tools for Trustworthy Smart Systems) and 2017TWRCNB SEDUCE (Designing Spatially Distributed Cyber-Physical Systems under Uncertainty).

T. Margaria and B. Steffen (Eds.): ISoLA 2022, LNCS 13703, pp. 266–282, 2022.
https://doi.org/10.1007/978-3-031-19759-8_17

(4) to ascertain how to respond to alerts from other robots (e.g., if already involved in one accident or on a low battery, a robot may simply forward the alert to other nearby robots).

Note that robots' behaviour depends on the physical environment (tasks (1) to (3)) as well as their local computational state (task (4)).

A possible expected global behaviour is that robots try to maximise the patrolled area while trying to avoid remaining isolated and to minimise the battery consumption. It is worth remarking that the global behaviour is not typically formalised *explicitly*; it should rather emerge from combining the behaviour of the single components. For instance, when designing the algorithm for the roaming of robots one could assume that a robot does not move towards an area where there are already a certain number of robots.

This paper applies behavioural specifications to the quantitative analysis of CAS. Using a simple, yet representative, robots scenario inspired by the example above, we show how to use behavioural specifications to study non-functional properties of CAS (emergent) behaviour. This exercise is instrumental for our contribution, which is a study of the relation between two complementary approaches to the performance analysis of CAS recently proposed. More precisely, we compare the approach based on generalised stochastic petri nets proposed in [28] with the one based on behavioural specifications proposed in [16]. These approaches support two rather different methodologies for the quantitative modelling and analysis of CAS.

The main difference between these two approaches is the following. The former is based on the analysis proposed in [28] where the designer must directly come up with a performance model using generalised stochastic petri nets. In this sense this is a *model-based* methodology. Instead, for the latter approach [16], the designer does not have to directly develop a model for the quantitative analysis; such model —a queueing network— is indeed "compiled" from the behavioural specification of the CAS. Hence, this is a *language-based* methodology.

This paper aims to compare such methodologies and to study their relative merits. More precisely we address the following two research questions:

RQ1. To what extent the approaches in [16] and in [28] support performance-aware design of CAS?

RQ2. How do the features of the approaches in [16] and in [28] compare?

For this comparison we will use a robot scenario that will allow us to highlight the respective strengths and weaknesses of the methodologies. As we will see, our analysis suggests an hybrid combination hinging on both approaches.

Outline. Section 2 describes the scenario used in the rest of the paper. We will consider two different architectures (i.e., independent and collaborative) for this scenario. Section 3 provides the models based on the specification language in [16] for both the architectures. Section 4 shows the performance analysis based on the proposed models of Sect. 3. The comparison between the approach in [28] and the one illustrated in Sect. 3 is discussed in Sect. 5. Final comments, related, and future work are in Sect. 6.

2   A Robot Scenario

Our analysis is conducted on a scenario where robots have the task to transport some equipment necessary in an emergency from an initial zone to a target location. In order to reach the target location, robots need to pass through two doors, or take an alternative longer route. Robots take the alternative route only if they find a door closed. When this happens on the second door, it will take more time for robots to reach the destination than if the alternative route had been taken at the start of the journey. After the delivery, robots return to the initial zone trying to follow the reverse path and the same constraints apply.

It is commonly accepted that the performance of a cyber-physical system varies with changes in the physical environment. Moreover, as experimentally confirmed in [28], it is possible to measure the impact of architectural patterns and dynamic space changes on the performance of cyber-physical systems. This type of analysis suggests that in this domain it is useful to factor performance at design time. Following [28], we will consider two architectural scenarios:

Independent. Robots do not cooperate with each other. In this architecture, robots simply detect the state of doors and behave as described above.
Collaborative. Robots behave exactly as above on open doors; instead, on closed doors, they send a message to nearby robots before taking the alternative route. In this way, every robot that receives such message can directly follow the alternative route.

The approach proposed in [28] is new and it hinges on Generalised Stochastic Petri Nets (GSPN) [4] as suitable models of cyber-physical systems. In this paper we apply such approach by adopting (i) a different modelling language, hinging on behavioural specifications and (ii) relying on queueing networks [18] for performance analysis. The modelling language used here has been advocated in [16] for specifying global behaviour of CAS. As shown in [16], this modelling language has a natural connection with queueing networks, therefore enabling performance analysis of CAS.

3   A Behavioural Specification Model

The behavioural specifications in [16] are inspired by AbC, a calculus of attribute-based communication [1]. The key feature of AbC is an abstract mechanism of addressing partners of communications by letting the specification of many-to-many communication between dynamically formed groups of senders and receivers. Informally, components expose domain-specific *attributes* used to address senders and receivers of communications according to *predicate* on such attributes. For instance, the robots in the scenarios in Sects. 1 and 2, may expose an attribute recording their physical position. This attribute can be used to specify communications among "nearby" robots through a suitable predicate so to determine the communication group as the set of robots satisfying such predicate. This mechanism is abstracted in [16] by *interactions* defined, in their most general form, as

$$A_|\rho \xrightarrow{\ e \quad e'\ } B_|\rho' \tag{1}$$

where A and B are *role names*, ρ and ρ' are logical formulae, e is a tuple of expressions, and e' is a tuple of *patterns*, that is expressions possibly including variables. The intuitive meaning of the interaction in (1) is

"*any* agent, say A, *satisfying* ρ generates an expression e for *any* agents satisfying ρ', dubbed B, provided that expression e' *matches* e." [16]

The conditions ρ and ρ' predicate over components' attributes. The payload of an output is a tuple of values e to be matched by receivers with the (tuple of) patterns e'; when e and e' match, the effect of the communication is that the variables in e' are instantiated with the corresponding values in e.

As said, a send operation targets components satisfying a given *predicate* on such attributes. For instance, if pos is the position attribute exposed by robots, the predicate

$$\rho \equiv \mathsf{abs}(\mathsf{self.pos} - \mathsf{pos}) < 5\,\mathsf{mt}$$

is satisfied by a receiving robot which is less than five meters away from the sending robot (i.e., the difference between the position self.pos of the receiver and the one pos of the sender is below five meters). Messages are disregarded if they do not satisfy ρ.

Role names A and B in (1) are pleonastic: they are used just for succinctness and may be omitted for instance writing $\rho \xrightarrow{\ e \quad e'\ } B_|\rho'$ or $\rho \xrightarrow{\ e \quad e'\ } \rho'$. Also, we abbreviate $A_|\rho$ with A when ρ is a tautology.

Interactions are the basic elements of an algebra of protocols [29] featuring iteration as well as non-deterministic and parallel composition. This algebra has an intuitive graphical presentation which we use here to avoid technicalities. In fact, we use *gates* to identify control points[1] of protocols:

- entry and exit points of loops are represented by ◇-gates,
- branching and merging points of a non-deterministic choice are represented by ◆-gates.

We remark that our behavioural model does not require fix in advance to the number of instances of agents. In fact, in our model:

- several agents can embody the same role at the same time; for instance, in our case study, an unspecified number of devices impersonate the robot role;
- instead of addressing senders and receivers by name, attribute-based communication by definition uses constraints to identify communication partners.

Therefore our model allows us to specify complex multiparty scenarios regardless the number of agents' instances.

The next sections give the architectures of our scenario in terms of the graphical notation sketched above.

---

[1] We do not consider forking and joining points of parallel composition (represented by □-gates) since this feature is not used in our case study.

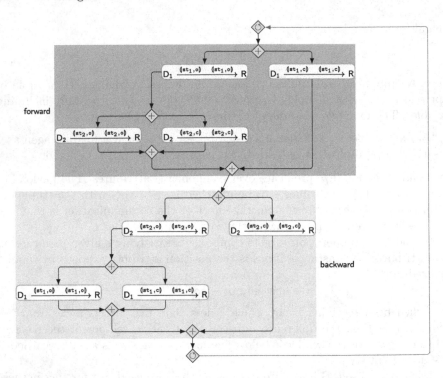

Fig. 1. A model for the independent architecture

3.1 Independent Architecture

Figure 1 gives a possible model capturing the independent architecture described in Sect. 2 in the graphical notation of our specification language. The model consists of a loop whose body is made by the sequential composition of the behaviour for the forward and the backward journey of robots. Robots try to go through the first door and then through the second one on their forward journey and try the opposite on their backward journey.

The model in Fig. 1 is rather simplistic and we will refine it soon; we use it to introduce our graphical notation. Interactions among doors and robots do not involve value passing; for instance, robots detect the status of the first door when they pattern match on the tuples $(\!|st_1, o)\!)$ and $(\!|st_1, c)\!)$ for open and closed doors respectively (an likewise for the second door). Robots detect the status of a door according to the format of the messages they intercept. For instance, on its forward journey a robot either pattern matches the tuple $(\!|st_1, o)\!)$ or the tuple $(\!|st_1, c)\!)$ from the first door. This choice is represented in Fig. 1 by ◇-gate immediately below the topmost ◇-gate. If the robot receives a $(\!|st_1, c)\!)$ tuple from the first door, it continues its journey on the alternative route after which it starts the backward journey. Otherwise, the robot approaches the second door and again goes through if $(\!|st_2, o)\!)$ is received otherwise takes the alternative route. The behaviour on the return journey is similar modulo the order in which robots approach doors.

As said, this model is simplistic. Let us refine it. In Fig. 1, we used role names D_1, D_2, and R for simplicity. However, this is not very precise. In fact, we would like to express that robots detect the status of a door only when they are "close enough" to it. To capture this behaviour let us assume that robots and doors expose the attribute ID yielding their identity. Then, we can define the conditions

$$\rho_d(x) \equiv abs(\text{self.pos} - pos(x)) < d$$

where $pos(x)$ is the position of the component with identifier x. Then we can replace in Fig. 1 the interactions $D_1 \xrightarrow{(\!|\text{st}_1, \text{o}|\!) \quad (\!|\text{st}_1, \text{o}|\!)} R$ with

$$\text{ID} = \text{d1} \xrightarrow{(\!|\text{self.ID}, \text{o}|\!) \quad (\!|x, \text{o}|\!)} \rho_d(x) \tag{2}$$

and similarly for the interactions $D_1 \xrightarrow{(\!|\text{st}_1, \text{c}|\!) \quad (\!|\text{st}_1, \text{c}|\!)} R$ and those involving D_2. Interaction (2) and the one for the closed status state that the door[2] with ID set to d_1 emits a tuple with their identity and the status. These tuples are intercepted by components whose state satisfy $\rho_d(x)$ where x is the variable instantiated with the identity of the sender. Other components would simply disregard those messages.

3.2 Collaborative Architecture

The collaborative architecture can be obtained by simply extending the independent one with the interactions among robots. A possible solution is given in Fig. 2 where for readability we only show the body of the loop and shorten $(\!|\text{self.ID}, \text{o}|\!)$ and $(\!|\text{self.ID}, \text{c}|\!)$ with o_{ID} and c_{ID} respectively, and $(\!|x, \text{o}|\!)$ and $(\!|x, \text{c}|\!)$ with x_o and c_o respectively.

As in the independent architecture, there are a forward and a backward phase. The only difference is that each time a robot detects a closed door, it will inform nearby robots that the door is closed. Once this communication is performed, the robot continues its journey on the alternative root. The fact that the adaptation is quite straightforward is due to the features offered by our modelling language. The attributes of components are indeed allowing us to just reuse the condition ρ_d also for coordinating inter-robots interactions.

There is however a crucial remark to be made. The behaviour of robots is to wait for three possible messages: the two sent by the door and one possibly coming from a robot which detected that the door was closed. In fact, there might be robots satisfying condition $\rho'(y, x)$ in Fig. 2, that is they are not close enough to the door but have a nearby robot, say r, aware that the door is closed. These robots should therefore be ready to receive the communication from robot r. Our model accounts for this type of robots but the graphical notion "hides" this since there are only two possibilities on branching $\diamond$-gates. As we will see in Sect. 4, this is a key observation for our performance analysis.

---

[2] The fact that identifiers are unique is not built-in in our model; in principle there could be more doors with the same identifier.

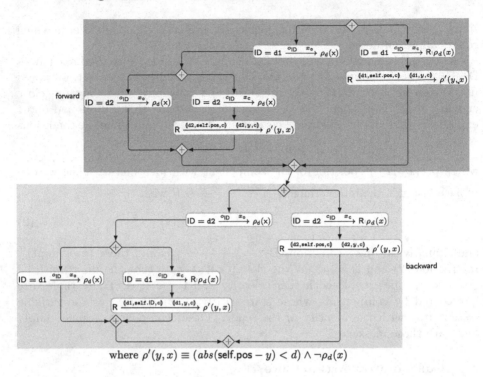

where $\rho'(y, x) \equiv (abs(\mathsf{self.pos} - y) < d) \wedge \neg\rho_d(x)$

Fig. 2. A model for the collaborative architecture

4   Quantitative Analysis

In [16] we relate our modelling language to Queueing Networks (QNs) [19], a widely used mathematical model to study waiting lines of systems represented as a network of queues [11,14]. Two main elements of QNs are *customers* (i.e., jobs, requests, or transactions) that need to be served by *service centres* (i.e., system resources). When a service centre is busy serving a customer, other jobs to be processed by the same resource wait in a queue for their turn. Also, QNs feature *routers* to dispatch customers to different centres and *delay stations* in order to model e.g., lags in the processing or "internal" computations not requiring further system resources. In [16], we provided some rules to automatically get QN performance models from a behavioural specification. The basic idea is to transform (i) an interaction into a service centre and (ii) a non-deterministic choice into a router. We will apply this construction to our robot scenario and its architectures.

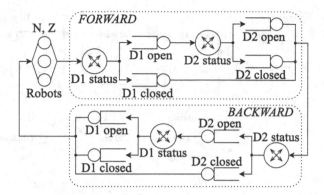

Fig. 3. QN of the independent architecture

We build on our recent experience [28] on using GSPN [4] performance models. A GSPN consists of places (represented as circles), tokens (represented as dots), transitions (represented as rectangles), and arcs that connect places to transitions and vice-versa. A token is removed from a place (and possibly added to another one) every time a transition fires. A transition is *enabled* when all the input places contain a number of tokens larger or equal to a pre-defined multiplicity (if not expressed it is equal to 1). There are two types of transitions in GSPN: *immediate transitions* and *timed transitions*. The former are graphically represented as thin black rectangles and fire when enabled, no timing is associated to the transition. The latter are graphically represented as thick white rectangles and fire following a randomly distributed time (in this paper we use exponential distributions), meaning that the transition implies some timing.

The analysis conducted in [28] shows that it is possible to measure the impact of architectural patterns and dynamic space changes on the performance of cyber-physical systems.

In the following we are interested in studying the applicability of GSPN in CAS and compare this approach to the one based on QNs. Both GSPN and QNs are analysed using JSIMgraph, i.e., the simulator of Java Modelling Tools (JMT) [7]. JSIMgraph discards the initial transient system behaviour and automatically stops when the desired confidence interval (i.e., the probability that the sample data lie within it, set to 99% for our experiments) is observed for all performance indices under analysis.

4.1 Independent Architecture

To address RQ1, we start by describing the approaches defined in [16] and in [28] to support performance-aware design of CAS. Let us focus on the independent architecture first.

The application of the rules introduced in [16] to the behavioural specification of Fig. 1 yields the QN depicted in Fig. 3. Specifically, the first and second non-deterministic choices in the forward box of Fig. 1 become respectively the D1

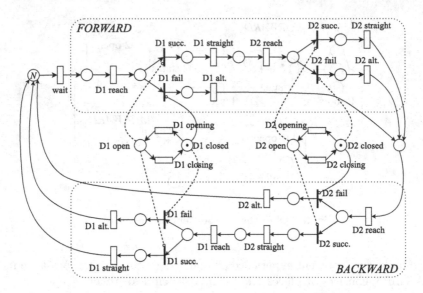

Fig. 4. GSPN of the independent architecture

status and D2 status router in the *FORWARD* box of Fig. 3. Interactions on the left (resp. right) branch of each choice in the forward box of Fig. 1 become the D1 open and D2 open (resp. D1 closed and D2 closed) service centres in the *FORWARD* box of Fig. 3. Similarly, the *BACKWARD* box in Fig. 3 is derived from the backward box in Fig. 1. A delay centre (i.e., Robots Fig. 3) represents the number of robots in the system and their *think time* is also added to the QN model as suggested in [16].

We assess the usefulness of the QN derived from the behavioural specification and rules defined in [16] by comparing it with the GSPN introduced in [28], and depicted in Fig. 4. Initially, there are N robots waiting for task assignment. When transition wait fires after an exponentially distributed time (i.e., when a task is assigned to a robot), a token is moved to the next place. This represents the fact that the robot starts moving towards the first door D1 reach. After some time, the robot reaches the door. If the door is closed (D1 fail) the robot has to take the alternative (and longer) route (D1 alt.); otherwise the robot goes through the first door (D1 succ.) and continues its journey towards the second door (D1 straight). After some time the robot approaches the second door (D2 reach). The status of each door is controlled by two places (e.g., D1 open and D1 closed for the first door) and two transitions. The door is initially closed (i.e., a token is in the D1 closed place). When the enabled transition fires, the token is removed from the D1 closed place and added to the D1 open place. Hence, the door stays open until the new enabled transition fires and the door status changes again.

Table 1. Numerical values used for GSPN and QN models of independent and collaborative architectures. *Direction* indicates **Forward** (F) or **Backward** (B), the parameter and its value are used. $S_{D* \ open}$ (QN) is obtained by summing $S_{D* \ reach}$ and $S_{D* \ straight}$ (GSPN). All timing parameters are in second.

GSPN			QN		
Parameter	Direction	Value	Parameter	Direction	Value
N		100	N		100
S_{wait}		10	Z		10
$S_{D* \ closing} + S_{D* \ opening}$		60	–	–	–
$S_{D* \ reach}$	F / B	5	$S_{D* \ open}$	F / B	10
$S_{D* \ straight}$	F / B	5			
$S_{D1 \ alt.}$	F	45	$S_{D1 \ closed}$	F	45
$S_{D2 \ alt.}$	F	60	$S_{D2 \ closed}$	F	60
$S_{D1 \ alt.}$	B	60	$S_{D1 \ closed}$	B	60
$S_{D2 \ alt.}$	B	45	$S_{D2 \ closed}$	B	45
$S_{D* \ follow}$	F / B	46	$S_{D* \ msg.}$	F / B	46
$S_{D* \ send}$	F / B	1	$S_{D* \ send}$	F / B	1

The two models are parameterized with values from the literature [32] as shown in Table 1. In our model the system response time is the time spent by each robot to complete a task and go back to the initial room.

To answer RQ2, we estimate the response time using both models against the probability that each door is open. The results of this analysis are given in the left histogram of Fig. 5 together with the confidence interval. Notice that extreme cases of 0.01 and 0.99 probabilities are reported instead of 0 and 1 since the latter ones are not probabilistic by definition, these values would imply doors are always either closed or open. We point out that our experimental results show high agreement in the performance predictions. The QN derived from the behavioural specification predicts the system response time with values similar to those predicted by the GSPN. As expected, the shortest response time of the system is observed when there is a high probability that both doors are open and

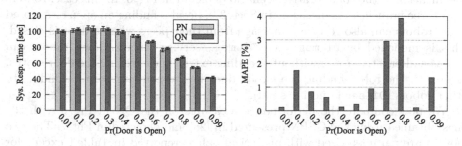

Fig. 5. Independent architecture – System response time (left) and MAPE (right) vs. Probability door is open

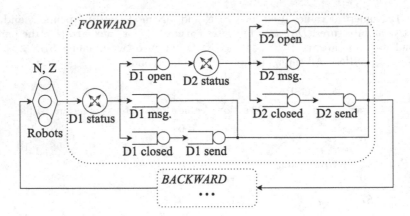

Fig. 6. QN of the collaborative architecture

robots can almost always take the fastest route. The longest system response time is observed for $0.2 \leq Pr(Door\ is\ Open) \leq 0.3$, when the probability of finding the first door open and the second one closed (or the second door open and the first on the backward journey) is higher. In this case, robots spend a longer time taking the alternative route, see Table 1. The QN predictions are further assessed in the right histogram of Fig. 5 via mean absolute percentage error (MAPE) calculated as

$$\text{MAPE}[\%] = \frac{|R_{GSPN} - R_{QN}|}{R_{GSPN}} \cdot 100$$

where R_{GSPN} and R_{QN} are the system response time estimated using GSPN and QN, respectively. The value of MAPE is always smaller than 4%, an excellent result when estimating the system response time [27].

4.2 Collaborative Architecture

We now repeat the previous exercise focusing on the collaborative architecture.

The application of the rules defined in [16] yields the QN from the behavioural specification of the collaborative scenario depicted in Fig. 6. In this case, routers have three branches. As discussed in Sect. 3.2, besides finding an open or a closed door, robots can also receive a message from their peers when a door is closed. This is modelled by D1 msg. and D2 msg. service centres. Now, robots can take the alternative route without spending extra time checking the door status. Moreover, the robot finding the closed door has to communicate its finding to other robots (D1 send and D2 send).

We now compare the performance measures on the QN in Fig. 6 with the ones obtained using the GSPN presented in [28] and depicted in Fig. 7. The two models are parameterized with numerical values reported in Table 1 except for probabilities used in the QN routers (i.e., D1 status and D2 status). Since the

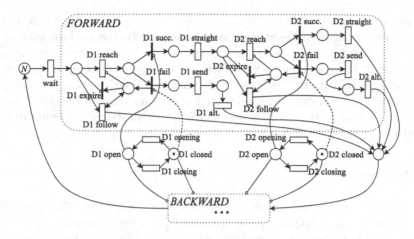

Fig. 7. GSPN of the collaborative architecture

probability of receiving a message from a peer depends on other characteristics of the system (e.g., the probability that doors are open, robots' position, and their speed), there is not an easy way to set router probabilities. To fairly compare QN results to GSPN ones, it is necessary to first analyse the GSPN model of the collaborative architecture given in Fig. 7. From this analysis we infer the probability values (i.e., for receiving a message from a peer under certain system circumstances) that are needed to properly parametrise the QN model.

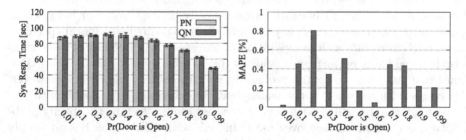

Fig. 8. Collaborative architecture – System response time (left) and MAPE (right) vs. Probability door is open

We now reconsider RQ2 for the collaborative architecture. Similarly to the independent architecture, we estimate the system response time using both models against the probability of doors being open. The response times of the system obtained with GSPN and QN are shown in Fig. 8. Also for the collaborative architecture, the QN parameterized as previously described allows us to obtain results that are close to those obtained with the GSPN. The response time of collaborative systems is generally shorter than the one observed for independent architectures since robots share knowledge about the state of the environment.

The only exception to this observation is for *Pr(Door is Open)* $\geq$ 0.9; in this case, a robot finding a closed door affects negatively the performance of its peers. Indeed, other robots take the alternative route after receiving the message. However, there is a high probability that the door will be open again when they will approach it. In this case, the value of MAPE is even smaller (i.e., less than 1%, see the right histogram of Fig. 8) than the one observed for the independent architecture. This is due to the router probabilities being directly derived from the GSPN used for comparison.

5   Discussion

Answering to our research questions, we can state that both QNs and GSPN are suitable for the performance analysis of CAS. Our experience shows that there is a trade-off between simplicity and expressiveness in the use of these models (RQ1). An interesting outcome of our simulations is that the two different model-based performance predictions match, the error is never larger than 4% denoting high agreement between the proposed performance abstractions (RQ2). Our experimental results confirm the expectation on the analysed scenarios. For instance, the system response time is minimised in case of doors open with a high probability. Collaboration among robots pays off, the collaborative architecture shows shorter response times since robots are informed before reaching doors and gain from promptly taking alternative paths.

The two modelling approaches offer different advantages which we discuss herafter. A main advantage of QNs is that they are conceptually simple: performance analysis is based on the probabilities assigned to observable events (e.g., door open). Moreover, QNs can be automatically derived from our behavioural specification of the system. A key observation is that our behavioural specification models introduce a clear separation of concerns: the modelling of the system is orthogonal to its performance analysis that is done by using the derived QNs; hence one just needs to fix the probabilities for the observable events. However, this comes with a cost: it is not usually easy to determine such probabilities.

Instead, the modelling with GSPN does not require to directly specify probabilities, a clear advantage over QNs. Indeed, with GSPN one has to simply select a suitable time distribution: this is therefore a more reliable approach compared to QNs. Besides, GSPN allow for controlling events with a same process; for instance, if a door is open in a direction, it must also be open in the other direction; this cannot be modelled using probabilities only. Overall, GSPN requires more expertise on building the performance model, but its parameterisation includes timing values only, hence they may also be used for monitoring (see e.g., [25]).

However, GSPN are more "rigid" than QNs because certain characteristics of the system are hardwired in the model itself. For instance, changing the number of doors robots have to traverse would require a more complex performance model. Moreover, this kind of generalisation will make the size of the model much larger, which can severely affect the performance of the analysis as the state space grows exponentially [4]. This is not the case for QNs derived from our behavioural specification because they permit to easily abstract away from the number of system components. On the other hand, GSPN allow to easily model other types of sophisticate coordination policies. For instance, in the collaborative architecture it is easy to let the robot first noticing the closed door wait for all nearby robots to take the alternative route before continuing its journey. This is not simple to model with our behavioural specification language or with QNs.

6 Conclusions, Related and Future Work

We proposed two approaches for the performance analysis of CAS. Our experimental observations are conducted on a simple case study of autonomous robots for which we consider two architectures. Our first approach is based on behavioural abstraction and QNs while the second is based on GSPN. Finally, we compare the two approaches by exploiting the models of the two architectures and observe a high level of agreement on model-based performance predictions.

Behavioural Abstractions. Coreographic models have been applied to Cyber-Phisical Systems [21,22], IoT [20] and robotics [24]. These papers focus on verification of correctness properties (e.g., deadlock freedom and session fidelity) and are not concerned with quantitative aspects or performance analysis. Some works in the literature exploits behavioural abstraction for cost analysis of message passing systems. Cost-aware session types [10] are multiparty session types annotated with size types and local cost, and can estimate upper-bounds of the execution time of participants of a protocol. Temporal session types [12] extend session types with temporal primitives that can be exploited to reason about quantitative properties like the response time. A parallel line of research studies timed session types [5,8,9], that is session types annotated with timed constraint in the style of timed automata [2]. They have been used for verification of timed distributed programs by means of static type checking [8,9] and runtime monitoring [6,25]. Despite the presence of timed constraints, which makes timed session types appealing for performance analysis, they have never been applied in such setting. Session types have been extended with probabilities [15] for verification of concurrent probabilistic programs, which is potentially useful for the CAS analysis. A common limitation of these approaches is that they do not easily permit to define the number of agents' instances embodying a specific role in the system specification. Our behavioural model instead allows it, as explained in the final remark of Sect. 3, hence it is suitable for performance analysis that indeed requires such a system workload information.

Quantitative Abstractions. Rigorous engineering of collective adaptive systems calls for quantitative approaches that drive the design and management of coordination actions, as recently advocated in [13]. Verification tools for CAS formation are surveyed in [17] and analysis techniques are considered still immature to deal with possible changes in decision-making, hence quantitative approaches that keep track of behavioural alternatives and their impact on system performance are of high relevance for CAS. Ordinary differential equations (ODEs) have been proposed in [30] as quantitative abstractions for CAS. The use of ODEs allows one to express large-scale systems that are analyzed through reaction network bisimulations. A limitation of the approach is that results are not reliable when the population of agents is small. A quantitative analysis of CAS is also pursued in [23] where the focus is on investigating the probabilistic behaviour of agents, and a specific language (i.e., CARMA) is introduced along with a simulation environment that provides quantitative information on CAS, however the scalability is limited and alternative (quantitative) semantics are claimed to be desirable to speed up the analysis. Performance characteristics of CAS are tackled in [31] where the goal is to select optimal (from a performance perspective) implementations of collective behaviour while preserving system functionalities and resiliency properties, however various implementations are required and the switch of identified alternatives cannot be executed at runtime. More recently, in [26] a design pattern, i.e., self-organising coordination regions, is proposed to partition system devices into regions and enable internal coordination activities. This supports our investigation of independent and collaborative architectures since their optimality relies on the physical space, as emerged by our quantitative analysis on the probability of doors being open/closed. As opposed to these approaches, we aim to automatically derive quantitative abstractions from the behavioural specification of CAS, thus simplifying the process to get performance indicators of interest.

Future Work. We plan to consider more complex application scenarios and investigate generalisations of our model-based performance analysis. In particular, we are interested to explore the possibility to automatically derive the structure of GSPN from our behavioural specifications. We conjecture that this could allow us to overcome some of the drawbacks of GSPN while avoiding the need to determine probabilities.

An interesting research direction to explore is the performance analysis of CAS in presence of dependencies among input parameters. For instance, in our scenario one could think of a synchronised behaviour of doors so that they change state in a coordinated way. This implies that the probability for a robot to find the second door open (after it crossed the first one) depends on its speed and the time when the robot went through the first door.

References

1. Abd Alrahman, Y., De Nicola, R., Loreti, M.: A calculus for collective-adaptive systems and its behavioural theory. Inf. Comput. **268**, 104457 (2019)
2. Alur, R., Dill, D.L.: A theory of timed automata. Theor. Comput. Sci. **126**(2), 183–235 (1994)
3. Apvrille, L., Tanzi, T., Dugelay, J.-L.: Autonomous drones for assisting rescue services within the context of natural disasters. In: URSI General Assembly and Scientific Symposium (URSI GASS), pp. 1–4 (2014)

4. Balbo, G., Ciardo, G.: On petri nets in performance and reliability evaluation of discrete event dynamic systems. In: Reisig, W., Rozenberg, G. (eds.) Carl Adam Petri: Ideas, Personality, Impact, pp. 173–185. Springer, Cham (2019). https://doi.org/10.1007/978-3-319-96154-5_22

5. Bartoletti, M., Cimoli, T., Murgia, M.: Timed session types. Log. Methods Comput. Sci. **13**(4) (2017)

6. Bartoletti, M., Cimoli, T., Murgia, M., Podda, A.S., Pompianu, L.: A contract-oriented middleware. In: Braga, C., Ölveczky, P.C. (eds.) FACS 2015. LNCS, vol. 9539, pp. 86–104. Springer, Cham (2016). https://doi.org/10.1007/978-3-319-28934-2_5

7. Bertoli, M., Casale, G., Serazzi, G.: JMT: performance engineering tools for system modeling. SIGMETRICS Perform. Evalu. Rev. **36**(4), 10–15 (2009)

8. Bocchi, L., Murgia, M., Vasconcelos, V.T., Yoshida, N.: Asynchronous timed session types. In: Caires, L. (ed.) ESOP 2019. LNCS, vol. 11423, pp. 583–610. Springer, Cham (2019). https://doi.org/10.1007/978-3-030-17184-1_21

9. Bocchi, L., Yang, W., Yoshida, N.: Timed multiparty session types. In: Baldan, P., Gorla, D. (eds.) CONCUR 2014. LNCS, vol. 8704, pp. 419–434. Springer, Heidelberg (2014). https://doi.org/10.1007/978-3-662-44584-6_29

10. Castro-Perez, D., Yoshida, N.: CAMP: cost-aware multiparty session protocols. Proc. ACM Program. Lang. **4**(OOPSLA), 155:1–155:30 (2020)

11. Cerotti, D., Gribaudo, M., Piazzolla, P., Pinciroli, R., Serazzi, G.: Multi-class queuing networks models for energy optimization. In International Conference on Performance Evaluation Methodologies and Tools (VALUETOOLS). EAI (2014)

12. Das, A., Hoffmann, J., Pfenning, F.: Parallel complexity analysis with temporal session types. Proc. ACM Program. Lang. **2**(ICFP), 91:1–91:30 (2018)

13. De Nicola, R., Jähnichen, S., Wirsing, M.: Rigorous engineering of collective adaptive systems. Int. J. Softw. Tools Technol. Transf. **22**(4), 389–397 (2020)

14. Gribaudo, M., Pinciroli, R., Trivedi, K.S.: Epistemic uncertainty propagation in power models. Electron. Notes Theor. Comput. Sci. **337**, 67–86 (2018)

15. Inverso, O., Melgratti, H.C., Padovani, L., Trubiani, C., Tuosto, E.: Probabilistic analysis of binary sessions. In: International Conference on Concurrency Theory (CONCUR), volume 171 of LIPIcs, pp. 14:1–14:21 (2020)

16. Inverso, O., Trubiani, C., Tuosto, E.: Abstractions for collective adaptive systems. In: Margaria, T., Steffen, B. (eds.) ISoLA 2020. LNCS, vol. 12477, pp. 243–260. Springer, Cham (2020). https://doi.org/10.1007/978-3-030-61470-6_15

17. Johari, M.H., Jawaddi, S.N.A., Ismail, A.: Survey on formation verification for ensembling collective adaptive system. In: Verma, P., Charan, C., Fernando, X., Ganesan, S. (eds.) Advances in Data Computing, Communication and Security. LNDECT, vol. 106, pp. 219–228. Springer, Singapore (2022). https://doi.org/10.1007/978-981-16-8403-6_19

18. Lazowska, E., Zahorjan, J., Scott Graham, G., Sevcik, K.: Computer System Analysis Using Queueing Network Models. Prentice-Hall Inc., Englewood Cliffs (1984)

19. Lazowska, E.D., Zahorjan, J., Graham, G.S., Sevcik, K.C.: Quantitative System Performance - Computer System Analysis Using Queueing Network Models. Prentice Hall, Englewood Cliffs (1984)

20. Lopes, L., Martins, F.: A safe-by-design programming language for wireless sensor networks. J. Syst. Archit. **63**, 16–32 (2016)

21. López, H.A., Nielson, F., Nielson, H.R.: Enforcing availability in failure-aware communicating systems. In: Albert, E., Lanese, I. (eds.) FORTE 2016. LNCS, vol. 9688, pp. 195–211. Springer, Cham (2016). https://doi.org/10.1007/978-3-319-39570-8_13

22. López, H.A., Heussen, K.: Choreographing cyber-physical distributed control systems for the energy sector. In: SAC, pp. 437–443. ACM (2017)
23. Loreti, M., Hillston, J.: Modelling and analysis of collective adaptive systems with CARMA and its tools. In: Bernardo, M., De Nicola, R., Hillston, J. (eds.) SFM 2016. LNCS, vol. 9700, pp. 83–119. Springer, Cham (2016). https://doi.org/10.1007/978-3-319-34096-8_4
24. Majumdar, R., Yoshida, N., Zufferey, D.: Multiparty motion coordination: from choreographies to robotics programs. Proc. ACM Program. Lang. 4(OOPSLA), 134:1–134:30 (2020)
25. Neykova, R., Bocchi, L., Yoshida, N.: Timed runtime monitoring for multiparty conversations. Formal Aspects Comput. 29(5), 877–910 (2017). https://doi.org/10.1007/s00165-017-0420-8
26. Pianini, D., Casadei, R., Viroli, M., Natali, A.: Partitioned integration and coordination via the self-organising coordination regions pattern. Futur. Gener. Comput. Syst. 114, 44–68 (2021)
27. Pinciroli, R., Smith, C.U., Trubiani, C.: Qn-based modeling and analysis of software performance antipatterns for cyber-physical systems. In: International Conference on Performance Engineering (ICPE), pp. 93–104. ACM (2021)
28. Pinciroli, R., Trubiani, C.: Model-based performance analysis for architecting cyber-physical dynamic spaces. In: International Conference on Software Architecture (ICSA), pp. 104–114 (2021)
29. Tuosto, E., Guanciale, R.: Semantics of global view of choreographies. J. Log. Algebr. Meth. Program. 95, 17–40 (2018)
30. Vandin, A., Tribastone, M.: Quantitative abstractions for collective adaptive systems. In: Bernardo, M., De Nicola, R., Hillston, J. (eds.) SFM 2016. LNCS, vol. 9700, pp. 202–232. Springer, Cham (2016). https://doi.org/10.1007/978-3-319-34096-8_7
31. Viroli, M., Audrito, G., Beal, J., Damiani, F., Pianini, D.: Engineering resilient collective adaptive systems by self-stabilisation. ACM Trans. Model. Comput. Simul. (TOMACS) 28(2), 1–28 (2018)
32. Weidinger, F., Boysen, N., Briskorn, D.: Storage assignment with rack-moving mobile robots in KIVA warehouses. Transp. Sci. 52(6), 1479–1495 (2018)

Programming Multi-robot Systems with X-KLAIM

Lorenzo Bettini[1] (ID), Khalid Bourr[2], Rosario Pugliese[1] (ID),
and Francesco Tiezzi[1](✉) (ID)

[1] Dipartimento di Statistica, Informatica, Applicazioni, Università degli Studi di
Firenze, Firenze, Italy
{lorenzo.bettini,rosario.pugliese,francesco.tiezzi}@unifi.it
[2] School of Science and Technology, Università di Camerino, Camerino, Italy
khalid.bourr@unicam.it

Abstract. Software development for robotics applications is still a
major challenge that becomes even more complex when considering a
Multi-Robot System (MRS). Such a distributed software has to perform
multiple cooperating tasks in a well-coordinated manner to avoid unsatis-
factory emerging behavior. This paper provides an approach for programming MRSs at a high abstraction level using the programming language
X-KLAIM. The computation and communication model of X-KLAIM,
based on multiple distributed tuple spaces, permits to coordinate with
the same abstractions and mechanisms both intra- and inter-robot interactions of an MRS. This allows developers to focus on MRS behavior,
achieving readable and maintainable code. The proposed approach can
be used in practice through the integration of X-KLAIM and the popular robotics framework ROS. We show the proposal's feasibility and
effectiveness by implementing an MRS scenario.

Keywords: Multi-robot systems · Multiple tuple spaces · X-KLAIM ·
ROS

1 Introduction

Autonomous robots are software-intensive systems increasingly used in many
different fields. Their software components interact in real-time with a highly
dynamic and uncertain environment through sensors and actuators. To complete tasks that are beyond the capabilities of an individual autonomous robot,
multiple robots are teamed together to form a *Multi-Robot System* (MRS). An
MRS can take advantage of distributed sensing and action, and greater reliability. On the other hand, an MRS requires robots to cooperate and coordinate to
achieve common goals.

This work was partially supported by the PRIN projects "SEDUCE" n. 2017TWR-
CNB and "T-LADIES" n. 2020TL3X8X, and the INdAM - GNCS Project "Proprietà
qualitative e quantitative di sistemi reversibili" n. CUP_E55F2200027001.

T. Margaria and B. Steffen (Eds.): ISoLA 2022, LNCS 13703, pp. 283–300, 2022.
https://doi.org/10.1007/978-3-031-19759-8_18

The development of the software controlling a single autonomous robot is still a challenge [24, 31, 49]. This becomes even more arduous in the case of MRSs [14, 25], as it requires dealing with multiple cooperating tasks to drive the robots to work as a well-coordinated team. To meet this challenge, various software libraries, tools and middlewares have been proposed to assist and simplify the rapid prototyping of robotics applications. Among them, nowadays, a prominent solution is ROS (Robot Operating System [52]), a popular framework largely used in both industry and academia for writing robot software. On the one hand, ROS provides a layer to interact with a multitude of sensors and actuators, for a large variety of robots, while abstracting from the underlying hardware. On the other hand, programming with ROS still requires dealing with low-level implementation details; hence, robotics software development remains a complex and demanding activity for practitioners from the robotic domain. To face this issue, many researchers have proposed using higher-level abstractions to drive the software development process and then resorting to tools for the automated generation of executable code and system configuration files. Many proposals in the literature are surveyed in [11, 13, 49, 50].

Along this line of research, we introduced in [5] an approach for programming a single-robot system. Specifically, we propose using the language X-KLAIM [7] to program the components of a robot's software. This choice is motivated by the fact that X-KLAIM provides mechanisms, based on distributed tuple spaces, for coordinating the interactions between these software components at a high level of abstraction. The integration of X-KLAIM with ROS permits the application of the approach in practice.

In this paper, we take a step forward in this direction by extending the approach in [5] to program MRSs. In fact, the X-KLAIM's computation and communication model is particularly suitable for dealing both with (i) the distributed nature of the architecture of each robot belonging to an MRS, where the software components dealing with actuators and sensors execute concurrently, and (ii) the inherent distribution of the MRS, which is formed by multiple interacting robots. Notably, the same tuple-based mechanisms are used both for intra- and inter-robot communication. This simplifies the design and implementation of MRS's software in terms of an X-KLAIM application distributed across both multiple threads of execution and multiple hardware platforms, resulting in a better readable, maintainable, and reusable code.

Our framework can be thought of as a proof-of-concept implementation for experimenting with the applicability of the tuple space-based paradigm to MRS software development. To show the execution of the generated code, we use a simulator of robot behaviors in complex environments. To illustrate the proposed approach, we consider a warehouse scenario, where an MRS involving an arm robot and two delivery robots manages the movement of items.

The rest of the paper is organized as follows. In Sect. 2, we provide some background notions concerning the X-KLAIM language, while in Sect. 3 we present our approach. In Sect. 4 we (partially) illustrate the implementation of a simple robotics scenario according to the proposed approach. In Sect. 5 we present a systematic analysis of the strictly related work, while in Sect. 6 we conclude and touch upon directions for future work.

2   The X-KLAIM Language

This section briefly describes the key ingredient of the approach we propose: the programming language X-KLAIM.[1] We refer the interested reader to the cited sources in the following for a complete account.

X-KLAIM is based on KLAIM (Kernel Language for Agents Interaction and Mobility, [15]), a formal language devised to design distributed applications consisting of (possibly mobile) software components deployed over the nodes of a network infrastructure. KLAIM generalizes the notion of *generative communication*, introduced by the coordination language Linda [33], to multiple distributed tuple spaces. A *tuple space* is a shared data repository consisting of a multiset of tuples. *Tuples* are *anonymous* sequences of data items that are associatively retrieved from tuple spaces using a *pattern-matching* mechanism. Tuple spaces are identified through *localities*, which are symbolic addresses of *network nodes* where processes and tuples can be allocated.

Processes can run concurrently, either at the same node or at different nodes, by executing actions to exchange tuples and to move processes. Action **out**(tuple)@nodeLocality adds the specified tuple to the tuple space of the target node identified by nodeLocality. A tuple is a sequence of actual fields, i.e., expressions, localities, or processes. Action **in**(template)@nodeLocality (resp., **read**(template)@nodeLocality) withdraws (resp., reads) tuples from the tuple space hosted at nodeLocality. The process is blocked until a matching tuple is found. *Templates* are sequences of *actual* and *formal* fields, where the latter are used to bind variables to values, localities, or processes. A template matches a tuple if both have the same number of fields and corresponding fields do match; two values/localities match only if they are identical, while formal fields match any value of the same type. Upon a successful matching, the template variables are replaced with the values of the corresponding actual fields of the accessed tuple. Action **eval**(Process)@nodeLocality sends Process for execution to nodeLocality. A process can use the reserved locality self to refer to its current hosting node.

The implementation of KLAIM consists of the Java package KLAVA (KLAIM in Java [4]), which provides the KLAIM concepts in terms of Java classes and methods, and X-KLAIM (eXtended KLAIM [7]), a Java-like programming language providing KLAIM constructs besides the typical high-level programming constructs. X-KLAIM is translated into Java code that uses the Java package KLAVA. An X-KLAIM program can smoothly access any Java type and Java library available in the project's classpath. X-KLAIM comes with a complete IDE support based on Eclipse. The syntax of X-KLAIM is similar to Java, thus it should be easily understood by Java programmers, but it removes much "syntactic noise" from Java.

3   The X-KLAIM Approach to Multi-robot Programming

In this section, we provide an overview of our approach, and the resulting software framework, for programming MRS applications using ROS and X-KLAIM.

---

[1] https://github.com/LorenzoBettini/xklaim.

A single autonomous robot has a distributed architecture, consisting of cooperating components, in particular sensors and actuators. Such cooperation is enabled and controlled by the ROS framework,[2] which provides tools and libraries for simplifying the development of complex controllers while abstracting from the underlying hardware. The core element of the ROS framework is the message-passing middleware, which enables hardware abstraction for a wide variety of robotic platforms. Although ROS supports different communication mechanisms, in this paper we only use the most common one: the anonymous and asynchronous publish/subscribe mechanism. For sending a message, a process has to publish it in a *topic*, which is a named and typed bus. A process that is interested in such message has to subscribe to the topic. Whenever a new message is published in the topic, the subscriber will be notified. Multiple publishers and subscribers for the same topic are allowed.

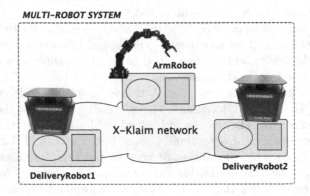

Fig. 1. Software architecture of an MRS in X-Klaim.

When passing from a single-robot system to an MRS, the distributed and heterogeneous nature of the overall system becomes even more evident. The software architecture for controlling an MRS reflects such a distribution: each robot is equipped with ROS, on top of which the controller software runs. This allows the robot to act independently and, when needed, to coordinate with the other robots of the system to work together coherently.

In X-Klaim the distributed architecture of the MRS's software is naturally rendered as a network where the different parts are deployed. As shown in Fig. 1, we associate an X-Klaim node to each robot of the MRS. In its turn, the internal distribution of the software controller of each robot is managed by concurrent processes that synchronize their activities using local data, i.e., tuples stored in the robot's tuple space. Inter-robot interactions rely on the same communication mechanism by specifying remote tuple spaces as targets of communication actions.

In practice, to program the behaviors of the robots forming an MRS, we enabled X-Klaim programs to interact with robots' physical components by

---

² https://www.ros.org/.

integrating the X-KLAIM language with the ROS middleware. The communication infrastructure of the integrated framework is based on ROS Bridge. This is a server included in the ROS framework that provides a JSON API to ROS functionalities for external programs. This way, the ROS framework installed in a robot receives and executes commands on the physical components of the robot, and gives feedback and sensor data. The use of JSON enables the interoperability of ROS with most programming languages, including Java. As an example, we report in Fig. 2 a message pose in the JSON format published on the ROS topic /goal, providing information for navigating a delivery robot to a given goal position. In our example, the goal is the position $(-0.21, 0.31)$, which is close to the position of the arm robot.

```
{ "topic":"/robot1/move_base_simple/goal",
   "msg":{ "header": { ... },
            "pose": { "position": { "x": -0.21, "y": 0.31, "z": 0.0 },
                      "orientation": { ... } } } }
```

Fig. 2. Example of a JSON message for the /goal topic.

X-KLAIM programs can indirectly interact with the ROS Bridge server, publishing and subscribing over ROS topics, via objects provided by the Java library *java_rosbridge*.[3] In its own turn, *java_rosbridge* communicates with the ROS Bridge server, via the WebSocket protocol, by means of the Jetty web server.[4]

ROS permits to check the execution of the code generated from an X-KLAIM program by means of the Gazebo[5] simulator. Gazebo [42] is an open-source simulator of robot behaviors in complex environments that is based on a robust physics engine and provides a high-quality 3D visualization of simulations. Gazebo is fully integrated in ROS; in fact, ROS can interact with the simulator via the publish-subscribe communication mechanism of the framework. The use of the simulator is not mandatory when ROS is deployed in real robots. However, even in such a case, the design activity of the MRS software may benefit from the use of a simulator, to save time and reduce the development cost.

Since the X-KLAIM compiler generates plain Java code, which depends only on KLAVA and a few small libraries, deploying an X-KLAIM application can be done by using standard Java tools and mechanisms. In the context of this paper, it is enough to create a jar with the generated Java code and its dependencies (KLAVA and *java_rosbridge*), that is, a so-called "fat-jar" or "uber-jar", and deploy it to a physical robot where a Java virtual machine is already installed. Under that respect, X-KLAIM provides standard Maven artifacts and a plugin to generate Java code outside Eclipse, e.g., in a Continuous Integration server. Moreover, the dependencies of an X-KLAIM application, including *java_rosbridge*, are only a few megabytes, which makes X-KLAIM applications suitable also for embedded devices like robots.

---

[3] https://github.com/h2r/java_rosbridge.
[4] Jetty 9: https://www.eclipse.org/jetty/.
[5] https://gazebosim.org/.

4   The X-KLAIM Approach at Work on an MRS Scenario

To illustrate the proposed approach, in this section, we show and briefly comment on a few interesting parts of implementing a warehouse scenario[6] involving an MRS that manages the movement of items. As shown in Fig. 3, the MRS is composed of an arm robot and two delivery robots, and the warehouse is divided into two sectors, each one served by a delivery robot. The arm robot, positioned in the center of the warehouse, picks up one item at a time from the ground, calls the delivery robot assigned to the item's sector, and releases the item on top of the delivery robot. The latter delivers the item to the appropriate delivery area, which depends on the item's color, and then becomes available for a new delivery.

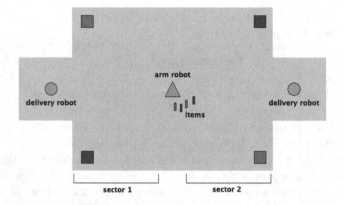

Fig. 3. Warehouse scenario.

In Fig. 4 we show a part of the network for our implementation of the scenario. Each robot is rendered as an X-KLAIM node, whose name represents its locality (see Sect. 2). We have one or several processes for each node implementing the robot's main tasks. Each node creates processes locally and executes them concurrently using the X-KLAIM operation `eval`. Processes are parametric concerning the URI of the ROS bridge WebSocket. As already discussed in Sect. 3, the execution of an X-KLAIM robotics application requires the ROS Bridge server to run, providing a WebSocket connection at a given URI. In the code of our example application, we consider the ROS Bridge server running on the local machine (0.0.0.0) at port 9090. Similarly, to execute the code in a simulated environment and obtain a 3D visualization of the execution, the Gazebo simulator has to be launched with the corresponding robot description. At this point, our application can be executed by running the Java class `Main`, which the X-KLAIM compiler has generated. A few processes require additional parameters like the robot and sector id and the locality of other nodes (e.g., the arm's node locality in `MoveToArm`).

---

[6] The complete source code of the scenario implementation, and a screencast showing its execution on Gazebo, can be found at https://github.com/LorenzoBettini/xklaim-ros-multi-robot-warehouse-example.

The code should be easily readable by a Java programmer. We mention a few additional X-KLAIM syntax features to make the code more understandable. Such types as `String` and `Double` are Java types, since, as mentioned above, X-KLAIM programs can refer directly to Java types. In the code snippets, we omitted the Java-like import statements. Variable declarations start with `val` or `var`, for final and non-final variables, respectively. The types of variables can be omitted if they can be inferred from the initialization expression. Here we also see the typical KLAIM operations, `read`, `in` and `out`, acting on possibly distributed tuple spaces. Formal fields in a tuple are specified as variable declarations, since formal fields implicitly declare variables that are available in the code occurring after `in` and `read` operations (just like in KLAIM).

In Fig. 4, the main processes of the nodes wait for specific matching tuples before starting a new loop. To make things simpler, the loop is infinite, but we could easily rely on a termination condition to stop the whole example's net. The main idea behind the implementation of our example is that processes coordinate themselves through the X-KLAIM tuple space-based communication. On the other hand, the processes still rely on the ROS bridge to coordinate the

```
net MRS {
  node Arm {
    val rosbridgeWebsocketURI = "ws://0.0.0.0:9090"
    while (true) {
      in("initialPosition")@self
      in("item", var String itemId, var String sector, var String itemType,
        var Double x, var Double y)@self
      eval(new GetDown(rosbridgeWebsocketURI,x,y))@self
      eval(new Grip(rosbridgeWebsocketURI))@self
      eval(new GetUp(rosbridgeWebsocketURI,x,y))@self
      eval(new Rotate(rosbridgeWebsocketURI,sector))@self
      eval(new Lay(rosbridgeWebsocketURI))@self
      eval(new Release(rosbridgeWebsocketURI,itemId,itemType))@self
      eval(new GoToInitialPosition(rosbridgeWebsocketURI))@self
    }
  }
  node DeliveryRobot1 {
    val rosbridgeWebsocketURI = "ws://0.0.0.0:9090"
    val robotId = "robot1"
    val sector ="sector1"
    while (true) {
      in("availableForDelivery")@self
      eval(new MoveToArm(rosbridgeWebsocketURI,robotId,sector,Arm))@self
      eval(new DeliverItem(rosbridgeWebsocketURI,robotId,Arm))@self
    }
  }
  node DeliveryRobot2 { ... }
  node SimuationHandler { ... }
}
```

Fig. 4. The X-KLAIM net of the warehouse scenario.

physical parts of the robots themselves. This approach can be seen in the code of two of the processes we comment on in this section.

In Fig. 5 we show the code of the process `Rotate`, executed in the node `Arm`. All the processes of this example start by waiting for a specific tuple before executing the main body. This way, the processes that execute in parallel (see the `eval` in Fig. 4) can coordinate themselves: a process will effectively begin its task only after the previous process terminated its task. Then, the process creates the ROS bridge and initializes a publisher for the topic related to the control of the arm movements. After creating the joint positions for the arm movement, the process publishes the trajectory to rotate the arm. The process also inserts a tuple, consisting of an identifier string and the sector, in its local tuple space. The presence of this tuple triggers the call for a delivery robot. In fact, as shown later in Fig. 6, such a tuple is consumed by the `MoveToArm` process, which is executed by the delivery robots. This form of tuple-based interaction between the two kinds of robots allows the arm's code not to depend on the number, the status, and the identities of the delivery robots. This way, the introduction of new delivery robots in the scenario would not affect the code of the arm robot.

```
proc Rotate(String rosbridgeWebsocketURI, String sector) {
    in("getUpCompleted")@self
    val bridge = new XklaimToRosConnection(rosbridgeWebsocketURI)
    val pub = new Publisher("/arm_controller/command",
            "trajectory_msgs/JointTrajectory", bridge)
    val jointPositions = #[−0.9546, −0.20, −0.7241, 3.1400, 1.6613, −0.0142]
    val JointTrajectory rotateTrajectory = new JointTrajectory().positions(jointPositions)
        .jointNames(#["joint1","joint2","joint3","joint4","joint5","joint6"])
    out("itemReadyForTheDelivery",sector)@self
    pub.publish(rotateTrajectory)
    bridge.subscribe(
        SubscriptionRequestMsg.generate("/arm_controller/state").
            setType("control_msgs/JointTrajectoryControllerState").
            setThrottleRate(1).setQueueLength(1),
        [ data, stringRep |
            val actual = data.get("msg").get("actual").get("positions")
            var delta = 0.0
            val tolerance = 0.008
            for (var i = 0; i < jointPositions.size; i++)
                delta += Math.pow(actual.get(i).asDouble() − jointPositions.get(i), 2.0)
            val norm = Math.sqrt(delta)
            if (norm <= tolerance) {
                out("rotationCompleted")@self
                bridge.unsubscribe("/arm_controller/state")
            }
        ])
}
```

Fig. 5. The X-KLAIM `Rotate` process.

The process then uses the Java API provided by *java_rosbridge* for subscribing to a specific topic (we refer to *java_rosbridge* documentation for the used API). The last argument is a lambda expression (i.e., an anonymous function). In X-KLAIM, *lambda expressions* have the shape [param1, param2, ... | body], where the types of the parameters can be omitted if they can be inferred from the context. The lambda will be executed when an event for the subscribed topic is received. In particular, the lambda reads some data from the event (in JSON format) concerning the "positions". ROS dictates the JSON message format. To access the contents, we use the standard Java API (data is of type JsonNode, from the jackson-databind library). The lambda calculates the delta between the actual joint positions and the destination positions to measure the arm movement's completeness. The if determines when the arm has completed the rotation movement, according to a specific tolerance. When that happens, the lambda activates the process responsible for raising the object (GetUp in our example, see Fig. 4). This is achieved, once again, by inserting a specific tuple in the local tuple space. Finally, we can unsubscribe from the topic so that this process will receive no further notifications from the ROS bridge.

```
proc MoveToArm(String rosbridgeWebsocketURI,String robotId,String sector,Locality arm) {
    val x = −0.21
    val y = 0.31
    in("itemReadyForTheDelivery",sector)@arm
    val bridge = new XklaimToRosConnection(rosbridgeWebsocketURI)
    val pub = new Publisher("/" + robotId + "/move_base_simple/goal",
            "geometry_msgs/PoseStamped", bridge)
    val destination = new PoseStamped().headerFrameId("world")
      .posePositionXY(x, y).poseOrientation(1.0)
    pub.publish(destination)
    bridge.subscribe(
      SubscriptionRequestMsg.generate("/" + robotId + "/amcl_pose").setType(
        "geometry_msgs/PoseWithCovarianceStamped").setThrottleRate(1).setQueueLength(1),
      [ data, stringRep |
        var mapper = new ObjectMapper()
        var rosMsgNode = data.get("msg")
        var current_position = mapper.treeToValue(rosMsgNode, PoseWithCovarianceStamped)
        val tolerance = 0.16
        var deltaX = current_position.pose.pose.position.x − destination.pose.position.x
        var deltaY = current_position.pose.pose.position.y − destination.pose.position.y
        if (deltaX <= tolerance && deltaY <= tolerance) {
          val pubvel = new Publisher("/" + robotId + "/cmd_vel",
            "geometry_msgs/Twist", bridge)
          pubvel.publish(new Twist())
          out("ready")@arm
          out("readyToReceiveTheItem")@self
          bridge.unsubscribe("/" + robotId + "/amcl_pose")
        }
    ])
}
```

Fig. 6. The X-KLAIM MoveToArm process.

In Fig. 6 we show the code of the process MoveToArm, executed in the node DeliveryRobot1. This process is responsible for moving the delivery robot to the arm to get the item deposited on the robot by the arm. The structure of this process is similar to the previous one. Since the arm robot has a fixed position in our scenario, the coordinates x and y are defined as constants. As anticipated above, this process first waits for a tuple deposited by the Rotate process (Fig. 5). Recall that the Rotate process deposits such a tuple at its locality, so the process MoveToArm retrieves a matching tuple at the locality of the node of the arm (passed as a parameter to the process). The process then publishes the destination position on the ROS bridge and waits until the destination is reached by subscribing to a specific topic. As before, we specify a lambda that decides when the destination has been reached. Also in this case, we use the published information as JSON messages. Once the lambda establishes that the delivery robot arrived at the arm robot's desired position, it stops the wheels (by publishing a Twist message). Then, it notifies the arm robot that the delivery robot is ready to receive the item (that is, the arm can drop the item), again, by inserting a tuple at the arm locality. The other tuple inserted in the local tuple space will be retrieved by the DeliverItem

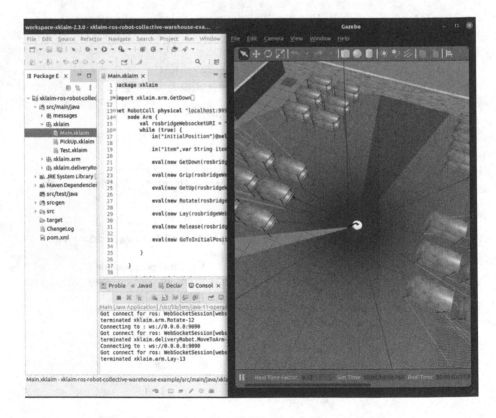

Fig. 7. Execution of an X-KLAIM robotics application.

process, not shown here. As usual, the lambda takes care of unsubscribing from the ROS bridge once done.

The screenshot in Fig. 7 shows our X-KLAIM robotics application in execution. On the left, the Eclipse IDE with our X-KLAIM code is shown (see the logged messages on the Console). On the right, the Gazebo simulator is shown, which visualizes on the center the arm ready to drop the item on top of the delivery robot's white plate.

5 Discussion and Related Work

Over the last years, researchers have attempted to define notations closer to the robotics domain to raise the abstraction level for enabling automated code generation, behavior analysis and property verification (e.g., safety and performance). In this section, we review several high-level languages and frameworks for modeling, designing and verifying ROS-based applications and some languages for coordinating collaborative MRSs. We summarize in Table 1 our considerations and comparison with the languages more strictly related to ours.

High-Level Languages and Frameworks. Many DSLs for component-based modeling of robotic systems are based on UML and target mostly the architectural aspect of robotic applications, e.g., RobotML [24], V³CMM [3], BRICS [9], RoboChart [48], and SafeRobots [53]. Some of them can be used to build ROS-based systems by either supporting a direct translation, e.g., Hyperflex [8], or serving as a base for other platforms. For example, in BRIDE [10], which relies on BRICS, the components are modeled using UML and converted to ROS meta-models to generate runnable ROS C++ code. Additional meta-models (i.e., deployment meta-model and experiment meta-model) for rapid prototyping component-based systems are provided in [43]. UML has also been used to model

Table 1. Features comparison of the related works.

DSL	Formal language	High-level language	Multi-robots	Heterogenous robots	Coordination	Decentralized coordination	Open-endedness	Compiler	IDE	ROS
ART2ool [28]		✓						✓		✓
ATLAS [39]		✓	✓		✓			✓		✓
BRIDE [10]		✓						✓	✓	✓
CommonLang [54]		✓						✓		✓
Drona [23]	✓	✓	✓		✓	✓		✓		✓
FLYAQ [12]		✓	✓							✓
Hyperflex [8]		✓						✓	✓	✓
ISPL [44]	✓	✓	✓		✓	✓		✓		
Koord [34]	✓	✓	✓	✓	✓	✓		✓		✓
PROMISE [32]		✓	✓							✓
RobotChart [48]	✓	✓						✓	✓	
ROSBuzz [55]	✓	✓	✓	✓	✓	✓		✓	✓	✓
RSSM [30]	✓							✓		✓
SCEL [21]	✓	✓	✓	✓	✓	✓	✓	✓		
X-Klaim	✓	✓	✓	✓	✓	✓	✓	✓	✓	✓

and design robotic tasks and missions, e.g., Art2ool [28] supports the development cycle of robotic arm tasks in which atomic tasks are abstracted with UML class diagrams. Textual languages, e.g., CommonLang [54], are another type of language used to model robotic systems. For example, in [2], a DSL based on the Python language is presented that can be used interactively, through the Python command-line interface, to create brand new ROS nodes and to reshape existing ROS nodes by wrapping their communication interfaces.

Some other contributions, to some extent, allow for the verification of ROS-based systems. ROSGen [47] takes a specification of a ROS system architecture as an input and generates a ROS node as an output. Using the theorem prover Coq, the generation process is amenable to formal verification. DeROS [1] permits describing a robot's safety rules (and their related corrective actions) and automatically generating a ROS safety monitoring node by integrating these rules with a run-time monitor. Another framework for run-time verification of ROS-based systems is described in [41], which allows generating C++ code for a monitoring node from user-defined properties specified in terms of event sequences. In [56], robot systems are modeled as a network of timed automata that, after verification in Uppaal, are automatically translated into executable C++ code satisfying the same temporal logic properties as the model. Finally, RSSM [30] permits to model the activities of multi-agent robot systems using Hierarchical Petri Nets and, once deadlock absence has been checked on this model, to generate C++ code for ROS packages automatically.

The approaches mentioned above have not been applied to such complex systems as MRSs, and some of them are not even suitable for such systems. Very few high-level languages for MRSs have been proposed. For example, FLYAQ [12] is a set of DSLs based on UML to specify the civilian missions for unmanned aerial vehicles. This work is extended in [26] for enabling the use of a declarative specification style, but it only supports homogeneous robots. ATLAS [39], which also provides a simulator-based analysis, takes a step further towards coordination of MRSs, but it only supports centralized coordination. PROMISE [32] allows specifying the missions of MRSs using Linear Temporal Logic operators for composing robotic mission patterns. Finally, RMoM [40] allows first using a high-level language for specifying various constraints and properties of ROS-based robot swarms with temporal and timed requirements and then automatically generating distributed monitors for their run-time verification.

Languages for Coordination. Coordination for MRSs has been investigated from several diverse perspectives, and nowadays there is a wide range of techniques that can be used to orchestrate the actions and movements of robots operating in the same environment [25,57]. Designing fully-automated and robust MRSs requires strong coordination of the involved robots for autonomous decision-making and mission continuity in the presence of communication failures [29]. Several studies recommend using indirect communication to cut implementation and design costs usually caused by direct communication. Indirect communication occurs through a shared communication structure that each robot can access in a distributed concurrent fashion. Some languages providing communication and coordination primitives suitable for designing robust MRSs are reviewed in [14]. In ISPL [44], communication is obtained as an indirect result of synchronization of multiple labeled transition systems on a specific action. In SCEL [21], a formal language for the description and verification of collective adaptive systems, communication is related to the concept of knowledge repositories, represented by tuple spaces. In Buzz [51], a language for programming heterogeneous robot swarms, communication is implemented as a distributed key-value store. For this latter language, integration with the standard environment of ROS has also been developed, which is named Rosbuzz [55]. Differently from X-KLAIM, however, Rosbuzz does not provide high-level coordination primitives, robots' distribution is not explicit, and permits less heterogeneity. Drona [23] is a framework for distributed drones where communication is somehow similar to the one used in ISPL. Koord [34] is a language for programming and verifying distributed robotic applications where communication occurs through a distributed shared memory. Differently from X-KLAIM, however, robots distribution is not explicit, and open-endedness is not supported. Finally, in [46] a programming model and a typing discipline for complex multi-robot coordination are presented. The programming model uses choreographies to compositionally specify and statically verify both message-based communications and jointly executed motion between robotics components in the physical space. Well-typed programs, which are terms of a process calculus, are then compiled into programs in the ROS framework.

6   Concluding Remarks and Future Work

In this paper, we have presented an approach for programming robotics applications based on the language X-KLAIM and the ROS framework. We have extended the approach introduced in [5] from single robot scenarios to MRS ones. X-KLAIM has proved expressive enough to smoothly implement MRSs' behaviors, and its integration with Java allowed us to seamlessly use the *java_rosbridge* API directly in the X-KLAIM code to access the publish/subscribe communication infrastructure of ROS.

We believe that the X-KLAIM computation and communication model is particularly suitable for programming MRSs' behavior. On the one hand, X-KLAIM natively supports concurrent programming, which is required by the distributed nature of robots' software. On the other hand, the organization of an X-KLAIM application in terms of a network of nodes interacting via multiple distributed tuple spaces, where communicating processes are decoupled both in space and time, naturally reflects the distributed structure of an MRS. In addition, X-KLAIM tuples permit to model both raw data produced by sensors and aggregated information obtained from such data; this allows programmers to specify the robot's behavior at different levels of granularity. Moreover, the form of communication offered by tuple spaces, supported by X-KLAIM, benefits the scalability of MRSs in terms of the number of components and robots that can be dynamically added. This would also permit to meet the open-endedness requirement (i.e., robots can dynamically enter or leave the system), which is crucial in MRSs.

Our long-term goal is to design a domain-specific language for the robotics domain that, besides being used for automatically generating executable code, is integrated with tools supporting formal verification and analysis techniques. These tools are indeed highly desirable for such complex and often safety-critical systems as autonomous robots [45]. The tools already developed for KLAIM, e.g., type systems [16,17,37,38], behavioral equivalences [18], flow logic [22], and model checking [19,20,27], could be a valuable starting point. A first attempt to define a formal verification approach for the design of MRSs using the KLAIM stochastic extension StoKlaim and the relative stochastic logic MoSL [19] has been presented in [36].

Runtime adaptation is another important capability of MRSs. In [35], we have shown that adaptive behaviors can be smoothly rendered in KLAIM by exploiting tuple-based higher-order communication to exchange code and possibly execute it. We plan to investigate to what extent we can benefit from this mechanism to achieve adaptive behaviors in robotics applications. For example, an X-KLAIM process (a controller or an actuator) could dynamically receive code from other possibly distributed processes containing the logic to continue the execution.

X-KLAIM has several other features that we did not use in this work. We list here the most interesting ones, which could be useful for future work in the field of MRSs. Non-blocking versions of in and read are available: in_nb and read_nb, respectively. These are useful to check the presence of a matching tuple without being blocked indefinitely. Under that respect, X-KLAIM also provides "timed" versions of these operations: as an additional argument, they take a timeout, which specifies how long the process executing such action is willing to wait for a matching tuple. If a matching tuple is not found within the specified timeout these operations return false, and the programmer can adopt counter-measures. In the example of this paper, we used the simplest way of specifying a *flat* and *closed* network in X-KLAIM. However, X-KLAIM also implements the hierarchical version of the KLAIM model as presented in [6], which allows nodes and processes to be dynamically added to existing networks so that modular programming can be achieved and *open-ended* scenarios can be implemented.

It is worth noticing that in this work we exploit both the tuple-based communication model, which X-KLAIM inherits from KLAIM, and the publish/subscribe one, supported by ROS and enabled in X-KLAIM by the *java_rosbridge* library. The former communication model is used to coordinate both the execution of concurrent processes running in a robot and the inter-robot interactions. The latter model, instead, is used to send/receive messages for given topics to/from the ROS framework installed in a single robot. In principle, the former model can be used to express the latter. However, this would require introducing inter-mediary processes that consume tuples and publish their data on the related topics and, vice-versa, generate a tuple each time an event for a subscribed topic is received. This would introduce significant overhead in the communication with the ROS framework, especially for what concerns the handling of the subscriptions (as topics related to sensors usually produce message streams). Nevertheless, we plan to investigate the definition of a programming framework to make transparent the use of the publish/subscribe mechanism as mentioned above, overcoming the performance issue by elevating the level of abstraction. The idea is not only to replace topics with tuples, but to provide ready-to-use processes acting as building blocks for creating robotics applications. The API for interacting with these processes will be tuples with given structures. These processes will hide the interactions with the ROS framework to the programmer, and produce tuples only when events relevant to the coordination of the MRS behavior occur (e.g., a robot reached a given position or a requested movement has been completed).

Finally, in this work we have used the version 1 of ROS as a reference middleware for the proposed approach, because currently this seems to be most adopted in practice. We plan anyway to investigate the possibility of extending our approach to the version 2 of ROS, which features a more sophisticated publish/subscribe system based on the OMG DDS standard.

Acknowledgements. We thank the anonymous reviewers for their useful comments.

References

1. Adam, S., Larsen, M., Jensen, K., Schultz, U.P.: Rule-based dynamic safety monitoring for mobile robots. J. Softw. Eng. Rob. **7**(1), 121–141 (2016)
2. Adam, S., Schultz, U.P.: Towards interactive, incremental programming of ROS nodes. In: Workshop on Domain-Specific Languages and models for Robotic systems (2014)
3. Alonso, D., et al.: V³CMM: a 3-view component meta-model for model-driven robotic software development. J. Softw. Eng. Rob. **1**, 3–17 (2010)
4. Bettini, L., De Nicola, R., Pugliese, R.: Klava: a Java package for distributed and mobile applications. Softw. Pract. Exp. **32**(14), 1365–1394 (2002)
5. Bettini, L., Bourr, K., Pugliese, R., Tiezzi, F.: Writing robotics applications with X-KLAIM. In: Margaria, T., Steffen, B. (eds.) ISoLA 2020. LNCS, vol. 12477, pp. 361–379. Springer, Cham (2020). https://doi.org/10.1007/978-3-030-61470-6_22
6. Bettini, L., Loreti, M., Pugliese, R.: An infrastructure language for open nets. In: SAC, pp. 373–377. ACM (2002)
7. Bettini, L., Merelli, E., Tiezzi, F.: X-KLAIM is back. In: Boreale, M., Corradini, F., Loreti, M., Pugliese, R. (eds.) Models, Languages, and Tools for Concurrent and Distributed Programming. LNCS, vol. 11665, pp. 115–135. Springer, Cham (2019). https://doi.org/10.1007/978-3-030-21485-2_8
8. Brugali, D., Gherardi, L.: HyperFlex: a model driven toolchain for designing and configuring software control systems for autonomous robots. In: Koubaa, A. (ed.) Robot Operating System (ROS). SCI, vol. 625, pp. 509–534. Springer, Cham (2016). https://doi.org/10.1007/978-3-319-26054-9_20
9. Bruyninckx, H., et al.: The BRICS component model: a model-based development paradigm for complex robotics software systems. In: SAC, pp. 1758–1764. ACM (2013)

10. Bubeck, A., et al.: BRIDE - a toolchain for framework-independent development of industrial service robot applications. In: ISR, pp. 137–142. VDE (2014)
11. Casalaro, G.L.: Model-driven engineering for mobile robotic systems: a systematic mapping study. Softw. Syst. Model. (2021). https://doi.org/10.1007/s10270-021-00908-8
12. Ciccozzi, F., et al.: Adopting MDE for specifying and executing civilian missions of mobile multi-robot systems. IEEE Access **4**, 6451–6466 (2016)
13. de Araújo Silva, E., Valentin, E., Carvalho, J.R.H., da Silva Barreto, R.: A survey of model driven engineering in robotics. Comput. Lang. **62**, 101021 (2021)
14. De Nicola, R., Di Stefano, L., Inverso, O.: Toward formal models and languages for verifiable multi-robot systems. Front. Rob. AI **5**, 94 (2018)
15. De Nicola, R., Ferrari, G.L., Pugliese, R.: KLAIM: a kernel language for agents interaction and mobility. IEEE Trans. Softw. Eng. **24**(5), 315–330 (1998)
16. De Nicola, R., Ferrari, G.L., Pugliese, R., Venneri, B.: Types for access control. Theor. Comput. Sci. **240**(1), 215–254 (2000)
17. De Nicola, R., Gorla, D., Pugliese, R.: Confining data and processes in global computing applications. Sci. Comput. Program. **63**(1), 57–87 (2006)
18. De Nicola, R., Gorla, D., Pugliese, R.: Basic observables for a calculus for global computing. Inf. Comput. **205**(10), 1491–1525 (2007)
19. De Nicola, R., Katoen, J., Latella, D., Loreti, M., Massink, M.: Model checking mobile stochastic logic. Theor. Comput. Sci. **382**(1), 42–70 (2007)
20. De Nicola, R., Loreti, M.: A modal logic for mobile agents. ACM Trans. Comput. Log. **5**(1), 79–128 (2004)
21. De Nicola, R., Loreti, M., Pugliese, R., Tiezzi, F.: A formal approach to autonomic systems programming: the SCEL language. ACM Trans. Auton. Adapt. Syst. **9**(2), 1–29 (2014)
22. De Nicola, R., et al.: From flow logic to static type systems for coordination languages. Sci. Comput. Program. **75**(6), 376–397 (2010)
23. Desai, A., Saha, I., Yang, J., Qadeer, S., Seshia, S.A.: Drona: a framework for safe distributed mobile robotics. In: 8th Internnational Conference on Cyber-Physical Systems, pp. 239–248 (2017)
24. Dhouib, S., Kchir, S., Stinckwich, S., Ziadi, T., Ziane, M.: RobotML, a domain-specific language to design, simulate and deploy robotic applications. In: Noda, I., Ando, N., Brugali, D., Kuffner, J.J. (eds.) SIMPAR 2012. LNCS (LNAI), vol. 7628, pp. 149–160. Springer, Heidelberg (2012). https://doi.org/10.1007/978-3-642-34327-8_16
25. Doriya, R., Mishra, S., Gupta, S.: A brief survey and analysis of multi-robot communication and coordination. In: International Conference on Computing, Communication, Automation, pp. 1014–1021 (2015)
26. Dragule, S., Meyers, B., Pelliccione, P.: A generated property specification language for resilient multirobot missions. In: Romanovsky, A., Troubitsyna, E.A. (eds.) SERENE 2017. LNCS, vol. 10479, pp. 45–61. Springer, Cham (2017). https://doi.org/10.1007/978-3-319-65948-0_4
27. Eckhardt, J., Mühlbauer, T., Meseguer, J., Wirsing, M.: Semantics, distributed implementation, and formal analysis of KLAIM models in Maude. Sci. Comput. Program. **99**, 24–74 (2015)
28. Estévez, E., et al.: ART2ool: a model-driven framework to generate target code for robot handling tasks. Adv. Manuf. Technol. **97**(1–4), 1195–1207 (2018)
29. Farinelli, A., Iocchi, L., Nardi, D.: Multirobot systems: a classification focused on coordination. IEEE Trans. Syst. Man Cybern. Part B (Cybern.) **34**(5), 2015–2028 (2004)

30. Figat, M., Zieliński, C.: Robotic system specification methodology based on hierarchical Petri nets. IEEE Access **8**, 71617–71627 (2020)
31. Frigerio, M., Buchli, J., Caldwell, D.G.: A domain specific language for kinematic models and fast implementations of robot dynamics algorithms. In: Proceedings of DSLRob 2011. CoRR, vol. abs/1301.7190 (2013)
32. García, S., et al.: High-level mission specification for multiple robots. In: 12th ACM SIGPLAN International Conference on Software Language Engineering, p. 127–140 (2019)
33. Gelernter, D.: Generative communication in linda. ACM Trans. Program. Lang. Syst. **7**(1), 80–112 (1985)
34. Ghosh, R., et al.: Koord: a language for programming and verifying distributed robotics application. Proc. ACM Program. Lang. **4**(OOPSLA), 1–30 (2020)
35. Gjondrekaj, E., Loreti, M., Pugliese, R., Tiezzi, F.: Modeling adaptation with a tuple-based coordination language. In: SAC 2012, pp. 1522–1527. ACM (2012)
36. Gjondrekaj, E., et al.: Towards a formal verification methodology for collective robotic systems. In: Aoki, T., Taguchi, K. (eds.) ICFEM 2012. LNCS, vol. 7635, pp. 54–70. Springer, Heidelberg (2012). https://doi.org/10.1007/978-3-642-34281-3_7
37. Gorla, D., Pugliese, R.: Enforcing security policies via types. In: Hutter, D., Müller, G., Stephan, W., Ullmann, M. (eds.) Security in Pervasive Computing. LNCS, vol. 2802, pp. 86–100. Springer, Heidelberg (2004). https://doi.org/10.1007/978-3-540-39881-3_10
38. Gorla, D., Pugliese, R.: Resource access and mobility control with dynamic privileges acquisition. In: Baeten, J.C.M., Lenstra, J.K., Parrow, J., Woeginger, G.J. (eds.) ICALP 2003. LNCS, vol. 2719, pp. 119–132. Springer, Heidelberg (2003). https://doi.org/10.1007/3-540-45061-0_11
39. Harbin, J., et al.: Model-driven simulation-based analysis for multi-robot systems. In: 24th International Conference on Model Driven Engineering Languages and Systems (MODELS) (2021)
40. Hu, C., Dong, W., Yang, Y., Shi, H., Zhou, G.: Runtime verification on hierarchical properties of ROS-based robot swarms. IEEE Trans. Reliabil. **69**(2), 674–689 (2019)
41. Huang, J., Erdogan, C., Zhang, Y., Moore, B., Luo, Q., Sundaresan, A., Rosu, G.: ROSRV: runtime verification for robots. In: Bonakdarpour, B., Smolka, S.A. (eds.) RV 2014. LNCS, vol. 8734, pp. 247–254. Springer, Cham (2014). https://doi.org/10.1007/978-3-319-11164-3_20
42. Koenig, N.P., Howard, A.: Design and use paradigms for Gazebo, an open-source multi-robot simulator. In: IROS, pp. 2149–2154. IEEE (2004)
43. Kumar, P., et al.: Rosmod: a toolsuite for modeling, generating, deploying, and managing distributed real-time component-based software using ros. In: International Symposium on Rapid System Prototyping (RSP) (2015)
44. Lomuscio, A., Qu, H., Raimondi, F.: Mcmas: an open-source model checker for the verification of multi-agent systems. Softw. Tools Technol. Transfer **19**(1), 9–30 (2017)
45. Luckcuck, M., Farrell, M., Dennis, L.A., Dixon, C., Fisher, M.: Formal specification and verification of autonomous robotic systems. ACM Comput. Surv. **52**, 1–41 (2020)
46. Majumdar, R., Yoshida, N., Zufferey, D.: Multiparty motion coordination: from choreographies to robotics programs. Proc. ACM Program. Lang. **4**(OOPSLA), 134:1–134:30 (2020)

47. Meng, W., Park, J., Sokolsky, O., Weirich, S., Lee, I.: Verified ROS-based deployment of platform-independent control systems. In: Havelund, K., Holzmann, G., Joshi, R. (eds.) NFM 2015. LNCS, vol. 9058, pp. 248–262. Springer, Cham (2015). https://doi.org/10.1007/978-3-319-17524-9_18
48. Miyazawa, A., et al.: RoboChart: modelling and verification of the functional behaviour of robotic applications. Softw. Syst. Model. **18**(5), 3097–3149 (2019)
49. Nordmann, A., Hochgeschwender, N., Wigand, D., Wrede, S.: A survey on domain-specific modeling and languages in robotics. Softw. Eng. Rob. **7**, 75–99 (2016)
50. Nordmann, A., Hochgeschwender, N., Wrede, S.: A survey on domain-specific languages in robotics. In: Brugali, D., Broenink, J.F., Kroeger, T., MacDonald, B.A. (eds.) SIMPAR 2014. LNCS (LNAI), vol. 8810, pp. 195–206. Springer, Cham (2014). https://doi.org/10.1007/978-3-319-11900-7_17
51. Pinciroli, C., Lee-Brown, A., Beltrame, G.: A tuple space for data sharing in robot swarms. EAI Endorsed Trans. Collab. Comput. **2**(9), e2 (2016)
52. Quigley, M., et al.: Ros: an open-source robot operating system. In: ICRA Workshop on Open Source Software (2009)
53. Ramaswamy, A., Monsuez, B., Tapus, A.: SafeRobots: a model-driven approach for designing robotic software architectures. In: Proceedings of CTS, pp. 131–134. IEEE (2014)
54. Rutle, A., Backer, J., Foldøy, K., Bye, R.T.: CommonLang: a DSL for defining robot tasks. In: Proceedings of MODELS18 Workshops. CEUR Workshop Proceedings, vol. 2245, pp. 433–442 (2018)
55. St-Onge, D., Varadharajan, V.S., Li, G., Svogor, I., Beltrame, G.: ROS and Buzz: consensus-based behaviors for heterogeneous teams. CoRR abs/1710.08843 (2017)
56. Wang, R.: A formal model-based design method for robotic systems. IEEE Syst. J. **13**(1), 1096–1107 (2018)
57. Yan, Z., Jouandeau, N., Ali, A.: A survey and analysis of multi-robot coordination. Int. J. Adv. Rob. Syst. **10**, 1 (2013)

Bringing Aggregate Programming
Towards the Cloud

Giorgio Audrito🆔, Ferruccio Damiani(✉)🆔, and Gianluca Torta🆔

Dipartimento di Informatica, Università di Torino, Turin, Italy
{giorgio.audrito,ferruccio.damiani,gianluca.torta}@unito.it

Abstract. Aggregate Programming (AP) is a paradigm for developing applications that execute on a fully distributed network of communicating, resource-constrained, spatially-situated nodes (e.g., drones, wireless sensors, etc.). In this paper, we address running an AP application on a high-performance, centralized computer such as the ones available in a cloud environment. As a proof of concept, we present preliminary results on the computation of graph statistics for centralised data sets, by extending FCPP, a C++ library implementing AP. This: *(i)* opens the way to the application of the AP paradigm to problems on large centralised graph-based data structures, enabling massive parallelisation across multiple machines, dynamically joining and leaving the computation; and *(ii)* represents a first step towards developing collective adaptive systems where computations dynamically move across the IoT/edge/fog/cloud continuum, based on mutable conditions such as availability of resources and network infrastructures.

Keywords: Distributed computing · Collective adaptive systems · Cloud computing · Graph algorithms

1 Introduction

In recent years, Aggregate Programming (AP) [14] has attracted significant attention as an innovative approach for the development of fully distributed systems [32]. The typical applications for which AP is particularly suited involve resource-constrained, spatially-situated nodes that coordinate through point-to-point, proximity-based communications. For example, AP has been adopted in simulations of domains such as swarm-based exploration [21], crowd safety management and monitoring [7,8,11], data collection from sensor networks [4], dynamic multi-agent plan repair [5,6].

The main implementations of AP can be understood as being combinations of two components: the first component provides full support for the constructs of the foundational language of AP, namely the Field Calculus (FC) [12]; the second component connects the FC program with the environment where the distributed system is deployed and executed. In particular, FC is currently supported by the following open-source implementations: the *FCPP* [3,10] library,

T. Margaria and B. Steffen (Eds.): ISoLA 2022, LNCS 13703, pp. 301–317, 2022.
https://doi.org/10.1007/978-3-031-19759-8_19

as a C++ internal Domain-Specific Language (DSL); *ScaFi (Scala Fields)* [20], as a Scala internal DSL; and *Protelis* [29], as a Java external DSL. The main execution environment provided by existing implementations consists of simulations that run on a single computer, simulating sets of nodes situated in a 2D or 3D space, their dynamics, and the point-to-point communications between neighbouring nodes. The *FCPP* library has an internal simulator, while *ScaFi* and *Protelis* exploit the Alchemist simulator [28]. Recently, the *FCPP* library has been adapted to deployment on physical Micro Controller Unit (MCU)-based boards in a simplified Industrial Internet of Things (IIoT) scenario [31], targeting Contiki on DecaWave boards. A further porting to Miosix [2] on WandStem boards is also currently in progress.

In this paper we start exploring a new direction for the application of AP, namely, the implementation and execution of distributed algorithms on high-performance, centralized computers such as the ones typically available in a cloud environment. Instead of a single CPU-based system, that can run multiple threads sharing the same memory, it can be interesting to consider clusters of such systems, communicating through high-speed links for sharing data. While we will discuss this possibility, the main purpose of the present work will be handling the execution on a single CPU, as a first preliminary step.

In particular, as a proof of concept, we will describe an extension of the *FCPP* library that allows it to ingest a centralized, large-scale graph structure, and compute some network statistics of its input graph. Preliminary results of experiments with the extended library will be presented. The ability of executing algorithms on large static graphs is per-se an important application [13], that could be further boosted by distribution over several CPU-based systems. Note that this contribution is different from the one described in [9], where AP was adopted to compute centrality statistics of *dynamic* networks, whose structure was induced by (simulated) spatial-based connectivity, using Alchemist and Protelis. In this paper, instead, we compute similar statistics for a *general static* graph (provided as a single file on disk) which does not arise from any spatial arrangement: in fact, as sample input data, we will use a (restricted) web graph.

In the long run, the possibility of a centralized (or locally distributed) execution of FC programs on graphs may allow the implementation of collective adaptive systems that exploit the IoT/edge/fog/cloud continuum. In fact, the same AP paradigm could be exploited for programming the far edge, constrained devices as well as the intermediate and most powerful nodes in the architecture, and this would simplify the dynamic migration of computations between different layers based on mutable conditions such as availability of resources and network infrastructures. In this paper, we devise a roadmap towards this aim, identifying the current paper's contribution as a first preliminary step.

The remainder of this paper is structured as follows. Section 2 presents the necessary background on aggregate programming, FCPP and the graph statistic application. Section 3 delineates a roadmap towards a IoT/edge/fog/-cloud continuum through AP. Section 4 presents the implementation of the first step, allowing graph-based data processing in FCPP. Section 5 experimentally evaluates the approach on graph statistic computation, and Sect. 6 concludes with final comments and remarks.

2 Background

2.1 Aggregate Programming and the FCPP DSL

AP [14,32] is an approach for programming networks of devices by abstracting away from individual devices behaviour and focusing on the global, aggregate behaviour of the collection of all devices. It assumes only local communication between neighbour devices, and it is robust with respect to devices joining/leaving the network, or failing; thus supporting an *open dynamic topology*. Beside communicating with neighbours, the devices are capable to perform computations. In particular, every device performs periodically the same sequence of operations, with an usually steady rate, asynchronously from other devices:

1. retrieval of received messages,
2. computation of the program;
3. transmission of resulting messages.

In case devices are equipped with sensors/actuators, they may use sensor data and provide instructions to actuators during the program execution. In AP, we assume that all device execute the *same* program. Note that this assumption does not restrict the realisable behaviour, as every device may follow different branches of the same program, resulting in a radically different behaviour.

AP is formally backed by FC [12], a small functional language for expressing aggregate programs. Few concrete implementations of FC exist to date: Proto, Protelis [29], Scafi [20], FCPP [3]. In this paper, we will focus on the latter and most recent, which is structured as a C++ internal DSL (i.e., library). The syntax of aggregate functions in FCPP is given in Fig. 1. It should be noted that, since FCPP is a C++ library providing an internal DSL, *an FCPP program is a C++ program* (so all the features of C++ are available). For compactness of presentation, we restrict here to a subset of the language with sufficient expressiveness for later examples. In the formal syntax, we use * to indicate an element that may be repeated multiple times (possibly zero).

An *aggregate function declaration* consists of keyword FUN, followed by the return type t and the function name d, followed by a parenthesized sequence of comma-separated arguments t x (prepended by the keyword ARGS), followed by *aggregate instructions* i (within brackets and after keyword CODE), followed by the *export description*, which lists the types that are used by the function in message-exchanging constructs.

Aggregate instructions always end with a *return* statement, reporting the function result. Before it, there may be a number of local variable declarations (assigning the result of an expression e to a variable x of type t), and for loops, which repeat an instruction i while increasing an integer index x until a condition e is met. The main types of *aggregate expressions* are:

| aggregate function declaration |
| F ::= FUN t d(ARGS, t x∗) {CODE i} FUN_EXPORT d_t = export_type<t ∗ >; |
| aggregate instructions |
| i ::= return e; \| t x = e; i \| for(LOOP(x, ℓ); e; ++x){i} i |
| aggregate expression |
| e ::= x \| ℓ \| t(e∗) \| ue \| e o e \| p(e∗) \| node.c(e∗) \| f(CALL, e∗) \| [&](t x∗)->t{i} \| e ? e : e |

type	aggregate function
t ::= T | bt | tt<t∗, ℓ ∗ >	f ::= b | d

| built-in aggregate functions |
| b ::= old \| nbr \| oldnbr \| spawn \| self \| mod_self \| map_hood \| fold_hood \| mux |

Fig. 1. Syntax of FCPP aggregate functions.

- a *variable* identifier x, or a C++ *literal value* ℓ (e.g. an integer or floating-point number);
- an *unary operator* u (e.g. $-$, $\sim$, !, etc.) applied to e, or a *binary operator* e o e (e.g. +, ∗, etc.);
- a *pure function call* p(e∗), where p is a basic C++ function which does not depend on node information nor message exchanges;
- an *aggregate function call* f(CALL, e∗), where f can be either a defined aggregate function name d or an aggregate built-in function b (see below);
- a *conditional branching* expression e_{guard} ? $e_\top$: $e_\perp$, such that $e_\top$ is evaluated and returned if e_{guard} evaluates to true, while $e_\perp$ is evaluated and returned if e_{guard} evaluates to false.

Finally, several aggregate built-in functions are provided, which allow implicit message exchange and state preservation across rounds. In this paper, we will mention the following ones:

- old(CALL,i,v), which returns the value passed for v to the function in the previous round, defaulting to i on the first call of this function;
- nbr(CALL,i,v), which returns the *field* (i.e., collection of) values passed for v to the function in the previous rounds of neighbour devices (including the current device, defaulting to i for it on the first call of this function);
- self(CALL, v) given a field v returns the value in v for the current device;
- fold_hood(CALL, f, v, i) given a field v and a function f, reduces the field to a single value by starting from i and repeatedly applying function f to each element of the collection and to the current partial result.

It is worth observing that the FCPP syntax uses a number of macros (e.g., CALL, CODE, etc.). These macros ensure that the aggregate context (i.e., the node object) is carried over throughout the program, also updating an internal representation of the stack trace for *alignment*. Thanks to alignment, the messages (implicitly) originating from a old or nbr construct are matched in future rounds

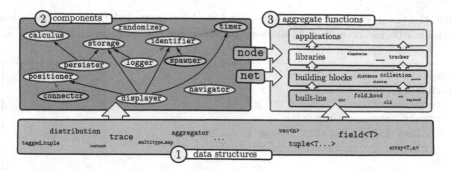

Fig. 2. The three main layers of the software architecture of FCPP: *data structures* for both other layers, and *components* which provide node and network abstractions to *aggregate functions.* Components that have been modified in this work are highlighted in magenta. Dependencies between components can be either *hard* (solid), for which the pointed component is always required as an ancestor of the other; or *soft* (dotted), for which the pointed component is required only in some settings.

(on the same or different devices) only to the *same* construct, that is, a construct called in the same position in the program syntax and in the stack trace. This mechanism allows to freely compose functions, and use recursion, without risking interferences of messages between different parts of the program.

2.2 FCPP Library Architecture

FCPP is based on an extensible software architecture, at the core of which are *components*, that define abstractions for single devices (*node*) and overall network orchestration (*net*), the latter one being crucial in simulations and cloud-oriented applications. In an FCPP application, the two types *node* and *net* are obtained by combining a chosen sequence of components, providing the needed functionalities in a mixin-like fashion.

The FCPP library architecture is divided in three main conceptual layers represented in Fig. 2: (*i*) C++ data structures of general use; (*ii*) components; (*iii*) aggregate functions. The first layer comprises data structures needed by the second layer either for their internal implementation or for the external specification of their options, but also data structures designed for the third layer. Some components are sufficiently general purpose to be used across different domains, including simulations and deployments (calculus, randomizer, storage and timer). Others may be useful only in certain domains (displayer, navigator, persister and spawner), or come with *variations* for different domains, sharing a common interface (connector, identifier, logger and positioner). For example, for simulations the *connector* component is given as a `simulated_connector`, which exchanges messages as pointers between objects in memory, determining if connection is possible based on simulated positions. For deployments, a `hardware_connector` is given, which instead exchanges physical messages through some provided networking interface. In order to handle processing of graph-based data, the timer and spawner components have been extended and a new variation of the connector component has been provided (cf. Sect. 4).

The basic structure of each component is as follows:

```
template <class... Ts>
struct my_functionality {
  template <class F, class P>
  struct component : public P {
    class node : public P::node { ... };
    class net : public P::net { ... };
  };
};
```

Thus, each component is a templated class with a variable number of type arguments, which are used to provide compile-time options to be used by the components to tune their behaviour. This options are empty templated types, wrapping the data of interest, such as `parallel<true>` to enable parallelism, or `connector<fixed<100>>` to specify that devices are to be connected within a fixed radius of 100 units. The outer class has a `component` template subclass with two type parameters: P, which represents the parent component composition, and F, the final outcome of the whole component composition, which is retrieved by the C++ template system thanks to the *Curiously Recursive Template Pattern* (CRTP, first introduced in [19]). Both the `node` and `net` classes are defined inside the component subclass to inherit from the corresponding classes in the parent composition P. The final outcome of the composition F may be used by those classes to mimic virtual-style calls that are resolved at compile-time.

The scenario originally supported by the first versions of FCPP is the simulation of distributed systems. Compared to the alternative implementations of FC (Protelis [29] and Scafi [33] with their simulator Alchemist [28]), it features additional simulation capabilities (3D environments, basic physics, probabilistic wireless connection models, fine-grained parallelism), while granting a significant reduction of the simulation cost in CPU time and memory usage, which comes with a corresponding speed-up of the development and test of new distributed algorithms.

2.3   Graph Statistics

Several techniques for collecting statistics from graph-based data have been investigated in the data mining community. In this section, we recall the statistics measuring centralities of the nodes of the graph considered in [9]. These are quite common and can be naturally implemented in FC. We will use them as a benchmark for the application of AP on graph algorithms.

Degree centrality is the historically first and conceptually simplest centrality measure. It is defined as the number of links incident upon a node (i.e. its degree): nodes with an higher number of links should be less prone to encounter network disconnections, so electing these nodes as communication hubs should be more effective than electing nodes with a lower degree. Degree centrality is simple and efficient to calculate. However, compared with other centrality measures, degree centrality is usually the least effective. In fact, in approximately homogeneous situated networks – where nodes at the edge of the network have lower degrees and all other nodes have similar degrees – selecting the node with the highest degree would correspond to select a random node which is not at the network edge.

PageRank [26] is an instance of the broader class of *eigenvector centrality measures*. This centrality measure has been first introduced for the Google search engine and it is quite popular in the data mining community. According to PageRank, the centrality score r_i of a node i is defined as the fixed point of the system of equations:

$$r_i = (1 - \alpha) + \alpha \sum_{j \in \text{neigh}(i)} \frac{r_j}{\deg(j)}$$

where α is a parameter (usually set at 0.85 [18]), $\deg(j)$ is the degree of node j and neigh(i) is the set of neighbour nodes j connected to i. PageRank has been proved effective on logical graphs as the web graph. It can be efficiently calculated by re-iterating the equations above for each node, starting from $r_i^0 = 1$.

Closeness Centrality and Harmonic Centrality are the most effective centrality measures that we consider [16]. They are both derivable from (variations of) the *neighbourhood function* of a graph, which is defined as follows.

Definition 1 (Neighbourhood Function). *Let $G = \langle V, E \rangle$ be a graph with n vertices and m edges. The generalized individual neighbourhood function $N_G(v, h, C)$, given $v \in V$, $h \geq 0$ and $C \subseteq V$, counts the number of vertices $u \in C$ which lie within distance h from v. In formulas, $N_G(v, h, C) = |\{u \in C : \text{dist}(v, u) \leq h\}|$.*

Many different questions – like graph similarity, vertex ranking, robustness monitoring, and network classification – can been answered by exploiting elaborations of the N_G values [16,27]. Unfortunately, exact computation of N_G is impractical: it requires $O(nm)$ time in linear memory and $O(n^{2.38})$ time in quadratic memory.

Fast algorithms approximating N_G up to a desired precision have been developed. In particular Vigna et al. [16] improved the original algorithm by: (i) exploiting *HyperLogLog counters* (a more effective class of estimators) [23]; (ii) expressing the "counter unions" through a minimal number of broadword operations; and (iii) engineering refined parallelisation strategies. HyperLogLog counters maintain size estimates with asymptotic relative standard deviation $\sigma/\mu \leq 1.06/\sqrt{k}$, where k is a parameter, in $(1 + o(1)) \cdot k \cdot \log \log(n/k)$ bits of space. Moreover, updates are carried out through k independent "max" operations on $\log \log(n/k)$-sized words. As a result, given a fixed precision, N_G can be computed in $O(nh)$ time and $O(n \log \log n)$ memory. This enables to apply it on very large graphs like, e.g., the Facebook graph [13].

We are now ready to present closeness centrality and harmonic centrality.

Closeness centrality of a node i, denoted by c_i, is defined as the reciprocal of the total distance to other nodes. It can be computed in terms of the neighbourhood function by the following equation:

$$\frac{1}{c_i} = \sum_{j \neq i} \text{dist}(i, j) = \sum_{h=1}^{D} h \left(N_G(i, h, V) - N_G(i, h-1, V) \right)$$

where D is the graph diameter (maximum distance between nodes in G).

Harmonic centrality of a node i, denoted by h_i, is defined as the sum of the reciprocals of distances to other nodes. It can be computed in terms of the neighbourhood function by the following equation:

$$h_i = \sum_{j \neq i} \frac{1}{\text{dist}(i, j)} = \sum_{h=1}^{D} \frac{N_G(i, h, V) - N_G(i, h-1, V)}{h}$$

where D is the graph diameter (maximum distance between nodes in G).

Nodes with high closeness/harmonic centrality are connected to many other vertices through a small number of hops. So, they are best-suited to be elected as leaders for coordination mechanisms.

3   Roadmap

In this section, we describe a roadmap to make the AP paradigm applicable beyond the level of a network of constrained devices. The first step has already been taken, and will be described in more detail in the rest of this paper. The other three steps, up to a hybrid deployment where computations can be dynamically moved between the devices (far edge) and a central infrastructure (cloud), will require further research and development efforts. However, we can at least sketch some concrete lines of work that shall be followed for their realization.

Step 1: Data Processing Support. In order to exploit cloud-based resources and integrate the AP paradigm with them, it is first of all necessary to provide a centralized, abstract view of the network in terms of a graph of nodes and their connections, allowing AP to centrally process this graph-based data. In this context, the notion of neighbourhood, which is fundamental for AP, can be derived from the graph structure, instead of being implicitly determined by the physical vicinity of devices. Note that AP simulators such as Alchemist and the simulator embedded in FCPP also have the necessity to represent the network of devices in a centralized structure. However, they assume that *(i)* the nodes are deployed in a 2D or 3D euclidean space; that *(ii)* possible connections are computed from the physical positions; that *(iii)* round scheduling is constrained by energy saving needs; and that *(ii)* the simulator can take full control of the nodes (position, velocity, etc.).

In a centralized AP computation, however, some or all of that assumptions may fail. Nodes may not be deployed in a physical space, or their position may be inaccessible due to lack of dedicated sensors. Connections between nodes should not be computed by the central application, but instead either read from a configuration file or induced by mirroring a physical deployment. Round scheduling should not be connected with energy saving needs, but instead tuned to get the best performance out of the available cloud resources. Finally, the amount of node control available in the central application may be limited.

In order to achieve this goals, we extended FCPP to be able to read and process locally available graph-based data, while allowing the schedule of rounds to be determined reactively in order to maximise performance. More details on this initial step and its implementation in FCPP are given in Sects. 4 and 5.

Step 2: Multi-CPU Distribution. The centralized AP computations can of course benefit of multi-core architectures by associating the nodes of the graph (and thus their computations) to multiple threads. This is already possible in the current implementation, and was relatively easy to implement by simply protecting with locks the (short) critical sections where nodes exchange messages with neighbours.

However, high-performance centralized infrastructures are often based on NUMA (Non-Uniform Memory Access) architectures, where multiple CPUs have (preferred) access to local memories. In such scenarios, the shared-memory model needed by multi-thread applications is not applicable, and a message-passing model must be adopted to connect computations carried by different CPUs. A promising approach consists in the adoption of MPI (Message-Passing Interface), the de-facto standard for message-passing on high-performance parallel architectures, which defines the syntax and semantics of a rich set of library routines. Several open-source implementations of MPI are available, in particular for the C++ language used by the FCPP implementation of the AP paradigm.

The main challenges we envision for integrating MPI with FCPP are: the automatic partition of the set of graph nodes on different CPUs so as to reduce as much as possible the cost of message-passing between different memories (we shall evaluate the applicability of graph partitioning algorithms such as [25]); and a software architecture that makes as transparent as possible the difference between shared memory communications (that should continue to be exploited by nodes assigned to the same CPU) and message-passing communications.

Step 3: Dynamic Multi-CPU Distribution. Up to now, we have assumed that the graph representing the AP network is static, but in general this is not the case: nodes and their connections can be added and removed dynamically, to reflect changes in the structure of the underlying distributed computation. In fact, dynamism in graph structure is already supported by the single-CPU implementation, as links can be inserted or removed through dedicated methods, as will be discussed in Sect. 4.

In multi-CPU scenarios, it is therefore of great importance to implement online mechanisms in charge of deciding if and which nodes should migrate from one CPU to another, in order to accommodate the changes in graph structure, while keeping the load balanced among CPUs for better performance. In order to implement this point, we predict that mainly two ingredients would be needed: a node migration mechanism, together with heuristic strategies guiding it.

Step 4: Hybrid and Mirror Systems. Until this point, the centralised AP-based system we proposed is described as fully logic, directly operating on graph-based data somehow available on the cloud. This data may have a purely logical origin as well, being for instance collected by a web crawler. However, it would also be crucial to consider data obtained by mirroring a physical network of IoT devices. In particular, we envision scenarios where virtual devices associated with physical IoT devices [22,30] perform their computations directly on the cloud, possibly inter-operating with physical IoT devices directly running the same AP system without mirroring.

For instance, a group of physical devices deployed at location *L1* may directly execute a FC program by communicating point to point with one another, while indirectly interacting with physical devices deployed at another location *L2*. Those may delegate their executions of the FC program to the cloud, since too many rounds of computation and communication would be needed to reach convergence of their results, which is too resource demanding to be handled locally. Further virtual nodes may also be present in the mirrored network in the cloud, that are derived fully logically without any physical mirror device, to perform further heavy assistive tasks (e.g. federated learning computations [24]).

In order to allow the integration of such a system within FCPP, given the infrastructure available from the previous steps, it would be necessary to add a component ensuring proper mirroring of a virtual device in the cloud with a physical IoT device. That may also require some routing mechanism in place, in case the IoT device to be mirrored does not have direct internet connection. After such a connection can be established, mirroring may be ensured by an external daemon process synchronizing the graph-based data on the cloud used by the centralised AP system with the data obtained from sensors on the mirror IoT device (possibly including messages listened from its neighbourhood), with a given frequency depending on energy requirements.

Step 5: Dynamic Hybrid Systems. Similarly to the dynamic distribution of nodes to different CPUs, it may be useful to enhance hybrid edge-cloud AP systems with the possibility of dynamically migrating some computations from the edge to the cloud and vice-versa, depending on the weight of the required computation, as well as on the current availability of resources. Given that the previous steps are all met, this could be implemented by proper heuristics guiding a migration mechanism, as for step 3.

4   A First Step: Extending FCPP to work with Graphs

In this section, we outline the extensions made to the FCPP library in order to allow FC programs to process centralized graphs. This new feature effectively constitutes a first step towards the goal of a self-organising edge-cloud application, as outlined in Sect. 3. Overall, these extensions will culminate into the definition of two new *component compositions*.

As mentioned in Sect. 2.2, an FCPP application is first specified through such a composition of components from the hierarchy shown in Fig. 2, which are then customised further with suitable parameters. For example, FCPP defines a batch simulation application as:

```
DECLARE_COMBINE(batch_simulator,
    simulated_connector, navigator, simulated_positioner, timer,
    logger, storage, spawner, identifier, randomizer, calculus);
```

exploiting the `DECLARE_COMBINE` macro to combine into the `batch_simulator` type all the components listed as the remaining parameters. The order of the specified components induces their parent relations, and must comply with compile-time restrictions enforced by the components themselves (depicted in Fig. 2). For example, in the `batch_simulator` combination, the `spawner` component has `identifier` as direct parent, and `randomizer` and `calculus` as further ancestors.

The new compositions we introduced are called `batch_data_processor` and `interactive_data_processor`, which differ from the existing `batch_simulator` in:

1. While the nodes of a simulation are situated in a 3D space, and thus have 3D position, velocity and acceleration vectors, the nodes of a graph do not have such attributes. This can be simply accommodated by omitting the `simulated_positioner` and `navigator` components from the mix.
2. In simulation, rounds are scheduled according to a programmatic policy. In data processing, we need rounds to be *reactively* scheduled when neighbours' values are updated. Since this feature may be relevant for classical simulated and deployed systems as well, we implemented it by extending the `timer` component in order to trigger reactive rounds after a message is received.
3. While in a simulation nodes are usually algorithmically generated across the simulated space, we need to generate them based on data read from a file. Since this feature could also be useful in 3D simulations, provided that position information is stored in the given file, we implemented it by extending the `spawner` component with options for file-based generation.
4. Finally, as the main structural difference, the neighbourhood of each node is not determined by the physical locations of nodes, but is given by the edges of the graph (also read from a separate file). This requires to introduce a new variant of the *connector* component, which we called `graph_connector`.

Based on this considerations, the mentioned combinations are defined as:

```
DECLARE_COMBINE(batch_data_processor,
    graph_connector, timer, scheduler, logger, storage,
    spawner, identifier, randomizer, calculus);
```

Note that this definition is remarkably similar to that of a batch simulation, i.e., we have been able to exploit several existing components. We also defined a `interactive_data_processor` combination providing a graphical user interface through which the network situation can be inspected (based on the existing similar `interactive_simulator` composition):

```
DECLARE_COMBINE(interactive_data_processor,
    displayer, graph_connector, simulated_positioner, timer, scheduler,
    logger, storage, spawner, identifier, randomizer, calculus);
```

The main responsibility of the *spawner* component is that of creating nodes with unique identifiers exploiting the `identifier` component (which is its parent). Formerly, that had to happen by algorithmic generation of node parameters. We extended the component to provide exactly the same function when the underlying system is a graph read from the disk. In particular: (i) the `net` constructor of the component handles the option `nodesinput` which specifies the name of the file where the nodes of the graph are stored; and (ii) each row of the nodes file is parsed according to a list `node_attributes` of expected attributes, which need to contain every mandatory argument needed for node construction (such as the `uid` attribute). All file-generated nodes are created at the execution start, but their first round can be scheduled arbitrarily later exploiting the `start` construction argument given by the *timer* component.

The *connector* component is in charge of handling the exchange of messages between neighbours. The `graph_connector` replaces the `simulated_connector` used in simulations by providing exactly the same function when the underlying system is a graph read from the disk. In particular:

1. it provides `connect` and `disconnect` methods to the `node`, so that nodes of the graph can be connected at start and disconnected at end by the component, while allowing dynamic connections to be also established through the program logic;
2. connections can be considered as directed or undirected by simply setting the Boolean option `symmetric`;
3. the `net` constructor of the component handles the option `arcsinput` which specifies the name of the file where the initial arcs of the graph are stored;
4. each row of the arcs file is parsed expecting a pair of node identifiers; and an arc between the two nodes is created by calling the `connect` method on the first node with the second node as a parameter;
5. it provides functionality to send messages to the outgoing neighbours of a node, i.e., the nodes reachable with an outgoing arc in the graph.

The *timer* component is in charge of scheduling rounds both a-priori and in the program logic. We extended it by: (i) adding a parameter `reactive_time`, that for every node sets a delay for triggering a round after a message is received; and (ii) through the function `node.disable_send()` provided by the *connector* component, messages can be blocked avoiding triggering rounds in neighbours whenever the results of the algorithm at hand are stable. By setting a reactive time that is much shorter than the non-reactive scheduling of rounds, we can ensure that nodes are reactively processed until convergence before any non-reactive rounds are scheduled.

In performing the extensions just described, we had to overcome some notable issues: (i) in data processing, fine-grained parallelism is necessary, and thus the implementation had to be designed so to avoid both data races and deadlocks, which is not trivial for graph-like structures; and (ii) by allowing reactive rounds, we broke an assumption of FCPP that the next event on a node is scheduled right after an event is executed. The *identifier* component keeps a queue of node events, executing them (in parallel) as necessary. Formerly, this queue could be updated by adding the next events right after each event is executed. In order to handle reactive rounds, we had to add an alternative way of updating the event queue: the identifier checks at each message received whether the next event changes, updating the queue accordingly. In particular, this introduced a new component dependency, requiring the timer to appear as parent of the identifier in order for this interaction to be captured.

5   Experimental Evaluation

5.1   Implementation

We evaluated our approach by implementing a case study on the computation of graph statistics, focusing on the centrality measures presented in Sect. 2.3. These statistics have been implemented as FC programs expressed in the FCPP DSL described in Sect. 2.1, similarly as previously done in the Protelis DSL in [9]. Differently than there, we enhanced the HyperANF algorithm to not require an upper bound of the diameter in input, computing the neighbourhood function up to a variable depth, stopping whenever no further nodes are found in the last level. The resulting code is shown with explanatory comments in Fig. 3.

The HyperANF algorithm is based on HyperLogLog counters, which we implemented in C++ with a `hyperloglog_counter` template class by mimicking the extremely efficient Java implementation described in [16]. The template parameters allow the specification of:

1. number of registers per HLL counter;
2. number of bits per register (defaulting to 4);
3. type of the counted data (defaulting to `size_t`, i.e., unsigned long integer);
4. hash function used to convert the counted data before HLL operations.

In particular, the implementation exploits *broadword programming* techniques to parallelize the union operations on all the registers contained in a word (e.g., 16 registers at a time, if the word is 64 bit and the register is 4 bits), thus significantly speeding-up the fundamental operations performed during the computation of N_G. In Fig. 3, type `hll_t` is used for those counters, which is defined as a specific instantiation of the `hyperloglog_counter` template.

5.2   Results

In order to evaluate the effectiveness of FCPP on centralised graph-based data processing, we compared our approach with the state-of-the-art WebGraph-based implementation [15,17] of the HyperANF algorithm computing harmonic

```
1   FUN tuple<real_t, real_t> hyperANF(ARGS) { CODE
2       real_t h = 0; // harmonic count
3       real_t c = 0; // closeness count
4       bool u = true; // are results unchanged from previous round?
5       hll_t l = hll_t(node.uid); // HLL counter of nodes up to a depth
6       real_t ps = 0; // size at the previous depth
7       real_t cs = l.size(); // size at the current depth
8       // loop over depths until no further nodes discovered
9       for (LOOP(depth, 1); ps < cs; ++depth) {
10          ps = cs; // current size becomes previous size
11          field<hll_t> nl = nbr(CALL, hll_t(), l); // neighbour HLLs
12          u = self(CALL, nl) == l and u; // check for change
13          // accumulate neighbour HLLs into l
14          fold_hood(CALL, [&](hll_t const& x, nullptr_t){
15              l.insert(x); // accumulate as side-effect
16              return nullptr; // dummy return value
17          }, std::move(nl), nullptr);
18          cs = l.size(); // new current size
19          h += (cs-ps)/depth; // update harmonic count
20          c += (cs-ps)*depth; // update closeness count
21      }
22      // notify neighbours with messages only if changes occurred
23      if (old(CALL, hll_t(), l) == l and u) node.disable_send();
24      return tuple<real_t, real_t>(h, c); // return counts
25  }
26  FUN_EXPORT hyperANF_t = export_list<hll_t>; // types used in messages
```

Fig. 3. Implementation of the HyperANF algorithm in FCPP.

and closeness centrality [16]. As reference graph, we used the *cnr-2000* test set [1] of moderate size, and run 10 executions for both implementations, in order to account for variability in execution times.

On a MacBook Pro with 2,4 GHz Intel Core i9 8 core CPU and 32 GB 2667 MHz RAM, the WebGraph implementation took from 28.263 s to 36.919 s to complete, with an average of 34.348 s. On the other hand, the FCPP implementation took from 111.230 s to 123.950 s to complete, with an average of 115.066 s. Even though the FCPP implementation was noticeably slower, requiring about $3\times$ time to complete, it has other advantages that compensate for this difference: most notably, the generality of the approach, which translates into much lower software development costs. In fact, the WebGraph implementation is highly specific to the problem at hand, and low-level optimised for it, so that it cannot be easily modified to accommodate any other task: the codebase needed to implement HyperANF is very large and complex, requiring high development costs. The FCPP codebase is also large and complex, however, it is sufficiently generic so that any other graph-based problem could be easily formulated in order to be executed with it, without direct intervention on that codebase. The development costs are thus limited to the AP formulation of the problem at hand, and are thus much lower as can be seen through the code snippet in Fig. 3.

We also remark that optimisations reducing execution times are planned for future releases of the FCPP implementation. These are likely to reduce the performance gap, although we do not expect this gap to be fully compensated. As the FCPP implementation is subject to the constraint of being able to run *any* aggregate program, in a way that is *inter-operable* with deployed self-organising systems running the same software, problem-specific optimisations are not possible, restricting leeway for improvements.

6   Discussion and Conclusions

In the present paper we have extended the FCPP implementation of FC in order to support a new execution environment, namely high-performance, centralized computers. In particular, FCPP can now ingest large-scale graph structures and execute FC programs as if the nodes of the graph were distributed devices, and the graph arcs represented the proximity-based communication links. The centrality statistics, chosen as a benchmark to test the extension, have been coded naturally with the FCPP DSL, and have shown more than decent performances compared with a state-of-the-art, carefully crafted Java implementation [16]. This extension has been carried out as a first step towards an AP-based IoT/edge/fog/cloud continuum, while also delineating a roadmap of 5 milestones to reach it, together with the main associated challenges to be overcome.

The evaluation of the extension presents some notable limitations that may be addressed in future work. First, the single problem of graph statistics computation was considered: the evaluation may be enhanced by considering more graph-related problems, such as routing, maximum flow or minimum spanning tree estimation. Furthermore, we carried the evaluation on a relatively small graph on a laptop computer: more accurate benchmarks could be obtained by performing a similar computation on larger graphs on an high-performance computer. In fact, such systems are sometimes equipped with Graphics Processing Unit (GPU)s beside multi-core CPUs: in the present paper we supported only CPU-based systems, since the Single Instruction, Multiple Data (SIMD) model of GPUs imposes restrictions on the computations that deserve a separate, in-depth analysis in future works.

References

1. Web crawl of the Italian cnr domain in year 2000. https://law.di.unimi.it/webdata/cnr-2000. Accessed 26 May 2022
2. Alongi, F., Ghielmetti, N., Pau, D., Terraneo, F., Fornaciari, W.: Tiny neural networks for environmental predictions: an integrated approach with miosix. In: IEEE International Conference on Smart Computing, (SMARTCOMP), pp. 350–355. IEEE (2020). https://doi.org/10.1109/SMARTCOMP50058.2020.00076
3. Audrito, G.: FCPP: an efficient and extensible field calculus framework. In: International Conference on Autonomic Computing and Self-Organizing Systems (ACSOS), pp. 153–159. IEEE (2020). https://doi.org/10.1109/ACSOS49614.2020.00037

4. Audrito, G., Casadei, R., Damiani, F., Pianini, D., Viroli, M.: Optimal resilient distributed data collection in mobile edge environments. Comput. Electr. Eng. **96**(Part), 107580 (2021). https://doi.org/10.1016/j.compeleceng.2021.107580

5. Audrito, G., Casadei, R., Torta, G.: Fostering resilient execution of multi-agent plans through self-organisation. In: ACSOS Companion Volume, pp. 81–86. IEEE (2021). https://doi.org/10.1109/ACSOS-C52956.2021.00076

6. Audrito, G., Casadei, R., Torta, G.: Towards integration of multi-agent planning with self-organising collective processes. In: ACSOS Companion Volume, pp. 297–298. IEEE (2021). https://doi.org/10.1109/ACSOS-C52956.2021.00042

7. Audrito, G., et al.: RM for users' safety and security in the built environment. In: VORTEX, pp. 13–16. ACM (2021). https://doi.org/10.1145/3464974.3468445

8. Audrito, G., Damiani, F., Stolz, V., Torta, G., Viroli, M.: Distributed runtime verification by past-ctl and the field calculus. J. Syst. Softw. **187**, 111251 (2022). https://doi.org/10.1016/j.jss.2022.111251

9. Audrito, G., Pianini, D., Damiani, F., Viroli, M.: Aggregate centrality measures for IOT-based coordination. Sci. Comput. Program. **203**, 102584 (2021). https://doi.org/10.1016/j.scico.2020.102584

10. Audrito, G., Rapetta, L., Torta, G.: Extensible 3d simulation of aggregated systems with FCPP. In: COORDINATION. Lecture Notes in Computer Science, vol. 13271, pp. 55–71. Springer (2022). https://doi.org/10.1007/978-3-031-08143-9_4

11. Audrito, G., Torta, G.: Towards aggregate monitoring of spatio-temporal properties. In: VORTEX, pp. 26–29. ACM (2021). https://doi.org/10.1145/3464974.3468448

12. Audrito, G., Viroli, M., Damiani, F., Pianini, D., Beal, J.: A higher-order calculus of computational fields. ACM Trans. Comput. Log. **20**(1), 5:1–5:55 (2019). https://doi.org/10.1145/3285956

13. Backstrom, L., Boldi, P., Rosa, M., Ugander, J., Vigna, S.: Four degrees of separation. In: Web Science 2012, WebSci 2012, Evanston, IL, USA, 22–24 June 2012, pp. 33–42 (2012). https://doi.org/10.1145/2380718.2380723

14. Beal, J., Pianini, D., Viroli, M.: Aggregate programming for the internet of things. IEEE Comput. **48**(9), 22–30 (2015). https://doi.org/10.1109/MC.2015.261

15. Boldi, P., Rosa, M., Santini, M., Vigna, S.: Layered label propagation: a multiresolution coordinate-free ordering for compressing social networks. In: World Wide Web (WWW), pp. 587–596. ACM (2011). https://doi.org/10.1145/1963405.1963488

16. Boldi, P., Rosa, M., Vigna, S.: Hyperanf: approximating the neighbourhood function of very large graphs on a budget. In: World Wide Web (WWW), pp. 625–634 (2011). https://doi.org/10.1145/1963405.1963493

17. Boldi, P., Vigna, S.: The webgraph framework I: compression techniques. In: World Wide Web (WWW), pp. 595–602. ACM (2004). https://doi.org/10.1145/988672.988752

18. Brin, S., Page, L.: The anatomy of a large-scale hypertextual web search engine. Comput. Netw. **30**(1–7), 107–117 (1998). https://doi.org/10.1016/S0169-7552(98)00110-X

19. Canning, P.S., Cook, W.R., Hill, W.L., Olthoff, W.G., Mitchell, J.C.: F-bounded polymorphism for object-oriented programming. In: 4th International Conference on Functional Programming Languages and Computer Architecture (FPCA), pp. 273–280. ACM (1989). https://doi.org/10.1145/99370.99392

20. Casadei, R., Viroli, M., Audrito, G., Damiani, F.: FScaFi?: a core calculus for collective adaptive systems programming. In: Margaria, T., Steffen, B. (eds.) ISoLA 2020. LNCS, vol. 12477, pp. 344–360. Springer, Cham (2020). https://doi.org/10.1007/978-3-030-61470-6_21

21. Casadei, R., Viroli, M., Audrito, G., Pianini, D., Damiani, F.: Engineering collective intelligence at the edge with aggregate processes. Eng. Appl. Artif. Intell. **97**, 104081 (2021). https://doi.org/10.1016/j.engappai.2020.104081

22. Datta, S.K., Bonnet, C.: An edge computing architecture integrating virtual iot devices. In: Global Conference on Consumer Electronics (GCCE), pp. 1–3 (2017). https://doi.org/10.1109/GCCE.2017.8229253

23. Flajolet, P., Fusy, É., Gandouet, O., Meunier, F.: Hyperloglog: the analysis of a near-optimal cardinality estimation algorithm. In: Analysis of Algorithms 2007 (AofA07), pp. 127–146 (2007)

24. Li, L., Fan, Y., Tse, M., Lin, K.Y.: A review of applications in federated learning. Comput. Ind. Eng. **149** (2020). https://doi.org/10.1016/j.cie.2020.106854

25. Liu, X., Zhou, Y., Guan, X., Shen, C.: A feasible graph partition framework for parallel computing of big graph. Knowl.-Based Syst. **134**, 228–239 (2017). https://doi.org/10.1016/j.knosys.2017.08.001

26. Page, L.: Method for node ranking in a linked database, 4 Sep 2001. US Patent 6,285,999

27. Palmer, C.R., Gibbons, P.B., Faloutsos, C.: ANF: a fast and scalable tool for data mining in massive graphs. In: International Conference on Knowledge Discovery and Data Mining (SIGKDD), pp. 81–90 (2002). https://doi.org/10.1145/775047.775059

28. Pianini, D., Montagna, S., Viroli, M.: Chemical-oriented simulation of computational systems with ALCHEMIST. J. Simul. **7**(3), 202–215 (2013). https://doi.org/10.1057/jos.2012.27

29. Pianini, D., Viroli, M., Beal, J.: Protelis: practical aggregate programming. In: Symposium on Applied Computing (SAC), pp. 1846–1853. ACM (2015). https://doi.org/10.1145/2695664.2695913

30. Sahlmann, K., Schwotzer, T.: Ontology-based virtual iot devices for edge computing. In: International Conference on the Internet of Things. Association for Computing Machinery (2018). https://doi.org/10.1145/3277593.3277597

31. Testa, L., Audrito, G., Damiani, F., Torta, G.: Aggregate processes as distributed adaptive services for the industrial internet of things. Pervasive Mob. Comput. **85** (2022). https://doi.org/10.1016/j.pmcj.2022.101658

32. Viroli, M., Beal, J., Damiani, F., Audrito, G., Casadei, R., Pianini, D.: From distributed coordination to field calculus and aggregate computing. J. Log. Algebraic Meth. Program. **109** (2019). https://doi.org/10.1016/j.jlamp.2019.100486

33. Viroli, M., Casadei, R., Pianini, D.: Simulating large-scale aggregate mass with alchemist and scala. In: Federated Conference on Computer Science and Information Systems (FedCSIS). Annals of Computer Science and Information Systems, vol. 8, pp. 1495–1504. IEEE (2016). https://doi.org/10.15439/2016F407

Ensemble-Based Modeling Abstractions for Modern Self-optimizing Systems

Michal Töpfer, Milad Abdullah, Tomas Bureš[(✉)], Petr Hnětynka,
and Martin Kruliš

Charles University, Prague, Czech Republic
{topfer,abdullah,bures,hnetynka,krulis}@d3s.mff.cuni.cz

Abstract. In this paper, we extend our ensemble-based component model DEECo with the capability to use machine-learning and optimization heuristics in establishing and reconfiguration of autonomic component ensembles. We show how to capture these concepts on the model level and give an example of how such a model can be beneficially used for modeling access-control related problem in the Industry 4.0 settings. We argue that incorporating machine-learning and optimization heuristics is a key feature for modern smart systems which are to learn over the time and optimize their behavior at runtime to deal with uncertainty in their environment.

Keywords: Self-adaptation · Ensembles · Machine-learning · Heuristics

1 Introduction

Modern smart systems increasingly aim at providing highly optimized behavior that copes with the high uncertainty and variability of their surrounding environment. This classifies them as representatives of *self-adaptive systems*, which are systems that monitor their performance and their ability to meet their goals and adapt their behavior to cope with changes in themselves and in their environment.

Modern smart systems are often composed of multiple components, which are required to coordinate their operation. This means that the system adaptation and optimization have to be done in a coordinated manner too.

Traditionally these systems have been designed by providing a set of adaptation rules that were supposed to identify principal states and changes in the environment and reconfigure the system. However, with more and more emphasis on data and with the increasing amounts of data the modern systems collect and are able to exploit in their operation, the specification using a fixed set of adaptation rules becomes increasingly more complex and hard to do (mainly due to the fact that the model behind the data is unknown and potentially changing).

A recent trend in modern smart systems is to use machine learning to help the system make adaptation and optimization decisions. However, machine learning is still used in a rather ad-hoc manner without having been systematically embedded in the architecture of the systems.

T. Margaria and B. Steffen (Eds.): ISoLA 2022, LNCS 13703, pp. 318–334, 2022.
https://doi.org/10.1007/978-3-031-19759-8_20

The main problem is that there is a lack of architectural models for the specification of system components that would provide abstractions for machine learning and other kinds of optimizations based on data observed by the system. As a result, every smart system that employs machine learning or some kind of optimization has to create its own architectural abstractions. This not only means duplicating the work but also requiring an expert in machine learning to be able to implement the abstractions correctly.

In this paper, we address this problem by providing a novel component model (called ML-DEECo) that features dedicated abstractions for machine learning (currently only supervised learning) and optimization heuristics (used mainly for coordination problems).

The ML-DEECo model is an extension of our previous DEECo component model [8]. Similar to DEECo, it is based on the concept of autonomic component ensembles, which are situation-based coordination groups of components that cooperate (within a given situation) to achieve a common goal.

In this paper, we demonstrate the main concepts of ML-DEECo on a use-case in the Industry 4.0 settings that stems from our previous project with industry.

We support the concepts of ML-DEECo by an implementation in Python, which can process the ML-DEECo abstractions and use them to automatically realize the complete learning loop (consisting of data collection, model training, and inference at runtime). By this, we show the usefulness of ML-DEECo as it saves not only the time needed to develop the learning loop but also the expertise needed to do that. The implementation is part of the replication package that comes along with the paper [2].

The structure of the text is as follows. Section 2 describes the running example and, based on the example, introduces ensemble-based component systems. Section 3 presents the machine-learning concepts of ML-DEECo while Sect. 4 discusses the application of heuristics. Section 5 evaluates the presented approach and Sect. 6 compares it with related work. Section 7 concludes the paper.

2 Running Example and Background

In this paper, we build on the running example from recent work on dynamic security rules by Al-Ali et al. [3]. The example is a simplified version of a real-life scenario concerning access to a smart factory and it is taken from our recent project with industrial partners.

The factory consists of several working places, each with an assigned shift of workers. The workers come to the factory in the morning. They have to go through the main gate to enter the factory. Then, they have to grab a protective headgear at a headgear dispenser inside the factory and they can continue to their workplace. The workers are not allowed to enter the workplaces of the other shifts in the factory.

To ensure security and safety in the factory, several rules are defined. For example, the workers are allowed to enter the factory at the earliest 30 min before their shift starts. The rule is enforced by a smart lock at the main gate.

Another rule defines that the worker can only enter his workplace if they are wearing the protective headgear. We can see that the security rules are dynamic as their effect depends on time (we allow workers to the factory at most 30 min before their shift) and on of workers (whether they wear the headgear or not).

The scenario further deals with replacing the workers who are late for their shift with standbys. For each shift in the factory, we have a defined set of standby workers. If a worker does not arrive at the factory sufficiently (16 min) before their shift starts, they are canceled for the day and a standby is called to replace them. As the actual time of arrival of the workers to the factory varies, it brings uncertainty to the system, which is an opportunity to use a machine-learning-based estimate to deal with it. Furthermore, the assignment of the standbys can be a hard optimization problem if the sets of standbys for the shifts overlap, so it can be dealt with using a heuristic approach.

2.1   Modeling Dynamic Security Rules with Components and Ensembles

We build our approach on the concept of autonomic component *ensembles*; in particular, we are using the abstractions of the DEECo ensemble-based component model [9]. In this section, we describe the concepts of ensembles that are necessary for understanding the paper.

Components represent the entities in our system (factory, rooms, dispenser, workers) and they are described by the component type. There are multiple instances (simply referred to as "components" in the paper) of each of the component types (i.e., multiple workers, rooms, etc.). Each of the components has a state represented as a set of data fields. Components that we cannot control directly (workers in our case) are referred to as "beyond control components". The state of these components is only observed or inferred.

Ensembles represent dynamically formed groups of components that correspond to a coordinated activity. As for the components, the ensembles are described by their ensemble type, which can be instantiated multiple times. A single component can be selected in multiple ensemble instances at the same time—we call this that the component is a "member" of the respective ensemble instance. The ensemble prescribes possible data interchange among the components in the ensemble and also the group-wise behavior (e.g., a coordinated movement).

Technically, an ensemble type specifies the (1) roles, (2) situation, and (3) actions.

The *roles* determine which components are to be included in the ensemble (i.e., components that should be members of the ensemble). Roles are either static or dynamic. The static ones are specified when the ensemble is instantiated and cannot change. They provide the identity to the ensemble instance (e.g., a shift for which the ensemble is instantiated). There cannot exist two ensemble instances of the same type that are equal in the assignment of their static roles.

The static roles are specified as a tuple: (i) type of component instances in the role, (ii) cardinality of the role.

The cardinality of the role is simply an interval determining the minimum and maximum number of component instances referred to by the role.

On the other hand, the dynamic roles are populated dynamically based on the situation in the system. The dynamic roles are specified as a triple: (i) type of component instances in the role, (ii) cardinality of the role, and (iii) condition over components in the role.

While the type and cardinality are the same as in the case of static roles, the condition further determines if a component may be selected for the role. The condition is parameterized by the component being selected for the dynamic roles and by the static roles (i.e. attributes of components in the static roles).

The situation is a condition over static roles that determines whether the ensemble should be instantiated.

The actions are activities to be executed when the ensemble is instantiated. They differ based on the target domain and have no influence on how ensembles are instantiated. In the case of our running example, we use two actions: *allow* and *notify*. The *allow* action assign some permission to a component. The *notify* action send a notification to a component (e.g. to let a standby worker know that they have been assigned to a shift).

Ensembles can be hierarchically nested, i.e., an ensemble can be defined as an inner one within another ensemble. This allows for the decomposition of complex conditions into simpler ones and thus makes the whole specification more easily manageable. Instances of an inner ensemble can be created only if there is an instance of the outer ensemble.

The ensembles are instantiated and dissolved dynamically and continuously as the state of the system changes. This instantiation of the ensembles and their dissolution is performed automatically by the ML-DEECo runtime framework.

An ensemble is instantiated for each possible assignment of static roles such that the situation condition is true and there exist components that can be assigned to the dynamic roles to satisfy the cardinality bounds and the dynamic role condition.

The instantiation is attempted periodically. In case of our running example, since this is run as a simulation, we perform the instantiation (and dissolution) of ensembles in every simulation step.

For our example, ensembles are used to express the security rules in the system. They dynamically grant/revoke access permissions to individual components.

Listing 1 shows a part of the specification of the running example. It represents the components and ensembles as illustrated in Fig. 1 There are 6 types of components: Door, Dispenser (of protective headgear), Factory, WorkPlace, Shift and Worker. Each of them is described by a set of their fields.

```
1 component type Door:
2    field position: Position
3
4 component type Dispenser:
```

```
 5    field position: Position
 6
 7  component type WorkPlace
 8    field position: Position
 9
10  component type Factory
11    field entryDoor: Door
12    field dispenser: Dispenser
13    field workplaces[*]: Workplace
14
15  component type Worker
16    field position: Position
17    field hasHeadgear: boolean
18
19  component Shift
20    field workPlace: WorkPlace
21    field startTime: Time
22    field endTime: Time
23    field assigned[*]: Worker # an original list of assigned workers
24    field workers[*]: Worker # a list of actually working workers
25    field standBys[*]: Worker
26
27  ensemble type AccessToFactory
28    static role shift: Shift
29    situation shift.startTime − 30 <= now <= shift.endTime + 30
30    dynamic role workers[*]: Worker
31      each worker in workers:
32      (worker in shift.assigned and not worker.canceled)
33        or worker in shift.calledStandbys
34    action allow workers enter factory
35
36  ensemble type CancelLateWorkers
37    static role shift: Shift
38    situation shift.startTime − 16 <= now <= shift.endTime
39    dynamic role lateWorkers[*]: Worker
40      each worker in lateWorkers:
41      worker in shift.assigned and not worker.isAtFactory
42    action notify lateWorkers with canceled
43    inner ensemble type ReplaceLateWithStandbys
44      dynamic role standBys[lateWorkers.size]: Worker
45        each worker in standBys:
46          worker in shift.standBys
47      action notify standBys with calledIn
```

Listing 1. An excerpt of the example specification

Further, ensemble types are specified. Due to the paper space limits, we show here only a few of them. In Fig. 1, sample instances of ensembles are represented as the hand-drawn oval shapes.

The AccessToFactory assigns to the workers the access-to-factory permission. The static role shift (line 28) determines the identity of the ensemble instance, i.e., the ensemble is instantiated for a selected shift and there is only one ensemble instance of AccessToFactory for a particular shift.

The situation (line 29) is a predicate determining under which conditions the ensemble has to be instantiated. In this particular case, the ensemble is instantiated from 30 min before the shift starts till 30 min after the shift ends.

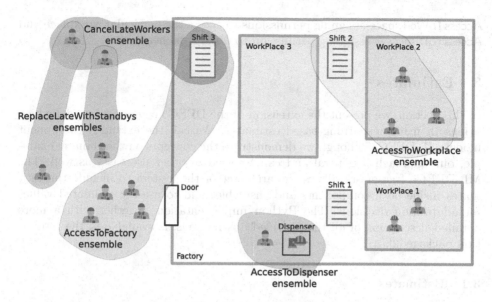

Fig. 1. Factory example

The dynamic role workers (line 30) selects all the workers which are assigned to the shift. These are workers that have been assigned to the shift and that have not been canceled due to being late, plus the standbys called to fill in for the late workers. This is stated on lines 32–33. The definition of the role specifies the cardinality, the type of components assigned to the role, and the condition that has to hold for each component in the role.

The workers selected in the dynamic role are assigned with permission to enter the factory (line 34).

Similar to the AccessToFactory, our specification contains ensembles AccessToDispenser and AccessToWorkplace, which differ only in what they regulate the access to. Since they are very similar, we omitted them in the paper.

The next ensemble—CancelLateWorker (line 36) serves for canceling workers that are late. The static role pins the ensemble instance to a shift. The dynamic role selects workers that are late (i.e., they are not in the factory 16 min before the shift start). Those workers are then canceled from the shift (line 42). This is done by notifying them and the system about being canceled.

To replace the canceled workers, there is a subensemble (ReplaceLateWithStandbys in line 43) of the CancelLateWorker ensemble. It selects the necessary number of standbys to fill in for the canceled workers. The cardinality of the standBys role is equal to the number of canceled workers. The standbys are notified by the ensemble about being called in.

All the described ensembles are illustrated in Fig. 1. The figure also shows other two ensembles (omitted from the listing due to the space constraints but defined in the complete example in the replication package). They are

AccessToWorkspace assigning permissions to access the particular workplace and AccessToDispenser assigning permission to obtain the headgear.

3   Estimates

In this section, we present the extension of the DEECo component model which brings in machine-learning-based estimates. We call the extended component model ML-DEECo. Though we demonstrate the concepts on the running example, our approach is general and can be used in other use cases as well. The ML-DEECo framework allows the architect of the system to include the estimates inside both components and ensembles and to use the estimated values for adaptation decisions. The Python implementation, together with a more detailed description of all the provided abstractions, is available in the replication package [2].

3.1   Estimates

In our recent projects, we have identified several use-cases, where machine learning would be beneficial to a proactive self-adaptation of the system. Several of these use cases exhibited the same patterns—we needed to predict a future state of a component or ensemble. The machine learning algorithms can easily be used in such situations as the future state will be known at some point in time in the future so we can formulate the problem as supervised learning and use the observed value for the training of the machine-learning-based estimate.

Based on our previous experience with designing ensemble-based systems and an analysis, we have identified the following three kinds of estimates based on where they can be applied in an architecture, i.e., on (i) a component, (ii) an ensemble, and (iiii) a component-ensemble pair.

In the first case, the estimate serves as a special field of the component and is parameterized by values of the regular fields. For instance, the Worker component can have an estimate predicting whether the particular worker would be willing to be activated as a "standby" (in the case the selection as a called-in standby is voluntary). The estimate would be parameterized by the current day-of-week and would be trained on the history of the particular worker's willingness to be activated as the standby.

In the second case, i.e., applying on an ensemble, an estimate is employed as the ensemble property and can be used in the ensemble conditions (in the situation and the dynamic role selectors). The estimate is parameterized by values obtained from global variables and static roles of the ensemble. For instance, if we extend the example by the automated planning of shifts (i.e., allocating workers to shifts), we can have an ensemble with the estimate that predicts the right number of workers in order to reach expected productivity goals. This prediction would be based on the day-of-week and start time of the shift (morning, afternoon, evening).

The last option—applying an estimate to the component-ensemble pair—is the most complex one. In this case, we associate the estimate with a component that has been dynamically selected in an ensemble. Since this is the most complex case, we will use it to showcase the ML-DEECo in the rest of the section.

As an example, we use machine learning for the adaptation of the replacement of late workers. A traditional rigid solution is to set a threshold for when the workers have to be inside the factory. In our case, the baseline approach is to cancel the workers if they are not present in the factory 16 min before the start of their shift. This, however, does not deal well with the uncertainty of the arrival of the workers. To replace the rigid approach, we suggest using a machine-learning-based estimate to predict whether a worker will come on time or not. This can be expressed as an estimate assigned to a dynamic role of an ensemble type as shown in Listing 2.

```
1  ensemble type CancelLateWorkers
2    static role shift: Shift
3    situation shift.startTime − 30 <= now <= shift.endTime + 30
4    dynamic role lateWorkers[*]: Worker
5      with value estimate willArrive:
6        output worker.isAtFactory @ T+<1,30>
7        input dayOfWeek
8        guard worker.shift == shift
9      each worker in lateWorkers
10        not worker.isAtFactory and not (willArrive @ shift.startTime)
11    action notify lateWorkers with cancelled
```

Listing 2. Machine-learning-enabled ensemble specification – Cancel late workers.

The dynamic role for finding late workers is specified on line 4. We assign an estimate to this role on line 5 to predict whether the worker will come to the factory or not. We use the prediction to determine whether we should cancel the worker or not. That is done on line 10 in the membership condition of the role – we use the estimate to predict whether the worker will be at the factory at the time the shift starts.

To be able to use the estimate, we need to specify its inputs and outputs. The output of the estimate is the future value of the worker.isAtFactory attribute (line 6). By T+<1,30>, we indicate that we want to construct a model which is able to predict this value in a range of 1 to 30 min into the future. The input of the model is the day of the week which the shift takes place on (line 7). Furthermore, we define a guard on line 8 which indicates the validity of the training data – here, as we have an instance of the ensemble for each shift, we only want to collect data about the workers from the one shift and not the other shifts.

3.2 Training of the Estimates

The specification of the estimate in the ensemble definition is enough to be able to automatically collect data and train the machine learning model, which is done by the ML-DEECo framework runtime. The semantics of the value estimate is as follows.

The estimate predicts an attribute from the future state of the system. In our example, the willArrive estimate predicts a future value of the isAtFactory attribute of the Worker component. We use the values of the attributes available at the time of prediction as inputs to the machine learning model—dayOfWeek in the example. Furthermore, we need to specify how far into the future we want to be able to predict—this is set by the T+<min_t,max_t> expression. This will influence what data we collect for training—we allow the time difference between inputs and outputs to be in the range $\langle min\_t, max\_t \rangle$.

To train the machine learning model, we need to collect training data. Our focus is on predictions of values, which can be observed at some point in the future. In the example, we predict whether the worker will come or not, and after some time, we can observe whether they really came or not. We thus need to observe these values and use them for the training of the model.

To collect the training data, we use the following procedure. In every time step of the simulation (every minute in the example), we check the guard and if it marks the data as valid, we collect the values of input attributes and tag them with the current time. After that, we collect the values of the output attributes for the current time step and link them with past inputs. Specifically, we go through all the allowed time differences $t \in \langle min\_t, max\_t \rangle$ and save the training example (t, inputs_at_now-t, outputs_now). The inputs are collected throughout the whole run of the simulation and the training is performed after the simulation finishes.

4   Heuristics

As mentioned in Sect. 2, after canceling late workers, it is necessary to select replacements from the standby workers. As this is not a prediction problem, we do not use machine learning (which we presented in the previous section). Rather we look for abstractions that allow us to specify component partitioning.

The problem here is that the assignment of standby worker is mutually exclusive – a standby worker cannot be assigned in place of two different late workers. This leads to an optimization problem, which has known inputs (i.e. components and their attributes, including the predicted ones) and known constraints.

An optimal selection of the standbys, considering for instance shared standbys among shifts, is an NP-complete problem. We faced this issue extensively in our previous work [9], where we were transforming ensembles to the constraint optimization problem. Even for small problem instances, the constraint optimization problem would soon become too computationally expensive to solve.

However, in this particular case, the optimal solution is not necessary (i.e., the correctness of the system here does not depend on whether the standbys are selected optimally but only that selections do not overlap—note that this is in strict contrast with the access permission assignment, where strict correctness is necessary). Fortunately, there are a number of heuristic algorithms that target such problems (i.e., NP-hard or complete problems). For example, a well-known and widely used heuristic algorithm is a k-means clustering method [22], which partitions n elements into k clusters in which each element belongs to the cluster with the nearest mean. By itself, the problem is NP-complete, but the k-means clustering method quickly converges to a local optimum.

In the case of the standbys selection, the exclusive choice method (e.g., [19]) can be used. Listing 3 shows the updated version of the ReplaceLateWithStandbys ensemble. Now, the selection of standbys is performed with the help of a special operation (line 5), where the exclusive choice heuristic method is implemented.

```
1  ensemble type CancelLateWorkers
2    # ... shortened here
3    inner ensemble type ReplaceLateWithStandbys
4      dynamic role standBys[lateWorkers.size]: Worker
5        exclusiveSelect worker from globalStandBys
6      action notify standBys with calledIn
```

Listing 3. Ensemble specification with heuristic operation

The above-mentioned k-means clustering method could be employed in our example, e.g., for clustering workers for optimized delivery of sensor data (i.e., workers are equipped with sensors, and to reduce the amount of communication, the measurements are not delivered directly, but they are aggregated by a worker that is "in-the-middle" of each cluster).

The downside of the use of heuristics is that they target individual problems. Therefore it is complicated to create a common "heuristics extension" for ML-DEECo, and particular heuristics need to be offered as specialized operations. However, our experience shows that there is only a limited number of problems in ensemble-based systems related to the assignment of components to ensembles: selection (exclusively select a fixed number of components for each ensemble instance), partitioning (split all components in a set among a set of known ensemble instances), clustering (split all components to an optimal unknown number of ensembles). For these, abstractions like the exclusiveSelect above can be created.

As a future work, we plan to create a detailed classification of problems related to ensemble-based systems and based on it, to design a set of common— at least to some extent—heuristics for ML-DEECo.

5 Evaluation

We center the evaluation around two arguments: (1) it saves on implementation effort to have machine learning abstractions part of the component model, (2) for certain situations allows the systems to perform better than just with fixed adaptation rules.

To this end, we have implemented a simulation of the running example using the ML-DEECo Python framework.

From the perspective of implementation effort, when using the abstractions of ML-DEECo realized by our Python implementation, the introduction of machine

learning consist essentially only in declaring the predictor and providing anno-
tations to component fields and ensemble roles. The exact code can be found in
the replication package [2]. All this amounts to approx. 25 lines of code. On the
other hand, custom implementation using TensorFlow or PyTorch frameworks
would amount to at least a hundred lines of code (taking into account the data
collection, pre-processing, training, retraining, and inference—all taken care of
by ML-DEECo).

In addition to the Industry 4.0 example presented in this paper, we have
used ML-DEECo to model also scenarios from smart farming. In all cases, the
abstractions featured by ML-DEECo proved to be expressive enough to cover
various supervised learning situations—including predictions of future states of
sensors (i.e., continuous data), prediction of the future state of a component (i.e.,
discrete data), predictions about the existence of an ensemble, and predictions
about which components will be members of an ensemble.

To illustrate that machine learning has the potential to outperform fixed
adaptation rules, we simulated the Industry 4.0 example described in the paper.
The configuration of the simulation is as follows. We assume that the workers
arrive by a bus which stops a few minutes from the main gate of the factory.
During business days, the bus arrives 24 min before the shift starts, and during
weekends, the bus arrives 30 min before the shift. Furthermore, we assume that
10% of the workers are late each day and they arrive by a later bus—18 min
before the start of the shift on business days and 15 min before the shift during weekends. To have more uncertainty in the environment, we add a random
delay (with exponential distribution) to each worker. If a worker is canceled and
replaced by a standby, we assume that it will take 30 min before the standby
arrives. We chose these values after careful deliberation to have something that
both illustrate the system and are close to what the reality would look like.

We ran the simulation with three shifts starting at the same time, each
with 100 workers, for three iterations. In the first iteration, we use the rigid
rule of canceling workers 16 min before their shift starts. In the following two
iterations, we use the machine-learning-based estimate described in Sect. 3 to
decide whether to cancel the worker. The results are shown in Fig. 2. The blue
points are the number of necessary standbys (averaged over the shifts) with a
blue line showing the average over the business days and weekends. The *lateness*
(shown in orange) is computed as the square of the delay of workers who arrive
late at their workplace. The ML-based estimate is trained after each iteration
(week)—first, we train it on the data collected while using the rigid rule (denoted
Training 1 in the figure), then, we update it using data collected in the second
week (Training 2). It is clear that for this configuration, the learned rules perform
significantly better than the rigid rule.

We have further inspected the outputs of the machine learning model to
see what the learned threshold for cancellation is. The outputs are shown in
Fig. 3. We observe that the learned threshold is different for business days and
for weekends (as we want it to be). The model is more forgiving to the workers
than the rigid rule—it allows them to enter the factory at latest 12 min before

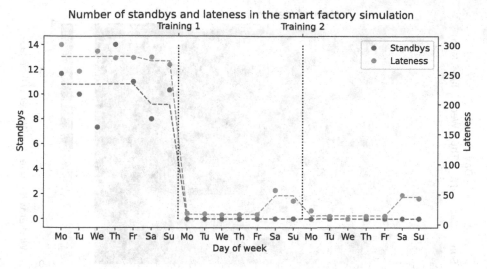

Fig. 2. Results of the simulation with 100 workers.

the shift starts on business days, and 7 min before the shift starts on weekends. It seems that it is beneficial to wait for the workers arriving by the later bus instead of calling the standbys which will take longer to arrive.

Furthermore, we have tried running the simulation with 20% and 30% of late workers to see the impact on the learning process. The results were very similar and the learned rule performed significantly better than the rigid one. For 30% of late workers, the difference in the cancellation time for business days and for weekends was not that big, but it is still clear that the network was capable of learning the pattern. The plots with results for 20% and 30% of late workers are available in the replication package [2].

In the example, we focused on a single source of uncertainty—the arrival of the workers. Other type of uncertainty in the example could be predicting whether a worker actually grabs the headgear. This is essentially an identical problem to the uncertainty of the workers arrival, only the predicted values are not continuous but discrete (and thus the underlaying neural network would differ only in the last layer that would use softmax, and in the loss function that would use categorical cross-entropy). For the sake of conciseness, we focused on a single example only.

Limitations and Threats to Validity: The evaluation we presented serves as an indication of an illustration of the potential of our approach. Due to the limited size of the use case, we refrain from claiming the generality of the approach. However, at least our indicative experiments show its potential.

We aimed at giving generality to the abstractions by constructing them independently of a particular use case. We based the abstractions on a taxonomy prediction (briefly discussed in Sect. 3)—i.e., associating predictions with a component, ensemble, or component-ensemble pair and classifying types of

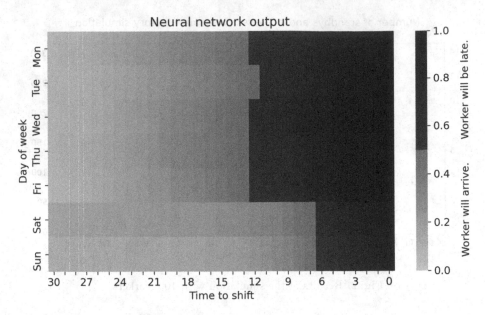

Fig. 3. Outputs of the neural network for predicting whether a worker will arrive to the factory before their shift starts (green) or not (red). (Color figure online)

predictions. This is independent of our use case and has been built as a combination of generally accepted abstractions.

Our work is limited to supervised learning only. We are currently in the process of extending ML-DEECO of reinforcement learning.

6   Related Work

In the paper, we have presented a component model targeting the development of adaptive systems and employing machine learning techniques directly at the level of a system architecture specification. Thus, the related areas are approaches defining explicit component models for adaptive systems and approaches combining adaptive systems with machine learning techniques—ideally, approaches combining both.

Using machine-learning techniques in adaptive systems is not a new approach. In [26], a systematic literature review (SLR) analyzes the employment of machine learning techniques in adaptive systems for the past 20 years. From the analysis, an apparent increasing trend in their usage can be seen, and the machine learning techniques are mainly employed in the adaptation phase. Also from the same area is the SLR in [16] which also confirms the increasing usage of machine learning techniques in adaptive systems—again mainly in the adaptation phase to optimize it and/or predict future actions. Nevertheless, most of the analyzed approaches use machine learning techniques "under-the-hood" in their implementation. This is in strict contrast with our approach, where we explicitly use and expose them for the architecture specification. In the text below, we discuss selected related approaches in more detail.

There are different uses for machine learning in self-adaptive systems ranging from predicting sensor values to reducing the space of adaptations. E.g., in [28] neural networks are employed for such a reduction. A similar approach [27] (by a similar group of authors) combines machine-learning techniques with a cost-based analysis to reduce the space and choose an adaptation with the best cost. In [17], a theorem defining a theoretical bound on the impact of applying a machine-learning method during adaptation was defined, and an approach for reducing an adaptation space was proposed. The paper [15] proposes a framework for the coevolution of an adaptive system together with its tests. Machine-learning is used for restrictions of an adaptation space in order to achieve a meaningful system as a result of an adaption step. An approach of a combination of machine-learning techniques and probabilistic model checking is described in the paper [11] and used for choosing the best adaptation and refusing unfeasible ones. The approach thus allows for fast convergence towards optimal decisions. Online reinforcement learning is used in [25] to deal with design-time uncertainty and automation of the development of the self-adaptation logic. Thanks to automation, there is thus no need for manual activities during the application of reinforcement learning. In the SARDE framework [18], machine learning is used for the selection of the best estimation approach and for optimization of the selected approaches. The whole framework then allows for self-adaptive resource demand estimation. In [23], machine-learning is utilized for forecasting values of QoS parameters and, therefore, for advanced and proactive selection of possible adaptation strategies.

As mentioned, the approaches in the paragraph above use machine-learning techniques internally for a particular functionality of a system/framework. This is in contrast with our approach, where we are targeting the creation of architectural abstractions allowing for the usage of machine-learning during the design of a self-adaptive system and direct use of machine-learning results at the architectural level.

This leads to the second area of related works—component models for adaptive systems and especially those that offer implementation in a common programming language. The Service Component Ensemble Language (SCEL) [24] laid the mathematical foundations and semantics for ensemble-based systems. Later, the concepts of SCEL were implemented in a Java-based runtime framework called jRESP [1]. Another implementation of the ensemble-based concepts can be found in Helena, which is a complete framework for developing ensemble-based systems [20]. An approach similar to ensembles can be found in the AbC calculus [5] that defines systems via attribute-based communication between components. The calculus has been formalized in [4]. Implementation of AbC is available as the Ab^aCuS framework [6]. Similar to our implementation of ML-DEECo, components in Ab^aCuS are modeled as classes, and processes (performing communication via component attributes similarly to ensembles) are also classes. Another implementation of AbC is ABEL [12] that is a DSL developed in the Erlang language. Dynamic logic for describing ensemble-based communication between components is defined in [21], and it is implemented in a variant of the *AbC* calculus. The DReAM framework [13] allows for specifications of dynamically reconfigurable architectures. Its architecture description language is based on an interaction logic and describes dynamic coordination among components. Static parts of the architecture are described using a propositional interaction logic, while DReAM describes dynamic coordination. The Java implementation of DReAM, similarly to our approach, maps components and coordination to classes. The BIP component model [7] is used as a basis for the propositional interaction logic employed in DReAM. BIP primarily focuses on the formal description of component behavior. A combination of UML components and BIP is proposed in [10], and it focuses on the description and verification of component behavior and inter-component communication. An extension of BIP is DR-BIP [14] that adds support for dynamic reconfigurations.

The approaches for modeling and implementing ensemble-based (and similar) architecture primarily focus on semantics but they do not introduce any machine-learning on the architectural (or even any other) level. This contrasts with our approach, where we enrich the ensemble-based systems with machine-learning techniques.

7   Conclusion

In this paper, we have presented ML-DEECo, a novel ensemble-based component model that features abstractions for machine learning (namely the supervised learning) and heuristics related to the assignment of tasks to components (realized by component membership in an ensemble). We illustrated the key abstractions on an example from our past project in Industry 4.0 domain.

In the future, we aim at featuring abstractions related to unsupervised and reinforcement learning, as they would cover situations when the ground trues cannot be observed at all (note that in this paper we assume that the ground trues cannot be observed at the time the prediction is performed but will be observable at a later point of time). Another direction for future work is to design a set of common heuristics for ML-DEECo.

Acknowledgment. This work has been partially supported by Charles University institutional funding SVV 260588, partially supported by the Czech Science Foundation project 20-24814J, and partially supported by the European Research Council (ERC) under the European Union's Horizon 2020 research and innovation programme (grant agreement No 810115).

References

1. jRESP: Java Runtime Environment for SCEL Programs. http://jresp.sourceforge.net/. Accessed 31 July 2022
2. Replication package (2022). https://github.com/smartarch/ml-deeco-security-isola

3. Al-Ali, R., et al.: Dynamic security rules for legacy systems. In: Proceedings of ECSA 2019, vol. 2, Paris, France (2019). https://doi.org/10.1145/3344948.3344974
4. Alrahman, Y.A., De Nicola, R., Loreti, M.: Programming interactions in collective adaptive systems by relying on attribute-based communication. Sci. Comput. Programm. **192** (2020). https://doi.org/10.1016/j.scico.2020.102428
5. Abd Alrahman, Y., De Nicola, R., Loreti, M.: On the power of attribute-based communication. In: Albert, E., Lanese, I. (eds.) FORTE 2016. LNCS, vol. 9688, pp. 1–18. Springer, Cham (2016). https://doi.org/10.1007/978-3-319-39570-8_1
6. Abd Alrahman, Y., De Nicola, R., Loreti, M.: Programming of CAS systems by relying on attribute-based communication. In: Margaria, T., Steffen, B. (eds.) ISoLA 2016. LNCS, vol. 9952, pp. 539–553. Springer, Cham (2016). https://doi.org/10.1007/978-3-319-47166-2_38
7. Bliudze, S., Sifakis, J.: The algebra of connectors-structuring interaction in BIP. IEEE Trans. Comput. **57**(10), 1315–1330 (2008). https://doi.org/10.1109/TC.2008.26
8. Bures, T., Gerostathopoulos, I., Hnetynka, P., Keznikl, J., Kit, M., Plasil, F.: DEECO: an ensemble-based component system. In: Proceedings of CBSE 2013, Vancouver, Canada, pp. 81–90. ACM (2013). https://doi.org/10.1145/2465449.2465462
9. Bures, T., et al.: A language and framework for dynamic component ensembles in smart systems. Int. J. Softw. Tools Technol. Transf. **22**(4), 497–509 (2020). https://doi.org/10.1007/s10009-020-00558-z
10. Chehida, S., Baouya, A., Bensalem, S.: Component-based approach combining uml and bip for rigorous system design. In: Salaün, G., Wijs, A. (eds.) FACS 2021. LNCS, vol. 13077, pp. 27–43. Springer, Cham (2021). https://doi.org/10.1007/978-3-030-90636-8_2
11. Cámara, J., Muccini, H., Vaidhyanathan, K.: Quantitative verification-aided machine learning: a tandem approach for architecting self-adaptive IoT systems. In: Proceedings of ICSA 2021, Salvador, Brazil, pp. 11–22. IEEE (2020). https://doi.org/10.1109/ICSA47634.2020.00010
12. De Nicola, R., Duong, T., Loreti, M.: ABEL - a domain specific framework for programming with attribute-based communication. In: Proceedings of COORDINATION 2019, Lyngby, Denmark. LNCS, vol. 11533, pp. 111–128. Springer (2019). https://doi.org/10.1007/978-3-030-22397-7_7
13. De Nicola, R., Maggi, A., Sifakis, J.: The DReAM framework for dynamic reconfigurable architecture modelling: theory and applications. Int. J. Softw. Tools Technol. Transf. **22**(4), 437–455 (2020). https://doi.org/10.1007/s10009-020-00555-2
14. El Ballouli, R., Bensalem, S., Bozga, M., Sifakis, J.: Programming dynamic reconfigurable systems. Int. J. Softw. Tools Technol. Transf. **23**(5), 701–719 (2021). https://doi.org/10.1007/s10009-020-00596-7
15. Gabor, T., et al.: The scenario coevolution paradigm: adaptive quality assurance for adaptive systems. Int. J. Softw. Tools Technol. Transf. **22**(4), 457–476 (2020). https://doi.org/10.1007/s10009-020-00560-5
16. Gheibi, O., Weyns, D., Quin, F.: Applying machine learning in self-adaptive systems: a systematic literature review. ACM Trans. Auton. Adapt. Syst. **15**(3), 9:1–9:37 (2021). https://doi.org/10.1145/3469440
17. Gheibi, O., Weyns, D., Quin, F.: On the Impact of applying machine learning in the decision-making of self-adaptive systems. In: Proceedings of SEAMS 2021, Madrid, Spain, pp. 104–110. IEEE (2021). https://doi.org/10.1109/SEAMS51251.2021.00023

18. Grohmann, J., et al.: SARDE: a framework for continuous and self-adaptive resource demand estimation. ACM Trans. Auton. Adapt. Syst. **15**(2), 1–31 (2021). https://doi.org/10.1145/3463369

19. Heinrich, B., Klier, M., Zimmermann, S.: Automated planning of process models: design of a novel approach to construct exclusive choices. Decis. Support Syst. **78**, 1–14 (2015). https://doi.org/10.1016/j.dss.2015.07.005

20. Hennicker, R., Klarl, A.: Foundations for ensemble modeling - the helena approach. In: Specification, Algebra, and Software, pp. 359–381. No. 8373 in LNCS, Springer (2014). https://doi.org/10.1007/978-3-642-54624-2_1

21. Hennicker, R., Wirsing, M.: A dynamic logic for systems with predicate-based communication. In: Proceedings of ISOLA 2020, Rhodes, Greece. LNCS, vol. 12477, pp. 224–242. Springer (2020). https://doi.org/10.1007/978-3-030-61470-6_14

22. Kanungo, T., Mount, D., Netanyahu, N., Piatko, C., Silverman, R., Wu, A.: An efficient k-means clustering algorithm: analysis and implementation. IEEE Trans. Pattern Anal. Mach. Intell. **24**(7), 881–892 (2002). https://doi.org/10.1109/TPAMI.2002.1017616

23. Muccini, H., Vaidhyanathan, K.: A machine learning-driven approach for proactive decision making in adaptive architectures. In: Companion Proceedings of ICSA 2019, Hamburg, Germany, pp. 242–245 (2019). https://doi.org/10.1109/ICSA-C.2019.00050

24. Nicola, R.D., et al.: The SCEL language: design, implementation, verification. In: Software Engineering for Collective Autonomic Systems, pp. 3–71. No. 8998 in LNCS, Springer (2015). https://doi.org/10.1007/978-3-319-16310-9_1

25. Palm, A., Metzger, A., Pohl, K.: Online reinforcement learning for self-adaptive information systems. In: Proceedings of CAiSE 2020, Grenoble, France. LNCS, vol. 12127, pp. 169–184. Springer (2020). https://doi.org/10.1007/978-3-030-49435-3_11

26. Saputri, T.R.D., Lee, S.W.: The application of machine learning in self-adaptive systems: a systematic literature review. IEEE Access **8**, 205948–205967 (2020). https://doi.org/10.1109/ACCESS.2020.3036037

27. Van Der Donckt, J., Weyns, D., Iftikhar, M.U., Buttar, S.S.: Effective decision making in self-adaptive systems using cost-benefit analysis at runtime and online learning of adaptation spaces. In: Evaluation of Novel Approaches to Software Engineering, LNCS, vol. 1023, pp. 373–403. Springer (2019). https://doi.org/10.1007/978-3-030-22559-9_17

28. Van Der Donckt, J., Weyns, D., Quin, F., Van Der Donckt, J., Michiels, S.: Applying deep learning to reduce large adaptation spaces of self-adaptive systems with multiple types of goals. In: Proceedings of SEAMS 2020, Seoul, South Korea, pp. 20–30. ACM (2020). https://doi.org/10.1145/3387939.3391605

Formal Analysis of Lending Pools
in Decentralized Finance

Massimo Bartoletti[1] , James Chiang[2] , Tommi Junttila[3],
Alberto Lluch Lafuente[2(✉)] , Massimiliano Mirelli[2] ,
and Andrea Vandin[2,4]

[1] Università degli Studi di Cagliari, Cagliari, Italy
bart@unica.it
[2] Technical University of Denmark, DTU Compute, Copenhagen, Denmark
{jchi,albl}@dtu.dk
[3] Aalto University, Espoo, Finland
tommi.junttila@aalto.fi
[4] Sant'Anna School of Advanced Studies, Pisa, Italy
andrea.vandin@santannapisa.it

Abstract. Decentralised Finance (DeFi) applications constitute an
entire financial ecosystem deployed on blockchains. Such applications
are based on complex protocols and incentive mechanisms whose financial safety is hard to determine. Besides, their adoption is rapidly growing, hence imperilling an increasingly higher amount of assets. Therefore,
accurate formalisation and verification of DeFi applications is essential
to assess their safety. We have developed a tool for the formal analysis
of one of the most widespread DeFi applications: Lending Pools (LP).
This was achieved by leveraging an existing formal model for LPs, the
Maude verification environment and the MultiVeStA statistical analyser.
The tool supports several analyses including reachability analysis, LTL
model checking and statistical model checking. In this paper we show
how the tool can be used to analyse several parameters of LPs that are
fundamental to assess and predict their behaviour. In particular, we use
statistical analysis to search for threshold and reward parameters that
minimize the risk of unrecoverable loans.

1 Introduction

Financial trading has recently shifted to virtual markets, platforms entirely regulated and controlled by novel protocols. *Decentralised Finance* (DeFi) [34] applications are deployed on blockchains like Ethereum [12,34], which offer distributed
infrastructures to execute *smart contracts* [18] without intermediaries. DeFi has
recently been employed by a growing community of users. As of April 2022,
the growth of the capital locked by DeFi applications has increased almost 10
times in the last two years: from approximately $9.78bn, on 1 April 2020, to

T. Margaria and B. Steffen (Eds.): ISoLA 2022, LNCS 13703, pp. 335–355, 2022.
https://doi.org/10.1007/978-3-031-19759-8_21

over \$83.51bn, on 1 April 2022 [29]. Even assuming the security guarantees ensured by the underlying blockchain, DeFi smart contracts have several vulnerabilities latent in their design [30,36]. Given the considerable amount of funds daily exchanged on DeFi platforms [1,16], even minor design flaws could determine massive and intolerable losses [21]. Notwithstanding the increasing interest of several research groups in this area [2,4,5,9,19,32], the complexity of DeFi protocols yields new interesting research problems. Formal verification of these systems is crucial, in order to ensure their correctness and security.

The verification tool proposed in this paper simulates and analyses *Lending Pools* (LPs), one of the most popular DeFi applications, whose two main features are lending and borrowing assets, to support various financial practices, including margin trading. Our verification tool is based on the formal model of LPs proposed in [6]. Such model encompasses the behaviour of the most widespread LPs, namely Aave [10] and Compound [24].

We craft an operational specification of the LP model of [6] in Maude [15], a specification language which is particularly suitable for highly concurrent systems such as LPs. Additionally, Maude provides a very extensive environment for both simulating and verifying the properties of the specified models. Given the complexity of the modelled systems, the analyses techniques offered by the Maude environment are not sufficient. Specifically, since the system may evolve by following an infinite number of execution paths, the traditional model checking methods result in being either ineffective or unviable. Therefore, the Maude-based LP simulator has been extended to support statistical analyses. This has been achieved by integrating the simulator with the MultiVeStA statistical analyser proposed in [31] and recently redesigned to focus on analyses of interest for of economical agent-based models [33]. The tool offers analysis techniques from the family of statistical model checking [3]. These statistical analyses, despite producing less accurate results, allow to observe the quantitative behaviour of large instances of the model, offering statistically-reliable results. In the case of lending pools, this approach allows to estimate parameters of the model so to increase its safety. Specifically, an essential safety property of the model is that the value of non-repayable loans is low.

This paper is based on the work done in [25] and proposes a Maude-based LP simulator (Sect. 3) capable of conducting several analyses of lending pools including LTL model checking and statistical analysis. The tool is open source and available at [26]. Additionally, the study showcases the usage of the tool by answering a still non-investigated research question, aiming at an enhancement of the analysed platforms' safety. In particular, the statistical analysis presented in Sect. 4 shows that a choice of the parameters used to instantiate the LP model reduces the amount of non-repayable loans.

2   Lending Pools and Price Models

Lending Pools. *Lending Pools* [35] are a class of DeFi applications which allow users to lend and borrow cryptoassets. At the time of writing, LPs are the most used DeFi applications, with the majority of them being deployed on Ethereum [29]. Deposited funds are pooled and lent on-demand to borrowers, only if they possess enough collateral (i.e. only if their account is over-collaterized). As blockchains typically do not provide strong identities, but pseudonyms [12], users' actions are difficult to be regulated under a jurisdiction, which makes collateralization the main protection mechanism against adversarial behaviours [27]: an agent can only borrow a quantity of tokens worth less than the amount of collateral they deposited. This mechanism and others (e.g. interest rates) is in place in order to incentivize borrowers to repay their loans.

We now recall details of the lending pools model in [6]. The basic components of the model are *agents* and *cryptoassets*. LP agents are the rational entities taking part in the protocol. Contrarily, LP cryptoassets are token types, each representing a different virtual currency. The model distinguishes two classes of token types: *free tokens* and *minted tokens*, denoted respectively by the sets $T_f = \{\tau_i\}_{i\in[1..k]}$ and $T_m = \{\tau'_i\}_{i\in[1..k]}$, where k is the number of cryptocurrencies available on the pool. The difference between these classes of token types is that free tokens have a value established by external markets, whereas minted tokens are assets coined by the protocol, hence holding value only in a specific LP environment. In other words, minted tokens are loyalty credits held by the agents actively joining the protocol. In fact, minted tokens are granted by the protocol to the agents in return for free tokens, hence each minted token τ' corresponds to a free token τ, also called its underlying token. We denote by T the set of all token types, i.e. $T = T_f \cup T_m$.

Given agents and assets, the LP model yields as a transition system where each state Γ is of the form $\Gamma = \sigma \mid \pi \mid p$:

1. The *wallets* function $\sigma : A \to (T \to \mathbb{R}_0^+)$ stores each agent's balance of tokens. For instance, the wallet of an agent A is expressed by the partial function σ_A, and the balance of its τ-typed tokens by $\sigma_A(\tau)$.
2. The *pool* component π is a triple (π_f, π_l, π_m). It is composed by three partial functions: $\pi_f : T_f \to \mathbb{R}_0^+$ storing the amount of free tokens deposited in the pool, $\pi_l : A \to (T_f \to \mathbb{R}_0^+)$ memorising the loans each agent owes to the pool and $\pi_m : T_f \to (T_m \times \mathbb{R}_0^+)$ keeping track of the minted tokens (also called the *collateral* or *credits*) purchased from the pool.
3. The *price* function $p : dom(\pi_f) \to \mathbb{R}_0^+$ stores the price of each free token available in the pool.

Given a partial map f, we denote by $f\{v/x\}$ the point-wise update of f at the point x to the value v. In order to add and remove tokens in the functions defined above, a partial binary operation $\circ : \mathbb{R}_0^+ \times \mathbb{R}_0^+ \to \mathbb{R}_0^+$, such as addition, is extended to them. Given a partial map $f : T \to \mathbb{R}_0^+$, a token type $\tau \in T$ and a value $v \in \mathbb{R}_0^+$, the partial map $f \circ v : \tau$ is defined as

$$f \circ v : \tau = \begin{cases} f\{f(\tau) \circ v/\tau\} \text{ if } \tau \in dom(f) \text{ and } f(\tau) \circ v \text{ is defined} \\ f\{v/\tau\} \text{ if } \tau \notin dom(f) \end{cases}$$

In order to describe the model evolution, some additional definitions shall be given. The following LP components may rely on the whole state Γ, or some of its components. This dependency is indicated by the means of subscripts. For instance, writing F_X means that F depends on the X component of the state.

The functions V_Γ^l and V_Γ^m define, respectively, value of tokens lent to a given agent, and the value of minted tokens owned by a given agent:

$$V_\Gamma^l(A) = \sum_{\tau \in \mathcal{T}_f} (\pi_l(A))(\tau) \cdot p(\tau) \qquad V_\Gamma^m(A) = \sum_{\tau' \in \mathcal{T}_m} \sigma_A(\tau') \cdot ER_\pi(\tau', \tau) \cdot p(\tau)$$

where $ER_\pi(\tau', \tau)$ is the exchange rate of minted tokens (see Sect. 3.1 of [6]).

The collateralization of an agent A is defined as $C_\Gamma(A) = V_\Gamma^m(A)/V_\Gamma^l(A)$. This is an essential indicator of agents' lending safety: in fact, a collateralization below a given threshold (C_{min}) entails an agent to be liquidated and hence to incur in a financial loss, as detailed later.

The behaviour of agents interacting with a lending pool is formalized as a set of rewriting rules, which define transitions between states. Such transitions are written as $\Gamma \xrightarrow{r_A(z^n)} \Gamma'$, where Γ is the starting state, Γ' is the target state, and $r_A(z^n)$ is the action (fired by A) which triggers the state transition. Actions have the form $r_A(z^n)$, where r is the action name, and z^n is an n-tuple of parameters.

Table 1. Summary of some of the lending pools actions from [6].

$Dep_A(v : \tau)$	A deposits v free-tokens of type τ from its wallet to the pool. Subsequently, the pool coins v' units of τ', with v' computed so to incentivize deposits only if the LP is lacking free tokens
$Rdm_A(v : \tau')$	A redeems v units of the minted token τ', as long as A's collateralization is greater than a threshold (C_{min}) and LP holds enough tokens of type τ'
$Bor_A(v : \tau)$	A borrows v units of a free token τ, assuming it has enough collateral
$Rep_A(v : \tau)$	A repays v units of its loan in the free token τ to the LP
$Liq_A(B, v : \hat{\tau}, \tau')$	A (liquidator) liquidates a variable amount of B's (borrower's) minted tokens τ', by paying v units of free tokens $\hat{\tau}$. Notably, $\hat{\tau} \in \mathcal{T}_f$ is in general different from τ, the underlying token of $\tau' \in \mathcal{T}_m$. This action can be executed only if the B's collateralization is below C_{min}, meaning B is undercollaterized
Int	The LP contract accrues interest on the existing loans. This disincentivizes borrowers from postponing their loans repayment
Price	Token prices are updated according to a given price evolution model

The main actions of lending pools are informally summarised in Table 1. Since the focus in this paper is on liquidations as one of the key incentive mechanisms, we will provide the details for such action only. Figure 1 provides a formal description of the rule. The essential preconditions to understand the rule are ④, ⑧, ⑨, ⑩ and ⑪.

(3) The amount of repayable loan is limited by a percentage factor $Maxliq$, as done in Aave [11] and Compound [28].

(4) computes the reward for the liquidating agent. This is based on the liquidated amount v and the reward factor r_{liq}. The idea is that A, by repaying part of B's loan, is reducing the likelihood of the protocol to become illiquid. This behaviour is incentivized by the platform by setting the aforementioned reward to a value strictly higher than 1. A common value for r_{liq} is 1.1.

(8), (9) update the involved agents' wallets, A repays v units of B's loan in $\hat{\tau}$ and is compensated with v' units of τ'

(10) ensures that the rule is executable only if B's collateralization is less than $C_{\min}$, which is often set to 1.5. This rule is the reason why agents' collateralization should be at least $C_{\min}$, so to avert the risk of being liquidated and incurring in the loss of the liquidation reward r_{liq}.

(11) prevents A from seizing a higher collateral amount than the one required for B to be considered safe (i.e. $C_\Gamma(B) \geq C_{\min}$).

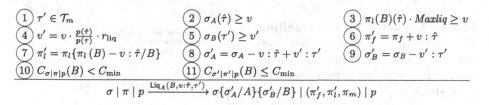

$$\boxed{1}\ \tau' \in \mathcal{T}_m \qquad \boxed{2}\ \sigma_A(\hat{\tau}) \geq v \qquad \boxed{3}\ \pi_l(B)(\hat{\tau}) \cdot Maxliq \geq v$$

$$\boxed{4}\ v' = v \cdot \tfrac{p(\hat{\tau})}{p(\tau)} \cdot r_{\mathrm{liq}} \qquad \boxed{5}\ \sigma_B(\tau') \geq v' \qquad \boxed{6}\ \pi'_f = \pi_f + v : \hat{\tau}$$

$$\boxed{7}\ \pi'_l = \pi_l\{\pi_l(B) - v : \hat{\tau}/B\} \qquad \boxed{8}\ \sigma'_A = \sigma_A - v : \hat{\tau} + v' : \tau' \qquad \boxed{9}\ \sigma'_B = \sigma_B - v' : \tau'$$

$$\boxed{10}\ C_{\sigma|\pi|p}(B) < C_{\min} \qquad \boxed{11}\ C_{\sigma'|\pi'|p}(B) \leq C_{\min}$$

$$\sigma \mid \pi \mid p \xrightarrow{\ \mathrm{Liq}_A(B,v:\hat{\tau},\tau')\ } \sigma\{\sigma'_A/A\}\{\sigma'_B/B\} \mid (\pi'_f, \pi'_l, \pi_m) \mid p$$

Fig. 1. The rule for liquidation.

Figure 2 illustrates the transition system for a simple running example, where three liquidate actions are executed. The figure shows six possible traces all originating from Γ_0 and having $\Gamma_{3,1}$ as final state. Each state in the figure is defined by a row in Table 2. Additionally, transitions, namely Liq actions performed by D, are indicated by different colours depending on the liquidated borrower in both the transition system and the table. Notably, assuming $C_{\min} = 1.5$ and $r_{\mathrm{liq}} = 1.1$, all borrowers in Γ_0, A, B and C, are undercollaterized. Specifically, A is marginally undercollaterized since $C_{\Gamma_0}(A) = 1.25 > 1.1 = r_{\mathrm{liq}}$, while B and C are strongly undercollaterized, being both $C_{\Gamma_0}(B)$ and $C_{\Gamma_0}(C)$ below 1.1. This allows D to seize the entire B and C's collateral, as evident from $\Gamma_{3,1}$ in Table 2. Contrarily A's collateralization is restored to $C_{\min}$.

As an example, consider transition $\Gamma_0 \xrightarrow{\ \mathrm{Liq}_D(B,91:\tau_1,\tau'_0)\ } \Gamma_{1,2}$. Agent D repays 91 units of τ_1, seizing $91 \cdot r_{\mathrm{liq}} \approx 100$ units of τ'_0 from agent B. This also affects π, in a way that the funds in τ_1 are incremented by 91 units, as illustrated by $\pi_f(\tau_1)$, while B's loan is decremented by 91 units, as shown by $\pi_l(B)(\tau_1)$. Contrarily, π_m is not modified by the transaction, as the 100 units of minted tokens τ'_0 are simply transferred from B's wallet to D's one.

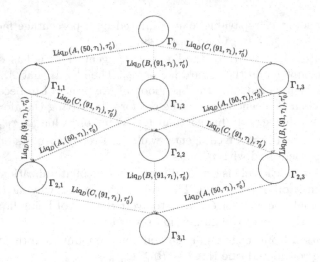

Fig. 2. Example transition system.

Stock Market Price Modelling.
We use the *geometric Brownian motion* (GBM) to define a predictive model for price evolution based on past stock market trends. A GBM is a continuous-time stochastic process $P_t = P_0 \cdot exp\left[\left(\mu - \frac{\sigma^2}{2}\right)t + \sigma W_t\right]$. The two constants μ and σ are respectively called *drift* and *volatility*, whereas W_t is a random variable following a *Weiner process*, i.e. a process $W_t = \epsilon\sqrt{dt}$ satisfying the following properties: (i) $\epsilon \sim N(0,1)$ and (ii) for any

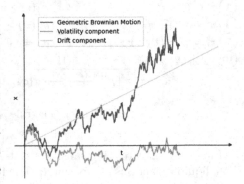

Fig. 3. GBM components.

given pair (t_0, t_0'), W_{t_0} and $W_{t_0'}$ are independent. In other words, a W_t is the component yielding the stochastic behaviour of a GBM. The geometric Brownian motion as a whole can be viewed as the harmonic result of its two components [20]: (i) the drift $\left(\mu - \frac{\sigma^2}{2}\right)t$ and (ii) the volatility σW_t. The effects of the two components on the resulting process is shown in Fig. 3. The drift component defines the trend of the resulting process, whereas the volatility component is a measure of the randomly sampled shocks. Intuitively, this signifies that negative values for μ yield to a downward prediction trend, whereas positive ones to a growth. Oppositely, the higher the σ is, the more significantly the prices predictions change. Ususall, μ and σ are estimated based on the daily log returns of the targeted stock market [17,20]. Given the closing prices of two consecutive trading days C_1 and C_2, the log return w.r.t. the second trading day is defined as $ln(C_2) - ln(C_1)$.

Table 2. States of the transition system in Fig. 2. For simplicity, the price function p is assumed to be constant such that $p(\tau_0) = p(\tau_1) = 1$ in every state. The values of the LP parameters are $C_{\min} = 1.5$, $r_{\text{liq}} = 1.1$ and $Maxliq = 1$.

Γ	π_f	π_l			σ_A		σ_B		σ_C		σ_D			C_Γ		
		A	B	C										A	B	C
	τ_1	τ_1	τ_1	τ_1	τ_1	τ'_0	τ_1	τ'_0	τ_1	τ'_0	τ_1	τ'_0	τ'_1	A	B	C
Γ_0^i	195	80	100	125	80	100	100	100	125	100	500	0	500	1.25	1	0.8
$\Gamma_{1,1}$	245	30	100	125	80	45	100	100	125	100	450	55	500	1.5	1	0.8
$\Gamma_{1,2}$	286	80	9	125	80	100	100	0	125	100	410	100	500	1.25	0	0.8
$\Gamma_{1,3}$	286	80	100	34	80	100	100	100	125	0	410	100	500	1.25	1	0
$\Gamma_{2,1}$	336	30	9	125	80	45	100	0	125	100	359	155	500	1.5	0	0.8
$\Gamma_{2,2}$	336	30	100	34	80	45	100	100	125	0	359	155	500	1.5	1	0
$\Gamma_{2,3}$	377	80	9	34	80	100	100	0	125	0	318	200	500	1.25	0	0
$\Gamma_{3,1}$	427	30	9	34	80	45	100	0	125	0	268	255	500	1.5	0	0

3 An LP Simulator for Liquidating Agents

We now lay the foundations for tackling a significant research problem for LPs: finding optimal $C_{\min}$ and r_{liq} parameters. This is achieved by instantiating the LP simulator to conduct statistical analyses of the model. The simulator comprises: the Maude specification of LPs [26]; a strategy for automating the behaviour of rational liquidators (Sect. 3.1); and a price evolution model for the three most widely employed cryptocurrencies (Sect. 3.2).

3.1 A Fully-Automated Liquidating Strategy

This section introduces a liquidating strategy causing the LP protocol to possibly reach unsafe states, where loans are not guaranteed to be repaid. We first give an intuitive understanding of aggressive liquidating behaviours, and then describe the proposed liquidating strategy.

The Impact of Liquidations On collateralization. Liquidate actions involve two agents: a liquidator, i.e. as an agent with enough tokens to fire liquidate actions, and a borrower with a collateralization below the threshold $C_{\min}$.

Liquidators have a fundamental role in the financial safety of LPs, as they supply free tokens whenever the pool is lacking them. On the other hand, excessively zealous liquidators could be harmful to the system, since they could disincentivize undercollaterized borrowers to repay their loans. This is exemplified in Fig. 4, where all the liquidating scenarios are outlined. The figure illustrates the agents' collateralization, detailing the outcomes of liquidate actions in every possible (non-trivial) state. The scenarios are also captured by the running example in Fig. 2.

Firstly, the three dashed lines in the figure correspond to the liquidation parameters specific to the instantiated pool. Their labels represent the respective line slopes. The line labelled 1 depicts the scenarios where the collateral value equals the loan value. Consequently, it can be intended as the loan repayment incentivizing threshold, i.e. the collateralization value below which borrowing agents should be considered to be disincentivized in repaying their loans as their outstanding loan debt exceeds their collateral in value. These residual loans are also called *non-recoverable*.

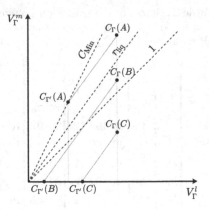

Fig. 4. Liquidation scenarios

Additionally, the three points indicate the initial collateralization of three liquidated borrowers. Each liquidation action is illustrated by a solid line drawn from $C_\Gamma(I)$ to $C_{\Gamma'}(I)$ for $I \in \{A, B, C\}$. Liquidations entail a decrease in the liquidated user's collateralization by a linear factor proportional to r_{liq} and ultimately determined by the liquidator. Note that the liquidation actions described in the figure follow the semantics of the liquidate action, as the resulting loan value must be greater than zero and the final collateralization must be at most C_{min}.

It is worth observing that the liquidations in the figure can be achieved by applying only one action if and only if two conditions hold. Firstly, the liquidator invests enough liquidity to seize the entire seizable collateral. Secondly, the liquidated borrower does not diversify the type of the loan. If either the first condition or the second does not hold, then the liquidations illustrated in the figure can be achieved uniquely by performing several liquidate actions on the borrower. This is frequently the case in the major LP implementations (Compound and Aave). In fact, these prevent the whole seizable collateral amount to be atomically liquidated, by setting *Maxliq* which is variable in Compound [28] and constant (equals to 0.5) in Aave [11]. Our model includes the parameter *Maxliq* as a constant following Aave, but it could be extended to a variable one.

The Proposed Liquidating Strategy. As shown in Fig. 4, the collateralization of A is re-established, whereas liquidations cause B and C to lose their entire collateral, disincentivizing them from repaying the loans. In light of this fact, a relevant research question is whether there exists an optimal pair $(C_{\text{min}}, r_{\text{liq}})$ such that the number of non-recoverable loans is minimal.

It is worth to observe that, ideally, the closer r_{liq} is to 1, the more the collateralization of a loan can drop and still be recoverable by liquidation. Thus a r_{liq} marginally greater than 1 is optimal in our model, since it would lead to the strongest recovery of user collateralization during liquidation. However, actual platforms deviate from such ideally optimal r_{liq} as the costs incurred by liquidators to execute actions have to be compensated by a suitable discount r_{liq} on the purchase of minted tokens from the liquidated borrowers. In order to investigate the effects of choices r_{liq} and C_{min}, we propose a strategy attempting to reproduce a rational behaviour for liquidators. The employed strategy simulates a *rational* behaviour where liquidators repay the entire borrowers' loan. The rationality of the behaviour we are going to study is based on the following key observations:

1. Fast liquidations have the advantage of restoring liquidity whenever the borrowers have collateralization slightly above r_{liq} (see agent A in Fig. 4).
2. On the other hand, fast liquidations may generate non-recoverable loans whenever the borrowers have collateralization slightly below r_{liq} (as for agents B and C in Fig. 4).
3. Price fluctuations can change the scenario between (1) and (2). For example, it could raise the collateralization of borrowers to r_{liq} allowing the liquidators to effectively restore the agents' collateralization to C_{min}, so that it would be convenient to delay liquidations.

The strategy used to implement the liquidator behaviour selects the liquidate input parameters, so to maximise the value of seized collateral. Specifically, given a liquidator L, the strategy computes the remaining four parameters of Liq: the borrower's agent identifier (B_r), the amount of loan to be repaid (v_r), the type of the asset to be repaid ($\hat{\tau}_r$) and the one of the asset to be seized (τ'_r). Because of space constraints, we refer to [25] for a detailed account of the strategy.

3.2 Price Modelling

This section describes the price model employed to predict cryptocurrencies prices, based on historical data. We start with an overview of the price model to motivate its adoption. Afterwards, we present the three model instantiation scenarios used in the subsequent statistical analysis.

Predicting Cryptocurrency Prices. The cryptoassets prices are derived from a statistical model representative of the past price behaviour based on the GBM. A GBM is instantiated by two parameters drift and volatility which can be estimated from the currency historical data. This makes the GBM the ideal stochastic process for modelling stock prices based on their past evolution [17].

Aiming at stress-testing the LP protocol and inspired by [19], we have designed three different scenarios, each comprising a pair of price trends. In practice, each scenario simulates the evolution of prices of a given collateral and loan assets, in a way that respectively when the former declines, the latter increases. In fact, assuming that each borrower B_0 owes a loan in only one asset type τ_l and similarly holds collateral of only one asset type τ_m, such a model for prices necessarily causes some borrowers to become undercollaterized, as shown in (1).

$$C_\Gamma(B_0) = \frac{V_\Gamma^m(B_0)}{V_\Gamma^l(B_0)} \xrightarrow{p(\tau_m) \to 0 \ p(\tau_l) \to V} 0, \text{with } V \gg 0 \qquad (1)$$

More precisely, prices modelling is achieved by opportunely gathering the data used to estimate the parameters (drift and volatility) for generating a growing, decreasing or relatively constant GBM process. In the literature, daily closing prices of stock markets are used since their samples generally tend to be normal, which allows to employ the GBM generic formula. Ultimately, since prices' predictions pairs should variate in a way that they simultaneously display an opposite behaviour, it is necessary to correlate them, as shown in [20].

Prices Model Instantiation. Given a collateral asset τ_m and a loan asset τ_l, the three prices evolution pairs are shown in Table 3.

Table 3. The three implemented prices evolution scenarios.

Scenario	τ_m	τ_l	$p(\tau_m)$	$p(\tau_l)$
ETH-WBTC	ETH	WBTC	Declining	Increasing
ETH-USDC	ETH	USDC	Declining	Constant
USDC-WBTC	USDC	WBTC	Constant	Increasing

The choice of the cryptocurrencies in the table is motivated by their closing price historical evolution in three different trimesters (shown in the Appendix, Fig. 9). By using those samples, it is possible to simulate the desired trends indicated in the columns named $p(\tau_m)$ and $p(\tau_l)$. This is achieved by estimating the expected price returns (μ) and the price volatility (σ), which are utilised as the drift and volatility instantiating the resulting GBM. The two parameters are estimated according to [20]. The drift μ is simply obtained by computing the mean over the closing prices. Contrarily, σ is calculated as $\sigma = \frac{s}{\sqrt{T}}$, where $T = \frac{91}{365}$, s indicates the standard deviation of the log returns and $\sqrt{T}$ is the annualisation constant.

The selected sampling time span (91 d, i.e. a trimester) is motivated by the fact that cryptoassets are subject to sudden fluctuations and, even though short samples might not be representative of the entire population, this is a consolidated practice [20]. Besides, the resulting price predictions span over the same time frames, as each price model instantiation produces 91 prices predictions, as illustrated in Sect. 3.2. Notably, the selected cryptocurrencies (ETH, USDC and WBTC) were among the four-most-utilised assets on the Compound market [16] at the moment of writing. Lastly, the selected closing price samples are suitable, since the derived log returns distributions tend to be normal.

Figure 5 shows an estimation of the GBM parameters (obtained from the close prices in the Appendix, Fig. 9), by the previously discussed methodology. The parameters are then utilised to instanti-ate the six GBM processes (each for price

Currency	μ	σ	P_0 (usd)
ETH	-0.012	0.12	3269.08
USDC	-7.84E-5	0.005	0.99
WBTC	0.012	0.094	57260.0

Fig. 5. GBM parameters

evolution), simulating the scenarios in Table 3. Finally, the asset initial price P_0 is a constant set to the actual price in USD of each asset on May 5th, 2021.

Expected Price predictions. We have used the MultiVeStA statistical analyzer to examine the prices predictions generated by the GBM in each of the scenarios explained in Sect. 3.2. The details are provided in the appendix (Fig. 10), and show the normalised trend of the price scenarios, discussed in Sect. 3.2. The figures in the appendix show that the expected behaviour, expressed in Table 3 is obtained in all the considered scenarios. Additionally, in Figs. 10a and 10b prices predictions are strongly correlated as it is expected. In fact, the GBMs pairs were instantiated as negatively correlated processes accordingly to [20], Sect. 14.5. Contrarily, Fig. 10b shows less correlated prices predictions. This is probably due to the fact that the computation was bounded to execute maximum 5,010 simulations. In fact, from experimental evidence, the approximation seem to converge at a very slow speed.

4   Statistical Analysis of Liquidation Scenarios

We have experimented with the LP model simulator described in Sect. 3 in order to answer the question: *given a specific scenario, what is the impact of the pair of LP parameters C_{min} and r_{liq}?*

We have considered scenarios generated by four factors. First, the liquidator logic defined in Sect. 3.1, determines immediate and quick liquidations, causing a significant financial loss to the liquidated party. Secondly, the agent to be liquidated is selected so to maximise the value of seized collateral, which is the most beneficial and rational option for liquidators. Thirdly, liquidators are assumed to hold an *unbounded* amount of resources, which allows them to repeat liquidations as long as there exists an undercollaterized agent. Finally, cryptoasset prices evolve following a trend aimed at causing borrowers to suddenly become undercollaterized.

We recall that the effect of the pair C_{min} and r_{liq} we are looking for is one that minimises the number of undercollaterized borrowers. We have explored the space of choices for the pair by executing MultiVeStA experiments for all C_{min} ranging, with step 0.1, from 1.2 to 1.5 and r_{liq} ranging from 1.1 to $C_{min} - 0.1$. These ranges were selected based on the values typically assigned to these parameters in the actual implementations: $C_{min} = 1.5$ and $r_{liq} = 1.1$ [6].

On these premises, we first illustrate the LP model initial configura-

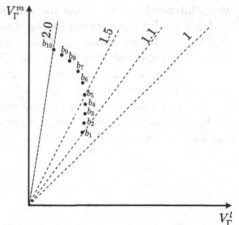

Fig. 6. Distribution of collateralization in initial configurations.

tions used for the subsequent experimentation. Next, we present the results of the performed experiments.

Initial Configurations. The initial configurations were designed to test the resistance of different borrowers' collateralization to becoming unrecoverable, when subject to repeated liquidations. Since the intention is to observe the model behaviour under three price models (Sect. 3.2), three different initial configurations are produced, each having a different price for collateral and loan assets. All the configurations share the same amount and types of agents. Specifically, a generic initial configuration comprises ten borrowers having collateralization ranging from 1.0 to 2.0, with step 0.1. This is depicted in Fig. 6, where b_i represents the generic borrower B_i's collateralization ($C_{\Gamma^i}(B_i)$), for Γ^i initial configuration. Additionally, an arbitrary number of liquidators (three) are added to each configuration.

Experimental Results. The results discussed here were obtained by performing MultiVeStA experiments of the LP simulator. Specifically, the inputs to the tool are: the LP simulator discussed in Sect. 3, a MultiQuaTEx property to express the desired measure to be estimated (the expected collateralization value at each liquidation round for each borrower), and a pair of statistical parameters defining the confidence interval (CI) of interest: the maximum confidence interval width δ and the confidence level $\alpha = 0.05$ which provides 95% statistical confidence that the estimated value is in the confidence interval. For each property, MultiVeStA will generate enough simulation to meet the required CI.

Figure 7 shows the per-borrower collateralization for varying liquidation rounds and choices of C_{min} and r_{liq} in the eth-wbtc prices scenario, with a fixed $r_{liq} = 1.1$. In this scenario, one can see that undercollaterized agents have a very different behaviour than overcollaterized ones. Specifically, the undercollaterized agents undergo very serious liquidations, which often lead them to unrecoverability, as their collateralization converges to a constant below C_{min}. Contrarily, overcollaterized agents do not incur in severe financial losses.

Additionally, our experiments (presented in detail in the Appendix, Figs. 11a to 11c) show that the C_{min} and r_{liq} having the least negative effects on undercollaterized balances is $C_{min} = 1.5$, $r_{liq} = 1.1$. This is also quantitatively confirmed by the numbers in Fig. 8. Intuitively, this is a consequence of the fact that when $C_{min} = 1.5$ and $r_{liq} = 1.1$ the collateralization of each agent b_1 to b_5 is higher on average than for any other C_{min} and r_{liq} pairs. As a result, the number of unrecoverable loans, the ones held by agents whose collateralization is below 1, is minimised.

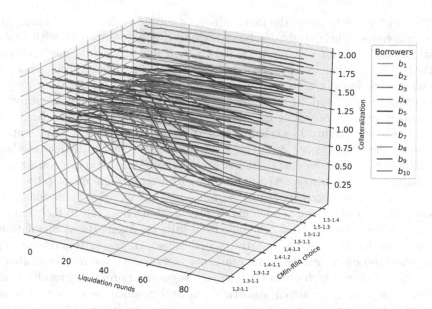

Fig. 7. Per-borrower collateralization (b_1 to b_{10}) in the ETH-WBTC prices scenario, for varying liquidation rounds and `CMin-Rliq` choices.

Finally, our experiments (presented in detail in the Appendix, Figs. 12a to 12c) show that over-collaterized borrowers could still incur in liquidations, in case the prices abruptly change as in the prices scenario ETH-WBTC. Dif-

Price scenario	(`CMin-Rliq`)		
	(1.5-1.1)	(1.4-1.1)	(1.3-1.1)
ETH-WBTC	0.7115	0.6518	0.6137
ETH-USDC	0.7106	0.6583	0.6231
USDC-WBTC	0.8381	0.7739	0.7299

Fig. 8. Minimum average $C_\Gamma(B_1)$

ferently, in the other scenarios, employing the stable coin USDC, overcollaterized agents are, on average, rarely liquidated.

5   Related Works

Verification of DeFi applications is a fairly recent research area where several techniques have been applied. We focus our discussion on works devoted to formal modelling and reasoning of DeFi applications, which typically follow two parallel directions: verification of the model properties [2,5,9,32], and statistical analysis of the model variables [4,13,14,19,22].

The work in [9] is one of the first addressing formal verification of smart contract properties. Their study combines a game-theoretic approach with probabilistic model checking, ultimately validating their results with the model checker PRISM [23]. Another example of research in this direction is Tolmach et al. [32] which developed the first multi-pools model and verified invariant properties initially formulated by [8]. Finally, [2] proposed a very relevant study on smart contracts, by modelling not only the contracts and the agents' behaviour but also the underlying blockchain using the BIP framework [7] and statistical model checking (as we do). The work in [2] employs statistical methods too. However, in their case, statistics is useful to estimate unknown variables of the analysed model, hence deriving desirable properties. The quantitative variables estimation is also achieved by performing Monte-Carlo simulations, with a more closely look at the behaviours displayed by agents [14]. In fact, most of this research in this line [4,13,22] bases its results on Agent-Based Simulations, which is employed to stress test the actual smart contracts implementations being executed on a *"custom-built Ethereum virtual machine that is written in C++"* [22]. This research direction, although suggesting promising results, is not ultimately supported by strong statistical guarantees, since the number of Monte Carlo simulations performed to run their analyses is arbitrarily chosen and not backed by a formal justification [19,22]. Nonetheless, a work relevant to ours is the analysis conducted in [22] on the Compound protocol scalability in face of high stock market prices volatility. Similarly to our work, their analysis models the prices by the use of the GBM. However, their data collection and analysis methodologies are very different. In fact, they do not sample entire historical periods as illustrated in Sect. 3.2 for estimating prices volatility. Contrarily, they simply evaluate the minimum and maximum volatility values ever observed and instantiate the GBM for different prices volatilities so to simulate several market environments. Finally, the prices model in Sect. 3.2 has been mostly inspired by [19]. Similarly to [22], they stress-test an LP model, not a specific implementation, by using the same price model explained in Sect. 3.2. Nonetheless, a remarkable difference is that they instantiate the predictions of the collateral and loan assets pairs with three different correlation parameters. We assume instead predictions of prices pairs to be strongly negatively correlated ($\rho = -1$), in order to simulate the worst-case scenario. Additionally, we reproduced [19]'s environment by using historical data of three different real cryptoassets on the market.

6   Conclusions

We have presented a tool for the analysis of lending pools, an archetypal DeFi application. Overall the tool consists of (i) an accurate LP simulator based on the model of [6] which can support both the study of vulnerabilities and attacks of LPs; (ii) a model checker capable of doing simple reachability analysis and verifying whether LTL properties hold of specific configurations; and (iii) a tool for statistical analysis backed by the statistical model checker MultiVeStA. In this paper, we have focused on (iii) and we have shown how to use it to optimize the LP parameters under specific scenarios. Details on (i) and (ii) as well as further examples, including reproduction of price oracle attacks using reachability analysis and LTL model checking are available in [25].

Future research supported by the developed tool could include the formalization of further attacks and properties of the model. Specifically, one could study resistance to illiquidity, as suggested by [22], or the behaviour of multi-pools configurations, each offering different market opportunities to agents, as proposed by [35] and partially developed in [32].

Acknowledgements. Massimo Bartoletti is partially supported by Conv. Fondazione di Sardegna & Atenei Sardi project F75F21001220007 *ASTRID*. James Hsin-yu Chiang is supported by the PhD School of DTU Compute. Alberto Lluch Lafuente is partially supported by the EU H2020-SU-ICT-03-2018 Project No. 830929 Cyber-Sec4Europe (cybersec4europe.eu). Andrea Vandin is partially supported by the DFF project REDUCTO 9040-00224B.

A   Figures

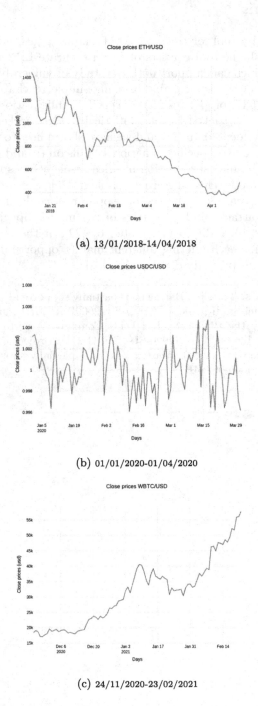

(a) 13/01/2018–14/04/2018

(b) 01/01/2020–01/04/2020

(c) 24/11/2020–23/02/2021

Fig. 9. Trimester closing prices, collected from CoinGecko APIs

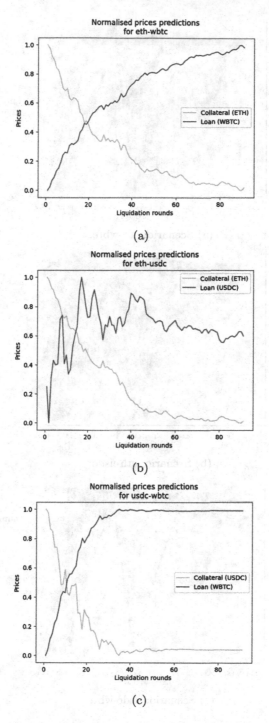

Fig. 10. Prices predictions produced, for each scenario in Table 3, by GBMs instantiated with the parameters in Fig. 5.

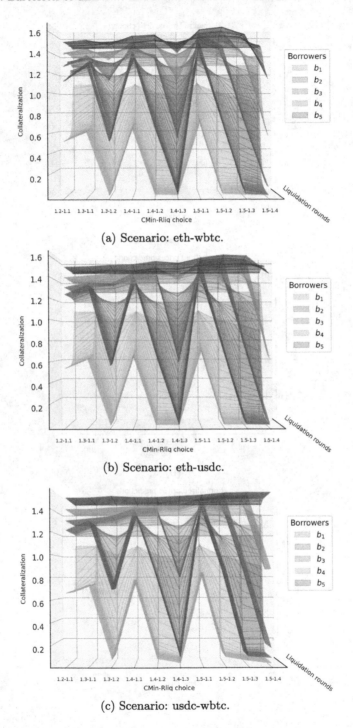

(a) Scenario: eth-wbtc.

(b) Scenario: eth-usdc.

(c) Scenario: usdc-wbtc.

Fig. 11. Per-borrower collateralization (b_1 to b_5) in the three prices scenarios, for varying CMin-rliq choices.

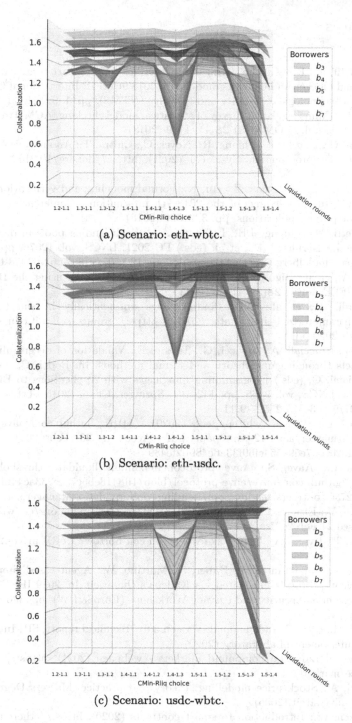

(a) Scenario: eth-wbtc.

(b) Scenario: eth-usdc.

(c) Scenario: usdc-wbtc.

Fig. 12. Per-borrower collateralization (b_3 to b_7) in the three prices scenarios, for varying CMin-rliq choices.

References

1. Aave, S.: Aave markets - webpage (2021). https://aave.com/
2. Abdellatif, T., Brousmiche, K.L.: Formal verification of smart contracts based on users and blockchain behaviors models. In: 2018 9th IFIP International Conference on New Technologies, Mobility and Security (NTMS), pp. 1–5. IEEE (2018)
3. Agha, G., Palmskog, K.: A survey of statistical model checking. ACM Trans. Model. Comput. Simul. (TOMACS) **28**(1), 1–39 (2018)
4. Angeris, G., Kao, H.T., Chiang, R., Noyes, C., Chitra, T.: An analysis of Uniswap markets. Cryptoeconomic Syst. (1) (2021). https://doi.org/10.21428/58320208.c9738e64
5. Bai, X., Cheng, Z., Duan, Z., Hu, K.: Formal modeling and verification of smart contracts. In: Proceedings of the 2018 7th International Conference on Software and Computer Applications, pp. 322–326 (2018)
6. Bartoletti, M., Chiang, J.H., Lafuente, A.L.: SoK: lending pools in decentralized finance. In: Bernhard, M., et al. (eds.) FC 2021. LNCS, vol. 12676, pp. 553–578. Springer, Heidelberg (2021). https://doi.org/10.1007/978-3-662-63958-0_40
7. Basu, A., et al.: Rigorous component-based system design using the BIP framework. IEEE Softw. **28**(3), 41–48 (2011)
8. Bernardi, T., et al.: WIP: finding bugs automatically in smart contracts with parameterized invariants (2020). https://groups.csail.mit.edu/sdg/pubs/2020/sbc2020.pdf
9. Bigi, G., Bracciali, A., Meacci, G., Tuosto, E.: Validation of decentralised smart contracts through game theory and formal methods. In: Bodei, C., Ferrari, G.-L., Priami, C. (eds.) Programming Languages with Applications to Biology and Security. LNCS, vol. 9465, pp. 142–161. Springer, Cham (2015). https://doi.org/10.1007/978-3-319-25527-9_11
10. Boado, E.: Aave whitepaper (2020). https://github.com/aave/protocol-v2/blob/master/aave-v2-whitepaper.pdf. Accessed 26 Feb 2021 - commit aeded1520c667e59a564cf69f33a6e489b2fe489
11. Boado, E., Aave, S.: Aave protocol maximum liquidate threshold (2021). https://github.com/aave/aave-protocol/blob/1ff8418eb5c73ce233ac44bfb7541d07828b273f/contracts/lendingpool/LendingPoolLiquidationManager.sol#L181
12. Buterin, V.: Ethereum whitepaper (2013). https://ethereum.org/en/whitepaper/. Accessed 24 Feb 2021
13. Chitra, T., Evans, A.: Why stake when you can borrow? CoRR arXiv:2006.11156 (2020)
14. Chitra, T., Quaintance, M., Haber, S., Martino, W.: Agent-based simulations of blockchain protocols illustrated via Kadena's chainweb. In: 2019 IEEE European Symposium on Security and Privacy Workshops (EuroS&PW), pp. 386–395. IEEE (2019)
15. Clavel, M., et al.: Maude manual (version 3.0). Technical report, SRI International Computer Science Laboratory (2020)
16. Compound Labs, I.: Compound markets - webpage (2021). https://compound.finance/markets
17. Dmouj, A.: Stock price modelling: theory and practice. Masters Degree Thesis, Vrije Universiteit (2006)
18. Entriken, W.: Introduction to smart contracts (2020). https://ethereum.org/en/developers/docs/smart-contracts/. Accessed 27 Feb 2021

19. Gudgeon, L., Perez, D., Harz, D., Livshits, B., Gervais, A.: The decentralized financial crisis. In: 2020 Crypto Valley Conference on Blockchain Technology (CVCBT), pp. 1–15. IEEE (2020)
20. Hull, J.C.: Options Futures and Other Derivatives. Pearson Education India (2003)
21. Jeffrey, G.: Compound price oracle attack (2020). https://news.bitcoin.com/100-million-liquidated-on-defi-protocol-compound-following-oracle-exploit/
22. Kao, H.T., Chitra, T., Chiang, R., Morrow, J.: An analysis of the market risk to participants in the Compound protocol. In: Third International Symposium on Foundations and Applications of Blockchains (2020)
23. Kwiatkowska, M., Norman, G., Parker, D.: PRISM 4.0: verification of probabilistic real-time systems. In: Gopalakrishnan, G., Qadeer, S. (eds.) CAV 2011. LNCS, vol. 6806, pp. 585–591. Springer, Heidelberg (2011). https://doi.org/10.1007/978-3-642-22110-1_47
24. Leshner, R., Hayes, G.: Compound: the money market protocol (2019). https://compound.finance/documents/Compound.Whitepaper.v04.pdf
25. Mirelli, M.: A formal verification tool for lending pools. Master's thesis, Aalto University. School of Science (2021). http://urn.fi/URN:NBN:fi:aalto-202108298504
26. Mirelli, M.: A maude simulator for lending pools (2021). https://github.com/MMirelli/maude-lp. Accessed 22 June 2022 - commit 2dae39b035938f5f9791040c53121fb473b4b7dd
27. Perez, D., Werner, S.M., Xu, J., Livshits, B.: Liquidations: DeFi on a knife-edge. In: Borisov, N., Diaz, C. (eds.) FC 2021. LNCS, vol. 12675, pp. 457–476. Springer, Heidelberg (2021). https://doi.org/10.1007/978-3-662-64331-0_24
28. Peterins, E., Flatow, J., Hayes, G., Wolff, M., Greenberg, A.: Compound protocol maximum liquidate threshold (2021). https://github.com/compound-finance/compound-protocol/blob/4e99ea3a64ab4f1bdf9c07c7a1bf325db09ab809/scenario/src/Event/ComptrollerEvent.ts#L170
29. Pulse: Defi pulse - webpage (2021). https://defipulse.com. Accessed 07 June 2021
30. Qin, K., Zhou, L., Livshits, B., Gervais, A.: Attacking the DeFi ecosystem with flash loans for fun and profit. In: Borisov, N., Diaz, C. (eds.) FC 2021. LNCS, vol. 12674, pp. 3–32. Springer, Heidelberg (2021). https://doi.org/10.1007/978-3-662-64322-8_1
31. Sebastio, S., Vandin, A.: Multivesta: Statistical model checking for discrete event simulators. Technical report, IMT Institute for Advanced Studies Lucca (2013)
32. Tolmach, P., Li, Y., Lin, S.W., Liu, Y.: Formal analysis of composable DeFi protocols. arXiv preprint arXiv:2103.00540 (2021)
33. Vandin, A., Giachini, D., Lamperti, F., Chiaromonte, F.: Automated and distributed statistical analysis of economic agent-based models. arXiv preprint arXiv:2102.05405 (2021)
34. Wackerow, P., Rhechler: Decentralized finance (DeFi) - webpage (2021). https://ethereum.org/en/defi/. Accessed 02 June 2021
35. Werner, S.M., Perez, D., Gudgeon, L., Klages-Mundt, A., Harz, D., Knottenbelt, W.J.: SoK: decentralized Finance (DeFi). CoRR arXiv:2101.08778 (2021)
36. Zhou, L., Qin, K., Cully, A., Livshits, B., Gervais, A.: On the just-in-time discovery of profit-generating transactions in DeFi protocols. In: IEEE Symposium on Security and Privacy, pp. 919–936. IEEE (2021). https://doi.org/10.1109/SP40001.2021.00113

A Rewriting Framework for Interacting Cyber-Physical Agents

Benjamin Lion[1], Farhad Arbab[1,2], and Carolyn Talcott[3(✉)]

[1] Leiden University, Leiden, The Netherlands
lion@cwi.nl
[2] CWI, Amsterdam, The Netherlands
arbarb@cwi.nl
[3] SRI International, Menlo Park, CA, USA
talcott@gmail.com

Abstract. The analysis of cyber-physical systems (CPS) is challenging due to the large state space and the continuous changes occurring in their constituent parts. Design practices favor modularity to help reducing this complexity. In a previous work, we proposed a discrete semantic model for CPS that captures both cyber and physical aspects as streams of discrete observations, which ultimately form the behavior of a component. This semantic model is denotational and compositional, where each composition operator algebraically models an interaction between a pair of components.

In this paper, we propose a specification of components as rewrite systems. The specification is operational and executable, and we study conditions for its semantics as components to be compositional. We demonstrate our framework by modeling a coordination of robots moving on a shared field. We show that our system of robots can be coordinated by a protocol in order to exhibit a desired emerging behavior. We use an implementation of our framework in Maude to give practical results.

1 Introduction

Cyber-physical systems are inherently concurrent. From a cyber point of view, the timing of a decision to sense or act on its physical environment impacts the resulting outcome. Moreover, several cyber entities may share the same physical environment, leading to race conditions. From a physical point of view, the ordering of events is not always possible, as some events may be independent. Moreover, two observers of the same physical phenomenon may order events differently. A concurrency protocol encapsulates the orderings of events acceptable to an application, and expressing protocols as separate, concrete modules (as in exogenous coordination [1]) helps to reduce the complexity in the design of cyber-physical systems.

T. Margaria and B. Steffen (Eds.): ISoLA 2022, LNCS 13703, pp. 356–372, 2022.
https://doi.org/10.1007/978-3-031-19759-8_22

More specifically, in this context, each part of a cyber-physical system (e.g., a car, a road, a battery, etc.) is represented as a module, and the system captures the concurrent and interactive execution of each module. We list the following benefits of such approach. First, it makes concurrency explicit at the level of modules, amenable to exogenous coordination, which provides the opportunity to reason about concurrency protocols directly as first-class objects (e.g., how much a move of a robot consumes energy, can two robots move 'simultaneously', etc.). Then, the representation of a system remains small. Often, a modular design allows composing constituent components statically to analyze the resulting system, or dynamically at runtime to keep the state space small for, e.g., simulating some runs. Finally, a component comes with a notion of an interface, that specifies what is visible and what is hidden from other components. This way, both discrete and continuous aspects of components have the same type of interface, containing the set of observations over time.

In [12] we present a model of components that captures timed-event sequences (TESs) as instances of their behavior. An observation is a set of events with a unique time stamp. A component has an interface that defines which events are observable, and a behavior that denotes all possible sequences of its observations (i.e., a set of TESs). Our component model is equipped with a family of operators parametrized with an interaction signature. Thus, cyber-physical systems are defined modularly, where each product of two components models the interaction occurring between the two components. The strength, as well as practical limitation, of our semantic model is its abstraction: there is no fixed machine specification that generates the behavior of a component. We give in this paper an operational description of components as rewrite systems.

Rewriting logic is a powerful framework to model concurrent systems [14, 15]. Moreover, implementations, such as Maude [3], make system specifications both executable and analyzable. Rewriting logic is suitable for specifying cyber-physical systems, as the underlying equational theory can represent both discrete and continuous changes. We give an operational specification for components as rewriting systems, and show its compositionality under some assumptions.

Finally, we apply our work to an example that considers two energy sensitive robots moving on a shared field. Each of the two robots aims at reaching the other robot's initial position which, by symmetry, may eventually lead to a crossing situation. The crossing of the two robots is the source of a livelock behavior which can lead to failure (i.e., no energy left in the battery). We show how, an exogenous coordination imposed by a protocol can coordinate the moves of the two robots to avoid the livelock situation. We demonstrate the result using our implementation of our framework in Maude.

We present the following contributions:

- an operational specification of components as rewrite systems;
- some conditions for the rewrite system's semantics to be compositional;
- an incremental, runtime implementation of composition;

- illustration of how a composed Maude specification can be used to incrementally analyze a system design using a case study involving the behavior of two coordinated robot agents roaming on a field.

The remainder of the paper is organized as follows. In Sect. 2, we recall some results on the algebra of components defined in [12], and give as examples the component version of a robot, a battery, and their product. In Sect. 3, we give an operational specification, using rewriting logic, of a product of components as a system of agents. We show compositionality: the component of a system of agents is equal to the product of each agent component. In Sect. 4, we detail the implementation in Maude of the operational specification given in Sect. 3 and analyse a system consisting of two robots, two private batteries, and a shared field.

2 Semantic Model: Algebra of Components

The design of complex systems becomes simpler if such systems can be decomposed into smaller sub-systems that interact with each other. In order to simplify the design of cyber-physical systems, we introduced in [12] a semantic model that abstracts from the internal details of both cyber and physical processes. As first class entities in this model, a component encapsulates a behavior (set of TESs) and an interface (set of events). We recall basic definitions and properties in this section. See [10] for additional examples.

2.1 Components

Preliminaries. A timed-event stream, TES, σ over a set of events E is an infinite sequence of *observations*, where its ith observation $\sigma(i) = (O, t)$, $i \in \mathbb{N}$, consists of a pair of a subset of events in $O \subseteq E$, called the *observable*, and a positive real number $t \in \mathbb{R}_+$ as time stamp. A timed-event stream (TES) has the additional properties that its consecutive time stamps are monotonically increasing and non-Zeno, i.e., if $\sigma(i) = (O_i, t_i)$ is the ith element of TES σ, then (1) $t_i < t_{i+1}$, and (2) for any time $t \in \mathbb{R}_+$, there exists an element $\sigma(i) = (O_i, t_i)$ in σ such that $t < t_i$. We use $\sigma^{(k)}$ to denote the k-th derivative of the stream σ, such that $\sigma^{(k)}(i) = \sigma(i + k)$ for all $i \in \mathbb{N}$. We refer to the stream of observables of σ as its first projection $\mathrm{pr}_1(\sigma) \in \mathcal{P}(E)^\omega$, and the stream of time stamps as its second projection $\mathrm{pr}_2(\sigma) \in \mathbb{R}_+^\omega$. We write $(O, t) \in \sigma$ if there exists $i \in \mathbb{N}$ such that $\sigma(i) = (O, t)$.

We write $\sigma(t) = O$ if there exists $i \in \mathbb{N}$ such that $\sigma(i) = (O, t)$, and $\sigma(t) = \emptyset$ otherwise. We use $dom(\sigma)$ to refer to the set of observable time stamps, i.e., the set $dom(\sigma) = \{t \in \mathbb{R}_+ \mid \exists i.\mathrm{pr}_2(\sigma)(i) = t\}$. Moreover, we use $\sigma \cup \tau$ to denote the stream such that, for all $t \in \mathbb{R}_+$, $(\sigma \cup \tau)(t) = \sigma(t) \cup \tau(t)$ and $dom(\sigma \cup \tau) = dom(\sigma) \cup dom(\tau)$.

A component denotes *what* observables are possible, over time, given a fixed set of events. We give three examples of components, which capture some cyber-physical aspects of concurrent systems.

Definition 1 (Component). A *component* $C = (E, L)$ is a pair of a set of events E, called its *interface*, and a *behavior* $L \subseteq TES(E)$.

Given component $A = (E_A, L_A)$, we write $\sigma : A$ for a TES $\sigma \in L_A$.

Example 1 (Battery). A battery component is a pair $(E_B(C), L_B(C))$ with events $read(l) \in E_B$ for $0\% \leq l \leq 100\%$, $charge(\mu) \in E_B$, and $discharge(\mu) \in E_B$ with μ a (dis)charging coefficient in % per seconds, and C a constant capacity in mAH. The battery displays its capacity with the event $capacity(C)$. The behavior L_B is a set of sequences $\sigma \in L_B$ such that there exists a piecewise linear function $f : \mathbb{R}_+ \to \mathcal{P}(E_B)$ with, for $\sigma(i) = (O_i, t_i)$,

- for $\sigma(0) = (O_0, t_0)$, $f([0; t_0]) = 100\%$, i.e., the battery is initially fully charged;
- if $O_i = \{read(l)\}$, then $f(t_i) = l$ and the derivation $f'_{[t_{i-1}, t_{i+1}]}$ of f is constant in $[t_{i-1}, t_{i+1}]$, i.e., the observation does not change the slope of f at time t_i;
- if $O_i = \{discharge(\mu)\}$, then $f_{[t_i, t_{i+1}]}(t) = \max(f(t_i) - (t - t_i)\mu, 0)$;
- if $O_i = \{charge(\mu)\}$, then $f_{[t_i, t_{i+1}]}(t) = \min(f(t_i) + (t - t_i)\mu, 100)$;

where $f_{[t_1; t_2]}$ is the restriction of function f on the interval $[t_1; t_2]$. There is *a priori* no restrictions on the time interval between two observations, as long as the sequence of timestamps is increasing and non-Zeno. □

Example 2 (Robot). A robot with identifier i is a component $R(i, T) = (E_R, L_R(T))$ with events $read(i, l) \in E_R$ for $0\% \leq l \leq 100\%$, $d(i, p) \in E_R$ with p the power requested by the robot for the move and d the direction, and T a period in seconds. For instance, the event $N(i, p)$ represents robot i moving North with power p. The robot reads the capacity of its battery with the event $getCapacity(i, C) \in E_R$, with C in mAH. Once the robot knows the capacity of the battery, the values read in percent can be converted to remaining power.

The behavior $L_R(T)$ contains any sequence of observations at fix period T, such that $\sigma \in L_R(T)$ if and only if $\sigma(i) = (O_i, t_i)$ implies $t_i = kT$ with $k \in \mathbb{N}$ and $O_i \subseteq E_R$ with $|O_i| = 1$. We assume that the robot does one action at a time: either a read of its sensors, or a move in some direction. □

2.2 Product and Division

Components describe which observations occur over time. When run concurrently, observable events from a component may relate to observable events of another component. This relation defines what kind of interaction occurs between the two components, as it may enforce two events to occur within the same observable at the same time (e.g., actuation of a wheel and changes of location of the robot), or it may prevent two events to occur simultaneously (e.g., two robots moving to the same physical location). Interaction constraints are therefore captured by an algebraic operator that acts on components. The result of forming the product of two components is a new component, whose behavior contains the composition of every pair of TESs, one from each product operand, that satisfies the underlying constraints imposed by that specific operator.

Let $A = (E_A, L_A)$ and $B = (E_B, L_B)$ be two components. We use the relation $R(E_A, E_B) \subseteq TES(E_A) \times TES(E_B)$ and the function $\oplus : TES(E) \times TES(E) \to TES(E)$, with $E = E_A \cup E_B$, to range over composability relations and composition functions, respectively. We use Σ to range over interaction signatures, i.e., pairs of a composability relation and a composition function.

Definition 2 (Product). The *product* of components A and B under interaction signature $\Sigma = (R, \oplus)$ is the component $C = A \times_\Sigma B = (E_A \cup E_B, L)$ where

$$L = \{\sigma \oplus \tau \mid \sigma \in L_A, \tau \in L_B, (\sigma, \tau) \in R(E_A, E_B)\}$$

For simplicity, we write $\times$ as a general product when the specific Σ is irrelevant.

Example 3. We define $\Sigma_{RB} = ([\kappa_{RB}], \cup)$ where $\cup$ unions two TESs as defined in the preliminaries, and $[\kappa_{RB}]$ specifies co-inductively (see [12] for details of the construction), from a relation on observations κ_{RB}, how event occurrences relate in the robot and the battery components of capacity C. More specifically, κ_{RB} is the smallest symmetric relation over observations such that $((O_1, t_1), (O_2, t_2)) \in \kappa_{RB}$ implies that $t_1 = t_2$ and

- the discharge event in the battery coincides with a move of the robot, i.e., $d(i, p) \in O_1$ if and only if $discharge(\mu) \in O_2$. Moreover, the interaction signature imposes a relation between the discharge coefficient μ and the required power p, i.e., $\mu = p/C$;
- the read value of the robot sensor coincides with a value from the battery component, i.e., $read(i, l) \in O_1$ if and only if $read(l) \in O_2$;
- the robot reads the capacity value that corresponds to the battery capacity, i.e., $getCapacity(i, c) \in O_1$ if and only if $capacity(c) \in O_2$.

The product $B \times_{\Sigma_{RB}} R(T, i)$ of a robot and a battery component, under the interaction signature Σ_{RB}, restricts the behavior of the battery to match the periodic behavior of the robot, and restricts the behavior of the robot to match the sensor values delivered by the battery.

As a result, the behavior of the product component $B \times_{\Sigma_{RB}} R(T, i)$ contains all observations that the robot performs in interaction with its battery. Note that trace properties, such as *all energy sensor values observed by the robot are within a safety interval*, does not necessarily entail safety of the system: some unobserved energy values may fall outside of the safety interval. Moreover, the frequency by which the robot samples may *reveal* some new observations, and such robot can safely sample at period T if, for any period $T' \leq T$, the product $B \times_{\Sigma_{RB}} R(T', i)$ satisfies the safety property. $\square$

3   System of Agents and Compositional Semantics

Components in Sect. 2 are declarative. Their behavior consists of all the TESs that satisfy some internal constraints. The abstraction of internal states in components makes the specification of observables and their interaction easier. The downside of such declarative specification lies in the difficulty of generating an element from the behavior, and ultimately verifying properties on a product expression.

An operational specification of a component provides a mechanism to construct elements in its behavior. An *agent* is the operational specification that produces finite sequences of observations that, in the limit, determine the behavior of a component. An agent is stateful, and has transitions between states, each labeled by an observation, i.e., a set of events with a time-stamp. We consider a finite specification of an agent as a rewrite theory, where finite applications of the agent's rewrite rules generate a sequence of observables that form a prefix of some elements in the behavior of its corresponding component. We restrict the current work to integer time labeled observations. While in the cyber-physical world, time is a real quantity, we consider in our fragment a countable infinite domain for time, i.e., natural numbers. The time interval between two tics is therefore the same for all agents, and may be interpreted as, e.g., seconds, milliseconds, femtoseconds, etc. We show how an agent may synchronize with a local clock that forbids actions at some time values, thus modeling different execution speeds.

An operational specification of a composite component provides a mechanism to construct elements in the behavior of a product expression. The product on components is parametrized by an interaction signature that tells *which* TESs can compose, and *how* they compose to a new TES. We consider, in the operational fragment of this section, interaction signatures each of whose composability relation is co-inductively defined from a relation on observations κ. Intuitively, such restriction enables a step-by-step operation to check that the head of each sequence is valid, i.e., extends the sequence to be a prefix of some elements in the composite component. Moreover, we require κ to be such that the product on component $\times_{([\kappa], \cup)}$ is commutative and associative (see [12]). By *system* we mean a set of agents that compose under some interaction signature $\Sigma = ([\kappa], \cup)$. A system is stateful, where each state is formed from the states of its component agents, and has transitions between states, each labeled by an observation, formed from the component agent observations. We consider a finite specification of a system as the composition of a set of rewriting theories (one for each agent), and a system rewrite rule that produces a composite observation complying with the relation κ. We prove compositionality: the system component is equal to the product under the interaction signature $\Sigma = ([\kappa], \cup)$ of every one of its constituent agent components.

In order to give to the agent a semantics as components, we recall some results and notations about TES transition systems $T = (Q, E, \rightarrow)$ (see [11] for more results on TES transition systems) where Q is a set of states, E a set of events, and $\rightarrow \subseteq Q \times (\mathcal{P}(E) \times \mathbb{R}_+) \times Q$ a set of transitions.

We write $q \xrightarrow{u} p$ for the sequence of transitions $q \xrightarrow{u(0)} q_1 \xrightarrow{u(1)} q_2 \ldots \xrightarrow{u(n-1)} p$, where $u = \langle u(0), \ldots, u(n-1) \rangle \in (\mathcal{P}(E) \times \mathbb{R}_+)^n$. We write $|u|$ for the size of the sequence u.

We use $\mathcal{L}^{\text{fin}}(T,q)$ to denote the set of finite sequences of observables labeling a finite path in T starting from state q, such that

$$\mathcal{L}^{\text{fin}}(T,q) = \{u \mid \exists q'.q \xrightarrow{u} q', \forall i < |u| - 1.u(i) = (O_i, t_i) \wedge t_i < t_{i+1}\}$$

Additionally, the set $\mathcal{L}^{\text{fin}*}(T,q)$ is the set of sequences from $\mathcal{L}^{\text{fin}}(T,q)$ postfixed with empty observations, i.e., the set

$$\mathcal{L}^{\text{fin}*}(T,q) = \{u\tau \in \mathit{TES(E)} \mid u \in \mathcal{L}^{\text{fin}}(T,q) \ and \ \tau \in \mathit{TES}(\emptyset)\}$$

We use $\mathcal{L}^{\text{inf}}(T,q)$ to denote the set of TESs labeling infinite paths in T starting from state q, such that

$$\mathcal{L}^{\text{inf}}(T,q) = \{\sigma \in \mathit{TES(E)} \mid \forall n.\sigma[n] \in \mathcal{L}^{\text{fin}}(T,q)\}$$

where, as introduced in Sect. 2, $\sigma[n]$ is the prefix of size n of σ.

Let $X \subseteq \mathit{TES(E)}$, we use $cl(X)$ to denote the set that contains the continuation with empty observations of any prefix of an element in X, i.e., $cl(X) = \{u\tau \in \mathit{TES(E)} \mid \tau \in \mathit{TES}(\emptyset) \ and \ \exists\sigma.\exists i.\sigma \in X \wedge \sigma[i] = u\}$. Given a component $C = (E, L)$, we write $cl(C)$ for the new component $(E, cl(L))$.

3.1 Action, Agent, and System

We give the operational counterparts of an observation, a component, and a product of components as, respectively, an action, an agent, and a system of agents. See [10] for proof sketches.

Action. Actions are terms of sort `Action`. An action has a name of sort `AName` and some parameters. We distinguish two typical actions, the idle action $\star$ and the ending action `end`. A term of sort `Action` corresponds to an observable, i.e., a set of events. The idle action $\star$ and the ending action `end` both map to the empty set of events. An example of an action is `move(R1,d)` or `read(R1, position, 1)` that, respectively, moves agent `R1` in direction `d` or reads the value 1 from the position sensor of `R1`. The semantics of action `move(R1, d)` consists of all singleton event of the form `{move(R1, d)}` with d a constant direction value. We use the operation $\cdot$: `Action Action` $\rightarrow$ `Action` to construct a composite action `a1 · a2` out of two actions `a1` and `a2`.

Agent. An agent operationally specifies a component in rewriting logic. We give the specification of an agent as a rewrite theory, and provide the semantics of an agent as a component. An agent is a four tuple $(\Lambda, \Omega, \mathcal{E}, \Rightarrow)$, each of whose elements we introduce as follow.

The set of sorts Λ contains the `State` sort and the `Action` sort, respectively for state and action terms. A pair of a state and a set of actions is called a configuration. The set of function symbols Ω contains ϕ : `State` $\times$ `Action` $\rightarrow$ `State`, that takes a pair of a state and an action term to produce a new state. The

(Λ, Ω)-equational theory $\mathcal{E}$ specifies the update function ϕ. The set of equations that specify the function ϕ can make ϕ both a continuous or discrete function.

The rule pattern in (1) updates a configuration with an empty set to a new configuration, i.e.,

$$(s, \emptyset) \Rightarrow (s', acts) \qquad (1)$$

with $acts$ a non-empty set of action terms, and s' a new state. We call an agent *productive* if, for any state $s :$ State, there exists a state s' with $(s, \emptyset) \Rightarrow (s', acts)$ and $acts$ non empty set. Such agent may eventually do the idling action $\star$.

We give a semantics of an agent as a component by considering the limit application of the agent rewrite rules. We construct a TES transition system $\mathcal{T}_\mathcal{A} = (Q, E, \to)$ as an intermediate representation for agent $\mathcal{A} = (\Lambda, \Omega, \mathcal{E}, \Rightarrow)$. The set of states $Q =$ State $\times \mathbb{N}$ is the set of pairs of a state of $\mathcal{A}$ and a time-stamp natural number. We use the notation $[s, t]$ for states in Q where $t \in \mathbb{N}$. The set of events E is the union of all observables labeling the transition relation $\to \subseteq Q \times (\mathcal{P}(E) \times \mathbb{N}) \times Q$, defined as the smallest set such that, for $t \in \mathbb{N}$:

$$\frac{(s, \emptyset) \Rightarrow (s', acts) \qquad a \in acts \qquad \phi(s', a) =_{\mathcal{E}} s''}{[s, t] \xrightarrow{(a, t+1)} [s'', t+1]} \qquad (2)$$

An agent that performs a rewrite moves the global time from one unit forward. All agents share the same time semantically, and we show some mechanisms at the system level to artificially run some agents *faster* than others.

Let $\mathcal{A} = (\Lambda, \Omega, \mathcal{E}, \Rightarrow)$ be an agent initially in state $s_0 \in S$ at time $t_0 \in \mathbb{N}$. The finite, respectively infinite, component semantics of $\mathcal{A}$ is the component $[\![\mathcal{A}([s_0, t_0])]\!]^* = (E, \mathcal{L}^{\mathrm{fin}*}(\mathcal{T}_\mathcal{A}, [s_0, t_0]))$, respectively the component $[\![\mathcal{A}([s_0, t_0])]\!] = (E, \mathcal{L}^{\mathrm{inf}}(\mathcal{T}_\mathcal{A}, [s_0, t_0]))$, with $E = \bigcup_{a \in \mathrm{Action}} a$.

Lemma 1 *(Closure). Let $\mathcal{A}$ be a productive agent initially in state $[s_0, t_0]$. Then $[\![A([s_0, t_0])]\!]^* = cl([\![A([s_0, t_0])]\!])$.*

Lemma 1 gives a condition under which a step by step execution of the agent is sound with respect to generating prefixes of elements in the component semantics. More precisely, if an agent $\mathcal{A}$ is productive, Lemma 1 ensures that finite sequences of rewrite rule applications generate finite sequences of observations each of which is a prefix of an element in the behavior of the component corresponding to $\mathcal{A}$. Alternatively, if $\mathcal{A}$ is not productive, a finite sequence of rule application may lead to a state for which no rule applies anymore. In such a case, there may not be any corresponding element in the agent component for which such finite sequence is a prefix.

System. A system gives an operational specification of a product of a set of components under $\Sigma = ([\kappa], \cup)$. The composability relation κ is fixed to be symmetric, so that the product $\times_\Sigma$ is commutative. We define $[\kappa]$ co-inductively, as in [11,12]. Formally, a system consists of a set of agents with additional sorts, operations, and rewrite rules. A system is a tuple $(\mathcal{A}, \Lambda, \Omega, \mathcal{E}, \Rightarrow_S)$ where $\mathcal{A}$ is a set of agents. We use $(\Lambda_i, \Omega_i, \mathcal{E}_i, \Rightarrow_i)$ to refer to agent $\mathcal{A}_i \in \mathcal{A}$.

The set of sorts Λ contains a sort $\texttt{Action} \in \Lambda$ which is a super sort of each sort $\texttt{Action}_i$ for $\mathcal{A}_i \in \mathcal{A}$. The set Ω contains the function symbol $\texttt{comp} : \texttt{Action} \times \texttt{Action} \to \texttt{Bool}$, which relates pairs of action terms. Given two actions $\texttt{a1,a2:Action}$, $\texttt{comp(a1,a2)} = \texttt{True}$ when the two actions $\texttt{a1}$ and $\texttt{a2}$ are *composable*. The set of equations $\mathcal{E}$ specifies the composability relation $\texttt{comp}$. First, we impose $\texttt{comp}$ to be symmetric, i.e., for all actions $\texttt{a1,a2:Action}$, $\texttt{comp(a1,a2)} = \texttt{comp(a2,a1)}$. Second, we assume that $\texttt{comp(a1} \cdot \texttt{a2, a3)}$ and $\texttt{comp(a1, a2)}$ hold if and only if $\texttt{comp(a2, a3)}$ and $\texttt{comp(a1, a2} \cdot \texttt{a3)}$ hold, for any actions $\texttt{a1, a2, a3}$ from disjoint agents. Given a set $\texttt{actions}$ of actions, we use the notation $\texttt{comp(actions)}$ for the predicate that is $\texttt{True}$ if all pairs of actions in $\texttt{actions}$ are composable, i.e., for all $\texttt{a1, a2}$ in $\texttt{actions}$, $\texttt{comp(a1,a2)}$ is $\texttt{True}$ and for all agent $\mathcal{A}_i$ such that there is no $\texttt{a3 : Action}_i \in \texttt{actions}$, then $\texttt{comp(a1,} \star_\texttt{i})$ is $\texttt{True}$. We call a set $\texttt{actions}$ of actions for which $\texttt{comp(actions)}$ holds, a *clique*. The conditions for a set of actions to form a clique models the fact that each action in the clique is independent from agent $\mathcal{A}_i$ with no action in that clique (see Sect. 4.1 for an instance of $\texttt{comp}$), and therefore composable with the silent action $\star_i$. The relation $\texttt{comp}$ can be graphically modelled as an undirected graph relating actions, where a clique is a connected component.

The rewrite rule pattern in (3) selects a set of actions, at most one from each agent, checks that the set of actions forms a clique with respect to $\texttt{comp}$, and applies the update accordingly. For $\{k_1, ..., k_j\} \subseteq \{1, ..., n\}$:

$$\{(s_{k_1}, acts_{k_1}), ..., (s_{k_j}, acts_{k_j})\} \Rightarrow_S \{(\phi_{k_1}(s_{k_1}, a_{k_1}), \emptyset), ..., (\phi_{k_j}(s_{k_j}, a_{k_j}), \emptyset)\} \quad (3)$$

if $\texttt{comp}(\bigcup_{i \in [1,j]}\{a_{k_i}\})$. As we show later, a system does not necessarily update all agents in lock steps, and an agent not doing an action may stay in the configuration $(s, \emptyset)$. As multiple cliques may be possible, there is non-determinism at the system level. Different strategies may therefore choose different cliques as, for instance, taking the largest clique.

We define the transition system for $\mathcal{S} = (\mathcal{A}, \Lambda, \Omega, \mathcal{E}, \Rightarrow_S)$ as the TES transition system $\mathcal{T}_S = (Q, E, \to)$ with $Q = \texttt{StateSet} \times \mathbb{N}$ the set of states, E the union of all observables labeling the transition relation $\to \subseteq Q \times (\mathcal{P}(E) \times \mathbb{N}) \times Q$, which is the smallest transition relation such that, for $\{k_1, ..., k_j\} \subseteq \{1, ..., n\}$:

$$\frac{\{(s_{k_i}, acts_{k_i})\}_{i \in [1,j]} \Rightarrow_S \{(\phi_{k_i}(s_{k_i}, a_{k_i}), \emptyset)\}_{i \in [1,j]} \quad \bigwedge_{i \in [1,j]} \phi_{k_i}(s_{k_i}, a_{k_i}) =_{\mathcal{E}_i} s''_{k_i}}{[\{s_i\}_{i \in [1,n]}, t] \xrightarrow{(\bigcup_{i \in [1,j]} a_{k_i}, t+1)} [\{s_1, ..., s''_{k_1}, ..., s''_{k_j}, ..., s_n\}, t+1]}$$

$$(4)$$

for $t \in \mathbb{N}$ and where we use the notation $\{x_i\}_{i \in [1,n]}$ for the set $\{x_1, ..., x_n\}$.

Remark 1. The top left part of the rule is a rewrite transition at the system level. As defined earlier, the condition for such rewrite to apply is the formation of a clique by all of the actions in the update. The states and labels of the TES transition system (bottom of the rule) are sets of states and sets of labels from the TES transition system of every agent in the system.

Let $\mathcal{A} = \{\mathcal{A}_1, ..., \mathcal{A}_n\}$ be a set of agents, and let $\mathcal{S} = (\mathcal{A}, \Lambda, \Omega, \mathcal{E}, \Rightarrow_S)$ be a system initially in state $\{(s_{0i}, \emptyset)\}_{i \in [1,n]}$ at time t_0 such that, for all

$i \in [1, n]$, $\mathcal{A}_i$ is initially in state s_{0i} at time t_0. The finite, respectively infinite, semantics of initialized system $\mathcal{S}([s_0, t_0])$, is the component $[\![\mathcal{S}([s_0, t_0])]\!]^* = (E, \mathcal{L}^{\text{fin}*}(\mathcal{T}_\mathcal{S}, [s_0, t_0]))$, respectively $[\![\mathcal{S}([s_0, t_0])]\!] = (E, \mathcal{L}^{\text{inf}}(\mathcal{T}_\mathcal{S}, [s_0, t_0]))$, where $E = \bigcup_{i \in [1,n]} E_i$ with E_i the set of events for the agent component $[\![\mathcal{A}([s_{0i}, t_0])]\!]$.

Given a composability relation comp, we define the interaction signature $\Sigma = ([\kappa_{\text{comp}}], \cup)$, with $\kappa_{\text{comp}}(E_1, E_2) \subseteq (\mathcal{P}(E_1) \times \mathbb{N}) \times (\mathcal{P}(E_2) \times \mathbb{N})$ to be such that, for ai : Action$_i$ and aj : Action$_j$:

- if comp(ai, aj), then $((a_i, n), (a_j, n)) \in \kappa_{\text{comp}}(E_i, E_j)$ for all $n \in \mathbb{N}$, i.e., two composable actions occur at the same time;
- if comp(ai, $\star_j$), then $((a_i, n), (a, k)) \in \kappa_{\text{comp}}(E_i, E_j)$ for all $(a, k) \in \mathcal{P}(E_j) \times \mathbb{N}$ with $k \geq n$, i.e., $\mathcal{A}_j$ may have an action at arbitrary future time.

with E_i the set of events of agent $\mathcal{A}_i$.

Lemma 2 (Composability). *If* Action$_i$ $\cap$ Action$_j$ $= \emptyset$ *for all disjoint agents i and j, then the product* $\times_{([\kappa_{comp}], \cup)}$ *is commutative and associative.*

Theorem 1 (Compositional semantics). *Let $\mathcal{S} = (\mathcal{A}, \Lambda, \Omega, \mathcal{E}, \Rightarrow_\mathcal{S})$ be a system of n agents with disjoint actions and $[\{s_{01}, ..., s_{0n}\}, t_0]$ as initial state. We fix $\Sigma = ([\kappa_{comp}], \cup)$. Then, $[\![\mathcal{S}([s_0, t_0])]\!] = \times_\Sigma \{[\![\mathcal{A}_i([s_{0i}, t_0])]\!]\}_{i \in [1,n]}$ and $[\![\mathcal{S}([s_0, t_0])]\!]^* = \times_\Sigma \{[\![\mathcal{A}_i([s_{0i}, t_0])]\!]^*\}_{i \in [1,n]}$.*

4 Application

We present the Maude implementation of the rewrite theories described in Sect. 3. We first describe our general framework as currently implemented in Maude, separating the agent modules, from the system module, and the composability relation. The framework is instantiated for a system consisting of two robot agents, each interacting with a (shared) field and a (private) battery agent (more details can be found in [10]). Finally, we run some analysis on the system using the Maude reachability search engine. The implementation of the framework in Maude can be found in [9].

4.1 General Framework

Actions. An action is a pair that contains the name of the action, and the set of agent identifiers on which the action applies. An agent action is identified by the source agent identifier, and is a triple ⟨id, (a; ids)⟩ where id is the agent doing the action with name a onto the set of agents ids, that we call resources of agent id for action named a.

```
fmod ACTION is
    inc STRING . inc BOOL . inc SET{Id} . ...
    sort AName Action AgentAction .
    op (_;_) : AName Set{Id} -> Action [ctor] .
    op (_,_) : Id Action -> AgentAction [ctor] .
    op mta : -> AgentAction .
endfm
```

Agent. The AGENT module in Listing 1.1 defines the theories on which an agent relies, the Agent sort, and operations that an agent instance must implement. The module is parametrized with a CSEMIRING theory, that is used to rank actions of an agent. Additionally, the AGENT includes modules that define state and action terms. A term of sort IdStates is a pair of an identifier and a map of sort MapKD.

A term of sort Agent is a tuple [id: C| state; ready?; softaction]. The identifier id is unique for each agent of the same class C. The state state of an agent is a map from keys to values. For instance, the state of a robot has three keys, position, energy, and lastAction, with values in Location, Status, and Bool. The flag ready? is of sort Bool and is True when the agent has submitted a possibly empty list of actions, and False otherwise. The pending actions softaction is a set of actions valued in the parametrized CSEMIRING. The use of a constraint semiring as a structure for action valuations enables various kinds of reasoning about preferences at the agent and system levels. We use the two operations of the csemiring, sum $+$ and product $\times$, as respectively modeling the choice and the compromise of two alternatives. See [6, 20, 21] for more details.

An agent instance implements four operations: computeActions, getOutput, getPostState, and internalUpdate. The operation computeActions, given a state:MapKD of agent id of class C, returns a set of valued actions in the parametrized CSEMIRING. The operation internalUpdate, given a state:MapKD of agent id of class C, returns a new state state':MapKD. For instance, an agent may record in its state, as an internal update, the outcome of computeActions and change the value that the key lastAction maps to. The getOutput operation, given an action name a:Name from agent identified by id2 applied to an agent id of class C in a state state, returns a collection of outputs outputs = getOutput(id, C, id2, an, state). The outputs generated by getOutput are of sort MapKD and therefore structured as a mapping from keys to values. For instance, the output of the action named read applied on a field agent has a key position that maps to the position value of the agent doing the read action. The operation getPostState, given an action name a:AName with inputs input:IdStates from agent identified by id2 applied on an agent id1 of class C in a state state, returns a new state state' = getPostState(id1, C, id2, an, input, state). The input input:IdStates is a collection of key to value mappings that results from collecting the outputs, i.e., with getOutput, of an action (id, an, ids) on all its resources in ids.

Listing 1.1. Extract from the AGENT Maude module.

```
fmod AGENT{X :: CSEMIRING} is
 inc IDSTATE .   inc ACTION .
 sort Agent .
 op [_:_|_;_;_] : Id Class MapKD Bool X$Elt -> Agent [ctor] .
 op computeActions : Id Class MapKD -> X$Elt .
 op internalUpdate : Id Class MapKD -> MapKD .
 op getPostState : Id Class Id AName IdStates MapKD -> MapKD
 op getOutput : Id Class Id AName MapKD -> MapKD .
endfm
```

The agent's dynamics are given by the rewrite rule in Listing 1.2, that updates the pending action to select one atomic action from the set of valued actions:

Listing 1.2. Conditional rewrite rule applying on agent terms.

```
crl[agent] : [sys [id : ac | state   ; false ; null]] =>
      [sys [id : ac | state' ; true  ; softaction]]
    if softaction + sactions := computeActions(id, ac, state)
      /\ state' := internalUpdate(id, ac, state) .
```

The rewrite rule in Listing 1.2 implements the abstract rule of Eq. 2. After application of the rewrite rule, the **ready?** flag of the agent is set to **True**. The agent may, as well, perform an internal update independent of the success of the selected action.

System. The SYSTEM module in Listing 1.3 defines the sorts and operations that apply on a set of agents. The sort **Sys** contains set of **Agent** terms, and the term **Global** designates top level terms on which the system rewrite rule applies (as shown in Listing 1.4). The SYSTEM module includes the **Agent** theory parametrized with a fixed semiring **ASemiring**. The theory **ASemiring** defines valued actions as pairs of an action and a semiring value. While we assume that all agents share the same valuation structure, we can also define systems in which such a preference structure differs for each agent. The SYSTEM module defines three operations: **outputFromAction**, **updateSystemFromAction**, and **updateSystem**. The operation **outputFromAction** returns, given an agent action (id, (an, ids)) applied on a system sys, a collection of identified outputs idOutputs = outputFromAction((id, (an, ids)), sys) given by the union of getOutput from all agents in ids. The operation **updatedSystemFromAction** returns, given an agent action (id, (an, ids)) applied on a system sys, an updated system sys' = updatedSystemFromAction((id, (an, ids)), sys). The updated system may raise an error if the action is not allowed by some of the resource agents in ids (see the battery-field-robot example in [10]). The updated system, otherwise, updates *synchronously* all agents with identifiers in ids by using the getPostState operation. The operation **updateSystem** returns, given a list of agent actions **agentActions** and a system term sys, a new system **updateSystem(sys, agentActions)** that performs a sequential update of sys with every action in **agentActions** using **updatedSystemFromAction**. The list **agentActions** ends with a delimiter action **end** performed on every agent, which may trigger an error if some expected action does not occur (see PROTOCOL in [10]).

Listing 1.3. Extract from the SYSTEM Maude module.

```
fmod SYS is
  inc AGENT{ASemiring} . sort Sys  Global .
  subsort Agent < Sys . op [_] : Sys -> Global [ctor] .
  op __ : Sys Sys -> Sys [ctor assoc comm id: mt] .   ...
  op outputFromAction : AgentAction Sys -> IdStates .
  op updatedSystemFromAction : AgentAction Sys -> Sys .
```

```
op updateSystem : Sys List{AgentAction} -> Sys .
endfm
```

The rewrite rule in Listing 1.4 applies on terms of sort `Global` and updates each agent of the system synchronously, given that their actions are composable. The rewrite rule in Listing 1.4 implements the abstract rule of Eq. 4. The rewrite rule is conditional on essentially two predicates: `agentsReady?` and `kbestActions`. The predicate `agentsReady?` is `True` if every agent has its `ready?` flag set to `True`, i.e., the agent rewrite rule has already been applied. The operation `kbestActions` returns a ranked set of cliques (i.e., composable lists of actions), each paired with the updated system. The element of the ranked set are lists of actions containing at most one action for each agent, and paired with the system resulting from the application of `updateSystem`. If the updated system has reached a `notAllowed` state, then the list of actions is not composable and is discarded. The operations `getSysSoftActions` and `buildComposite` form the set of lists of composite actions, from the agent's set of ranked actions, by composing actions and joining their preferences.

Listing 1.4. Conditional rewrite rule applying on system terms.

```
crl [transition] : [sys]  => [sys']
  if agentsReady?(sys)  /\ saAtom := getSysSoftActions(sys) /\
    saComp := buildComposite(saAtom , sizeOfSum(saAtom)) /\
    p(actseq, sys') ; actseqs := kbestActions(saComp, k, sys) .
```

Composability Relation. The term `saComp` defines a set of valued lists of actions. Each element of `saComp` possibly defines a clique. The operation `kbestActions` specifies which, from the set `saComp`, are cliques. We describe below the implementation of `kbestActions`, given the structure of action terms.

An action is a triple (`id`, (`an`, `ids`)), where `id` is the identifier of the agent performing the action `an` on resource agents `ids`. Each resource agent in `ids` reacts to the action (`id`, (`an`, `ids`)) by producing an output (`id'`, `an`, `O`) (i.e., the result of `getOutput`). Therefore, $comp((id, (an, ids)), a_i)$ holds, with $a_i : Action_i$ and $i \in ids$, only if a_i is a list that contains an output (`i`, `an`, `O`), i.e., an output to the action. If one of the resources outputs the value (`i,notAllowed(an)`), the set is discarded as the actions are not pairwise composable. Conceptually, there are as many action names `an` as possible outputs from the resources, and the system rule (2) selects the clique for which the action name and the outputs have the same value. In practice, the list of outputs from the resources get passed to the agent performing the action.

4.2   Analysis in Maude

We analyze in Maude two scenarios. In one, each robot has as strategy to take the shortest path to reach its goal. As a consequence, a robot reads its position, computes the shortest path, and submits a set of optimal actions. A robot can sense an obstacle on its direct next location, which then allows for sub-optimal lateral moves (e.g., if the obstacle is in the direct next position in the West direction, the robot may go either North or South). In the other scenario, we add a protocol that swaps the two robots if robot id(0) is on the direct next location on the west of robot id(1). The swapping is a sequence of moves that ends in an exchange of positions of the two robots. See [10] for details on the TROLL, FIELD, BATTERY, and PROTOCOL agents specified in Maude, and for the specification of the init term for both scenarios.

In the two scenarios, we analyze the behavior of the resulting system with two queries. The first query asks if the system can reach a state in which the energy level of the two batteries is 0, which means that its robot can no longer move:

```
search [1] init =>* [sys::Sys
    [ bat(1) : Battery | k(level) |-> 0 ; true ; null],
    [ bat(2) : Battery | k(level) |-> 0 ; true ; null]] .
```

The second query asks if the system can reach a state in which the two robots successfully reached their goals, and end in the expected locations:

```
search [1] init =>* [sys::Sys  [ field : Field | k(( 5 ; 5 ))
    |-> d(id(0)), k(( 0 ; 5 )) |-> d(id(1)) ; true ; null]] .
```

As a result, when the protocol is absent, the two robots can enter in a livelock behavior and eventually fail with an empty battery:

```
Solution 1 (state 80)
states: 81   rw: 223566 in 73ms cpu (74ms real) (3053554 rw/s)
```

Alternatively, when the protocol is used, the livelock is removed using exogenous coordination. The two robots therefore successfully reach their end locations, and stop before running out of battery:

```
No solution. states: 102
rewrites: 720235 in 146ms cpu (145ms real) (4920041 rw/s)
```

In both cases, the second query succeeds, as there exists a path for both scenarios where the two robots reach their end goal locations. The results can be reproduced by downloading the archive at [9].

5   Related Work

Real-time Maude. Real-Time Maude is implemented in Maude as an extension of Full Maude [18], and is used in applications such as in [8]. There are two ways to interpret a real-time rewrite theory, called the pointwise semantics and the continuous semantics. Our approach to model time is similar to the pointwise semantics for real-time Maude, as we fix a global time stamp interval before execution. The addition of a composability relation, that may discard actions to occur within the same rewrite step, differs from the real-time Maude framework.

Models Based on Rewriting Logic. In [21], the modeling of cyber-physical systems from an actor perspective is discussed. The notion of event comes as a central concept to model interaction between agents. Softagents [20] is a framework for specifying and analyzing adaptive cyber-physical systems implemented in Maude. It has been used to analyze systems such as vehicle platooning [4] and drone surveillance [13]. In Softagents agents interact by sharing knowledge and resources implemented as part of the system timestep rule.

Softagents only considers compatibility in the sense of reachability of desired or undesired states. Our approach provides more structure enabling static analysis. Our framework allows, for instance, to consider compatibility of a robot with a battery (i.e., changing the battery specification without altering other agents in the system), and coordination of two robots with an exogenous protocol, itself specified as an agent.

Algebra, Co-algebra. The algebra of components described in this paper is an extension of [12]. Algebra of communicating processes [5] (ACP) achieves similar objectives as decoupling processes from their interaction. For instance, the encapsulation operator in process algebra is a unary operator that restricts which actions may occur, i.e., $\delta_H(t \parallel s)$ prevents t and s to perform actions in H. Moreover, composition of actions is expressed using communication functions, i.e., $\gamma(a, b) = c$ means that actions a and b, if performed together, form the new action c. Different types of coordination over communicating processes are studied in [2].

Discrete Event Systems. Our work represents both cyber and physical aspects of systems in a unified model of discrete event systems [1,17]. In [7], the author lists the current challenges in modelling cyber-physical systems in such a way. The author points to the problem of modular control, where even though two modules run without problems in isolation, the same two modules may block when they are used in conjunction. In [19], the authors present procedures to synthesize supervisors that control a set of interacting processes and, in the case of failure, report a diagnosis. An application for large scale controller synthesis is given in [16]. Our framework allows for experiments on modular control, by adding an agent controller among the set of agents to be controlled. The implementation in Maude enables the search of, for instance, blocking configurations.

6   Conclusion

We give an operational specification of the algebra of components defined in [12]. An agent specifies a component as a rewrite theory, and a system specifies a product of components as a set of rewrite theories extended with a composability relation. We show compositionality, i.e., that the system specifies a component that equals to the product, under a suitable interaction signature, of components specified by each agent.

We present an implementation of our framework in Maude, and instantiate a set of components to model two energy sensitive robots roaming on a shared field.

We analyze the behavior of the resulting system before and after coordination with a protocol, and show how the protocol can prevent livelock behavior.

The modularity of our operational framework and the interpretation of agents as components in interaction add structure to the design of cyber-physical systems. The structure can therefore be exploited to reason about more general properties of CPSs, such as compatibility, sample period synthesis, etc.

Acknowledgement. Talcott was partially supported by the U. S. Office of Naval Research under award numbers N00014-15-1-2202 and N00014-20-1-2644, and NRL grant N0017317-1-G002. Arbab was partially supported by the U. S. Office of Naval Research under award number N00014-20-1-2644.

References

1. Arbab, F.: Puff, the magic protocol. In: Agha, G., Danvy, O., Meseguer, J. (eds.) Formal Modeling: Actors, Open Systems, Biological Systems. LNCS, vol. 7000, pp. 169–206. Springer, Heidelberg (2011). https://doi.org/10.1007/978-3-642-24933-4_9

2. Bergstra, J.A., Klop, J.W.: Process algebra for synchronous communication. Inf. Control **60**(1), 109–137 (1984)

3. Clavel, M., et al.: All About Maude - A High-Performance Logical Framework. LNCS, vol. 4350. Springer, Heidelberg (2007). https://doi.org/10.1007/978-3-540-71999-1

4. Dantas, Y.G., Nigam, V., Talcott, C.: A formal security assessment framework for cooperative adaptive cruise control. In: IEEE Vehicular Networking Conference, pp. 1–8. IEEE (2020)

5. Fokkink, W.J.: Introduction to Process Algebra. TTCS, Springer, Heidelberg (2000). https://doi.org/10.1007/978-3-662-04293-9

6. Kappé, T., Lion, B., Arbab, F., Talcott, C.: Soft component automata: composition, compilation, logic, and verification. Sci. Comput. Program. **183**, 102300 (2019)

7. Lafortune, S.: Discrete event systems: modeling, observation, and control. Ann. Rev. Control Robot. Auton. Syst. **2**(1), 141–159 (2019)

8. Lee, J., Kim, S., Bae, K., Ölveczky, P.C.: HYBRID SYNCHAADL: modeling and formal analysis of virtually synchronous CPSs in AADL. In: Silva, A., Leino, K.R.M. (eds.) CAV 2021. LNCS, vol. 12759, pp. 491–504. Springer, Cham (2021). https://doi.org/10.1007/978-3-030-81685-8_23

9. Lion, B.: Cyber-physical framework in maude (2022). https://doi.org/10.5281/zenodo.6587173

10. Lion, B., Arbab, F., Talcott, C.: A rewriting framework for interacting cyber-physical agents (2022)

11. Lion, B., Arbab, F., Talcott, C.: Runtime composition of systems of interacting cyber-physical components (2022)

12. Lion, B., Arbab, F., Talcott, C.: A semantic model for interacting cyber-physical systems. In: Lange, J., Mavridou, A., Safina, L., Scalas, A. (eds.) Proceedings 14th Interaction and Concurrency Experience, ICE 2021, 18 June 2021, volume 347 of EPTCS, pp. 77–95 (2021)

13. Mason, I.A., Nigam, V., Talcott, C., Brito, A.: A framework for analyzing adaptive autonomous aerial vehicles. In: Cerone, A., Roveri, M. (eds.) SEFM 2017. LNCS, vol. 10729, pp. 406–422. Springer, Cham (2018). https://doi.org/10.1007/978-3-319-74781-1_28

14. Meseguer, J.: Conditioned rewriting logic as a united model of concurrency. Theor. Comput. Sci. **96**(1), 73–155 (1992)

15. Meseguer, J.: Twenty years of rewriting logic. J. Log. Algebraic Methods Program. **81**(7–8), 721–781 (2012)

16. Moormann, L., van de Mortel-Fronczak, J.M., Fokkink, W.J., Maessen, P., Rooda, J.E.: Supervisory control synthesis for large-scale systems with isomorphisms. Control. Eng. Pract. **115**, 104902 (2021)

17. Nivat, M.: Behaviors of processes and synchronized systems of processes. In: Broy, M., Schmidt, G. (eds.) Theoretical Foundations of Programming Methodology. NATO Advanced Study Institutes Series, vol. 91, pp. 473–551. Springer, Netherlands, Dordrecht (1982). https://doi.org/10.1007/978-94-009-7893-5_14

18. Ölveczky, P.C.: Real-time Maude and its applications. In: Escobar, S. (ed.) WRLA 2014. LNCS, vol. 8663, pp. 42–79. Springer, Cham (2014). https://doi.org/10.1007/978-3-319-12904-4_3

19. Sampath, M., Lafortune, S., Teneketzis, D.: Active diagnosis of discrete-event systems. IEEE Trans. Autom. Control **43**(7), 908–929 (1998)

20. Talcott, C., Arbab, F., Yadav, M.: Soft agents: exploring soft constraints to model robust adaptive distributed cyber-physical agent systems. In: De Nicola, R., Hennicker, R. (eds.) Software, Services, and Systems. LNCS, vol. 8950, pp. 273–290. Springer, Cham (2015). https://doi.org/10.1007/978-3-319-15545-6_18

21. Wirsing, M., Denker, G., Talcott, C.L., Poggio, A., Briesemeister, L.: A rewriting logic framework for soft constraints. Electr. Notes Theor. Comput. Sci. **176**(4), 181–197 (2007)

Model Checking Reconfigurable Interacting Systems

Yehia Abd Alrahman, Shaun Azzopardi(✉), and Nir Piterman

University of Gothenburg, Gothenburg, Sweden
{yehia.abd.alrahman,shaun.azzopardi,nir.piterman}@gu.se

Abstract. Reconfigurable multi-agent systems consist of a set of autonomous agents, with integrated interaction capabilities that feature opportunistic interaction. Agents seemingly reconfigure their interactions interfaces by forming collectives, and interact based on mutual interests. Finding ways to design and analyse the behaviour of these systems is a vigorously pursued research goal. We propose a model checker, named R-CHECK (Find the associated toolkit repository here: https://github.com/dsynma/recipe.), to allow reasoning about these systems both from an individual- and a system- level. R-CHECK also permits reasoning about interaction protocols and joint missions. R-CHECK supports a high-level input language with symbolic semantics, and provides a modelling convenience for interaction features such as reconfiguration, coalition formation, and self-organisation.

1   Introduction

Reconfigurable Multi-agent systems [17,20], or Reconfigurable MAS for short, have emerged as new computational systems, consisting of a set of autonomous agents that interact based on mutual interest, and thus creating a sort of opportunistic interaction. That is, agents seemingly reconfigure their interaction interface and dynamically form groups/collectives based on run-time changes in their execution context. Designing these systems and reasoning about their behaviour is very challenging, due to the high-level of dynamism that Reconfigurable MAS exhibit.

Traditionally, model checking [11,22] is considered as a mainstream verification tool for reactive systems [5] in the community. A system is usually represented by a low-level language such as NuSMV [9], reactive modules [7,16], concurrent game structures [8], or interpreted systems [14]. The modelling primitives of these languages are very close to their underlying semantics, e.g., predicate representation, transition systems, etc. Thus, it makes it hard to model and reason about high-level features of Reconfigurable MAS such as reconfiguration, group formation, self-organisation, etc. Indeed, encoding these features

This work is funded by the ERC consolidator grant D-SynMA (No. 772459) and the Swedish research council grants: SynTM (No. 2020-03401) and VR project (No. 2020-04963).

T. Margaria and B. Steffen (Eds.): ISoLA 2022, LNCS 13703, pp. 373–389, 2022.
https://doi.org/10.1007/978-3-031-19759-8_23

in existing formalisms would not only make it hard to reason about them, but will also create exponentially large and detailed models that are not amenable to verification. The latter is a classical challenge for model checking and is often termed as *state-space explosion*.

Existing techniques that attempt to tame the state-space explosion problem (such as BDDs, abstraction, bounded model checking, etc.) can only act as a mitigation strategy, right-level of abstraction to compactly model and reason about high-level features of Reconfigurable MAS.

MAS are often programmed using high-level languages that support domain-specific features of MAS like emergent behaviour [2,6,23], interactions [3], intentions [12], knowledge [14], etc. These descriptions are very involved to be directly encoded in plain transition systems. Thus, we often want programming abstractions that focus on the domain concepts, abstract away from low-level details, and consequently reduce the size of the model under consideration. The rationale is that reasoning about a system requires having the right level of abstraction to represent its behaviour. Thus, there is a pressing demand to extend traditional model checking tools with support for reasoning about high-level features of Reconfigurable MAS. This suggests supporting an intuitive description of programs, actions, protocols, reconfiguration, self-organisation, etc.

RECIPE [3,4] is a promising framework to support modelling and verification of reconfigurable multi-agent system. It is supported with a symbolic semantics and model representation that permits the use of symbolic representation to enable efficient analysis. However, writing models in RECIPE is very hard and error prone. This is because RECIPE models are encoded in a predicate-based representation that is far from how we usually program. In fact, the predicate representation of RECIPE supports no programming primitives to control the structure of programs, and thus everything is encoded using state variables.

In this paper, we present R-CHECK, a model checking toolkit for verifying and simulating reconfigurable multi-agent systems. R-CHECK supports a minimalistic high-level programming language with symbolic semantics based on the RECIPE framework. The syntax of the language was first presented briefly, along with a short case study, in [1]. Here we formally present the syntax and semantics of R-CHECK language and use it to model and reason about a non-trivial case study from the realm of reconfigurable and self-organising MAS. We provide two types of semantics: structural semantics in terms of automata to recover information about interaction actions and message exchange, and an execution semantics based on RECIPE. The interaction information recovered in the structural semantics is recorded succinctly in the execution semantics, and thus permits reasoning about interaction protocols and message exchange.

We integrate R-CHECK with NUXMV and enable LTL symbolic and bounded model checking. This specialised integration provides a powerful tool that permits verifying high-level features of Reconfigurable MAS. Indeed, we can reason about systems both from an individual and a system level. We show how to reason about synchronisations, interaction protocols, joint missions, and how to express high-level features such as channel mobility, reconfiguration, coalition formation, self-organisation, etc.

The structure of this paper: In Sect. 2, give a background on RECIPE [3, 4], the underlying theory of R-CHECK. In Sect. 3, we present the language of R-CHECK and its symbolic semantics. In Sect. 4, we provide a nontrivial case study to model autonomous resource allocation. In Sect. 5 we discuss the integration of R-CHECK with NUXMV and we demonstrate our development using high-level properties. Finally, we report concluding remarks in Sect. 6.

2   RECIPE: A Model of Computation

We present the underlying theory of R-CHECK. Indeed, R-CHECK accepts a high-level language that is based on the symbolic RECIPE formalism [3,4]. We briefly present RECIPE agents and their composition to generate a system-level behaviour. Formally, agents rely on a set of common variables CV, a set of data variables D, and a set of channels CH containing the broadcast one $\star$. Common variables CV are used by agents to send messages that indirectly specify constraints on receivers. Each agent relates common variables to their local variables through a re-labelling function. Thus, agents specify constraints anonymously on common variables which are later translated to the corresponding receiver's local variables. That is, when messages are delivered, a receiver checks the satisfaction of the constraints re-labeled with CV; D are the actual communicated values in the message; CH define the set of channels that agents use to communicate.

Definition 1 (Agent). *An agent is $A_i = \langle V_i,\ f_i,\ g_i^s,\ g_i^r,\ \mathcal{T}_i^s,\ \mathcal{T}_i^r, \theta_i \rangle$,*

- *V_i is a finite set of typed local variables, each ranging over a finite domain. A state s^i is an interpretation of V_i, i.e., if $\mathsf{Dom}(v)$ is the domain of v, then s^i is an element in $\prod_{v \in V_i} \mathsf{Dom}(v)$. The set V' denotes the primed copy of V and Id_i to denote the assertion $\bigwedge_{v \in V_i} v = v'$.*
- *$f_i : \mathrm{CV} \to V_i$ is a function, associating common variables to local variables. The notation f_i is used for the assertion $\bigwedge_{cv \in \mathrm{CV}} cv = f_i(cv)$.*
- *$g_i^s(V_i, \mathrm{CH}, \mathrm{D}, \mathrm{CV})$ is a send guard specifying a condition on receivers. That is, the predicate, obtained from g_i^s after assigning s^i, ch, and $\mathbf{d}$ (an assignment to D), which is checked against every receiver j after applying f_j.*
- *$g_i^r(V_i, \mathrm{CH})$ is a receive guard describing the connectedness of an agent to a channel ch. We let $g_i^r(V_i, \star) = \mathsf{true}$, i.e., every agent is always connected to the broadcast channel. Note, however, not all messages are received by all agents, and that receiving a broadcast message could have no effect on an agent.*
- *$\mathcal{T}_i^s(V_i, V_i', \mathrm{D}, \mathrm{CH})$ and $\mathcal{T}_i^r(V_i, V_i', \mathrm{D}, \mathrm{CH})$ are assertions describing, respectively, the send and receive transition relations. We assume that an agent is broadcast input-enabled, i.e., $\forall v, \mathbf{d}\ \exists v'$ s.t. $\mathcal{T}_i^r(v, v', \mathbf{d}, \star)$.*
- *θ_i is an assertion on V_i describing the initial states, i.e., a state is initial if it satisfies θ_i.*

Agents exchange messages of the form $m = (ch, \mathbf{d}, i, \pi)$. A message is defined by the channel it is sent on ch, the data it carries $\mathbf{d}$, the sender identity i, and the assertion describing the possible local assignments to common variables of receivers π. The predicate π is obtained from grounding the sender's send guard on the sender's current state ($s^i \in \prod_{v \in V_i} \mathsf{Dom}(v)$), ch and $\mathbf{d}$.

A set of agents agreeing on common variables CV, data variables D, and channels CH define a *system*, defined as follows. We use $\uplus$ for disjoint union.

Definition 2 (Discrete System). *Given a set* $\{A_i\}_i$ *of agents, a system is* $S = \langle \mathcal{V}, \rho, \theta \rangle$, *where* $\mathcal{V} = \underset{i}{\uplus} V_i$, *a state of the system* s *is in* $\prod_i \prod_{v \in V_i} \mathsf{Dom}(v)$ *and the initial assertion* $\theta = \bigwedge_i \theta_i$. *The transition relation* ρ *of* S *is as follows:*

$$
\rho = \exists ch \, \exists \mathrm{D} \bigvee_k \mathcal{T}_k^s(V_k, V_k', \mathrm{D}, ch) \wedge
$$
$$
\bigwedge_{j \neq k} \left(\exists \mathrm{CV}. f_j \wedge \left(\begin{array}{l} g_j^r(V_j, ch) \wedge g_k^s(V_k, ch, \mathrm{D}, \mathrm{CV}) \wedge \quad \mathcal{T}_j^r(V_j, V_j', \mathrm{D}, ch) \\ \vee \qquad\qquad\qquad\qquad\qquad\qquad \neg g_j^r(V_j, ch) \wedge \mathsf{Id}_j \\ \vee \qquad \neg g_k^s(V_k, ch, \mathrm{D}, \mathrm{CV}) \wedge ch = \star \wedge \mathsf{Id}_j \end{array} \right) \right).
$$

The transition relation ρ describes two modes of interactions: blocking multicast and non-blocking broadcast. Formally, ρ relates a system state s to its successors s' given a message $m = (ch, \mathbf{d}, k, \pi)$. Namely, there exists an agent k that sends a message with data $\mathbf{d}$ (an assignment to D) with assertion π (an assignment to g_k^s) on channel ch and all other agents are either (a) connected to channel ch, satisfy the send predicate π, and participate in the interaction (i.e., has a corresponding receive transition for the message), (b) not connected and idle, or (c) do not satisfy the send predicate of a broadcast and idle. That is, the agents satisfying π (translated to their local state by the conjunct $\exists \mathrm{CV}. f_j$) and connected to channel ch (i.e., $g_j^r(s^j, ch)$) get the message and perform a receive transition. As a result of interaction, the state variables of the sender and these receivers might be updated. The agents that are *not connected* to the channel (i.e., $\neg g_j^r(s^j, ch)$) do not participate in the interaction and stay still. In case of broadcast, namely when sending on $\star$, agents are always connected and the set of receivers not satisfying π (translated again as above) stay still. Thus, a blocking multicast arises when a sender is blocked until all *connected* agents satisfy $\pi \wedge f_j$. The relation ensures that, when sending on a channel different from $\star$, the set of receivers is the full set of *connected* agents. On the broadcast channel agents not satisfying the send predicate do not block the sender.

R-CHECK adopts a symbolic model checking approach that directly works on the predicate representation of RECIPE systems. Technically speaking, the behaviour of each agent is represented by a first-order predicate that is defined as a disjunction over the send and the receive transition relations of that agent. Moreover, both send and receive transition relations can be represented by a disjunctive normal form predicate of the form $\bigvee(\bigwedge_j \text{assertion}_j)$. That is, a disjunct of all possible send/receive transitions enabled in each step of a computation.

In the following, we will define a high-level language that can be used to write user-friendly programs with symbolic computation steps. We will also show how to translate these programs to RECIPE predicate representation.

```
1       agent name
2           local: var_name:type , ···, var_name:type
3           init: θ_T
4           relabel: common_var <− Exp
5                ...
6                    common_var <− Exp
7           receive−guard: g^r(V_T, CH)
8           repeat: P
```

Fig. 1. Agent type.

3   The R-CHECK Language

We formally present the syntax of R-CHECK language and show how to translate it to the RECIPE predicate representation. We start by introducing the type **agent**, its structure, and how to instantiate it; we introduce the syntax of the agent behaviour and how to create a system of agents.

The type **agent** is reported in Fig. 1. Intuitively, each agent type has a **name** that identifies a specific type of behaviour. That is, we permit creating multiple instances/copies with the same type of behaviour. Each agent has a local state **local** represented by a set of local variables V_T, each of which can be of a type boolean, integer or enum. The initial state of an agent **init:** θ_T is a predicate characterising the initial assignments to the agent local variables. The section **relabel** is used to implement the relabelling function of common variables in a RECIPE agent. Here, we allow the relabelling to include a boolean expression **Exp** over local variables V_T to accommodate a more expressive relabelling mechanism, e.g., $cv_1 \leftarrow (\text{length} \geq 20)$. The section **receive-guard** specifies the connectedness of the agent to channels given a current assignment to its local variables. The non-terminating behaviour of an agent is represented by **repeat:** P, which executes the process P indefinitely.

Before we introduce the syntax of agent behaviour, we show how to instantiate an agent and how to compose the different agents to create a system. An agent type of name A can be instantiated as follows $A(id, \theta)$. That is, we create an instance of A with identity id and an additional initial restriction θ. Here, we take the conjunction of θ with the predicate in the **init** section of the type A as the initial condition of this instance. We use the parallel composition operator $\|$ to inductively define a system as in the following production rule.

$$(\text{System}) \qquad S ::= \quad A(id, \theta) \quad | \quad S_1 \| S_2$$

That is, a system is either an instance of agent type or a parallel composition of set of instances of (possibly) different types. The semantics of $\|$ is fully captured by ρ in Definition 2.

The syntax of an R-CHECK process is inductively defined as follows.

$$\begin{aligned}
\text{(Process)} \quad & P ::= \quad P; P \quad | \quad P + P \quad | \quad \textsf{rep}\ P \quad | \quad C \\
\text{(Command)} \quad & C ::= \quad l : C \quad | \quad \langle \varPhi \rangle\ ch\ !\ \pi\ \mathbf{d}\ \textsf{U} \quad | \quad \langle \varPhi \rangle\ ch\ ?\ \textsf{U}
\end{aligned}$$

A process P is either a sequential composition of two processes $P; P$, a non-deterministic choice between two processes $P + P$, a loop $\textsf{rep}\ P$, or a command C. There are three types of commands corresponding to either a labelled command, a message-send or a message-receive. A command of the form $l : C$ is a syntactic labelling and is used to allow the model checker to reason about syntactic elements as we will see later. A command of the form $\langle \varPhi \rangle\ ch\ !\ \pi\ \mathbf{d}\ \textsf{U}$ corresponds to a message-send. Intuitively, the predicate $\varPhi$ is an assertion over the current assignments to local variables, i.e., is a pre-condition that must hold before the transition can be taken. As the names suggest, ch, π and (respectively) $\mathbf{d}$ are the communication channel, the sender predicate, and the assignment to data variables (i.e., the actual content of the message). Lastly, $\textsf{U}$ is the next assignment to local variables after taking the transition. We use ! to distinguish send transitions. A command of the form $\langle \varPhi \rangle\ ch\ ?\ \textsf{U}$ corresponds to a message-receive. Differently from message-send, $\varPhi$ can also predicate on the incoming message, i.e., the assignment $\mathbf{d}$. We use ? to distinguish receive transitions.

Despite the minimalistic syntax of R-CHECK, we can express every control flow structure in a high-level programming language. For instance, by combining non-determinism and pre-conditions of commands, we can encode every structure of IF-statement. Similarly, we can encode finite loops by combining $\textsf{rep}\ P$ and commands C, e.g., $(\textsf{rep}\ C1 + C_2)$ means: repeat C_1 or block until C_2 happens.

3.1   The Semantics of R-CHECK

We initially give a structural semantics to R-CHECK process using a finite automaton such that each transition in the automaton corresponds to a symbolic transition. Intuitively, the automaton represents the control structure of an R-CHECK process. We will further use this automaton alongside the agent definition to give an R-CHECK agent an execution semantics based on the symbolic RECIPE framework. This two-step semantics will help us in verifying structural properties about R-CHECK agents.

Definition 3 (Structure automaton). *A structure automaton is of the form* $G = \langle S,\ \Sigma,\ s_i,\ E,\ s_f \rangle$*, where*

- *S is a finite set of states;*
- *$s_i, s_f \in S$: are two states that, respectively, represent the* initial *state and the* final *state in G (though the automaton does not terminate);*
- *Σ is the alphabet of G;*
- *$E \subseteq S \times \Sigma \times S$: is the set of edges of G.*

We use (s_1, σ, s_2) to denote an edge $e \in E$ such that s_1 is the source state of e, s_2 is the target state of e and the letter σ is the label of e.

Now, everything is in place to define the structure semantics of R-CHECK processes. We define a function $(\!| \, . \, |\!)^{[s_i, s_f]} : P \to 2^E$ which takes an R-CHECK process P as input and produces the set of edges of the corresponding structure automaton. The function $(\!| \, . \, |\!)^{[s_i, s_f]}$ assumes that each process has unique initial state s_i and final state s_f in the structure automaton. Please note that the states of the structure automaton only represent the control structure of the process, and an agent can have multiple initial states depending on θ_T while starting from s_i. The definition of the translation function $(\!| \, . \, |\!)^{[s_i, s_f]}$ is reported below.

$$(\!|\text{repeat} : P|\!)^{[s_i, s_f]} \triangleq (\!|P|\!)^{[s_i, s_i]}$$

$$(\!|P_1; P_2|\!)^{[s_i, s_f]} \triangleq (\!|P_1|\!)^{[s_i, s_1]} \bigcup (\!|P_2|\!)^{[s_1, s_f]} \qquad \text{for a fresh } s_1$$

$$(\!|P_1 + P_2|\!)^{[s_i, s_f]} \triangleq (\!|P_1|\!)^{[s_i, s_f]} \bigcup (\!|P_2|\!)^{[s_i, s_f]}$$

$$(\!|\text{rep } P|\!)^{[s_i, s_f]} \triangleq (\!|P|\!)^{[s_i, s_i]}$$

$$(\!|C|\!)^{[s_i, s_f]} \triangleq \{(s_i, C, s_f)\}$$

Intuitively, the structure semantics of $(\!|\text{repeat} : P|\!)^{[s_i, s_f]}$ corresponds to a self-loop in the structure automaton (with s_i as both the source and the target state) and where P is repeated indefinitely. Moreover, the semantics $(\!|P_1; P_2|\!)^{[s_i, s_f]}$ is the union of the transitions created by P_1 and P_2 while creating a fresh state in the graph s_1 to allow sequentiality, where P_1 starts in s_i and ends in s_1 and later P_2 continues from s_1 and ends in s_f. That is, the structure of the process is encoded using an extra memory. Differently, the non-deterministic choice $(\!|P_1 + P_2|\!)^{[s_i, s_f]}$ does not require extra memory because the execution of P_1 and P_2 is independent. The semantics of $(\!|\text{rep } P|\!)^{[s_i, s_f]}$ is similar to $(\!|\text{repeat} : P|\!)^{[s_i, s_f]}$ and is introduced to allow self-looping inside a non-terminating process. Finally, the semantics of a command C in corresponds to an edge $\{(s_i, C, s_f)\}$ in the structure automaton. This means that the alphabet Σ of the automaton ranges over R-CHECK commands. Note how the translation is completely syntactic and does not enumerate variable values, resulting in a symbolic automaton.

To translate an R-CHECK agent into a RECIPE agent, we first introduce the following functions: typeOf, varsOf, predOf and guardOf on a command C. That is, typeOf(C) returns the type of a command C as either ! or ?. For example, typeOf($\langle \Phi \rangle\, ch \, ! \, \pi \, \mathbf{d} \, \mathsf{U}$) = !. varsOf($C$) returns the set of local variables that are updated in C, while the predOf(C) returns the predicate characterising C in terms of local variables V_T, the primed copy V'_T, the channel ch and the data variables D (excluding π). For instance, predOf($\langle \mathsf{Link} = \mathsf{c} \rangle \star ! \pi(\mathsf{MSG} := \mathsf{m})[\mathsf{Link} := \mathsf{b}]$) is $(\mathsf{Link} = \mathsf{c}) \wedge (ch = \star) \wedge (\mathsf{MSG} = \mathsf{m}) \wedge (\mathsf{Link}' = \mathsf{b})$. Finally guardOf($C$) returns the send predicate π in a send command and false otherwise.

Moreover, we use $keep(X)$ to denote that the set of local variables X is not changed by a transition (either send or receive). More precisely, $keep(X)$ is equivalent to the assertion $\bigwedge_{x \in X} x = x'$, where x' is the primed copy of x.

Next we define how to construct a RECIPE agent from an R-CHECK agent with structure semantics interpreted as a structure automaton.

Definition 4 (from R-CHECK to ReCiPe). *Given an instance of agent type T as defined in Fig. 1 with a structure semantics interpreted as a structure automaton $G = \langle S, \Sigma, s_i, E, s_f \rangle$, we can construct a RECIPE agent $A = \langle V, f, g^s, g^r, \mathcal{T}^s, \mathcal{T}^r, \theta \rangle$ that implements its behaviour.*
We construct A as follows:

- $V = V_T \cup \{\mathsf{st}\}$*: that is, the union of the set of declared variables V_T in the* local *section of T in Fig. 1 and a new state variable* st *ranging over the states S in G of the structure automaton, representing the control structure of the process of T. Namely, the control structure of the behaviour of T is now encoded as an additional variable in A;*
- *the initial condition $\theta = \theta_T \wedge (\mathsf{st} = s_i)$: that is the conjunction of the initial condition θ_T in the* init *section of T in Fig. 1 and the predicate $\mathsf{st} = s_i$, specifying the initial state of G.*
- *f and g^r have one-to-one correspondence in section* relabel *and section* receive-guard *respectively of T in Fig. 1.*
- $g^s = \bigvee\limits_{\sigma \in \Sigma:\ \mathsf{typeOf}(\sigma) =\ !} \mathsf{guardOf}(\sigma)$

- $\mathcal{T}^s = \bigvee\limits_{(s_1,\sigma,s_2) \in E:\ \mathsf{typeOf}(\sigma) =\ !} \left(\begin{array}{c} \mathsf{predOf}(\sigma) \wedge (\mathsf{st} = s_1) \wedge (\mathsf{st}' = s_2) \wedge \\ keep(V_T \backslash \mathsf{varsOf}(\sigma)) \end{array} \right)$

- $\mathcal{T}^r = \bigvee\limits_{(s_1,\sigma,s_2) \in E:\ \mathsf{typeOf}(\sigma) =\ ?} \left(\begin{array}{c} \mathsf{predOf}(\sigma) \wedge (\mathsf{st} = s_1) \wedge (\mathsf{st}' = s_2) \wedge \\ keep(V_T \backslash \mathsf{varsOf}(\sigma)) \end{array} \right).$

4   Case Study: Autonomous Resource Allocation

We model a scenario where a group of clients are requested to jointly solve a problem. Each client will buy a computing virtual machine (VM) from a resource manager and use it to solve its task. Initially, clients know the communication link of the manager, but they need to self-organise and coordinate the use of the link anonymously. The manager will help establishing connections between clients and available machines, and later clients proceed interacting independently with machines on private links learnt when the connection is established.

There are two types of machines: high performance machines and standard ones. The resource manager commits to provide high performance VMs to clients, but when all of these machines are reserved, the clients are assigned to standard ones. The protocol proceeds until each client buys a machine, and then all clients have to collaborate to solve the problem and complete the task.

A client uses the local variables cLink, mLink, tLink, role to control its behaviour, where cLink is a link to interact with the manager, mLink is a placeholder for a mobile link that can be learnt at run-time, tLink is a link to synchronise with other clients to complete the task, and role is the role of the client. A client's initial condition θ_c is: cLink $=$ c $\wedge$ mLink $=$ empty $\wedge$ tLink $=$ t $\wedge$ role $=$ client, specifying that the resource manager is reachable on c, the mobile link is empty, the task link is t and the role is client.

Note that the interfaces of agents are parameterised to their local states and state changes may create dynamic and opportunistic interactions. For instance, when cLink is set to empty, the client does not connect to channel c; also when a channel is assigned to mLink, the client starts receiving messages on that channel.

Clients may use broadcast or multicast; in a broadcast, receivers (if exist) may anonymously receive the message when they are interested in its values (and when they satisfy the send predicate). Otherwise, an agent may not participate in the interaction. In multicast, all agents listening on the multicast channel must participate to enable the interaction.

Broadcast is used when agents are unaware of the existence of each other while (possibly) sharing some resources while multicast is used to capture a more structured interaction where agents have dedicated links to interact. In our example, clients are not aware of the existence of each other while they share the resource manager channel c. Thus they may coordinate to use the channel anonymously by means of broadcast. A client reserves the channel c by means of a broadcast message with a predicate targeting other clients. All other clients self-organise and disconnect from c and wait for a release message.

A message in R-CHECK carries an assignment to a set of data variables D. In our scenario, $D = \{LNK, MSG\}$ where LNK is used to exchange a link with other agents, and MSG denotes the label of the message and takes values from $\{reserve, request, release, buy, connect, full, complete\}$.

Agents in this scenario use one common variable cv ranging over roles to specify potential receivers. Remember that every agent i has a relabelling function $f_i : CV \rightarrow V_i$ that is applied to the send guard once a message is delivered to check whether it is eligible to receive. For a client, $f_c(cv) = role$. The send guard of a client appears in the messages that the client sends, and we will explain later. In general, broadcasts are destined to agents assigning to the common variable cv a value matching the role of the sender, i.e., client; messages on cLink are destined to agents assigning mgr to cv; and other messages are destined to everyone listening on the right channel.

The receive guard g_c^r is $(ch = \star) \vee (ch = cLink) \vee (ch = tLink)$. That is, reception is always enabled on broadcast and on a channel that matches the value of cLink or tLink. Note that these guards are parameterised to local variables and thus may change at run-time, creating a dynamic communication structure.

```
1    repeat: (sReserve: <cLink==c > *! (cv==role)(MSG := reserve)[]
2              + rReserve: <cLink==c && MSG == reserve> *? [cLink := empty]);
3           ( (sRequest: <cLink!=empty> cLink! (cv==mgr)(MSG := request)[];
4             rConnect: <mLink==empty && MSG == connect> cLink? [mLink := LNK];
5             sRelease: <TRUE> *! (cv==role)(MSG := release)[cLink := empty];
6             sBuy: <mLink!=empty> mLink! (TRUE)(MSG := buy)[mLink := empty];
7             (sSolve: <TRUE> tLink!(TRUE)(MSG := complete)[]
8                + <MSG == complete> tLink? [])
9           ) + rRelease: <cLink==empty && MSG == release> *? [cLink := c])
```

Fig. 2. Client behaviour.

The behaviour of the client is reported in Fig. 2. In this example, we label each command with a name identifying the message and its type (i.e., s for send and r for receive). For instance, the send transition at Line 1 is labelled with sReserve while the receive transition at Line 2 is labelled with rReserve. We use these later to reason about agent interactions syntactically.

Initially in Lines 1–2, every client may either broadcast a reserve message to all other clients (i.e., (cv = role)) or receive a reserve message from one of them. This is to allow clients to self-organise and coordinate to use the common link. That is, a client may initially reserve an interaction session with the resource manager by broadcasting a reserve message to all other clients, asking them to disconnect the common link c (stored in their local variable cLink); or receive a reserve message, i.e., gets asked by another client to disconnect from channel c. In either case, the client progress to Line 3. Depending on what happened in the previous step, the client may proceed to establish a session with the resource manager (i.e., (cv = mgr)) and a machine (Lines 3–8) or gets stuck waiting for a release message from the client, currently holding the session (Line 9). In the latter case, the client gets back in the loop to (Line 1) after receiving a release message and attempts again to establish the session.

In the former case, the client uses the blocking multicast channel c to send a request to the resource manager (Line 3) and waits to receive a private connection link with a virtual machine agent on cLink (Line 4). When the client receives the connect message on cLink, the client assigns its mLink variable the value of LNK in the message. That is, the client is now ready to communicate on mLink. On Line 5, the agent releases the common link c by broadcasting a release message to all other clients (with (cv = role)) and proceeds to Line 6 and starts communicating privately with the assigned VM agent. The client buys a service from the VM agent on a dedicated link stored in mLink by sending a buy to the VM agent to complete the transaction. The client proceeds to line 7 and wait for other clients to collaborate and finish the task. Thus, the client either initiates the last step and sends a complete message when the rest of clients are ready (Line 7) or receives a complete message from another client that is ready (Line 8).

We now specify the manager and the virtual machine, and show how reconfigurable multicast can be used to cleanly model a point-to-point interaction.

The resource manager's local variables are hLink, sLink, cLink, role, where hLink and sLink store channel names to communicate with high- and standard-performance VMs respectively and the rest are as defined before.

The initial condition θ_m is: hLink $= g_1 \wedge$ sLink $= g_2 \wedge$ cLink $= c \wedge$ role $=$ mgr. Note that the link g_1 is used to communicate with the group of high performance machines while g_2 is used for standard ones.

The send guard for a manager is always satisfied, (i.e., g_m^s is true) while the receive guard specifies that a manager only receives broadcasts or on channels that match with cLink or hLink, i.e., g_m^r is (ch $= \star$) $\vee$ (ch $=$ cLink) $\vee$ (ch $=$ hLink).

The behaviour of the agent manager is reported in Fig. 3. In summary, the manager initially forwards requests received on channel c (Line 1) to the high performance VMs first as in (Line 2). The negotiation protocol with machines is

```
1    repeat: rRequest: <MSG == request> cLink? [];
2             sForward: <TRUE> hLink! (TRUE)(MSG := request)[];
3             (rConnect: <MSG == connect> cLink? []
4             + rep (rFull: <MSG == full> hLink? [];
5                     sRequest: <TRUE> sLink! (TRUE)(MSG := request)[]))
```

Fig. 3. Manager behaviour.

reported in Lines 3–5. The manager can receive a connect message and directly enable the client to connect with the virtual machine as in (Line 3) or receive a full message, informing that all high performance machines are fully occupied (Line 4). In the latter case, the requests are forwarded to the standard performance machines on sLink as in (Lines 4–5). The process repeats until a connect message is received (Line 4) and the manager gets back to (Line 1) to handle other requests. Clearly, the specifications of the manager assumes that there are plenty of standard VMs but not a lot of high performance ones. Thus it only expects a full message to be received on channel hLink. Note also that the manager gets ready to handle the next request once a connect message is received on channel c and leaves the client and the selected VM to interact independently.

The virtual machine's local variables are: gLink, pLink, cLink, asgn, where asgn indicates if the VM is assigned, gLink is a group link, pLink is a private link and gLink is as before; the initial condition θ_{vm} is $\neg$asgn $\wedge$ cLink = empty (note gLink and pLink will be machine specific), where initially virtual machines are not listening on the common link cLink. Depending on the group that the machine belong to, the gLink will either be assigned to high performance machine group g_1 or the standard one g_2. Moreover, each machine has a unique private link pLink. A VM's send guard is always satisfied, (i.e., g_{mv}^s is true) while its receive guard specifies that it always receives on broadcast, pLink, gLink and cLink, i.e., g_{vm}^r is ch = $\star$ $\vee$ ch = gLink $\vee$ ch = pLink $\vee$ ch = cLink.

```
1    repeat: rForward: <cLink==empty && MSG == request> gLink? [cLink:= c];
2             (sConnect: <cLink==c && !asgn> cLink! (TRUE)(MSG := connect, LNK := pLink)
             [cLink:= empty, asgn:= TRUE]
3             + sFull: <cLink==c && asgn> gLink! (TRUE)(MSG := full)[cLink:= empty]
4             + rConnect: <cLink==c && MSG == connect> cLink? [cLink:= empty]
5             + rFull: <cLink==c && asgn && MSG == full> gLink? [cLink:= empty]
6             ) + rBuy: <MSG == buy> pLink? []
```

Fig. 4. Machine behaviour.

The behaviour of the virtual machine agent is reported in Fig. 4. Intuitively, a VM either receives the forwarded request on the group channel gLink (Line 1) and thus activating the common link and also a nondeterministic choice between connect and full messages (Lines 2–5) or receives a buy message from a client on the private link pLink (Line 6). In the latter case, the VM agent agrees to sell the service and stays idle. In the former case, a VM sends connect, with its private link pLink carried on the data variable LNK, on cLink if it is not assigned (Line

2), or sends full on gLink otherwise (Line 3). Note that a full message can only go through if all VMs in group gLink are assigned. Note that reception on gLink is always enabled by the receive guard g_{vm}^r and the receive transition at Line 3 specifies that a machine enables a send on a full message only when it is assigned. For example, if gLink = g_1 then only when all machines in group g_1 are assigned, a full message can be enabled.

Furthermore, a connect message will also be received by other VMs in the group cLink (Line 4). As a result, all other available VMs (i.e., ¬asgn) in the same group do not reply to the request. Thus, one VM is non-deterministically selected to provide a service and a point-to-point like interaction is achieved. Note that this easy encoding is possible because agents change communication interfaces dynamically by enabling and disabling channels.

Now, we can easily create an R-CHECK system as follows.

$$
\begin{aligned}
\text{system} = {}& \text{Client}(\text{client1}, \text{TRUE}) \parallel \text{Client}(\text{client2}, \text{TRUE}) \\
& \parallel \text{Client}(\text{client3}, \text{TRUE}) \parallel \text{Manager}(\text{manager}, \text{TRUE}) \\
& \parallel \text{Machine}(\text{machine1}, \text{gLink} = \text{g1} \wedge \text{pLink} = \text{vmm1}) \\
& \parallel \text{Machine}(\text{machine2}, \text{gLink} = \text{g1} \wedge \text{pLink} = \text{vmm2}) \\
& \parallel \text{Machine}(\text{machine3}, \text{gLink} = \text{g2} \wedge \text{pLink} = \text{vmm3})
\end{aligned}
\tag{1}
$$

This system is the parallel composition (according to Definition 2) of three copies of a client {$client_1, \ldots, client_3$}; a copy of a manager {manager}; and finally three copies of a machine {$machine_1, \ldots, machine_3$}, each belongs to a specific group and a private link. For instance, $machine_1$ belongs to group g_1 (the high performance machines) and has a private link named vmm1.

5   Model-Checking Through NUXMV

We describe the integration of R-CHECK with the NUXMV model checker [10] to enable an enhanced symbolic LTL model-checking. We also demonstrate our developments using examples, and show how the combined features of R-CHECK, the symbolic LTL model-checking, and NUXMV provides a powerful tool to verify high-level features of reconfigurable and interactive systems.

From R-CHECK to NUXMV. We give individual R-CHECK agents a symbolic semantics based on the RECIPE framework as shown in Sect. 3.1 and Definition 4. Notably, we preserve the labels of commands (i.e., $l : \sigma$) and use them as subpredicate definitions. For instance, given a labeled edge $(s_1, l : \sigma, s_2)$ in the structure automaton G in Definition 3, we translate it into the following predicate in RECIPE as explained in Definition 4: $l := \text{predOf}(\sigma) \wedge (\text{st} = s_1) \wedge (\text{st}' = s_2) \wedge keep(V_T \backslash \text{varsOf}(\sigma))$.

The only difference here is that the label l is now a predicate definition and its truth value defines if the transition $(s_1, l : \sigma, s_2)$ is feasible. Since every command is translated to either message-send or message-receive, we can use these labels now to refer to message exchange syntactically inside LTL formulas.

Moreover, we rename all local variables of agents to consider the identity of the agent as follows: for example, given the cLink variable of a client, we generate the variable client − cLink. This is important when different agents use the same identifier for local variables. We also treat all data variables D and channel names CH as constants and we construct a RECIPE system $S = \langle \mathcal{V}, \rho, \theta \rangle$ as defined in Definition 2 while considering subpredicate definitions and agent variables after renaming. Technically, a RECIPE system S has a one-to-one correspondence to a NUXMV module M. That is, both S and M agrees on local variables $\mathcal{V}$ and the initial condition θ, but are slightly different with respect to transition relations. Indeed, the transition relation ρ of S as defined in Definition 2 is translated to an equivalent transition relation $\hat{\rho}$ of M as follows: $\hat{\rho} = \rho \vee (\neg \rho \wedge keep(\mathcal{V}))$. That is, NUXMV translates deadlock states in S into stuttering (sink) states in M where system variables do not change.

R-CHECK provides an interactive simulator that allows the user to simulate the system either randomly or based on predicates that the user supplies. For instance, starting from some state in the simulation, the user may supply the constraint next(client1−cLink) = c to ask the simulator to select the transition that leads to a state where the next value of client1−cLink equals c. If such constraint is feasible (i.e., there exists a transition satisfying the constraint), the simulator selects such transition, and otherwise it returns an error message. Users can also refer to message -send and -receive using command labels in the same way. A constraint on a send transition like client1−sReserve, to denote the sending of the message reserve in Fig. 2, Line 2, means that this transition is feasible in the current state of simulation. However, a constraint on a receive transition client−rReserve, like on the message in Fig. 2, Line 4, means that this transition is already taken from the previous state of simulation. This slight difference between send and receive transitions is due to the fact that receive transitions cannot happen independently and only happen due to a joint send transition. Finally, R-CHECK is supported with an editor, syntax highlighting and visualising tool. For instance, once the model of the scenario in Sect. 4 is compiled, R-CHECK produces the corresponding labelled and symbolic structure automata in Fig. 5, which the user may use to reason about interactions.

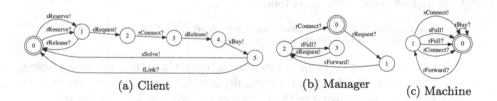

(a) Client   (b) Manager   (c) Machine

Fig. 5. Symbolic structure automata.

Symbolic Model Checking. R-CHECK supports both symbolic LTL model checking and bounded LTL model checking. We illustrate the capabilities of R-CHECK by several examples. In this section, we will use Eq. 1, Sect. 4 and the corresponding structure automata in Fig. 5 as the system under consideration.

We show how to verify properties about agents both from individual and interaction protocols level by predicating on message exchange rather than on atomic propositions. It should be noted that the transition labels in Fig. 5 are not mere labels, but rather predicates with truth values changing dynamically at run-time, introducing opportunistic interaction. For instance, we can reason about a client and its connection to the system as follows.

$$G \text{ (client1−sReserve } \rightarrow \text{ F client1−sRequest)} \quad (1)$$
$$G \text{ (client1−sReserve } \rightarrow \text{ F client1−sRelease)} \quad (2)$$
$$G \text{ (client1−sRequest } \rightarrow \text{ F client1−rConnect)} \quad (3)$$

The liveness condition (1) specifies that the client can send a request to the manager after it has already reserved the common link c; the liveness condition (2) specifies that the client does not hold a live lock on the common link c. Namely, the client releases the common link eventually. The liveness condition (3) specifies that the *system* is responsive, i.e., after the client's request, other agents collaborate to eventually supply a connection.

We can also reason about synchronisation and reconfiguration in relation to local state as in the following.

$$G \text{ (manager−sForward } \rightarrow \text{ X machine1−rForward)} \quad (4)$$
$$F \text{ (client1−sRelease \& } G(!client1−rConnect)) \quad (5)$$
$$G \text{ ((!machine1−asgn \& machine1−rForward) } \rightarrow \text{ machine1−sConnect)} \quad (6)$$

In (4), we refer to synchronisation, i.e., the manager has to forward the request before the machine can receive it. Note that this formula does not hold for $machine_3$ because sForward is destined for group g_1; we can refer to reconfiguration in (5), i.e., eventually the client disconnects from the common link c, and it can never be able to receive connection on that link; moreover, in (6) the machine sends a connection predicated on its local state, i.e., if it is not assigned. Note that (6) does not hold because $machine_1$ might lose the race for $machine_2$ in group g_1 to execute connect message.

We can also specify channel mobility and joint missions from a declarative and centralised point of view, as follows.

$$F(\text{client1−mLink} \neq \text{empty}) \text{ \& } F \text{ (client2−mLink} \neq \text{empty)} \text{ \& } F \text{ (client3−mLink} \neq \text{empty)}$$
$$\longrightarrow F \text{ (client1−sSolve } | \text{ client2−sSolve } | \text{ client3−sSolve)}$$

That is, each client eventually receiving a mobile link (i.e., mLink $\neq$ empty), which is used to buy a VM, means eventually one client will initiate the mission's termination by synchronising with the others to solve the joint problem.

We are unaware of a model-checker that enables reasoning at such a high-level.

6   Concluding Remarks

We introduced the R-CHECK model checking toolkit for verifying and simulating reconfigurable multi-agent system. We formally presented the syntax and semantics of R-CHECK language in relation to the RECIPE framework [3, 4], and we used it to model and reason about a nontrivial case study from the realm of reconfigurable and self-organising MAS. Our semantics approach consisted of two types of semantics: structural semantics in terms of automata to recover information about interaction features, and execution semantics based on RECIPE. The interaction information recovered in the structural semantics is recorded succinctly in the execution one, and thus permits reasoning about interaction protocols and message exchange. R-CHECK is supported with a command line tool, a web editor with syntax highlighting and visualisation.

We integrated R-CHECK with NUXMV to enable LTL verification through symbolic, bounded, and IC3 model checking. We showed that this specialised integration provides a powerful tool that permits verifying high-level features such as synchronisations, interaction protocols, joint missions, channel mobility, reconfiguration, self-organisation, etc.

Our work is focused on multi-agent systems, which is a special case of collective adaptive systems. The difference here is that the number of agents is usually smaller, and thus the issue of scalability is not our main concern. Indeed, if we consider a large number of agents then qualitative reasoning with LTL would not be sufficient and probabilistic techniques, like statistical model checking [21], would be more appropriate.

Related Works. We report on closely related model-checking toolkits.

MCMAS is a successful model checker that is used to reason about multi-agent systems and supports a range of temporal and epistemic logic operators. It also supports ISPL, a high-level input language with semantics based on *Interpreted Systems* [14]. The key differences with respect to R-CHECK are: (1) MCMAS models are enumerative and are exponentially larger than R-CHECK ones; (2) actions in MCMAS are merely synchronisation labels while command labels in R-CHECK are predicates with truth values changing dynamically at run-time, introducing opportunistic interaction; (3) lastly and most importantly R-CHECK can model and reason about dynamic communication structure with message exchange and channel mobility while in MCMAS the structure is fixed.

MTSA toolkit [13] is used to reason about labelled transition systems (LTS) and their composition as in the simple multiway synchronisation of Hoare's CSP calculus [18]. MTSA uses *Fluent Linear Temporal logic (FLTL)* [15] to reason about actions, where a fluent is a predicate indicating the beginning and the end of an action. As the case of MCMAS, the communication structure is fixed and there is no way to reason about reconfiguration or even message exchange.

SPIN [19] is originally designed to reason about concurrent systems and protocol design. Although SPIN is successful in reasoning about static coordination protocols, it did not expand its coverage to multi-agent system features. Indeed, the kind of protocols that SPIN can be used to reason about are mainly related to static structured systems like hardware and electronic circuits.

Finally, NUXMV [10] is designed at the semantic level of transition systems. NUXMV implements a large number of efficient algorithms for verification. This makes NUXMV an excellent candidate to serve as a backbone for special-purpose model checking tools. For this reason, we integrate R-CHECK with NUXMV.

Future Works. We plan to integrate LTOL, from [4], to R-CHECK. Indeed, the authors in [4] provide a PSPACE algorithm for LTOL model checking (improved from EXPSPACE in [3]). This way, we would not only be able to refer to message exchange in logical formulas, but also to identify the intentions of agents in the interaction and characterise potential interacting partners. Moreover, we would like to equip R-CHECK with a richer specification language that allows reasoning about the knowledge of agents and the dissemination of knowledge in distributed settings. For this purpose, we will investigate the possible integration of R-CHECK with MCMAS [22] to make use of the specialised symbolic algorithms that are introduced for knowledge reasoning.

References

1. Abd Alrahman, Y., Azzopardi, S., Piterman, N.: R-CHECK: a model checker for verifying reconfigurable MAS. In: Proceedings of the 21st International Conference on Autonomous Agents and Multiagent Systems, AAMAS 2022, pp. 1518–1520. International Foundation for Autonomous Agents and Multiagent Systems, Richland, SC (2022). https://doi.org/10.5555/3535850.3536020
2. Abd Alrahman, Y., De Nicola, R., Loreti, M.: A calculus for collective-adaptive systems and its behavioural theory. Inf. Comput. **268**, 104457 (2019). https://doi.org/10.1016/j.ic.2019.104457
3. Abd Alrahman, Y., Perelli, G., Piterman, N.: Reconfigurable interaction for MAS modelling. In: Seghrouchni, A.E.F., Sukthankar, G., An, B., Yorke-Smith, N. (eds.) Proceedings of the 19th International Conference on Autonomous Agents and Multiagent Systems, AAMAS 2020, Auckland, New Zealand, 9–13 May 2020, pp. 7–15. International Foundation for Autonomous Agents and Multiagent Systems (2020). https://doi.org/10.5555/3398761.3398768
4. Abd Alrahman, Y., Piterman, N.: Modelling and verification of reconfigurable multi-agent systems. Auton. Agents Multi Agent Syst. **35**(2), 47 (2021). https://doi.org/10.1007/s10458-021-09521-x
5. Aceto, L., Ingólfsd'ottir, A., Larsen, K.G., Srba, J.: Reactive Systems: Modelling, Specification and Verification. Cambridge University Press, Cambridge (2007). https://doi.org/10.1017/CBO9780511814105
6. Alrahman, Y.A., Nicola, R.D., Loreti, M.: Programming interactions in collective adaptive systems by relying on attribute-based communication. Sci. Comput. Program. **192**, 102428 (2020). https://doi.org/10.1016/j.scico.2020.102428
7. Alur, R., Henzinger, T.: Reactive modules. Formal Methods Syst. Des. **15**(1), 7–48 (1999)
8. Alur, R., Henzinger, T., Kupferman, O.: Alternating-time temporal logic. J. ACM **49**(5), 672–713 (2002). https://doi.org/10.1145/585265.585270
9. Cimatti, A., et al.: NuSMV 2: an OpenSource tool for symbolic model checking. In: Brinksma, E., Larsen, K.G. (eds.) CAV 2002. LNCS, vol. 2404, pp. 359–364. Springer, Heidelberg (2002). https://doi.org/10.1007/3-540-45657-0_29
10. Cimatti, A., Griggio, A.: Software model checking via IC3. In: Madhusudan, P., Seshia, S.A. (eds.) CAV 2012. LNCS, vol. 7358, pp. 277–293. Springer, Heidelberg (2012). https://doi.org/10.1007/978-3-642-31424-7_23
11. Clarke, E.M., Grumberg, O., Peled, D.A.: Model Checking. MIT Press, Cambridge (2000)

12. Cohen, P.R., Levesque, H.J.: Intention is choice with commitment. Artif. Intell. **42**(2–3), 213–261 (1990). https://doi.org/10.1016/0004-3702(90)90055-5
13. D'Ippolito, N., Fischbein, D., Chechik, M., Uchitel, S.: MTSA: the modal transition system analyser. In: 23rd IEEE/ACM International Conference on Automated Software Engineering (ASE 2008), L'Aquila, Italy, 15–19 September 2008, pp. 475–476. IEEE Computer Society (2008). https://doi.org/10.1109/ASE.2008.78
14. Fagin, R., Halpern, J., Moses, Y., Vardi, M.Y.: Reasoning about Knowledge. MIT Press, Cambridge (1995)
15. Giannakopoulou, D., Magee, J.: Fluent model checking for event-based systems. In: Proceedings of the 9th European Software Engineering and 11th ACM SIGSOFT International Symposium on Foundations of Software Engineering, pp. 257–266. ACM (2003)
16. Gutierrez, J., Harrenstein, P., Wooldridge, M.: From model checking to equilibrium checking: reactive modules for rational verification. Artif. Intell. **248**, 123–157 (2017). https://doi.org/10.1016/j.artint.2017.04.003
17. Hannebauer, M. (ed.): Autonomous Dynamic Reconfiguration in Multi-Agent Systems. LNCS (LNAI), vol. 2427. Springer, Heidelberg (2002). https://doi.org/10.1007/3-540-45834-4
18. Hoare, C.A.R.: Communicating sequential processes. In: Jones, C.B., Misra, J. (eds.) Theories of Programming: The Life and Works of Tony Hoare, pp. 157–186. ACM/Morgan & Claypool (2021). https://doi.org/10.1145/3477355.3477364
19. Holzmann, G.J.: The model checker spin. IEEE Trans. Software Eng. **23**(5), 279–295 (1997)
20. Huang, X., Chen, Q., Meng, J., Su, K.: Reconfigurability in reactive multiagent systems. In: Kambhampati, S. (ed.) Proceedings of the Twenty-Fifth International Joint Conference on Artificial Intelligence, IJCAI 2016, New York, NY, USA, 9–15 July 2016, pp. 315–321. IJCAI/AAAI Press (2016). http://www.ijcai.org/Abstract/16/052
21. Legay, A., Lukina, A., Traonouez, L.M., Yang, J., Smolka, S.A., Grosu, R.: Statistical model checking. In: Steffen, B., Woeginger, G. (eds.) Computing and Software Science. LNCS, vol. 10000, pp. 478–504. Springer, Cham (2019). https://doi.org/10.1007/978-3-319-91908-9_23
22. Lomuscio, A., Qu, H., Raimondi, F.: MCMAS: an open-source model checker for the verification of multi-agent systems. STTT **19**(1), 9–30 (2017)
23. Wooldridge, M.J.: An Introduction to MultiAgent Systems, 2nd edn. Wiley, New York (2009)

Formal Methods Meet Machine Learning

Formal Methods Meet Machine Learning (F3ML)

Kim Larsen[1], Axel Legay[2], Gerrit Nolte[3], Maximilian Schlüter[3(✉)],
Marielle Stoelinga[4], and Bernhard Steffen[3]

[1] Aalborg University, Aalborg, Denmark
kgl@cs.aau.dk
[2] Université Catholique de Louvain, Louvain-la-Neuve, Belgium
axel.legay@uclouvain.be
[3] TU Dortmund University, Dortmund, Germany
{gerrit.nolte,maximilian.schlueter,bernhard.steffen}@tu-dortmund.de
[4] University of Twente, Enschede, The Netherlands
m.i.a.stoelinga@utwente.nl

Abstract. The field of machine learning focuses on computationally efficient, yet approximate algorithms. On the contrary, the field of formal methods focuses on mathematical rigor and provable correctness. Despite their superficial differences, both fields offer mutual benefit. Formal methods offer methods to verify and explain machine learning systems, aiding their adoption in safety critical domains. Machine learning offers approximate, computationally efficient approaches that let formal methods scale to larger problems. This paper gives an introduction to the track "Formal Methods Meets Machine Learning" (F3ML) and shortly presents its scientific contributions, structured into two thematic subthemes: One, concerning formal methods based approaches for the explanation and verification of machine learning systems, and one concerning the employment of machine learning approaches to scale formal methods.

1 Preface

During recent decades, machine learning has risen to an immense level of prominence in the realm of computer science. From language processing [6] and computer vision [12, 40] to playing complex games [39] and self driving cars [36], machine learning has found success in domains where it is almost impossible to succeed with traditional, handwritten programs. At its core, the promise of machine learning is an attractive one: Given enough data and enough computational resources, complex problems can be trivially solved by an autonomously learning machine without requiring human work.

On the flipside of this utopian vision of machine learning stands the reality of its opaqueness and its common lack of reliability. The solutions that machine learning offers, while powerful, are sometimes heavily flawed, often unreliable and almost always incomprehensible. As machine learning solutions are trained from necessarily incomplete data, their behavior is largely uncontrolled in situations that are unlike those they encountered during training.

T. Margaria and B. Steffen (Eds.): ISoLA 2022, LNCS 13703, pp. 393–405, 2022.
https://doi.org/10.1007/978-3-031-19759-8_24

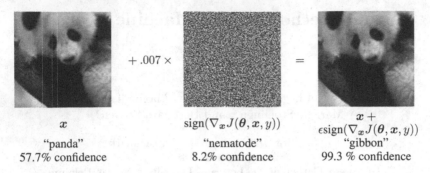

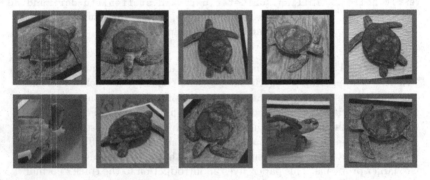

Fig. 1. Popular adversarial example of Goodfellow et al. [14]. Adding a small fine-tuned noise to a correctly classified image can change the classification at-will of the attacker.

Fig. 2. Popular example of an adversarial object from Athalye et al. [2]. The 3D printed turtle is incorrectly classified as a riffle throughout multiple images with different backgrounds and object rotations.

This situation is further complicated by the fact that machine learning solutions do not usually adhere to human intuition. Unlike code written by a human, that usually obeys reason and logic, machine learning systems are entirely unrestrained. Phenomena such as adversarial attacks [42], where machine learning systems can be fooled by an almost imperceptible change in their input, showcase just how big the gap between human reasoning and machine learning systems can be. Popular examples include the panda-gibbon adversarial example by Goodfellow et al. [14] (cf. Fig. 1) and the turtle-rifle adversarial object by Athalye et al. [2] (cf. Fig. 2). This erratic and unintuitive nature of machine learning decision making makes it especially hard to achieve machine learning systems that are *trustworthy* enough to be deployed in real world scenarios.

Disturbing issues with regards to both social fairness [31] and safety critical applications [26] are direct consequences of these properties and have repeatedly halted the adoption of machine learning systems in practical applications beyond the minimal-risk domains where they can currently be employed.

As machine learning transforms the world, formal methods play a key role in ensuring that learned systems are well-understood, fair and safe.

This landscape, while challenging, represents a fruitful soil for the application of formal methods. From model checking [8, 32] of large reactive systems to verifying large code bases [44], the formal methods community has in the past routinely provided reliable, mathematically sound approaches to analyze and verify large, complex systems. Conceptually, this is precisely what is needed to enable the widespread adoption of machine learning systems in practical domains where safety and security become imperative.

However, there is still a noticeable gap between machine learning and formal methods. The challenging nature of machine learning systems requires approaches that are specifically tailored to the system at hand to achieve scalability, comprehensibility and reliability. Symmetrically, the field of formal methods also stands to benefit from novel approaches in machine learning.

Formal methods, at present, offer mathematically precise and rigorous analyses of complex systems. As a consequence, formal methods play a significant role in the adoption of computer systems into safety critical industries, from healthcare to aerospace applications and finance [45]. However, when applying formal methods to large scale systems in practice, issues with scalability arise frequently. Even relatively fundamental techniques of formal methods such as SMT solving [4] and model checking [32] are challenging to scale to large problems.

In this respect, the profiles of formal methods and machine learning are diametrically opposed: Formal methods are mathematically rigorous and well founded while often incurring scaling issues. Machine learning approaches lack mathematical rigor in favor of approximate, statistical solutions that, in turn, are easy to scale to large problems. This motivates the introduction of machine learning approaches to the field of formal methods. By leveraging probabilistic methods from the field of machine learning, the scalability of formal methods can be improved.

The challenge is to integrate machine learning approaches which are inherently imprecise into the field of formal methods without losing their mathematical rigor.

The track "Formal Methods Meet Machine Learning" (F3ML) aims to bridge the gap between the communities of formal methods and machine learning. By nature of its theme, F3ML can be split into two distinct subthemes, one regarding the application of formal methods in the context of machine learning and one, conversely, regarding the application of machine learning techniques in the realm of formal methods.

The first subtheme contains multiple interesting approaches covering a wide spectrum of machine learning systems that, broadly speaking, *make machine learning systems trustworthy* using formal methods. This includes:

- Approaches that leverage formal methods to verify, explain and/or analyze machine learning systems in a mathematically rigorous manner.
- Approaches that construct machine learning systems in a manner that is *by construction* more trustworthy, either by enforcing safety standards during construction or constructing systems that are more easily explained or verified.
- Approaches that leverage statistical methods or methods from traditional test suite design to yield test suites that can either be used to give probabilistic bounds on error probabilities of a given system or which ensure that a certain degree of the systems behavior is properly covered.

The approaches presented here concern a wide variety of machine learning systems that are relevant in practical use.

The second subtheme addresses the application of machine learning techniques in formal methods. This includes work that, in any way, incorporates statistical, probabilistic or approximate methods from machine learning to formal methods to achieve scalability under the constraint that the resulting method is mathematically rigorous or at least such that its probabilistic error can be tightly controlled.

In the following, we will briefly introduce each paper belonging to either subtheme and sketch their respective contributions.

2   Formal Methods for Machine Learning

The presentation of the nine contributions of the track can be structured in the following three sections that roughly focus on explanation, verification, and testing, respectively:

2.1   Explanations of Machine Learning Systems

Explaining a machine learning system entails giving conceptual reasoning as to how the system works and how it makes its decisions in a way that is *comprehensible to humans* [10]. The following three contributions represent different flavors of explainability: The first paper presents an "explainable-by-construction" approach, aiming to construct a machine learning system that is by virtue of its structure comprehensible to humans. The second paper presents an approach that changes the representation of a machine learning system, transforming a previously black-box system into a comprehensible, white-box system that serves as an explanation. The third contribution combines formal methods and machine learning to increase the dependability of AI and increase their robustness. Central to their approach is the modeling of uncertainty—that is inherent to almost all machine learning systems—using formal methods.

Learning Explainable Controllers. In their paper "Algebraically Explainable Controllers: Decision Trees and Support Vector Machines Join Forces" [22]

Jüngermann, Křetínský, and Weininger use two machine learning models—Support Vector Machines (SVMs) [35] and Decision Trees [33]—to encode a previously constructed controller in a new model that is easier to comprehend, analyse, and verify, and that also has a smaller memory footprint for usage in e.g. embedded systems. Their approach highlights the benefits of Decision Trees:

• They are human comprehensible and are therefore widely regarded as explainable structures in XAI research [17, 46].
• They encode shared predicates efficiently reducing memory footprint.

Generally, a drawback of using Decision Trees as a machine learning (ML) model is that they are either greatly limited in their expressiveness in comparison to other ML models or that their training is very inefficient (several aspects of optimal decision tree construction are NP complete [33, Chapter 6.1]). The inefficiency is a result of the learning algorithm of Decision Trees: At each node all possible splits are ranked using one of many established measures. Thus, the training time is mostly influenced by the class of predicates used. While the space of simpler (axis-aligned) predicates is finite and can easily be explored completely, more expressive predicates (like linear, polynomial, and algebraic predicates) cannot be ranked efficiently.

The authors instead propose the usage of SVMs to find proper predicates. An SVM works by finding the best separating hyperplane between two classes of points and is therefore a natural candidate for finding linear predicates. Additionally, the so-called kernel trick is almost always applied to SVMs. A kernel is a non-linear projection of the original data into a higher dimensional space that can be efficiently computed. As a result, linear predicates found by the SVM in the higher dimensional space correspond to algebraic predicates when observed in the original space. Combining this trick with domain knowledge, the authors derive a problem specific higher-dimensional space that yields polynomial predicates of second degree (quadratic equations) as found frequently in physical applications.

Further, the authors present a series of post-processing steps that can be applied to predicates to improve their comprehensibility making the model an even better explanation. With their running example "cruise control" the authors show how their approach can capture the behavior of a controller using a Decision Tree with just 13 predicates (the same number of predicates another team reached with a handcrafted solution).

Explaining Neural Networks via Decision Structures. It is a well-known fact that, despite their widely renowned success in practice, neural networks are regarded as opaque models (so-called black-box models), whose behavior still evades human intuition [11]. The paper "Towards Rigorous Understanding of Neural Networks via Semantics-preserving Transformation" [38] by Schlüter, Nolte, and Steffen presents a conceptual approach that opens the metaphorical black-box by transforming a (piece-wise linear) neural network into a fully semantically equivalent white-box model in the form of a *Typed Affine Decision Structure* (TADS). TADS are also structurally similar to Decision Trees, utilizing again the explainable nature of Decision Trees [17,46] as in the previous paper. Therefore TADS constitute a suitable model for correct, sound, and complete explanations of neural network behavior.

Conceptually, TADS are obtained from a given piece-wise linear neural network using symbolic execution [5,25] yielding complete explanations for neural network behavior. The authors transform the resulting structure into a decision tree specialized to the profile of neural networks: For example, the predicates derived from neural networks are usually unique, rendering aggregation and variable ordering unnecessary (techniques used extensively in Decision Diagrams and Random Forests). On the other hand, new techniques are applied like infeasible path elimination [15,34] that greatly reduce the size of TADS while preserving semantics. Moreover, much like in the case of Algebraic Decision Diagrams [3], the authors show that TADS also inherit the algebraic properties of the underlying algebra of the terminal nodes (which is for TADS a real-valued vector space). This can be used to elegantly decide a wide array of questions regarding neural networks, most notably whether two neural networks represent the same function or whether they represent functions that differ by only a small amount. The paper contains a running example that illustrates how TADS can be used to precisely explain, verify and compare smaller-sized neural networks.

Robust and Dependable Artificial Intelligence. In his talk "Robust and Dependable Artificial Intelligence" Nils Jansen presents his vision of foundational and application-driven research in artificial intelligence (AI). He takes a broad stance on AI that brings together machine learning, control theory, and formal methods, in particular formal verification. As part of his research line, he studies problems inspired by autonomous systems, planning in robotics, and direct industrial applications. A shared key aspect in these problems is a thorough understanding of the uncertainty that may occur when machine learning agents operate in the real world. He details the following goals and the inherent real-world challenges that are central to his efforts:

- Increase the dependability of AI in safety-critical environments.
- Render AI models robust against uncertain knowledge about their environment.
- Enhance the capabilities of verification to handle real-world problems using learning techniques.

As a concrete research highlight, Nils Jansen presents a method that directly integrates techniques from machine learning with formal verification. He uses partially observable Markov decision processes (POMDPs) as formal model for planning under uncertainty, and recurrent neural networks (RNNs) as policy representations for these POMDPs. He trains RNN-based policies and then automatically extracts a so-called finite-state controller (FSC) from the RNN. Such FSCs offer a convenient way to verify temporal logic constraints. His method exploits so-called counterexamples as diagnostic information to either adjust the complexity of the extracted FSC, or to improve the policy by performing focused retraining of the RNN. The method synthesizes policies that satisfy temporal logic specifications for POMDPs with up to millions of states.

2.2 Verification of Machine Learning Systems

The following three contributions are each concerned with different flavors of machine learning verification. Broadly speaking, the considered verification approaches entail any approach that can either prove or disprove properties of machine learning systems in a mathematically rigorous manner, ensuring their safe deployment in safety critical domains.

Formal Verification for Neural Networks. The current renaissance in artificial intelligence (AI) has led to the advent of data-driven machine learning (ML) methods deployed within components for sensing, actuation, and control in safety-critical cyber-physical systems (CPS). While such learning-enabled components (LECs) are enabling autonomy in systems like autonomous vehicles and robots, ensuring that such components operate reliably in all scenarios is extraordinarily challenging, as demonstrated in part through recent accidents in semi-autonomous/autonomous CPS and by adversarial ML attacks.

In his talk "Formal Verification for Neural Networks in Autonomous Cyber-Physical Systems" Taylor Johnson discusses formal methods for assuring specifications—mostly robustness and safety—in autonomous CPS and subcomponents thereof using the software tools NNV and Veritex, developed as part of an ongoing DARPA Assured Autonomy project. These tools have been evaluated in CPS development with multiple industry partners in automotive, aerospace, and robotics domains, and allow for analyzing neural networks and their usage in closed-loop systems. Further, Taylor Johnson discusses his ongoing community activities that are relevant in this context, such as the Verification of Neural Networks Competition (VNN-COMP) held with the International Conference on Computer-Aided Verification (CAV) the past few years, as well as the AI and Neural Network Control Systems (AINNCS) category of the hybrid systems verification competition (ARCH-COMP) also held the past few years. The talk concludes with a discussion of future directions in the broader safe and trustworthy AI domain, such as in new projects verifying neural networks used in medical imaging analysis.

Property Directed Verification of Recurrent Neural Networks. In their paper "Analysis of Recurrent Neural Networks via Property-Directed Verification of Surrogate Models" [24], Leucker et al. present a novel approach to the property directed verification of Recurrent Neural Network (RNN) classifiers such as Gated Recurrent Units (GRUs) and Long Short-Term Memory networks (LSTMs) [7,19]. RNNs operate on input sequences of variable length making them a suitable model for e.g. speech recognition tasks. Assigning a label to any given input allows one to model the behaviour of a binary classifier in terms of a deterministic automaton. As end-to-end verification of RNNs would require unrolling the network multiple times, standard neural network verification techniques would be overly expensive. This motivates the need for a different approach tailored specifically to their profile by building on active automata learning.

The authors use L*, a well understood and rigorous algorithm that can learn an unknown automaton by actively probing it [1], to iteratively learn an automaton that acts as a surrogate model of the RNN at hand. This yields an elegant and effective verification loop that repeatedly refines the surrogate model until it mirrors the neural network closely to reveal potential erroneous behavior. An especially important facet of this approach is the *targeted* refinement of the surrogate model, actively inspecting it for property violations and checking whether these violations transfer from the surrogate model to the actual system. The paper also presents experimental results underlining the scalability and utility of this approach, showing that it compares favorably to existing approaches at the task of verifying LSTMs.

Connecting Reinforcement Learning and Model Checking. In the setting of reinforcement learning, a machine learning agent is tasked with learning how to operate in some environment, formalized as a Markov Decision Process, to maximize some form of reward [23,41]. This setting is of huge practical interest as it models the learning process of humans that learn through experience how to operate in the real world. As a consequence, there exist many different approaches to solving these problems, some from the realm of machine learning and some being based upon formal methods and mathematical rigor.

The differences, similarities and synergies between these approaches are highlighted in the paper "The Modest State of Learning, Sampling, and Verifying Strategies" [18] by Hartmanns, and Klauck. The paper connects probabilistic model checking and statistical model checking with scheduler sampling, as well as traditional Q-learning with value iteration methods and deep Q-learning. Further, the authors present theoretical and empirical comparisons between these methods. An especially interesting observation is made regarding symmetry between the formal methods approaches and the reinforcement learning approaches. Q-learning and probabilistic model checking work relatively similar, both converging to the optimal strategy via a fixed-point based iteration scheme. Both methods incur huge memory costs as the problem becomes more complex. Deep Q-learning and statistical model checking with scheduler sampling are both used to remedy this issue, providing easier scalability at the cost of precision. The authors also discuss corresponding tool support for statistical model checking [29] and how it can be applied to machine learning in the form of deep statistical model checking [16].

2.3   Test-Based Validation of Machine Learning Systems

In many cases, verification of neural networks is computationally too expensive to be feasible. In such cases, it is natural to *test* the neural network at hand. While not as rigorous as formal verification, software testing is a cornerstone of ensuring trustworthiness of software [13], but its extension to machine learning systems is challenging. The following paper is concerned with the transfer of traditional testing strategies to neural networks.

Neural Network Testing. As neural networks do not generally adhere to human intuition, it is much more difficult to evaluate whether a given test suite adequately covers enough of the neural networks behavior to give confidence in its reliability. In their paper "An Overview of Structural Coverage Metrics for Testing Neural Networks" [43] Pasareanu et al. discuss various coverage metrics for testing neural networks.

The authors present multiple different coverage metrics from existing literature, some adapted from traditional testing, some specifically designed for neural networks. Especially for the coverage metrics that are adapted from traditional testing, it is not obvious whether they adapt well to neural networks. Therefore, the authors conduct an experimental study where they examine the link between coverage metrics and the quality of the corresponding test suite. In particular, they show that some existing coverage metrics are inadequate as an indicator for a good coverage of the neural networks behavior, revealing a potential gap in existing research.

The authors also present DNNCov, a tool that automatically generates coverage reports for a given test suite and a given neural network, indicating the coverage achieved by said test suite on said network. The same tool can also be used for other purposes such as the reduction of test suites and the pruning of unused neurons.

3   Machine Learning for Formal Methods

In the previous section, we already discussed the paper "The Modest State of Learning, Sampling, and Verifying Strategies" [18] which discusses, among other topics, the applicability of statistical model checking to the task of verifying neural network based reinforcement learning systems. Thus, it interprets statistical model checking as a formal method that is applied to machine learning systems.

However, it is important to note that statistical model checking plays a twofold role in this context. While statistical model checking has its roots in formal methods, it relies on probabilistic methods and is thus technologically closely aligned with the field of machine learning. In that way, statistical machine learning can be considered as an approach that leverages tools from machine learning to achieve scalability of formal methods.

The following papers present improvements in the realm of statistical model checking, incorporating tools from probability theory and statistics to improve reliability and accuracy of statistical model checking.

Importance Splitting in Statistical Model Checking. Statistical model checking consists of learning the probability that the execution of a system will satisfy a given property [29,30]. The approach elegantly combines (1) a simulation-based algorithm for learning the probability distribution of satisfying the property by observing a fixed number of its executions with (2) runtime verification algorithms applied on these executions.

The efficiency of the SMC depends on the number of executions needed to obtain an estimate while minimizing the error rate. The most common SMC learning algorithm is that of Monte Carlo. When it comes to validating a property that has a high chance of being satisfied, Monte Carlo is considered efficient. In this case, the algorithm minimizes the number of simulations and guarantees a low error rate. The situation changes when one must estimate probability distributions of rarer events such as the probability that an execution contains a bug. This situation comes from the uniform character of the Monte Carlo simulation which does not aim to find the bug. It therefore takes too many simulations to influence the variance of the distribution. To overcome this problem, several authors have proposed learning algorithms that guide the simulations. These techniques, called "importance splitting" [21], orient the execution simulation according to the intermediate results of the runtime verification algorithm. This helps to isolate simulations and identify the bug. These techniques have been deployed in many contexts ranging from automotive to computational biology. Most of the existing work is limited to prototypes and pure probabilistic systems. Except for very restricted situations [20], real-time is not considered. This limits the applicability of the approaches to concrete problems. The paper "Importance Splitting in UPPAAL" [27] proposes a new importance splitting approach for systems that combine both probabilistic and timed aspects. This work extends existing work on the topic by (1) adding real-time aspects into the sampling process, and (2) providing a professional implementation within the UPPAAL toolset. The efficiency of the approach is illustrated on two concrete problems, one of them being an estimate of the spread of the contagion of the COVID-19 epidemic.

Statistical Model Checking for Variability-Intensive Stochastic Systems. Software product lines are sets of computer systems that share many common behaviors and that differ in identified functionalities. For a set of n functionalities one can generally create 2^n different systems. Checking each system individually would introduce an explosion of time. To overcome these problems, researchers have proposed compact product line representations [9]. These representations make it possible to check all the products in one pass. For nearly 10 years, these approaches were limited to purely Boolean systems. Recently, this approach has been extended to stochastic systems. In this case, one must calculate the probability that a product satisfies the property. This calculation is generally done by extending classical exhaustive algorithms such as those implemented in PRISM (see [37] for an example). The contribution of the article "Verification of Variability-Intensive Stochastic Systems with Statistical Model Checking" [28] is to extend SMC to learn the probability distribution of each product by simulating the structure which gathers the behaviors of the set of products. This approach has a double advantage:

1. The SMC simulation is more efficient than the exhaustive model checking algorithm.
2. The simulations are done at once on all the products by exploiting the efficiency.

The authors implemented their approach in a prototype and proved its effectiveness on concrete case studies.

Acknowledgements. As organisers of the track, we would like to thank all authors for their contributions. We would also like to thank all reviewers for their insights and helpful comments and all participants of the track for asking interesting questions, giving constructive comments and partaking in lively discussions.

References

1. Angluin, D.: Queries and concept learning. Mach. Learn. **2**(4), 319–342 (1988)
2. Athalye, A., Engstrom, L., Ilyas, A., Kwok, K.: Synthesizing robust adversarial examples. In: Dy, J., Krause, A. (eds.) Proceedings of the 35th International Conference on Machine Learning, Proceedings of Machine Learning Research, vol. 80, pp. 284–293. PMLR (2018). https://proceedings.mlr.press/v80/athalye18b.html
3. Bahar, R.I., et al.: Algebric decision diagrams and their applications. Formal Methods Syst. Des. **10**(2), 171–206 (1997)
4. Barrett, C., Tinelli, C.: Satisfiability modulo theories. In: Clarke, E., Henzinger, T., Veith, H., Bloem, R. (eds.) Handbook of Model Checking, pp. 305–343. Springer, Cham (2018). https://doi.org/10.1007/978-3-319-10575-8_11
5. Boyer, R.S., Elspas, B., Levitt, K.N.: Select-a formal system for testing and debugging programs by symbolic execution. ACM SigPlan Not. **10**(6), 234–245 (1975)
6. Brown, T., et al.: Language models are few-shot learners. Adv. Neural. Inf. Process. Syst. **33**, 1877–1901 (2020)
7. Chung, J., Gulcehre, C., Cho, K., Bengio, Y.: Empirical evaluation of gated recurrent neural networks on sequence modeling. arXiv preprint arXiv:1412.3555 (2014)
8. Clarke, E.M.: Model checking. In: Ramesh, S., Sivakumar, G. (eds.) FSTTCS 1997. LNCS, vol. 1346, pp. 54–56. Springer, Heidelberg (1997). https://doi.org/10.1007/BFb0058022
9. Cordy, M., et al.: A decade of featured transition systems. In: ter Beek, M.H., Fantechi, A., Semini, L. (eds.) From Software Engineering to Formal Methods and Tools, and Back. LNCS, vol. 11865, pp. 285–312. Springer, Cham (2019). https://doi.org/10.1007/978-3-030-30985-5_18
10. Doran, D., Schulz, S., Besold, T.R.: What does explainable AI really mean? A new conceptualization of perspectives. arXiv preprint arXiv:1710.00794 (2017)
11. Došilović, F.K., Brčić, M., Hlupić, N.: Explainable artificial intelligence: a survey. In: 2018 41st International Convention on Information and Communication Technology, Electronics and Microelectronics (MIPRO), pp. 0210–0215. IEEE (2018)
12. Dosovitskiy, A., et al.: An image is worth 16x16 words: transformers for image recognition at scale. arXiv preprint arXiv:2010.11929 (2020)
13. Everett, G.D., McLeod Jr., R.: Software testing. Testing Across the Entire (2007)
14. Goodfellow, I.J., Shlens, J., Szegedy, C.: Explaining and harnessing adversarial examples. arXiv preprint arXiv:1412.6572 (2014)
15. Gossen, F., Steffen, B.: Algebraic aggregation of random forests: towards explainability and rapid evaluation. Int. J. Softw. Tools Technol. Transf. (2021). https://doi.org/10.1007/s10009-021-00635-x
16. Gros, T.P., Hermanns, H., Hoffmann, J., Klauck, M., Steinmetz, M.: Deep statistical model checking. In: Gotsman, A., Sokolova, A. (eds.) FORTE 2020. LNCS, vol. 12136, pp. 96–114. Springer, Cham (2020). https://doi.org/10.1007/978-3-030-50086-3_6

17. Guidotti, R., Monreale, A., Ruggieri, S., Turini, F., Giannotti, F., Pedreschi, D.: A survey of methods for explaining black box models. ACM Comput. Surv. **51**(5) (2018). https://doi.org/10.1145/3236009

18. Hartmanns, A., Klauck, M.: The modest state of learning, sampling, and verifying strategies. In: Margaria, T., Steffen, B. (eds.) ISoLA 2022. LNCS, vol. 13703, pp. 406–432. Springer, Cham (2022)

19. Hochreiter, S., Schmidhuber, J.: Long short-term memory. Neural Comput. **9**(8), 1735–1780 (1997)

20. Jegourel, C., Larsen, K.G., Legay, A., Mikučionis, M., Poulsen, D.B., Sedwards, S.: Importance sampling for stochastic timed automata. In: Fränzle, M., Kapur, D., Zhan, N. (eds.) SETTA 2016. LNCS, vol. 9984, pp. 163–178. Springer, Cham (2016). https://doi.org/10.1007/978-3-319-47677-3_11

21. Jegourel, C., Legay, A., Sedwards, S.: Importance splitting for statistical model checking rare properties. In: Sharygina, N., Veith, H. (eds.) CAV 2013. LNCS, vol. 8044, pp. 576–591. Springer, Heidelberg (2013). https://doi.org/10.1007/978-3-642-39799-8_38

22. Jüngermann, F., Kretínský, J., Weininger, M.: Algebraically explainable controllers: decision trees and support vector machines join forces. Int. J. Softw. Tools Technol. Transf. (2022, to appear)

23. Kaelbling, L.P., Littman, M.L., Moore, A.W.: Reinforcement learning: a survey. J. Artif. Intell. Res. **4**, 237–285 (1996)

24. Khmelnitsky, I., et al.: Analysis of recurrent neural networks via property-directed verification of surrogate models. Int. J. Softw. Tools Technol. Transf. (2022, to appear)

25. King, J.C.: Symbolic execution and program testing. Commun. ACM **19**(7), 385–394 (1976)

26. Kohli, P., Chadha, A.: Enabling pedestrian safety using computer vision techniques: a case study of the 2018 Uber Inc. self-driving car crash. In: Arai, K., Bhatia, R. (eds.) FICC 2019. LNNS, vol. 69, pp. 261–279. Springer, Cham (2020). https://doi.org/10.1007/978-3-030-12388-8_19

27. Larsen, K.G., Legay, A., Mikučionis, M., Poulse, D.B.: Importance splitting in uppaal. In: Margaria, T., Steffen, B. (eds.) ISoLA 2022. LNCS, vol. 13703, pp. 433–447. Springer, Cham (2022)

28. Lazreg, S., Cordy, M., Legay, A.: Verification of variability-intensive stochastic systems with statistical model checking. In: Margaria, T., Steffen, B. (eds.) ISoLA 2022. LNCS, vol. 13703, pp. 448–471. Springer, Cham (2022)

29. Legay, A., Delahaye, B., Bensalem, S.: Statistical model checking: an overview. In: Barringer, H., et al. (eds.) RV 2010. LNCS, vol. 6418, pp. 122–135. Springer, Heidelberg (2010). https://doi.org/10.1007/978-3-642-16612-9_11

30. Legay, A., Lukina, A., Traonouez, L.M., Yang, J., Smolka, S.A., Grosu, R.: Statistical model checking. In: Steffen, B., Woeginger, G. (eds.) Computing and Software Science. LNCS, vol. 10000, pp. 478–504. Springer, Cham (2019). https://doi.org/10.1007/978-3-319-91908-9_23

31. Mehrabi, N., Morstatter, F., Saxena, N., Lerman, K., Galstyan, A.: A survey on bias and fairness in machine learning. ACM Comput. Surv. (CSUR) **54**(6), 1–35 (2021)

32. Müller-Olm, M., Schmidt, D., Steffen, B.: Model-checking. In: Cortesi, A., Filé, G. (eds.) SAS 1999. LNCS, vol. 1694, pp. 330–354. Springer, Heidelberg (1999). https://doi.org/10.1007/3-540-48294-6_22

33. Murthy, S.K.: Automatic construction of decision trees from data: a multidisciplinary survey. Data Min. Knowl. Discov. **2**(4), 345–389 (1998)

34. Murtovi, A., Bainczyk, A., Nolte, G., Schlüter, M., Bernhard, S.: Forest gump: a tool for veriification and explanation. Int. J. Softw. Tools Technol. Transf. (2022, to appear)
35. Noble, W.S.: What is a support vector machine? Nat. Biotechnol. **24**(12), 1565–1567 (2006)
36. Rao, Q., Frtunikj, J.: Deep learning for self-driving cars: chances and challenges. In: Proceedings of the 1st International Workshop on Software Engineering for AI in Autonomous Systems, pp. 35–38 (2018)
37. Rodrigues, G.N., et al.: Modeling and verification for probabilistic properties in software product lines. In: 16th IEEE International Symposium on High Assurance Systems Engineering, HASE 2015, Daytona Beach, FL, USA, 8–10, January 2015, pp. 173–180. IEEE Computer Society (2015). https://doi.org/10.1109/HASE.2015.34
38. Schlüter, M., Nolte, G., Steffen, B.: Towards rigorous understanding of neural networks via semantics preserving transformation. Int. J. Softw. Tools Technol. Transf. (2022, to appear)
39. Silver, D., et al.: Mastering the game of go without human knowledge. Nature **550**(7676), 354–359 (2017)
40. Simonyan, K., Zisserman, A.: Very deep convolutional networks for large-scale image recognition. arXiv preprint arXiv:1409.1556 (2014)
41. Sutton, R.S., Barto, A.G.: Reinforcement Learning: An Introduction. MIT Press, Cambridge (2018)
42. Szegedy, C., et al.: Intriguing properties of neural networks. arXiv preprint arXiv:1312.6199 (2013)
43. Usman, M., Sun, Y., Gopinath, D., Dange, R., Manolache, L., Pasareanu, C.: An overview of structural coverage metrics for testing neural networks. Int. J. Softw. Tools Technol. Transf. (2022, to appear)
44. Vardi, M.Y., Wolper, P.: An automata-theoretic approach to automatic program verification. In: 1st Symposium in Logic in Computer Science (LICS). IEEE Computer Society (1986)
45. Woodcock, J., Larsen, P.G., Bicarregui, J., Fitzgerald, J.: Formal methods: practice and experience. ACM Comput. Surv. (CSUR) **41**(4), 1–36 (2009)
46. Xu, F., Uszkoreit, H., Du, Y., Fan, W., Zhao, D., Zhu, J.: Explainable AI: a brief survey on history, research areas, approaches and challenges. In: Tang, J., Kan, M.-Y., Zhao, D., Li, S., Zan, H. (eds.) NLPCC 2019. LNCS (LNAI), vol. 11839, pp. 563–574. Springer, Cham (2019). https://doi.org/10.1007/978-3-030-32236-6_51

The Modest State of Learning, Sampling, and Verifying Strategies

Arnd Hartmanns[1]([✉])[iD] and Michaela Klauck[2]([✉])[iD]

[1] University of Twente, Enschede, The Netherlands
a.hartmanns@utwente.nl
[2] Saarland University, Saarbrücken, Germany
klauck@cs.uni-saarland.de

Abstract. Optimal decision-making under stochastic uncertainty is a core problem tackled in artificial intelligence/machine learning (AI), planning, and verification. Planning and AI methods aim to find good or optimal strategies to maximise rewards or the probability of reaching a goal. Verification approaches focus on calculating the probability or reward, obtaining the strategy as a side effect. In this paper, we connect three strands of work on obtaining strategies implemented in the context of the Modest Toolset: statistical model checking with either lightweight scheduler sampling or deep learning, and probabilistic model checking. We compare their different goals and abilities, and show newly extended experiments on Racetrack benchmarks that highlight the trade-offs between the methods. We conclude with an outlook on improving the existing approaches and on generalisations to continuous models, and emphasise the need for further tool development to integrate methods that find, evaluate, compare, and explain strategies.

1 Introduction

In many everyday interactions, but also in almost every system where software interfaces with and controls physical processes, decisions must be made in the presence of uncertainty about the possible actions' outcomes and the environment they interact with. In most cases, the uncertainty can be captured by randomisation: In casino card games, human players would like to maximise their chances of winning, or the expected return, against a randomly shuffled deck of cards. In travel planning, we have to choose between transport options that are often unreliable, and would like to maximise the probability of arriving on time. Our travel plans often include fallback options: the choices to make to recover when one step has gone wrong. Software controlling industrial processes

Authors are listed alphabetically. This work was supported by the German Research Foundation (DFG) under grant No. 389792660 as part of TRR 248, by the EU's Horizon 2020 research and innovation programme under MSCA grant agreement 101008233 (MISSION), and by NWO VENI grant no. 639.021.754.

T. Margaria and B. Steffen (Eds.): ISoLA 2022, LNCS 13703, pp. 406–432, 2022.
https://doi.org/10.1007/978-3-031-19759-8_25

must keep the process safe while optimising for, e.g., product completion time or throughput. Network routing over unreliable links must find routes that achieve a reasonable compromise between message delivery probability and expected delivery time. In autonomous driving, the car must react safely to unpredictable outside actors, imprecise measurements, and imperfect actuators without excessively inflating travel time. To appropriately deal with these kinds of situations, we need to find optimal, safe, or sufficiently performant *strategies*[1] describing the action to choose for every possible *state* of the system and/or environment.

The fundamental mathematical model for such scenarios are Markov decision processes (MDP). In MDP, the system jumps in discrete time steps from one discrete state to another. In every state, a *nondeterministic* choice (controllable or adversarial) over the available actions is followed by a *probabilistic* (i.e., random) choice of the next state. Various extensions cover continuous-time [16,36,79] and continuous-state [40,42,99] scenarios. The core problem, however, is always the same: *Find a strategy satisfying the stated objectives.* We focus on maximising the probability to eventually reach a set of goal states: *probabilistic reachability*.

Over the past decades, two broad types of solutions have been developed and implemented in tools. The *verification* approaches build on probabilistic and statistical model checking (PMC and SMC, respectively). PMC [8,77] runs an iterative numeric algorithm on a representation of the full MDP to ϵ-approximate the maximal reachability probability. While the corresponding strategy can be extracted from the algorithm's data structures upon termination, doing so has traditionally not been the focus of PMC. The strategy itself is typically represented as a list mapping (all reachable) states to chosen actions. SMC [1,66,80,105] applies Monte Carlo simulation to a concise executable specification of an MDP—typically given in a higher-level modelling language such as Modest [16,54] or JANI [22]—to estimate the probability under a given strategy. While highly effective in *evaluating* (the quality of) a strategy, it needs to be combined with a method to *find* an (optimal or good-enough) strategy in the first place. In contrast to PMC, SMC does not suffer from state space explosion: its memory usage is constant in the size of the MDP, as it only needs to store the current and next states obtained via the executable specification. It is thus a good partner for strategy-finding methods with similarly constant or moderate memory usage.

The first such method that we use in this paper is *lightweight scheduler sampling* (LSS) [81]: It randomly picks m strategies, applies an SMC-based heuristic to find the best one, and returns an SMC estimate under this strategy as an underapproximation of the maximum reachability probability. The key idea and advantage of LSS is its use of a constant-memory representation of a strategy as a fixed-size integer. It thus finds and evaluates a strategy in constant memory.

Finding good strategies is the focus of methods developed in (probabilistic) planning [26,72,104] and artificial intelligence/machine learning. A prominent success is *reinforcement learning* (RL) [100], in particular Q-learning [84,85]. Here, again a concise specification of the MDP is executed in an initially random

---

[1] Depending on context, strategies are also called adversaries, policies, or schedulers.

manner, storing and over time improving a measure of the quality of every state-action pair that is executed. Similar to PMC, the strategy obtained by RL is a list mapping each *visited* state to the (best-quality) chosen action.

Deep neural networks (NNs) are responsible for astounding advances across applications as diverse as image classification [76], natural language processing [67], and playing games [98]. *Deep reinforcement learning* (deep RL) algorithms that use deep NNs to store the quality measure have exhibited unprecedented performance in various tasks [85]. At the cost of losing the eventual convergence to the optimum, deep RL reduces the memory usage of RL, possibly to constant (if we use a fixed-size NN independent of the size of the MDP or its executable specification). The combination of deep RL for finding strategies with SMC for their evaluation is *deep statistical model checking* (DSMC) [44].

So far, these methods have been presented, implemented, and benchmarked mostly in isolation. A wide range of PMC variants is available to users in tools such as PRISM [78], STORM [64], and the MODEST TOOLSET [57]. The latter, which is the focus of this paper, also includes the statistical model checker MODES [21] with support for LSS. The quantitative verification benchmark set (QVBS) [60] provides the standard set of models for benchmarking and comparisons of PMC and SMC tools. RL and in particular deep RL approaches, on the other hand, are often evaluated on training environments specified implicitly in the form of simulation code. In the academic context, the Arcade Learning Environment is widely used, which provides game simulators for different ATARI 2006 benchmarks [12]. For reinforcement learning, these training environments are then often interfaced with the learning algorithm via the OpenAI Gym API [19]. It is used by algorithms interacting with the interface [35,47,68,89,97], as well as benchmarks that implement (and sometimes extend) it [10,27,37,102,103,106]. We use the OpenAI Gym API via MOGYM [45] to train NN and then evaluate their quality with DSMC.

This paper contributes a uniform presentation of PMC, SMC with LSS, and deep RL with DSMC, spanning the range from verification approaches delivering optimal strategies at the cost of state space explosion to AI-based methods using deep NN approximations for limiting memory usage at the cost of losing optimality guarantees. We spell out the consequences that the differing goals of these methods have for obtaining and ultimately explaining strategies. Our new experimental comparison in Sect. 4 confirms the expected differences, but also highlights the particularities and similarities of the approaches. For example, the effectiveness of LSS appears to be an indicator for the (startup) difficulty of RL on our models. We use different variants of Racetrack benchmarks embodying a simplistic autonomous driving scenario. They are easy to visualise and understand, yet can flexibly be configured to provide various kinds of difficulties for the methods we study. Their action space is also very regular, which is currently a prerequisite for deep RL to be effective.

2   Preliminaries

For any nonempty set S we let $\mathcal{D}(S)$ denote the set of discrete probability distributions over S, i.e., of functions $\mu \colon S \to [0,1]$ such that the support $spt(\mu) = \{\, s \in S \mid \mu(s) > 0 \,\}$ is countable and $\sum_{s \in spt(\mu)} \mu(s) = 1$.

Definition 1. *A finite Markov decision process (MDP) [13,69,92] is a tuple*

$$\mathcal{M} = \langle \mathcal{S}, \mathcal{A}, \mathcal{T}, \mathcal{R}, s_0, \mathcal{S}_* \rangle$$

consisting of a finite set of states $\mathcal{S}$, a finite set of actions $\mathcal{A}$, the partial transition probability function $\mathcal{T} \colon \mathcal{S} \times \mathcal{A} \rightharpoonup \mathcal{D}(\mathcal{S})$, a reward function $\mathcal{R} \colon \mathcal{S} \times \mathcal{A} \times \mathcal{S} \to \mathbb{R}_{\geq 0}$ assigning a reward to each triple of state, action, and target state, an initial state $s_0 \in \mathcal{S}$, and a set of goal states $\mathcal{S}_* \subseteq \mathcal{S}$. For every state $s \in \mathcal{S}$, there is at least one action $a \in \mathcal{A}$ such that $\mathcal{T}(s,a)$ is defined.

An action $a \in \mathcal{A}$ is *applicable* in a state $s \in \mathcal{S}$ if $\mathcal{T}(s,a)$ is defined. In this case, we also write $\mathcal{T}(s,a,t)$ for the probability $\mu(t)$ of going to state t according to $\mathcal{T}(s,a) = \mu$. $\mathcal{A}(s) \subseteq \mathcal{A}$ is the set of all actions that are applicable in state s. An infinite sequence of states connected via transitions with applicable actions, $\zeta = (s_i)_{i \in \mathbb{N}}$, is a *path*.

The reward function assigns to every transition from one state to another a reward depending on the start and destination state as well as the action. This enables us, e.g., to reason about the sum of the rewards obtained when taking multiple transitions in a row. Rewards, while not influencing reachability probabilities, are an important concept in RL that we come back to in Sect. 3.3.

Definition 2. *Given an MDP $\mathcal{M}$ as above, a function*

$$\sigma \colon \mathcal{S} \to \mathcal{A}$$

satisfying $\sigma(s) \in \mathcal{A}(s)$ for all states s is a (deterministic) memoryless strategy.

A strategy determines the action to take for every state. Restricting MDP $\mathcal{M}$ to the choices made by strategy σ results in an *induced* discrete-time Markov chain (DTMC) $M|_\sigma$: an MDP where $\forall s \in \mathcal{S} \colon |\mathcal{A}(s)| = 1$. Intuitively, the probability that a certain path (or prefix of it) is taken in a DTMC can be calculated as the product over the transition probabilities of the path (prefix). Formally, since the set of paths is uncountable, the cylinder set construction [77] can be used to obtain a probability measure P over paths such that in particular the set $\Pi_{\mathcal{S}_*}$ of paths that contain a state in $\mathcal{S}_*$ is measurable. Then $P(\Pi_{\mathcal{S}_*})$ is the *reachability probability* $p_{\mathcal{S}_*}$ in the DTMC. In an MDP, each strategy σ induces a DTMC $M|_\sigma$ and consequently a reachability probability $p_{\mathcal{S}_*}^\sigma$. Then $p_{max} \stackrel{\text{def}}{=} \sup_\sigma p_{\mathcal{S}_*}^\sigma$ is the maximum reachability probability that we are looking for; and an *optimal strategy* σ_{max} such that $p_{max} = p_{\mathcal{S}_*}^{\sigma_{max}}$ in fact exists [14].

3   Finding Strategies

To find strategies that satisfy stated criteria, e.g., (near-)optimality or suitability for a certain purpose, various approaches have been developed in the fields of probabilistic verification and artificial intelligence (AI). In this section, we contrast (i) the traditional verification approach of probabilistic model checking, (ii) the more recent lightweight scheduler sampling method that lifts statistical model checking from DTMC to MDP, (iii) the core AI technique of reinforcement learning, and (iv) its variant using deep neural networks to approximate the Q-function combined with statistical model checking.

All approaches start with a succinct executable specification of an MDP. This is either a model specified in a (textual or graphical) modelling language, for which execution support is provided by some tool's state space exploration engine, or a computer program directly implementing the model. For simplicity, we only assume that we have an interface with the following functions:

- `initial()` to obtain s_0,
- `actions`(s) to obtain $\mathcal{A}(s)$,
- `sample`(s, a) to (pseudo-)randomly select a next state s' according to $\mathcal{T}(s, a)$,
- `distr`(s, a) to obtain the distribution $\mu = \mathcal{T}(s, a)$, e.g., as a list of pairs of probabilities p and next states s' such that $p = \mu(s')$, and
- `goal`(s) that returns *true* if $s \in \mathcal{S}_*$ and *false* otherwise.

Not all functions will be needed by all approaches; e.g., probabilistic model checking uses `distr` but not `sample` whereas reinforcement learning does the opposite.

3.1   Probabilistic Model Checking

Traditional exhaustive probabilistic model checking (PMC) starts by constructing a complete in-memory representation of the MDP: from a call to `initial`, it performs a graph search by iteratively following all transitions via calls to `actions` and `distr` until no new states are discovered. The resulting MDP as in Definition 1 can be stored as an *explicit-state* graph-like data structure or sparse matrix, or *symbolically* using multi-terminal binary decision diagrams [88].

The next step in PMC is to calculate p_{max}. One approach is to convert the MDP into a linear program, with one variable per state, which in turn is solved using any linear programming solver. The value of the variable corresponding to the initial state will then be p_{max}. Although this approach can in principle deliver exact results (though usually up to some floating-point precision), it needs to store the MDP in memory twice (as in Definition 1 and in suitably-encoded form for the LP solver), and most LP solvers so far do not scale well to large MDP. Therefore, most PMC tools default to using iterative numeric algorithms based on value iteration. Value iteration computes a sequence of values $v_i(s)$ for every state $s \in \mathcal{S}$ that converges to the maximum reachability probability *from each state* (i.e. as if that state was the initial state). It does so by, starting from the trivial underapproximation where $\forall i: v_i(s) = 1$ if $s \in \mathcal{S}_*$ and $v_0(s) = 0$ if $s \notin \mathcal{S}_*$, applying the Bellman equation

$$v_{i+1}(s) = \max_{a \in \mathcal{A}(s)} \sum_{s' \in spt(\mathcal{T}(s,a))} \mathcal{T}(s, a, s') \cdot v_i(s)$$

for all states $s \notin \mathcal{S}_*$. Then $\lim_{i \to \infty} v_i(s_0) = p_{max}$. Value iteration lacks a stopping criterion to determine the i where $v_i(s_0)$ is close enough to the true value (e.g., within a user-specified relative error ϵ) [48]. Thus sound PMC tools today use variants of value iteration that provide such a stopping criterion, e.g., interval iteration [18,49], sound value iteration [93], or optimistic value iteration [59].

Strategy Representation. Once iterations stop at some i, a (near-)optimal strategy has implicitly been obtained, too: it is, assuming no end components here,

$$\sigma_{max} = \{ s \mapsto \arg\max_{a \in \mathcal{A}(s)} \sum_{s' \in spt(\mathcal{T}(s,a))} \mathcal{T}(s, a, s') \cdot v_i(s) \}.$$

The PMC tools PRISM, STORM, and MCSTA of the MODEST TOOLSET all offer an option to not only report p_{max}, but also write σ_{max} to file as a list of state-action pairs, with as many entries as there are states in the MDP. With typical ϵ-correct relative-error implementations of sound value iteration variants, PMC tools guarantee that, when stopped,

$$|v_i(s_0) - p_{max}|/p_{max} \le \epsilon$$

(assuming non-zero p_{max}; probability-zero states can be determined by graph-based precomputations [38]). The value of ϵ is specified by the user, and typically 10^{-3} or 10^{-6} by default.

Modest Tools. In the MODEST TOOLSET, the MCSTA tool implements PMC. It is an explicit-state model checker that can use secondary storage (i.e., hard disks and SSDs) to mitigate state space explosion to some degree at the cost of runtime [58]. Its focus is on providing correct results; for this purpose, it implements interval iteration, sound value iteration, and optimistic value iteration, and recently gained the ability to obtain results that are guaranteed to be free of errors due to imprecisions and rounding in floating-point calculations [56]. It was the first tool to implement practically efficient methods for reward-bounded properties [50], includes a novel symblicit engine to handle very large structured models [51], and provides methods that work with only a partial exploration of the state space [4,18]. Beyond MDP, it has state-of-the-art support for Markov automata [24] and stochastic timed automata [53]. The QComp 2020 and 2021 competitions [23,52] showed that MCSTA performs well.

Related Methods. Other alternatives to linear programming and value iteration are policy iteration [70] and variants such as topological value iteration [28] that may deliver significant speedups for MDPs with appropriately-sized strongly connected components. To mitigate state space explosion, we can attempt to only explore a part of the state space that is likely to be reached [18]; then we obtain an upper bound on the reachability probability by assuming all unexplored "border states" to be goal states, and a lower bound by assuming them to be non-goal states. Often referred to as (being based on) BRTDP [83], an approach from probabilistic planning, implementations nowadays—such as the one in MCSTA—are rather different from the original BRTDP technique and better described as partial exploration-based PMC [4]. A similar approach also known from probabilistic planning called LRTDP [17] in combination with FRET [75] has recently been extended to be applicable to all established property types, except long-run averages and nested properties, on MDP structures with positive and zero-valued rewards [73]. With this technique, often only a fraction of the state space—the part sufficient to calculate the property at hand—has to be visited. The technique is implemented in MODYSH in the MODEST TOOLSET.

3.2   Statistical Model Checking with Scheduler Sampling

Given our interface to an MDP and a function $\mathtt{schedule}(s)$ implementing a strategy σ to return $\sigma(s)$, statistical model checking (SMC) estimates the reachability probability on the DTMC induced by σ up to a statistical error. It does so by sampling the indicator function on paths

$$\mathbb{1}_{\Pi_{\mathcal{S}_*}} \overset{\text{def}}{=} \{\, \pi \mapsto 1 \text{ if } \pi \text{ contains a state in } \mathcal{S}_* \text{ else } 0 \,\}$$

n times as follows:

1. Initialise $s := \mathtt{init}()$.
2. If $\mathtt{goal}(s)$, return 1; if the probability to reach a goal state from s is 0, return 0.
3. Select an action $a := \mathtt{schedule}(s)$ and sample the next state: $s := \mathtt{sample}(s, a)$.
4. Go to step 2.

That is, SMC generates n *simulation runs*. Let k be the number of runs where 1 is returned; then the sample mean $\hat{p}_{\mathcal{S}_*} \overset{\text{def}}{=} k/n$ is an unbiased estimator for $p_{\mathcal{S}_*}^{\sigma}$. This basic approach can be modified in various ways to incorporate different statistical methods that quantify the error to be expected from an SMC analysis. Popular methods are to compute confidence intervals given n and either a desired interval width or confidence level; to perform sequential testing using Wald's sequential probability ratio test [101], thereby dynamically determining n as the samples come in; or to use the Okamoto bound [87] that provides a formula relating n, the confidence level δ, and the error ϵ a priori such that

$$\mathbb{P}(|\hat{p}_{\mathcal{S}_*} - p_{\mathcal{S}_*}| > \epsilon) < 1 - \delta$$

with typical default values of δ being 0.95 or 0.99. For a more extensive overview of statistical methods for SMC, we refer the interested reader to the survey by Reijsbergen et al. on hypothesis testing and its references [94]. The development of efficient methods to determine whether a state has probability 0 of reaching a goal state in step 2 is a topic of ongoing research [5]. When p_{S_*} is small, ϵ must also be small for the result to be useful. Then the n required to achieve the same confidence grows quickly, leading to a runtime explosion. This is the *rare events* problem faced by SMC, for which various *rare event simulation* [95] methods exist as mitigation.

As specified above, SMC requires a strategy to be given in order to be applicable to MDP. Many SMC tools do not provide support for user-specified strategies, but instead implicitly use the uniform random strategy that, every time schedule(s) is called, uniformly at (pseudo-)random samples a new action from $\mathcal{A}(s)$. The result consequently is *some* probability *somewhere* between maximum and minimum. UPPAAL SMC [34] notably defines a "stochastic semantics" for probabilistic timed automata that makes continuously uniformly- or exponentially-distributed choices over time delays followed by discretely uniform choices over actions. The resulting non-nondeterministic model is sometimes referred to as stochastic timed automata, not to be confused with the earlier formalism of the same name of [16] that is a proper extension of probabilistic timed automata preserving their nondeterminism.

Lightweight scheduler sampling identifies a strategy by a fixed-size (typically 32-bit) integer value. It

1. (pseudo-)randomly selects m such *strategy identifiers*, then
2. applies a heuristic involving SMC runs as described above under the sampled strategy to try to find the one that induces the highest probability, and finally
3. performs another SMC analysis for the selected strategy (statistically independent from step 2) to obtain an estimate of the probability it induces.

The result is an underapproximation of p_{max}, up to statistical errors. LSS may or may not find a strategy better than the uniform random one, but often does so. Its ability to find a near-optimal strategy depends only on the probability mass of near-optimal strategies in the space of strategies sampled from.

The key idea that makes LSS work, in constant memory in the size of the MDP, lies in its implementation of schedule. It uses a hash function $\mathcal{H}$ that takes an arbitrary-length bitstring and returns a 32-bit integer such that, ideally, (i) small changes in the input result in unpredictable and significant changes in the output, and (ii) for uniformly random inputs (e.g., of a fixed length), the outputs appear uniformly distributed over the output space. Then it implements schedule(s) for strategy identifier $\mathfrak{s} \in \mathbb{Z}_{32}$ by selecting the $(\mathcal{H}(s.\mathfrak{s}) \bmod |\mathcal{A}(s)|)$-th element of a fixed ordering of $\mathcal{A}(s)$, where $s.\mathfrak{s}$ is the concatenation of the bitstring representations of s and $\mathfrak{s}$. In this way, schedule implements a memoryless strategy as required and sufficient for unbounded probabilistic reachability, but also other types of strategies—such as history-dependent or partial-information strategies [29]—are easy to implement by appropriately changing the input of $\mathcal{H}$.

We use LSS with a simplified variant of the *smart sampling* [32] heuristics for step 2. In addition to m, it is parametrised by $n_r \geq m$, the simulation budget per round. In the first round, we perform $\lfloor n_r/m \rfloor$ runs for each of the m strategy identifiers. Usually, n_r is not much larger than m, so this first round produces a very coarse estimation of the quality of each sampled strategy. We then drop the worst-performing half of the strategies before proceeding with the second round, where $\lfloor n_r/2m \rfloor$ runs are performed per strategy, providing a somewhat better estimation. This process, dropping the worst half of the remaining strategies in every round, continues until only one strategy remains. In this way, we can evaluate a large number of strategies with moderate simulation effort.

Strategy Representation. SMC with LSS returns the estimate of the reachability probability under the best strategy, and the 32-bit integer identifying that strategy. By itself, this integer is useless: it does not describe the strategy's decisions directly. However, given a state of the MDP and the known implementation of `schedule` used during the LSS process, we can recompute the strategy's decision at any time. We thus get a memory-efficient strategy representation that is not explanatory in any way.

Modest Tools. In the MODEST TOOLSET, the MODES statistical model checker [21] implements SMC with LSS as described above. It has dedicated simulation algorithms for MDP, Markov automata, singular stochastic hybrid automata, and general stochastic hybrid automata: as the modelling formalism becomes more expressive, simulation becomes computationally more involved, with more and more complex computations needed for every transition (up to numeric integration to approximate the non-linear dynamics in general stochastic hybrid automata). To mitigate the rare events problem, MODES implements rare event simulation by means of importance splitting in a highly automated fashion [20].

Related Methods. Prior to implementing LSS, MODES used partial order [15] and confluence reduction [61] checks to identify whether the nondeterministic choices in an MDP it simulates are non-spurious, i.e., whether they influence the probability being estimated. If not, these choices would be resolved randomly; otherwise, simulation would abort with an error indicating the presence of possibly non-spurious nondeterminism. Where UPPAAL SMC implicitly applies a specific strategy—its stochastic semantics—the more recent UPPAAL Stratego tool [33] combines SMC with the computation of (most permissive) strategies.

3.3   Reinforcement Learning

Reinforcement learning is an AI approach to train agents to take actions maximising a reward in uncertain environments. Mathematically, the agent in its environment can be described as an MDP: the agent chooses actions; the environment determines the states and is responsible for the probabilistic outcomes of the actions. In this paper, we follow the *Q-learning* approach: We maintain a Q-function $Q \colon \mathcal{S} \times \mathcal{A} \to [0,1]$ initialised arbitrarily, or to 0 everywhere. Using a learning rate parameter α, a discounting factor $\gamma \in (0,1]$, and a probability ϵ that is initially 1, n learning *episodes* are performed as follows:

1. Set $s := \texttt{init}()$.
2. Perform option a) with probability ϵ and b) with probability $1 - \epsilon$:
    a) Select a from $\texttt{actions}(s)$ uniformly at random (exploration).

    b) Select $a := \arg\max_{a' \in \texttt{actions}(s)} Q(s, a')$ (exploitation).

3. Sample $s' := \texttt{sample}(s, a)$ and set $r := 1$ if $\texttt{goal}(s')$ and 0 otherwise.
4. Update $Q(s, a) := Q(s, a) + \alpha \cdot (r + \gamma \cdot \max_{a' \in \texttt{actions}(s')} Q(s', a') - Q(s, a))$.
5. Set $s := s'$; if $\texttt{goal}(s)$ or s has probability 0 of reaching a goal state, end the episode; else go to step 2.

An episode is very similar to a simulation run, except that we update the Q-function to estimate the "quality" of taking action a from state s as $Q(s, a)$ and follow an "ϵ-greedy" strategy: initially, when $\epsilon = 1$, we explore randomly; over time, we make it more and more likely to follow what looks like the best action to improve our estimate of its quality. RL traditionally optimises for expected discounted rewards, thus the discounting factor γ; for unbounded reachability probabilities, we set γ to 1 and only obtain a reward upon reaching a goal state (as above). As long as we are guaranteed to visit every state infinitely often, $\max_{a \in \mathcal{A}(s_0)} Q(s_0, a)$ converges towards p_{max}. Like in value iteration, there is no stopping criterion that would ensure a specified error.

Strategy Representation. The (near-)optimal strategy obtained when we end the learning process is directly given by the Q-function: It is

$$\sigma_{max} = \{\, s \mapsto \arg\max_{a \in \mathcal{A}(s)} Q(s, a) \,\}.$$

Like in PMC, if we have an explicit in-memory representation of the Q-function, we can write this strategy to file as a list of state-action pairs.

Modest Tools. RL with an explicit representation of the Q-function is implemented in the MODEST TOOLSET's MODES tool to find strategies in non-linear stochastic hybrid automata, where classic PMC techniques cannot be applied due to the continuous nature of the state space [86].

Related Methods. The first use of RL for formal models known to us is in the work of Henriques et al. [63], which however neglects the statistical error incurred by performing repeated tests. The first sound formal use of RL is in [18]. For probabilistic reachability, the rewards are very sparse: only when we hit a goal state we do receive a reward. This tends to make RL inefficient; for linear-time properties, denser reward structures can automatically be created, see, e.g., [55].

3.4 Deep Statistical Model Checking

Deep Reinforcement Learning. In RL as described above, we need to store the Q-function in memory; as we visit more states in large MDP, this will lead to state space explosion as in PMC. To avoid this scalability limitation, the use of function approximators to store an inexact representation of the Q-function has become popular in recent years. In particular, when we use deep neural networks as a function approximator with RL, we perform *deep reinforcement learning* resp. deep Q-learning [39,85]. This use of artificial neural networks

(NN) to learn strategies in large systems has seen dramatic successes, exhibited by the abilities of today's AI systems to play, win, and solve games such as Atari games [85], Go and Chess [98], and Rubic's cubes [2].

NN consist of neurons: atomic computational units that apply a (non-linear) *activation function* to a weighted sum of their inputs [96]. We consider feed-forward NN, where neurons are arranged in a sequence of layers. Inputs are provided to the first (input) layer, and the computation results are propagated through the layers in sequence until reaching the final (output) layer. In every layer, every neuron receives as inputs the outputs of all neurons in the previous layer. For a given set of possible inputs $\mathcal{I}$ and (final layer) outputs $\mathcal{O}$, a neural network can be considered as an efficient-to-query total function $\pi \colon \mathcal{I} \to \mathcal{O}$. For the problems discussed in this paper, one can assume that this function constitutes the strategy σ: the inputs are the states $\mathcal{S}$ and the outputs are actions from $\mathcal{A}$. *Deep* neural networks consist of many layers.

Strategy Representation. A NN represents a Q-function, and thus a strategy. The NN used in deep RL are typically initialised with random weights, representing a random initial Q-function. As we learn more and more episodes, the decisions determined as optimal by the NN tend to converge towards a good, often optimal, strategy. However, in contrast to the exact Q-learning of Sect. 3.3, deep RL does not *need to* converge in this way, and in practice rarely behaves monotonically. That is, more episodes can (temporarily) make the NN represent a worse strategy. To preserve the memory advantage of NN over explicit representations, at the end of the learning process, we store the NN itself (i.e., its structure and weights) as the strategy instead of turning it into a list of state-action pairs (which would require a full state space exploration). The disadvantage of this representation is that, similar to the scheduler identifiers of LSS, the NN definition itself neither makes the strategy's decisions explicit nor explains them.

Deep Statistical Model Checking. In contrast to Q-learning with an exact representation of the Q-function, we cannot rely on the value returned by the NN for the initial state being in any formal way related to p_{max} [44]. One approach to assess the quality of strategies given by NN is *deep statistical model checking* (DSMC) [44], which bridges machine learning and verification: first, deep RL delivers a strategy σ in the form of an NN trained to act and achieve a certain goal in an environment described by a formal model. Second, SMC, as a verification technique, assesses the quality of the strategy defined by the NN. This is done by implementing the `schedule` function in SMC as described in Sect. 3.2 by querying the NN as a black-box oracle: The NN receives the state descriptor s as input, and it returns as output a decision $\sigma(s)$ determining the next step. Hence, at the core of DSMC is a straightforward variation of SMC, applied to an MDP, together with an NN that has to take the decisions. The DSMC approach furthermore allows assessing the progress of the NN during learning. As shown in works on DSMC [44,46], the quality assessment of an agent during training is not trivial and cannot always be derived from the observed training returns.

Modest Tools. The DSMC functionality of using a previously trained NN to resolve the nondeterminism during SMC is implemented in a branch of MODES [44] that will be integrated into the official version of the MOD-EST TOOLSET soon. In addition, this DSMC extension of MODES is used in MoGYM [45]. MoGYM is a toolbox that bridges the gap between formal methods and RL by enabling (a) formally specified training environments to be used with machine-learned decision-making agents, and (b) the rigorous assessment of the quality of learned agents. For (a), it implements and extends the OpenAI Gym API [19]. MoGYM is based on Momba [74], a Python toolbox for dealing with quantitative models from construction to analysis centred around JANI. MoGYM can process JANI models for the description of a training environment and, based on the induced formal MDP semantics, makes it possible to train agents using popular RL algorithms. For (b), the environment format itself is accessible to state-of-the-art model checkers. This enables to perform DSMC by using MODES directly in MoGYM. The DSMC extension of MODES is also integrated in *DSMC evaluation stages* [46], where DSMC is applied during deep RL to determine state space regions with weak performance to concentrate on during the learning process. To visualise the SMC results of MODES when executing DSMC on Racetrack benchmarks, the tool *TraceVis* has been implemented [43]. It takes the traces generated by MODES as input, visualises and clusters them, and provides information on the goal probability when starting on a predefined position.

Related Methods. Other works combining formal methods with NN, for example, study strategy synthesis for partially observable MDPs (POMDPs) using recurrent neural networks (RNN). The RNN is then used to construct a Markov chain for which the temporal property can be checked using PMC [25]. Furthermore, an iterative learning procedure consisting of SMT-solving and learning phases has been used to construct controllers for stochastic and partially unknown environments [71]. In addition, a reinforcement learning algorithm has been invented to synthesize policies which fulfil a given linear-time property on an MDP [62]. By expressing the property as a limit deterministic Büchi Automaton, a reward function over the state-action pairs of the MDP can be defined such that the policy is only constructed by considering the part of the MDP which fulfils the property. This is of special interest when working on sparse reward models. To be able to add features to NN acting as a controller without retraining and losing too much performance, quantitative run-time shields have been devised [7]. This method can easily be implemented as an extension of DSMC. The shields may alter the command given by the controller before passing it to the system under control. To generate these shields, reactive synthesis is used.

3.5   Summary

The four approaches we presented provide distinct characteristics and advantages as well as drawbacks: PMC delivers precise results up to a user-specified error ϵ, and RL eventually converges to the true result as well with statistical guarantees [18], whereas SMC with LSS and deep RL in DSMC cannot be guaranteed to eventually obtain a near-optimal strategy. In all but PMC (using sound algorithms such as interval iteration), there is no unconditional stopping criterion to determine when ϵ is reached. PMC is thus the only technique that can guarantee optimality. This comes at the cost of memory usage: the state space explosion problem. RL faces the same issue, where it however can be avoided by using NN trained with deep RL in DSMC—at the cost of the eventual convergence guarantee. Where PMC needs the `distr` method of our MDP interface, `sample` suffices for the others. That is, PMC requires a white-box model, whereas the other methods only need sampling access—a much simpler requirement for practical applications. Rare events are no issue for PMC, but lead to a runtime explosion in SMC, and similarly hinder RL and DSMC, where the learning process will be very unlikely to ever explore a path leading to one of the rare goal states. Finally, in terms of the representation of the strategy, PMC and RL deliver explicit and complete strategies, which however may be unmanageably large, whereas LSS and DSMC provide compact yet opaque representations.

4   Experiments

We compare the approaches presented above on a set of six Racetrack benchmarks differing in the track shape. Originally Racetrack is a pen and paper game [41]: A track is drawn with a start line and a goal line on a sheet of squared paper. A vehicle starts with velocity 0 from some position on the start line, with the objective to reach the goal as fast as possible without crashing into a wall. Nine possible actions modify the current velocity vector by one unit (up, down, left, right, four diagonals, keep current velocity). This simple game lends itself naturally as a benchmark for sequential decision making. Like Barto et al. [11], we consider a noisy version of Racetrack that emulates slippery road conditions: actions may *fail* with a given probability, in which case the action does not change the velocity and the vehicle instead continues driving with unchanged velocity vector. In particular, when extending the problem with noise, we obtain MDP that do not necessarily allow the vehicle to reach the goal with certainty. In a variety of such noisy forms, Racetrack was adopted as a benchmark for MDP algorithms in the AI community [11,17,82,90,91]. Because of its analogy to autonomous driving, Racetrack has recently also been used in multiple verification and model checking contexts [9]. Due to the velocity vector only taking integer values, Racetrack benchmarks are discrete-state models; by definition, they are discrete-time.

Experimental Setup. We performed our experiments on Racetrack benchmarks with a noise probability of 10%. For each Racetrack instance, given as a JANI model, we use PMC, SMC with LSS, and deep RL with DSMC to find a good or optimal strategy for reaching the goal line from a certain start position and compute its induced probability. For PMC, we used MCSTA on an Intel Core i7-6600U system (2 cores, 4 threads) with 16 GB of RAM running 64-bit Windows 10. For SMC with LSS, we used MODES on an Intel Core i7-4790 system

(4 cores, 8 threads) with 8 GB of RAM running 64-bit Ubuntu Linux 18.04. For deep RL and DSMC, we used MoGym, internally calling the DSMC functionality of MODES, on an AMD Ryzen 9 5950X system (16 cores, 32 threads) with 124 GB of RAM running 64-bit Ubuntu Linux 22.04. All runtimes we report in our tables are in seconds.

SMC-LSS Specifics. Since MODES does not implement sophisticated methods for detecting probability-zero states, we used step-bounded properties for SMC with LSS: we asked for the probability to reach the goal line via at most 100, 200, 400, and 800 transitions. We also computed the true probabilities for these modified properties via PMC with MCSTA for comparison, and used SMC without LSS but with the uniform random strategy ("SMC/unif." in our tables). To obtain reproducible results, we fixed the seeds for the pseudo-random number generators in LSS and SMC, and disabled multi-threading. That is, we used one simulation thread only. SMC and LSS are easy to speed up by parallelisation, so this puts them at an unnatural disadvantage. We compare three different "families" of strategies (indicated by "fam." in our tables): one sampled with seed 1, one with seed 2, and one with seed 3. For each family, we run LSS sampling $m = 10,000$, $100,000$, and $1,000,000$ strategies. Due to the fixed seeds, the first 10,000 strategies sampled when $m = 100,000$ are the same as for $m = 10,000$ in the same family, etc. The same applies over the different step bounds.

Deep RL with DSMC Specifics. Usually, learning NN is done on GPUs [43–46], but for a reasonable runtime comparison, we used a CPU infrastructure here. In addition, the *random start* setup [44]—during learning, the agent starts randomly from one of the free road cells instead of always from the same start cell—leads to significantly better learning performance. This is because the agent then has the chance to start closer to the goal and learn earlier where the goal is and how to reach it. But since the other methods we compare to can only start from a fixed cell, we used the *normal start* setup during learning for this paper, where the agent also starts its exploration runs from a single start position always. The NN we trained have an input layer of 15 neurons, two hidden layers of 64 neurons each and an output layer of 9 neurons encoding the nine possible acceleration values, as done in other case studies on Racetrack [43,44,46].

4.1   The *barto-small* Track

We start with the *barto-small* track shown in Fig. 1. The start position is on the far left, highlighted in green; the goal line is shown in red on the top right. On this track, the vehicle must make a 90-degree left turn at the right point. We show our experimental results in Tables 1 and 3. First, in Table 1, we show the results for PMC and DSMC, which use the original unbounded probabilistic reachability

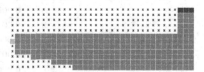

Fig. 1. The *barto-small* track.

Table 1. *barto-small* results, unbounded.

Method	p	Time	Episodes
PMC	1.000	362	–
DSMC	0.000	600	4,000
	0.981	5,280	44,000

Table 2. Results for *maze*.

Method	p	Time	Episodes
PMC	0.968	1,305	–
DSMC	0.000	600	14,000
	0.000	55,800	981,000
SMC-LSS	0.000	684	–

property. This model has only 44,231,073 states, which MCSTA easily handles in 16 GB of memory, and thus finds the optimal result (and strategy) with a probability close to 1 in 6 min. In deep RL with DSMC, on the other hand, the NN has not learnt any useful strategy at this point, after 4,000 learning episodes. After 88 min, however, it has found action choices that result in a near-optimal probability of 0.981. In Table 3, we see how the uninformed sampling employed by LSS performs in comparison. We underline the best results found for each value of m. Using a population of $m = 100,000$ strategies, LSS already finds some that lead the vehicle to the goal, albeit with a probability of at most 0.281. Once we extend the population to 1,000,000 strategies, the success probability increases to about 0.35. We observe limited returns in sampling larger numbers of strategies: with $m = 10,000,000$ for family 3, we get a probability of approx. 0.426 after 192 min—another increase of around 0.07 for a tenfold increase of m (and 20× of runtime). So in runtime comparable to PMC, LSS finds non-trivial strategies, but unlike for deep RL with DSMC, additional time does not lead to significant further improvements. Our use of different step bounds highlights a peculiar effect here: although strategies exist that reach the goal with a high probability in 100 steps (as found by PMC), LSS fails to find these; the reasonable strategies it finds need at least 200 steps, but do not improve when given more steps to reach the goal. As a baseline, the uniform random strategy is clearly useless, essentially never allowing the vehicle to reach the goal.

Table 3. Results for *barto-small*, step-bounded analysis.

Method	m	fam.	100 steps		200 steps		400 steps		800 steps	
			p	Time	p	Time	p	Time	p	Time
PMC			0.913	172	1.000	231	1.000	335	1.000	335
SMC-LSS	10,000	1	0.000	2	0.004	3	0.004	4	0.004	5
		2	0.000	2	0.000	3	0.000	3	0.000	5
		3	0.000	3	<u>0.028</u>	3	<u>0.027</u>	4	<u>0.032</u>	5
	100,000	1	0.000	24	0.041	35	0.044	43	0.043	58
		2	0.000	23	<u>0.281</u>	39	<u>0.281</u>	48	<u>0.281</u>	62
		3	0.000	26	0.225	39	0.225	47	0.225	58
	1,000,000	1	0.286	264	0.343	396	0.343	476	0.343	630
		2	0.318	250	0.317	398	0.317	481	0.317	620
		3	<u>0.351</u>	258	<u>0.351</u>	394	<u>0.350</u>	470	<u>0.349</u>	601
	10,000,000	3							0.426	11,513
SMC/unif.			0.000	0	0.000	0	0.000	0	0.000	0

4.2 The *barto-medium* and *barto-big* Tracks

We next consider the three variants of an R-shaped track shown in Fig. 2: the original *barto-big* track on the right, and two versions of reduced size. We use these variants of presumably increasing difficulty to find the point where our three methods stop being able to find non-trivial strategies. The MDP for track *barto-medium-small* has 35,149,687 states, *barto-medium-large* has 69,918,581, and *barto-big* has 330,872,263. The experimental results are shown in Table 4. For PMC, MCSTA manages to check the two *barto-medium* benchmarks without running out of memory, but on *barto-big*, 16 GB of memory do not suffice. In its "hybrid" disk-based mode, where the MDP and all value vectors are kept in memory-mapped files, MCSTA manages even this largest model, at a significant runtime cost. Deep RL for DSMC again does not manage to learn a useful NN in up to 30 min for all sizes of the *barto* tracks but is able to deliver a near-optimal strategy after 741,000 episodes for *barto-medium-small*. The slightly increased difficulty of *barto-medium-large* is already enough such that the NN has still a poor performance with a goal probability of 0.002 after 641,000 episodes which took 18 h and 40 min. *barto-big* is then too difficult to learn a strategy reaching the goal even after 29 h with 665,000 training episodes when using the normal start setting. From other works we know finding a good strategy is no issue for deep RL in the random start setting [44,46]. For LSS, we only show the best result achieved among the three families with $m = 1,000,000$ and a bound of 800 steps. The *barto-medium-small* track is the last one where LSS manages to find non-trivial strategies, however these strategies already perform very poorly. Our

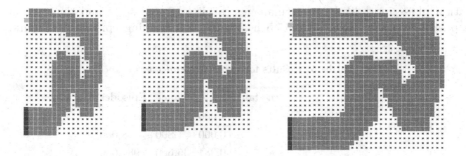

Fig. 2. The *barto-medium-small*, *barto-medium-large*, and *barto-big* tracks.

Table 4. Results for the two *barto-medium* tracks and the *barto-big* track.

Method	barto-medium-small			barto-medium-large			barto-big		
	p	Time	Episodes	p	Time	Episodes	p	Time	Episodes
PMC	0.999	156	–	1.000	402	–	1.000	17,413	–
DSMC	0.000	600	8,000	0.000	600	8,000	0.000	600	5,000
	0.000	1,800	21,000	0.000	1,800	18,000	0.000	1,800	11,000
	0.946	50,400	741,000	0.002	67,200	641,000	0.000	104,400	665,000
SMC-LSS	0.023	670	–	0.000	742	–	0.000	1,048	–

explanation for this result, despite the *barto-medium* models having a similar number of states as *barto-small*, is that the tracks require much more specific behaviour to navigate the R shape, i.e., fewer strategies are successful and thus the probability mass of successful strategies becomes too low for LSS. In essence, LSS hits a "rare strategy problem". We do not show the uniform random strategy, which again does not manage to hit the goal; in fact, it does not manage to do so for any of our examples in this section.

4.3   The *maze* Track

The *maze* track is depicted in Fig. 3. The MDP for this track consists of 156,967,073 states. The results of the experiments are summarized in Table 2. MCSTA implementing PMC solves the benchmark in around 22 min. While we do not need to use its hybrid disk-based mode, it still needs more than 16 GB of memory at certain points and is thus slowed down by the operating system swapping memory contents to disk. Because of the very narrow streets on the track, LSS has no chance: any useful strategy needs to pick a long sequence of exactly the right actions to not crash into a wall, which is very unlikely to be sampled. Consequently, we only see probability-zero strategies in our experiments. The same issue makes it infeasible to learn an NN of reaching the goal with deep RL in the normal start setting: the random exploration phase most likely never manages to hit any goal state and thus obtain a positive reward. Even after 15.5 h and 981,000 training episodes, we found

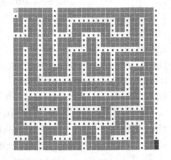

Fig. 3. The *maze* track.

Table 5. Results for *river-deadend-narrow*.

Method	m	fam.	p	Time	Episodes
PMC	–	–	1.000	1,563	–
DSMC	–	–	0.000	1,800	18,000
	–	–	0.984	36,600	981,000
SMC-LSS	10,000	1	0.483	11	–
		2	0.111	12	–
		3	0.007	16	–
	100,000	1	0.547	139	–
		2	0.427	145	–
		3	0.590	159	–
	1,000,000	1	0.590	1,476	–
		2	0.587	1,446	–
		3	0.609	1,490	–

no strategy reaching the goal. We remark that deep RL has no issues with this track in the random start setting [46].

4.4 The *river-deadend-narrow* Track

Finally, we consider the *river-deadend-narrow* track (Fig. 4) in the shape of a river delta. The experimental results are shown in Table 5. The MDP of this model has 175,783,293 states. MCSTA can find a policy with a goal probability of 0.984 in 26 min (again slightly slowed down by swapping). As before, deep RL is not able to find a useful strategy in up to 30 min but delivers a nearly optimal strategy in around 10 h

Fig. 4. The *river-deadend-narrow* track.

after 981,000 training episodes. SMC with LSS, for which we show the results for time bound 800 in Table 5 (since the time bound does not lead to a difference in results here), finds strategies that are successful up to 60 % of the time. While still far from the optimum, these are the best results that LSS achieves across the tracks we experiment with. We hypothesise that this is because no "complex navigation" is required to reach the goal; strategies that are mild variants of moving straight ahead are reasonably successful here. Of these, enough appear to exist for LSS to do reasonably well.

4.5 Summary

We observe that the Racetrack benchmarks are non-trivial in terms of decision-making, with the uniform random strategy being completely useless. MCSTA manages to analyse all of them with PMC, at the cost of white-box model access—and we intentionally selected tracks that are not too large to be able to make useful comparisons. LSS only works when the decisions need not be too specific. It appears to be an indicator of where learning, including deep RL with normal start, has difficulties starting up. Compared to deep RL, LSS is fast. Deep RL learned near-optimal strategies for all but the *maze* and the larger *barto* tracks, at a massive computational effort. In practice, the burden of this effort is on the GPU, making runtimes more acceptable. For the Racetrack cases, we could have significantly sped up deep RL (and made it work for all tracks) with the random start approach. Random start is clearly crucial for efficient deep RL; however it is only so easy to apply to intuitively structured models like Racetrack maps. For arbitrary verification models as, e.g., in the quantitative verification benchmark set [60], suitable random start procedures (e.g., by sensibly assigning non-initial values to the model's variables) still need to be developed.

5 Outlook

Our survey of verification- and AI-based approaches for finding strategies highlights their very different characteristics in terms of the required model interface, memory usage, and runtime, which in turn depend on the structure of the MDP. We have seen that all three methods can be effective in finding reasonable, good, or even (near-)optimal strategies in suitable cases. All three methods also have tool support in the MODEST TOOLSET to apply them to verification models such as those from the quantitative verification benchmark set [60]. However, various challenges remain to make these approaches work better, interconnect them, and make the strategies they find useful and accessible to domain expert users.

Informed Exploration. We saw how crucial the random start process is to bootstrap the exploration phase in learning. For LSS, the uninformedness of the search is inherent: it simply picks many random strategies (in the sense of randomly chosen fixed decisions, *not* randomised decisions resampled every time as in the uniform random strategy). We speculate that, given a suitable heuristic indicating, e.g., the distance to the goal, the currently monolithic LSS strategies could be split into segments that could be individually sampled and combined, going backwards from the goal. A random start-like process for LSS may lead to *robust* strategies that work well not only for a single starting point.

Interconnecting Tools Through Strategies. Currently, specific connections exist between strategy-finding methods like LSS or deep RL and strategy-evaluation methods like SMC or PMC: the final phase of LSS is an SMC evaluation, and DSMC brings NN into MODES. Other works connect deep RL with PMC [25]. All of these are specific to a pair of strategy-finding and strategy-evaluation implementations. This is because today's verification tools do not treat strategies as first-class objects. At the least, we should be able to apply a strategy found with any method to the model (determinising it) in the evaluation using any other method (such as PMC or SMC). This will require standardised formats or interfaces to represent or dynamically query strategies (similar to JANI), and further implementation work in tools to take strategies as input wherever possible.

Explaining Strategies. Each of the strategy-finding methods delivers its result in a specific format: lists of state-action pairs for PMC, an integer strategy identifier for LSS, and a NN definition for deep RL. None of them helps the user to understand and implement the strategy. Without understanding, especially in safety-critical situations, it is hard for users to trust the verification or AI tool's result. A promising way out is to convert the strategy into an (often small and human-readable) decision tree, using as input an NN from deep RL [3] or a state-action pair list from PMC [6]. Ideally, we would integrate such a method directly into our verification and learning tool ecosystem around the MODEST TOOLSET, which poses technical but also conceptual challenges to, e.g., obtain a decision tree from an LSS scheduler identifier without having to exhaustively enumerate all of the MDP's states and thus negating the memory advantage of the SMC-LSS approach. And in the end, while such approaches may make the strategy understandable, they still do not explain why the strategy at hand is (near-)optimal and should be the one to be implemented. A different approach is visualisation, which works well for illustrative benchmarks like Racetrack or other cyber-physical systems. A first such tool is TraceVis [43], visualising the DSMC results and traces. An extension of the tool towards visualisation of the NN internals and the learning process is currently under development.

Beyond Discrete Markov Models. Models with general probability distributions, such as stochastic automata [31], are desirable to more realistically represent phenomena such as time-to-failure distributions or combinations of failures, inspections, repairs, and attacks. Continuous dynamics specified by differential equations, as in hybrid automata [65], allow the inclusion of models of physical processes and thus the analysis of cyber-physical systems. SMC also effectively works for non-Markovian and hybrid formalisms, as evidenced by MODES' support for stochastic hybrid automata, however LSS does not [30]. We have recently combined SMC for such models with RL, but used explicitly stored Q-functions and discretisation for learning [86]. PMC approaches for such models are the subject of active research, with simple approaches based on interval abstractions provided by the MODEST TOOLSET today [53,54]. NN, on the other hand, can in principle handle continuous inputs and outputs just as well as discrete ones. In light of these various advances of learning and verification into non-Markovian continuous-time and continuous-state models, a coherent toolchain that supports verification models with a focus on strategies is still lacking today.

Future Racetracks. We are working on a continuous version of the Racetrack benchmark where the car does not move in a discrete grid. We also continuously extend the benchmark with features like tanks to restrict fuel consumption, different engine types, and other variants [9]. The current developments of Racetrack can always be found online at racetrack.perspicuous-computing.science.

Data Availability. A dataset with models, tools, and scripts from our experimental evaluation is archived and available at DOI https://doi.org/10.4121/20669646.

Acknowledgments. The authors thank Timo P. Gros and Maximilian A. Köhl for their work on the tools we build on.

References

1. Agha, G., Palmskog, K.: A survey of statistical model checking. ACM Trans. Model. Comput. Simul. **28**(1), 6:1–6:39 (2018). https://doi.org/10.1145/3158668
2. Agostinelli, F., McAleer, S., Shmakov, A., Baldi, P.: Solving the Rubik's cube with deep reinforcement learning and search. Nat. Mach. Intell. **1**, 356–363 (2019)

3. Alamdari, P.A., Avni, G., Henzinger, T.A., Lukina, A.: Formal methods with a touch of magic. In: 2020 Formal Methods in Computer Aided Design, FMCAD 2020, Haifa, Israel, 21–24 September 2020, pp. 138–147. IEEE (2020). https://doi.org/10.34727/2020/isbn.978-3-85448-042-6_21

4. Ashok, P., Butkova, Y., Hermanns, H., Křetínský, J.: Continuous-time Markov decisions based on partial exploration. In: Lahiri, S.K., Wang, C. (eds.) ATVA 2018. LNCS, vol. 11138, pp. 317–334. Springer, Cham (2018). https://doi.org/10.1007/978-3-030-01090-4_19

5. Ashok, P., Daca, P., Křetínský, J., Weininger, M.: Statistical model checking: black or white? In: Margaria, T., Steffen, B. (eds.) ISoLA 2020. LNCS, vol. 12476, pp. 331–349. Springer, Cham (2020). https://doi.org/10.1007/978-3-030-61362-4_19

6. Ashok, P., Jackermeier, M., Křetínský, J., Weinhuber, C., Weininger, M., Yadav, M.: dtControl 2.0: explainable strategy representation via decision tree learning steered by experts. In: Groote, J.F., Larsen, K.G. (eds.) TACAS 2021. LNCS, vol. 12652, pp. 326–345. Springer, Cham (2021). https://doi.org/10.1007/978-3-030-72013-1_17

7. Avni, G., Bloem, R., Chatterjee, K., Henzinger, T.A., Könighofer, B., Pranger, S.: Run-time optimization for learned controllers through quantitative games. In: Dillig, I., Tasiran, S. (eds.) CAV 2019. LNCS, vol. 11561, pp. 630–649. Springer, Cham (2019). https://doi.org/10.1007/978-3-030-25540-4_36

8. Baier, C., de Alfaro, L., Forejt, V., Kwiatkowska, M.: Model checking probabilistic systems. In: Clarke, E., Henzinger, T., Veith, H., Bloem, R. (eds.) Handbook of Model Checking, pp. 963–999. Springer, Cham (2018). https://doi.org/10.1007/978-3-319-10575-8_28

9. Baier, C., et al.: Lab conditions for research on explainable automated decisions. In: Heintz, F., Milano, M., O'Sullivan, B. (eds.) TAILOR 2020. LNCS (LNAI), vol. 12641, pp. 83–90. Springer, Cham (2021). https://doi.org/10.1007/978-3-030-73959-1_8

10. Bard, N., et al.: The Hanabi challenge: a new frontier for AI research. Artif. Intell. **280**, 103216 (2020)

11. Barto, A.G., Bradtke, S.J., Singh, S.P.: Learning to act using real-time dynamic programming. Artif. Intell. **72**(1–2), 81–138 (1995)

12. Bellemare, M.G., Naddaf, Y., Veness, J., Bowling, M.: The arcade learning environment: an evaluation platform for general agents. J. Artif. Intell. Res. **47**, 253–279 (2013)

13. Bellman, R.: A Markovian decision process. J. Math. Mech. **6**(5), 679–684 (1957)

14. Bianco, A., de Alfaro, L.: Model checking of probabilistic and nondeterministic systems. In: Thiagarajan, P.S. (ed.) FSTTCS 1995. LNCS, vol. 1026, pp. 499–513. Springer, Heidelberg (1995). https://doi.org/10.1007/3-540-60692-0_70

15. Bogdoll, J., Ferrer Fioriti, L.M., Hartmanns, A., Hermanns, H.: Partial order methods for statistical model checking and simulation. In: Bruni, R., Dingel, J. (eds.) FMOODS/FORTE -2011. LNCS, vol. 6722, pp. 59–74. Springer, Heidelberg (2011). https://doi.org/10.1007/978-3-642-21461-5_4

16. Bohnenkamp, H.C., D'Argenio, P.R., Hermanns, H., Katoen, J.: MODEST: a compositional modeling formalism for hard and softly timed systems. IEEE Trans. Software Eng. **32**(10), 812–830 (2006). https://doi.org/10.1109/TSE.2006.104

17. Bonet, B., Geffner, H.: Labeled RTDP: improving the convergence of real-time dynamic programming. In: ICAPS, pp. 12–21 (2003)

18. Brázdil, T., et al.: Verification of Markov decision processes using learning algorithms. In: Cassez, F., Raskin, J.-F. (eds.) ATVA 2014. LNCS, vol. 8837, pp. 98–114. Springer, Cham (2014). https://doi.org/10.1007/978-3-319-11936-6_8
19. Brockman, G., et al.: OpenAI gym. CoRR arXiv:abs/1606.01540 (2016)
20. Budde, C.E., D'Argenio, P.R., Hartmanns, A.: Automated compositional importance splitting. Sci. Comput. Program. **174**, 90–108 (2019). https://doi.org/10.1016/j.scico.2019.01.006
21. Budde, C.E., D'Argenio, P.R., Hartmanns, A., Sedwards, S.: An efficient statistical model checker for nondeterminism and rare events. Int. J. Softw. Tools Technol. Transf. **22**(6), 759–780 (2020). https://doi.org/10.1007/s10009-020-00563-2
22. Budde, C.E., Dehnert, C., Hahn, E.M., Hartmanns, A., Junges, S., Turrini, A.: JANI: quantitative model and tool interaction. In: Legay, A., Margaria, T. (eds.) TACAS 2017. LNCS, vol. 10206, pp. 151–168. Springer, Heidelberg (2017). https://doi.org/10.1007/978-3-662-54580-5_9
23. Budde, C.E., et al.: On correctness, precision, and performance in quantitative verification. In: Margaria, T., Steffen, B. (eds.) ISoLA 2020. LNCS, vol. 12479, pp. 216–241. Springer, Cham (2021). https://doi.org/10.1007/978-3-030-83723-5_15
24. Butkova, Y., Hartmanns, A., Hermanns, H.: A Modest approach to Markov automata. ACM Trans. Model. Comput. Simul. **31**(3), 14:1–14:34 (2021). https://doi.org/10.1145/3449355
25. Carr, S., Jansen, N., Wimmer, R., Serban, A.C., Becker, B., Topcu, U.: Counterexample-guided strategy improvement for POMDPs using recurrent neural networks. In: Kraus, S. (ed.) Proceedings of the Twenty-Eighth International Joint Conference on Artificial Intelligence, IJCAI 2019, Macao, China, 10–16 August 2019, pp. 5532–5539 (2019). https://doi.org/10.24963/ijcai.2019/768. https://www.ijcai.org/
26. Chung, T.H., Burdick, J.W.: A decision-making framework for control strategies in probabilistic search. In: 2007 IEEE International Conference on Robotics and Automation, ICRA 2007, Roma, Italy, 10–14 April 2007, pp. 4386–4393. IEEE (2007). https://doi.org/10.1109/ROBOT.2007.364155
27. Côté, M.-A., et al.: TextWorld: a learning environment for text-based games. In: Cazenave, T., Saffidine, A., Sturtevant, N. (eds.) CGW 2018. CCIS, vol. 1017, pp. 41–75. Springer, Cham (2019). https://doi.org/10.1007/978-3-030-24337-1_3
28. Dai, P., Mausam, Weld, D.S., Goldsmith, J.: Topological value iteration algorithms. J. Artif. Intell. Res. **42**, 181–209 (2011). http://jair.org/papers/paper3390.html
29. D'Argenio, P.R., Fraire, J.A., Hartmanns, A.: Sampling distributed schedulers for resilient space communication. In: Lee, R., Jha, S., Mavridou, A., Giannakopoulou, D. (eds.) NFM 2020. LNCS, vol. 12229, pp. 291–310. Springer, Cham (2020). https://doi.org/10.1007/978-3-030-55754-6_17
30. D'Argenio, P.R., Hartmanns, A., Sedwards, S.: Lightweight statistical model checking in nondeterministic continuous time. In: Margaria, T., Steffen, B. (eds.) ISoLA 2018. LNCS, vol. 11245, pp. 336–353. Springer, Cham (2018). https://doi.org/10.1007/978-3-030-03421-4_22
31. D'Argenio, P.R., Katoen, J.P.: A theory of stochastic systems part I: stochastic automata. Inf. Comput. **203**(1), 1–38 (2005). https://doi.org/10.1016/j.ic.2005.07.001
32. D'Argenio, P.R., Legay, A., Sedwards, S., Traonouez, L.M.: Smart sampling for lightweight verification of Markov decision processes. Int. J. Softw. Tools Technol. Transf. **17**(4), 469–484 (2015). https://doi.org/10.1007/s10009-015-0383-0

33. David, A., Jensen, P.G., Larsen, K.G., Mikučionis, M., Taankvist, J.H.: UPPAAL STRATEGO. In: Baier, C., Tinelli, C. (eds.) TACAS 2015. LNCS, vol. 9035, pp. 206–211. Springer, Heidelberg (2015). https://doi.org/10.1007/978-3-662-46681-0_16

34. David, A., Larsen, K.G., Legay, A., Mikučionis, M., Wang, Z.: Time for statistical model checking of real-time systems. In: Gopalakrishnan, G., Qadeer, S. (eds.) CAV 2011. LNCS, vol. 6806, pp. 349–355. Springer, Heidelberg (2011). https://doi.org/10.1007/978-3-642-22110-1_27

35. Doshi-Velez, F., Kim, B.: Towards a rigorous science of interpretable machine learning. arXiv preprint arXiv:1702.08608 (2017)

36. Eisentraut, C., Hermanns, H., Zhang, L.: On probabilistic automata in continuous time. In: Proceedings of the 25th Annual IEEE Symposium on Logic in Computer Science, LICS 2010, Edinburgh, UK, 11–14 July 2010, pp. 342–351. IEEE Computer Society (2010). https://doi.org/10.1109/LICS.2010.41

37. Fan, L., et al.: Surreal: open-source reinforcement learning framework and robot manipulation benchmark. In: Conference on Robot Learning, pp. 767–782. PMLR (2018)

38. Forejt, V., Kwiatkowska, M., Norman, G., Parker, D.: Automated verification techniques for probabilistic systems. In: Bernardo, M., Issarny, V. (eds.) SFM 2011. LNCS, vol. 6659, pp. 53–113. Springer, Heidelberg (2011). https://doi.org/10.1007/978-3-642-21455-4_3

39. François-Lavet, V., Henderson, P., Islam, R., Bellemare, M.G., Pineau, J.: An introduction to deep reinforcement learning. Found. Trends Mach. Learn. **11**(3–4), 219–354 (2018). https://doi.org/10.1561/2200000071

40. Fränzle, M., Hahn, E.M., Hermanns, H., Wolovick, N., Zhang, L.: Measurability and safety verification for stochastic hybrid systems. In: Caccamo, M., Frazzoli, E., Grosu, R. (eds.) Proceedings of the 14th ACM International Conference on Hybrid Systems: Computation and Control, HSCC 2011, Chicago, IL, USA, 12–14 April 2011, pp. 43–52. ACM (2011). https://doi.org/10.1145/1967701.1967710

41. Gardner, M.: Mathematical games. Sci. Am. **229**, 118–121 (1973)

42. Gribaudo, M., Remke, A.: Hybrid Petri nets with general one-shot transitions. Perform. Eval. **105**, 22–50 (2016). https://doi.org/10.1016/j.peva.2016.09.002

43. Gros, T.P., Groß, D., Gumhold, S., Hoffmann, J., Klauck, M., Steinmetz, M.: TraceVis: towards visualization for deep statistical model checking. In: Margaria, T., Steffen, B. (eds.) ISoLA 2020. LNCS, vol. 12479, pp. 27–46. Springer, Cham (2021). https://doi.org/10.1007/978-3-030-83723-5_3

44. Gros, T.P., Hermanns, H., Hoffmann, J., Klauck, M., Steinmetz, M.: Deep statistical model checking. In: Gotsman, A., Sokolova, A. (eds.) FORTE 2020. LNCS, vol. 12136, pp. 96–114. Springer, Cham (2020). https://doi.org/10.1007/978-3-030-50086-3_6

45. Gros, T.P., Hermanns, H., Hoffmann, J., Klauck, M., Köhl, M.A., Wolf, V.: MoGym: using formal models for training and verifying decision-making agents. In: CAV 2022 (2022, to appear)

46. Gros, T.P., Höller, D., Hoffmann, J., Klauck, M., Meerkamp, H., Wolf, V.: DSMC evaluation stages: fostering robust and safe behavior in deep reinforcement learning. In: Abate, A., Marin, A. (eds.) QEST 2021. LNCS, vol. 12846, pp. 197–216. Springer, Cham (2021). https://doi.org/10.1007/978-3-030-85172-9_11

47. Haarnoja, T., Zhou, A., Abbeel, P., Levine, S.: Soft actor-critic: off-policy maximum entropy deep reinforcement learning with a stochastic actor. In: International Conference on Machine Learning, pp. 1861–1870. PMLR (2018)

48. Haddad, S., Monmege, B.: Reachability in MDPs: refining convergence of value iteration. In: Ouaknine, J., Potapov, I., Worrell, J. (eds.) RP 2014. LNCS, vol. 8762, pp. 125–137. Springer, Cham (2014). https://doi.org/10.1007/978-3-319-11439-2_10

49. Haddad, S., Monmege, B.: Interval iteration algorithm for MDPs and IMDPs. Theor. Comput. Sci. **735**, 111–131 (2018). https://doi.org/10.1016/j.tcs.2016.12.003

50. Hahn, E.M., Hartmanns, A.: A comparison of time- and reward-bounded probabilistic model checking techniques. In: Fränzle, M., Kapur, D., Zhan, N. (eds.) SETTA 2016. LNCS, vol. 9984, pp. 85–100. Springer, Cham (2016). https://doi.org/10.1007/978-3-319-47677-3_6

51. Hahn, E.M., Hartmanns, A.: Symblicit exploration and elimination for probabilistic model checking. In: Hung, C., Hong, J., Bechini, A., Song, E. (eds.) The 36th ACM/SIGAPP Symposium on Applied Computing, SAC 2021, Virtual Event, Republic of Korea, 22–26 March 2021, pp. 1798–1806. ACM (2021). https://doi.org/10.1145/3412841.3442052

52. Hahn, E.M., et al.: The 2019 comparison of tools for the analysis of quantitative formal models. In: Beyer, D., Huisman, M., Kordon, F., Steffen, B. (eds.) TACAS 2019. LNCS, vol. 11429, pp. 69–92. Springer, Cham (2019). https://doi.org/10.1007/978-3-030-17502-3_5

53. Hahn, E.M., Hartmanns, A., Hermanns, H.: Reachability and reward checking for stochastic timed automata. Electron. Commun. Eur. Assoc. Softw. Sci. Technol. **70**, 1–15 (2014). https://doi.org/10.14279/tuj.eceasst.70.968

54. Hahn, E.M., Hartmanns, A., Hermanns, H., Katoen, J.: A compositional modelling and analysis framework for stochastic hybrid systems. Formal Methods Syst. Des. **43**(2), 191–232 (2013). https://doi.org/10.1007/s10703-012-0167-z

55. Hahn, E.M., Perez, M., Schewe, S., Somenzi, F., Trivedi, A., Wojtczak, D.: Faithful and effective reward schemes for model-free reinforcement learning of omega-regular objectives. In: Hung, D.V., Sokolsky, O. (eds.) ATVA 2020. LNCS, vol. 12302, pp. 108–124. Springer, Cham (2020). https://doi.org/10.1007/978-3-030-59152-6_6

56. Hartmanns, A.: Correct probabilistic model checking with floating-point arithmetic. In: Fisman, D., Rosu, G. (eds.) TACAS 2022. LNCS, vol. 13244, pp. 41–59. Springer, Cham (2022). https://doi.org/10.1007/978-3-030-99527-0_3

57. Hartmanns, A., Hermanns, H.: The Modest Toolset: an integrated environment for quantitative modelling and verification. In: Ábrahám, E., Havelund, K. (eds.) TACAS 2014. LNCS, vol. 8413, pp. 593–598. Springer, Heidelberg (2014). https://doi.org/10.1007/978-3-642-54862-8_51

58. Hartmanns, A., Hermanns, H.: Explicit model checking of very large MDP using partitioning and secondary storage. In: Finkbeiner, B., Pu, G., Zhang, L. (eds.) ATVA 2015. LNCS, vol. 9364, pp. 131–147. Springer, Cham (2015). https://doi.org/10.1007/978-3-319-24953-7_10

59. Hartmanns, A., Kaminski, B.L.: Optimistic value iteration. In: Lahiri, S.K., Wang, C. (eds.) CAV 2020. LNCS, vol. 12225, pp. 488–511. Springer, Cham (2020). https://doi.org/10.1007/978-3-030-53291-8_26

60. Hartmanns, A., Klauck, M., Parker, D., Quatmann, T., Ruijters, E.: The quantitative verification benchmark set. In: Vojnar, T., Zhang, L. (eds.) TACAS 2019. LNCS, vol. 11427, pp. 344–350. Springer, Cham (2019). https://doi.org/10.1007/978-3-030-17462-0_20

61. Hartmanns, A., Timmer, M.: Sound statistical model checking for MDP using partial order and confluence reduction. Int. J. Softw. Tools Technol. Transf. **17**(4), 429–456 (2015). https://doi.org/10.1007/s10009-014-0349-7

62. Hasanbeig, M., Abate, A., Kroening, D.: Logically-correct reinforcement learning. CoRR arXiv:1801.08099 (2018)

63. Henriques, D., Martins, J.G., Zuliani, P., Platzer, A., Clarke, E.M.: Statistical model checking for Markov decision processes. In: Ninth International Conference on Quantitative Evaluation of Systems, QEST 2012, London, UK, 17–20 September 2012, pp. 84–93. IEEE Computer Society (2012). https://doi.org/10.1109/QEST.2012.19

64. Hensel, C., Junges, S., Katoen, J.P., Quatmann, T., Volk, M.: The probabilistic model checker Storm. Int. J. Softw. Tools Technol. Transf. (2021). https://doi.org/10.1007/s10009-021-00633-z

65. Henzinger, T.A.: The theory of hybrid automata. In: Proceedings of 11th Annual IEEE Symposium on Logic in Computer Science, New Brunswick, New Jersey, USA, 27–30 July 1996, pp. 278–292. IEEE Computer Society (1996). https://doi.org/10.1109/LICS.1996.561342

66. Hérault, T., Lassaigne, R., Magniette, F., Peyronnet, S.: Approximate probabilistic model checking. In: Steffen, B., Levi, G. (eds.) VMCAI 2004. LNCS, vol. 2937, pp. 73–84. Springer, Heidelberg (2004). https://doi.org/10.1007/978-3-540-24622-0_8

67. Hinton, G., et al.: Deep neural networks for acoustic modeling in speech recognition: the shared views of four research groups. IEEE Signal Process. Mag. **29**(6), 82–97 (2012)

68. Ho, J., Ermon, S.: Generative adversarial imitation learning. Adv. Neural. Inf. Process. Syst. **29**, 4565–4573 (2016)

69. Howard, R.A.: Dynamic Probabilistic Systems: Semi-Markov and Decision Processes. Dover Books on Mathematics, vol. 2. Dover Publications, Mineola (2013)

70. Howard, R.A.: Dynamic Programming and Markov Processes. MIT Press, Cambridge (1960)

71. Junges, S., Jansen, N., Dehnert, C., Topcu, U., Katoen, J.-P.: Safety-constrained reinforcement learning for MDPs. In: Chechik, M., Raskin, J.-F. (eds.) TACAS 2016. LNCS, vol. 9636, pp. 130–146. Springer, Heidelberg (2016). https://doi.org/10.1007/978-3-662-49674-9_8

72. Keller, T., Eyerich, P.: PROST: probabilistic planning based on UCT. In: McCluskey, L., Williams, B.C., Silva, J.R., Bonet, B. (eds.) Proceedings of the Twenty-Second International Conference on Automated Planning and Scheduling, ICAPS 2012, Atibaia, São Paulo, Brazil, 25–29 June 2012. AAAI (2012). http://www.aaai.org/ocs/index.php/ICAPS/ICAPS12/paper/view/4715

73. Klauck, M., Hermanns, H.: A Modest approach to dynamic heuristic search in probabilistic model checking. In: Abate, A., Marin, A. (eds.) QEST 2021. LNCS, vol. 12846, pp. 15–38. Springer, Cham (2021). https://doi.org/10.1007/978-3-030-85172-9_2

74. Köhl, M.A., Klauck, M., Hermanns, H.: Momba: JANI meets Python. In: TACAS 2021. LNCS, vol. 12652, pp. 389–398. Springer, Cham (2021). https://doi.org/10.1007/978-3-030-72013-1_23

75. Kolobov, A., Mausam, Weld, D.S., Geffner, H.: Heuristic search for generalized stochastic shortest path MDPs. In: Bacchus, F., Domshlak, C., Edelkamp, S., Helmert, M. (eds.) Proceedings of the 21st International Conference on

Automated Planning and Scheduling, ICAPS 2011, Freiburg, Germany, 11–16 June 2011. AAAI (2011). http://aaai.org/ocs/index.php/ICAPS/ICAPS11/paper/view/2682

76. Krizhevsky, A., Sutskever, I., Hinton, G.E.: ImageNet classification with deep convolutional neural networks. In: NIPS, pp. 1097–1105 (2012)

77. Kwiatkowska, M., Norman, G., Parker, D.: Stochastic model checking. In: Bernardo, M., Hillston, J. (eds.) SFM 2007. LNCS, vol. 4486, pp. 220–270. Springer, Heidelberg (2007). https://doi.org/10.1007/978-3-540-72522-0_6

78. Kwiatkowska, M., Norman, G., Parker, D.: PRISM 4.0: verification of probabilistic real-time systems. In: Gopalakrishnan, G., Qadeer, S. (eds.) CAV 2011. LNCS, vol. 6806, pp. 585–591. Springer, Heidelberg (2011). https://doi.org/10.1007/978-3-642-22110-1_47

79. Kwiatkowska, M.Z., Norman, G., Segala, R., Sproston, J.: Automatic verification of real-time systems with discrete probability distributions. Theor. Comput. Sci. **282**(1), 101–150 (2002). https://doi.org/10.1016/S0304-3975(01)00046-9

80. Legay, A., Delahaye, B., Bensalem, S.: Statistical model checking: an overview. In: Barringer, H., et al. (eds.) RV 2010. LNCS, vol. 6418, pp. 122–135. Springer, Heidelberg (2010). https://doi.org/10.1007/978-3-642-16612-9_11

81. Legay, A., Sedwards, S., Traonouez, L.-M.: Scalable verification of Markov decision processes. In: Canal, C., Idani, A. (eds.) SEFM 2014. LNCS, vol. 8938, pp. 350–362. Springer, Cham (2015). https://doi.org/10.1007/978-3-319-15201-1_23

82. McMahan, H.B., Gordon, G.J.: Fast exact planning in Markov decision processes. In: ICAPS, pp. 151–160 (2005)

83. McMahan, H.B., Likhachev, M., Gordon, G.J.: Bounded real-time dynamic programming: RTDP with monotone upper bounds and performance guarantees. In: Raedt, L.D., Wrobel, S. (eds.) Machine Learning, Proceedings of the Twenty-Second International Conference (ICML 2005), Bonn, Germany, 7–11 August 2005. ACM International Conference Proceeding Series, vol. 119, pp. 569–576. ACM (2005). https://doi.org/10.1145/1102351.1102423

84. Mnih, V., et al.: Playing Atari with deep reinforcement learning. arXiv preprint arXiv:1312.5602 (2013). Accessed 15 Sept 2020

85. Mnih, V., et al.: Human-level control through deep reinforcement learning. Nature **518**, 529–533 (2015)

86. Niehage, M., Hartmanns, A., Remke, A.: Learning optimal decisions for stochastic hybrid systems. In: Arun-Kumar, S., Méry, D., Saha, I., Zhang, L. (eds.) 19th ACM-IEEE International Conference on Formal Methods and Models for System Design, MEMOCODE 2021, Virtual Event, China, 20–22 November 2021, pp. 44–55. ACM (2021). https://doi.org/10.1145/3487212.3487339

87. Okamoto, M.: Some inequalities relating to the partial sum of binomial probabilities. Ann. Inst. Stat. Math. **10**(1), 29–35 (1959)

88. Parker, D.A.: Implementation of symbolic model checking for probabilistic systems. Ph.D. thesis, University of Birmingham, UK (2003)

89. Pathak, D., Agrawal, P., Efros, A.A., Darrell, T.: Curiosity-driven exploration by self-supervised prediction. In: International Conference on Machine Learning, pp. 2778–2787. PMLR (2017)

90. Pineda, L.E., Lu, Y., Zilberstein, S., Goldman, C.V.: Fault-tolerant planning under uncertainty. In: IJCAI, pp. 2350–2356 (2013)

91. Pineda, L.E., Zilberstein, S.: Planning under uncertainty using reduced models: revisiting determinization. In: ICAPS (2014)

92. Puterman, M.L.: Markov Decision Processes: Discrete Stochastic Dynamic Programming. Wiley, New York (1994)

93. Quatmann, T., Katoen, J.-P.: Sound value iteration. In: Chockler, H., Weissenbacher, G. (eds.) CAV 2018. LNCS, vol. 10981, pp. 643–661. Springer, Cham (2018). https://doi.org/10.1007/978-3-319-96145-3_37

94. Reijsbergen, D., de Boer, P., Scheinhardt, W.R.W., Haverkort, B.R.: On hypothesis testing for statistical model checking. Int. J. Softw. Tools Technol. Transf. **17**(4), 377–395 (2015). https://doi.org/10.1007/s10009-014-0350-1

95. Rubino, G., Tuffin, B. (eds.): Rare Event Simulation Using Monte Carlo Methods. Wiley, New York (2009). https://doi.org/10.1002/9780470745403

96. Sarle, W.S.: Neural networks and statistical models (1994)

97. Schulman, J., Wolski, F., Dhariwal, P., Radford, A., Klimov, O.: Proximal policy optimization algorithms. arXiv preprint arXiv:1707.06347 (2017)

98. Silver, D., Hubert, T., Schrittwieser, J., Antonoglou, I., Lai, M., Guez, A., Lanctot, M., Sifre, L., Kumaran, D., Graepel, T., Lillicrap, T., Simonyan, K., Hassabis, D.: A general reinforcement learning algorithm that masters chess, shogi, and go through self-play. Science **362**(6419), 1140–1144 (2018)

99. Sproston, J.: Decidable model checking of probabilistic hybrid automata. In: Joseph, M. (ed.) FTRTFT 2000. LNCS, vol. 1926, pp. 31–45. Springer, Heidelberg (2000). https://doi.org/10.1007/3-540-45352-0_5

100. Sutton, R.S., Barto, A.G.: Reinforcement Learning: An Introduction. Adaptive Computation and Machine Learning, 2nd edn. The MIT Press, Cambridge (2018)

101. Wald, A.: Sequential tests of statistical hypotheses. Ann. Math. Stat. **16**(2), 117–186 (1945)

102. Waschneck, B., et al.: Optimization of global production scheduling with deep reinforcement learning. Procedia CIRP **72**, 1264–1269 (2018)

103. Xia, F., Zamir, A.R., He, Z., Sax, A., Malik, J., Savarese, S.: Gibson env: real-world perception for embodied agents. In: Proceedings of the IEEE Conference on Computer Vision and Pattern Recognition, pp. 9068–9079 (2018)

104. Yoon, S.W., Fern, A., Givan, R.: FF-replan: a baseline for probabilistic planning. In: Boddy, M.S., Fox, M., Thiébaux, S. (eds.) Proceedings of the Seventeenth International Conference on Automated Planning and Scheduling, ICAPS 2007, Providence, Rhode Island, USA, 22–26 September 2007, p. 352. AAAI (2007). http://www.aaai.org/Library/ICAPS/2007/icaps07-045.php

105. Younes, H.L.S., Simmons, R.G.: Probabilistic verification of discrete event systems using acceptance sampling. In: Brinksma, E., Larsen, K.G. (eds.) CAV 2002. LNCS, vol. 2404, pp. 223–235. Springer, Heidelberg (2002). https://doi.org/10.1007/3-540-45657-0_17

106. Yu, T., et al.: Meta-world: a benchmark and evaluation for multi-task and meta reinforcement learning. In: Conference on Robot Learning, pp. 1094–1100. PMLR (2020)

Importance Splitting in Uppaal

Kim Guldstrand Larsen[1], Axel Legay[2]($\boxtimes$), Marius Mikučionis[1],
and Danny Bøgsted Poulsen[1]

[1] Department of Computer Science, Aalborg University, Aalborg, Denmark
{kgl,marius,dannybpoulsen}@cs.aau.dk
[2] Université catholique de Louvain, Louvain-la-Neuve, Belgium
axel.legay@uclouvain.be

Abstract. Statistical Model Checking is a simulations-based verification technique that has gathered increased focus in the past ten years, due to its applicability to handle much larger models compared to exhaustive verification techniques used in model checking. Statistical Model Checking is also applicable to a larger class of systems than exhaustive methods—in particular its ability to handle hybrid systems is important. To apply statistical model checking we must however accept that verification results are probabilistic, and simulations exercise only the most likely behaviour of models. Unfortunately the events we are often interested in finding/estimate the probability of are *rare*. In its core form, Statistical Model Checking cannot reliably estimate such events.

In this work we investigate how to incorporate the rare event simulating technique *importance splitting* into Uppaal SMC.

1 Introduction

Stochastic Timed Automata refines Timed Automata [1] by assigning probabilities to the non-deterministic choices of the timed automata: delays are drawn from a probability density distribution (exponential or uniform) while non-deterministic actions are selected using probabilistic choice. The stochastic behaviour of a composed system is given by races between components, resulting in nested integrals over uniform and exponential distributions for to step-bounded reachability probabilities. In principal, it could be possible to calculate the probability of reaching a given set of goal states by symbolically exploring the state space to find all paths leading to the set and subsequently solve the integral of all those paths. In practice, however, solving the integrals are nontrivial. Therefore the probabilities are usually estimated using Statistical Model Checking (SMC) [5,13].

Statistical Model Checking consists of learning the probability that the execution of a system will satisfy a given property. The approach elegantly combines (1) a simulation-based algorithm for learning the probability distribution of satisfying the property by observing a fixed number of its executions with (2) runtime verification algorithms applied on these executions. Those runtime verification algorithms naturally depend on the nature of the property to be validated.

T. Margaria and B. Steffen (Eds.): ISoLA 2022, LNCS 13703, pp. 433–447, 2022.
https://doi.org/10.1007/978-3-031-19759-8_26

The efficiency of SMC depends on the number of executions needed to obtain an estimate while minimising the error rate. The most common SMC learning algorithm is that of Monte Carlo. When it comes to validating a property that has a high chance of being satisfied, Monte Carlo is considered efficient. In this case, the algorithm minimises the number of simulations and guarantees a low error rate. The situation changes when one must estimate probability distributions of rarer events such as the probability that an execution contains a bug.

This situation comes from the uniform character of the Monte Carlo simulation which does not aim to find the bug. It therefore takes too many simulations to influence the variance of the distribution. To overcome this problem, several authors have proposed learning algorithms that guide the simulations. These techniques, called *importance splitting* [12], orient the execution simulation according to the intermediate results of the runtime verification algorithm. This helps to isolate simulations and identify the bug. These techniques have been deployed in many contexts ranging from automotive to computational biology.

In the paper we explore importance splitting techniques for stochastic timed automata via an implementation in state-of-the-art tool UPPAAL [5] The efficiency of the approach is illustrated on two concrete problems, one of them being an estimate of the spread of the contagion of the COVID-19 epidemic.

2   Stochastic Timed Transition Systems

In the following we present the semantical foundation of stochastic timed automaton, in a step-wise fashion. First we present classic timed transition systems, and afterwards see how to refine a timed transition system by assigning probabilities to the transitions. Although our works major contribution is about incorporating importance splitting into UPPAAL, we will not be presenting how stochastic timed automata are given stochastic semantics using stochastic timed transition systems. For this we refer to [5].

Let L be a finite set of symbols called channels. Channels are the communication pathways of two transition systems. From these labels we construct the set of output actions $\Sigma^!(L) = \{a_0! \mid a_0 \in L\}$ and the set of input actions $\Sigma^?(L) = \{a_0? \mid a_0 \in L\}$. For the set of all actions over L we let $\Sigma^{!\cup?}(L) = \Sigma^!(L) \cup \Sigma^?(L)$. Given a set of actions $\Sigma^{!\cup?}$ we use the notation to $\Sigma^{!\cup?}\!\downarrow$ to get the set of synchronisation labels.

Definition 1. *A timed transition system (tts) is a tuple* $\langle S, \blacktriangleright, \Sigma^!, \Sigma^?, \rightarrow, P, \mathcal{P} \rangle$ *where*

- S *is a set of states,*
- $\blacktriangleright \in S$ *is the initial state,*
- $\Sigma^!$ *is a set of output actions,*
- $\Sigma^?$ *is a set of input actions,*
- $\rightarrow \subseteq S \times (\Sigma^! \cup \Sigma^? \cup \mathbb{R}_{\geq 0}) \times S$ *is a transition relation,*
- P *is a finite set of propositions,*
- $\mathcal{P} : S \rightarrow 2^P$ *assign propositions to individual states.*

To simplify notation we adopt a convention of writing $s \xrightarrow{a} s'$ whenever $(s, a, s') \in \rightarrow$, $s \not\xrightarrow{a}$ if there exists no $s' \in S$ such that $(s, a, s') \in \rightarrow$, and $s \rightarrow$ if for some $s' \in S$ and action $a \in \Sigma^? \cup \Sigma^! \cup \mathbb{R}$ we have $s \xrightarrow{a} s'$. As a slight abuse of notation we also write $s \in P$ as a short hand for $\mathcal{P}(s) \subseteq P$. We will generally assume that all transition systems are

- *input-enabled* meaning that for all states $s \in S$ and all input-actions $a_0? \in \Sigma^?$ it should be the case that $s \xrightarrow{a_0?}$.
- *input-deterministic* meaning that if $s \xrightarrow{a_0?} s'$ and $s \xrightarrow{a_0?} s''$ then $s' = s''$,

For a tts $\mathcal{T} = \langle S, \blacktriangleright, \rightarrow, P, \mathcal{P} \rangle$ we call a sequence of states and delays $\omega = s_0(d_0, a_0!)s_1(d_1, a_1!) \ldots, s_n$, where for all i, $s_i \in S$ and $s_i \xrightarrow{d_i} \xrightarrow{a_0!} s_{i+1}$, a run of $\mathcal{T}$ from s_0. To simplify notation we let $|\omega| = n$, let $\omega[i]$ index into the states of a run i.e. $\omega[i] = s_i$ and let $\omega[i]^\delta$ index into the delay i.e. $\omega[i]^\delta = d_i$. We denote all runs of $\mathcal{T}$ from s_0 by $\Omega(\mathcal{T}, s_0)$. Since we are interested in time-bounded reachability we need the set of timed runs with a duration less than some upper bound τ. Thus in the following we let $\Omega^{\leq\tau}(\mathcal{T}, s) = \{\omega \in \Omega(\mathcal{T}, s) \mid \sum_{i=0}^{|\omega|} \omega[i]^\delta \leq \tau\}$. For all runs starting from the initial state we omit the state signifier and let $\Omega(\mathcal{T}) = \Omega(\mathcal{T}, \blacktriangleright)$.

Definition 2 (Stochastic Timed Transition System). *A stochastic Timed Transition System is a tuple $\langle \mathcal{T}, \mu \rangle$ where $\mathcal{T} = \langle S, \blacktriangleright, \Sigma^!, \Sigma^?, \rightarrow, P, \mathcal{P} \rangle$ is a transition system and $\mu : S \rightarrow \mathbb{R} \times \Sigma^!(\rightarrow)\mathbb{R}$ assigns a density to delay-action pairs such that for all states $s \in S$*

- *$\mu(s)$ is a probability density function i.e. $(\int_{\geq 0} \sum_{a \in \Sigma^!} \mu(s)(d, a))dt = 1$ and*
- *$\mu(s)$ only assign densities to possible actions i.e. $\mu(s)(d, a) \neq 0 \implies s \xrightarrow{d} \xrightarrow{a}$.*

For a stochastic timed transitions system $\mathcal{K} = \langle \langle S, \blacktriangleright, \rightarrow, P, \mathcal{P} \rangle, \mu \rangle$ we define a *cylinder* of traces to be a structure $\pi = P_0 I_0 P_1 I_1 \ldots P_n$ where for all i, I_i is an interval with rational end points. A timed run $\omega = s_0(d_0, a_0!)s_1(d_1, a_1!) \ldots, s_n \ldots$ belongs to the cylinder π if for all i, $\mathcal{P}(s_i) = P_i$ and $d_i \in I_i$. Using the probability-density μ we can now define the probability measure of π from state s recursively as

$$\mu_{[s]}(\pi) = \left(\begin{cases} 1 & \text{if } P_0 = \mathcal{P}(s_i) \\ 0 & \text{otherwise} \end{cases} \right) \cdot \int_{t \in I_0} \sum_{a_1! \in !} (\mu(t, a_1!)) \mu_{[s]^{t,a_1!}}(\pi^1)$$

where $\pi^1 = P_1 I_1, P_2 I_2, \ldots P_n$ and $[s]^{t,a_1!}$ is the unique state such that $s \xrightarrow{t} \xrightarrow{a_1!} [s]^{t,a_1!}$.

Reachability Probability. The problem we consider is from a starting state s to find the probability of reaching a state where a set of propositions ☺ are true state s— denoted $\mathbb{P}_s(\lozenge_{\leq t}\odot)$. The set of simulations for which s reaches $\odot$ we define as

$$\text{Reach}(\odot, t) = \{s_0(d_0, a_0!)s_1(d_1, a_1!)\ldots, s_n \in \Omega^{\leq \tau}(T, s) \mid s_n \in \odot\}$$

and can define the probability $\mathbb{P}_s(\lozenge_{\leq t}\odot)$ as the Lebesque-integral:

$$\mathbb{P}_s(\lozenge_{\leq t}\odot) = \int_{\Omega^{\leq \tau}(T,s)} \left(\begin{cases} 1 & \text{if } \omega \in \text{Reach}(\odot, t) \\ 0 & \text{otherwise} \end{cases} \right) \cdot \mu_s d(\omega)$$

Composition. The semantics for a composition of stochastic timed transition system is usually given in terms of repeated races between the individual systems. The definition used for STTSs in this paper, however, allows composing transition systems by defining a new stochastic transition system that captures these races. Let $\mathcal{K}_1, \mathcal{K}_2, \ldots \mathcal{K}_n$ be a stochastic transition systems where for all i, $\mathcal{K}_i = \langle T_i, \mu_i \rangle$, $T_i = \langle S_i, \blacktriangleright_i, \Sigma_i^!, \Sigma_i^?, \to^i, \mathrm{P}_i, \mathcal{P}_i \rangle$ and $\Sigma_i^? = \cup_{j \neq i} \Sigma^?(\Sigma_j^! \downarrow)$.[1] Then we define the their composition $\mathcal{K}_1 \| \mathcal{K}_2 \| \ldots \mathcal{K}_n$ to be the stochastic transition system

$$\mathcal{K}_{\mathcal{J}} = \langle S_1 \times S_2 \times S_n, (\blacktriangleright_1, \ldots \blacktriangleright_n), \uplus_{i=1\ldots n}\Sigma_i^!, \emptyset, \to^{\mathcal{J}}, \mathrm{P}_{\mathcal{J}}, \mathcal{P}_{\mathcal{J}} \langle \rangle, \mu_{\mathcal{J}} \rangle$$

with

- $(s_1, s_2, \ldots s_n) \xrightarrow{a_0!} (s_1', s_2', \ldots, s_n')$ if $s_i \xrightarrow{a_0!} s_i'$ and for all $j \neq i$ $s_j \xrightarrow{a_0?} s_j'$,
- $(s_1, s_2, \ldots s_n) \xrightarrow{d} (s_1', s_2', \ldots, s_n')$, $d \in \mathbb{R}$ if for all i $s_i \xrightarrow{d} s_i'$,
- $\mathrm{P}_{\mathcal{J}} = \uplus_{i=1\ldots n}\mathrm{P}_i$
- $\mathcal{P}_{\mathcal{J}}((s_1, s_2, \ldots s_n)) = \uplus_{i=1\ldots n}\mathcal{P}_i(s_i)$ and

$$\mu_{\mathcal{J}}((s_1, s_2, \ldots s_n))(d, a_0!) = \mu_i(s_i)(d, a_0!) \prod_{j \neq i} \int_{\tau > d} \sum_{a_1! \in \Sigma_j^!} \mu_j(s_j)(\tau, a_1!),$$

for $a_0! \in \Sigma_i^!$. The construction is for the most part the *standard composition* of timed transition systems, and only the definition of the probability density may require some further explanation: it essentially says that the density of performing an action $a_0!$ after a delay of time d is found by first taking the density of the component i^{th} component owning that action multiplied by the probability all other components choose a delay longer than d. It thus embeds the *race semantics* of David et al. [4] into the definition of the density functions.

---

[1] The latter requirement captures that all components of the compositions uses the other components outputs as input.

3   Importance Splitting

The overarching idea of *importance splitting* is to split a (rare) reachability goal into sub-goals that must be reached on the way to the overall goal. That is, we define a series of intermediate goals (called levels) $\mathbb{O}_1, \mathbb{O}_2, \ldots, \mathbb{O}_n$ where $\mathbb{O}_n = \mathbb{O}$. For each run $\omega \in \text{Reach}(\mathbb{O}, t)$ it should be the case that for all i there exists a j such that $\omega[j] \in \mathbb{O}_i$, Given such a series of goals importance splitting proceeds by n successive conditional probability estimations (see Algorithm 2). First, a number of states (m_1) is sampled uniformly from the set of initial states. For each of these states a simulation is generated. At the moment a simulations reaches $\mathbb{O}_1$ it is stopped, and the resulting state added to a set NStates_1. An estimate of reaching the first level is thus $\frac{|\text{NStates}_1|}{m_1}$. The probability of reaching $\mathbb{O}_2$ is now estimated by starting m_2 new simulations from a state $s \in \text{NStates}_1$ as starting point. Simulations are terminated when they reach $\mathbb{O}_2$ and the resulting states added to a set NStates_2. The probability of reaching $\mathbb{O}_2$ is estimated by $\frac{|\text{NStates}_2|}{m_2}$ Repeating this process for all n finally yields an estimate of

$$\mathbb{P}(\mathbb{O}) = \prod_{i=1}^{n} \frac{|\text{NStates}_i|}{m_i}$$

One thing to be aware of is that we in addition to sub-goals also need a stopping criterion for when to stop simulations i.e. some way of telling the simulations that there is no chance of reaching the next level. One (trivial) stopping criterion is exceeding the time bound of the reachability query. For simplicity we characterise these as a set of states $\mathbb{O}_i$.

Until now we have left it open how we sample states for estimating a level. There are at least two strategies for this sampling:

Fixed Effort. In a fixed effort scheme each level is estimated using a fixed amount of simulations (the *effort*) n. The starting state of the n simulations for level i is selected uniformly from NStates_{i-1}.

Fixed Splitting. In a fixed splitting each simulation reaching a level i is given a pre-determined fixed amount offspring simulations k. That means level i is estimated using $m_i = |\text{NStates}_{i-1}| \cdot k$ simulations.

Remark 1. The fixed effort approach has the major advantage of having predicable behaviour in regards to computing powers. No matter the level, it will always use the same number of traces n thus if there are m levels then $m \cdot n$ simulations will be used. On the other hand, fixed effort needs to store n states in memory for each level estimation. The Fixed Splitting approach is less predictable, and if we select our levels unwisely we might face an exponential growth of traces per level. It does, however, have the huge advantage that it may be implemented in a recursive fashion and only keep one state per level at a time.

Example 1. Consider the simple automaton in Fig. 1 and consider the probability of reaching A with x >= 100. Obviously this is possible by the automaton taking

---

Algorithm 1. Generate Trace

1: **procedure** GENERATE($s_0, \smiley, \frownie$)   ▷ start state, set of goal states, states to avoid
2:    $i \leftarrow 0$
3:    $s_c = s_0$
4:    **while** $s_c \notin \frownie_i$ **do**
5:        **if** $s_r \in \smiley$ **then return** s_a
6:        **end if**
7:        $(d_i, a_i) \sim \mu(s_c)$
8:        Let s_r be such that $s_c \xrightarrow{d_i} \xrightarrow{a_i} s_r$
9:        $s_c \leftarrow s_r$
10:    **end while**
11:    **return** $\langle \perp, \rangle$
12: **end procedure**

Algorithm 2. Importance Splitting

1: **procedure** IMPORTANCE SPLIT($s_0, \smiley_1 \ldots \smiley_n \frownie,$) ▷ start state, sub-goals, states to avoid
2:    NStates $= \{(s_0)\}$
3:    **for** $i \leftarrow 1 \ldots n$ **do**
4:        States $\leftarrow$ RESAMPLE(NStates)
5:        NStates $= \{\}$
6:        **for all** $s_c \in$ States **do**
7:            $s_n \leftarrow$ GENERATETRACE($s_c, \smiley_i, \frownie, d$)
8:            **if** $s_n \neq \perp$ **then**
9:                NStates $\leftarrow$ NStates $\cup \{(s_n, \delta)\}$
10:            **end if**
11:        **end for**
12:        $p_i \leftarrow \frac{|\text{NStates}|}{|\text{States}|}$
13:    **end for**
        return $\prod_{i=1}^{n} p_i$
14: **end procedure**

---

the looping transition *at least* 100 times before going to B. Since the choice of the transitions is independent at each step the probability is obviously $0.5^{100} = 7.88 \times 10^{31}$. A statistical model checker like UPPAAL SMC is however unlikely to properly assess this probability since it needs to generate too many samples. It would need an expected number of $2^{100} = 1.26 \times 10^{30}$ samples just to find one satisfying case.

The realisation with *importance splitting* is that although reaching $\langle A, x >= 100 \rangle$ from $\langle A, x == 0 \rangle$ is very unlikely, it is actually quite likely from $\langle A, x >= 99 \rangle$. Likewise reaching $\langle A, x >= 99 \rangle$ from $\langle A, x = 0 \rangle$ is very unlikely, but

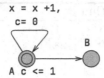

Fig. 1. Timed Automaton with a rare event

from $\langle A, x >= 98 \rangle$ it is very likely. Using basic probability theory it is easy to realise that

$$\mathbb{P}(\Diamond \langle A, x >= 100 \rangle) = \mathbb{P}(\Diamond \langle A, x >= 100 \rangle | \Diamond \langle A, x >= 99 \rangle) \cdot$$
$$\mathbb{P}(\Diamond \langle A, x >= 99 \rangle | \Diamond \langle A, x >= 98 \rangle)$$

$$\cdot \vdots$$

$$\mathbb{P}(\Diamond \langle A, x >= 1 \rangle | \Diamond \langle A, x = 0 \rangle),$$

and thus we have reduced our estimation problem to evaluate these (more likely) conditional probabilities. In the grey column in Table 1 we show some of these conditional probabilities.

Score Function. A natural way of defining the intermediate goal-states required by importance splitting is defining a *score* function. A score function is a mapping from the state space to the reals i.e. it is a function $\Delta : S \to \mathbb{R}$. It should assign a higher score to states more likely to reach the final goal, and should attain its highest value for the set of goal states. Formally, for a sequence of levels $\Theta_1, \Theta_2, \ldots, \Theta_n$ a score function (Δ) should ensure that if $s_i \in \Theta_i$, $s_j \in \Theta_j$ and $i < j$ then $\Delta(s_i) < \Delta(s_j)$. In the

X	Success	Effort	Probability
1	509	1000	0.509
2	517	1000	0.517
3	499	1000	0.499
4	499	1000	0.499
5	481	1000	0.481
6	510	1000	0.51
7	478	1000	0.478

Table 1. Estimates of $\mathbb{P}(\Diamond \langle A, x >= X \rangle | \Diamond \langle A, x >= X - 1 \rangle)$

remainder of this paper we will define the levels needed by importance splitting in terms of a score function and threshold values $\tau^1, \tau^2 \ldots \tau^n$ for crossing into a new level i.e. we let $\Theta_i = \{ s \in S \mid \tau^i \leq \Delta(s) < \tau^{i+1} \}$. For easening notation later, we lift the score function to finite traces by letting $\Delta(\omega)$ for a trace ω be the maximal score attained at any point i.e.

$$\Delta(\omega) = \max\{\Delta(\omega[0], \Delta(\omega[1] \ldots, \Delta(\omega[|\omega|]\}.$$

The practical applicability of importance splitting highly depends on the definition of the score function, and on the thresholds for transitioning from one level to the next. Defining the score function is oftentimes the easiest part of

---

Algorithm 3. Adaptive Algorithm

1: **procedure** IMPORTANCE SPLIT(s_0, Δ, τ, N_k)   ▷ start state, score function, final level score, simulations to Keep
2:     NStates $= \{(s_0, 0)\}$
3:     $\tau_c = \Delta(s_0)$
4:     **while** $\tau_c < \tau$ **do**
5:         States $\leftarrow$ RESAMPLE(NStates)
6:         NStates $= \emptyset$
7:         Simus $\leftarrow \{$GENERATEFULLTRACE(s_c)$|s_c \in$ States$\}$
8:         Let τ_c be the maximal value such that $|\{\Delta(\omega) \geq \tau_c\})|\omega \in$ Simus$\})| \geq N_k$
9:         Selected $= \{\omega \in$ Simus$|\Delta(\omega) \geq \tau_c\}$
10:         NStates $\leftarrow \cup_{\omega \in \text{Selected}}\{\omega[i] \mid i = \min\{0 \leq j < |\omega| \mid \Delta(\omega[j]) \geq \Delta(\omega)\}\}$
11:         $p_i \leftarrow \frac{|\text{NStates}|}{|\text{States}|}$
12:     **end while**
        return $\prod_{i=1}^{n} p_i$
13: **end procedure**

---

applying importance splitting: many models have an inherent *progress measure* that can be used as the level—in Example 1 a natural progress measure is the value of X thus the value of X can be used as the *score* function. The thresholds are more difficult to define. According to Rubino and Tuffin [12] we should strive towards thresholds that ensure the conditional probability of going from one level to the next is the same for all levels i.e. that $\mathbb{P}(\copyright_1) = \mathbb{P}(\copyright_2|\copyright_1) = \mathbb{P}(\copyright_3|\copyright_2) = \ldots$. In order to take advantage of this principle of defining good thresholds, we would need to know the probabilities in advance, but then there would be no point in doing importance splitting. It is however still advantageous to know this principle as we with proper model knowledge we might be able to use it to define levels that adhere to the principle. Also, the principle is used by algorithms for finding the level thresholds automatically.

3.1   Adaptive Levels Algorithm

Our discussion of importance splitting has so far required users to define the score function, and define the level thresholds. The latter is a time-consuming part of using importance splitting as it involves lots of trial and errors from a human user. Jégourel et al. [7] tried to overcome this problem by developing an algorithm that automatically finds the thresholds during simulation. Intuitively this adaptive algorithm (Algorithm 3) works by iteratively generating a number, say N, of full traces[2]. The N simulations are scored by their highest score at any point during the simulation. The algorithm then finds the N_k best states and retains those for the next iterations. It terminates when the N_k best states has a score higher than the final levels value.

---

[2] Traces that reaches on overall timebound.

4   Importance Splitting in Uppaal

A major contribution of the current paper is integrating the three importance splitting methods into the mainstream verification tool UPPAAL. The implemented techniques are the *fixed effort* and *fixed splitting* algorithms and the *adaptive level* algorithm by Jégourel et al. [7]. UPPAAL [5] is established as a key player in regards to verification timed automata models, and has since ten years also established itself as a major player in Monte-Carlo based verification techniques (for timed automata systems). The SMC engine has, however, since its inception missed an easy to use rare-event simulation technique. In the past, Jégourel et al. [8] integrated importance sampling into the engine. It required extensive modifications to the trace sampling method of the engine. Another nuisance with the importance sampling method was its dependence on a symbolic reachability analysis—drastically limiting the systems for which rare event simulation could be applied. Importance splitting is less invasive to the sampling engine as it only requires the ability to copy states and restart sampling from those copied states.

The overarching design philosophy of integrating importance splitting into UPPAAL has been to make minimal changes to the user experience. Users should be able to model systems exactly as they are used to, and use all features of UPPAAL. The only thing a modeller should learn is two new queries

Interaction with External Libraries. UPPAAL has the ability to interact with external libraries which allows modellers to keep parts of the simulation state external to UPPAAL. This has been previously used to analyse worst case execution time of binaries [3] and integrating an LLVM simulator into UPPAAL [10]. Having the actual simulation engine residing in an external library means UPPAAL can no longer easily copy states as needed for the importance splitting algorithms. Therefore external libraries wishing to use the importance splitting algorithms must implement three C-functions an for storing and recalling states:

- `int32_t uppaal_store_state ()`; save the current state and return an identifier for the state. Called by UPPAAL when it has reached a level.
- `int32_t uppaal_recall_state (int32_t i)` ; restore the state identified by i .Called by UPPAAL when it restarts simulations from a state.
- `void uppaal_delete_state (int32_t i)` ; delete the state identified by i. This is called by UPPAAL when it has finished estimating the probability of one level.

4.1   Queries

Fixed Effort and Fixed Splitting. The *fixed effort* and *fixed splitting* algorithms are integrated as a single query inside UPPAAL. The exact algorithms is selected as a configuration option. Likewise the *effort* and *offspring* parameters are defined as an option. The structure of the query is

```
Pr[<=T]   (<>)levels levelExpr {T1,T2,T3...TN}
```

```
$ verifyta --splitting.algorithm 1 --splitting.offspring 40 -q
    running.xml

Verifying formula 1 at /nta/queries/query[1]/formula
 -- Formula is satisfied.
Pr(<> ...) in 6.48834e-31.
Level 0 (1)    52 / 100
Level 1 (5)    120 / 2080
Level 2 (10)   143 / 4800
Level 3 (15)   173 / 5720
Level 4 (20)   225 / 6920
Level 5 (25)   283 / 9000
Level 6 (30)   348 / 11320
Level 7 (35)   405 / 13920
Level 8 (40)   489 / 16200
Level 9 (45)   613 / 19560
Level 10 (50)  740 / 24520
Level 11 (55)  948 / 29600
Level 12 (60)  1209 / 37920
Level 13 (65)  1452 / 48360
Level 14 (70)  1754 / 58080
Level 15 (75)  2250 / 70160
Level 16 (80)  2770 / 90000
Level 17 (85)  3535 / 110800
Level 18 (90)  4482 / 141400
Level 19 (95)  5701 / 179280
Level 20 (100) 7134 / 228040

Values in [39.0316,60.6699] mean=49.9625 steps=0.0404454: 80 0 0 0 0
    40
```

Listing 1.1. Running importance splitting in the terminal

where `levelExpr` is an arithmetic UPPAAL expression defining the current level , `T1,...,TN` are constant arithmetic expression defining the level thresholds and `T` is an integer defining the bound within which `levelExpr >= TN` should be reached.

Example 2. Let us briefly return to Fig. 1. In this model it is quite natural to express the score in terms of the value of x. Thus we can estimate the probability of $\mathbb{P}(\Diamond\langle A, x >= 100\rangle)$ by posing the query

```
Pr[<=100] (<>) levels x  {1,5,10,15,20,25,30,35,40,45,50,55,
                          60,65,70,75,80,85,90,95,100}
```

Listing 1.1 shows an example of running this query using the fixed splitting approach, and using 40 offsprings per level.

In the result, we are first and foremost shown what the estimated probability is $(6.48834 \times 10^{-31})$. UPPAAL also tells us how many simulations reached each level and how many simulations were used to estimate each level—a line `Level 4 (20) 225/6920` tells us that 225 runs reached level 4, the threshold of level 4 was 20 and we used 6920 simulations for this estimation. Table 1 is in fact created by parsing the output from UPPAALverification.

Adaptive Levels. The adaptive algorithm in UPPAAL is triggered by simply posing a query: `Pr[<=T] (<>) adaptive levelExpr -> Thres`. Here T is a time limit, `levelExpr` is an arithmetic expression defining the level function and `Thres` is an arithmetic expression defining the final level.

5 Experiments

We have been experimenting with our implementation in UPPAALfor two cases. The models and results reported on in the following sections is available at https://github.com/dannybpoulsen/splitting_rep.git.

5.1 JobShop

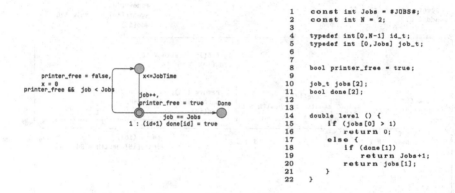

```
1   const int Jobs = #JOBS#;
2   const int N = 2;
3
4   typedef int[0,N-1] id_t;
5   typedef int [0,Jobs] job_t;
6
7
8   bool printer_free = true;
9
10  job_t jobs[2];
11  bool done[2];
12
13
14  double level () {
15      if (jobs[0] > 1)
16          return 0;
17      else {
18          if (done[1])
19              return Jobs+1;
20          return jobs[1];
21      }
22  }
```

Fig. 2. JobShop worker

In this first example (Fig. 2) we apply our importance splitting implementation to a simple instance of the JobShop problem: we have two Workers each with n jobs they need to finish. The workers need a shared resource to complete their jobs, so before processing a job they first need to acquire the resource. There is no scheduler in this setup, so the two processes are racing to acquire the resource. After finishing a task, the worker release the resource and enters a new race to acquire the resource before processing the next task. The two workers are very similar in their behaviour except that Worker(0) is quicker than Worker(1) to acquire the resource. The property we are interested in about this is whether Worker(1) can finish all of its jobs before Worker(0) has finished it's first task. Obviously this is possible, but it is—as we will see—a very rare event. In UPPAAL we have defined a level function `level` which returns zero if Worker(0) has finished and otherwise returns what job number Worker(1) has finished last. That is, we use the number of finished jobs as our level.

Table 2. Probability estimates for the JobShop scheduling example for increasing number of jobs.

Jobs	Fixed effort	Fixed splitting	Adaptive
1	2.8700×10^{-1}	2.8700×10^{-1}	3.2000×10^{-1}
6	5.0355×10^{-3}	4.9783×10^{-3}	1.8517×10^{-2}
11	3.4196×10^{-5}	3.6162×10^{-5}	1.1466×10^{-3}
16	1.9653×10^{-7}	1.9709×10^{-7}	2.9288×10^{-5}
21	9.7140×10^{-10}	1.0437×10^{-9}	1.1031×10^{-6}
26	4.4231×10^{-12}	5.2293×10^{-12}	2.9549×10^{-8}
31	2.3099×10^{-14}	2.4707×10^{-14}	1.4558×10^{-9}
36	1.6732×10^{-16}	1.4214×10^{-16}	1.2020×10^{-10}
41	3.2620×10^{-19}	6.4069×10^{-19}	1.2734×10^{-12}
46	5.2512×10^{-21}	2.5757×10^{-21}	4.1715×10^{-14}

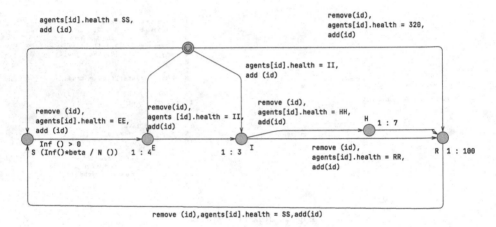

Fig. 3. Covid health template

In UPPAAL we verify the property with both adaptive levels algorithm and the classic importance splitting algorithms for varying amount of jobs (1 through 46). The results are shown in Table 2.

5.2 Epidemic Simulation

The emergence of Covid19 lead researchers in communities not normally working with epidemic modelling to apply their methods to this new use case [2,6,9,11]. In the current work we integrate a pandemic SEIRH-model inside UPPAAL. An SEIRH-model divides a population into five different stage of disease progression:

- *Susceptible* (S) are individuals that have not yet contracted the disease,
- *Exposed* (E) are individuals that have contracted the disease but have not developed symptoms and cannot infect other,

Table 3. Levels for the pandemic model

Level	Threshold	Satisfied	Effort	Probability
0	1796	102	1000	0.102
1	1857	120	1000	0.12
2	1887	111	1000	0.111
3	1918	113	1000	0.113
4	1939	101	1000	0.101
5	1949	122	1000	0.122
6	1961	119	1000	0.119
7	1969	209	1000	0.209
8	1977	116	1000	0.116
9	1980	595	1000	0.595
10	1982	108	1000	0.108
11	1991	142	1000	0.142
12	1996	102	1000	0.102
13	2003	112	1000	0.112

- *Infectious* (I) are individuals that may infect a susceptible person,
- *Recovered* (R) are individuals that have recovered from the disease,
- *Hospitalised* (H) are individuals that are so seriously ill that they have to be hospiltalised.

Figure 3 shows one UPPAAL template modelling the health of one agent in a world.

There would be such template a per agent and another template for controlling where an agent is. A person transits from S to E via interactions with an infected individual on their present location. Assuming a well-stirred environment this happens with a exponential rate of Inf() * beta/N(). Here Inf() is the number of infectious at the agents current environment while N() is the total number of agents in the environment. Afterwards an agent transit from E to I, I to R or H and H to R. The time at which these transitions happen are governed by exponential distributions in Fig. 3. In practice

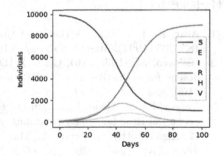

Fig. 4. Simulations of the pandemic model. Top: S,E,R,H-trajectories for one simulation. Bottom: H trajectories from ten simulations.

we do not use these exact parameters: SEIRH-models are very general and can be instantiated to model any epidemic by proper adjustment of the transition time between individual health states. Also we have actually "out-sourced" the SEIRH modelling to an external library as this allows us to easily scale the model to thousands or millions of agents. Thus UPPAAL mainly functions as an orhestrator of verification queries. In Fig. 4 we show trajectories from a simulation with 10.000 agents. It was obtained using the UPPAAL query

```
simulate [<=100] {S (),E (),I(),R (),H()}
```

The function calls are calls to the external solver for information about the counts of different health states. Looking at several plots of this kind shows that we often experience a peek at around 1700 exposed individuals. It should, however, be possible to get more than 2000 exposed individuals—it is just highly unlikely. To estimate exactly how unlikely it is we use our adaptive levels implementation and run the query

```
Pr[<=200] (<>) adaptive E() -> 2000
```

UPPAAL estimates the probability to be 2.9918×10^{-11} and found the levels in Table 3.

6   Conclusion

In this work we have presented our work to integrate rate event simulation into UPPAAL. We use three different algorithms fixed splitting, 1. fixed effort, and 2. an adaptive level algorithm. We have applied these techniques to two cases: a variation on the JobShop problem and an epidemic model. Since the epidemic model is quite large the simulation itself is offloaded to an external library which UPPAAL interacts with.

References

1. Alur, R., Dill, D.L.: A theory of timed automata. Theor. Comput. Sci. **126**(2), 183–235 (1994). https://doi.org/10.1016/0304-3975(94)90010-8
2. Bisiacco, M., Pillonetto, G.: COVID-19 epidemic control using short-term lockdowns for collective gain. CoRR, abs/2109.00995 (2021). https://arxiv.org/abs/2109.00995
3. Cassez, F., de Aledo, P.G., Jensen, P.G.: WUPPAAL: computation of worst-case execution-time for binary programs with UPPAAL. In: Aceto, L., Bacci, G., Bacci, G., Ingólfsdóttir, A., Legay, A., Mardare, R. (eds.) Models, Algorithms, Logics and Tools. LNCS, vol. 10460, pp. 560–577. Springer, Cham (2017). https://doi.org/10.1007/978-3-319-63121-9_28
4. David, A., et al.: Statistical model checking for networks of priced timed automata. In: Fahrenberg, U., Tripakis, S. (eds.) FORMATS 2011. LNCS, vol. 6919, pp. 80–96. Springer, Heidelberg (2011). https://doi.org/10.1007/978-3-642-24310-3_7
5. David, A., Larsen, K.G., Legay, A., Mikučionis, M., Poulsen, D.B.: UPPAAL SMC tutorial. Int. J. Softw. Tools Technol. Transf. **17**(4), 397–415 (2015). https://doi.org/10.1007/s10009-014-0361-y
6. Großmann, G., Backenköhler, M., Wolf, V.: Importance of interaction structure and stochasticity for epidemic spreading: a COVID-19 case study. In: Gribaudo, M., Jansen, D.N., Remke, A. (eds.) QEST 2020. LNCS, vol. 12289, pp. 211–229. Springer, Cham (2020). https://doi.org/10.1007/978-3-030-59854-9_16

7. Jegourel, C., Legay, A., Sedwards, S.: An effective heuristic for adaptive importance splitting in statistical model checking. In: Margaria, T., Steffen, B. (eds.) ISoLA 2014. LNCS, vol. 8803, pp. 143–159. Springer, Heidelberg (2014). https://doi.org/10.1007/978-3-662-45231-8_11

8. Jegourel, C., Larsen, K.G., Legay, A., Mikučionis, M., Poulsen, D.B., Sedwards, S.: Importance sampling for stochastic timed automata. In: Fränzle, M., Kapur, D., Zhan, N. (eds.) SETTA 2016. LNCS, vol. 9984, pp. 163–178. Springer, Cham (2016). https://doi.org/10.1007/978-3-319-47677-3_11

9. Jensen, P.G., Jørgensen, K.Y., Larsen, K.G., Mikučionis, M., Muñiz, M., Poulsen, D.B.: Fluid model-checking in UPPAAL for Covid-19. In: Margaria, T., Steffen, B. (eds.) ISoLA 2020. LNCS, vol. 12476, pp. 385–403. Springer, Cham (2020). https://doi.org/10.1007/978-3-030-61362-4_22

10. Kulczynski, M., Legay, A., Nowotka, D., Poulsen, D.B.: Analysis of source code using UPPAAL. In: Proença, J., Paskevich, A. (eds.) Proceedings of the 6th Workshop on Formal Integrated Development Environment, F-IDE@NFM 2021, Held Online, 24–25th May 2021, volume 338 of EPTCS, pp. 31–38 (2021). https://doi.org/10.4204/EPTCS.338.5

11. Pejó, B., Biczók, G.: Games in the time of COVID-19: promoting mechanism design for pandemic response. CoRR, abs/2106.12329 (2021). https://arxiv.org/abs/2106.12329

12. Rubino, G., Tuffin, B. (eds.): Rare Event Simulation using Monte Carlo Methods. Wiley, Hoboken (2009). ISBN 978-0-470-77269-0. https://doi.org/10.1002/9780470745403

13. Younes, H.L.S., Simmons, R.G.: Probabilistic verification of discrete event systems using acceptance sampling. In: Brinksma, E., Larsen, K.G. (eds.) CAV 2002. LNCS, vol. 2404, pp. 223–235. Springer, Heidelberg (2002). https://doi.org/10.1007/3-540-45657-0_17

Verification of Variability-Intensive Stochastic Systems with Statistical Model Checking

Sami Lazreg[1], Maxime Cordy[1(✉)], and Axel Legay[2]

[1] University of Luxembourg, Esch-sur-Alzette, Luxembourg
{sami.lazreg,maxime.cordy}@uni.lu
[2] UCLouvain, Louvain-La-Neuve, Belgium
axel.legay@uclouvain.be

Abstract. We propose a simulation-based approach to verify Variability-Intensive Systems (VISs) with stochastic behaviour. Given an LTL formula and a model of the VIS behaviour, our method estimates the probability for each variant to satisfy the formula. This allows us to learn the products of the VIS for which the probability stands above a certain threshold. To achieve this, our method samples VIS executions from all variants at once and keeps track of the occurrence probability of these executions in any given variant. The efficiency of this algorithm relies on Algebraic Decision Diagram (ADD), a dedicated data structure that enables orthogonal treatment of variability, stochasticity and property satisfaction. We implemented our approach as an extension of the ProVeLines model checker. Our experiments validate that our method can produce accurate estimations of the probability for the variants to satisfy the given properties.

Keywords: Software product lines · Variability · Statistical Model Checking · Markov chains · Stochastic systems

1 Introduction

When deployed in the field, the correct behaviour of software systems is often put at risk because of unpredictability in the environment (e.g., users or natural phenomena) these systems interact with. That is, the state evolution of the environment is stochastic and this, in turn, entails random non-determinism in the system behaviour. In face of this stochasticity, engineers must provide confidence that the system they build will behave correctly in various situations they cannot control. The difficulty of this task vastly increases when the same engineers develop not a standalone system, but a *Variability-Intensive System (VIS)*.

VISs, such as software product lines [11] and configurable systems [26,28], are systems that one can derive into multiple variants (or configurations). The term variability refers to all the ways in which the variants can differ. In software

T. Margaria and B. Steffen (Eds.): ISoLA 2022, LNCS 13703, pp. 448–471, 2022.
https://doi.org/10.1007/978-3-031-19759-8_27

product lines, such variation points are usually named *features*. Therefore, system variants are uniquely identified by their set of features. Variability makes development activities inherently harder for VISs than for single system development. This is due to the necessity of handling features and their effects throughout all development steps, including verification and validation. Therefore, quality assurance techniques must ensure that *all* system variants that will run in the fieldwork correctly.

VIS variants share many common behaviors and that differ in identified functionalities. For a set of n functionalities one can at worst create 2^n different systems. Checking each system individually would introduce an explosion of time. To overcome these problems, researchers have proposed compact product line representations. These representations make it possible to check all the products in one pass. For nearly 10 years, these approaches were limited to purely Boolean systems. Recently, we have extended the approach to stochastic systems. In this case, we must calculate the probability that a product satisfies the property. This calculation is generally done by extending classical exhaustive algorithms such as those implemented in PRISM.

The variability of VISs and their stochasticity call for dedicated techniques to estimate the *probability* that *any* VIS variant satisfies intended requirements over its behaviour. Engineers should be able to quickly answer questions like *"what is the probability that all variants satisfy a given requirement"*, *"which variants satisfy a given requirement with a desired degree of confidence"*, or *"which variants are the most likely to satisfy a given set of requirements"*. One straightforward way to answer such questions is to apply classical quality assurance techniques to each variant separately to derive an accurate ranking of the variants' likeliness to comply with a requirement. However, getting an accurate answer for all variants may prove difficult, time-consuming and, in turn, even falsify the ranking of these variants with respect to their probability to satisfy the requirements.

In this paper, we propose a method to learn the probability that VIS variants satisfy a given property. Compared to state-of-the-art methods, our approach (a) allows engineers to explicitly model the stochastic distribution of environment events and (b) can effectively assess probabilistic properties across multiple variants. As a side effect, our approach is able to learn the variants of the VIS for which the probability to satisfy the property stays above a given threshold. To achieve this, we lean on Statistical Model Checking (SMC) – a type of verification algorithms that relies on execution sampling and statistical tests to assess model properties [21,22,34]. Statistical model checking consists of learning the probability that the execution of a system will satisfy a given property. The approach elegantly combines (1) a simulation-based algorithm for learning the probability distribution of satisfying the property by observing a fixed number of its executions with (2) runtime verification algorithms applied on these executions. Those runtime verification algorithms naturally depend on the nature of the property to be validated. We develop a novel SMC algorithm that is *family-based*, i.e. it can sample executions from all variants at once *and* keep track of the occurrence probability of these executions in any given variant. The effectiveness of this algorithm relies on Algebraic Decision Diagram (ADD) [2], a dedicated data structure that enables an orthogonal treatment of variability, stochasticity and property satisfaction.

We conduct a preliminary validation of our approach based on case studies from the literature. Our results confirm that our family-based approach produces reliable estimations of the probability for the variants to satisfy given properties. We discuss the factors that influence the effectiveness of our method – i.e., its capability to compute estimations that preserve the differences between the variants – compared to alternatives that analyze each variant separately.

2   Background

2.1   Markov Chains and Variability

We model stochastic system behaviours into Discrete-Time Markov Chains (DTMCs). In such models, (1) the state space S of the system is countable, (2) time elapses at discrete steps and (3) the transitions between states $T \subseteq S \times S$ are stochastic. Hence, one can see DTMCs as a Kripke structure where each transition between two states has a probability to occur at each discrete time step. These probabilities are defined such that they satisfy the usual probability axioms. By Markov's property, the probability of occurrence of a transition depends only on the current state and not on the previously executed transitions. Therefore, the probability for the DTMC to follow a k-length path $\rho = s_0 \ldots s_{k-1}$ is equal to the product of the state transition probabilities.

Rodrigues et al. [27] have extended DTMC with variability. The resulting formalism – named *Featured DTMC* (FDTMC) – associates each transition $t \in S \times S$ of the Markov chain with a *probability profile* Π_t that encodes the probability for each variant v to execute t. Such profiles list the set of variants that are following the transitions as well as the probability to take such a transition for a given variant. Precisely, given a set V of variants, Π_t is a function from V to $[0, 1]$. For any $t = (s, s')$ and $v \in V$, $\Pi_t(v) = 0$ means that the variant v cannot execute t, whereas $\Pi_t(v) = 1$ means that, when in state s, v surely executes t at the next discrete time step. For an FDTMC to be consistent, for any state $s \in S$ the probability profile associated to the transitions leaving s must satisfy the probability axioms for all variants. That is, for any $v \in V$, $s \in S$, we have $\sum_{t \in \{(s,s') \in T\}} \Pi_t(v) = 1$. A variant v is typically represented as a set of features (aka variation points) such as $v \in \mathbb{B}^F$.

The product of two probability profiles Π_t and $\Pi_{t'}$ is defined as $(\Pi_t \otimes \Pi_t)(v) = \Pi_t(v)\Pi_{t'}(v)$. The sum $\oplus$ and the division $/$ of two probability profiles are defined similarly. We denote by $\mathbf{0}$ (resp $\mathbf{1}$) the *fixed* profile that associates a value i to every variant ($\forall v \in V, \Pi_{(v)} = i$). Then for 0 (resp. 1) a complement of Π_t is defined as $(-\Pi_t)$, with $(-\Pi)(v) = 1 - \Pi(v)$, and we also note it $1 - \Pi$.

Based on probability profiles, we define an FDTMC as a tuple (S, ν, V, Π) where S is a countable, non-empty set of states; ν is a vector of size $|S|$ that records the initial probability distribution of every state; V is the set of variants;

$\Pi : (S \times S) \rightarrow (V \rightarrow [0,1])$ is the transition probability function, which assigns a probability profile to each transition. The fact that variant v cannot execute a transition from s to s' is encoded as $\Pi(s,s')(v) = 0$. Note that the probability that any variant executes a k-length path $\rho = s_0, s_1, \ldots, s_k$ in the FDTMC is given by $\Pi_{(s_0,s_1)} \otimes \cdots \otimes \Pi_{(s_{k-1},s_k)}$.

An FDTMC is a concise representation for a set of DTMCs, that is, one per valid variant (or product). The DTMC modelling a particular variant v is obtained by *projecting* the probability profile of each transition onto v. The transition probability function of the resulting DTMC is defined as $P : S \times S \rightarrow [0,1] : P(s,s') = \Pi(s,s')(v)$.

We provide an example of FDTMC in Fig. 1 and a projection of this FDTMC in Fig. 2. This model considers two exclusive features I and J and an optional feature K. The 4 resulting variants can then be expressed in the following feature combinations $\{\{I\}, \{I,K\}, \{J\}, \{J,K\}\}$.

Each transition has either a *fixed* probability value (e.g. the Markov chain transits from s_0 to s_1 with a *fixed* probability profile of **0.5**) or a profile that depends on the variant features. For example, from state s_0, all variants can transit to s_1 (or s_2) with probability 0.5. All variants can also transit from s_1 to state s_0 but with different probabilities (i.e., 0.5 for variants with feature I, 0.2 for ones with J).

Furthermore, only some variant can execute some transitions. For example, only variants with feature J can loop over s_2 while only variants with feature I can loop over s_1. Having a variant that cannot execute a transition t is similar to $\Pi_t(v) = 0$. Similarly, a variant with a probability of 1 to execute a transition is equivalent to a non-stochastic transition (e.g., s_4 to s_3 for variants without K feature).

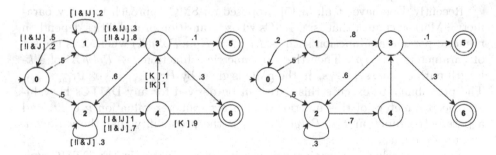

Fig. 1. An illustrative example of stochastic VIS represented as a FDTMC.

Fig. 2. DTMC resulting from the $FDTMC_{|\{J \wedge \neg I \wedge \neg K\}}$ projection.

2.2 Probabilistic Linear Temporal Logic

We formulate requirements over stochastic systems in the Linear-Time Logic (LTL) [25]. We form LTL formulae according to the following grammar:

$$\phi ::= \top \mid a \mid \phi \wedge \phi \mid \neg \phi \mid \bigcirc \phi \mid \phi \; U \; \phi$$

where a is an atomic state property; $\bigcirc$ is the next operator; and U is the until operator. From the until operator, one can derive $\Diamond \phi$, which means that the system must eventually reach a state that satisfies ϕ; and $\Box \phi$, which means that the ϕ should always hold.

In this work, given that we employ simulation-based approaches that return finite traces, it may happen that we cannot conclude the satisfaction or the violation of an LTL formula (that involves the until operator) from finite traces. This happens, e.g., for $a \; U \; b$, when the finite system execution always satisfies a without ever satisfying b. In such a case, we conclude that the trace does not satisfy the property. We discuss ideas to improve our method in such cases in Sect. 8.

2.3 Statistical Model Checking

Statistical Model Checking (SMC) is a family of algorithms to estimate the probability that a stochastic system satisfies an LTL property ϕ [34]. The idea is to sample a set E of bounded executions of the system and to associate each execution $e \in E$ with a Bernoulli variable b_e (1 if the execution satisfies the property, 0 otherwise). Then, one can estimate the overall probability that the system satisfies ϕ as $\sum_{e \in E} \frac{b_e}{|E|}$. SMC also applies to non-stochastic systems by assuming an implicit uniform probability distribution on each state successor.

Recently, Delahaye et al. [3,15] proposed an SMC approach to verify parametric Markov chains, that is, DTMCs whose transition probabilities depend on numeric parameters function such as $Pr : S \times S \to Poly(\mathbb{X})$ where $\mathbb{X}$ is the set of parameters $p_0, ..., p_n$. Then the – parametric – function $f \in Poly(\mathbb{X})$ of a k-length path $\rho = s_0, s_1, \ldots, s_k$ in the pMC is given by $Pr_{(s_0, s_1)} \otimes \cdots \otimes Pr_{(s_{k-1}, s_k)}$. The probability to execute this path can be derived for any DMTCs by valuate the parameters of this function. Given a parameter valuation $\nu \in \mathbb{R}^{\mathbb{X}}$ and a parametric function $f \in Poly(\mathbb{R}), f(\nu)$ is the probability that the variant ν executes the path.

This approach is interesting because it samples paths in the DTMC uniformly and accumulates a parametric function that encodes the – parametric – probability of this path to be executed for any valuation (aka variants). The approach also associates every sampled execution with a reward (e.g., 1 if the execution satisfies the checked property; 0 otherwise). Then, the probability that a given parameter valuation satisfies the property is estimated as the average of all rewards weighted with the value of the associated parametric function corresponding to the parameter valuation. Delahaye et al. [15] demonstrate the soundness of their method theoretically and experimentally on three examples.

There are three fundamental differences between these parametric Markov chains and FDTMCs that impede the direct application of Delahaye et al.'s approach. First, FDTMCs include Boolean parameters, whereas parametric Markov chains include real parameters. Second, these Boolean parameters represent VIS features and determine the existence of transitions within the different variants, whereas Delahaye et al. assume that all transitions are available regardless of any particular parameter values. Third and last, VIS features are interdependent and it is necessary to filter out feature combinations that do not correspond to any existing (valid) variants. However, these two approaches can be both used to verify every variants (or valuations) of a stochastic VIS because:

$$FDTMC_{|v\in\mathbb{B}^F} = pMC_{|\nu\in\mathbb{R}^X} \iff \forall t \in T, \Pi_t(v) = Pr_t(\nu).$$

Therefore, our work takes inspiration from the principles of Delahaye et al. [3,15] but develops a novel SMC approach to verify FDTMCs. The implementation of our algorithms relies on a dedicated data structure – based on Algebraic Decision Diagrams (ADDs) [2] – to account for the binary nature and relationships of FDTMCs parameters. Indeed, the advantage of our data structure over Delahaye's parametric approach is that ADDs can record (1) which variants can (or cannot) execute a given FDTMC path and (2) with which probability – and it can do so while keeping its structure concise as it accumulates more probability profiles. The other advantage of our approach is that we can directly embed constraints between the features within the decision diagram that can also act as constraints between transition probabilities. [8,12]. By doing so, we discard invalid combinations of features by constructions – whereas parametric approaches would invoke a solver to determine the set of valid combinations. Overall, our solution fits specifically well to the problem of verifying stochastic VISs, whereas Delahaye's method is more appropriate for classical parametric models.

3   Statistical Model Checking for Featured DTMC

We consider the problem of checking an LTL formula on a featured discrete-time Markov chain. The traditional SMC method of Younes et al. [34] can work only on a single variant. One straightforward way to address our problem is, therefore, to compute the projections of the FDTMC onto each variant $\forall v \in V, FTMC_{|v}$ and apply traditional SMC to each resulting DTMC. For example, the projection in Fig. 2 results in 6 states with two states (5 and 6) that accept the LTL formula ϕ. The traditional SMC method will sample n paths of k steps (arbitrary values). In this example, some possible paths of 3 steps are: $\rho_1 = (0, 1, 3, 2)$, $\rho_2 = (0, 2, 2, 4)$, $\rho_3 = (0, 2, 4, 3)$, $\rho_4 = (0, 1, 0, 1)$, $\rho_5 = (0, 1, 3, 5)$ and $\rho_6 = (0, 1, 3, 6)$. The two last paths ρ_5 and ρ_6 reach an accepting state. This mean that they violate the safety property (i.e., $\rho_{i\in\{5,6\}} \not\models \phi$). The probability that the system will produce these behavior is $P[\rho_5] = .5 \times .8 \times .1 = .04$ and $.12$ for ρ_6. More probable paths are for example ρ_1 where $P[\rho_1] = .24$ or ρ_3 $(.35)$.

Given 6 samples P of 3 steps, lets say the one described $\rho_1, ..., \rho_6$, the probability $\mathbb{E}$ that the system violates the property is

$$\mathbb{E} = \frac{\sum_{\rho \in P, \rho \not\models \phi} P[\rho]}{\sum_{\rho \in P} P[\rho]} = \frac{.04 + .12}{.24 + .105 + .35 + .05 + .04 + .12} = 0.176$$

Although this procedure is simple, it suffers from the exponential blow-up inherent to variability [9], that is, the number of variants tends to increase exponentially in the number of features.

Instead, we propose a new SMC method that can sample executions from all variants at once (i.e., directly in the FDTMC) regardless of the probabilistic differences across the variants. We rely on the theoretical results of Delahaye et al. [3, 15] and adapt their principles to FDTMC verification. Hence, our algorithm performs a uniform random walk to sample a path in the FDTMC. That is, at each step, the next transition to execute is selected uniformly regardless of the number of variants that can execute it and with which probability.

For each sample path ρ, we record three pieces of information:

- The probability profile Π_ρ associated to ρ, which records the probability that each variant executes it. In our implementation, we encode a probability profile into an ADD. We also record the set of variants V_ρ that can execute ρ. We can compute this set from Π_ρ a posteriori, such that $v \in V_\rho \Leftrightarrow \Pi_\rho(v) > 0$.
- A Boolean value b_ρ that indicates whether ρ satisfies or not the checked formula, that is, the reward of ρ according to Delahaye et al.'s terminology.
- The probability p_ρ that the uniform random walk samples ρ.

A number n of repeated applications of Algorithm 1 produce a set of tuples $\{(\rho_1, \Pi_1, b_1, p_1) \dots (\rho_n, \Pi_n, b_n, p_n)\}$. Then, leaning on Delahaye et al.'s theory [15] for parametric DTMC estimation, we can compute an estimator of the probability that any system variant satisfies the property. For a given variant v, this estimator is the average reward of the paths ρ_i sampled from the FTDMC projection onto v, weighted by the probability that v executes ρ_i, that is, $\mathbb{E}_{b_v} = \frac{1}{n_v} \times \sum_i (b_i \times \Pi_i(v))$ where n_v is the number of paths sampled in the projection onto v such as $\forall v \in V, n_v = \sum_{i=1}^{n} \Pi_i(v) > 0$. The idea is that for a large number n of samples, this expected reward converges towards the real probability that v satisfies the property. Our uniform random walk approach, however, cannot directly produce such an estimator because it samples paths uniformly, irrespective of the real probabilities that the variants can execute these paths. We, therefore, follow Delahaye et al.'s parametric approach and *normalize* the weighted average reward $\mathbb{E}_{b_v}$ with the probability with which the random walk sampled each path ρ_i. Hence, we compute the estimator as

$$\tilde{\Pi} = \frac{1}{\mathbf{n}} \otimes \left(\frac{b_1}{p_1} \otimes \Pi_1 \oplus \dots \oplus \frac{b_n}{p_n} \otimes \Pi_n \right) \tag{1}$$

where $\frac{1}{\mathbf{n}}$ is the probability profile that associates $\frac{1}{n_v}$ to each variant v. Then, for sufficient numbers $\{n_v\}$, $\tilde{\Pi}(v)$ is the estimated probability that the variant

v satisfies ϕ. We can reduce the demonstration of this result to Delahaye et al.'s proofs for parametric DTMC [3,15], by transforming our FDTMC into a parametric DTMC (c.f. Fig. 3), such that each parameter corresponds to a feature and takes either the value 1 (the feature is enabled) or 0 (the feature is disabled). Then, in probability profile a positive literal over a feature f is simply encoded as f (e.g., $f \times 0.4$ corresponds to $\Pi(f) = 0.4$) and a negative literal over f is encoded as $(1 - f)$ (e.g., $(1 - f) \times 0.4$ corresponds to $\Pi(\neg f) = 0.2$). In the end, the only difference in our working assumptions – which has no incidence on the proof – is that the number of paths that each variant can execute can differ. This is taken into account with the profile $\frac{1}{n}$ and is equivalent to having paths that some variants executes with a zero probability. For the sake of conciseness, we do not replicate the proof of Delahaye et al. here.

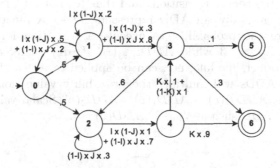

Fig. 3. Parametric DTCM resulting from the FDTMC illustrative example.

Algorithm 1 implements our random walk method for properties of the form $\Diamond a$ with $a \in AP$. The reasons we present the algorithm for these simple properties are the clarity of the presentation and because the key principle of our method is how we accumulate probability information during the random walk.

The algorithm selects an initial state of the FDTMC according to the initial state distribution ν (Line 1). Then, it enters an iterative process to select the successive states that the FDTMC goes through (Lines 7–17)). If the current state s satisfies the atomic property a then the current path ρ satisfies $\Diamond a$ – in this case, the algorithm stops and returns ρ and the associated probability profile Π_ρ that describes the probability for each variant to execute ρ (Line 19). Otherwise, the algorithm picks the next state s' from the reachable set of successors with a uniform probability (Line 12–13). In order to sample a relevant path, we consider only states s' that at least one variant can reach from s with a non-zero probability. The algorithm also updates the probability profile of ρ by multiplying it with the probability profile of the transition from s to s' (noted $\Pi_{(s,s')}$ – see Line 15). The algorithm iterates until it executes k steps or finds a state satisfying a.

The generalization to any LTL property is straightforward. It consists of executing the trace into the Büchi automaton equivalent to ϕ. Then the trace satisfies the property if and only if the execution loops over an accepting state of the automaton. Concretely, this generalization is obtained by removing Lines 9–11 and add after Line 18 the execution of the trace into the automaton. The implementation of this execution is a standard model checking procedure and is omitted here for conciseness.

The most important design decision for our algorithm is the representation we use for probability profiles and their accumulation. We propose to encode probability profiles using Algebraic Decision Diagram (ADD) data structure. ADD are a generalization of Binary Decision Diagram (BDD). BDDs are traditionally used for non-stochastic VISs and encode efficiently [9] which variants can or cannot execute the transitions. We propose ADD to also encode variants probability to execute transitions and thus to capture VISs with stochastic nature. More formally, an ADD represents $\mathbb{B}^n \to \mathbb{R}$ function. Such function can capture the probability to execute a transition for every variant. $ADD_{s_1,s_3}(I, \neg J, K) = .3$ while $ADD_{s_1,s_3}(\neg I, J, \neg K) = .8$, etc. Operations such as sum, product, modulo, etc. can be applied to ADDs. In our case, the product of two ADDs will multiply the probability values for every variants $\forall v \in V, (ADD_1 \otimes ADD_2)(v) = ADD_1(v) \otimes ADD_2(v)$. Scalar value i can also be considered as an ADD such as $\forall v \in V, ADD(v) = i$.

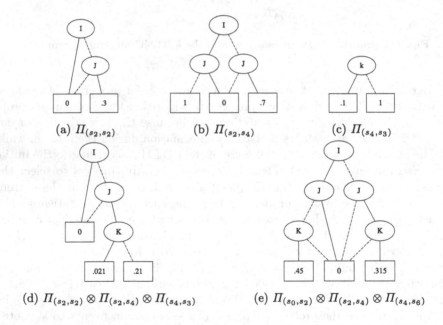

(a) $\Pi_{(s_2,s_2)}$ (b) $\Pi_{(s_2,s_4)}$ (c) $\Pi_{(s_4,s_3)}$

(d) $\Pi_{(s_2,s_2)} \otimes \Pi_{(s_2,s_4)} \otimes \Pi_{(s_4,s_3)}$ (e) $\Pi_{(s_0,s_2)} \otimes \Pi_{(s_2,s_4)} \otimes \Pi_{(s_4,s_6)}$

Fig. 4. Probability profiles of some transitions and paths encoded as ADDs.

Figures 4a, 4b and 4c illustrate probability profiles of some *featured* stochastic transitions as ADDs. While the (s_2, s_2) transition is only possible for variants with $\{\neg I \wedge J\}$. Such variants have .3 probability to fire this transitions (.7 to fire another one). Other variants cannot fire this transition. The (s_2, s_4) is a XOR ADD over I and J. $I \wedge \neg J$ variants can and will fire this transition as the probability is 1. Similarly, (s_4, s_3) transition is mandatory for K variants while $\neg K$ variants have .9 probability to not fire it. Figure 4d and 4e are two examples of probability profile of path (s_2, s_2, s_4, s_3) and (s_0, s_2, s_4, s_6). The first one is the product of the probability profiles of transitions illustrated in Fig. 4.

Figure 5 Illustrates our method with two sampled paths using Algorithm 1. The first path is: $\rho_1 = (s_0, s_1, s_3, s_2)$. The second is $\rho_7 = (s_0, s_2, s_4, s_6)$. As explained, Algorithm 1 returns a triplet containing the path probability profile (i.e., encoding the probability to execute the path given each variant. The Boolean value that indicates if the path violates or not the given formula $\rho_1 = 0$ while $\rho_7 = 1$, and the uniform probability to sample the path (.055 for ρ_1 and .125 for ρ_7). Then for each samples path, the average reward to violate the formula is:

$$\frac{1}{n} \otimes (\frac{0}{.055} \otimes \Pi_1 \oplus \frac{1}{.125} \otimes \Pi_7).$$

The profile n is the number of executable sampled paths for each variant. For instance, while $\{\neg I \wedge J \wedge K\}$ or $\{I \wedge \neg J \wedge K\}$ variants or can executes the two sampled paths, $\{\neg I \wedge J \wedge \neg K\}$ or $\{I \wedge \neg J \wedge \neg K\}$ can only execute ρ_1.

Note that in this example, the final (rightmost) ADD does not represent a probability (the terminal values are greater than one). This is because the number of samples is insufficient for these values to converge to the real probability values. Here, the terminal values are greater than one because the corresponding variants have a real probability to sample the paths that is greater than the probability of sampling these paths uniformly. Through additional repetitions of our algorithm, we would likely obtain other paths that the variants are less likely to execute and, ultimately, the final ADD will converge. Nevertheless, this example already illustrates the capability of our family-based approach to exploit common behaviour shared across multiple variants: by sampling only two paths in the FDTMC, we manage to get information about four different variants.

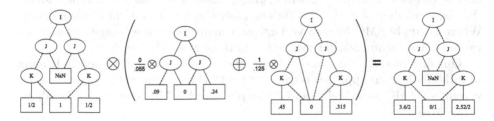

Fig. 5. Illustration of the Eq. 1, $\tilde{\Pi} = \frac{1}{n} \otimes (\frac{b_1}{p_1} \otimes \Pi_1 \oplus ... \oplus \frac{b_n}{p_n} \otimes \Pi_n)$ with two sampled paths.

Input: An FDTMC $m = (S, \nu, V, \Pi)$;
An LTL formula $\phi = \Diamond_k a$.
Output: a random path ρ with maximum length k;
a binary variable b, equal to 1 if and only if $\rho \models \phi$;
Π, the probability profile of ρ;
p_ρ is the probability that uniform sampling returns ρ

```
1  s ← pick from S with probability νₛ;
2  depth ← 0;
3  b ← 0;
4  ρ ← s;
5  Πρ ← 1;
6  pρ ← 1;
7  while b = 0 ∧ depth < k do
8  |    depth ← depth + 1;
9  |    if s ⊨ a then
10 |    |   b ← 1;
11 |    end
12 |    Succ ← {s′ ∈ S|∃v ∈ V : Π₍ₛ,ₛ′₎(v) > 0};
13 |    s′ ← pick from Succ with probability  1/|Succ|;
14 |    ρ ← ρs′;
15 |    Πρ ← Πρ ⊗ Π₍ₛ,ₛ′₎;
16 |    pρ ← pρ × 1/|Succ|;
17 |    s ← s′;
18 end
19 return (ρ, b, Πρ, pρ)
```

Algorithm 1: Uniform Random Walk in FDTMC

4   Evaluation

4.1   Objectives and Methodology

We conduct experiments that assess the effectiveness of our method in estimating correctly the probability of each variant to satisfy given properties. Our experiments consider a scenario where engineers have a limited simulation budget, that is, a number of SMC runs (in our case, a run is a uniform random walk). When we apply SMC to each variant, we equally share the budget between all variants. We decompose our evaluation in three research questions.

Our first research question evaluates the soundness of our approach. It aims to validate that our approach is consistent with (1) classical SMC applied to each variant's DTMC separately and (2) the parametric SMC approach of Delahaye et al. [3, 15].

RQ1: Is our approach consistent with other probability estimation methods?

To demonstrate this consistency, we reuse a toy example, called "Parametric Toy", that comes from Delahaye et al.'s paper [15]. It is a simple parametric model that we transformed into an equivalent FDTMC where each variant corresponds to a parameters valuation. We consider 26 such different variants. The reason we use this example is that its small size gives us confidence that our translation has preserved the original semantics of the model. We set the simulation bound k to 15, which is sufficient to for this small model. The setting of k depends on various factors such as the ones mentioned in Sect. 4.2.

To compare the approaches, we compute the correlation between (1) our ground truth containing the probability of each variant to satisfy the given property and (2) the same probabilities estimated by the method. We computed this ground truth from a very large number of simulations run for each separate variant to precisely estimate the probabilities (10^6 simulations per variant). We use the Kendall coefficient to measure the correlation because, as an ordinal association metric, it focuses on how well each method ranks the variants according to their probability (irrespective of the actual probability values). A high Kendall correlation means that the method preserves the ranking of the variants according to their probability to satisfy the property. To complement our analysis, we also use the Pearson's correlation coefficient, which captures linear relationships between two variables (here, the ground truth versus the probability values estimated by each method). Thus, a high Pearson correlation would indicate that the method can also preserve the difference in probability between the variants.

Our second research question evaluates the benefits of factorizing the analysis over all variants at once:

RQ2: Does family-based analysis improve effectiveness?

To answer this question, we compare the effectiveness of (1) our family-based approach with (2) our uniform random walk applied to each variant separately. Since both approaches use the same sampling strategy (uniform sampling), any observable difference would show the benefit of factorizing the sampling across all variants.

We measure effectiveness as the capability of each method to estimate properly the satisfaction probability of these variants. As mentioned before, we get an aggregated view of effectiveness by computing the Kendall and Pearson correlations. That is, we measure the capability of SMC methods to rank variants properly (using Kendall) and to preserve the relative difference between the estimated probability of the variants (using Pearson).

To conduct these experiments, we use two models that are bigger than Parametric Toy. The first is the Body Sensor Network from [24] and the second is a minepump VIS [9,20]. We check both models against the property originally described in their respective papers. As for the simulation bound k, we set it to 30 for the Body Sensor Network and to 50 for the Minepump. Those values are sufficient to find violations of the properties.

Finally, we check how our uniform sampling approach compares to a product-by-product sampling that considers the transition probability values to guide the random walk (i.e., the standard way to apply SMC to probabilistic systems). The difference between this "guided" random walk and uniform random walk is that the former asymptotically produces better estimates since it directly samples from the DTMC transition function. However, this guided approach may miss rare property violations in case of insufficient sampling budget, which may affect the conclusions of SMC. Hence, our research question is:

RQ3: Is guided random walk more effective than uniform random walk?

To answer this question, we repeat our RQ2 experiments (same protocol and settings) using SMC with guided random walk applied to each variant individually.

4.2   Datasets and Parameters

To conduct our experiments, we use two models from the literature. The first is the Body Sensor Network from [24]. This system consists of a set of medical sensors that monitor a person's vital signs. Sensors and other elements exhibit variation points from which 10 variants can be derived. This system has only one property to satisfy, which is that it should never reach a failure state.

The second model is a minepump VIS [9,20] with 448 variants. The underlying FTS comprises 250,561 states[1]. We have modified this model to introduce probability over non-deterministic transitions (e.g. those that modify the level of water and the presence of methane), such that the probability mass is distributed uniformly over alternative transitions. For this model, we consider the four properties described in Table 1.

We set respectively, the simulation bound to 30 for BSN and 50 for minepump. The setting of the simulation bound k often depends on the case study. It requires knowledge about the case study but also about external factors such as system requirements, system execution context, etc. This expertise usually came from the system engineers. For example, k may depend on the property to check, such as what is the probability of having a system failure by some given time t. That is, it requires knowledge about how long the system should run before it can be considered safe.

Higher simulation bound allows finding more (but usually less probable) violations of the properties. The simulation bound may also depend on the system itself and its future usage. A more complex system will likely require a higher simulation bound because a bigger state space must be checked. If interested in rare events or if the system will run during a long time period before maintenance, the simulation bound can be increased as well. Similarly, the number of samples (or simulation runs) also depends on the case study. Basically, a complex system with a lot and/or longer paths will likely require a more significant number of samples to have a precise enough idea of the probability to satisfy the property.

---

[1] The state space of all variants taken individually reaches 889,124 states.

Table 1. Minepump properties that we use in our experiments.

Property number	Property formula
minepump #16	$\neg((\Box\Diamond methane) \wedge (\Box\Diamond\neg methane))$
minepump #18	$\Box(methane \Rightarrow (\Diamond stateMethanestop))$
minepump #26	$\Box((highWater \wedge \neg methane) \Rightarrow \Diamond pumpOn)$
minepump #30	$\neg\Diamond\Box(\neg pumpOn \wedge highWater)$

4.3   Implementation

We implemented our family-based SMC algorithm and the classical product-by-product SMC algorithm into ProVeLines[2] [12], a state-of-the-art model checker for VIS. The tool takes as input (a) an FDTMC – modelled in an extension of the Promela language [19] where transitions are associated with a probability distribution and can be guarded with features, (b) an LTL formula, and (c) a s sample budget of k steps. Then it runs simulations (using the available budget) and returns the probability of variants that satisfied the property. Therefore, we compare our algorithm and classical SMC on common technical ground.

To efficiently encode the probability profiles Π_ρ that our algorithm manipulates and returns, we extended the Algebraic Decision Diagrams [2] data structure. ADDs are like binary decision diagrams [5] except that leaf nodes can receive a real value. In our case, branches represent features of the VIS. Therefore, an ADD path represents a set of variants, and the value of the leaf is the probability associated to this set. Equation 1 is implemented by using two extended ADDs. ADD_p that iteratively capture the output of each path sampled by Algorithm 1 (i.e., $\frac{b}{p} \otimes \Pi_\rho$) and $ADD_\sim$ that accumulate them such $ADD_\sim = \sum_{p=0}^{n} ADD_p$. We implemented our ADD extension into the efficient CuDD library [29]. The extension allows to store multiple real values as leaves in order to optimize the implementation.

As for the parametric approach, we reuse the prototype Python implementation of Delahaye et al.[3] [15]. Unfortunately, this prototype does not support concurrent systems (i.e., multiple processes/modules) and a very limited subset of the Prism language. Consequently, it cannot verify Body Sensor Network nor Minepump case studies.

We run all our experiments on a Dell Latitude i7 16 GB 1.8 GHz. To account for random variations, we execute 10 runs of each experiment and report the average accuracy. Body Sensor Network and Minepump ground truth computations took, respectively, 6 min and 50 min approximately. The different case studies took a few seconds for Body Sensor Network and few minutes for Minepump. The memory consumption of ProVeLines was around a dozen of MB. We do not notice differences in performance between the methods implemented in ProVeLines.

---

[2] https://bitbucket.org/SamiLazregSuidi/provelines-stc/src/master/.
[3] https://github.com/paulinfournier/MCpMC.

5   Results

We present our experimental results for the three research questions hereafter.

5.1   RQ1: Soundness

We show in Table 2 the correlation analysis for the Parametric Toy exemplar, the only model we could model equivalently in Delahaye et al.'s tool [15] and in ours. We show the correlations for Delahaye et al.'s approach (*Parametric*), our family-based algorithm, and the product-by-product uniform random walk. For each method, we show the correlation between the probability values that the method estimated and the ground truth. As a reminder, the ground truth was computed from a very large number of simulations run for each variant to precisely estimate the probabilities (10^6 simulations per variant). Interestingly, we observe that each method achieves extremely strong correlations (above 0.89). This indicates that both the approach of Delahaye et al. [15] and our novel SMC algorithm can produce suitable estimates to compare and rank the variants of the Parametric Toy.

We can observe that the variation of the number of simulations does not drastically influence the correlation of any of the methods. This indicates that even the smallest simulation budget we considered (10^3) is enough to cover rare behaviors specific to few variants of the Toy exemplar. This also suggests that our uniform normalisation function is adequate for this system [15].

> These positive results indicate that our approach can produce suitable estimations. This allows us to have confidence in its correctness and capabilities.

This successful preliminary validation encourages us to pursue our endeavour on larger models and more complex properties, which we investigate in the next research questions.

5.2   RQ2: Benefits of Family-Based

We study the correlations achieved by our approach ("Family-based") compared to the product-by-product random walk ("PbyP: Classical"), on larger models than the parametric toy exemplar. Table 3 shows the results for Body Sensor Network (BSN) and for Minepump. It has to be noted that the two models have significantly different characteristics. The state-space of Minepump is larger than BSN and requires, therefore, longer explorations (in terms of simulation bound k) to sample relevant path prefixes. BSN, however, presents an extreme factor of complexity: all its stochastic transitions are featured, i.e., the transition probabilities change with the system features. This means that the stochastic behaviour of two variants can differ significantly and do so early during the simulation.

In the BSN case (Table 3), we observe that, for all sampling budgets, both approaches achieve very strong Pearson correlation (>0.93) and strong Kendall correlation (>0.77). This means that they are both effective in estimating the ranking of variants (wrt. their property violation probability) and even more in estimating the relative differences (in violation probability) between these variants.

In both cases, increasing the budget improves the correlation values. This indicates that, in spite of its reasonable state space size, BSN remains challenging to simulate due to the divergence in the variants' stochastic behaviour. We actually observe that, though our family-based approach strongly correlate with the ground truth, the product-based alternative is better in this case.

In the Minepump case (Table 3), we observe again that the two approaches are overall effective: they both achieve very strong Pearson correlation (>0.90) and strong Kendall correlation (>0.64) for all properties and sampling budget. There are, however, observable differences between the two techniques.

First, the family-based approach achieves better Kendall correlations than the product-by-product method (up to 0.13 difference), but worse Pearson correlation (up to 0.07). This means that the product-by-product estimates the relative difference between variants slightly better. However, it has more failures when it comes to ranking these variants. This can be explained by the fact that, in Minepump, multiple variants can have very close violation probabilities. In this case, the product-by-product method can fail to rank them due to the inherent estimation error. By contrast, the family-based approach estimates the probability of these variants at once; therefore, it applies the same estimation error to all variants, which does not impact the rankings.

Second, increasing the sampling budget increases the correlation values for the product-by-product method, but has no significant effect on the family-based approach. This indicates that our method can provide its maximal benefits even with a small sampling budget. We explain these results by the fact that the minepump variants differ more by their unique transitions than in their probabilities to execute common transitions. In such a case, the factorization capability of our family-based method is optimally used and enables the production of accurate estimation even with a low number of sampled paths.

The main benefit of our approach is to effectively estimate the ranking of the different variants according to the probability to violate the property. Our method is more effective at ranking variants than product-by-product approaches, especially at low sampling budgets.

5.3   RQ3: Guided Sampling

Our last research question investigates whether a product-by-product sampling approach that is guided by transition probabilities brings benefits over uniform sampling. Results for this approach are again shown in Table 3 (column "PbyP: Guided").

In the BSN case, we observe that this new approach achieves very strong Pearson correlation (>0.96) – it is as effective as the product-by-product uniform sampling approach – and strong Kendall correlations (>0.73) – though, overall, less strong than the two uniform approaches. Interestingly, we observe that these Kendall correlations can significantly increase or decrease with the sampling budget, whereas one would expect the correlation to improve monotonically with the sampling budget. Because it is guided, this sampling approach inherently favours common execution paths over rare paths. In case these rare paths are violating, this biased sampling introduces random factors in the ranking of the variants.

In the Minepump case, the guided approach achieves lower Pearson and Kendall correlations compared to the two uniform approaches, though these correlations remain strong (>0.73). As we previously observed on the uniform product-by-product method, the guided approach improves its estimations with an increasing the sampling budget, though it never manages to perform better than our family-based method.

> Our uniform sampling method performs better at low sampling budgets. This indicates that guided sampling methods tend to be more sensitive to path rarity, which can deteriorate the estimations.

These results demonstrate the importance of path rarity in accurately estimating all variants' violation probability. This importance, in turn, motivates the use of uniform sampling and normalization methods that we have proposed in this paper.

Table 2. Correlation between each method and the ground truth (10^6 simulations run for each variant). In each cell, left number is Pearson's correlation; right number is Kendall's. In the table, "Parametric" refers to Delahaye et al.'s approach. "Family-based" is our novel SMC algorithm. "PbyP: Classical" means uniform random walk SMC applied to each variant separately.

	Sample budget	Family-based		PbyP: Classical		Parametric	
Param. Toy	10^3	0.9655	0.9294	0.9964	0.8928	0.9570	0.9983
Param. Toy	10^4	0.9630	0.9230	0.9972	0.9733	0.9539	0.9984
Param. Toy	10^5	0.9627	0.9231	0.9998	0.9733	0.9539	0.9984

6 Threats to Validity

The first threat to validity is the models we use. We used only two VIS models from the literature that we could easily adapt to become stochastic VIS. These models do not exhibit a real-world level of complexity (i.e., hundreds of variants and hundreds of thousands of states). But even if the case studies are relatively simple compared to real-world VISs, the preliminary results of

Table 3. Correlation between each method and the ground truth (10^6 simulations run for each variant). In each cell, left number is Pearson's correlation; right number is Kendall's. In the table, "Family-based" is our novel SMC algorithm. "PbyP: Classical" means uniform random walk SMC applied to each variant separately. "PbyP: Guided" means guided SMC applied to each variant separately.

	Sample budget	Family-based		PbyP: Classical		PbyP: Guided	
BodySensorNet.	10^2	0.9386	0.7778	0.9675	0.809	0.9673	0.7333
BodySensorNet.	10^3	0.9594	0.7778	0.9984	0.8667	0.9976	0.9556
BodySensorNet.	10^4	0.9672	0.9111	0.9999	0.9111	0.9982	0.9111
BodySensorNet.	10^5	0.966	0.9556	1.0	0.9556	0.9994	0.8222
minepump#16	250	0.9586	0.778	0.9762	0.6412	0.8284	0.756
minepump#16	500	0.9617	0.7791	0.9873	0.6753	0.8274	0.7601
minepump#16	1000	0.9602	0.7697	0.9922	0.6852	0.8292	0.7606
minepump#16	2000	0.9603	0.7766	0.9953	0.7152	0.8292	0.761
minepump#18	250	0.9574	0.7651	0.9856	0.7171	0.837	0.7424
minepump#18	500	0.9576	0.7775	0.991	0.737	0.8366	0.7544
minepump#18	1000	0.958	0.7699	0.995	0.7752	0.8381	0.7518
minepump#18	2000	0.9578	0.7823	0.9969	0.781	0.837	0.7563
minepump#26	250	0.909	0.8434	0.9509	0.7841	0.8445	0.733
minepump#26	500	0.9085	0.8453	0.9677	0.7912	0.8493	0.7579
minepump#26	1000	0.909	0.8445	0.9751	0.7958	0.8526	0.7804
minepump#26	2000	0.9085	0.8469	0.9809	0.811	0.8552	0.7832
minepump#30	250	0.9027	0.8583	0.9591	0.7859	0.7799	0.7498
minepump#30	500	0.9028	0.8719	0.9745	0.8277	0.7847	0.8074
minepump#30	1000	0.9014	0.8788	0.9773	0.833	0.7856	0.8064
minepump#30	2000	0.9038	0.8765	0.9832	0.8365	0.7859	0.8323

our evaluation show that our method is a promising direction for verification of VISs. As future work, we plan to collect several real-world stochastic systems from different industries such as space, automotive and biomedical to further develop our method.

Our second threat to validity is that the effectiveness of our method may depend on the system to verify. Indeed, a basic assumption is that systems with many common behaviors across the variants will provide better results. This is what we can observe with our models. The effectiveness of our method also depends on the property to check. For example, our method provides worst Pearson but better Kendall correlations for the last two minepump properties #26 and #30. The other case studies share similar results. However, further research and investigations will be required to characterize how different systems and properties will impact our method.

Similarly, the choice of the normalization function and the simulation bound k may highly impact the results of our method. We show that the uniform normalization function outperforms the traditional guided sampling in giving accurate estimations. However, as the convergence speed can be affected by the choice of the normalization function [15], this choice may also depend on the case study. For the simulation bound, our k settings find violations for every variant with reasonable probability of happening (higher than 0.0001). Indeed, in our models, a lower k produces fewer behaviors (but more probable) that violate the property, while higher k will find more violations (but with a lower probability of happening). Nevertheless, setting precisely the simulation bound (similar to simulation run length) requires knowledge about the case study and external factors such as system requirements, system execution context, etc. This expertise usually came from the system engineers.

Another threat concerns the way we computed out ground truth that is used as real probabilities that each variant has to violate the property. We propose to compute this ground truth using a very high number of samples compared to the one used for the experiment. For example, for minepump, 10^6 samples were used to compute the ground truth. In comparison, 20^2 samples is the budget to assess a method. We also repeated the computation of ground truth multiple times to see if this high number is sufficient to avoid random variations. We observed slight probability variations from 10^{-6} to 10^{-9} (depending on the case study). These variations are too small to impact product ranking. Another way to compute the ground truth is to apply exhaustive bounded probabilistic model checking on each variant. This computation method differs from the one we propose in this paper and might not be a relevant comparison.

Finally, a construct validity comes from the metrics we use to measure effectiveness. Kendall and Pearson coefficients are established statistical methods to measure the correlation between two variables (here, the ground truth and the estimations). We reused standard libraries to compute them and are therefore confident that our computation is correct. Still, these coefficients assess to what extent the estimations preserve the real differences between variants (be it of raking or of value) and do not precisely reflect the estimation errors. Overall, these coefficients are meaningful if the goal is to compare products rather than get extremely accurate probability estimations.

7   Related Work

7.1   VIS Verification

There are numerous models proposed for VIS verification. For instance, Classen et al. proposed *Featured Transition System* [9] (FTS) formalism which is an automata-based model that relies on transitions labelled by a features expression. Consequently, this formalism determines which variants can exercise the transition. Using this information, the fact that variants have behaviour in common could be exploited, leading to significant speedup in terms of verification time.

Accordingly, Classen et al. proposed variability-aware *exhaustive* algorithms to model-check FTS.

In addition to FTS, other models have been extended to capture the behaviour of multiple variants such as modal transition system [30], product-line-CCS [18], featured Petri-nets [23]. Each formalism has a different syntax and semantics. Modal transition systems or modal I/O automata use optional "may" transitions to model variability. Similarly, product-line-CSS is a process algebra with alternative choice operators between two processes to model the behavior of a set of variants. All these approaches are reasonable solutions for VIS verification. However, most of them are isolated efforts that do not come with mature companion tools. Our work is, therefore, based on FTS. Ter Beek et al.'s [30] solution based on modal transition systems is another mature approach. However, it requires the use of a separate logic to link variants to their behaviour in the model, which we found to be less practical than the explicit variability information contained in FTS. This information makes it easy and efficient to determine the variants that can execute a given buggy behaviour [10].

There also exist VIS models that include probabilistic information, such as FDTMCs [27] and Markov decision processes [7]. These models come with dedicated generalization of exact probabilistic model checking algorithms to compute precise probability values to satisfy given properties. By contrast to all the above methods, our approach is non-exhaustive and samples paths from the model to estimate the probabilities of the stochastic VIS while reducing the verification effort. Our work, therefore, trades off the exactness of the verification results for an increased efficiency. This compromise is essential to verify VIS with large state space.

A related line of work concerns the selection of a DTMC from a family of candidate DTMCs. Ceska et al. [6] approach this problem from three angles: feasibility (does there exist a family member that satisfies the property), threshold (which family members satisfy the property within a given probability threshold, and which ones do not), and optimality (which family member optimizes the probability to satisfy the property). They propose a solution to answer these three questions based on an abstraction-refinement scheme over Markov decision processes. Our objectives differ in that we aim to estimate the violation probability of each family member, a more precise information that is not necessary (but is sufficient) to answer the above questions. The exploration of using SMC and combine it with Ceska et al.'s abstraction approach is an interesting direction for future work.

7.2   SMC for VIS

Recent work has applied SMC in the context of VIS. Vandin et al. [31,32], proposed an algebraic language to formally model behaviour with dynamic variability (i.e. where the system can adapt its configuration during its execution). Vandin et al. also proposed a product-based SMC approach to check properties on the reconfigurable system. Contrary to this work, our approach assumes static variability (the variants are distinct systems) and relies on family-based algorithms to reason more efficiently on the whole set of variants.

Dubslaff et al. [17] and Nunes et al. [27] have studied VIS subject to stochastic behaviour and proposed exhaustive model-checking algorithms to check the probabilistic properties of such systems. These algorithms suffer from scalability limitations because of their exhaustive nature and the inherent computational cost of stochastic model checking approaches. To overcome this scalability issue, Delahaye et al. applied SMC to stochastic parametric systems [16]. Their approach opens the possibility to verify stochastic VIS, where each variant is a valuation of the parameters. More precisely, Delahaye et al. target the verification of quantitative reachability properties. By contrast, we support non-quantitative but more general properties (expressed in a fragment of LTL).

In a series of recent works [31], ter Beek et al. proposed a simulation-based approach for software product lines with stochastic behaviours. The approach relies on an algebra to describe sets of variants and on SMC [21,22,34] to compute the probability of each variant to satisfy a given bounded LTL property.

In this paper, we reconciled the approaches of [31] and of [15] by proposing a family-based extension of SMC for FDTMC. We sketched the theory and proposed an implementation in the ProVeLines model checker [12]. We then show that our approach is more effective than the traditional, guided, product-by-product SMC method. It is, furthermore, sample-efficient as its factorization capability enables the production of suitable estimations with a low sample budget.

8   Conclusion

There are two majors difficulties with the verification of VISs. The first is to find a compact representation for a set of variants that share a common basis of behaviours, but also differ by their unique behaviours. The second is to exploit this representation to evaluate each variant efficiently.

In this paper, we consider VISs whose behaviours depend on stochastic information. As seen in [27], such systems can be represented with FDTMC. That is to say with transition systems whose transitions are extended with probability profiles. Such profiles list the set of variants that are following the transitions as well as the probability to take such a transition for a given variant.

Interestingly, we got some promising results that our family-based approach produces consistent results and could precisely estimate the rank of the different variants, especially at very low simulation budgets. Product-based approaches seem to suffer from a fundamental limitation. The amount of estimations errors sums up between the different variants reducing thus ranking capabilities. Consequently, they may require more significant simulation budgets to outperform our method.

Over the last years, verifying FDTMC has been the subject of intense studies (see e.g., [17,27]). Some of the verification techniques that have been proposed are family-based; that is, exploiting the compact structure of FDTMC to avoid redundant work. Other approaches enumerate and perform verification on each variant represented by the FDTMC. All those studies rely on extensions of probabilistic model checking algorithms. While such algorithms are precise, they eventually suffer from the state-space explosion problem.

This paper is the beginning of a new thread of results on applying SMC to VISs. There are various directions for future research. The first direction is to consider variants with both stochastic and non-deterministic aspects. This could be done by combining the result of the present paper with the smart sampling approach for non-deterministic behaviours proposed in [14]. Another extension concerns the properties that we can verify. The present paper is restricted to bounded executions. The problem is that verifying full LTL over infinite executions is incompatible with a simulation-based approach. Indeed, the main hypothesis of such an approach is that the property can be decided on each simulation after a finite number of steps. This is a contradiction with the liveness fragment of LTL that requires monitoring unbounded executions. Several authors have proposed solutions to this problem. These solutions either require to have computed to the full state space of the model, or they drastically increase the number of simulations [13,33]. We plan to investigate a novel approach based on three-valued LTL. The idea would be to use the work in [4] that offers a finite-word automata-based representation to monitor LTL properties. Given a finite execution, the approach can either decide if it satisfies the property by comparing the outcomes of two finite automata, or return an undefined value in case the comparison is inconclusive. Such a three-valued approach cannot be handled by classical Monte Carlo algorithms, but promising extensions exist [1] and can inspire our work.

References

1. Arora, S., Legay, A., Richmond, T., Traonouez, L.-M.: Statistical Model Checking of Incomplete Stochastic Systems. In: Margaria, T., Steffen, B. (eds.) ISoLA 2018. LNCS, vol. 11245, pp. 354–371. Springer, Cham (2018). https://doi.org/10.1007/978-3-030-03421-4_23

2. Bahar, R.I., Frohm, E.A., Gaona, C.M., Hachtel, G.D., Macii, E., Pardo, A., Somenzi, F.: Algebric decision diagrams and their applications. Formal Methods Syst. Des. 10(2), 171–206 (1997). https://doi.org/10.1023/A:1008699807402

3. Bao, R., Attiogbe, C., Delahaye, B., Fournier, P., Lime, D.: Parametric Statistical Model Checking of UAV Flight Plan. In: Pérez, J.A., Yoshida, N. (eds.) FORTE 2019. LNCS, vol. 11535, pp. 57–74. Springer, Cham (2019). https://doi.org/10.1007/978-3-030-21759-4_4

4. Bauer, A., Leucker, M., Schallhart, C.: Monitoring of Real-Time Properties. In: Arun-Kumar, S., Garg, N. (eds.) FSTTCS 2006. LNCS, vol. 4337, pp. 260–272. Springer, Heidelberg (2006). https://doi.org/10.1007/11944836_25

5. Bryant, R.E.: Symbolic boolean manipulation with ordered binary-decision diagrams. ACM Comput. Surv. 24(3), 293–318 (1992)

6. Češka, M., Jansen, N., Junges, S., Katoen, J.-P.: Shepherding Hordes of Markov Chains. In: Vojnar, T., Zhang, L. (eds.) TACAS 2019. LNCS, vol. 11428, pp. 172–190. Springer, Cham (2019). https://doi.org/10.1007/978-3-030-17465-1_10

7. Chrszon, P., Dubslaff, C., Klüppelholz, S., Baier, C.: ProFeat: feature-oriented engineering for family-based probabilistic model checking. Formal Aspects of Computing **30**(1), 45–75 (2017). https://doi.org/10.1007/s00165-017-0432-4

8. Classen, A., Cordy, M., Heymans, P., Schobbens, P.Y., Legay, A.: Snip: an efficient model checker for software product lines. Technical report, University of Namur (FUNDP) (2011)

9. Classen, A., Cordy, M., Schobbens, P.Y., Heymans, P., Legay, A., Raskin, J.F.: Featured transition systems: foundations for verifying variability-intensive systems and their application to LTL model checking. Trans. Softw. Eng. **39**, 1069–1089 (2013)

10. Classen, A., Heymans, P., Schobbens, P.Y., Legay, A., Raskin, J.F.: Model checking lots of systems: efficient verification of temporal properties in software product lines. In: ICSE'10, pp. 335–344. ACM (2010)

11. Clements, P.C., Northrop, L.: Software Product Lines: Practices and Patterns. SEI Series in Software Engineering, Addison-Wesley (2001)

12. Cordy, M., Schobbens, P.-Y., Heymans, P., Legay, A.: Provelines: a product-line of verifiers for software product lines. In: SPLC'13, pp. 141–146. ACM (2013)

13. Daca, P., Henzinger, T.A., Kretínský, J., Petrov, T.: Faster statistical model checking for unbounded temporal properties. ACM Trans. Comput. Log. 18(2), 12:1–12:25 (2017)

14. D'Argenio, P.R., Legay, A., Sedwards, S., Traonouez, L.: Smart sampling for lightweight verification of markov decision processes. CoRR, abs/1409.2116 (2014)

15. Delahaye, B., Fournier, P., Lime, D.: Statistical model checking for parameterized models. working paper or preprint (2019)

16. Delahaye, B., Fournier, P., Lime, D.: Statistical model checking for parameterized models (2019)

17. Dubslaff, C., Klüppelholz, S., Baier, C.: Probabilistic model checking for energy analysis in software product lines. In: Binder, W., Ernst, E., Peternier, A., Hirschfeld, R., (eds.) 13th International Conference on Modularity, MODULARITY '14, Lugano, Switzerland, 22–26 April, 2014, pp. 169–180. ACM (2014)

18. Gruler, A., Leucker, M., Scheidemann, K.: Modeling and Model Checking Software Product Lines. In: Barthe, G., de Boer, F.S. (eds.) FMOODS 2008. LNCS, vol. 5051, pp. 113–131. Springer, Heidelberg (2008). https://doi.org/10.1007/978-3-540-68863-1_8

19. Holzmann, G.J.: The SPIN Model Checker: Primer and Reference Manual. Addison-Wesley (2004)

20. Kramer, J., Magee, J., Sloman, M., Lister, A.: Conic: an integrated approach to distributed computer control systems. Comput. Digit. Tech. IEE Proc. E **130**(1), 1–10 (1983)

21. Legay, A., Delahaye, B., Bensalem, S.: Statistical Model Checking: An Overview. In: Barringer, H., Falcone, Y., Finkbeiner, B., Havelund, K., Lee, I., Pace, G., Roşu, G., Sokolsky, O., Tillmann, N. (eds.) RV 2010. LNCS, vol. 6418, pp. 122–135. Springer, Heidelberg (2010). https://doi.org/10.1007/978-3-642-16612-9_11

22. Legay, A., Lukina, A., Traonouez, L.M., Yang, J., Smolka, S.A., Grosu, R.: Statistical Model Checking. In: Steffen, B., Woeginger, G. (eds.) Computing and Software Science. LNCS, vol. 10000, pp. 478–504. Springer, Cham (2019). https://doi.org/10.1007/978-3-319-91908-9_23

23. Muschevici, R., Clarke, D., Proenca, J.: Feature petri nets. In: Proceedings of the 14th International Software Product Line Conference (SPLC 2010), vol. 2. Lancaster University, Lancaster, United Kingdom (2010)

24. Nunes, V., Fernandes, P., Alves, V., Rodrigues, G.: Variability management of reliability models in software product lines: an expressiveness and scalability analysis. In: SBCARS '12, pp, 51–60 (2012)
25. Pnueli, A.: The temporal logic of programs. In: FOCS'77, pp. 46–57 (1977)
26. Raatikainen, M., Soininen, T., Männistö, T., Mattila, A.: A Case Study of Two Configurable Software Product Families. In: van der Linden, F.J. (ed.) PFE 2003. LNCS, vol. 3014, pp. 403–421. Springer, Heidelberg (2004). https://doi.org/10.1007/978-3-540-24667-1_30
27. Rodrigues, G.N., et al.: Modeling and verification for probabilistic properties in software product lines. In: HASE 2015, Daytona Beach, FL, USA, 8–10 January, 2015, pp. 173–180 (2015)
28. Sabin, D., Weigel, R.: Product configuration frameworks-a survey. IEEE Intell. Syst. Appl. **13**(4), 42–49 (1998)
29. Somenzi, F.: Cudd: Cu Decision Diagram Package-Release 2.4. 0. University of Colorado at Boulder (2012)
30. ter Beek, M.H., Fantechi, A., Gnesi, S., Mazzanti, F.: Modelling and analysing variability in product families: model checking of modal transition systems with variability constraints. J. Logical Algebraic Methods Program. **85**(2), 287–315 (2016)
31. ter Beek, M.H., Legay, A., Lluch-Lafuente, A., Vandin, A.: A framework for quantitative modeling and analysis of highly (re)configurable systems. IEEE Trans. Softw. Eng. **46**(3), 321–345 (2020)
32. Vandin, A., ter Beek, M.H., Legay, A., Lluch Lafuente, A.: QFLan: A Tool for the Quantitative Analysis of Highly Reconfigurable Systems. In: Havelund, K., Peleska, J., Roscoe, B., de Vink, E. (eds.) FM 2018. LNCS, vol. 10951, pp. 329–337. Springer, Cham (2018). https://doi.org/10.1007/978-3-319-95582-7_19
33. Younes, H.L.S., Clarke, E.M., Zuliani, P.: Statistical Verification of Probabilistic Properties with Unbounded Until. In: Davies, J., Silva, L., Simao, A. (eds.) SBMF 2010. LNCS, vol. 6527, pp. 144–160. Springer, Heidelberg (2011). https://doi.org/10.1007/978-3-642-19829-8_10
34. Younes, H.L.S., Simmons, R.G.: Probabilistic Verification of Discrete Event Systems Using Acceptance Sampling. In: Brinksma, E., Larsen, K.G. (eds.) CAV 2002. LNCS, vol. 2404, pp. 223–235. Springer, Heidelberg (2002). https://doi.org/10.1007/3-540-45657-0_17

Author Index

Abd Alrahman, Yehia   373
Abdullah, Milad   318
Alberts, Elvin   231
Altmann, Philipp   249
Arbab, Farhad   356
Audrito, Giorgio   301
Azzopardi, Shaun   373

Bae, Kyungmin   47
Bartoletti, Massimo   335
Basile, Davide   142
Bergenti, Federico   165
Bettini, Lorenzo   283
Bortolussi, Luca   30
Bourr, Khalid   283
Bozga, Marius   13
Brandstätter, Andreas   97
Bureš, Tomáš   215, 318

Cairoli, Francesca   30
Chiang, James   335
Ciancia, Vincenzo   142
Cordy, Maxime   448

Damiani, Ferruccio   301
De Nicola, Rocco   3, 82
Di Stefano, Luca   82

Fettke, Peter   65

Gabor, Thomas   249
Gerostathopoulos, Ilias   231
Grosu, Radu   97

Hahner, Sebastian   215
Hartmanns, Arnd   406
Heinrich, Robert   215
Hennicker, Rolf   110
Hnětynka, Petr   215, 318

Inverso, Omar   82

Jähnichen, Stefan   3
Junttila, Tommi   335

Khalyeyev, Danylo   215
Klauck, Michaela   406
Klein, Cornel   249
Klein, Julia   181
Knapp, Alexander   110
Kruliš, Martin   215, 318

Larsen, Kim   393
Larsen, Kim Guldstrand   433
Lazreg, Sami   448
Lee, Jaehun   47
Legay, Axel   393, 433, 448
Leguizamon-Robayo, Alexander   199
Linnhoff-Popien, Claudia   249
Lion, Benjamin   356
Lluch Lafuente, Alberto   335

Mikučionis, Marius   433
Mirelli, Massimiliano   335
Monica, Stefania   165
Murgia, Maurizio   266

Nolte, Gerrit   393

Ölveczky, Peter Csaba   47

Paoletti, Nicola   30
Petrov, Tatjana   181
Phan, Thomy   249
Pinciroli, Riccardo   266
Piterman, Nir   373
Plášil, František   215
Poulsen, Danny Bøgsted   433
Pugliese, Rosario   283

Reisig, Wolfgang   65
Ritz, Fabian   249

Sanders, J. W.   127
Sauer, Horst   249
Schlüter, Maximilian   393
Schmid, Reiner   249
Sedlmeier, Andreas   249
Seifermann, Stephan   215

Sifakis, Joseph   13
Smolka, Scott A.   97
Steffen, Bernhard   393
Stoelinga, Marielle   393
Stoller, Scott D.   97

Talcott, Carolyn   356
ter Beek, Maurice H.   142
Tiezzi, Francesco   283
Tiwari, Ashish   97
Töpfer, Michal   318
Torta, Gianluca   301
Trubiani, Catia   266

Tschaikowski, Max   199
Tuosto, Emilio   266

Valiani, Serenella   82
Vandin, Andrea   335

Walter, Maximilian   215
Wieghardt, Jan   249
Wirsing, Martin   3, 110

Yifeng, Chen   127

Zambonelli, Franco   165

Printed in the United States
by Baker & Taylor Publisher Services